EXAM PREP

PHR

Professional in Human Resources

Cathy Lee Gibson

PHR Exam Prep: Professional in Human Resources

International Standard Book Number: 0-7897-3450-8

Library of Congress Catalog Card Number: 2005930376

Printed in the United States of America

First Printing: December 2005

09 08 07   6 5 4 3

Trademarks

All terms mentioned in this book that are known to be trademarks or service marks have been appropriately capitalized. Que Publishing cannot attest to the accuracy of this information. Use of a term in this book should not be regarded as affecting the validity of any trademark or service mark.

Warning and Disclaimer

Every effort has been made to make this book as complete and as accurate as possible, but no warranty or fitness is implied. The information provided is on an "as is" basis. The authors and the publisher shall have neither liability nor responsibility to any person or entity with respect to any loss or damages arising from the information contained in this book or from the use of the CD or programs accompanying it.

Bulk Sales

Que Publishing offers excellent discounts on this book when ordered in quantity for bulk purchases or special sales. For more information, please contact

U.S. Corporate and Government Sales

1-800-382-3419

corpsales@pearsontechgroup.com

For sales outside the U.S., please contact

International Sales

international@pearsoned.com

PUBLISHER
Paul Boger

EXECUTIVE EDITOR
Jeff Riley

ACQUISITIONS EDITOR
Steve Rowe

MANAGING EDITOR
Charlotte Clapp

PROJECT EDITOR
Seth Kerney

COPY EDITOR
Ben Berg

INDEXER
Chris Barrick

PROOFREADER
Lisa Wilson

TECHNICAL EDITOR
Bob Prescott

PUBLISHING COORDINATOR
Cindy Teeters

MULTIMEDIA DEVELOPER
Dan Scherf

INTERIOR DESIGNER
Gary Adair

COVER DESIGNER
Anne Jones

PAGE LAYOUT
Toi Davis

Contents at a Glance

Table of Contents

About the Author

Cathy Lee Gibson (SPHR) is the Director of Human Resources Programs at Cornell University's School of Industrial and Labor Relations in New York City. Cathy has nearly 20 years of progressively responsible generalist, specialist, and management experience in the field of human resources, and has worked at small and large organizations, in educational settings, in the for-profit, and in not-for-profit sectors.

Cathy leads professional development programs for managers and human resources professionals on interviewing and performance management—and how to ensure that those functions have a more strategic impact on organizations. In that spirit, Cathy wrote a book in 2004 titled *Performance Appraisals* for Silver Lining Publications, a division of Barnes & Noble. She has also co-authored online workshops titled "Effective Interviewing," "Performance Management and Appraisal," "Managing Performance," and "Fundamentals of Compensation."

Outside of work, Cathy focuses on her family. She is also actively committed to encouraging living and non-living organ donation, and has spoken nationally on this topic. Cathy has also co-authored an e-learning course that—in at least one state—must be completed before a driver's license will be issued.

You can reach Cathy at Cathy@CathyLeeGibson.com

Dedication

For my parents, Jean and Phil Pantano...

*Though I can find enough words to fill a book (and then some), I cannot find
the words to adequately thank you.... So, in the slightly modified lyrics of Celine Dion,
please know that this book was written for you...*

*For all those times you stood by me
For all the truth that you made me see
For all the joy you brought to my life
For all the wrongs that you made right
For every dream you made come true
For all the love I found in you
I'll be forever thankful
You're the ones who held me up
Never let me fall
You're the ones who saw me through, through it all
You were my strength when I was weak
You were my voice when I couldn't speak
You were my eyes when I couldn't see
You saw the best there was in me
Lifted me up when I couldn't reach
You gave me faith 'cause you believed
You gave me wings and made me fly
You touched my hand, I could touch the sky
I lost my faith, you gave it back to me
You said no star was out of reach
You stood by me and I stood tall
I had your love I had it all
I'm grateful for each day you gave me
Maybe I don't know that much
But I know this much is true
I was blessed because I was loved by you
You were always there for me
The tender wind that carried me
A light in the dark shining your love into my life
You've been my inspiration
Through the lies you were the truth
My world is a better place because of you.*

Acknowledgments

I've learned many things from writing this book—one of which is that I'll never again skip past the "Acknowledgments" section of a book that I'm reading. I've come to realize that an author—at least this author—is a person fortunate enough to be surrounded by a team of talented and committed individuals without whom there would be no book—and therefore without whom there would be no authorship.

So, in recognition of those who wove together the tapestry that you now hold in your hand, I would like to express my appreciation to the following individuals:

- ▶ Steve Rowe, development editor: For so many things… for the opportunity to write this book, for his direction and open-mindedness, for his unwavering commitment and support, and for his patience and flexibility throughout unique and trying circumstances. Steve, you understood where this book needed to go, and you made sure it got there.

- ▶ Bob Prescott, technical editor: For his guidance, perspective, discernment, and insight—along with his willingness to be a sounding board—all of which yielded far better ideas and results than I could have generated on my own. Drawing upon his decades of experience as a practitioner, academic professional, and author, Bob kept me on the technical straight and narrow.

- ▶ Jeff Riley, executive editor: For his leadership, expertise, and sound advice throughout the editorial transition and the actual publication of this book.

- ▶ Editors Seth Kerney and Ben Berg: For their eagle-eyed scrutiny, and for their simultaneous—yet single-minded—attention to the "forest" as well as to the "tree."

- ▶ Larry Phillips, SPHR Exam Prep author: For his collaboration, wisdom, experience, and level-headed horse sense (or, in recognition of his lakeside companions, perhaps I should say "dog sense").

- ▶ Jon Laskowitz: For enlightening me many years ago to the importance and vitality of living a well-examined life, and to always choosing a conscious response.

- ▶ Dawn Sugarman and James (owner of "Pasta la Vista"): For the many even-better-than-homemade dinners—so "delicious and nutritious for the family that I love…."

- ▶ Eve: For keeping me company while I burned the midnight oil.

- ▶ Maribeth, Tara, and Jamie: For the peace of mind that comes from knowing my kids are happy, well cared for, and well-loved.

▶ Dennis: For all the sage advice and good counsel he has given me over the years, for invariably being able to see the humor and irony in almost any situation, and for some truly great lawyer jokes.

▶ Those managers and decision makers who have opened professional doors along the way—including (but not limited to) Tom Turbyne, Cindy Albanese, Carol Riley, Susan Brecher, and Tony Panos.

▶ The many family members, friends, and colleagues who, in myriad ways, have made a difference in my personal and professional life and who helped make this book possible (including the Mahers, the Meyers, and our beloved Nanny Panny).

▶ Catherine Thibedeau and Ken Jones: For teaching me to love, respect, appreciate, and never grow tired of language.

▶ Ceil: For showing me the way.

▶ Susan: For her friendship and for "keeping me grounded."

▶ Aunt Barbara, Diana, Michael, and "the boys:" For being our family, and for providing me with my heart's home (not to mention an occasional much-needed victory in "Krazy Bee Rummy").

▶ Philicia, Leah, Alex, and Emmie: For their love, their support, their genuine interest and inquisitiveness, and for reminding me how important it is to keep the chairs at the same height.

▶ And last, but not least, Michael: For his gifts of love, support, encouragement, belief, respect, time, commitment, humor, understanding, acceptance, open-mindedness, and fresh perspective.

We Want to Hear from You!

As the reader of this book, *you* are our most important critic and commentator. We value your opinion and want to know what we're doing right, what we could do better, what areas you'd like to see us publish in, and any other words of wisdom you're willing to pass our way.

As an executive editor for Que Publishing, I welcome your comments. You can email or write me directly to let me know what you did or didn't like about this book—as well as what we can do to make our books better.

Please note that I cannot help you with technical problems related to the topic of this book. We do have a User Services group, however, where I will forward specific technical questions related to the book.

When you write, please be sure to include this book's title and author as well as your name, email address, and phone number. I will carefully review your comments and share them with the author and editors who worked on the book.

Email: feedback@quepublishing.com

Mail: Jeff Riley
          Executive Editor
          Que Publishing
          800 East 96th Street
          Indianapolis, IN 46240 USA

For more information about this book or another Que Certification title, visit our website at www.examcram.com. Type the ISBN (excluding hyphens) or the title of a book in the Search field to find the page you're looking for.

Introduction

Welcome to *PHR Exam Prep*! Whether this is the first Exam Prep book you've ever picked up, or whether you've used our test prep resources before, you'll find that this book will provide important information, critical insights, and valuable suggestions as you prepare to take the PHR examination.

This introduction will explain the PHR (Professional in Human Resources) exam in a general sense and will explore all the ways this Exam Prep can help you as you prepare to take the test. It will also begin to give you an idea of the various topics we'll be exploring in greater detail in the book, as well information about how the book is structured.

About the Test

In many organizations, performing HR-related transactions well is important—but it may not be enough. Those who truly wish to succeed in the HR profession must master the HR body of knowledge and must be able to implement that knowledge in effective, meaningful, and appropriate ways.

The PHR test is administered by the Human Resource Certification Institute (HRCI), an affiliate of the Society for Human Resource Management (SHRM). SHRM is one of the most—if not *the* most—preeminent professional organizations with which HR professionals can align themselves, and HRCI enjoys the full measure of respect that comes along with that association. Since 1976, HRCI has certified nearly 70,000 HR professionals through its various programs, and in so doing has contributed greatly to the advancement of the profession.

Successfully completing the PHR exam and earning the certification that goes along with it will unequivocally affirm—for you, for your employer, and even for potential employers—that you possess the knowledge and can demonstrate the skills needed to perform as a competent HR generalist. It is an important part of what makes this profession a true profession, and it is a well-recognized, well-respected indication of achievement. By selecting this book, you have taken an important first step toward earning the distinction that accompanies a PHR designation.

About This Book

Most PHR test preparation materials on the market today don't separate test prep for the PHR exam from test prep for the SPHR (Senior Professional in Human Resources) exam. We do. Why? Because the tests are different (see Chapter 1). It's our belief that since the PHR and SPHR tests are designed and constructed differently, your preparation should be different, as well. By tailoring your preparation specifically to what will be covered on the PHR exam, you have a better chance of focusing on those areas that matter most.

We'll start the book off with a chapter that covers everything you need to know about the exam—how to apply for it, prepare for it, and what to expect before, during, and after the actual test. We'll also provide you with the information you'll need to determine whether you actually qualify to take the PHR exam, or whether you might want to consider taking the SPHR exam, instead.

Chapter 2 will explore the underlying knowledge and principles of HR—important building blocks you'll need as you move into more specific disciplinary areas. You'll then devote a chapter to each of the functional areas covered in the PHR exam, specifically

- ▶ Strategic management

- ▶ Workforce planning and employment

- ▶ HR development

- ▶ Compensation and benefits

- ▶ Employee and labor relations

- ▶ Occupational health, safety, and security

At the end of the book, we'll provide you with a complete practice PHR exam, as well as an answer key and explanations about why each choice was—or wasn't—the best possible response.

Exam Prep books are aimed strictly at test preparation and review. They do not teach you everything you need to know about a topic. Instead, we'll present and dissect some of the types of questions and problems we've found that you're likely to encounter on a test. We've worked to bring together as much information as possible about the PHR exam—as well as lists of resources where you can get more information about a particular topic.

Once you've read the book, you can brush up on a certain area by using the index or the table of contents to go straight to the topics and questions you want to reexamine. We've tried to use the headings and subheadings to provide outline information about each given topic. After you've taken the PHR we think you'll find this book useful as a tightly focused reference that you can use in the future, as well.

Chapter Formats

Each Exam Prep chapter follows a regular structure, along with graphical cues about especially important or useful material. The structure of a typical chapter is as follows:

▶ **Objectives List**—Each chapter begins with a listing of the PHR objectives the chapter will cover. There will also be a short, descriptive paragraph that sheds some light on what is expected for that objective.

▶ **Chapter Outline**—Next you will find an outline of the chapter's topics complete with the page number of where that topic is found. This is a handy feature that can help you quickly locate the topics that interest you most.

▶ **Study Strategies**—This section offers you some helpful tips and hints as to how you can effectively study and interact with the chapter's content.

▶ **Topical Coverage**—After the opening items, each chapter covers the topics related to the chapter's subject.

▶ **Exam Alerts**—Throughout the topical coverage section, we highlight material most likely to appear on the exam by using a special Exam Alert layout that looks like this:

EXAM ALERT

This is what an Exam Alert looks like. An Exam Alert stresses concepts, terms, or activities that will most likely appear in one or more exam questions. For that reason, we think any information found off-set in Exam Alert format is worthy of unusual attentiveness on your part.

Even if material isn't flagged as an Exam Alert, *all* the content in this book is associated in some way with test-related material. What appears in the chapter content is critical knowledge.

▶ **Notes**—This book is an overall examination of the topics covered on the PHR. As such, we'll dip into many aspects of employee relations, understanding employment law, organization development, and so on. Where a body of knowledge is deeper than the scope of the book, we use notes to indicate areas of concern or specialty training. The following is an example of a note.

NOTE

Passing the PHR exam will help you earn a valuable credential, but that alone won't make you a competent HR practitioner. Although you can try to memorize just the facts you need in order to pass the PHR exam, you'll be much better off spending time understanding the underlying concepts and relating topics to your own professional experiences.

▶ **Tips**—We provide tips that will help you to build a better foundation of knowledge or focus your attention on an important concept that will reappear later in the book. Tips provide a helpful way to remind you of the context surrounding a particular area of a topic under discussion. The following shows you what a tip looks like.

TIP

This is what tips look like. The intent of tip elements is to provide you with alternative ways to approach duties HR professionals do in the real-world. These may be quicker ways of doing tasks or new methods that are not as well known. These elements help us bring real-world HR content into the boundaries of an exam prep book, too!

▶ **Review Breaks and Chapter Summaries**—Crucial information is summarized at various points in the book, in lists of key points you need to remember. Each chapter ends with an overall summary of the material covered in that chapter as well.

▶ **Key Terms**—A list of key terms appears at the end of each chapter.

▶ **Exercises**—Found at the end of each chapter in the "Apply Your Knowledge" section, the exercises include additional tutorial material and more chances to practice the skills that you learned in the chapter.

▶ **Review Questions**—These open-ended, short answer/essay-type questions will elicit your explanation of important chapter concepts.

▶ **Exam Questions**—This section presents a short list of test questions related to the specific chapter topic. The practice questions highlight the areas found to be important on the exam.

▶ **Review and Exam Question Answers and Explanations**—The next two sections will include the answers and explanations for the Review Questions and Exam Questions.

▶ **Suggested Readings and Resources**—Each chapter concludes with a listing of suggested books, websites, or other media that will offer you the opportunity to explore more on the topics covered in that particular chapter.

The bulk of the book follows this chapter structure, but there are a few other elements that we would like to point out:

▶ **Objectives Quick Reference**—This jump-table is found at the beginning of the book. This organizes the important PHR objectives and puts them alongside the page numbers where each objective can be found in the book. This is great for quickly finding items you want to see immediately.

- **Study and Exam Tips**—This section helps you develop study strategies. It also provides you with valuable exam-day tips and information. You should read it early on, so that is why we have placed this near the front of this book.

- **Practice Test** —The practice test, which appears toward the end of this book, is a very close approximation of the types of questions you are likely to see on the current PHR exam.

- **Answer Key** —This provides the answers to the practice exam, complete with explanations of both the correct responses and the incorrect responses.

- **Glossary**—This is an extensive glossary of important terms used in this book.

Contacting the Author

Together with my editors and colleagues, we've tried to create a real-world tool that you can use to prepare for and pass the PHR exam. In that spirit, we're all interested in any feedback you would care to share about this book, especially if you have ideas about how we can improve it for future test-takers. We'll consider everything you say carefully and will respond to all reasonable suggestions and comments. You can reach me via email at Cathy@CathyLeeGibson.com.

For instance, let us know if you found this book to be helpful in your preparation efforts. We'd also like to know how you felt about your chances of passing the exam *before* you read the book and then *after* you read the book. We're also interested in hearing your suggestions for changes or additions that should be made to this book. And, of course, we'd love to hear that you passed the PHR exam, so even if you just want to share your triumph, we'd be happy to hear from you!

Thanks for choosing us as your personal test prep coaches. Enjoy the book. We would wish you luck on the exam, but we know that if you read through all the chapters and work with the sample exams, you won't need luck—you'll do well on the strength of your knowledge, skills, and your ability to apply those skills to real-life workplace situations.

Study and Exam Prep Tips

Imagine yourself in this situation: It's the day before you're scheduled to take the PHR exam. Your legs, arms and fingertips tingle as you experience a rush of adrenaline. Beads of sweat dot your forehead. If you've scheduled the exam on a workday, or on a day that follows a workday, you may find yourself dreading the tasks you normally enjoy because, in the back of your mind, you're wishing you could read just a few more pages…or review your notes just one more time…or complete just a couple more practice questions….

Fear not—if you use this book, along with your other preparation resources, you can develop an evenly paced study plan that will help you avoid (most of) these pre-test day jitters.

This section of the book provides you with some general guidelines for preparing for any certification exam, and for the Professional in Human Resources (PHR) exam in particular. It's organized into three sections. The first section addresses learning styles and how they impact how you should prepare for the exam. The second section covers exam-preparation activities as well as general study and test-taking tips. This is followed by a closer look at the PHR certification exam, including PHR-specific study and test-taking tips.

Learning Styles

To best understand the nature of test preparation, it is important to understand the learning process. You're probably already aware of how you best learn new material and, if you're not, now's a great time to figure it out. You might find that outlining works best for you. If you're more of a visual learner, you might need to "see" things in order for them to "sink in." If you're a kinesthetic learner, a hands-on approach will serve you best.

Whatever your preferred learning style, test preparation is always more effective when it takes place over a period of time. You obviously wouldn't start studying for a certification exam by "pulling an all-nighter" the night before the exam, or even postpone your study until the week before the exam. But solid preparation means even more than that. It requires *consistent* preparation—at a steady pace, over a period of months, not days or weeks. As you begin your preparation, it's important to really appreciate that learning is a developmental process. It will help you focus on what you know well, on what you need to know better, and on what you still need to learn.

Learning takes place when you incorporate new information into your existing knowledge base. And remember, with confidence, that even if this book is the first PHR study tool you've looked at so far, you *do* have an existing knowledge base! How can you be certain of that? Because you're required to have two years of exempt-level experience in order to sit for the PHR exam. So you've already got a start.

> **NOTE**
>
> Don't rely on any single resource—even this book—to prepare for the PHR exam. No matter how good a resource might be, it only provides one perspective, and it can only provide a limited amount of material. This Exam Prep should serve as a supplement to your other study resources, not as a replacement for them. There is more knowledge and skill required to pass the PHR exam than could ever be found in this book, or any other single book. And nothing, of course, can replace practical experience.

As you prepare for the PHR exam, this book (along with all other study materials you use) will serve three purposes:

- ▸ First, it will add incrementally to your existing knowledge base.

- ▸ Second, it will facilitate the process of drawing meaningful connections between the test content and your own professional experience.

- ▸ Third, it will enable you to restructure your existing knowledge and experience into a format that's consistent with the PHR exam.

So, perhaps without even realizing it, you'll be adding new information into your existing knowledge base—all of which will then be organized around the framework of the six functional areas of HR around which the exam is designed. This process will lead you to a more comprehensive understanding of important concepts, relevant techniques, and the human resources profession in general. Again, all of this will only happen as a result of a repetitive process, not as the product of a single study session.

Keep this model of learning in the forefront of your mind as you prepare for the PHR exam. It will help you make better decisions about what to study and about how much more studying you need to do.

General Study Tips

There's no one "best" way to study for any exam. There are, however, some general test preparation strategies and guidelines that have worked well for many test-takers, and that might work well for you, too.

Study Strategies

Although each of us learns and processes information somewhat differently, certain basic learning principles apply to everyone. As you develop your own personal study plan, try to incorporate some of the strategies that are built upon these principles.

One of these principles is that learning can be broken into various depths:

▶ Recognition (of terms, for example) exemplifies a rather surface level of learning in which you rely on a prompt of some sort to elicit recall.

▶ Comprehension or understanding (of the concepts behind the terms, for example) represents a deeper level of learning than recognition.

▶ The ability to analyze a concept and apply your understanding of it in a new way represents further depth of learning.

This is not to say that recognition isn't important. It is—especially for the PHR exam. However, in addition to ensuring that you will recognize terms, your study strategy should also ensure that you "absorb" the material at a level or two deeper than that. In this way, you'll know the material so thoroughly that you'll be able to perform well on questions that require you to apply your knowledge to problems, as well as on recognition-level types of questions—both of which appear on the PHR exam.

Macro and Micro Study Strategies

One strategy that can enhance and support learning at multiple levels of depth is outlining. Creating your own outline that covers all of the objectives and subobjectives of the PHR exam will support your efforts to absorb and understand the content more fully. Specifically, it will help you make connections between the 19 core areas of knowledge, HR-related responsibilities, and HR-related knowledge associated with each of the six functional areas on the PHR exam. It will also help you dig a bit deeper into the material by including a level or two of detail beyond what you might find on most generic, summary-style study tools. You can add even more to your outline by expanding it to include a statement of definition—or a summary of a particular approach—for each point in the outline.

An outline provides two approaches to studying. First, you can study the outline by focusing on the organization of the material. As you build the points and subpoints of your outline, you'll be able to better appreciate how they relate to one another. You'll also gain a better understanding of how each of the main objective areas for the PHR exam is similar to—and different from—the other main objective areas. Then, do the same thing with the subobjectives; be sure you understand how subobjectives pertain to each objective and how they relate to one another. It's also important to understand how each of the HR-related responsibilities is similar to—or different from—the others. The same also holds true for the HR-related knowledge required for each of the functional areas and the 19 core areas of knowledge that span the six functional areas.

Next, work through your completed outline. Focus on learning the details. Take time to memorize and understand terms, definitions, facts, laws, cases, and so forth. In this pass-through of the outline, you should attempt to learn detail rather than the big picture (you focused on that as you built your outline).

Research has shown that attempting to assimilate both types of information (macro and micro) at the same time interferes with the overall learning process. If you separate your studying into these two approaches, you are likely to perform better on the exam.

Active Study Strategies

The process of writing down and defining objectives, subobjectives, terms, facts, and definitions promotes a more active learning strategy than merely reading the material does. In human information-processing terms, writing forces you to engage in more active encoding of the information. Simply reading over the information leads to more passive processing. Using this study strategy, focus on writing down the items that are highlighted in the book's bulleted or numbered lists, exam alerts, notes, cautions, and review sections.

Another active study strategy involves applying the information you have learned by creating your own examples and scenarios. Think about how or where you could apply the concepts you are learning. You could even try your hand at writing your own questions, which you could then consider sharing with a study partner or group. Once again, write everything down to help you process the facts and concepts in an active fashion.

The multiple review and exam questions at the end of each chapter provide additional opportunities to actively reinforce the concepts you are learning…so don't skip them!

Common-sense Strategies

Follow common-sense practices when studying: Study when you are alert; reduce or eliminate distractions; and take breaks when you become fatigued.

Design Your Own Personal Study Plan

And do it now. There is no single "best" way to prepare for any exam. Different people learn best in different ways, so it's important to develop a personal study plan that's right for you. As you do so, establish long-term and short-term goals for yourself. Know exactly what you will accomplish, and by what date. You'll experience a sense of accomplishment each time you reach a milestone—so allow yourself the opportunity to celebrate! You will have earned the right to revel a bit—plus, taking a little celebratory break will help you feel more refreshed as you move into the next stage of your prep.

Questions to Ask Yourself

As you develop your personal study plan, ask yourself the following questions:

- ▶ How much time do I have to invest in preparing for the exam?

- ▶ How much money do I have to invest in preparing for the exam?

- ▶ Do I learn better on my own, or when I have the chance to interact with others? Or, does some combination of both work best for me?

- ▶ Am I comfortable with an online study environment, or do I prefer a traditional classroom setting?

- ▶ Does my schedule afford me the opportunity to attend regularly scheduled classroom-based workshops?

- ▶ What is/are my preferred learning style/s?

- ▶ If I've taken this test before and didn't pass, what was effective about my original study plan? What was ineffective?

Pretesting

One of the most important aspects of learning is what has been called *meta-learning*. Meta-learning has to do with realizing when you know something well or when you need to study some more. In other words, you recognize how thoroughly (or not) you have learned the material you are studying.

For most people, this can be difficult to assess independently, in the absence of study tools. Pretesting allows you to assess the overall effectiveness of your study strategies. Pretesting tools such as review questions, practice questions, and practice tests are useful in that they objectively assess what you have successfully learned, as well as what you have not yet learned.

You can then use the insights you obtain from assessment tools to guide and direct your studying, since developmental learning takes place as you cycle through studying. So, assess how well you have learned a particular topic. Use that assessment to decide what you need to review more. Then, conduct another assessment, followed by more review. Repeat this cycle until you feel ready to take the exam.

You might have already noticed that there is a practice exam included in this book. You should use it as part of your learning process. The test-simulation software included on this book's CD-ROM also provide you with a tool with which to assess your knowledge.

Set a goal for your pretesting. A reasonable goal would be to score consistently in the 90% range.

See Appendix A, "CD Contents and Installation Instructions," for further explanation of the test-simulation software.

General Test-taking Tips

▶ Taking exams can be stressful! This is especially true if it's been a while since you've been in school or taken tests. As you prepare for the test—and answer lots of practice questions—your comfort level with test-taking will likely increase. Be patient with yourself; your "rustiness" will fade away.

▶ The structure, format, and style of the exam may be unfamiliar to you. Test taking is a skill all on its own, and every test is different. This is why so many individuals offer test-preparation services. You've probably seen the advertisements—SAT, LSAT, GRE, GMAT—the alphabet soup of test taking goes on and on. The specific attributes of each exam, however, are unique. Be patient with yourself.

PHR-specific Information, Study, and Test-taking Tips

We've all heard of "the fear of the unknown." Well, knowledge dispels fear (or at least it helps). Knowing as much as possible about how the PHR exam is designed, formatted, administered, and delivered will help you as you prepare to take the exam.

How Is the PHR Exam Administered?

HRCI contracts with the Professional Examination Service (PES) to handle a variety of administrative responsibilities, including

▶ Determining if PHR, SPHR, and GPHR candidates meet exam eligibility requirements

▶ Handling payments

▶ Issuing Authorization to Test (ATT) letters once a candidate's eligibility to take the test and earn the credential has been confirmed (the letter you need to bring with you to the test site)

▶ Tabulating and communicating (in writing) PHR, SPHR, and GPHR test scores

HRCI contracts with Thomson Prometric for exam delivery services. These services include scheduling, administering, and proctoring exams.

How Is the PHR Exam Put Together?

It's helpful to understand how the PHR exam was developed—and how it's updated. This insight can help you maintain your focus on what's truly most important to study.

Since 1976, HRCI has defined the HR body of knowledge for the PHR exam. This body of knowledge has evolved and changed over time, and the PHR exam has evolved and changed with it. This body of knowledge also translates directly into the PHR exam test specifications.

EXAM ALERT

At times, the changes to the PHR exam have been relatively subtle. Such changes can result from information gleaned through literature review and/or environmental scans. Four times since 1976, however, the body of knowledge has been completely revised. Make sure you periodically check the HRCI website to monitor whether—and how—the PHR exam test specifications have changed or evolved, and then modify your preparation accordingly.

PHR Exam Format

In addition to studying each of the six functional areas, you also need to be familiar with the format of the PHR exam.

The PHR exam is a computerized test consisting of 225 multiple-choice questions. You'll have four hours to complete the exam, which is administered only in English.

Of the 225 test questions, only 200 are actual exam questions that will count towards your overall score. Twenty-five of the 225 questions are being "tested" for possible use in future exams. Your responses to these pretest questions will not count toward your overall score. Pretest questions, however, aren't identified as such. You won't know which questions will count toward your overall score, and which won't—so your best bet is to assume that every question is a scored question.

Each question has four possible answers. Often, more than one answer will make sense, or may initially seem correct. You must, however, choose the "best possible answer."

EXAM ALERT

It has been said that "close only counts in horseshoes and hand grenades." Close doesn't count on the PHR exam, either. Take your time and evaluate all four options before selecting the "best possible answer."

Be particularly careful not to choose the response that is the closest to how your employer would handle a particular situation. Every organization has its own way of handling HR-related situations; however, *your* employer's way of handling a situation isn't necessarily the *best* way.

Examples of multiple-choice questions appear at the end of each chapter in this book.

PHR Preparation Options

There are many options from which to choose as you prepare for the PHR exam. Here is a sampling of some of those options:

- **Classroom Courses**: A variety of classroom options exist, including

  - *College/University Preparatory Courses*: More than 200 colleges/universities offer the SHRM preparatory course. The SHRM Learning System—valued at over $500—is included with most of these programs. Visit www.shrm.org to find a college/university program offered near you.

  - *SHRM Certification Test Courses*: SHRM sponsors intensive three-day preparatory courses throughout the country. This "immersion" program allows a condensed training opportunity for test takers, and may offer a valuable option for those who cannot attend a semester-long college/university-based program. The SHRM Learning System—valued at $500—is included with this three-day program.

  - *Chapter-level Courses*: From time to time, some SHRM chapters offer PHR preparatory courses (a "chapter" is a local or regional-based group of SHRM members who benefit from the opportunity to network and collaborate on a regular basis). Contact your local chapter to find out if it offers the preparatory course. A list of SHRM-affiliated chapters can be found at http://www.shrm.org.

  - *In-house Company Courses*: If there are enough individuals at your employer who are interested in earning PHR or SPHR certification, your employer may decide to bring SHRM on-site to deliver a preparatory course to you and your co-workers. Normally, only individuals within the sponsoring organization can participate in these programs (the "sponsoring" organization is the one that has brought SHRM on site to conduct the prep course).

- **Online Courses**: You may wish to consider a college/university-based online prep course instead, especially if a traditional classroom setting is not the most appropriate option for you. Through the Internet, you'll become part of a "virtual class" that prepares together for the PHR exam.

CAUTION

Check out online college/university programs carefully before signing up, to ensure that you choose a format that's right for you. Be particularly alert to real-time participation requirements if you have limited time availability, or if you are only available to study during non-traditional classroom hours.

▸ **Self-study**: If being part of a cohort group isn't the best choice for you, you might want to consider a "self-study" option. SHRM offers a self-study learning system, which contains prep books on each functional area as well as software that includes

  ▸ A diagnostic pretest

  ▸ Application exercises for each module

  ▸ Electronic flashcards

  ▸ Electronic glossary

  ▸ A diagnostic post

  The self-study format allows you maximum flexibility to prepare for the PHR at a time and a place that's most convenient for you.

▸ **Study Buddies**: Whether you're preparing for the PHR using a classroom, online, or self-study format, you may find it helpful to find another test-taker with whom you can partner as you prepare for the test. Ideally, you'll want to find someone whose schedule and learning style is similar to your own. Even more importantly, look for a buddy who has strengths in those functional areas in which you need the most development, and who needs someone to help him or her in those functional areas in which you are strongest. You can look for a buddy to work with in person, or someone with whom you will confer online. Buddies can be found through colleagues at work, through a prep course, or through other reputable sources.

▸ **Online Study Groups:** If you're an SHRM member (and who shouldn't be?), check out www.shrm.org to look for others with whom you can form a study group that's right for you.

PHR-specific Test Preparation Tips

Make no mistake: The PHR exam challenges your knowledge, your HR skills, *and* your test-taking abilities. Here are some tips to help you as you prepare for the PHR exam:

▸ Be prepared to combine your skill sets with your experience, and to identify solutions. The PHR exam tests your knowledge as well as your skill. You will be called upon to resolve problems that may involve different dimensions of the material covered. For example, you could be presented with a realistic workplace scenario about a layoff that requires you to understand when—and how—the Age Discrimination in Employment Act (ADEA) needs to be taken into consideration. Why is this type of question likely to appear? Because it's reflective of real life. And it's necessary to be able to make these applications if you're going to be an effective HR professional. In this particular example, it's one thing to know the provisions of the ADEA, but it's something else entirely to understand its application and relevance to a layoff situation.

▶ Practice delving into minute details. Each exam question can incorporate a multitude of details. Some of this information is ancillary. Some of it will help you rule out possible answers, but not necessarily enable you to identify the best possible response. Some of it will provide you with a more complete picture. Still, you may be called upon to combine this information with what you know and what you have experienced in order to identify the best possible response. If you don't pay attention to how the information that you're given helps you to eliminate certain responses, the best possible answer might elude you.

▶ Practice with a time-limit. The PHR exam must be completed within four hours. To get used to the time limits, use a timer when you take practice tests. Learn to pace yourself.

▶ Peruse the HRCI website (www.hrci.org) for valuable information and materials, such as the PHR/SPHR/GPHR Handbook.

▶ Talk with others who have already taken the PHR exam—whether or not they passed. Although PHR test-takers are prohibited from sharing specific parts of the exam with you, they can tell you about their experiences with it. You may find that their information, ideas, and suggestions might help as you get ready to take the test.

Strategies and Tips for PHR Exam Day

Your studying is done, you've familiarized yourself with the test center (online "virtual tools" are available), you're wearing comfortable clothing, and you've arrived at least 30 minutes early with ID in hand. Now what? First, breathe. Remember that you have thoroughly prepared yourself for the PHR exam. You are ready for this.

Now, prepare yourself mentally. Focus on your feelings of confidence. There's no one "right" way to do this. Some people, however, find it helpful to consider one (or perhaps both) of the following two mindsets:

"If you can see it, you can be it." Visualize yourself confidently answering test questions. See yourself leaving the test center, a smile on your face, just having learned that you have passed the exam.

"What's the worst that can happen?" Remind yourself that the worst thing that could possibly happen is that you do not pass the exam. If that does happen, there are many choices available to you, the most obvious of which is retaking the test. So, even if the worst possible thing happens, you'll get through it.

Here are some additional suggestions to consider as you sit down to take the PHR exam:

- **Take your time**—Determine how much time you can spend on each question, while still allowing yourself time to check your responses afterward. Most importantly, read every question—and every answer—deliberately and completely. You need to identify the best response, not just a good response.

- **Collect yourself**—Once you actually sit down at the computer terminal, take a few moments to collect yourself before you jump right into the test. Once again, breathe. Set aside any internal distractions and focus on the exam.

- **Take a break if you need one**—You have four hours to complete the exam, so give yourself some time to get some air, stretch your legs, and just reenergize yourself.

- **Remember that you might be audiotaped or videotaped**—Don't allow this to distract you; instead, just remember that taping test-takers is "business as usual" for Prometric testing facilities. Don't take it personally. Just let it go. You have more important things to focus on than a camera or microphone.

- **Don't rush, but don't linger too long on difficult questions, either**—The questions vary in degree of difficulty. Don't let yourself be flustered by a particularly difficult, wordy, or (seemingly) tricky question.

- **Read every word of every question**—Just like in real life, one word or one minute detail can make all the difference in selecting the "best possible answer."

- **Don't look for patterns in answer selections**—There aren't any.

- **Don't assume the longest answer is the best answer**—Don't assume the shortest answer is the best answer, either.

- **Answer every question**—Unanswered questions are 100% likely to be wrong. If you make a guess, you have a 25% chance of getting it right. If, however, you can narrow down your choices to three possible responses, you've can double or triple your chances of answering the question correctly.

- **Take advantage of the fact that you can "mark," return to and review skipped or previously answered questions**—When you reach the end of the exam, return to the more difficult questions.

- **If you have session time remaining after you complete all the questions, review your answers**—Pay particular attention to questions that contain a lot of detail.

- **When rechecking your responses, you may be tempted to question every answer you've made. Don't second-guess yourself too much**—If you read the question carefully and completely, and you felt like you knew the right answer, you probably did. If, however, as you check your answers, a response clearly stands out as incorrect, change it. You also might want to consider changing a response if you missed, misread, or misinterpreted details in the questions the first time around, or if you jumped to a clearly incorrect conclusion. If you are at all unsure, however, go with your first impression.

PART I

Exam Preparation

CHAPTER ONE

The HR Profession and the PHR Exam

Study Strategies

Note that in this chapter you won't find content that you will be tested on, per se. What you will find here is a chapter with information about the background of HR, the PHR exam, and information that is essential for successful performance on the exam. Use this chapter to prepare your mind for what the coming chapters will present you and to mentally prepare you for the journey of exam preparation on which you are embarking.

Introduction

For well over 50 years, Human Resources (HR) practitioners have struggled with how to define and establish themselves as members of a true—and recognized—profession. (Of course, we weren't always called "HR professionals", or even "HR practitioners"). In 1948, Herbert Heneman, Jr., Ph.D., opened the discussion of certification for our professional ancestors when he wrote an article titled, "Qualifying the Professional Industrial Relations Worker." The discussion was picked up by ASPA (American Society for Personnel Administration), which was renamed SHRM (Society for Human Resource Management) in 1989.

In 1967, ASPA co-sponsored a conference with Cornell University's School of Industrial & Labor Relations "Cornel-ILR." The purpose of this conference was to define "personnel" as a profession and to identify HR's "body of knowledge." One year later, Cornell-ILR and ASPA reconvened and identified the following five defining criteria of a profession:

- A profession must be full-time.
- Schools and curricula must be aimed specifically at teaching the basic ideas of the profession, and there must be a defined common body of knowledge.
- A profession must have a national professional association.
- A profession must have a certification program.
- A profession must have a code of ethics.

ASPA felt that personnel already met three of the five criteria. Two critical elements remained—identifying a body of knowledge and establishing a certification program.

By 1975, that body of knowledge was identified. The certification exam was not far behind; it was administered by AAI (ASPA Accreditation Institute) less than a year later. Test exemptions were granted to 2100 individuals—the first of whom was the very same Herbert Heneman, Jr., Ph.D., who had begun the discussion around certification more than a quarter of a century earlier.

The PHR (Professional in Human Resources) and SPHR (Senior Professional in Human Resources) certification exams have been modified many times since, reflecting a continuous commitment to quality, relevance, and the ever-evolving nature of our profession. These exams are administered by HRCI (the Human Resource Certification Institute), the modern-day version of AAI. HRCI is a separate organization from SHRM, the largest HR professional association in the world. The two organizations are, however, closely affiliated.

The PHR certification exam will test your knowledge about the HR body of knowledge. It will also test many of the HR-specific skills you'll need to perform successfully as an HR professional. In addition, however, the PHR exam will go well beyond what you know and what you can do; it's specifically designed to determine how well you can actually apply that knowledge and those skills to the workplace. It is this ability to combine knowledge and skill—along with solid preparation and relevant experience—that will enable you to pass the PHR exam and to perform successfully as an HR professional.

What Is SHRM, and What Does It Mean to You?

As you prepare for the exam, it's important to have a general understanding of SHRM (nicknamed, and pronounced, "sherm"). SHRM now boasts nearly 200,000 HR professionals in more than 100 countries—making it the largest professional association for HR practitioners in the world. In addition to being the largest, SHRM is considered by many to be one of the foremost professional organizations with which HR professionals can affiliate themselves.

Membership Information

While you're not required to be a SHRM member to take an HRCI certification exam, membership will prove to be of invaluable assistance as you prepare for the exam and as you grow in your career. Visit the "Join/Renew" section at SHRM's website (www.shrm.com) for guidelines that will help you determine the type of membership that's most appropriate for you.

> **NOTE**
>
> SHRM membership is individual, not corporate. Wherever you go, your SHRM membership will go with you.

Benefits of Membership

SHRM's membership benefits are many are varied and fall into the following five categories:

- **Professional Resources**: Tools, directories, forums, webcasts, chats—even an online job listing service.

- **Publications**: Weekly, monthly, and quarterly updates on a variety of critical HR issues including legislative updates, workplace issues, and a host of other HR-related topics.

- **Research**: Original surveys, reports, and analyses on a wide spectrum of emerging workplace issues.

- **Professional Development**: SHRM provides a wide array of online, classroom, and self-study resources.

▶ **Conferences**: Regional, state, and national conferences provide virtually limitless learning and networking opportunities. While non-members can attend conferences, SHRM members will enjoy deeply discounted prices. Be sure to visit SHRM's website to keep up to date on when and where their conferences occur.

> **CAUTION**
>
> Since membership in SHRM is individual and non-transferable, only SHRM members can avail themselves of designated member benefits. Many portions of the website, for instance, are "members only." Access by non-members is considered an ethical violation—and it may also constitute theft.

What Is HRCI?

HRCI is the modern-day version of AAI. Although closely affiliated with SHRM, technically HRCI and SHRM are two separate organizations. HRCI is responsible for certifying—and recertifying—individuals seeking professional certification in the field of HR.

The number of individuals attaining certification in the HR profession has increased dramatically, particularly during the last five years. HRCI offers three different certification exams: PHR, SPHR, and GPHR (Global Professional in Human Resources). Later in this chapter, we'll give you information and suggestions to help you decide which—if any—of these certifications might be appropriate for you.

Why Is Certification Important?

Successfully passing an HRCI certification exam (and thereby becoming certified) constitutes a significant personal and professional accomplishment. An HRCI credential speaks volumes about you to your current—and to your potential—employers.

> **NOTE**
>
> More and more organizations are beginning to indicate a strong preference in job postings and advertisements for HRCI certification, particularly the PHR or SPHR designations. Earning this credential, therefore, can enhance your appeal to potential employers, while at the same time increasing your value to your current employer.

Certification affirms that

▶ You have, at minimum, two years of exempt-level HR work experience.

▶ You are committed to your profession, to your professional development, and to your career.

▶ You have demonstrated mastery of the HR body of knowledge, and how that body of knowledge is applied in the workplace.

▶ You've demonstrated your commitment to maintaining currency in our ever-changing profession through the recertification process, in which you'll participate every three years.

NOTE

HRCI requires certified professionals to "recertify" every three years. More information on recertification is available on the HRCI website.

Should I Go for Certification Now?

There is no doubt that HRCI certification has value. This alone, however, doesn't automatically mean that taking the PHR exam at this time is the best option for you. There are any number of reasons you may choose to wait until a different time to seek certification. On a practical level, perhaps you don't have the required HR exempt-level experience, and therefore don't meet HRCI's minimum qualifications. Or, perhaps you simply don't have sufficient time right now to prepare adequately to take the exam. Taking the test—and preparing to take it—also requires commitment of financial resources, which may not be realistic for you at this time.

Another consideration worth thinking about is this: Test-taking requires risk-taking. If you take the test, you are opening yourself up to the possibility that you will pass the test and earn an HRCI credential. You are also, however, opening yourself up to the possibility that you may *not* pass the test and may *not* earn an HRCI credential—*at this time*. Before you commit to taking the test, be sure that is an outcome you would be prepared to accept.

CAUTION

Becoming a "certified HR professional" through HRCI is completely different from earning an "HR certificate," and it's critical to understand the difference between the two.

The only way to become a certified HR professional is to successfully pass the PHR exam or the SPHR exam. Completing a prep course of any type does not equate to passing the test, or to earning HR certification. In addition to being the only way you can become certified, passing the test is the only way you earn the right to use the "PHR" or "SPHR" designation after your name.

Gaps in Employment—Certification Can Help

Many of us, at one point or another, will experience a gap in employment. Whether your gap in employment is planned or unplanned, and whatever the reason for that gap in employment may be, you can use this "gap in your employment" to fill in a "gap in your credentials." For many, the time between jobs may present an ideal opportunity to prepare for—and take—an HRCI certification exam.

The most obvious benefit of doing this is that you will earn an HRCI credential—and that you will enjoy all of the benefits that accrue from earning that credential. There are, however, less immediately obvious benefits to earning HRCI certification during a gap in employment:

▶ *"I need to do something for myself, too."* Whatever the reason is that you're on an unplanned leave, chances are that it demands either a lot of your time or a lot of your energy. Perhaps it demands both. In circumstances like these, it can be beneficial—and even healthy—to do something for yourself. Working toward a goal may also help you to focus your attention on your own positive growth and development from time to time—regardless of whatever else is happening around you.

▶ *"What did you do while you were on leave?"* When you decide to return to the work-place, and are asked that seemingly inevitable question about what you did while you were on leave, you'll be able to respond in a professional context.

Earning an HRCI certification is an investment in yourself and an investment in your future. It validates your commitment to return to the workplace, both to you as well as to potential employers.

What Tests Does HRCI Administer, and Which One Is Right for Me?

Once you decide to work toward HRCI certification, the next step you need to take is to determine which of HRCI's certification exams is most appropriate for you to take. The following highlights the exams offered.

GPHR (Global Professional in Human Resources)

The GPHR exam, HRCI's newest certification offering, is designed for HR professionals whose work has a decidedly global focus. Typical job responsibilities for GPHR candidates might include developing and implementing global strategy, overseeing international assignments, or managing an overseas HR operation. If your responsibilities don't include these sorts of functions, this GPHR exam probably is not for you. If your role does have an

27

What Tests Does HRCI Administer, and Which One Is Right for Me?

international focus, you might want to consider the GPHR exam, as well as either the PHR or SPHR exams.

PHR and SPHR Exams—The Similarities

The PHR and SPHR exams share a number of common characteristics. First, both tests focus on the same six functional areas:

▶ **Strategic Management**: Strategic HR management speaks to HR's overall commitment, in both word and deed, to meeting the ever-evolving short-term, long-term, and strategic objectives of the organization.

▶ **Workforce Planning and Employment**: Workforce planning and employment speaks to HR's responsibility to ensure integrated, seamless, and effective recruitment, hiring, orientation, and exit processes that support the short-term, long-term, emerging, and strategic objectives of the organization.

▶ **Human Resource Development**: Human resource development employs effective training, development, change management, and performance management functions and initiatives to ensure that the skills, knowledge, abilities, and performance of the workforce will meet the short-term, long-term, emerging, and strategic objectives of the organization.

▶ **Compensation and Benefits**: Compensation and benefits speaks to HR's responsibility to ensure that an organization's total compensation and benefits programs, policies, and practices support the short-term, long-term, emerging and strategic objectives of the organization.

▶ **Employee and Labor Relations**: Employee and labor relations encompass every dimension of relationships at the workplace, with the overall objective of balancing employee's rights with the employer's need to attain short-term, long-term, emerging, and strategic objectives.

▶ **Occupational Health, Safety, and Security**: Occupational health, safety, and security promotes employees' physical and mental well-being while maintaining a safe and non-violent work environment, all in support of the employer's short-term, long-term, emerging, and strategic objectives.

Other similarities exist between the PHR and SPHR. They

▶ Both require two years of exempt-level HR experience

▶ Both are taken in testing centers

▶ Both constitute valuable, well-respected credentials that speak to your knowledge and skill as an HR professional

▶ Both will garner respect from your current employer

▶ Both represent an increasingly important "preferred" credential by many potential employers

PHR and SPHR Exams—The Differences

There are a number of key distinctions between the PHR and SPHR exams:

▶ **Relative Weights of Functional Areas**: One of the most important differences between the two exams is the relative emphasis that each exam places on the six previously listed functional areas (and, consequently, the number of questions that are asked about each of these areas). Table 1.1 highlights these differences.

TABLE 1.1   Relative Weight of Functional Areas for the PHR and SPHR

Functional Area	PHR	SPHR
Strategic Management	12%	26%
Workforce Planning and Employment	26%	16%
Human Resource Development	15%	13%
Compensation and Benefits	20%	16%
Employee and Labor Relations	21%	24%
Occupational Health, Safety, and Security	6%	5%

Since the SPHR exam places a significantly stronger emphasis on the more strategic areas of HR, those test-takers with less experience or who have been siloed in one particular discipline of HR should consider taking the PHR exam, instead.

EXAM ALERT

No amount of study can replace practical experience. Even if you take a course, engage in self-study, join a study group, and complete every practice PHR exam that has ever been written, taking either of these exams without sufficient experience is strongly discouraged.

▶ **Focus on Management Practices**: Approximately one fourth of the SPHR exam questions relate in some way to sound general management practices and principles. Candidates who lack hands-on management experience may find the SPHR exam more difficult in this way as well, in addition to the more strategic emphasis that results from the relative weight placed on each functional area.

PHR and SPHR Candidates—The Differences

You've explored how the PHR and SPHR exams are different. Now, let's take a look at some of the key distinctions between the people who take those exams. Table 1.2 highlights some of the more important differences.

TABLE 1.2   Key Differences Between PHR and SPHR Candidates

Difference	Explanation
Length of Experience	HRCI recommends that PHR candidates should ideally have four years exempt level HR experience, and that SPHR candidates have should ideally have eight years of exempt level HR experience.
Breadth of Experience	PHR candidates are more likely to have experience in only one or two HR disciplines, whereas SPHR candidates are more likely to have held positions in a variety of HR disciplines. SPHR candidates are also more likely to have served in a generalist capacity.
Depth of Experience	PHR candidates are more likely to hold jobs that requires a more tactical/"hands on" approach, while SPHR candidates' jobs are more likely to have a more strategic focus.
Level of Responsibility	PHR candidates are more likely to hold positions that are at a "lower level" in the HR departmental hierarchy, while SPHR candidates are more likely to have greater overall responsibility and accountability within HR and throughout the organization.
Sphere of Impact	PHR candidates are more likely to hold positions that allow them to have an impact within the HR function and on the overall performance of the HR department, while SPHR candidates are more likely to hold jobs that enable them to have greater organization-wide impact.

PHR or SPHR—Which Should You Take?

Deciding whether to take the PHR or the SPHR should be just that—a *conscious* decision. Like any decision, it needs to be made carefully, logically, and unemotionally. The following sections will help you in determining which exam is best for you.

Factors to Consider As You Make This Decision

As you go through the decision-making process, there are many things to keep in mind. For instance, be cognizant of whom you allow to influence your decision. For instance, be careful not to allow the decisions of others who are opting for the PHR or SPHR to have an undue influence on you. Many test-takers have shied away from the SPHR because of the lack of confidence expressed by people at work, in their study groups, or in their prep classes. Similarly, many have also opted to take the SPHR because of undue—and largely irrelevant and unhelpful—peer pressure.

Although the opinions of your family and friends are important, they shouldn't be the deciding factor. It's time to do some soul searching at this point. Ask yourself some difficult questions, answer them honestly, and record your answers in writing:

▶ Have I compared myself to typical PHR and SPHR candidates? To which group am I more similar?

▶ Am I confident that I have enough exempt level HR experience, both in terms of *how much* experience I have, and also in terms of the *relative value* of that experience?

▶ Is my experience diverse? Have I been "siloed" in one or two particular HR disciplines, or have I had exposure to other areas of HR, as well?

▶ Do I have exposure to different HR philosophies, approaches, and practices, or am I only familiar with the philosophies, approaches, and practices of my own organization?

▶ Am I confident that my organization employs "best practices," and have I had a chance to implement those?

▶ Have I sought the advice of a trusted mentor, or an objective "outsider"? What did that person suggest in terms of HRCI certification?

▶ Have I allowed my decision-making process to be overly, or inappropriately, influenced by those around me?

▶ Have I allowed my desire to "shoot for the stars" to lead me away from setting a more realistic goal for myself (such as "shooting for the basketball hoop," instead of "shooting for the stars")? In other words, do I want to take the SPHR examination simply because it exists, and because it represents the pinnacle of professional achievement with respect to HR certification?

▶ Have I explored the HRCI website and other available materials for current statistics and information on the test, and on the test-takers?

▶ With what degree of risk am I comfortable?

Add any other questions that you feel are relevant to your particular situation. Be sure to write your answers down—this will help you honestly and objectively assess where you stand as you decide whether to seek PHR or SPHR certification.

Perhaps most importantly, remember that deciding to take the PHR exam instead of the SPHR exam would not constitute a less-desirable choice. You would not be "settling." This decision would not reflect personal or professional inexperience, incompetence, or any other sort of deficiency.

You wouldn't even be saying "no" to the SPHR exam. In reality, all you'd be saying is "not right now."

Assessment Exam

It's often suggested to HRCI candidates that they may want to take an assessment exam. While there is certainly value in doing so, that value may not extend to helping you decide whether to take an HRCI certification exam, or which one to take. Why not? In short, how well you perform on the assessment test may not be an accurate indicator of how you will perform on the actual test, especially if it has been a while since you've taken an exam. Be patient with yourself, and recognize that your comfort with—and performance on—the test will increase with study, with familiarity, and with time.

In one way, test taking is similar to interviewing. Just because a candidate doesn't perform well on an interview doesn't mean that he or she isn't the best-qualified candidate for the position. So too, poor performance on an HRCI assessment test doesn't mean that you shouldn't take an HRCI certification exam, and it doesn't mean that you wouldn't pass it.

Going Forward with the PHR Exam

If, at this point, you have decided to take the SPHR exam, congratulations! You may want to also consider purchasing the *SPHR Exam Prep*. The SPHR version was designed specifically with the SPHR candidate in mind, and reflects the more strategic and policy-level focus of the SPHR.

If, on the other hand, you have decided to take the PHR exam, congratulations! You've engaged in one of the most challenging activities of all—self-scrutiny. You haven't allowed your desire to attain the "highest" level of recognition offered in our profession to misdirect you from seeking what may constitute a more appropriate choice.

As a PHR candidate, you'll find this book will assist you in preparing for the exam by helping you to identify those areas where you are strong, and those areas in which you need more preparation. It will also provide you with a series of suggestions, tips, study tools, and ideas to increase the likelihood that you will successfully pass the PHR examination. And, perhaps most importantly, it will direct you toward other resources that will help you dig more deeply into each of the specific functional areas.

Registering for the PHR Exam

Now that you've decided to take the PHR exam, the next step is to register for it. The following sections describe eligibility requirements and timetable considerations you need to be aware of when registering.

Eligibility Requirements

U.S. PHR candidates must have at least two years of HR exempt-level experience in order to qualify to take the PHR exam, and to subsequently earn the PHR credential. Specific requirements for U.S.-based and non-U.S.-based PHR candidates can be found at www.hrci.org.

> **NOTE**
>
> What is meant by the term *HR exempt-level work experience*? The term *exempt-level* can be loosely defined as "professional level" but, in reality, there's nothing "loose" about this term. "Exempt" and "non-exempt" refer to the overtime provisions of the Fair Labor Standards Act (FLSA) and its amendments. The FLSA is an involved and complicated law, and the subject of much public and legislative debate and discussion. It's also an important part of the Compensation and Benefits portion of the PHR exam, so now is as good a time as any for you to refresh your understanding of this law. You can learn more about "exempt" and "non-exempt" status at the U.S. Department of Labor's website at www.dol.gov/elaws/flsa.htm.

> **NOTE**
>
> Special requirements also exist for students and recent graduates. If you are currently an undergraduate student, or if you have earned your bachelor's degree within the past year, please review "For Students or Recent Grads" at http://www.hrci.org/Certification/RECENT/

Timeframes to Keep in Mind

Timetables for registering for the exam, and for actually taking the exam, can be found at www.hrci.org. Applications for the PHR exam can be completed online or submitted on paper.

> **CAUTION**
>
> Whether you are applying online or by paper, be sure to provide all of the requested information, particularly relative to documenting your exempt work experience. Failure to do so can result in being ruled ineligible to take the exam—and determinations of ineligibility are final.

What to Expect the Day of Your Test

In "the old days," the PHR exam was administered at a particular time, on a particular day, in a particular place. Today, however, the PHR exam is administered in a computerized format, during particular time frames (up to two months long) at hundreds of possible test sites. This gives you a lot more flexibility relative to when and where you take the PHR exam.

The Test Centers

PHR testing is conducted at Thomson Prometric test sites, located in all 50 states and throughout the world. Currently, there are more than 250 test sites conveniently located throughout the U.S., U.S. territories, and Canada.

> **CAUTION**
>
> Thomson Prometric testing centers provide testing services for organizations ranging from A (Air Conditioners Contractors of America) to Z (Zimmer, an orthopedics company). To allow yourself maximum choice and flexibility with respect to the time, date, and place of your test, be sure to schedule your exam as early as possible.

First and foremost, be sure you bring a government-issued signature-bearing photo ID with you. Just as importantly, make sure you bring the Authorization to Test (ATT) letter you received after your eligibility to take the PHR test was reviewed and approved by the Professional Examination Service (PES), HRCI's testing vendor. Also, be sure to arrive at least half an hour before you are scheduled to begin your test.

The more you know about what to expect once you arrive at the test center, the more comfortable you'll be once you actually get there. Check out www.prometric.com to take a virtual tour of a test site, and to see a list of frequently asked questions, and their answers.

What Happens After You Complete the Exam?

One of the best things about taking the PHR exam at a computerized Thomson Prometric testing center is that you'll know whether you passed the test before you leave the center.

No more running to the mailbox to see if that long awaited letter arrived…and no more wondering (and worrying?) for up to six weeks. You'll have your answer immediately.

The minimum possible score on the PHR exam is 100 and the maximum possible score is 700. The passing score is 500, based on a scaled score.

"What If I Don't Pass the Exam?"

Okay, it's not a positive thought—but it happens. And it happens a lot. And it can even happen to you. Test-taking requires risk-taking, and failing the test is a possibility.

Realistically, it's important to keep in mind that a considerable number of individuals don't pass the PHR exam. According to HRCI, approximately one third of the individuals who take the PHR exam don't pass it. After all, if it were that easy to earn the PHR credential, it wouldn't be nearly as valuable.

There is no shame in not passing the PHR exam. More importantly, not passing the exam does not in any way preclude you from taking it again. There's always the second time around. It could just turn out that the knowledge, insight, and experience you gain from taking the exam the first time could equip you to pass the test the next time around.

Chapter Summary

In this chapter, you learned about HR as a profession. You also learned about two important organizations that exist to support our profession, and the importance of becoming a certified HR professional.

You also reviewed information that helped you determine whether this is the right time for you to take an HR certification exam. If it is, you reviewed information that helped you decide which test is right for you. Lastly, you were provided with information that will assist you with registering for the exam, and detailed information about what will happen the day of your exam.

Key Terms List

▶ ASPA

▶ SHRM

▶ PHR

▶ SPHR

▶ HRCI

▶ Strategic Management

▶ Workforce Planning and Employment

▶ Human Resource Development

▶ Compensation and Benefits

▶ Employee and Labor Relations

▶ Occupational Health, Safety and Security

▶ PES

CHAPTER TWO

HR: A Body of Underlying Knowledge and Principles

Study Strategies

This chapter explores each of the 19 core areas of knowledge. Knowing each area is important, as is knowing how the areas relate to each other, and to the six functional areas of HR knowledge identified by HRCI.

▶ Create 19 large index cards (for instance, 8-1/2 by 5-1/2) and write down key notes about each of these functional areas. Ensure that your notes are general enough that they describe or define the core area of knowledge in a way that does not limit it to one or two specific functional areas.

▶ As you review each functional area, create a list of the ways in which each of the core areas of knowledge (as appropriate) applies to that area.

Introduction

As discussed in chapter 1, HRCI has identified and classified the HR body of knowledge, which consists of the following six functional areas:

- ▶ Strategic management

- ▶ Workforce planning and employment

- ▶ HR development

- ▶ Compensation and benefits

- ▶ Employee and labor relations

- ▶ Occupational health, safety, and security

Underlying these six functional areas are 19 areas of core knowledge that HRCI has identified as essential for all HR professionals. These core areas of knowledge have relevance, application, and impact across all six functional areas within HR. Possessing knowledge in each of these areas is mandatory for successful performance on the PHR exam. More importantly, being able to readily recall that knowledge and apply it to a seemingly unlimited variety of workplace situations is foundational to being an effective HR professional.

While our profession consists of countless critical areas of responsibility, we cannot simply break our function down into a list of tasks and duties. Nor can we limit ourselves to memorizing definitions, models, or fact patterns and outcomes of relevant legal cases. Instead, we must establish a backdrop...an infrastructure, in one sense, within which we can knowledgeably approach the intricacies of our multifaceted profession.

This chapter will provide a brief overview of each of the core areas of knowledge. While this chapter will not provide you with all of the information you will need as you prepare to take the PHR exam, it will help you identify those areas in which you need additional preparation and study. More importantly, this chapter will encourage you to approach the HR profession with a more holistic and integrated perspective.

Each of these knowledge areas will be addressed to varying degrees in subsequent chapters. At this point in your PHR test preparation process, however, use this introduction as a way of framing out and making connections between the six functional HR areas.

Needs Assessment and Analysis

"Needs assessment and analysis" is the first step in "ADDIE," a process model often used in the area of instructional design. "ADDIE" is actually an acronym that stands for

- ▶ A: Needs *Assessment/Analysis* (cited differently in different sources)

- ▶ D: *Design*

- ▶ D: *Development*

- ▶ I: *Implementation*

- ▶ E: *Evaluation*

We're going to take a much closer look at ADDIE in Chapter 5, "HR Development," but for now, let's just address the idea of needs assessment and analysis. Needs assessment and analysis is a way of defining problems. Taking this a step further, a "problem" could be defined as the difference between a situation or condition as it currently is compared to what that situation or condition should be.

Ask Questions and Listen to the Answers

Managers—and even other HR professionals—may come to you with definite ideas of how to resolve a particular problem. When this happens, pause, ask questions, and—above all—listen. It's critical at this point to collaboratively identify the actual—rather than the perceived—problem, and to ascertain the underlying causes of that problem. Therein lies a difference between "assessment" (identifying the problem) and "analysis" (identifying the causes of that problem). Skipping either of those steps is likely to impact the effectiveness of the remaining steps in ADDIE process.

> **CAUTION**
>
> Solutions that are predicated on faulty needs analysis and assessment are, by definition, likely to be faulty, as well.

Third-Party Contract Management

More and more organizations are deciding to have certain services performed by individuals or entities that are external to the organization, rather than by employees. Welcome to the ever-expanding world of "third-party" contracts.

Third-party relationships are no longer a "phenomenon"; rather, they are progressively becoming a standard—and even expected—way of conducting business. Some services that are outsourced represent new initiatives or projects. At other times, work that is currently being performed by employees is outsourced to individuals or entities outside the organization.

Functions Often Outsourced

Different organizations may choose to outsource different functions. Many (and some people would argue "any") functions within an organization can be outsourced.

Many HR departments outsource significant functions, as well. Some of the HR functions that are often partially—or fully—outsourced include

- 401(k) or 403(b) programs
- Pensions/benefits

- ▶ Stock option administration
- ▶ Health benefits
- ▶ Learning and development
- ▶ Payroll
- ▶ Safety and security

Strategic Outsourcing

Decisions about outsourcing should be made within a broader strategic context. This context should extend beyond those considerations that relate specifically to the HR function that is being considered for outsourcing. Instead, that function must be looked at from a more holistic perspective that encompasses the entire HR function—as well as the organization as a whole. For instance, before outsourcing the training function, an organization should weigh many factors, just one of which would be "perceived credibility":

- ▶ **Possible Disadvantage to Outsourcing**: Would an outside trainer be perceived as having diminished credibility, since he or she does not have prior experience within the organization?
- ▶ **Possible Advantage to Outsourcing**: Would an outside trainer be perceived as having added credibility, since he or she is less subject to organizational dictates? In other words, since "no one is a prophet in his or her own town," could an outsider be more highly valued for his or her untainted "perspective"?

Request for Proposal (RFP)

The RFP ("Request for Proposal") is a written document that invites contractors to propose written solutions that address the organization's needs—all within a price that the customer is willing to pay. Developing a solid and carefully constructed RFP is critical; a poorly designed or overly vague RFP may yield proposed solutions that do not address the organization's actual problems. Worse yet, those solutions may appear to be workable and appropriate—until they have been implemented.

Communication Strategies

In the course of performing our jobs, HR professionals need to possess and demonstrate a wide variety of skills and abilities—analytical, problem solving, decision making, interpersonal, intrapersonal, conflict resolution—just to name a few. Underscoring all of these is the ability to communicate effectively and strategically. Once again, this concept spans all six areas of HR. Doing our jobs well just isn't enough—we have to ensure that the work that we do is appropriately communicated to, and understood by, the people we serve. For instance, we might design a compensation program that is designed to "lead the market" (see Chapter 6, "Compensation and Benefits," for more information on what this means). We might accomplish that posture by establishing competitive base pay rates, along with an incentive program that is—potentially—very lucrative for employees who meet or exceed certain goals. If we don't communicate with managers and employees about how we designed the program, however, and about how the incentive program really puts us ahead of our labor market competitors in terms of compensation, the impact and power of our design might be unappreciated or, even worse, misunderstood.

One way to look at this is to consider the five "Ws" and one "H" questions that news reporters seek to answer:

▶ **Why communicate**: First, think about why you are communicating this message. If you don't clearly convey a reason for the message, others within the organization will undoubtedly ascribe a reason. Not surprisingly, that reason will not always be accurate or positive.

▶ **What to communicate**: Balancing employees' "need to know" (and some would say "right to know") against the organization's legal and/or ethical obligations relative to the dissemination of information presents a delicate and precarious situation. If you find yourself in a situation like this (and it is likely that—sooner or later—you will), be truthful. Lies or half-truths will always surface. And, once lost, credibility can rarely be regained. Even then, it must be earned—a slow and costly process. Sometimes, telling the truth means that you can't reveal every detail of every situation—and that you might need to acknowledge this.

CAUTION

Confidential information is just that—confidential! This may especially true if you have "friends" within the organization who may come to you looking for confidential information. Reminding employees (regardless of the nature of your personal relationship with them) of your commitment to maintaining confidentiality is part of truth telling, as well.

▶ **When to communicate**: Timing may not be "everything" when it comes to communication, but it is critically important. First, consider the content of the message you will be communicating. How much urgency is there for communicating the message? Is there a benefit to waiting? Think about other considerations, as well. In a micro sense, be aware of the day of the week and the time of the day when you choose to communicate a message. In a macro sense, consider what's going on in the organization, in the industry, in society, and even in the world before you share critical information.

▶ **Where to communicate**: Think about where you want people to be when they receive the message: Attending a face-to-face meeting, which is largely presentation-driven? Or, participating from a satellite location in teleconference that permits questions and answers? Or, alone, behind their computers, reading an email?

▶ **Who will communicate, and to whom**: Sometimes HR professionals prepare messages that they will communicate directly. At other times, HR professionals will collaborate with managers to put together a particular message that the managers will deliver personally. Or, HR professionals deliver messages that—in some form or fashion—others have created for us. And of course, there are times when we "ghost write" information that someone else will actually communicate.

There's no one right answer for any situation, so think through the "cast of characters"—those who will construct the message, deliver the message, and receive the message—thoroughly and carefully.

▶ **How to communicate**: It's not enough to rely upon one method of communication. Identify multiple ways to communicate important messages. There are different media available to you—in-person, print, electronic mail, teleconference, and live streaming video, to name just a few.

"How to communicate" addresses another important consideration: the directional flow of communication. Are methods in place within the organization to ensure that information can flow up, as well as down? Can individuals across difference units or divisions of the organization communicate with each other? And are meaningful feedback mechanisms in place to enable you to accurately gauge the impact and effectiveness of your communication efforts?

"I'm a People Person"

The answers to the questions "why, where, when, who, and how" can communicate just as powerfully as "what" the message is. HR professionals must be keenly aware not only of what they communicate, but that "how" one communicates, by itself, constitutes another level of communication. You must be keenly aware of the nuance of these underlying messages and approach them in a strategic manner.

This approach constitutes a significant departure from the stereotypical image of the HR professional as a "people person." That image evokes, in part, the idea of a "touchy feely" person, a shoulder to cry on.

In reality, there is nothing "soft" or "natural" about communicating in one's role as an HR professional, and there is much justification for HRCI to identify it as a core area of knowledge. With respect to the ways in which you communicate as an HR professional, you must be "an ear to listen," not "a shoulder to cry on."

Documentation Requirements

Within an organization, maintaining documentation is dreaded my many, enjoyed by few, and viewed suspiciously by others. HR's role in maintaining legal and effective documentation is particularly pivotal.

Some documentation basics that HR professionals need to think about include

▶ **Knowing what needs to be documented**: This includes federal, state, and local requirements—as well as documentation mandated by collective bargaining agreements, employment contracts, and/or performance management programs.

▶ **Knowing how to document**: Many forms must be completed in accordance with specific, detailed, and mandatory guidelines. Those specific requirements can also impact the ways in which documents are maintained, stored, retrieved, and distributed.

▶ **Knowing what not to document**: Documentation takes two main forms—*documentation that pertains to collecting and maintaining legally mandated record keeping*, and *documentation that pertains to performance management*. For purposes of the core areas of knowledge, this discussion will focus on the first type of documentation.

CAUTION

There's an old joke that goes something like this:

Question: "What's the difference between true love and employment litigation?"

Answer: "Employment litigation is forever."

In truth, there is nothing funny about employment litigation. However, there's a valuable reminder that can be taken away from this joke—any documentation you create, in any form, is—for all intents and purposes—forever subject to subpoena. This is particularly true for electronic communications—emails and even instant messages. Our most contemporary communications are, in some ways, even more permanent than stone tablets of ages gone by—so be extremely prudent and careful about the documentation you maintain. You may one day have the opportunity to review it again—in a courtroom, in front of a jury.

Adult Learning Processes

Two realities: First, organizations continually change and evolve, thereby demanding more and different things from the people they employ. Second, those employees must be willing and able to learn new skills in order to perform their expanding roles in a fully proficient manner. With respect to an employee's performance within the organization, maintaining one's current level of performance often equates to stagnation, or even degradation.

This is true for employees who wish to grow into higher-level positions within the organization, as well as for employees who wish to continue successfully performing in their current

positions. Even the "Steady Eddies" and "Steady Bettys" within orga
they must learn and grow within their jobs in order to keep them. Few i
they are performing their current job in the same way they performed i
ago. During those years much has been learned, and most likely more wi
remain employed with the organization. This will require the organization
learners and the realities of teaching adults new skills.

Adults learn very differently, however, from children (see Chapter 5, "HR Development"). HR professionals must understand these differences and incorporate them into the instructional design of training programs the organization is offering. Training, like documentation and so many other areas of core knowledge, is more than just a function. It will have a tremendous impact on how you are perceived, and how your role—both individually and as a member of HR—is defined within the organization. Treat a roomful of employees or managers like children and you'll have a captive audience—but not in a good sense. They'll be looking for ways to duck out early for breaks, surreptitiously answer emails on a handheld wireless device under the table, or—worse yet—just leave and not return. Training provides an opportunity to partner. Be cautious to guard against unintentionally patronizing. Training can help define you as an inspiring and motivating facilitator, or it can reinforce negative adage that "those who can't do, teach."

Motivation Concepts and Applications

Motivation cuts across all six functional areas. Motivation, for instance, is often associated with why—and how—employees learn. It's also highly relevant, however, to how employees perceive and value salaries, wages, and benefits, and to establishing and sustaining positive relationships in the workplace.

Motivation theory directly impacts employee performance in the workplace. As such, HR professionals need a keen understanding of the various motivation theories in order to incorporate them—in a practical sense—into their initiatives and into their consulting relationships with managers. Some of the key theories in which HR professionals must be well versed are

- ▶ Maslow's Hierarchy of Needs
- ▶ B.F. Skinner—Operant Conditioning
- ▶ Frederick Herzberg—Motivation-Hygiene Theory
- ▶ Douglas McGregor—Theory X and Theory Y
- ▶ David McClelland—Acquired Needs Theory
- ▶ J. Stacy Adams—Equity Theory
- ▶ Victor Vroom—Expectancy Theory

following subsections will describe each of these theories in order to help you build your knowledge of these critical theories.

Maslow's Hierarchy of Needs—1954

Maslow's theory presents five levels of need experienced by humans. People move from fundamental to higher levels of need as lower levels of need are sufficiently satisfied. Those levels, from most basic to most evolved, are

▶ **Basic physical needs**: Basic physical needs include food, water, shelter, acceptable working conditions, and other fundamental, foundational needs.

▶ **Safety and security**: Safety and security needs speak to the need to live and work in an environment that feels—and is—safe.

▶ **Belonging and love**: In the workplace, this need can manifest itself through membership in a department, a profession, a division, clubs, affinity groups, or simply through friendships and relationships.

▶ **Esteem**: Esteem manifests in two dimensions: *self* and *others*. Self-esteem refers to valuing one's own self, personally and/or professionally. Esteem from others relates to receiving recognition and approval from others.

▶ **Self-actualization**: Through self-actualization, individuals want to, and strive to, reach their full potential. Self-actualization may be its own reward.

Maslow at Work

HR professionals need to look for creative ways to address the motivational needs identified by Maslow—even though employees may not be fully aware of them.

"Addressing needs" doesn't mean trying to move everyone to the next level. It is important not to impose expectations on employees that they do not wish to embrace. It is equally important to afford workplace-appropriate opportunities for those who do.

On that note, be sure to keep all applications of Maslow's theory firmly grounded in the workplace. Link it clearly and unambiguously to performance—of the organization, the department, and the individual. Always maintain your focus on the organization's goals, and always be prepared to articulate job related reasons for motivation-based initiatives.

Lastly, as you focus on creating opportunities that enable employees to move to higher need levels, don't lose track of whether and how well employee's lower level needs are being met. A compensation system, for instance, that allows employees to meet their basic physical needs at one point in time may eventually become problematic, and fall well below what labor market competitors are paying, if insufficient attention is paid to appropriate range movement, merit budgets, and the like.

B.F. Skinner, Operant Conditioning—1957

B.F. Skinner's theory of operant conditioning assumes that the ways people choose to behave in the future are a function of the consequences that have resulted from their past behavior. Skinner identifies four different types of consequences:

▶ **Positive Reinforcement**: Demonstrating desired behavior results in a desirable outcome or consequence. This may encourage the individual to choose to engage in desired behaviors again.

   Workplace example: A customer service supervisor observes as a customer service representative skillfully resolve a complaint from an irate customer, and immediately praises that person for successfully defusing a potentially volatile situation.

▶ **Negative Reinforcement (or "avoidance")**: When an individual believes that specific behaviors will result in a specific undesirable outcome or consequence, he or she may choose not to demonstrate that undesired behavior again.

   Workplace example: An employee decides not to use his or her company's email system for jokes and/or other correspondence that could be viewed as inappropriate for the workplace, so as not to violate the company's recently distributed policies—and thereby risk being written up or terminated.

▶ **Punishment**: Demonstrating undesired behavior results in an undesirable outcome or consequence. This may encourage the individual to choose not to engage in that undesired behavior again.

   Workplace example: An employee who continues to answer incoming personal cell phone calls during a training session even after being asked to stop is asked to leave the training session, and is not permitted to register for a "make up" program for at least three months.

▶ **Extinction**: An individual's behavior—whether desired or undesired elicits *no* outcomes or consequences at all. The individual may choose not to demonstrate that behavior again.

   Workplace example: An employee persists in trying to engage co-workers in counterproductive conversations about other co-workers ("gossip"). If the co-workers do not join in, the employee might choose not to initiate these sorts of conversations again.

Frederick Herzberg, Motivation-Hygiene Theory— 1959

Herzberg identified two separate and distinct types of needs:

▶ **Motivation Factors**: Motivation factors relate specifically to the job itself—for instance, the nature of the work, the challenge inherent to the work, the perceived or real value of the work.

▶ **Hygiene Factors**: Hygiene factors relate to everything else an employee might experience in the workplace…everything associated *with* the work, but *not the work itself*. This includes—but is not limited to—pay, benefits, nature of supervision, relationships with co-workers, and so forth.

Dubbed "The Father of Job Enrichment," Herzberg distinguished between factors that can generate positive feelings about work (the motivation factors) and factors that can result in negative feelings about work (hygiene factors). So, while unacceptable motivation factors won't cause an employee to be unhappy at work, unacceptable hygiene factors could. Conversely, acceptable or positive motivation factors will cause an employee to be happy at work, but acceptable or positive hygiene factors won't. However, motivation factors will have a positive impact on an employee's motivation level *if, and only if*, hygiene factors are acceptable.

Herzberg's theory challenged employers—and "personnel" departments—to look at employees' satisfaction at work in a completely new and different way. No longer was "job satisfaction" viewed as existing along a single continuum. Herzberg newly defined it as a function of two related, but wholly different, factors—both of which warranted attention.

Douglas McGregor, Theory X and Theory Y—1960

Building on Maslow's work, Theory X and Theory Y refers to two different approaches to management:

▶ Theory X managers manage in accordance with the general belief that employees are uncommitted, uninterested, hesitant to assume any additional responsibility, and essentially lazy.

▶ Theory Y managers manage in accordance with the general belief that employees will take on—and even look for—additional work if the employee perceives that the work is satisfying and rewarding.

David McClelland, Acquired Needs

McClelland's theory identified and focused on one particular nee
McClelland, achievement is not a universal motivator for everyc
varies from individual to individual.

Individuals who experience—or, perhaps more appropriately, posses
ment are neither risk-averse nor risk-lovers. More frequently, they tak   .ue road"
approach when it comes to risk—calculated, and conscious. Those mo   _u by the need for
achievement, therefore, will assume a level of risk that allows the opportunity for upside potential, confident all the while that their skills, abilities, and contributions will have the greatest
impact in determining the outcome of a situation. Interestingly, individuals with a high
achievement need are less concerned with the rewards of achievement than they are with the
actual attainment of that achievement.

With respect to performance management, individuals who have a high need for achievement
may gravitate toward "stretch goals," to be explored further in Chapter 5, "HR Development."
They would also be more likely to focus on the "goals" portion of a performance management
system or form than the "competencies" portion.

J. Stacy Adams, Equity Theory—1963

Equity theory, as the name implies, is predicated on the assumption that people want to be
treated fairly, particularly when compared to how others around them are treated. Such comparisons will be made frequently.

In the context of employment, equity theory asserts that employees will compare their "inputs"
(everything they bring to the job and invest in the job) and "outputs" (how they are rewarded—
both intrinsically and extrinsically—for what they invest in the job) to others' inputs and outputs. If employees come away from this process feeling as though they are being treated fairly
in comparison to others, they will continue to put forth effort. Conversely, employees who
come away from this process with the belief that they are being treated unfairly will seek to
make a change. That change might include trying to change their own inputs, trying to change
their own outputs, or trying to change the inputs or outputs of others. Any of these efforts could
manifest themselves in either productive or unproductive ways. Alternatively, of course, that
same employee could quit—the most dramatic way that an employee can change inputs.

Victor Vroom, Expectancy Theory—1964

Vroom's expectancy theory is all about weighing options and making choices. It asserts, in
essence, that people will put forth effort when they believe that it will result in an outcome,
and that that outcome is worthwhile. This theory is comprised of three key elements and
resulting questions that individuals (in this case, employees) ask themselves:

ancy: "How likely is it that I'll be able to attain a particular goal (in this case, a tain level of performance) if I put forth the required effort?"

▸ **Instrumentality**: "Assuming that I do attain this level of performance, how likely it is that I'll be recognized or rewarded in some way?"

▸ **Valence**: "Assuming that I am recognized or rewarded, what is that recognition or reward really worth to me?"

Training Methods

HR professionals, in collaboration with the clients within the organizations we serve, can choose from many training approaches (see Chapter 5, "HR Development"). Having familiarity with as many of these methods as possible will enable the HR professional to develop a training solution that is most appropriate for each unique problem, while taking into account individual, departmental, and organizational considerations.

TIP

Not every situation requires a training solution. However, HR professionals (particularly those with a background in learning and development) often default to a training solution before exploring all possible options. It's critical for HR professionals to develop a solution that addresses each particular problem, not a solution that seems most readily available or most closely matches one's own background and skill set.

EXAM ALERT

Be prepared to identify, describe, and address case study issues regarding both active and passive training methods and techniques including (but not limited to)

Passive: Conference, lecture, presentation, and so on.

Active: Case studies, demonstrations, facilitated discussions, exercises, role play, self-paced study, and so on.

Be familiar with the advantages and disadvantages of each, as well as different situations in which each approach would be most effective.

Leadership Concepts and Applications

Developing leaders within the organization is a key objective for HR professionals, specifically for those who are involved in organization development.

Leadership is difficult to define, as many different individuals have set forth just as many different definitions. Leadership is also very different from management, although those terms are often (mis)used interchangeably. In simplest terms, leadership can be defined as the ability to encourage "followership" to attain specific objectives. Without followers, there can be no leaders. Without effective leaders, there will be no followers, and there will be no organized, implemented strategy for attaining organizational objectives.

Over time, the following four different theories have emerged on the subject of leadership, each evolving from the prior.

▶ Trait Theories

▶ Behavioral Theories

▶ Situational Leadership Theories

▶ Contingency Theories

Trait Theories

Trait theories support the idea that leaders are born, not made. Being a great leader, then, was more a function of "nature" than "nurture." It had to do with being a great person—and being born that way. Research in support of this theory, however, was neither consistent nor complete. For instance, no one set of leadership traits could be identified. Additionally, different leaders using very different approaches in different situations could all effect a successful outcome. Enter behavioral theories.

Behavioral Theories

Beginning in the 1940s, a new school of thought on leadership began to emerge: Leadership can be taught. All it would take to develop non-leaders into leaders would be a willing student who would receive proper instruction relative to essential and appropriate leadership behaviors.

Ohio State University and the University of Michigan both conducted considerable research on behavioral management theories. Their research yielded similar results by identifying two critical dimensions of leadership behavior:

▶ **Consideration (Ohio State) or Employee-Centered (University of Michigan):** Refers to the interpersonal, trust, respect, and social dimensions of leadership.

▶ **Initiating Structure (Ohio State) or Job-Related (University of Michigan):** Refers to factors related to the work itself—specifically, what employees need to do, and how they need to do it, in order to attain objectives.

As with trait theories, questions about leadership still remained unanswered by the behavioral theory approach. Situation leadership theories represented the next evolution of thought.

Situational Leadership Theories

Situational leadership theories demonstrate a greater appreciation for the complexity of the leadership role. They suggest that no single leadership approach is right for every situation. Situational leadership theories also suggest that part of being a good and effective leader is having the ability to select and utilize the most effective leadership approach for each specific situation.

The following sections will present three key situational leadership theories.

Paul Hersey and Ken Blanchard's Situational Leadership Theory

How does a leader encourage followership? According to Paul Hersey and Ken Blanchard, "it depends." Hersey and Blanchard's theory of situational leadership suggests that leaders must use different approaches, at different times, with different employees. These approaches will depend upon each employee's "maturity" and proficiency at performing specific functions. Maturity or proficiency relate to the technical skills required to perform a particular task, as well as the non-technical skills (or "behavioral competencies") required to bring a task to its successful conclusion.

Hersey and Blanchard identify four different approaches:

- **Telling**: Leaders must provide the employee with precise instruction and fairly close supervision while the employee is learning to perform the new task. Feedback must be specific and frequent.

- **Selling**: As the employee begins to develop proficiency at the new task, an effective leader will begin to provide additional background information and/or explanation relative to the nuances of the task. At this stage, the employee has moved beyond "the basics," and can function with a bit less supervision.

- **Participating**: By now, the employee has developed a certain level of skill at performing the task and can comprehend many of the underlying principles of the task. They still, however, require support, encouragement, and reinforcement. In this phase, leaders need to make the employee more aware of what they *can* do, and encourage him or her to perform the tasks in an increasingly confident, independent, and self-sufficient manner.

- **Delegating**: By now, in addition to being able to perform the technical aspects of the task, the employee also possesses the behavioral competencies required to bring the task to a successful conclusion. The leader needs to communicate the goal (ideally, after collaboratively developing it with the employee), and must allow the employee to accomplish it independently. In short, at this point, an effective leader lets go.

See Figure 2.1, which demonstrates this theory further.

BLANCHARD SITUATIONAL LEADERSHIP MODEL	
LEADER BEHAVIOR CATEGORIES	
DIRECTIVE BEHAVIOR	**SUPPORTIVE BEHAVIOR**
• One-way communication • Followers' roles spelled out • Close supervision of performance	• Two-way communication • Listening, providing support & Encouragement • Facilitate interaction • Involve follower in decision making

FIGURE 2.1 The Hersey-Blanchard Situational Leadership Model

Each of these quadrants also represents a different relationship between "task" and "relationship." As described previously, each of these considerations will be "low" or "high" depending upon the maturity and proficiency of the employee. In other words, the emphasis that a leader should place on task and relationship considerations will be different for each quadrant.

NOTE

It is important to note that—at any one point in time—the same employee can function in different quadrants for different tasks. An employee should not be "assigned" to or identified as performing in a particular quadrant. Rather, each individual task performed by the employee may fall into a different quadrant, and therefore warrant a different leadership approach.

Robert R. Blake and Jane S. Mouton's Situational Leadership Theory

Blake-Mouton's situational leadership theory depicts leadership behavior along a two-axis grid:

► Concern for people (vertical axis)

► Concern for task/production (horizontal axis)

Each axis uses a one-to-nine scale on which to chart the degree of concern that leaders demonstrate for each dimension (see Figure 2.2).

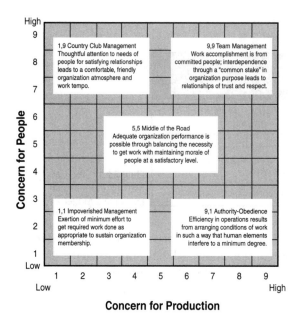

High

9

1,9 Country Club Management
Thoughtful attention to needs of people for satisfying relationships leads to a comfortable, friendly organization atmosphere and work tempo.

9,9 Team Management
Work accomplishment is from committed people; interdependence through a "common stake" in organization purpose leads to relationships of trust and respect.

5,5 Middle of the Road
Adequate organization performance is possible through balancing the necessity to get work with maintaining morale of people at a satisfactory level.

1,1 Impoverished Management
Exertion of minimum effort to get required work done as appropriate to sustain organization membership.

9,1 Authority-Obedience
Efficiency in operations results from arranging conditions of work in such a way that human elements interfere to a minimum degree.

Concern for People

Low

1   2   3   4   5   6   7   8   9

Low   High

Concern for Production

From Blake, R.R., and J.S. Mouton, The Managerial Grid. Gulf Publishing, Houston, 1964.
RMW 2/10/02

FIGURE 2.2 The Blake-Mouton Situational Leadership Model

Unlike Hersey and Blanchard's model, there is room for gradations within each of the four quadrants in this model. Looking at the extremes, however, does afford insight into the leadership style that each of the four quadrants (to one degree or another) represents:

▸ **Task managers** (nine on task, one on people) are demanding and authoritarian. They rarely, if ever, admit to being wrong. They shift blame away from themselves. They focus entirely on "what" needs to be attained, with little concern for the human dimensions that speak to "how" the task will be attained.

▸ **Team Leaders** (nine on task, nine on people) focus on attaining tasks as well as maintaining and enhancing relationships with those who will be performing those tasks.

▸ **Country Club Managers** (one on task, nine on people) are more like "cheerleaders" than "coaches." They focus almost exclusively on cultivating positive relationships with employees—within a positive work environment—and pay little if any attention to the tasks at hand. Relationships become the exclusive goal; organizational objectives become irrelevant.

▸ **Impoverished Managers** (one on task, one on people) take the "laissez faire" management style to an unproductive extreme. They delegate work (the task), and are often not seen again until there is more work to be delegated. They are "absentee leaders" in every sense—with respect to what needs to get done, who will do it, and how it will get done.

Contingency Theories

Evolving out of situational leadership theory, the fourth stage in this evolutionary process involves contingency theories, the best known of which was developed by Fred Fiedler. Like some of the earlier theories, Fiedler devised a method of ascertaining the degree to which leaders were concerned with tasks and the degree to which leaders were concerned with people. Fiedler then used that measure to determine situations in which different leaders would be most effective; or in other words, the situations that would be most favorable for specific leadership styles.

The factors that determine that level of favorableness are

- **Leader-members relations**: How strong, and how significant, are the relationships between the leader and the team members? To what degree will those relationships make the leader more, or less, effective and influential?

- **Task structure**: How structured is the work that the team members are performing?

- **Position Power**: How much power or influence does the leader's position hold, or how much can it exert? To what degree can the leader ensure accountability for performance and authority to delegate?

A leader's effectiveness will be impacted by the relative strength or weakness of these three factors. In general, the higher the factors, the more effective the leader will be.

Leadership Styles

Though leadership styles vary widely, they can be grouped into two primary categories:

- **Transactional leadership**: The transactional leadership style is characterized by the possibility of rewards and the threat of punishment. This is a "no news is good news" approach to leadership—leaders get involved when goals are not met or when employees are not adhering to stated rules.

- **Transformational leadership**: Transformational leaders are coaches, not enforcers. They model the behavior they expect the group to emulate, and they focus on relationships as well as tasks. These two concerns are not mutually exclusive; rather, they co-exist and are complementary. Both are essential, and neither is expendable.

EXAM ALERT

Be prepared to speak to the differences between "leadership" and "management," as each pertains to specific organizational roles, functions, and activities. In addition, be familiar with the differences between dictatorial (authoritarian), democratic, and laissez-fair leadership styles, and appropriate applications of each.

Project Management Concepts and Applications

In the vernacular of "project management," a project is a "special" and temporary undertaking designed to accomplish a specific goal and yield a specific output. The "management" portion of this term speaks to the overall process required for ensuring the successful accomplishment of this goal, rather than the goal itself.

Projects are usually deadline driven. Though the project timeline may be demanding, it is not uncommon for projects not to have additional resources devoted to their accomplishment.

As HR professionals, it is likely that we will undertake projects in addition to our regular responsibilities, rather than being afforded a temporary "hiatus" from those responsibilities. Balancing day-to-day workload, therefore, while working to complete a "special project" can be challenging and requires a unique skill set—one that is often separate and distinct from the skills needed to execute the project itself.

Like HR, project management is a profession. Although HR managers may not be members of this profession, we still must develop many of the unique skills associated with project management in order to successfully accomplish our objectives—which, once again, will span all six functional areas of HR. Some of those skills will include

▶ Clarifying goals

▶ Analyzing a project and developing a workable plan to complete it on time

▶ Managing the project according to the plan

▶ Ensuring that other work expectations are still met

Diversity Concepts and Applications

Diversity is a workplace issue. Diversity is also a performance issue. Creating a workplace that recognizes and values diversity is essential for organizational health, growth, and (often) survival. Diversity is sometimes confused with affirmative action or equal employment opportunities. Although it falls on the same spectrum, however, diversity is *not* the same thing.

Diversity is in no way limited to the protected classes that are identified in EEO law—categories such as gender, age, religion, national origin, sexual orientation, color, veteran status, or disability status. Diversity also reaches out to recognize differences in communication styles, thinking styles, and a wide range of other factors that make each of us, as humans, unique.

Human Relations Concepts and Applications

Workplaces are composed of people, with all of the unique attributes and foibles that humans possess. Although this may seem obvious to us today, it wasn't until the establishment of the Industrial Relations Association of America (later renamed the American Management Association) in the 1920s that any real legitimacy was granted to the study of workplaces as social—as well as economic—organizations.

This concept touches upon all six functional areas and all HR disciplines. It directly relates to the topics of motivation, productivity, and a host of other issues, and will be addressed throughout this book.

HR Ethics and Professional Standards

SHRM has developed and published standards for ethical behavior for the HR profession. The six dimensions of this code can be summarized as follows:

▶ **Professional Responsibility**: As HR professionals, we serve as more than just individual contributors to our organizations. Instead, we are representatives of and ambassadors for our profession. In that spirit, we must demonstrate personal and professional accountability for every decision we make, and for every action we take. We must behave in a manner that consistently demonstrates personal and professional credibility and creates organizational value.

▶ **Professional Development**: As HR professionals, we must commit ourselves—both formally and informally—to learning about, and contributing to, our profession's ever-expanding knowledge base. We must never allow ourselves to professionally stagnate.

▶ **Ethical Leadership**: As HR professionals, we must "walk the walk" of ethical leadership. We must always hold ourselves to the highest standards of ethical behavior and, through this, serve as role models of ethical behavior for current, emerging, and future leaders.

▶ **Fairness and Justice**: As HR professionals, we must promote fairness and ensure justice for all employees within the organizations in which we work. This commitment extends beyond adhering to specific legal mandates; rather, it encompasses the cultivation workplaces that foster dignity, respect, diversity, and inclusion.

▶ **Conflicts of Interest**: As HR professionals, we must ensure that we avoid any and all situations where a real or perceived conflict of interest could exist. This includes any situation in which we have—or in which it appears as though we could—benefit materially or financially from the positions we hold within our organizations.

▶ **Use of Information**: As HR professionals, we have an obligation to protect the proprietary organizational and personal information with which we are entrusted on a regular basis.

Technology and Human Resource Information Systems (HRIS) to Support HR Activities

An organization's HRIS (human resource information system) is both a repository of vast amounts of data and a tool for extracting, manipulating, and deriving information from that data. How that information will ultimately be used will be a function of the system itself, as well as of the individuals who are responsible for its initial implementation and ongoing maintenance.

Selecting an HRIS

Selecting an HRIS is a critical business decision that will have long-term ramifications for the business—not just for the HR department. HR issues must reflect organizational issues, so the HRIS must be designed to store, retrieve, summarize, and report information in a way that enables HR professionals to address the organization's needs.

As with any other business decision, the process of selecting an HRIS must start with conducting a needs assessment and analysis (the "A" in ADDIE). In the IT field, this step is also referred to as a *requirements assessment* or *requirement gathering*. An early step in that analysis will include identifying the functions that the HRIS will be expected to support, which could include

▶ Affirmative action reporting

▶ Applicant flow

▶ Benefits administration and enrollment

▶ Candidate database

- ▶ Compensation administration

- ▶ EEO reporting

- ▶ Payroll administration

- ▶ Skills database—employees

- ▶ Training programs administration

In addition to identifying the ways in which you plan to use an HRIS, other considerations need to be taken into account, as well. These should include, but not necessarily be limited to questions such as:

- ▶ What are the system requirements?

- ▶ What limits are, or will be, in place on the system?

- ▶ What are our key data security concerns, and how must a system address those concerns?

- ▶ How much do you anticipate your company will grow?

- ▶ What financial resources can you commit to purchasing and implementing the system?

- ▶ What human and capital resources will be required to support implementation of the system?

- ▶ What financial, human, and capital resources will be required to support and maintain the system?

- ▶ How will cutover from the existing HRIS, if any, be handled?

- ▶ How will the new system interface with other existing systems such as payroll?

- ▶ Is the system easily upgradeable?

- ▶ Is Internet-based employee self-service one of the organization's objectives?

Conducting a needs analysis is one step, and selecting an HRIS is another. A third key step is implementing the system. The most carefully selected and technologically advanced HRIS system can devolve into a nightmarish fiasco if the implementation phase of the project is underestimated, or poorly executed.

Qualitative and Quantitative Methods and Tools for Analysis, Interpretation, and Decision-Making Purposes

As stated throughout the chapter, and as is true for our profession, HR decisions are business decisions. As such, they mandate a structured and deliberate "businesslike" analysis.

An early part of any analysis is identifying the problem that needs to be solved. This is not always as easy as it seems, as symptoms often disguise themselves as problems. From there, careful data collection and data analysis is undertaken, and conclusions are drawn.

Different types of analyses can be clustered into two categories:

▶ Quantitative Analysis

▶ Qualitative Analysis

Quantitative Analysis

Numeric, mathematical models are utilized in conducting qualitative analysis. Historical data is measured and scrutinized in order to extract objective and meaningful insights. Correlation and measures of central tendency are two items of quantitative analysis you should know.

Correlation

Quantitative analysis involves measuring *correlation*. Through measurement and comparison, correlation mathematically determines whether there is a demonstrated relationship between two different factors or entities. A "positive correlation" or "negative correlation" indicates that a relationship does exist. The "correlation coefficient" is a number between –1 and +1 that defines the strength of that relationship. The closer that coefficient is to zero, the weaker the relationship between the two factors.

> **EXAM ALERT**
>
> Understand, and be able to articulate, the difference between a positive correlation and a negative correlation. In addition, become familiar with scattergrams, and be able to indicate whether a particular scattergram represents a positive correlation, a negative correlation, or no correlation.

Measures of Central Tendency

When it comes to quantitative analysis, it's important to look beyond—and even within—what we commonly think of as an "average." Three measures of central tendency with which HR professionals need to be familiar are

- ▶ **Mean**: *Mean* most closely corresponds to what people intend when they use the word "average." The mean of a set of numbers of calculated as follows:

  The total of all the values (or "numbers") in a set divided by the number of values that are in that set.

  EXAMPLE: For the set: 57, 64, 15, 37, 11, 99, 1, 1, and 19, the mean is calculated as follows:

  Total of all values in the set: (57+64+15+37+11+99+1+1+19) = 304

  Number of values in the set: 9

  Mean: 304/9 = 33.78

- ▶ **Median**: The *median* is derived by putting a set of data in numeric order, from lowest to highest, and identifying the value that is in the middle.

  EXAMPLE: For the set: 57, 64, 15, 37, 11, 99, 1, 1, and 19, the median is determined as follows:

  Values in numeric order, lowest to highest:

  1, 1, 11, 15, 19, 37, 57, 64, 99

  Median (middle value): 19

- ▶ **Mode**: The "mode" is the value that appears most frequently in a set.

  EXAMPLE: For the set: 57, 64, 15, 37, 11, 99, 1, 1, and 19, the mode is "1", as that is the value that appears most frequently.

- ▶ **Weighted Average**: Sometimes, not all factors or pieces of data that are being quantitatively analyzed are equally important. Weighted averages allow certain pieces of data to be multiplied by a particular factor to give them greater "weight," or importance.

Qualitative Analysis

Qualitative analysis does not involve mathematical modeling or calculations. It is based more on judgments that are subjective in nature.

An Added Value of Analysis

There is a place in HR for both qualitative and quantitative analysis. Rely too heavily on qualitative analysis and you may be accused of not having "facts" to back up your assumptions. Rely exclusively on quantitative analysis and you may be undervaluing the knowledge and expertise of your seasoned colleagues. Both of these approaches, when used exclusively, can damage relationships with your clients, and can also damage your professional credibility within the organization.

Each chapter in this book will identify ways in which the ability to conduct accurate and meaningful quantitative and qualitative analyses will strengthen your effectiveness as an HR professional. Once again, this is representative of the ways in which HR has evolved into a true profession, and supports the important reality that it's simply not enough to be a "people person."

Change Management

Change is inevitable—for individuals, for organizations, and for society. Change is multifaceted, complex, and often unpredictable. Its fluid nature precludes the possibility of preparing for "all possible contingencies." It impatiently demands our immediate attention and focus when it happens. Sometimes change occurs because of initiatives created within the organization, and sometimes it is foisted upon us. Change is universal and omnipresent. Change is here to stay.

There is no dimension of the six HR functional areas that can remain untouched by change, just as there is no area of the business that is immune from change. While change cannot be prevented, it can be managed—and HR plays a key role in that process. This role will be more fully developed and explored in Chapter 5.

The Winds of Change Can Also Be the Wind Beneath Your Wings

Change is neither inherently good nor inherently bad. The way in which an organization handles change will, however, produce outcomes that *will* ultimately be viewed as positive or negative.

HR must *seek* out opportunities to play a proactive and integral role before, during, and after times of abundant change. Such an approach will require HR professionals to muster all the skills in their repertoire—particularly employee relations skills, analytical skills, and communication skills. The demands of such a response represent a valuable long-term investment: In addition to playing a significant role during the change that is currently evolving, HR professionals can also use this experience to bolster relationships throughout the organization. Demonstrate your ability to interact in a manner that is consultative, rather than directive. In short, times of change afford you the opportunity to make a choice: Will you function in a manner that is transactional? Strategic? Ideally, you will be able to navigate yourself to a carefully balanced combination of both. The choice is yours—so choose consciously.

Liability and Risk Management

Proactively identifying and preventing costly legal actions is a practice known as *risk management*. Let's start by looking at the potential scope of liability and risk management so that we can begin to develop an appreciation of the unique role that HR professionals can play with respect to risk management.

Organizations face potential exposure in many different employment-related areas—allegations can be made relative to sexual harassment, wrongful discharge, unlawful discrimination, or negligent hiring and retention, just to name a few.

Legal actions stemming from employment-related issues cost organizations untold dollars in attorneys' fees, court fees, settlements, and judgments. These monetary costs do not even begin to recognize other costs that are far more difficult to calculate—costs resulting from diminished employee morale, decreased productivity, dedication of internal resources, and perhaps even the organizations' reputation as a labor market competitor, vendor, or community member.

HR professionals are uniquely positioned to anticipate, identify, and intervene before problems become "cases." Look for areas of potential exposure. In our roles, we see more, hear more, and know more about situations that have the potential to escalate. De-escalation of potentially litigious situations constitutes one of the most valuable contributions that HR professionals can make to their organizations.

TIP

When it comes to litigation, even if you win, you lose.

Look for areas of potential exposure. Use all your skills and knowledge to find them. Then, build on the collaborative relationships you have developed with managers to work through these challenges.

NOTE

Don't "just say no." Employment-related decisions are business decisions. This holds true even for those decisions that can potentially have legal ramifications. Depending on the culture of your organization, decisions are frequently "owned" by the individuals who make them—not by HR. Saying "no" may undermine your effectiveness, and even your credibility, if your "no" is ultimately overruled. Treat this situation as you would any other business decision, and utilize your best consultative skills.

Job Analysis and Job Description Methods

Like every other core area of knowledge, conducting a job analysis and creating job descriptions are functions that impact every dimension of the six functional areas of HR. Job analysis, for instance, generates job specifications, which relate directly to the skills, knowledge, and abilities that are required for successful performance of the position. This contributes directly to determining the qualifications that must be assessed for each candidate during the recruiting process ("Workplace Planning and Employment"). Job analysis also provides information that will be used to determine appropriate compensation for each position and each person ("Compensation and Benefits"). Job analysis may also identify chemicals to which the employee will be exposed at work, which in turn triggers the need for MSDS (Material Data Safety Sheets) ("Occupational Health, Safety, and Security"). Similar links could be made to the three other functional areas of HR, as well.

Job Analysis

Job analysis is the process by which an inventory of data about a position is collected. The elements that comprise each job in the organization are identified through this process. These elements often include

- ► Responsibilities, duties, and tasks performed by the position incumbent.

- ► How those responsibilities, duties, and tasks relate to each other and to other jobs within the organization. This includes how frequently each of those activities is performed, as well as how activities relate to each other in terms of importance.

Job analysis also identifies the KSAs required for successful performance of the position:

- ► **Knowledge**: What you need to know to perform in a position; the body of information with which the incumbent must be familiar with or fluent to successful perform a position.

- ► **Skills**: The ability to perform certain tasks or functions that are required for successful performance of the position.

- ► **Abilities**: Personal characteristics or capabilities that are required by the incumbent to perform the job successfully.

Although someone within HR usually leads job analysis initiatives within HR, "leadership" must not become confused with "ownership." HR professionals perform job analysis on behalf of clients. The clients are the ones who own the initiatives, and who must live with the results. HR must function in a consultative manner to ensure support and buy-in by our internal clients.

Job analysis is not about completing a form. It is also not just about the job description that will be produced as a result of that analysis. Rather, it is like every other core competency, it is a building block as you continue to form relationships with your internal clients. It will either enhance or diminish how others within your organization perceive you.

> **CAUTION**
>
> There is a temptation to define a job according to the skills, abilities, or abilities that the current—or former—incumbent brings to it. Job analysis must focus, however, on the *job, not on the individual* who holds, or held, that particular position.

How to Conduct Job Analysis

There are many ways to collect information that will be used in conducting a job analysis. Depending on what is appropriate in your organization, consider

- ▶ Interviewing the incumbent, or the prior incumbent, if that person is available.
- ▶ Interviewing the person who supervises the position.
- ▶ Interviewing the supervisor's supervisor.
- ▶ Interviewing co-workers.
- ▶ Interviewing direct reports, if applicable.
- ▶ Interviewing clients or customers with whom the position interacts.
- ▶ Interviewing vendors with whom the position interacts.
- ▶ Observing the incumbent performing the position, if possible and appropriate.
- ▶ Reviewing work product.
- ▶ Reviewing any documentation, reports, and/or performance-related statistics or records generated by—or about—the position.

> **TIP**
>
> Take a "360 degree" approach to the position. Consider collecting input from everyone with whom the position interacts.

Conducting Job Analysis Interviews

Interviews can be conducted in-person, through written or emailed surveys, or by a combination of both. Either way, be sensitive to the amount of time you ask people to invest in this process. Work to ensure that this process remains as streamlined and efficient as possible, while still ensuring that you collect the information you need.

Interviews/questionnaires may vary in length and content, depending upon the nature and amount of involvement and contact that the "interviewee" has with the position. Also be certain that you explain the purpose of the interview/questionnaires and the way in which participating in this process will ultimately benefit the interviewee.

Job Descriptions

One of the primary results generated by a job analysis is a *job description*. A job description is an "inventory" of important information gathered about the position during the job analysis process.

EXAM ALERT

It's important to understand the differences between job analysis, job descriptions, and job evaluation—as well as the relationships and connections that exist between them.

Different organizations structure their job descriptions differently. In large part, this is a function of the job evaluation system that will be used (see Chapter 6, "Compensation and Benefits"). Job descriptions, however, incorporate stylistic as well as substantive considerations. They reflect, to a degree, the culture of the organization.

However the job description is designed, certain elements should be included:

- ▶ Job title
- ▶ Date on which the description was completed
- ▶ Name of person preparing the description
- ▶ Department, unit, and/or division
- ▶ Supervisory reporting relationship(s)
- ▶ Direct reporting relationships, if applicable
- ▶ Essential functions
- ▶ Non-essential functions

- ▸ Working conditions and environment

- ▸ Physical requirements of the position

- ▸ Degree of financial accountability

- ▸ Qualifications required to perform the position

Employee Records Management

With respect to record keeping, HR is responsible for maintaining much of the information and documentation required to ensure compliance with federal, state, and local laws. A few examples of some of these record-keeping requirements include, but are in no way limited to, tax information, applicant flow data, veteran status, and I9 reporting. We'll take a closer look at recordkeeping requirements within the context of each functional area.

Maintaining documentation is, in a sense, a "Catch-22" for HR professionals. By definition, the actions associated with maintaining documentation are transactional. They are not strategic in nature. They are also driven, in large part, by compliance requirements. But if we don't perform this portion of our job well, it is unlikely that we will be given the opportunity to perform more strategic functions. Why? The first reason is fairly self-evident: If we cannot demonstrate the ability to successfully execute tasks of a mundane and administrative nature, it is unlikely that we will be entrusted with initiatives that are more strategic or visible. The second reason can become painfully obvious: Documentation, when mishandled, can lead to very real and tangible costs (human, as well as monetary) to the organization.

Documentation Strategies for HR Professionals

So what can you do to attain both of these objectives, and to ensure that they don't become mutually exclusive? Here are some ideas:

- ▸ Set up streamlined processes and procedures for handling routine and repetitive documentation requirements.

- ▸ Incorporate "fail safe" mechanisms into those processes. Even in the best-designed systems, it's inevitable that things will go wrong. Make sure there is a way to identify and resolve insufficient and/or non-compliant documentation.

- ▸ Look for ways to use existing documentation more strategically. Ascertain how you can turn "data" into "information," and how you can use that information as you work to earn, or maintain, a "seat at the table."

Interrelationships Among HR Activities and Programs Across Functional Areas

The six functional areas of HR are clearly delineated for purposes of the PHR exam. In reality, however, these aren't very clear, and they aren't very delineated, either. The lines between them are blurred, as evidenced by these 19 core areas of knowledge. They overlap, entwine, and weave themselves into unique workplace tapestries, as do the six HR functional areas. This is part of what makes HR such an interesting and challenging profession, and part of what mandates our commitment to continuous professional development. For just when we think we have "seen it all," we are presented with a new—and until that point unpredictable—set of circumstances.

Chapter Summary

This chapter provided an overview of each of the 19 core areas of knowledge identified by HRCI. More importantly, it provided you with the tools you will need to look for ways to integrate and link these core areas of knowledge to each other, and to each functional area, as you proceed through the rest of your test preparation.

In summary, in addition to addressing concepts and defining terms that you'll need to know for the PHR test, this chapter helped you practice another key skill that will be required for success on the PHR exam—the ability to think, look, and analyze across functional and disciplinary lines.

Key Terms List

▶ Needs assessment and analysis

▶ Third-party contract management, including development of requests for proposals (RFP's)

▶ Communication strategies

▶ Documentation requirements

▶ Adult learning processes

▶ Motivation concepts and applications

▶ Training methods

▶ Leadership concepts and applications

▶ Project management concepts and applications

▶ Diversity concepts and applications

▶ Human relations concepts and applications (for example, interpersonal and organizational behavior)

▶ HR ethics and professional standards

▶ Technology and human resource information systems (HRIS) to support HR activities

▶ Qualitative and quantitative methods and tools for analysis, interpretation and decision making purposes

▶ Change management

▶ Liability and risk management

▶ Job analysis and job description methods

▶ Employee records management (for example, retention, disposal)

▶ The interrelationships among HR activities and programs across functional areas

Apply Your Knowledge

Exercises

The following exercises present some scenarios you might encounter in your duties as an HR professional. Give each of these a try and later in the chapter you will find the answer and explanation of the correct answer.

1. A competitor has recently hired three of your company's employees. An email is sent to all remaining employees reminding them of their obligation to protect proprietary information to which they are exposed during the performance of their jobs, and that disciplinary action up to and including termination could result as a result of violating this policy. Shortly thereafter, a fourth employee interviews with a different competitor. The employee knows that he or she could present him or herself better by discussing current research and development projects on which he is working. The employee decides, however, not to discuss information about these projects with the interviewers.

This represents an example of:

- ○ **A.** Negative Reinforcement
- ○ **B.** Positive Reinforcement
- ○ **C.** Punishment
- ○ **D.** Extinction

2. An organization conducts an employee survey and finds that many employees are bored with their jobs, unhappy with their pay, and feel as though they don't get enough vacation time. If the organization's primary goal is to motivate employees, what is the first step that should be taken?

- ○ **A.** Conduct a survey to determine pay rates and vacation allotments among labor market competitors.
- ○ **B.** Identify ways in which employees' jobs can be enriched, and implement them.
- ○ **C.** Give everyone an across-the-board raise, and let employees know that you will be conducting a salary survey to see if further adjustments are needed.
- ○ **D.** Conduct another employee survey to see if the results of this survey are consistent with the results of the first survey.

3. A manager with whom you have not previously worked comes to you for help with implementing two different solutions she has come up with to fix a turnover problem in her department. This manager is highly regarded—and highly visible—in the organization. You are eager to perform well on this project, because you are confident it will help you forge a relationship with this

manager. You are also certain that the manager will tell her peers about her experience with you, which makes it particularly critical that you handle yourself well. Your first response should be to

- ○ **A.** Communicate your commitment to implementing the manager's solution.

- ○ **B.** Offer alternative solutions based on experience you have had with similar situations.

- ○ **C.** Ask questions to obtain more information about the problems the manager is experiencing.

- ○ **D.** Ask questions to obtain information that will help you implement the manager's solution more effectively.

4. You've been asked to make a recommendation relative to a new HRIS for your organization, and you need to collect information to assist you in formulating that recommendation. During the HRIS needs assessment, it would be important for you to ask all of the following questions except

- ○ **A.** To what degree are current employees familiar with the new system?

- ○ **B.** What financial resources can you commit to purchasing and implementing the system?

- ○ **C.** What human and capital resources will be required to support implementation of the system?

- ○ **D.** What financial, human, and capital resources will be required to support and maintain the system?

Review Questions

1. Would transactional leaders be best described as coaches, directors, enforcers, or captains? Why?

2. What are some important considerations to keep in mind about confidentiality?

3. How do "affinity groups" relate to Maslow's hierarchy of needs?

4. According to Fred Fiedler's Contingency theory, what three factors contribute to determining a situation's level of favorableness for a particular leadership style?

5. What sources of information should be considered when conducting a job analysis?

Exam Questions

1. Which of the following is not a key element of the ADDIE model?

   ○ **A.** Needs Assessment / Analysis

   ○ **B.** Evaluation

   ○ **C.** Data collection

   ○ **D.** Design

2. Which of the following functions is least likely to be outsourced?

   ○ **A.** Learning and development

   ○ **B.** Recruiting

   ○ **C.** Employee relations

   ○ **D.** Retirement benefits

3. Which of the following does Maslow identify as each person's most fundamental need?

   ○ **A.** Basic physical needs

   ○ **B.** Esteem

   ○ **C.** Recognition

   ○ **D.** A living wage

4. Which of the following statements about RFPs is true?

   ○ **A.** RFPs should be written in a broad and open-ended manner.

   ○ **B.** RFPs should not initially request information relative to the vendor's estimated costs.

   ○ **C.** Only government contractors or subcontractors need to use RFPs.

   ○ **D.** RFPs can be used relative to a variety of organizational problems.

5. Which of the following statements about motivation-hygiene theory is accurate?

   ○ **A.** Victor Vroom developed it.

   ○ **B.** "Motivation factors" refer to non-work related factors such as pay, benefits, and relationships with co-workers.

   ○ **C.** Acceptable hygiene factors won't cause an employee to be happy at work, but unacceptable motivation factors will.

   ○ **D.** Acceptable or positive motivation factors won't cause an employee to be happy at work, but acceptable or positive hygiene factors will.

6. Blake-Mouton's situational leadership theory

- ⃝ **A.** Measures and assesses concern for the needs of direct reports and concern for the accomplishment of tasks.
- ⃝ **B.** Identifies "impoverished managers" as ones who have not been given the opportunity to engage in training opportunities designed to enhance essential supervisory skills.
- ⃝ **C.** Uses a 10-point scale along each axis.
- ⃝ **D.** Builds upon Hersey and Blanchard's model.

7. In the "selling" quadrant of Hersey and Blanchard's situational leadership model, employees

- ⃝ **A.** Have mastered the technical aspects of the job and can function independently.
- ⃝ **B.** Have shifted their focus from learning a specific task to instructing and/or mentoring others in the organization on how to perform the function.
- ⃝ **C.** Have developed basic skills related to the task, and can benefit from additional background and information about the task.
- ⃝ **D.** Need to focus on developing self-confidence in their abilities—selling themselves, in a sense, on their own ability to perform a particular task.

8. Which of the following is not one of the six key elements of the HR Code of Ethics?

- ⃝ **A.** Professional Development
- ⃝ **B.** Commitment to Workplace Diversity
- ⃝ **C.** Fairness and Justice
- ⃝ **D.** Use of Information

9. Trait theories

- ⃝ **A.** Support the belief that leaders are born, not made.
- ⃝ **B.** Support the belief that individuals can be trained to be effective leaders.
- ⃝ **C.** Support the belief that different situations require different leadership styles.
- ⃝ **D.** Support the belief that relationship dimensions of leadership style are more important than task dimensions of leadership style.

10. The transformational leadership style

- ○ **A.** Places greater emphasis on relationships than on tasks.
- ○ **B.** Places greater emphasis on tasks than on relationships.
- ○ **C.** Is characterized by the possibility of rewards, and by the threat of punishment.
- ○ **D.** Encourages a coaching style of leadership.

Answers to Exercises

1. **Answer A is the best response.** This employee is trying to avoid negative consequences that could result from revealing proprietary information. The other answers refer to the three other possible consequences identified through Skinner's operant conditioning theory.

2. **Answer A is the best response.** According to Herzberg's Motivation-Hygiene theory, motivation factors will have a positive impact on an employee's motivation level *if, and only if,* hygiene factors are acceptable. In this situation, it appears as though neither motivation nor hygiene factors are acceptable. It's important to deal first with addressing hygiene factors to ensure that motivation factors will have a positive impact. Answer B jumps straight to motivation factors. Answer C takes a "ready, fire, aim" approach—although employees appear to be unhappy with their pay, that does not necessarily mean that pay levels are inappropriate, that they need to be increased, or that 5% is the right number to use. Answer D is not the best choice; although it will probably be necessary to collect more information (perhaps through follow up meetings), it would not be effective to ask employees to give you the same information in the same way.

3. **Answer C is the best response.** HR adds value to this process by asking questions that help us ascertain the underlying problems—and that help distinguish problems from symptoms. Answer A is not the best choice because although a manager may be convinced of what his or her problem is, and/or of what the solution should be, the manager's assessment is not necessarily correct, so you shouldn't commit to implementing it. Answer B is not the best choice for a related reason—you don't know what the problem is, so it is not possible to suggest a solution. Additionally, if you use this approach, you are dismissing the manager's opinions and experience—and risk damaging your relationship with the manager. Answer D is not the best choice because it assumes that the manager's assessment of the problem is correct, and that the proposed solution is the best possible intervention.

4. **Answer A is the best response.** The degree to which current employees are familiar with the new system is relatively unimportant, as long as communication is effective, training is provided, and support is available. Answers B, C, and D each represent important questions to ask before selecting an HRIS.

Answers to Review Questions

1. Of these four choices, the term "enforcer" would best characterize transactional leaders. Transactional leaders use a system built on "the carrot and the stick"—and mainly the stick. "Coaching" doesn't reflect this approach, and instead is more characteristic of the transformational leadership style. The image of a "captain" might more closely reflect the role a leader plays in the "selling" quadrant of Hersey and Blanchard's situational leadership model. A "director" could imply a wider variety of leadership approaches under transactional as well as transformational styles.

2. Confidential information should be communicated in a manner consistent with the law, and on a strict "need to know" basis. Using that standard, it's important to remember that not all HR professionals within an organization should be granted access to all confidential work-related information. Communicating outside the physical workplace does not negate the fact that the information you are communicating is confidential.

3. Organizational affinity groups bring together people who share common interests, goals, or backgrounds. As such, they primarily address the need that Maslow identified as "belonging and love." It is possible, however, that members of affinity groups might derive benefits that impact their esteem or that enable them to self-actualize.

4. Fred Fiedler identified three factors of favorableness. He asserted that the relative strength or weakness of these factors would impact a leader's effectiveness. The three factors are

   Leader-members relations: This factor looks at how strong, and how significant, relationships between the leader and the team members are. It considers the degree to which those relationships make the leader more, or less, effective and influential.

   Task structure: This factor ascertains the degree to which the work that the team members perform is structured.

   Position Power: This factor looks at the degree to which the leader's position holds, or can exert, power or influence. It also looks at the degree to which the leader can ensure accountability for team members' performance, and the degree to which the leader has the authority to delegate.

5. Depending on what is appropriate in your organization, consider using the following sources of information when conducting a job analysis:

   ▸ The incumbent, or the prior incumbent, if that person is available.

   ▸ The person who supervises the position incumbent.

   ▸ The supervisor's supervisor.

   ▸ Co-workers.

- ▶ Direct reports, if applicable.

- ▶ Clients or customers with whom the position's incumbent interacts.

- ▶ Vendors with whom the position's incumbent interacts.

- ▶ Work product.

- ▶ Documentation, reports, and/or performance-related statistics or records generated by—or about—the position.

Answers to Exam Questions

1. **Answer C is the best response.** The five key elements of ADDIE are Needs Assessment/Analysis, Design, Development, Implementation, and Evaluation. While "data collection" would be a part of needs assessment and analysis, it does not constitute one of the five key elements (and, therefore, doesn't stand for either of the "Ds" in the acronym ADDIE).

2. **Answer C is the best response.** Currently within HR, transactional functions are more likely to be outsourced than non-transactional functions. In part, this is because non-transactional (including tactical and strategic) functions provide HR professionals with the greatest opportunities to add value to the organization. Of these four choices, employee relations is the least transactional function. This information also highlights the need for HR professionals to recognize opportunities for performing seemingly transactional functions in a more strategic manner. Among the choices offered here, "recruiting" is the function that—while most likely to be performed in a transactional manner—offers the most untapped opportunity for strategic contribution.

3. **Answer A is the best response.** Esteem is the second highest need on Maslow's hierarchy. Esteem encompasses both "self" and "other" components, recognition falling into the category of "other." Although it could be argued that a living wage falls under the category of basic physical needs, it is not—by definition—the same as basic physical needs. In part, this is because the concept of a living wage did not exist when Maslow developed his hierarchy. Additionally, earning a living wage does not ensure that *all* of the dimensions of a person's basic physical needs will be met.

4. **Answer D is the best response.** RFPs can be used relative to any function, task, or project that the organization is considering outsourcing. Answer A is not the best choice because writing RFPs in a highly structured manner increases the likelihood that the proposed solutions are responsive to the organization's specific needs. A structured approach also facilitates the process of comparing RFPs that are submitted from multiple vendors. Answer B is not the best choice because seeking information about pricing ensures that a company will not waste time by entertaining solutions that are

cost-prohibitive. Answer C is not the best choice because RFPs should be used by all organizations that are considering any kind of outsourcing; the process is unrelated to whether or not the organization is a government contractor or subcontractor.

5. **Answer C is the best response.** Vroom developed the Expectancy Theory, and Herzberg developed the Motivation-Hygiene theory. *Motivation factors* refer to work related factors (such as the nature of the work, and the challenge inherent to the work), while *hygiene factors* refer to the non-work related factors identified in answer B. Lastly, acceptable or positive motivation factors will cause an employee to be happy at work, but acceptable or positive hygiene factors won't.

6. **Answer D is the best response.** Blake-Mouton's situational leadership theory measures and assesses concern for people and concern for task/production. It identifies "impoverished managers" as those who delegate responsibility, then demonstrate no real concern for either people or task/production. This model uses a nine-point scale along each axis.

7. **Answer C is the best response.** An employee who falls into the "selling" quadrant with respect to one particular task has not fully mastered the technical aspects of the position, and cannot yet function in a fully independent manner. None of the four quadrants in this model addresses the efforts on developing others. Additionally, employees in this quadrant have not yet developed their skills or knowledge relative to a particular skill to the point where they should focus their efforts on developing confidence; they need to continue working on practicing and honing their own skill level.

8. **Answer B is the best response.** Although workplace diversity is one of the core areas of knowledge for HR professionals, it is not one of the six specific dimensions identified in the HR Code of Ethics. It is, however, one expression of the ethical mandate for "fairness and justice."

9. **Answer A is the best response.** The concept of training people to be leaders was introduced as part of behavior theories, introduced in the 1940s. The idea that different situations require different leadership styles emerged under situational leadership theories. None of the leadership theories specifically asserts that relationship dimensions of leadership style are universally more important than task dimensions of leadership style.

10. **Answer D is the best response.** Transformational leaders concern themselves with relationship as well as task dimensions—neither is emphasized to the exclusion of the other. The transactional leadership style is characterized by the possibility of rewards and the threat of punishment, while the transformational leadership style focuses on coaching rather than enforcement (or threats of enforcement).

Suggested Readings and Resources

Bohlander, George W. and Snell, Scott. *Managing Human Resources*. ISBN 0324184050.

Pell, Arthur R. *The Complete Idiot's Guide to Human Resource Management*. ISBN 0028641949.

Mazin, Rebecca A. and Smith, Shawn A. *HR Answer Book, The: An Indispensable Guide for Managers and Human Resources Professionals*. ISBN 0814472230.

CHAPTER THREE

Strategic Management

Study Strategies

Although the PHR exam is multiple choice, try writing and answering your own "essay-based" questions. Write open-ended questions that require a response of at least a full paragraph—and try writing your answers without looking back at your study materials. The process of actually writing down your answers will reinforce what you already know, and will highlight what you need to study more. It will also likely help you as you work to recall this same information when you answer related multiple choice questions on the actual PHR exam.

Introduction

There is a familiar saying that goes something like this: "Some people make things happen, some people watch things happen, and some people wonder what happened." In our profession, we are fortunate to have the opportunity to choose which of those paths we will follow. While this choice holds true for every chapter of this book (and therefore for every functional area within HR), it is particularly true of this one.

In each of the following sections, we will look a bit more closely at some of the key, underlying concepts and how they can support our efforts to function more strategically in our roles as HR professionals. Some of the areas will provide a step-by-step approach to the concepts being presented. Others will identify, define, and/or offer a brief explanation about other items that it's important for HR professionals to know, but that aren't fully explored in this chapter.

EXAM ALERT

Perhaps more than for any of the six functional areas, PHR candidates are strongly urged to supplement the material presented in this chapter with other sources. Although the wisdom of seeking ancillary materials holds true for all of the functional areas, doing so is particularly important for strategic management, for a number of reasons. First, the concepts covered in this area are prone to a variety of interpretations, which may differ slightly from each other.

Additionally, though the functional area of strategic management represents a relatively small percentage of the PHR exam (12%), it covers a significant volume of information and spans a wide array of theories, disciplines, and practices. The SPHR exam, in fact, devotes 26% of its questions to this functional area—*more than twice the percentage found on the PHR exam*.

With such a large amount of territory to cover, it's impossible to predict what will be on the exam—so don't try. Give yourself plenty of time, curl up with a good periodical or two, and prepare to learn a lot. This approach will increase the likelihood that you will perform better on the PHR exam. Perhaps even more importantly, it will help you function more effectively in your role as an HR professional, as well.

The Evolving Role of HR

As explored in Chapter 1, HR has been on a long and sometimes challenging journey through which it has redefined itself as a profession and redefined itself with respect to its role in the organization.

A Brief Historical Scan of HR

Much has changed about our profession during the last 50+ years, during which an ongoing discussion around professionalism and certification has continued to evolve. Perhaps the most outwardly recognizable sign of the struggle in which we have been engaging is how we refer to our profession.

Originally, it was known as "Industrial Relations" (the "I" and the "R" in Cornell's "ILR" come from "industrial relations"; the "L" comes from "labor"). Sometime back in the 1950s, it started to be called "Personnel." Today, for the most part, we know it as "Human Resources." Tomorrow, who knows what it will be called; in some organizations, a "Chief People Officer" or a "VP of People" already leads our function.

One thing is certain—our name hasn't changed just to "keep up with the times." Rather, these changes reflect the transformation of our role from a "job" or a "support function" to a bona fide profession—from administrative support roles to strategic organizational partners.

Of course, just as the name of our department has not changed in all organizations, so too our role has not evolved at an even pace in all organizations. Let's take a closer look at what this means, and at what its true impact is on how we carry out our roles.

HR As It Was, and HR As It Is (or Can Be)

As mentioned previously, the way in which HR professionals carry out their functions has changed and evolved over the years. Table 3.1 highlights these:

TABLE 3.1   HR: Then and Now

Then	Now
Reactive	Proactive
Gatekeeper (or gate closer)	Facilitator
Policy enforcer	Policy strategy consultant
Authoritarian	Consultative
Focused on HR, and its goals	Focused on the organization, and its mission
Employee advocate (from managers' perspective)	"Truth advocate" ® (Mary Rudder, Rx Management)
Management advocate (from employees' perspective)	

The distinctions between "then" and "now," however, aren't always quite as absolute as this chart may indicate.

- ▶ Many organizations fall somewhere along the spectrum between "then" and "now" in terms of how their HR departments function in an overall sense.

- ▶ Other organizations might more closely resemble "then" with respect to some HR functions, and more closely resemble "now" with respect to others.

- ▶ So, too, each of us might function in some ways closer to the "then" end of the spectrum, and function in other ways closer to the "now" end of the spectrum.

This can be true on an organizational, functional, or even individual level.

Dimensions of HR—Three Legs of a Stool

Just as our role has evolved, so too the ways in which we need to carry out that role have evolved.

Leg #1: Administrative

These are the transactions—the things that need to be done. Over the years, some of the transactions we used to perform have gone away. More often, however, those functions simply take a dramatically different form today than they did yesterday, or are being handled in different (and often more streamlined and/or more technologically sophisticated) ways (such as self sever kiosks, Intranets, HRIS applications, outsourcing, and so on).

Leg #2: Strategic

The difference between the administrative functions in HR and the strategic functions in HR is like the difference between being a person who designs automobiles and being a passenger. Both are important and, ultimately, each needs the other. Were there no automobile designers, the current generation of cars would become the future generation of cars, leaving certain safety and efficiency needs unmet (not to mention ever-changing stylistic trends). Were there no passengers, there would be little need for cars in the first place, and certainly no need for anyone to invest time and energy in looking toward the future.

Strategic HR takes a long-term, future-focused approach to the ways in which it will work with the organization to attain its organizational mission. It looks at business and organizational issues, rather than "HR issues." It fosters and cultivates change, rather than maintenance of the status quo. It is dynamic, effective, consultative and ever-evolving—just like our profession itself.

Leg #3: Operational / Tactical

Somewhere in between the administrative functions that must be performed and the inventive and creative life force that is part of strategic management lies the operational—or tactical—dimension of the HR function.

One definition of the word "tactical" offers a militaristic reference, which might help to explain its particular relevance to the HR profession. *The American Heritage Dictionary of the English Language* defines "tactical" as follows:

- ▶ (a) Of, relating to, used in, or involving military or naval operations that are smaller, closer to base, and of less long-term significance than strategic operations.

- ▶ (b) Carried out in support of military or naval operations: *tactical bombing*.

This definition aligns well with the application of this term in the HR profession. The operational, tactical, or day-to-day performance and execution of the HR role can be accomplished in many different ways—some of which do more to define us toward the administrative end of the spectrum, while others demonstrate more vividly how, and whether, the overarching strategic objectives of HR (and, therefore, of the organization) are being brought to life. In the metaphor used previously, the tactical area might be depicted by the role of the driver. We wouldn't get anywhere without drivers—even if a car had the most evolved designs and finest appointments imaginable. Also, the performance and safety features that were woven into the design will only come to life in the hands and feet of the driver—who plays a more active and involved role than any of his or her passengers.

Understanding Your Clients' Management Functions

To be an effective strategic business partner, it's also critical to have an understanding of some of the foundational underpinnings of management.

Principles of Management

Perhaps an unlikely guru, Henri Fayol was hired at the age of 19 to work as an engineer for a French mining company. He worked there for many years, ultimately serving as its managing director from 1888 to 1918. Based on the experience he gained at the mining company, Fayol—known as the Father of Modern Management—identified five functions of a manager, which he referred to as

- ▶ Prevoyance
- ▶ To organize
- ▶ To command
- ▶ To coordinate
- ▶ To control

In modern parlance, these five functions are often referred to as *planning*, *organizing*, *coordinating*, *directing*, and *controlling*. Let's take a closer look at each of these so as to better understand organizational structure and the context within our clients carry out their roles.

Planning

Planning lays the groundwork for how managers will work toward accomplishing the organization's goals. Through planning, managers decide what needs to get done, when it needs to get done, who will do it, how it will get done, and where it will be done. In the absence of planning, the organization—and the people in it—will lack direction, and perhaps even just "coast along." In other words, to quote the immortal words of the great philosopher (and baseball

"Hall of Famer") Yogi Berra, "If you don't know where you are going, you will end up somewhere else."

Organizing

Organizing speaks to the ways in which the manager obtains and arranges the resources that he or she needs to implement the plans (the output of the "planning" function). Those resources could include people, facilities, materials, and so on. During the organizing function, the manager must also decide reporting relationships within the organization. In short, the linkages between people, places, and things must be established.

Coordinating

Through the coordinating function, the manager brings together all of the resources that he or she has organized to accomplish the stated plan. The manager must also ensure that "the pieces fit."

Directing

During the directing phase, the "rubber hits the road." The actual work is performed—goods are produced or services are provided. In addition to ensuring that things go smoothly from a technical perspective, in the directing phase, the manager must also focus attention on leading and motivating the human resources who are actually performing the work.

Controlling

Controlling assumes more of an oversight role, and in some senses an evaluative role. In this phase, the manager ascertains the degree to which the planning he or she engaged in actually produced the desired results. If the manager determines that there is a gap between the targeted goals and the actual results, the manager must then focus on ways to bridge that gap.

Fayol subsequently broke these five functions further down into fourteen principles of management:

1. Division of work

2. Authority and responsibility

3. Discipline

4. Unity of command

5. Unity of direction

6. Subordination of individual interests to general interests

7. Remuneration of personnel

8. Centralization

9. Scalar chain

10. Order

11. Equity

12. Stability of tenure of personnel

13. Initiative

14. Esprit de corps (union is strength)

Project Management—A Valuable Tool

More and more, work is project based. For many of us, and for many of our clients, project management is a critical skill needed to perform our own work and to support the work that our clients are performing, as well.

A common difficulty of project-based work is the inherent challenge of balancing day-to-day workload with efforts to complete high priority "special" projects. Projects are frequently delegated to individuals with nothing more than a deadline—and with no additional resources. Understandably, the person to whom the project has been delegated will seek assistance in undertaking the project from people and from equipment that is already being utilized to carry out the day-to-day responsibilities of the operation. In addition to slowing down productivity relative to the regular workload, it is also quite possible that the project may not be accomplished within its stated time frame. Enter "project management."

Project Management: Definition and Processes

"Project management" is interesting and somewhat unique in that it is both a means to an end as well as an end (and a profession) unto itself (sounds a bit like human resources, doesn't it?).

The Project Management Institute (PMI) defines project management as "the application of knowledge, skills, tools, and techniques to a broad range of activities in order to meet the requirements of a particular project." Project managers seek to accomplish their objectives by gaining control over five factors: *time*, *cost*, *quality*, *scope*, and *risk*. To do this, those who undertake a project must clarify the needs and scope of the project, work out a plan for meeting those needs, and manage the project according to that plan. These steps, however, are sometimes easier to talk about than they are to execute.

PMI goes on to identify five distinct (yet overlapping) processes within project management:

- **Initiation Processes**: Initiation processes are those processes that secure approval and/or authorization to undertake the project.

- **Planning Processes**: Through planning processes, objectives are established, as are the best alternatives that will support the attainment of those objectives.

▶ **Executing Processes**: Everything comes together through the executing processes—the scope, the objectives, and the deliverables all fall into place. In order to attain this level of successful execution, the right resources need to be in the right place at the right time.

▶ **Controlling Processes**: Controlling processes include managing the scope of the project and making sure the project stays in line with the original objectives. A significant degree of follow-up is required to carry out controlling processes.

▶ **Closing Processes**: Closing processes involve "signoff" processes and mark the end of the project. As part of closing processes, stakeholders must determine whether and to what degree the project met its obligations.

These processes, while separate, are interrelated. The output from one set of processes contributes significantly to the inputs used for other processes. While the processes are not wholly finite and discrete, they are more or less sequential, in the order presented here. Perhaps the best way to describe these processes is that they are "interdependent," while still separate.

EXAM ALERT

Be familiar with important project planning terms and concepts, including, but not necessarily limited to

▶ Project manager

▶ Project sponsor

▶ Project charter

▶ Project team

▶ Project plan

▶ Project schedule

▶ Work breakdown structure (WBS)

▶ Gantt chart

▶ Program evaluation and review technique (CHART) charts

HR's Role in Change Management

It has been said that the only constant is change. That is perhaps particularly—and at times poignantly—true in the workplace.

Organizationally, change is all around us and can take many forms: downsizings, redeployments, introductions of new processes, reassignment among staff, mergers and acquisitions…the list goes on and on. Without a doubt, HR plays a major role with respect to managing that change productively (in those organizations where HR has truly earned a "seat at the table," HR will ideally have an important role with respect to shaping change, as well).

HR's role, in this regard, is inextricably linked to the attainment of organizational objectives and the furtherance of the organization's mission. During times of change, HR is called upon to lead people management processes. HR professionals—individually and collectively within the organization—must align their people management efforts with the strategic goals of the organization. HR must also be prepared to measure the degree of success that has been attained (see "Measuring HR Effectiveness").

To meet the ever-accelerating pace of change, HR professionals must understand change as well as the environments that cause change. This understanding will be particularly important when HR is called upon to adapt the organization's people management practices to new workplace-based realities while maintaining and improving upon current levels of organizational performance. As such, successfully designing, aligning, and implementing adaptive people management practices is an essential component of being a strategic HR partner.

EXAM ALERT

Although these areas extend beyond the scope of this book, they don't extend beyond the scope of your potential responsibilities as an HR professional. Let this book serve as a starting point for your PHR exam prep, as well as for your continued growth and development as an HR professional.

Change theory and process is addressed more thoroughly in Chapter 5, "HR Development."

Outsourcing

Outsourcing—otherwise known as the use of "third-party contractors"—is a growing trend that has directly impacted, and that will continue to directly impact, HR's role. That impact has two distinct dimensions: First, HR is an area that has, in many organizations, experienced partial or significant outsourcing of its components. Second, HR facilitates—and sometimes oversees or even orchestrates—outsourcing that takes place within other parts of the organization.

Outsourcing Defined

Let's take a step back, however, and take a closer look at the concept of outsourcing. Outsourcing can be described as the reassignment of responsibilities, functions, or jobs that had been performed *within the organization* to now be carried out by resources that are *outside the organization*.

NOTE

"Offshoring" is a specific type of outsourcing that seeks vendors that are *way* outside the organization—specifically, these third-party providers are located overseas.

How to Outsource: An Outline

Outsourcing is a complex process that can have a significant impact on the organization, the people who work within the organization, the attainment of organizational goals, and even the organization's reputation in the marketplace. The decision to outsource should not be made lightly, and the "three step process" outlined here is in no way intended to "dummy down" the required course of action. Like so many other components of this book, this three step process is intended to provide you with a starting point—an overarching framework that will help you identify those areas in which you would benefit from additional information.

Question #1: Is outsourcing appropriate?

In addressing this question, a number of factors need to be taken into consideration, a few of which are

▶ Internal costs versus the costs associated with outsourcing

▶ Internal abilities and talents versus abilities and talents available through outsourcing

▶ The importance and complexity of the function that is being considered for outsourcing

▶ The degree of variability in transaction volume of the function that is being considered for outsourcing

Question #2: If outsourcing is appropriate, how will we select a vendor?

There are many factors to take into consideration, and questions to ask, when choosing a vendor. Here are a few that are particularly important to consider:

▶ **Technological strength**: Do the vendor's technological resources and capabilities meet or exceed your project requirements? If so, by how much? Are there appropriate backup systems and redundancies in place?

▶ **Scale**: How much growth do you anticipate? Is the vendor prepared to meet your growth expectations and requirements?

▶ **Experience**: Does the vendor have related *and recent* experience? How closely does that experience resemble the current project in terms of scope, complexity, and so forth?

▶ **Costs**: What are the up-front costs that you would incur with this vendor? Up-front costs could include training, program design, IT setup, and many others. Additionally, what hidden costs might you incur, perhaps as a function of attrition, telecommunications charges, and the like?

▶ **Quality**: What is the vendor's commitment to quality? How does it manifest itself, and how can it be measured? On average, how much time does it take for the vendor to resolve concerns that originate from customers and/or clients? What are current client/customer satisfaction rates with those resolutions?

▶ **Communications**: What is the nature and frequency of the communication that you can expect to engage in with the vendor? If appropriate, will someone (an individual with appropriate authority) be available 24/7 throughout the life of the project?

▶ **Success Record**: What is the vendor's track record with *recent* clients? To find out, talk with recent clients *of your choosing*. Ask them what went well in their experiences with the vendor and what didn't. Ask about lessons that the vendor learned and how well (and quickly) the vendor was able to incorporate and apply those lessons. Also ask about communication—as the relationship went on, did the nature and frequency of communication deviate from what the vendor had initially committed to at the beginning of the relationship (or project)?

Question #3: Once we select a vendor, how will we manage the vendor, and our relationship with the vendor?

▶ If possible, start out with a pilot program and see how it unfolds before devoting all necessary resources to the endeavor.

▶ Set clear and reasonable expectations (SMART performance management objectives—specific, measurable, action-oriented, realistic, and timebound—work well with vendors, as well. See Chapter 5).

▶ Observe, monitor, measure, and evaluate actual performance.

▶ Give the vendor constructive and positive feedback (BASIC—behavioral, as soon as possible, specific, interactive and consistent—see Chapter 5).

▶ As appropriate and possible, coach the vendor.

▶ As appropriate and possible, incorporate upside potential and downside risk into your negotiated agreements with vendors.

EXAM ALERT

Other outsourcing related terms with which you should familiarize yourself before taking the PHR exam are

▶ Request for proposal (RFP) (see Chapter 2)

▶ Third party vendor

HR Technology Concerns/Opportunities

Technology touches indirectly or perhaps quite directly all dimensions of the human resource function and profession. The speed with which this transformational impact has taken place has increased exponentially, and will likely continue to do so into the foreseeable future.

Many organizations, both small and large, now use a human resource information system (HRIS) to better manage HR-related data. An HRIS is an integrated computer-based system that collects, processes, analysis, stores, maintains, and retrieves information relating to all dimensions of the HR function.

EXAM ALERT

Before taking the PHR exam, familiarize yourself with the various ways in which an HRIS can support each of the various functional areas of HR.

HRISs have redefined, in many ways, how HR professionals perform their jobs. When utilized to its fullest extent, an HRIS can even help HR professionals move from the "then" end of the spectrum to the "now" end of the spectrum (see this chapter's section titled "HR As It Was, and HR As It Is (or Can Be"). This is possible because an HRIS can help to free us from some of HR's required, albeit mundane, administrative responsibilities, and thus can afford us time that we may be able to use to address more strategic issues.

It is not enough, however, for an HRIS to make our lives easier. Instead, we must ensure that the HRIS we choose will truly address business needs, not just HR-specific concerns. By this, for example, we mean that an HRIS must be a tool that can be used to support initiatives that contribute to attainment of overall organizational objectives. For instance, an HRIS should provide us with information that will ultimately facilitate and support

- ▶ Increasing overall employee productivity
- ▶ Identifying and rewarding top performers
- ▶ Investing in ongoing employee development
- ▶ Placing the right people in the right jobs at the right times
- ▶ Ensuring readiness to identify and appropriately respond to changing business strategies

Changes on the Horizon—and How They May Impact HR

In many ways, HR trends are best identified by looking for business/organizational, industry, and societal trends. As a microcosm of the outside world, organizations are directly impacted by what happens in the external environment. It logically follows that since HR exists to support the attainment of organizational objectives, it is impossible—or at least extremely ill-advised—for us to isolate ourselves.

> **NOTE**
>
> Keep your finger on the pulse of the world around you, and the world at large. Workplaces can change almost instantaneously, and trends can develop almost as quickly.
>
> One devastatingly illustrative example of this can be found in the aftermath of Hurricane Katrina. In 2004, many of us gathered for the national SHRM conference at the New Orleans conference center to learn, to network, to groove to the music of the Doobie Brothers, and to be moved and inspired by the now stilled—but never silenced—voice of Christopher Reeve. Slightly more than one year later, that same building in which we congregated was literally overflowing with individuals displaced from their jobs, their homes, their loved ones, and nearly every other recognizable dimension of their lives. Hurricane Katrina and its aftermath thrust many concerns to the forefront—issues that may not have been on everyone's radar screen just a few weeks earlier.

Here are just a few of the trends that all HR professionals should monitor and revisit on a regular basis:

- ▶ Globalization
- ▶ Technology
- ▶ Safety and security
- ▶ Terrorism
- ▶ Aging workforce
- ▶ Multi-generational workplaces
- ▶ Work/life balance
- ▶ Changing technology
- ▶ Contingent workforce

Strategic Planning

Strategic planning is a step-by-step process through which organizations engage in two types of activities. Specifically, the organization

1. Identifies where it wants to be and what it wants to accomplish long-term (often 3–5 years).

2. Begins to map out how its vision and mission for those years will be attained.

In an oversimplified sense, strategic planning is the process of looking into the future, painting a picture of where we want to be and what we want to achieve in that future, and ascertaining how we will get there. It is a type of "extreme proactivity" rather than reactivity…of planning for the future rather than simply responding to it as it unfolds.

There are a number of compelling reasons for organizations to engage in a strategic planning process, just a few of which are

▶ By methodically looking towards the future, the organization creates an opportunity to proactively shape and influence its own future.

▶ The organization will develop a clearer awareness of how it is positioned externally, and how it "measures up" internally.

▶ It either creates or reaffirms the overall vision, mission, and values of the organization, and refocuses attention on how to bring them to life.

▶ It engages individuals throughout the organization in a meaningful and effective initiative.

Strategic Planning—A Four-Phase Process

Many theorists describe and define the strategic planning process in different ways, and as containing different steps and components. The following is one way of looking at the strategic planning process.

Phase 1: Establish a Foundation for the Strategy

To be effective, the strategic planning process must be grounded in the organization's mission, vision, and values.

▶ **Vision:** An organization's vision is a brief yet comprehensive descriptive and inspirational statement that articulates where the organization wants to be and what it wants to become in the future. The vision should resonate in the hearts, minds, and day-to-day endeavors of the organization's employees. It should give those employees an awareness that they have a meaningful opportunity to be part of something bigger than themselves. It must motivate them to aspire to the legacy that the vision can create and that it ultimately can leave behind.

▶ **Mission**: An organization's mission statement articulates, in essence, its reason for being. It may speak to the nature of the organization's business or purpose, its customers, and sometimes even its employees and its role in the community. A mission statement should be broad (but not overly generalized), brief, clear, unambiguous, and designed to last for "the long haul." The goals of an organization must be based on the mission, so the mission is therefore far bigger than any goal—and thus must be able to withstand the test of time.

▶ **Values**: Values are the beliefs on which the organization has been built. They are the tenets that shape and guide strategic and day-to-day decision making, as well as the behaviors that are exhibited in the organization. Organizations identify values, in part, as a way to clearly guide those decisions and behaviors. Values are often represented in terms and principles such as integrity, honesty, respect, and so on.

Phase 2: Develop the Strategic Plan

Formulating a strategy on the basis of deliberately crafted statements that articulate the mission, vision and values of the organization is critical, but it's only the first step. The next step is to actually develop the strategic plan.

There are several key components to the development phase of the strategic plan.

SWOT Analysis (Strengths, Weaknesses, Opportunities, and Threats)

A SWOT analysis is conducted to ascertain the strengths and weaknesses that are inherent to an organization, as well as the opportunities and threats that it faces from external forces. Though it sounds relatively simple and straightforward, the process of conducting a SWOT analysis can become challenging, in part because it is often difficult for organizations—as it is for people—to see themselves objectively.

When examining "strengths" and "weaknesses," it is necessary for analysis to be directed inward. This clear and objective assessment would ascertain the resources of the organization, including, but not necessarily limited to

▶ Human

▶ Financial

▶ Technological

▶ Capital

▶ Brand image

Opportunities and threats, conversely, look outward at factors such as competition, economic trends, customer needs and wants, and legislative or regulatory activity. This process, known as environmental scanning, is explored more thoroughly in "Environmental Scanning—An External Perspective," later in this chapter.

> **EXAM ALERT**
>
> Familiarize yourself with SWOT—what it stands for and what it consists of. SWOT analysis is particularly critical to our development as strategic organizational partners, and thus is likely to appear on the PHR exam.

Generate Strategic Objectives

Once the SWOT analysis is completed, the outputs of that analysis can and should be scrutinized and, to the degree possible, addressed. Once that process has been completed—or at least has been begun—it's time to begin generating ideas that will eventually grow, develop, and be cultivated until they take the shape of organizational objectives.

These organizational objectives must be translated into specific strategies that enable each department, division, or other organizational unit to contribute directly to the attainment of the organization's overall objectives. In order for this to happen, a top-down/bottom-up approach similar to that described in the performance management process must be implemented throughout the organization (see Chapter 5). To oversimplify the process, like any pyramidal structure—and even like Maslow's hierarchy of needs (see Chapter 2)—goals at the "lower," more functional levels of the organization must be attained in support of the more overarching objectives of the organization. Keep this process building and you'll be well on your way to bringing the vision, mission, and values of the organization to life in a highly tangible and visible manner.

Phase 3: Implement the Strategic Plan

Similar to Fayol's "directing" stage, the implementation phase is, once again, where "the rubber meets the road." Strategies become tactics and tactics become operationalized. Management functions—from planning through controlling—are used to make the strategies a part of the day-to-day fabric and functioning of the organization. Since, at this level, we have also reached the point at which individuals will have a very real, albeit somewhat indirect, impact on whether the organization's objectives are attained, performance management principles become critical, as well (see Chapter 5).

Three factors that are critical to successfully implementing any strategic plan are commitment, credibility, and communication.

Commitment

It is absolutely critical to secure the support and commitment of leaders at all levels of the organization—particularly the upper levels—before even entertaining the idea of creating (let alone implementing) a strategic plan. This commitment can and should encompass everything from seeing the strategic process through to its conclusion, to striving to achieve the goals and implementing the changes that are generated through this process.

In short, strategic plans that sit on a shelf are useless. Talking the talk is not enough. Walking the walk is mandatory. Without commitment, a strategic plan is not only useless—it might even do more harm than good.

Credibility

Credibility is created and sustained through representative participation from all levels of the organization, through a commitment to follow through on every step of the process (rather than "short cutting" the process), and through clear, complete, and appropriate documentation of the process.

Phase 4: Evaluate the Plan, Process, and Performance

Evaluating how well a strategic plan was envisioned, designed, and implemented is an involved process, as any evaluative process is. In Chapter 5, we provide a more in depth discussion of any evaluative process as explored through ADDIE. Revisit the "E" in ADDIE, and also seek other sources and ideas for evaluating a plan, the process for developing that plan, and the overall performance against that plan.

Perhaps most importantly, be prepared to incorporate changes, insights, and revisions. Holding on to a flawed design or an ineffective implementation process is like "spending good money after bad." In an organization, the "currency" in question may be your own reputation and credibility, so be prepared to flex.

REVIEW BREAK

Strategic planning helps the organization look towards the future, and to begin to shape how it will position itself for that future.

One element of strategic planning that was mentioned in the last section was "external scanning." Let's take a closer look at that particular component.

Environmental Scanning—An External Perspective

Environmental scanning is the process through which organizations maintain awareness of the opportunities and threats presented by the surroundings—both macro and micro—within which they operate.

For information that is obtained through an environmental scan to be truly valuable, leaders within the organization must use the data that is collected to modify—as appropriate—organizational objectives or strategies. The *ability* to demonstrate organizational agility in response to environmental information is essential; the *willingness* to act upon that information is perhaps even more important.

Some organizations conduct environmental scans on an ad hoc basis, often in response to crises or other unexpected events. Other organizations plan to conduct environmental scans on a more regular basis. Still other organizations choose to conduct scanning on a continuous basis—always collecting, processing, and analyzing data. While there is no one right answer for every organization, in today's highly turbulent (and sometimes even volatile) business and organizational environments, it may be prudent to consider conducting environmental scanning more frequently, as opposed to less frequently.

External Trends—Things to Keep an Eye On

Organizations need to monitor trends of a wide and varying nature, including, but in no way limited to

- ▶ Economic trends
- ▶ Competitive trends
- ▶ Political trends
- ▶ Global trends
- ▶ Business trends
- ▶ Industry trends
- ▶ Employment trends
- ▶ Technological trends
- ▶ Demographic trends

Organizations: Structure, Design, and Partnership

As we've reiterated numerous times, in order to be effective in our profession, we have to be businesspeople—not just HR professionals. Our profession is our craft. We need to be prepared to knowledgeably practice that craft within the organizations we support. In order to do so, one of the many things we need to understand is how organizations are structured.

As we begin to take a look at how organizations are functionally organized, let's go back and revisit Henri Fayol. Fayol identified six functional groups within organizations, and suggested that all organizational activities can fit into one of those six functional areas:

- ▶ Technical activities
- ▶ Commercial activities: sales and marketing
- ▶ Financial activities
- ▶ Security activities
- ▶ Accounting activities
- ▶ Managerial activities

Despite the ongoing validity of Fayol's theories, a few things have changed since Fayol's time. One is the role of human resources in the organization, which at first glance is not well-reflected in these six areas. Another is information technology, non-existent in the early twentieth century when Fayol set forth his ideas. Something that can be said to hold true for both of these areas is that while each is its own independent function, each also supports and reinforces the efforts of every other area. This is important, in and of itself, since it reinforces the idea that these areas—while illustrative—are not necessarily as clearly dichotomized as they were when Fayol originally set forth his ideas.

What HR Professionals Need to Know About the Organizations They Support

As HR professionals, there is specific business-related information we should know about the various structural elements of organizations. While any of these items could conceivably be on the PHR exam, discussing them goes beyond the scope of (and the page allocation for) this book. What we will do, then, is to set forth the concepts that are important for you to know and encourage you (in the strongest possible terms) to seek out, familiarize yourself with, learn, and (when appropriate) memorize facts, information, and formulas relating to the following:

- ▶ Technical activities/operations:
  - ▶ Capacity
  - ▶ Standards
  - ▶ Scheduling
  - ▶ Inventory
  - ▶ Control

- ▶ Commercial Activities—Sales and Marketing
  - ▶ The 4 Ps:
    - ▶ Product
    - ▶ Place
    - ▶ Price
    - ▶ Promotion
- ▶ Finance and Accounting Activities
  - ▶ Budgeting:
    - ▶ Incremental budgeting
    - ▶ Formula budgeting
    - ▶ Zero-based budgeting
    - ▶ Activity based budgeting
  - ▶ Assets
  - ▶ Liability
  - ▶ Equity
  - ▶ Accounts payable
  - ▶ Accounts receivable
  - ▶ Balance sheet

- ▶ Income statement

- ▶ Gross profit margin

- ▶ Statement of cash flows

- ▶ Financial ratios:

    - ▶ Business activity ratios

    - ▶ Profitability ratios

    - ▶ Debt ratios

    - ▶ Liquidity

    - ▶ Current ratio

- ▶ Acid test

Balanced Scorecard

In the early 1990s, a new approach to strategic management was developed by Dr. Robert Kaplan and Dr. David Norton. Called the "balanced scorecard," this new approach sought increased clarity and specificity by offering a clear and unequivocal prescription of what companies should measure in order to appropriately balance financial measures of success against *non-financial* measures of success.

In addition to being a measurement system, the balanced scorecard is also a management system. It turns strategic planning into a hands-on, reality driven, highly effective tool. It is important to note, however, that in creating and describing the balanced scorecard, Kaplan and Norton do not denounce the value of traditional financial measures. They do, however, share their premise that financial measures by themselves are not enough. Other perspectives must be incorporated in order to obtain a more accurate assessment of organizational performance.

The balanced scorecard embodies the following four perspectives:

- ▶ **Learning and Growth Perspective**: This perspective looks at employee training, as well as attitudes toward individual and corporate growth. It emphasizes the criticality of the knowledge worker, of people as the organization's primary resource, and of the need for employees to continually grow and learn so as to be able to perform in a manner that will truly support the attainment of organizational goals.

- ▶ **Business Process Perspective**: This perspective scrutinizes key internal business processes so as to measure and ascertain how well those processes generate business results (such as products and services) that meet customer expectations. The business process perspective ascertains performance levels through specific measures that are unique to each particular organization.

▸ **The Customer Perspective**: This perspective focuses on the criticality of customer focus and customer satisfaction—for *every* business and organization. Dissatisfied customers will eventually look to others who will meet their needs and expectations (often without ever sharing their reasons for doing so), which, if the numbers are large enough, can ultimately lead to organizational decline.

▸ **The Financial Perspective**: The financial perspective is the most traditional of Kaplan's and Norton's four perspectives. As previously indicated, financial considerations cannot be overlooked—they simply have to be supplemented with other meaningful organizational measures.

Organizational Life Cycle

It's particularly important for HR professionals to be familiar with organizational life cycles, since each phase will warrant different interventions. These phases or stages roughly approximate the phases of life experienced by humans—thereby further bolstering the perspective of the organization as a living, breathing entity.

The four stages of the lifecycle—though referred to slightly differently by different experts—are as follows:

▸ **Stage 1: Introduction (or "birth").** Excitement and energy are high and cash flow may be low. Struggling start-ups often find themselves searching for solid footing—financially as well operationally. The core group of highly talented employees may focus fixedly on the founder as a source of direction, wisdom, and inspiration.

In the introduction phase, employees may find themselves paid above market rates as a reflection of the founder's desire to "lure" them on board. Alternatively, if money is in short supply, employees in the introduction phase may earn less cash compensation, and have those diminished earnings offset by other non-cash rewards (equity, intrinsic rewards, and so on).

Depending upon the organization, HR may or may not have a presence in this phase of the organizational life cycle.

▸ **Stage 2: Development (or "growth").** The organization grows in so many ways during the development phase—market share, facilities, equipment, revenues, and the number of employees are all likely to expand, to varying degrees. Along with that growth, the organization is likely to experience some "growing pains."

Though it may be a challenging process for some organizations—one that might meet with resistance—it is important that policies and procedures are formalized, as a way of fostering equity, compliance, and consistency.

▶ **Stage 3**: **Maturity.** The growing pains have passed, and the culture is well established. In fact, it's important to ensure that certain elements of the culture do not become a bit *too* well-established. If this were to happen, an "entitlement mentality" could begin to emerge relative to pay, benefits, and/or other terms and conditions of employment. The organizational structure could evolve in a somewhat rigid manner, and resistance to OD and change initiatives could be high.

As is the case with us humans, organizations must resist the onset of inertia during these years of maturity lest they begin to atrophy. In concert with senior leadership, HR must play a key role in ensuring that this doesn't happen.

▶ **Stage 4**: **Decline.** If that inertia does set in, and if the atrophy does begin, decline is likely not far behind. There are many examples of the demise of long-standing organizations—retailers, in particular—"anchors" in our local and national communities that just weren't able to "keep up with these changing times." This can happen for any number of reasons such as salaries that are beyond what the organization can truly afford to pay, inflexible management, disengaged workers…the list goes on and on. In the wake of such decline, downsizing is likely to occur—either in pockets or across the organization as a whole.

Organizational Structure

Organizational structure refers to the various ways in which organizations can be designed to attain maximum levels of effectiveness and efficiency.

EXAM ALERT

As you prepare for the PHR exam, familiarize yourself with terms and concepts relating to organizational structure, including

▶ Formalization, or formal authority

▶ Departmentalization ("departmentation")

▶ Functional structure

▶ Division structure

▶ Matrix structure

▶ Chain of command

▶ Span of control

▶ Centralization

▶ Decentralization

▶ Simple structure organization model

▶ Bureaucratic organization model

▶ Virtual organization model

▶ Boundaryless organization model

▶ Mechanistic organizations

▶ Organic organizations

▶ Concentrated structures

In addition to representing information that is likely to show up somewhere on the PHR exam, this list also reflects information that you need to know and understand as an HR professional.

Measuring HR Effectiveness

HR's effectiveness can no longer be measured according to non-specific, non-quantifiable, "soft" assessments. Instead HR must be able to unequivocally demonstrate the effectiveness with which it is executing its various roles and the degree to which it is meeting the needs of its clients.

This discussion leads us to a critical—and foundational—distinction between "effectiveness" and "efficiency." Effectiveness is the degree to which carefully established (and, in our case, strategically aligned) goals are met. Efficiency, however, is a ratio of "outputs" to "inputs." Another way of putting it is that efficiency is "doing things right," while effectiveness is "doing the right things."

It's quite possible, therefore, that HR professionals can be effective without being efficient, or that they can be efficient without being effective. HR measures help to ensure that we will achieve efficiency as well as effectiveness.

There are a variety of HR measurement tools with which HR professionals need to be familiar.

HR Audits

The HR audit is the primary tool that many HR departments utilize in an effort to assess their own effectiveness and efficiency. Whether conducted in-house or by an outside vendor, HR audits have a number of purposes and produce a variety of results. Ultimately, however, the overall purpose is to ascertain how well the HR department—through all of its various functional areas—has aligned itself with the organization's strategic objectives.

More specifically, HR audits will scrutinize and draw conclusions relative to

▶ The degree to which the organization complies with legal requirements

▶ The degree to which HR services are "user friendly"

▶ Grievances, their causes, and their impact

▶ The degree to which the organization complies with I-9 requirements

▶ The degree to which core competencies have been identified and defined

▶ The degree to which recruiting, selection, and retention processes reflect the organization's core competencies

▶ The degree to which the organization achieves the ways it has chosen to position itself in the marketplace with respect to compensation and benefits (lead, lag, or match)

▶ The usefulness, appropriateness, and effectiveness of the employee handbook

▶ The degree to which existing OD initiatives, including training programs, meet the company's current and emerging human capital needs

▶ The degree to which the organization's safety program complies with federal, state, and local guidelines, and the degree to which it supports the company's objectives.

Other HR Measurement Techniques

There are a variety of other measurement techniques with which HR professionals need to be familiar.

▶ Return on investment (ROI)

▶ Cost-benefit analysis

▶ Break-even analysis

> **EXAM ALERT**
> Be familiar with how these techniques can be used to generate meaningful HR measurement tools.

Research

Oftentimes, ascertaining the effectiveness and efficiency of HR practices is best accomplished through research. Research, in simple and decidedly "unacademic" terms, refers to finding answer to questions. In practice, research is a bit more involved.

Research can be either "primary" or "secondary." Primary research involves collecting data first-hand, from the original source from which it emanates. Secondary research, conversely, involves collecting information "second-hand"—meaning not directly from the original source of the data. Secondary research assimilates data that has already been collected by others, and thus allows those secondary researchers to "stand on the shoulders" of those who conducted the primary research.

One type of primary research with which HR professionals need to be familiar is the scientific method. The scientific method is a systematic approach of testing hypotheses and using the knowledge generated to strengthen the degree to which HR can support the overall objectives of the organization.

The five steps in the scientific method are as follows:

1. Question, and observe. Formulate a question that addresses the problem you want to study and to solve.

2. Develop a hypothesis. A hypothesis is an "educated guess" about the outcomes that you think the research will produce.

3. Design a method: This is the step where you'll outline the specific steps that you'll take while conducting the experiment (your research).

4. Collect your data, which are the unexamined results of your research.

5. Analyze your data and reach a conclusion. State why you think the experiment (your research) turned out the way it did and ascertain whether the results supported your initial hypothesis.

Ethical Considerations for HR Professionals

All too frequently, headlines broadcast the latest local and national corporate scandals. Whether it's cover-ups, money laundering, insider trading, outright theft, corrupt practices, or conflicts of interest, there is no shortage of highly public and highly publicized documentation of ethical lapses within this nation's corporations.

This phenomenon, however, is not limited to the private sector. The words just look a little different when we talk about ethical lapses in the public sector, where we might find ourselves reading headlines that talk about, for instance, "misappropriation of public funds." In both school and governmental settings, there have been far too many examples of employees engaging in lavish and unauthorized spending, illegally financed personal trips, and corruption.

Ironically, approximately 90% of business schools offer ethics courses. In many curricula, those programs are not only offered—they are required. Yet, the headlines are still being printed. And in the organizations from which these headlines emanate, it is often HR professionals who find themselves in the middle of the fray.

What Is Ethics?

Ethics has been defined in a number of ways. One way to look at ethics is as a shared values-based system that serves to guide, channel, shape, and direct the behavior of individuals in organizations in an appropriate and productive direction.

Taking this definition one step further, business ethics could be defined as a shared values-based system designed to inculcate within the organization's population a sense of how to conduct business properly.

HR's Role in Ethics

HR must play a leadership role in establishing, encouraging, and ensuring ongoing ethical behavior within organizations. HR cannot, however, "own" ethics, or even own the organization's ethical initiative. Like other programs that are viewed as "HR's responsibility" (for instance, performance management, interviewing, and the like), ethics must be operationalized so that ownership and responsibility are truly shared by all.

In her article "The Ethical Enabler: Empowering Employees To Become Chief Ethics Officers," Susan Alevas speaks of the process of promulgating and inculcating ethical values in the organization as follows:

> When it comes to combating ethical complacency, governing board members, chief executive officers and senior management need to become "ethical enablers," the folks who encourage, support, and champion their employees to become "Chief Ethics Officers." Moreover, there's nothing stopping organizations from also bestowing their vendors and customers with the "Chief Ethics Officer" role.

Why Ethics?

Maintaining an ethical organization isn't about "being nice" or even "being good." Instead, there are a number of business-driven reasons for cultivating an ethical organization. In short, an erosion of ethics can lead to an erosion of the organization. Just a few of the reasons why it is critical to ensure that our organizations remain ethical are discussed in the following sections.

To Prevent Erosion of Trust

Successful organizations are based on a network of trust—trust that their members will "do the right thing." When that doesn't happen, or when negative actions are tolerated (or worse, encouraged), employees stop trusting. They may then begin to rationalize inappropriate and unethical behaviors. As the results of this erosion become more visible, employees with a strong sense of personal integrity may leave, and potential employees who do uphold high ethical standards might be difficult to attract.

To Prevent Cynicism

Some people describe skepticism as "healthy," and perhaps some small measure of it is...unless it begins to degenerate into cynicism. The negativity that comes along with cynicism can poison the culture of an organization. Those who cannot tolerate that atmosphere will likely leave—which makes the atmosphere of the remaining organization even more toxic.

To Prevent Dysfunctional Manifestations of Politics

Politics, to some degree, is inevitable within organizations. In unethical organizations, however, politics will likely become increasingly dysfunctional and perhaps even destructive.

To Prevent Aggression/Violence

The anger that can fester when employees perceive that the leaders of an organization have acted in an unjust or inequitable manner often must have an outlet somewhere. Sadly, even tragically, that outlet is not always productive, and can even be highly destructive, as we have all witnessed in well-publicized cases of workplace violence, such as the 1992 Royal Oak Post Office shooting. According to a letter written 10 years later by Charlie Withers, chief steward of the Royal Oak Post Office:

> This tragedy was the result of a hostile work environment, created by postal management and condoned by those in higher positions within the postal service. This militaristic autocratic management style was allowed to go unchecked, even though the Royal Oak District was feeling the "backlash" in service to its patrons…. The workforce through-out the Royal Oak District was under attack by overzealous managers who used whatever tactics needed to disrupt their lives…. This same group of managers had been investigated in a GAO (Government Accounting Office) investigation done in Indianapolis for the same problems 3 years prior…and nothing was done!!

Aggression can also manifest itself through less violent—and thus perhaps less easily identifi-able—forms, such as theft, lying, tampering or vandalism—all in an effort to "get even" with those in power who are treating them unfairly. Aggressive acts such as these have financial as well as non-financial costs to the organization that might exponentially increase if the organ-ization permits or perpetuates an unethical culture.

Cultivating an Ethical Organization

One important element of creating an ethical culture comes from establishing an organiza-tional code of ethics. That code, which ideally should have an introduction from the CEO, should reaffirm the organization's commitment to the code. The code itself needs to start with the mission, vision, and values of the organization. Together, these three go a long way toward setting the framework for ethics. From there, an organization's code of ethics needs to address myriad issues from the perspectives employees, customers, shareholders, suppliers, and the community at large.

The Code of Ethics: A Living Document

The process of writing a code of ethics is only the beginning. It cannot simply be written and forgotten. Instead, the code of ethics needs to have "life," and it needs to have "teeth"—clear statements relative to how the code—along with and the policies that emanate from the code—will be implemented and upheld.

Once the code is established, individuals at *all* levels of the organization must be held to its standards. A single standard must apply to all within the organization. Nothing will erode a code of ethics faster than the revelation that it has been applied or enforced inconsistently. It is simply not possible to "overlook" certain ethical violations from a certain person while making an example of the ethical violations of others.

> **EXAM ALERT**
>
> SHRM has established its own code of ethics specifically for HR professionals. This is a likely topic for inclusion on the PHR exam, so review it beforehand.

Legislative Framework, Considerations, and Opportunities

At the introduction of this chapter, we referenced a familiar saying: "Some people make things happen, some people watch things happen, and some people wonder what happened." This is perhaps no more apparent than in our legislative process, created hundreds of years ago, yet perhaps more vibrant and vital now more than ever before.

As HR professionals, understanding the legislative process helps us to more effectively impact that process. It is both our right and our responsibility to do this. Why? Because the employment-related laws that are passed in our nation directly impact our profession, the organizations for which we work, and the way we perform our jobs (hint: think HIPAA, FMLA, and so forth).

How a Bill Becomes a Law

Some readers may recall the *Schoolhouse Rock* series from the '70s and '80s that explained—quite entertainingly—how a bill becomes a law. Although "I'm Just a Bill" may not grace our televisions anymore, the following 13-step process still accurately describes how laws are passed. It's a process that is worth revisiting now, as we reaffirm our commitment to being strategic and effective business and organizational partners.

Although anyone can draft a bill, only a member of Congress can actually introduce legislation. In so doing, that member of Congress becomes the sponsor of the bill.

There are four basic types of legislation: bills, joint resolutions, concurrent resolutions, and simple resolutions.

The legislative process officially begins when a bill or resolution is given a number (the number is preceded by "H.R." if it is a House bill, and "S." if it is a Senate bill). Once a number is assigned, the following steps will ensue:

1. **Referral to Committee**: Bills are usually referred to standing committees in the House or Senate according to carefully delineated rules of procedure.

2. **Committee Action**: One of three things can happen to a bill once it reaches a committee: It can be sent to a subcommittee, it can be considered by the committee as a whole, or it can be ignored (at which point the bill dies, or is killed, depending upon one's point of view).

3. **Subcommittee Review**: Bills are often referred to subcommittee for study and hearings. Hearings provide the opportunity to put views of the executive branch, experts, other public officials, supporters, and opponents officially "on the record." Testimony can be in person or submitted in writing.

4. **Mark Up**: When the hearings are completed, the subcommittee may meet to "mark up" the bill; that is, make changes and amendments prior to recommending the bill to the full committee. If a subcommittee votes not to report legislation to the full committee, the bill dies.

5. **Committee Action to Report a Bill**: After receiving a subcommittee's report on a bill, the full committee has two choices: It can conduct further study and hearings, or it can vote on the subcommittee's recommendations and any proposed amendments. The full committee then votes on its recommendation to the House or Senate. This procedure is called "ordering a bill reported."

6. **Publication of a Written Report**: After a committee votes to have a bill reported, the chairman instructs staff to prepare a report on the bill. This report describes the intent and scope of the legislation, impact on existing laws and programs, position of the executive branch, and views of dissenting members.

7. **Scheduling Floor Action**: After a bill is reported back to the chamber where it originated, it is placed in chronological order on the calendar. In the House, there are several different legislative calendars, and the speaker and majority leader largely

determine if, when, and in what order bills come up. In the Senate there is only one legislative calendar.

8. **Debate**: When a bill reaches the floor of the House or Senate, there are rules or procedures governing the debate. These rules determine the conditions and amount of time that will be allocated for debate.

9. **Voting**: After the debate and the approval of any amendments, the bill is passed or defeated by the members voting.

10. **Referral to Other Chamber**: When a bill is passed by the House or the Senate, it is referred to the other chamber, where it usually follows the same process through committee and floor action. This chamber can choose from four courses of action: approve the bill as is, reject the bill, ignore the bill, or change the bill.

11. **Conference Committee Action**: If only minor changes are made to a bill by the other chamber, it is common for the legislation to go back to the first chamber for concurrence. However, when the actions of the other chamber significantly alter the bill, a conference committee is formed to reconcile the differences. If the conferees cannot reach agreement, the legislation dies. If agreement is reached, a conference report describing the committee members' recommendations for changes is prepared. Both the House and the Senate must approve the conference report.

12. **Final Actions**: After the House and Senate have approved a bill in identical form, it is sent to the president. At this point, there are two ways in which the legislation can become law:

   ▶ If the president approves of the legislation, he or she signs it and it becomes "the law of the land."

   ▶ If the president takes no action for 10 days while Congress is in session, the legislation automatically becomes law.

   Alternatively, if the president opposes the bill, he or she can veto it; or, if he or she takes no action after the Congress has adjourned its second session, it is considered a "pocket veto" and the legislation dies.

13. **Overriding a Veto**: If the president vetoes a bill, Congress may attempt to override the veto. This requires a two-thirds roll call vote of the members who are present in sufficient numbers for a quorum.

Be Heard—Reach Out to Your Elected Officials

There are a variety of ways to reach out to the members of Congress and other elected officials who represent you.

Write (Early, But Not Too Often)

Morris K. Udall (1922–1998), a congressman from Arizona, composed "The Right to Write—Some Suggestions on Writing to Your Representative in Congress." Although Udall retired from Congress in 1991 before the advent of the Internet as a popular method of day-to-day communication, his suggestions are as valid today as they were years ago:

- Address your correspondence properly (for instance, when writing to a member of Congress, address it to "The Honorable _____ _____").

- Use the correct physical address.

- Identify the bill or issue you're writing about, ideally using the bill number as well as the name by which it is popular known.

- Send letters in a timely manner, while there is still time for your member of Congress to consider your input.

- Communicate with those members of Congress who represent you.

- Be brief, and be legible. Our elected officials are busy, and receive a great deal of communication to sort through.

- Personal letters may have greater impact than form letters, or petitions.

- Be specific about why you hold your opinion, and about how the legislation would impact you.

- When possible, offer suggestions.

- If you have expertise in a particular area, say so—and then share it.

- Provide your elected officials with positive, as well as constructive, feedback.

Udall offers some basic "don'ts" as well

- Don't threaten.

- Don't promise.

- Don't engage in name-calling.

- Speak for others, not for others for whom you claim to represent (unless you actually do).

- Don't become a "pen pal."

- Don't demand commitment—especially before all the facts are in.

Lobbying

Lobbying is the process of reaching out to your elected officials to express your beliefs and opinions with the hope of influencing a governmental body.

NOTE

Before you begin lobbying, do your homework. Know the subject matter and draft your message clearly and concisely. Be firm, be knowledgeable, and be confident. Know the issue, explain your concerns relative to the consequences of the issue, and suggest a specific course of action. In addition, consider coordinating your efforts with others who share a similar viewpoint.

Personal Visits

Consider meeting with your elected official, or perhaps with one of his or her staff members.

Stay Informed

Perhaps most importantly, stay up to date on the issues that can potentially impact the HR profession, the organization in which you work, or the ways in which you will carry out the role of HR. Affiliate with organizations—such as SHRM—that are committed to shaping the laws that impact our profession and our workplaces. Sign up to receive "e-alerts"—legislative updates from organizations. And don't stop paying attention after a law is passed—court interpretations can also have a big impact on how you execute your role.

Chapter Summary

Functioning effectively requires a number of areas of knowledge and expertise, all of which could be grouped into three critical categories: knowing our business (organization), knowing our profession (craft), and knowing our customers. Though simply stated, much goes into mastering these three areas, if they are to be performed at a highly efficient and effective level.

This chapter addressed some of the specific areas of knowledge with which HR professionals need to become fluent. It is intended as a starting point, not an ending point. Strategic management is also an area that many HR professionals will more fully understand, appreciate, and excel at as they gain experience and expertise within their organization, as well as within their craft.

Key Terms

- Strategic management
- Industrial relations
- Personnel
- Human resources
- Administrative HR functions
- Strategic HR functions
- Operational/tactical HR functions
- Henri Fayol
- Planning function
- Organizing function
- Coordinating function
- Directing function
- Controlling function
- Project management
- Initiating processes
- Planning processes
- Executing processes
- Controlling processes

- Closing processes
- Project manager
- Project sponsor
- Project charter
- Project team
- Project plan
- Project schedule
- Work breakdown structure (WBS)
- Gantt chart
- Program evaluation and review technique (PERT) charts
- Change management
- Outsourcing
- Offshoring
- Request for proposal (RFP) (see Chapter 2)
- Third party vendor
- HRIS
- Globalization

- Technology
- Safety and security
- Terrorism
- Aging workforce
- Multi-generational workplaces
- Work/life balance
- Changing technology—and not losing relations
- Contingent workforce
- Strategic planning
- Vision
- Mission
- Values
- SWOT analysis (strengths, weaknesses, opportunities, threats)
- Environmental scanning
- Capacity
- Standards
- Scheduling
- Inventory
- Control
- The 4 P's:
  - Product
  - Place
  - Price
  - Promotion
- Budgeting:
  - Incremental budgeting
  - Formula budgeting
    - Zero-based budgeting
    - Activity based budgeting
- Assets
- Liability
- Equity
- Accounts payable
- Accounts receivable
- Balance sheet
- Income statement
- Gross profit margin
- Statement of cash flows
- Financial ratios:
  - Business activity ratios
  - Profitability ratios
  - Debt ratios
- Liquidity
- Current ratio
- Acid test
- Gross profit margin
- Balanced scorecard
- Learning and growth perspective
- Business process perspective
- Customer perspective
- Financial perspective
- Organizational lifecycle
- Introduction/birth
- Development/growth
- Maturity

- Decline
- Organizational structure
- Formalization, or formal authority
- Departmentalization ("departmentation")
- Functional structure
- Division structure
- Matrix structure
- Chain of command
- Span of control
- Centralization
- Decentralization
- Simple structure organization model
- Bureaucratic organization model
- Virtual organization model
- Boundaryless organization model
- Mechanistic organizations

- Organic organizations
- Concentrated structures
- HR audits
- Return on investment (ROI)
- Cost-benefit analysis
- Break-even analysis
- Research
- Primary research
- Scientific method
- Secondary research
- Ethics
- Business ethics
- Bills
- Joint resolutions
- Concurrent resolutions
- Simple resolutions
- Lobbying

Apply Your Knowledge

This chapter focuses on issues relating to strategic management. Complete the following review questions and exam questions as a way of reviewing and reinforcing the knowledge and skills you'll need to perform your responsibilities as an HR professional, and to increase the likelihood that you will pass the PHR examination.

Review Questions

1. Describe the managerial function "planning."

2. Describe what is meant by the "mission" of an organization.

3. What is a code of ethics, and why is it important to an organization?

4. Describe the "introduction" phase of the organizational life cycle.

5. Describe the controlling processes of project management.

Exam Questions

1. Which of the following is *not* a category of processes within project management?

   ○ **A.** Planning

   ○ **B.** Executing

   ○ **C.** Coordinating

   ○ **D.** Controlling

2. Which of the following statements about change is *most* true?

   ○ **A.** HR professionals must proactively seek to understand change and what causes change.

   ○ **B.** HR must serve as an employee advocate during times of change.

   ○ **C.** HR must ensure that the pace of change does not exceed the organization's ability to adapt to it.

   ○ **D.** HR must serve as a management advocate during times of change.

3. Which of the following statements about values is *not* true?

   ○ **A.** Values are often expressed through terms such as "communication" and "decision making."

   ○ **B.** Values impact behaviors that are exhibited on a day-day-to-day basis in the workplace.

   ○ **C.** Values are the beliefs on which an organization is built.

   ○ **D.** Values shape and guide strategic—as well as day-to-day—decision making.

4. The first step in the scientific method is

   ○ **A.** Develop a hypothesis.

   ○ **B.** Question and observe.

   ○ **C.** Scan existing secondary research.

   ○ **D.** Conduct a needs analysis.

5. The primary purpose of an HR audit is

    ○ **A.** To ascertain how well the HR department—through all of its various functional areas—has aligned itself with the organization's strategic objectives.

    ○ **B.** To ascertain the degree to which the HR department has complied with all legal requirements, and the potential financial exposure associated with existing levels of non-compliance.

    ○ **C.** To ascertain the performance of the HR department with respect to the nature and quality of the consultative services it provides to its internal clients.

    ○ **D.** To ascertain the degree to which the HR department is poised to meet the current, future, and emerging human capital and talent needs of the organization.

6. Which of the following is not one of the four perspectives of the balanced scorecard?

    ○ **A.** The financial perspective

    ○ **B.** The external perspective

    ○ **C.** The learning and growth perspective

    ○ **D.** The business process perspective

7. Effectiveness can be defined as

    ○ **A.** A ratio of "inputs" to "outputs"

    ○ **B.** The degree to which goals are met

    ○ **C.** The degree to which goals reflect desired outputs

    ○ **D.** A ratio of "outputs" to "inputs"

8. Which of the following is not specifically recognized as being critically important to successfully implementing any strategic plan?

    ○ **A.** Commitment

    ○ **B.** Credibility

    ○ **C.** Collaboration

    ○ **D.** Communication

9. Project managers seek to accomplish their objectives by gaining control over five factors, one of which is:

○ **A.** Regulatory compliance

○ **B.** Risk

○ **C.** Reward structures

○ **D.** Staffing

10. All of the following are compelling reasons for organizations to engage in a strategic planning process except:

○ **A.** Developing a clearer awareness of how the organization "measures up" internally and externally

○ **B.** Engaging individuals throughout the organization in a meaningful organizational effort

○ **C.** Enabling employees to prepare themselves to react positively and constructively to future events

○ **D.** Creating—or reaffirming—the vision, mission, and values of the organization

Answers to Review Questions

1. Planning, the first of five managerial functions, lays the groundwork for how managers will work toward accomplishing the organization's goals. Through planning, managers decide what needs to get done, when it needs to get done, who will do it, how it will get done, and where it will be done. In the absence of planning, the organization—and the people in it—will lack direction, and perhaps even just "coast along."

2. An organization's mission statement articulates, in essence, its reason for being. It may speak to the nature of the organization's business or purpose, its customers, and sometimes even its employees and its role in the community. A mission statement should be broad (but not overly generalized), brief, clear, unambiguous, and designed to last for "the long haul." Since the goals of an organization must be based on the mission, the mission is far bigger than any goal—and thus must be must be able to withstand the test of time.

3. Establishing an organizational code of ethics is one important part of creating an ethical culture. The ethics code should begin with an introduction from the CEO that reaffirms the organization's commitment to the code. The code itself needs to start with the mission, vision, and values of the organization. From there, an organization's code of ethics needs to address myriad issues from the varying perspectives of employees, customers, shareholders, suppliers, and the community at large.

4. "Introduction" (or "birth") is the first step in the organizational lifecycle. During this phase, excitement and energy run high, and cash flow may be quite tight. Struggling start-ups often find themselves searching for solid footing—financially as well operationally. The core group of highly talented employees who are part of a start-up operations may focus fixedly on the founder as a source of direction, wisdom, and inspiration.

In the introduction phase, employees may find themselves paid above market rates as a reflection of the founder's desire to "entice" them to come on board. Alternatively, if money is in short supply, during the introduction phase of the lifecycle employees may earn less cash compensation and have those diminished earnings offset by other non-cash rewards (equity, intrinsic rewards, and so on).

Depending upon the organization, HR may or may not have a formal presence in this phase of the organizational life cycle.

5. Controlling processes include managing the scope of the project and making sure the project stays in line with the original objectives. A significant degree of follow-up is required to carry out controlling processes.

Answers to Exam Questions

1. **Answer C is the best choice.** "Coordinating" is a management function, not a project management process. Answers A, B, and D are not the best choices, since they each identify a project management process (those processes include initiation, planning, executing, controlling, and closing).

2. **Answer A is the best choice.** HR professionals must seek to understand change and what causes change—ideally before change descends upon the organization. Change, itself, brings considerable challenges of its own—and often does not afford HR professionals with the luxury of time to "study" change theory or process (those are lessons that HR professionals need to undertake in advance). Answer C is not the best choice, since HR's role is not to regulate the pace of change. At times, the pace of change may not be controllable. At other times, the pace of change may, in fact, be controllable, but the organization's leaders may decide that it is not appropriate or advisable to slow the pace of change. Answers B and D are not the best choices; HR must serve as a "truth advocate®" during times of change (in fact, at all times), not as dedicated advocates of management *or* employees.

3. **Answer A is the best choice.** Words like "communication" and "decision making" are terms that are often used to describe competencies (also called success factors), not values. Answers B, C, and D are not the best choices, since each makes a true statement about values.

4. **Answer B is the best choice.** "Question and observe" is, in fact, the first step in the scientific method. Answer A is not the best choice, since developing a hypothesis is the second step in the scientific method. Answer C is not the best choice, since the scientific method is a form of primary research, and is therefore separate and distinct from secondary research. Answer D is not the best choice, since "conducting a needs analysis and assessment" is the first step in the ADDIE process, not the scientific method.

5. **Answer A is the best choice.** The primary and overarching purpose of an HR audit is to ascertain how well the HR department has aligned itself with the organization's strategic objectives. Answers B, C, and D are not the best responses; while each identifies a possible component of an HR audit, none of these is broad enough to encompass the overarching purpose of an HR audit.

6. **Answer B is the best choice.** Though various elements of the balanced scorecard take external factors into consideration, the "external perspective" is not one of the four specific perspectives. Answers A, C, and D are not the best choices, since they each identify one of the perspectives of the balanced scorecard.

7. **Answer B is the best choice.** Effectiveness is a measure of the degree to which goals—carefully established goals—are met.

8. **Answer C is the best choice.** While collaboration is an important element of the strategic planning process, it is not recognized as on one of the "three Cs"—the most important keys to successful strategic planning. Those "three Cs" are commitment (answer A), credibility (answer B), and communication (answer D).

9. **Answer B is the best choice.** The five factors over which project managers seek to establish control are time, cost, quality, scope, and risk (answer B is "risk"). Project managers do not specifically seek to establish control over regulatory compliance (answer A), reward structures (answer C), or staffing (answer D), although all of those elements will be considerations as they work to attain their objectives.

10. **Answer D is the best choice.** The focus of strategic planning is on "proactivity," not "reactivity." Therefore, through strategic planning, the organization creates an opportunity for individuals at all levels of the organization to proactively shape and influence the future, rather than just react to it. Answers A, B, and C are not the best responses, since each one articulates a compelling reason to engage in strategic planning.

Suggested Readings and Resources

"HR as a strategic partner: What does it take to make it happen?" An article from *HR. Human Resource Planning*, by Edward E. Lawler, III, Susan A Mohrman.

The HR Value Proposition (hardcover) by Dave Ulrich, Wayne Brockbank, David Ulrich

Human Resource Champions (hardcover) by David Ulrich

"The Ethical Enabler: Empowering Employees To Become Chief Ethics Officers." An article by Susan F. Alevas, Esq., President, Alevas Consulting Group, Inc.

Organizational Architecture: Designs for Changing Organizations (Jossey Bass Business and Management Series) (hardcover), by David A. Nadler, Marc S. Gerstein, Robert B. Shaw

Know Your Responsibilities: Ethics & Fiduciary Duties for HR (HR Executive Special Reports) (hardcover), by Anne H. Williams

The HR Scorecard: Linking People, Strategy, and Performance (hardcover), by Brian E. Becker, Mark A. Huselid, Dave Ulrich

Get Them On Your Side (hardcover), by Samuel B. Bacharach

Designing Dynamic Organizations: A Hands-On Guide for Leaders at All Levels (paperback), by Jay Galbraith, Diane Downey, Amy Kates.

CHAPTER FOUR

Workforce Planning and Employment

Study Strategies

Use index cards (ideally, of different sizes and different colors) to help you study:

▶ Prepare large index cards for each of the laws. Make note of important facts, dates, and details relating to each law. On the back of the card, in pencil, jot down names of relevant cases.

▶ Prepare small index cards for case law. On each card, write the name of each court case that is relevant to this functional area (don't forget to include cases that were decided after this book was published).

▶ On a third—and slightly larger set of index cards—jot down key learning points from each case. Like you did with the larger set of cards, write the name of each case in pencil on the back of the card.

▶ Match the three sets of cards together. Of course, don't look at the back of the cards until you've matched all of the cards—then, check to see if you've done so correctly.

▶ Try writing out your own multiple choice test questions. Writing out the questions along with detailed answers can go a long way toward reinforcing what you are studying. If you've got a study partner, trade questions with that person.

▶ Although the PHR exam is multiple choice, try writing and answering your own "essay based" questions. Write open-ended questions that require a response of at least a full paragraph—and write your answers without looking back at your study materials. The process of actually writing down your answers will reinforce what you already know, and will highlight what you need to study more. It will also likely help you as you work to recall this same information when you answer related multiple choice questions on the actual PHR exam.

▶ While many HR professionals have experience in the areas of employment, that experience may more closely reflect their organization's practices rather than "best practices." It's possible, therefore, that—while you're going through this chapter (and your other related study materials) and trying to match your experience to the materials—you may find some areas in which there is a disconnect between your personal experience and what you're reading. For purposes of the PHR exam test, stick with the recommended practices that are written here and in your other prep materials. When you are actually on the job, look for ways to reconcile these best practices with "the way I've always done it" or "the way it's always been done around here." Seek to incorporate ideas that can revitalize the ways in which you carry out the workforce planning and employment function.

▶ As with each of the six functional areas of HR, determine what you already know and what you don't know. Then, work to prepare yourself. Conduct research. Use the Internet to find relevant articles and white papers. Peruse textbooks that provide guidance relative to those particular areas. Be sure to find several real-life examples to ensure that you gain a variety of perspectives and insights. This is particularly important for the skill-based, rather than fact-based, components of this functional area.

Introduction

An organization's overall success will be determined to a significant degree by its ability to have the right people, with the right skills, in the right places at the right times. It sounds somewhat straightforward, but let's take a closer look at what this statement actually means.

"*Having*" in this context can refer to hiring employees to work a traditional work arrangement, hiring employees to work some sort of non-traditional work arrangement, or retaining non-employees to perform services on an as-needed basis ("consultants"). Most organizations secure most of their "people resources" through traditional employment relationships, which may be augmented by non-traditional arrangements or consulting services.

"*The right people, with the right skills*" refers to employing or contracting with individuals who possess and demonstrate the skills, knowledge, abilities, and competencies needed to support the organization's mission and to attain the organization's objectives. Employing individuals who don't have the necessary skills can be problematic (or, at the very least, challenging). So is employing—and retaining—individuals who possess skills that they want to put to use but that aren't needed.

"*In the right places, at the right times*" speaks to the importance of analyzing short-term and long-term organizational needs in order to ensure that the organization is neither overstaffed nor understaffed at any time. In this context, the terms "overstaffing" and "understaffing" can refer to the number of people employed, as well as the skills that those individuals bring to the organization.

Achieving this delicate balance requires a considerable amount of planning. It also requires that HR professionals continually maintain awareness of the organization's mission, as well as of its short term, long term, and emerging goals. In this way, HR professionals—in close collaboration with the leaders and managers of the organization—can determine how to strategically support the organization's goals.

In order to formulate and execute these plans, HR professionals must be well-versed in those laws that affect our profession and that affect the ways in which we source, hire, promote, and terminate employees. Equal employment opportunity is the foundation upon which these laws have been built, and therefore constitutes a critical element of every HR professional's knowledge base. Laws are not static, however. As they are continually interpreted and reinterpreted by the courts, HR professionals also have a mandate to know important cases from the past and to monitor new cases so as to understand and appreciate new interpretations of these laws and how they will affect the workplace.

This chapter will explore these areas with a specific eye toward how they affect the way we perform our jobs.

Equal Employment Opportunity: The Basics

As mentioned previously, a commitment to ensure equal opportunities throughout all dimensions of the employment relationship serves as the backdrop to employment-related legislation. In order to be effective, HR professionals need to have an understanding of certain fundamental concepts.

Protected Class

A group of people who share a common characteristic and who are protected from discrimination and harassment on the basis of that shared characteristic are said to belong to a "protected class."

Discrimination

Discrimination, in the truest sense of the word, is not necessarily illegal. To discriminate is to make a distinction, or to discern. When distinctions or discernments are made on the basis of factors, traits, or characteristics that are protected by law, however, discrimination becomes unlawful.

Types of Unlawful Discrimination

HR professionals must be knowledgeable about the following types of discrimination:

- Disparate (or "adverse") treatment
- Disparate (or "adverse") impact
- Perpetuating past discrimination

Disparate (or "Adverse") Treatment

Disparate (or "adverse") treatment is a type of unlawful discrimination that occurs when an employer *intentionally* treats applicants or employees differently on the basis of their race, color, sex, religion, national origin, age, disability, or any other characteristic protected by law. The following would constitute examples of disparate treatment:

- ▶ Candidates who indicate on their employment application that they speak Spanish are interviewed in Spanish, while all other candidates are interviewed in English.

- ▶ Female members of a team or department are asked to take meeting minutes or provide refreshments, while male members are not.

- ▶ The quality or quantity or work that is performed by employees who request a modified schedule so as to be able to attend religious services is closely scrutinized, while the quality or quantity of work performed by employees who do not make such a request is not scrutinized as closely.

Disparate (or "Adverse") Impact

Disparate (or adverse) impact occurs when a seemingly neutral policy or practice has a disproportionately negative impact upon a member of a protected class. Policies or practices that are not job related and that have a statistically significant impact upon members of a protected class may constitute unlawful discrimination. For instance:

- ▶ An organization requires that all newly hired employees have a college degree, even though a degree is not required to perform some of the jobs that exist within the organization. If members of protected classes are "screened out" at a statistically higher rate, an allegation of disparate impact might be upheld.

- ▶ An organization requires that all newly promoted managers must spend the first six months on the job working at six different—and geographically dispersed—locations throughout the country. If members of a protected class are eliminated from consideration for employment at a statistically higher rate because of this policy, and if this policy is found to be unrelated to successful performance of the position, an allegation of disparate impact might be upheld.

EXAM ALERT

Know how to mathematically determine whether adverse impact exists. In addition, know what options and choices exist in the event that adverse impact does exist.

While disparate treatment is an intentional form of discrimination, disparate impact may be either intentional *or* unintentional. However, it doesn't matter. Lack of intent does not alter or excuse the fact that unlawful discrimination has occurred.

Perpetuating Past Discrimination

A third type of unlawful discrimination occurs when an employer's *past* discriminatory practices are perpetuated through *current* policies or practices—even those that appear to be non-discriminatory. When linked in some way with past discrimination, seemingly non-discriminatory practices can have a discriminatory effect.

One of the most commonly recognized examples of how past discrimination is perpetuated can be found in the use of employee referral programs. For instance, if discriminatory hiring decisions have been made in the past, an employer's workforce may now be primarily white…or male…or young…. If that same employer uses referrals from current employees as the primary means of recruiting new employees, it is likely that the individuals who will subsequently be brought into the workforce may also be primarily white…or male…or young—thus perpetuating the discriminatory decisions that were made in the past.

Harassment—Another Form of Unlawful Discrimination

Unlawful workplace harassment can also manifest itself as harassment on the basis of a person's membership in protected class. While most of the landmark court cases and media coverage on this topic focus on sexual harassment, HR professionals must be cognizant of the fact that harassment on the basis of *any* protected class—not just sex—may constitute unlawful discrimination.

Sexual Harassment

Sexual harassment is a form of sex discrimination that was rendered illegal by Title VII of the Civil Rights Act of 1964 (see Title VII of the Civil Rights Act [1964] in this chapter). The EEOC defines sexual harassment as follows:

"Unwelcome sexual advances, requests for sexual favors, and other verbal or physical conduct of a sexual nature constitute sexual harassment when:

1. "Submission to such conduct is made either explicitly or implicitly a term or condition of an individual's employment."

2. "Submission to or rejection of such conduct by an individual is used as the basis for employment decisions affecting such individual."

3. "Such conduct has the purpose or effect of unreasonably interfering with an individual's work performance or creating an intimidating, hostile, or offensive working environment."

There are two categories of sexual harassment:

▶ **Quid Pro Quo**: As previously articulated in point number 2, quid pro quo harassment occurs when an individual's submission to or rejection of sexual advances or conduct of a sexual nature is used as the basis for employment-related decisions. Quid pro quo harassment, therefore, originates from a supervisor, or from others who have the authority to influence or make decisions about the employee's terms and conditions of employment.

▶ **Hostile Work Environment**: As partially articulated, hostile work environment harassment occurs when unwelcome sexual conduct unreasonably interferes with an individual's job performance or creates a hostile, intimidating, or offensive work environment. Hostile work environment harassment can be found to exist whether or not the employee experiences (or runs the risk of experiencing) tangible or economic work-related consequences. By definition, hostile work environments can be created by virtually anyone with whom an employee might come in contact in the workplace (or "workspace," in the event of remote harassment through electronic means such as emails, faxes, instant messages (IMs), and so on.

EEO Reporting Requirements

By September 30 of each year, annual EEO reports must be filed by all employers with 100 or more employees. Additionally, federal contractors with at least 50 employees and federal contracts of at least $50,000 per year must also file an annual report.

EXAM ALERT

Don't limit your knowledge of EEO compliance to requirements that apply to your current organization. Familiarize yourself with all EEO reporting requirements. Specifically, be sure to familiarize yourself with the nine job categories listed in the EEO reporting forms and with the different EEO reporting requirements for different industries.

Applicant Flow Data

Employers also need to be cognizant of the need to maintain applicant flow data.

CAUTION

The EEOC's definition of an "applicant" is different from the OFCCP's definition of an applicant. Employers—and HR professionals—need to know which definition to use, and when.

Employers who are covered by EO 11246 have particular obligations with respect to maintaining applicant flow data (and, for that matter, with appropriately defining the term "applicant").

With this foundational understanding of EEO and employment law, HR professionals are then better prepared to engage in the workforce planning and employment process in a more knowledgeable—and therefore a more responsible and effective—manner.

Equal Opportunity for Whom?

Ensuring equal employment opportunity (EEO) is an ever-evolving concept. As such, it might be more accurate to say that as of today these laws ensure equal opportunities for "most," rather than for "all."

There are still individuals who—at a federal level—can be excluded from consideration for employment on the basis of shared characteristics or traits—even though those characteristics or traits are completely unrelated to the position. For instance, there is no federal law prohibiting employment discrimination on the basis of sexual orientation or on the basis of marital status, even though certain states do offer those additional protections.

This chapter is based under the premise that all workforce planning and employment decisions should be based on job-related factors. This will help ensure that we do not run afoul of the law. Additionally—and perhaps just as importantly—this will also ensure that we do not eliminate qualified individuals on the basis of factors that have nothing to do with whether or not they can perform the job.

Related Legislation: Workforce Planning and Employment

Congress has passed numerous pieces of federal legislation specifically designed to eradicate discrimination on the basis of a variety of factors. Though there are a host of factors covered, they all share one thing in common—none of them has any impact on a person's ability to do the job. Each piece of legislation, therefore, has brought the workplace one step closer to ensuring that hiring, promotional, and all other employment-related decisions are based solely on job-related factors.

> **EXAM ALERT**
>
> Be familiar with laws designed to protect employee privacy, including the Privacy Act of 1974.

> **EXAM ALERT**
>
> When responding to questions on the PHR exam, be certain to answer on the basis of federal laws, not state or local laws that might govern your particular employer (and with which you might be more familiar)

> **CAUTION**
>
> When it comes to employment law, HR professionals must tread carefully. In order to function effectively, we need a solid understanding of the laws that affect our profession, our clients, and our organization. We must maintain currency with respect to how the courts interpret—and reinterpret—existing laws, and we must understand the impact of new laws. There is, however, a line over which we cannot cross—under penalty of law. Ultimately, a person who is not an attorney cannot practice law or dispense legal advice. We must be cautious that our efforts do not unintentionally encroach upon this domain.

Title VII of the Civil Rights Act (1964)

Though not the first anti-discrimination law, Title VII of the Civil Rights Act of 1964 was a landmark piece of legislation prohibiting employment discrimination on the basis of race, color, religion, sex, or national origin. The most inclusive piece of anti-discrimination legislation up to that time (and perhaps even up through this time), Title VII radically changed the workplace and the way we interact within it.

The Civil Rights Act of 1964 established the first "protected classes," and created the Equal Employment Opportunity Commission (EEOC). As published on its website, the EEOC's mission is "to promote equal opportunity in employment through administrative and judicial enforcement of the federal civil rights laws and through education and technical assistance."

Title VII of the Civil Rights Act of 1964 prohibited discrimination in all aspects of the employment relationship, including

- ▸ Hiring and firing
- ▸ Compensation, assignment, or classification of employees
- ▸ Transfer, promotion, layoff, or recall
- ▸ Job advertisements
- ▸ Recruitment
- ▸ Testing
- ▸ Use of company facilities
- ▸ Training and apprenticeship programs
- ▸ Fringe benefits
- ▸ Pay, retirement plans, and disability leave
- ▸ Other terms and conditions of employment

Title VII also prohibits retaliating against an employee who files a charge of discrimination, participates in an investigation, or opposes discriminatory practices.

Title VII covers

- ▸ All private employers
- ▸ Federal, state and local governments
- ▸ Education institutions that employ 15 or more individuals
- ▸ Private and public employment agencies
- ▸ Labor organizations
- ▸ Joint labor management committees controlling apprenticeship and training

Under rare circumstances, exceptions can be made to Title VII requirements. Table 4.1 includes some of these exceptions.

TABLE 4.1   Exceptions to Title VII

Type of Exception	Definition	Example
Bona fide occupational qualification (BFOQ)	Certain job requirements that are mandated by business necessity may have an unintended discriminatory (disparate) impact upon applicants or employees on the basis gender, religion, or national origin.	Hiring females to be bathroom attendants in a women's restroom. Hiring a person of a particular religious denomination to be a minister to members of that faith.
Professionally developed test of skill or ability	Job-related tests that ascertain skills or abilities may have an unintended discriminatory (disparate) impact upon people on the basis of gender, religion, or national origin.	Strength or physical agility tests if those tests assess skills that have been shown to be necessary for successful performance of a particular position—as determined by the actual performance of current or former employees.
Seniority systems	Bona fide seniority or merit-based systems that are not intended or designed to discriminate unlawfully.	Bona fide collective bargaining agreements.
Piece-rate systems	Compensation programs under which individuals are paid according to their production volume.	Certain assembly line or factory assignments.

Executive Order 11246 (1965)

Unlike laws, which are passed by Congress, Executive Orders are enacted by the president. They do carry, however, the same weight as a law. Executive Orders provide guidance and assistance to federal agencies relative to the execution of their duties and to employers relative to what they must do in order to be in compliance with the executive order.

HR professionals need to be familiar with Executive Orders pertaining to employment issues. These EOs are administered by the Department of Labor—specifically, the Office of Contract Compliance Programs (OFCCP).

EO 11246, the first employment-related EO, established two key requirements for federal contractors and subcontractors that have contracts in excess of $10,000 during any one-year period:

▶ First, these employers are prohibited from discriminating in employment decisions on the basis of race, creed, color, or national origin. This requirement reconfirmed the non-discrimination requirements established by Title VII of the Civil Rights Act of 1964.

▶ Second, these employers must take affirmative steps—or actions—in advertising open positions, recruiting, employment, training, promotion, compensation, and termination of employees to ensure the elimination of employment barriers for women and minorities (people who we might refer to today as "people of color").

In addition, federal contractors and subcontractors with $50,000 or more in contracts during any 12-month period are also required to design and implement formal affirmative action plans (AAPs).

NOTE

In 1967, EO 11375 was enacted, adding sex to the list of protected classes. In 1969, EO 11478 was enacted, adding age and people with a "handicap" to the list of protected classes. In 1998, EO 13087 was enacted, adding sexual orientation to the list of protected classes. Parental status was added as a protected class in 2000 through EO 13152.

Affirmative Action Plans

On November 13, 2000, 41 CFR Part 60-2 (the portion of the federal register that addresses affirmative action) was significantly revised, with the overall intention of reducing the size and complexity of written AAPs. Some of the key AAP-related changes resulted in the following:

▶ Replaced the workforce analysis with a one-page organizational profile.

▶ Reduced the eight-factor availability analysis to two factors (those with requisite skills within a "reasonable recruitment area"; and those in the contractor workforce who are "promotable," "transferable," or "trainable").

▶ Reduced the number of "additional required elements" of the written AAP from 10 to 4.

▶ Reaffirmed that AAPs don't establish quotas; rather, they establish goals that are pursued through good faith efforts.

▶ Established an Equal Opportunity survey, designed to collect information on a contractor's federal government contracts and affirmative action programs, personnel activity, and compensation data. This survey is sent annually to certain contractors, who must then complete it.

▶ Granted employers with fewer than 150 employees permission to prepare a job group analysis that uses EEO-1 categories as job groups.

It's important to familiarize yourself with all of the elements of an AAP, and, specifically, with how to prepare each of them. Some of the elements that are required to be in an AAP are

▶ **Designation of Responsibility**: This person—identified by name—is often an HR professional. He or she must have the necessary authority and resources to implement the AAP successfully. This must include the support of and access to top management. This is particularly important since the DOL is quite direct in its position that commitment to affirmative action should be an integral part of the organization's functioning, rather than an administrative "add-on."

▶ **Organizational Display or Workforce Analysis**: Non-construction contractors must prepare an organizational profile, which can be presented as either the new "organizational display" or the older workforce analysis. The proposed organizational profile is a shorter, simpler format, which in most cases would be based upon the contractor's existing organizational chart(s) to provide a depiction of the contractor's workforce. This profile is essentially an organizational chart that includes summary information about incumbents' race, gender, and wages.

▶ **Job Group Analysis**: Non-construction contractors must also prepare a "job group analysis," intended to begin the process of comparing the employer's representation of women and minorities to the estimated availability of qualified women and minorities who are available to be employed.

▶ **Availability Analysis**: The new regulations still require contractors to determine the availability of minorities and women for jobs in their establishments, compare incumbency to availability, declare underutilization, and must set goals to eliminate the underutilization.

▶ **Utilization Analysis**: Availability is then compared to incumbency, and if the percentage of minorities or women is lower than the availability—"less than would reasonably be expected given their availability percentage in that particular job group"—the contractor must establish a "placement goal" (41 C.F.R. §60-2.15); that is, the contractor must set placement goals to correct the underutilization.

▶ **Placement Goals**: Placement goals are established for areas in which underutilization exists. Placement goals must be pursued through good faith efforts—not through the establishment of quotas. The "bottom line" is that, when underutilization exists, the placement goal must be set at an annual percentage rate equal to the availability figure for women or minorities (it may be necessary, at times, to set goals for particular minority groups where significant underutilization exists).

▶ **Action-Oriented Programs**: The employer must develop and execute action-oriented programs that are specifically designed to correct any problem areas and to attain established placement goals. These action-oriented programs cannot just be "more of the same" ineffective procedures that resulted in these problem areas in the first place. Instead, the employer must demonstrate good faith efforts to remove identified barriers, expand employment opportunities, and produce measurable results.

▶ **Identification of Problem Areas**: The contractor must perform in-depth analyses of its total employment process to determine whether and where impediments to equal employment opportunity exist.

▶ **Internal Audit and Reporting System**: The contractor must develop and implement an auditing system that periodically measures the effectiveness of its total affirmative action program. The following actions are identified by the DOL as key to a successful affirmative action program:

1. Monitor records of all personnel activity—including referrals, placements, transfers, promotions, terminations, and compensation—at all levels to ensure the nondiscriminatory policy is carried out.

2. Require internal reporting on a scheduled basis as to the degree to which equal employment opportunity and organizational objectives are attained.

3. Review report results with all levels of management.

4. Advise top management of program effectiveness and submit recommendations to improve unsatisfactory performance.

EXAM ALERT

It's important to familiarize yourself with all of the elements of an AAP and with how to prepare each of them.

EXAM ALERT

It's also important to become familiar with compliance reviews: who is most likely to be audited and what happens before, during, and after audits. Be particularly cognizant of the fact that audits can—and do—vary significantly depending upon a variety of factors, so it's important not to draw conclusions based only upon your personal experiences with the OFCCP.

Age Discrimination in Employment Act (1967)

The ADEA prohibits discrimination on the basis of age for individuals age 40 and above. There is no upper cap on age limit (although there initially was).

ADEA covers private employers with 20 or more employees, state and local governments (including school districts), employment agencies, and labor organizations.

EXAM ALERT

Be familiar with the exceptions and requirements under ADEA, particularly as they apply to benefits plans and coverages and early retirement incentives.

Rehabilitation Act (1973)

The Rehabilitation Act of 1973 prohibits discrimination on the basis of physical and mental disabilities.

Section 503 of the Act requires affirmative action and prohibits employment discrimination by federal government contractors and subcontractors with contracts of more than $10,000.

Section 504 of the Act states that "no otherwise qualified individual with a disability in the United States...shall...be excluded from the participation in, denied the benefits of, or be subjected to discrimination under any program or activity receiving Federal financial assistance or activity conducted by any Executive agency or by the United States Postal Service."

Section 508 requires that federal agencies' electronic and information technology is accessible to people with disabilities, including employees and members of the public.

Vietnam Era Veterans' Readjustment Assistance Act (VEVRAA) (1974)

VEVRAA requires employers with federal contracts or subcontracts of $25,000 or more to provide equal opportunity and affirmative action for Vietnam era veterans, special disabled veterans, and veterans who served on active duty during a war or in a campaign or expedition for which a campaign badge has been authorized.

EXAM ALERT

Don't let the acronym mislead you—VEVRAA affords protection to veterans in addition to those who served during the Vietnam era. Be familiar with the definitions of "special disabled veteran," Vietnam era veterans, and all other veterans covered by VEVRAA.

For purposes of VEVRAA, a Vietnam era veteran is a person who (1) served on active duty for a period of more than 180 days, any part of which occurred between August 5, 1964 and May 7, 1975, and was discharged or released with other than a dishonorable discharge; (2) was discharged or released from active duty for a service connected disability if any part of such active duty was performed between August 5, 1964 and May 7, 1975; or (3) served on active duty for more than 180 days and served in the Republic of Vietnam between February 28, 1961 and May 7, 1975.

VEVRAA requires employees with federal contracts or subcontracts of $100,000 or more must file a VETS-100 report by September 30 each year.

> **NOTE**
>
> The threshold for filing a VETS-100 report was raised from $25,000 to $100,000 for contracts awarded on or after December 1, 2003.

Federal contractors and subcontractors are required to list with the local state employment service all employment openings except for executive and top management jobs; jobs which the contractor expects to fill from within; and jobs lasting 3 days or less. The intention is that preference will be given to veterans.

Pregnancy Discrimination Act (1978)

The Pregnancy Discrimination Act of 1978 amended Title VII of the Civil Rights Act of 1964. Specifically, this Act prohibits discrimination on the basis of pregnancy, childbirth, or related medical conditions. In short, it requires that employers treat applicants or employees who are pregnant or otherwise affected by related conditions in the same manner as other applicants or employees with other short-term conditions.

Uniform Guidelines on Employee Selection Procedures (1978)

The Uniform Guidelines on Employee Selection Procedures was intended to address the need to establish a uniform set of principles relative to all elements of the selection process—including but not limited to interviewing, pre-employment testing, and performance appraisal.

A key purpose of the Uniform Guidelines is to deal with the concept of "adverse impact" (also known as "disparate impact") as this concept pertains to the employment process, and to ensure that interview and selection processes are reliable (consistent) and valid.

> **CAUTION**
>
> Maintain careful and consistent records of your organization's employment selection procedures.

Reliability

The degree to which a selection process or instrument is consistent will determine the degree to which that instrument is reliable.

All interviews for a position should generate consistent information for decision-making—even if several interviewers are involved, and even when all interviewers don't meet every candidate.

In this context, one important function of a well-defined and well-documented interviewing process is to ensure the most consistent and reliable results possible, even given the inevitable differences between interviewers. This is one reason why it is critical that interviewers prepare and consistently use a list of job-related questions that will be asked of all candidates for a particular position.

Validity

Employment interviews measure applicants' skills. Valid interviews ensure that those skills relate meaningfully and clearly to the skills that are required to perform a particular job.

Validity establishes and demonstrates a clear relationship between performance on the selection procedure and performance on the job. Although it is very difficult to establish good measures of validity, it is possible to make a case for validity if the interview has the following characteristics:

- ▶ It is based on job analysis.

- ▶ It contains questions that provide evidence about important job-related skills.

- ▶ Interview information is systematically related to a specific job.

HR professionals need to be familiar with at least four different types of validity:

- ▶ **Content Validity**: A selection procedure has content validity if it assesses a candidate's ability to perform representatively sampled significant parts of the job.

   Example: A typing test for an administrative assistant's position would demonstrate content validity.

- ▶ **Criterion-Related Validity**: A selection procedure has criterion-related validity if scores achieved by incumbents correlate highly with their respective job performance.

   Example: A requirement that candidates have fluency in a particular foreign language would have criterion-related validity if it were shown that people who demonstrate fluency in that language actually perform better on the job than those who do not demonstrate fluency.

▶ **Construct Validity**: A selection procedure has construct validity if it measures the degree to which the test-taker possesses a particular psychological trait (if, of course, it can be shown that the trait is required for successful performance of the position). More specifically, according to the EEOC Uniform Employee Selection Guidelines, "Evidence of the validity of a test or other selection procedure through a construct validity study should consist of data showing that the procedure measures the degree to which candidates have identifiable characteristics which have been determined to be important in successful performance in the job for which the candidates are to be evaluated."

Example: An instrument that assesses the degree to which candidates for a car salesperson's position are persistent would demonstrate construct validity.

▶ **Predictive Validity**: A selection procedure has predictive validity if the predictions that it makes actually manifest themselves in the test-takers' subsequent performance.

Example: An instrument that is designed to assess the degree to which candidates for a position possess and demonstrate empathy would have predictive validity if individuals who scored well on this test demonstrated, after being hired, that they actually did possess and demonstrate this characteristic.

Immigration Reform and Control Act (IRCA) (1986)

IRCA accomplishes a number of objectives. Specifically, IRCA

▶ Prohibits discrimination against job applicants on the basis of national origin. IRCA also, however, specifically prohibits giving employment preference to U.S. citizens.

▶ Creates penalties for knowingly hiring illegal aliens (people who are referred to by some individuals and organizations as "undocumented workers," rather than "illegal aliens").

IRCA accomplishes these objectives through several means. The most visible process requires employers to review and record information/documentation submitted by employees that establish that employee's identity and eligibility to work in the United States. The form used to record this information is known as the I-9 form. The I-9 form must be completed within three business days of the employee's date of hire (but not before the employer starts). Certain portions of the I-9 must be completed by the employee and certain portions must be completed by the employer.

CAUTION

The I-9 lists acceptable documents for establishing identity and eligibility to work in the United States. Employees must provide either one document from Column A or one document each from Column B and Column C. Under no circumstances can an employer express preference for any particular document.

Employer penalties for non-adherence to hiring and recordkeeping requirements—even wholly intentional ones—are steep. Ensure that you are in compliance with both the letter and the spirit of the law.

Worker Adjustment and Retraining Notification Act (WARN) (1988)

As its name implies, the Worker Adjustment and Retraining Notification Act (WARN) is designed to give displaced workers time to make arrangements for other employment. "Arrangements," in this sense, span a spectrum of possibilities from transferring to another worksite to participating in retraining programs, or anything in between.

WARN covers employers with 100 or more full-time employees (or the equivalent—100 or more full-time and part-time employees who work a combined total of 4,000 or more hours per week).

EXAM ALERT

Exceptions and clarifications abound when it comes to determining whether an employer is covered by WARN. Review www.dol.gov for more information about how to make this determination.

WARN requires these employers to give employees at least 60 days' written notice before either a "mass layoff" or "plant closing."

According to WARN, a "mass layoff" occurs when either of the following two events happens within a 30-day period at a single worksite:

▶ 500 full-time employees are laid off

▶ At least 33 percent of the workforce is laid off (if and only if that 33% includes 50-499 full-time employees)

The DOL—the federal agency responsible for administering WARN—defines a "plant closing" as happening when "a facility or operating unit is shut down for more than six months, or when 50 or more employees lose their jobs during any 30-day period at a single site of employment." In this context, the DOL defines "losing one's job" or "employment loss" as

▶ An employment termination, other than a discharge for cause, voluntary departure, or retirement

▶ A layoff exceeding six months

▶ A reduction in hours of work of individual employees of more than 50% during each month of any 6-month period

Under WARN, notice must be given to

▶ Affected employees or their representatives (such as a collective bargaining unit)

▶ The State Dislocated Worker Unit

▶ The appropriate local government unit

CAUTION

Exceptions to this and other portions of WARN have been built into the Act (relating, for instance, to job retraining programs, bankruptcies, and so on). In addition, be aware that some states such as California have "baby WARN" laws in effect, which may have different notification thresholds and/or requirements. So, as always, be sure to check for—and ensure you are in adherence with—any relevant state laws.

Americans with Disabilities Act (ADA) (1990)

The EEOC proudly describes the ADA as "the world's first comprehensive civil rights law for people with disabilities," and likens it to the Emancipation Proclamation for people with disabilities.

Title I of the ADA prohibits employment discrimination against people with disabilities. Title V of the ADA provides additional instructions with respect to its enforcement of the ADA by the EEOC, the federal agency charged with enforcing the employment provisions of the ADA.

The ADA prohibits discrimination against a qualified person with a disability, who has a record of a disability, or who is regarded as having a disability. HR professionals must understand these terms and definitions in order to effectively implement the provisions of the ADA.

Qualified Person

To be a "qualified person," a candidate must meet minimum job requirements (education, experience, licenses, and so forth) and must be able to perform the essential functions of the position with or without reasonable accommodation.

Reasonable Accommodation

A "reasonable accommodation" represents a change in the way that one (or more) responsibilties relating to the execution of a position is performed, so as to enable a person with a disability to perform the essential functions of the position. Accomodations, however, do not have to be adopted if they cause undue hardship to the organization.

Undue Hardship

An "undue hardship" is one that creates significant difficulty (enough to disrupt business operations); results in a significant financial outlay; or changes something about the essential nature of the business.

> **CAUTION**
>
> Don't unilaterlally make a determination about what constitutes undue hardship. Confer with legal counsel, client managers, and/or senior HR colleagues, as appropriate.

Disability

The ADA defines a current "disability" as a medical condition or disorder (called an "impairment") that substantially limits a person's ability to perform basic activities (called "major life activities").

Major Life Activities

According to the EEOC, "major life activities" include but are not necessarily limited to walking, seeing, hearing, breathing, caring for oneself, performing manual tasks, sitting, standing, lifting, learning, and thinking.

> **EXAM ALERT**
>
> The ADA is a multifaceted, multi-layered law. In addition to those items discussed here, ensure that you understand related concepts including, but not limited to, direct threat; current and past drug and alcohol use; and so on.

Civil Rights Act (1991)

The Civil Rights Act of 1991 significantly expanded upon employees' rights and remedies under Title VII of the Civil Rights Act of 1964. First, it established the right for plaintiffs to enjoy jury trials when bringing charges of discrimination. Second, it allowed for the awarding of compensatory and punitive damages. Total damages cannot exceed $300,000 per employee, and could be capped as low as $50,000 per employee depending upon the number of people employed by the employer. In short, the larger the workforce, the higher the cap on damages.

Compensatory damages are designed to "make the employee whole" with respect to lost wages, benefits, and other expenses and losses. Punitive damages, as the name implies, are intended to punish employers who violate the Act.

Congressional Accountability Act (CAA) (1995)

Touted on the informational poster as "advancing safety, health, and workplace rights in the legislative branch," the Congressional Accountability Act expanded coverage of the following 12 laws to Congressional employees:

- Fair Labor Standards Act (FLSA) (1938)
- Title VII of the Civil Rights Act of 1964, as amended
- Age Discrimination in Employment Act of 1967
- Occupational Safety and Health Act of 1970
- Rehabilitation Act of 1973
- Civil Service Reform Act of 1978
- Employee Polygraph Protection Act of 1988
- Worker Adjustment and Retraining Notification Act of 1988
- Americans with Disabilities Act of 1990
- Family and Medical Leave Act of 1993
- Veterans Reemployment Act of 1994
- Uniformed Services Employment and Reemployment Rights Act of 1994

Workforce Planning: Where Are We Going?

Effective workforce planning ensures that the organization has the "people resources" in place that will enable it to fulfill its mission and achieve its objectives. It encompasses myriad activities relating to how employees enter into—and exit from—the organization. It looks at these functions primarily from the perspective of meeting the organization's needs, and ideally takes a long-term approach.

By effectively performing responsibilities relating to workforce planning and development, HR professionals can grasp another opportunity to forge a strategic partnership with their client managers. In order for this to happen, HR professionals must take a deliberate and consistent approach to workforce planning that starts with the organization's strategic plan and with how HR can align its efforts with that plan.

Workforce Planning: What Will We Need to Get There?

Determining what and who the organization needs to achieve its goals is more involved than it might appear. Accurate forecasting requires selecting from among numerous non-mathematical (qualitative) as well as mathematical (quantitative) analyses.

Non-mathematical Forecasting Techniques

In most organizations, qualitative judgments are made all the time. These judgments can relate to a whole host of issues—marketing, product development, philanthropy, staffing, or any other business-related issues. These judgments can be structured or unstructured, informal or formal.

Management Forecasts

Sometimes, individuals who perform qualitative analysis draw upon the knowledge and experience of the organization's managers—and the institutional knowledge that those managers have acquired in their roles. Savvy managers—especially those who couple their awareness of the organization with awareness of the industry and of the economy in general—can provide HR with a wealth of information. As a caution, however, it's also important to remember that the information derived through this somewhat unstructured approach may not always be accurate. Relying too heavily on managerial predictions can result in significant errors in judgment, and therefore must be coupled with other more structured mathematical and non-mathematical approaches.

The Delphi Technique

The Delphi technique is an example of a structured non-mathematical technique in which expert opinions from a variety of individuals are sought, distilled, and distilled again. An objective, neutral, uninvolved leader recaps what the experts submit, summarizes that information, and condenses it into a more concise format. (The leader is not one of the "experts" and does not inject his or her opinions or interpretations into the process.) This happens several times until a final position is identified—one that incorporates the input of many individuals, but that does not unduly reflect any one position or viewpoint.

A distinguishing—and critical—element of the Delphi technique is that the "experts" from whom opinions are sought, and whose ideas are culled down, never meet in person and never discuss their submissions—all of which are made in writing. Rather, their submissions are collected and processed by an objective third party. In this way, the Delphi technique ensures that factors such as group dynamics, overpowering personalities, or just plain politics do not taint the assessment process. The anonymity of the process further encourages individuals to "take a risk" and submit their ideas without fear of reprisal, retribution, or judgment—even if none of those outcomes would ever happen. The sanitized nature of this process puts expert contributors on a more even footing, further ensuring the integrity of this process.

Nominal Group Technique

Like the Delphi technique, the nominal group technique takes a non-mathematical approach to forecasting. The nominal group technique is also similar to the Delphi technique in that it calls upon the expertise and predictive ability of experts. Most of the similarities between the two techniques, however, end there. With the nominal group technique, experts meet in person and process their ideas as a group. Led by a facilitator, the meeting begins by each expert writing down and presenting his or her ideas to the group. Discussion of ideas, however, is not permitted at this point—only presentation is acceptable. The group then comes together to discuss each others' ideas, after which each individual group member is called upon to independently rank the ideas. The meeting facilitator will then combine all of the individual rankings to determine which are the most important to the group. Through this process, the forecast is made.

Mathematical Forecasting Techniques

Mathematical—or quantitative—forecasting techniques are predicated on the belief that the best predictor of future performance is past performance.

Trend Analysis

Trend analysis looks at and measures how one particular factor changes over a period of time. Trend analysis can provide information—albeit unrefined—that can be helpful in developing a better understanding of business cycles, which in turn will affect staffing needs.

Ratio Analysis

Ratio analysis is similar to trend analysis, in that it examines changes, movements, and trends over a period of time. Instead of looking at just one variable alone, however, it looks at two variables (one of which relates to staffing levels) and how the relationship between those two variables has evolved over time. This becomes the basis for a number of applications, including forecasting staffing needs.

As an example, a rental car company might look at how the number of cars rented per day, or per shift, compares to the number of employees assigned to work per day or per shift. This might help the car rental company predict future staffing requirements.

> **NOTE**
>
> Ratio analysis assumes that the relationship between the two factors being looked at will hold constant. In this example it also assumes that there will not be any turnover, which, of course, is not usually a reasonable assumption. Other assumptions may be operating, as well. Since the degree to which those assumptions are sound will significantly affect the overall quality of the ratio analysis, these underlying (and sometimes unrecognized) assumptions must be identified and factored into the analysis. Also, ratio analysis—like any other analysis—usually should not be the only type of analysis that you use. A combination of factors will generally yield a more reliable result.

Turnover Analysis

Turnover measures the percentage of the workforce that has left the organization during a specified period of time. Most often expressed on an annual basis, turnover is calculated as follows:

$$\frac{\text{\# of terminations during a specified period of time}}{\text{the average \# of employees in the workforce during that same period of time}}$$

This information can be used in a number of ways—one of which is to help predict future turnover rates, which can affect staffing needs. Turnover can be voluntary (for instance, an employee accepts employment at another organization) or involuntary (for instance, an employee is laid off). Turnover can be broken down in any number of ways:

- Total for the entire organization
- Total for one—or more—particular departments
- FLSA (exempt or non-exempt) status
- Length of service

> **NOTE**
>
> Despite popular opinion, turnover is not inherently bad. Just like cholesterol, there is "good turnover" and "bad turnover." An example of good turnover might be an individual who accepts a more challenging or appropriate position in a different unit or division within that same organization. An example of "bad turnover" might be a relatively new employee who quits after two weeks because he or she did not accurately understand the job requirements of the position for which he or she was hired.
>
> Whether turnover is deemed "good" or "bad," of course, involves making value judgments, which will vary from organization to organization. In one organization, for instance, an employee resigning to pursue higher education on a full-time basis or to serve the nation (through military service or the Peace Corps, for instance) might be counted as "good" turnover. In other organizations, these same reasons might be counted as "bad" turnover. Some organizations use the terms "acceptable" and "unacceptable" rather than "good" or "bad," so as to downplay the value judgments inherent to these labels. It's also possible to look at turnover in terms of "controllability." Controllable turnover might include voluntary terminations, and non-controllable turnover might include death or retirement.

Simple Linear Regression

Simple linear regression provides a different way of looking at statistical relationships. It examines the past relationship between two factors (in this case, one of which is staffing), determines the statistical strength of that relationship, and—on the basis of that analysis—projects future conditions. In the previous example of the rental car company, the relationship between car rentals and staffing levels would be measured, and—on the basis of the strength of that relationship—would be extrapolated into the future.

Multiple Linear Regression

Multiple linear regression is similar to simple linear regression, except that several factors are taken into consideration. In the rental car example, for instance, other factors that could be looked at in addition to staffing levels might be the number of vehicles that were actually available to be rented, the number of customers that "no-showed," or the number of potential customers who were turned away.

Simulations

Simulations create scenarios through which different "realities" can be tested out mathematically to see what could happen under a variety of changing conditions.

Workforce Planning: What Jobs Will Need to Be Performed?

Once you have made an estimate relative to the number of employees it will take to accomplish the organization's short-term, long-term, and emerging staffing needs, the next step is to determine functionally—and on a job-by-job basis—what these employees will need to do in order to move the organization to where it needs to go. It is in this context that we will look at jobs.

NOTE

Not all organizations conduct this process in exactly the same order. It's more important to ensure that all these steps are taken in a logical way that will yield solid results than it is to mandate a particular process.

Job Analysis

As stated in Chapter 2, a job analysis is the process by which information about a specific position is collected (refer back to Chapter 2 for additional information). Job analysis produces three important outputs that are critical to the workforce planning process:

▶ Job description

▶ Job specifications

▶ Job competencies

Job Description

Job descriptions are a key tool for many of the functions that HR professionals perform. Though they can take many different formats, most job descriptions share several elements in common:

▶ **Identifying information**: Such as job title, department and/or division name, reporting relationship, FLSA status, the date on which the description was written, the name of the person who wrote it, and so on.

▶ **Scope information**: The area of responsibility for, over, or within which this position has authority and/or responsibility.

▶ **Responsibility for supervision, if applicable**: Any positions who the incumbent supervises.

▶ **Physical work conditions and/or physical demands**: Though easy to overlook, it's critical to include this information in the job description.

▶ **Minimum requirements**: Often, this refers to experience, education, and or other mandatory "credentials" required to perform the position successfully. These are often the factors that will be initially used to "screen" candidates in or out during the résumé review process, and to determine who will be interviewed.

▶ **Knowledge, skills, and abilities required**: Acceptable levels of knowledge, skills, and abilities (also known as KSAs). These go beyond the "minimum requirements" noted previously, and may include items that organizations or interviewers sometimes mistakenly take for granted and do not explore enough with candidates during the selection process.

    ▶ **Knowledge**: Simply stated, what the incumbent "needs to know" about a specific body of information in order to be able to perform the position successfully. For instance, an instructor who conducts training on-site at a particular organization may need to have knowledge of organizational dynamics. An automotive mechanic may need to have knowledge of mechanical, electronic, and computer technology.

    ▶ **Skills**: A skill refers to the "the ability to" perform a particular task. For instance, the instructor may need to possess the ability to engage participants in facilitated discussions about the workshop topics. The automotive mechanic may needs to possess the ability to drive a standard (or "stick") shift.

▶ **Abilities**: Abilities refer to specific traits or "behavioral characteristics" required to perform successfully in a position. For instance, the instructor may need the ability to perform effectively in unfamiliar environments, with people with whom he or she is not acquainted. The automotive mechanic might need to be mechanically inclined.

▶ **Overall purpose of the position**: A short (usually less than a paragraph, and maybe even as short as a sentence) statement summarizing why the position exists and what it is intended to accomplish.

NOTE

Some organizations also choose to include the mission of the organization on each job description, as a way of ensuring that the mission of the position is—and remains—meaningfully linked to and aligned with the mission of the organization.

▶ **Duties and responsibilities**: Tasks and functions that the incumbent is expected to perform. Sometimes, job descriptions also indicate the percentage of time that is spent on each major responsibility, or group of responsibilities (which may or may not correlate to the importance of the responsibility).

NOTE

For ADA and other purposes, duties and responsibilities must be divided into two categories: essential and non-essential job functions.

CAUTION

The ADA states that "consideration shall be given to the employer's judgment as to what functions of a job are essential, and if an employer has prepared a written description before advertising or interviewing applicants for the job, this description shall be considered evidence of the essential functions of the job." Failure to have a job description in place, therefore, could diminish the strength of the employer's position in defending an allegation that an employee or applicant has been discriminated against on the basis of disability. In short, employers can't make up (or look like they are making up) requirements "after the fact."

Essential functions are those that are inherently fundamental and necessary to a position. Together—and perhaps even on their own—they constitute part or all of the reason the job exists. Often, an essential function cannot be performed by many—or perhaps even any—other employees in the organization.

Conversely, non-essential functions are more peripheral to the position. They generally constitute a small and relatively unimportant part of the position and could fairly easily be performed by other employees.

> **CAUTION**
>
> Confer with managers, senior HR staff, and counsel—as appropriate—relative to delineating essential from non-essential functions.

Job Specifications (or "Specs")

Job specifications refer to the qualifications that a successful candidate must possess and/or demonstrate in order to perform effectively in a position. They do not refer to the qualifications that the best-qualified candidate might possess; instead, they refer to what it will take to get the job done in a manner that fully meets expectations of the position.

Job specs can be expressed as

- ▶ KSAs

- ▶ Credentials (years of experience, educational requirements, and so forth)

- ▶ Physical and or mental requirements

> **CAUTION**
>
> Credentials, while important to establish and consider, can be misleading in real life. Specifically, a person who possesses or has earned a particular credential doesn't necessarily have the knowledge or skills that one might assume go along with that credential. Earning a four-year degree in accounting, for instance, doesn't necessarily mean that a candidate can perform certain accounting functions. Alternatively, the greatest accomplishment of a candidate who has five years of related professional-level experience may, in fact, be that he or she was not terminated during those five years, he or she might have one year's worth of professional level experience that he or she has repeated five times. The bottom line—don't make assumptions. Credentials should be a starting point, not an ending point.

Job Competencies

Job competencies speak to broad categories of behavioral characteristics that are required to perform successfully in a particular position, department, or organization. They are often embraced by organizations with terms such as "key success factors," "competencies for success," or "performance factors." They could include things such as "communication skills," "teamwork," and/or "initiative." The same competencies may manifest themselves differently in different positions throughout the organization.

Employment: Recruiting Candidates

"Recruiting and selection" are often thought of as a single process. In fact, however, they are two separate components of the staffing process and need to be approached accordingly. "Recruiting" is the process of attracting and creating a pool of qualified candidates. "Selection" is the process of identifying the candidate(s) to whom the position will be offered.

Employer Branding

Before an employer goes out in search of new employees, it needs to consider how potential candidates in the labor market will perceive the organization. Organizations create a "brand" as an employer in much the same way they create a "brand" for the product or service that they market to their customers. So, just as an organization markets its products or services deliberately and intentionally, it must deliberately and intentionally decide upon a marketing strategy that will be used to promote the employer brand within the labor market.

Selection Criteria

The first step that must be taken in order to begin the process of creating a pool of qualified candidates is to identify and develop selection criteria for the position. Selection criteria can be likened to a "shopping list" of what you're looking for in the individuals who will populate your candidate pool (and, ultimately, the employee who will join the organization). This could—and often will—include KSAs, job specifications, and specific requirements stemming from the job competencies.

Never Go Shopping—or Recruiting—Without a List

If you go grocery shopping without a list, you can lose your focus, forget items you need, or be attracted to items that are marketed well but that might lack substance. If this happens when you're going grocery shopping, it's no big deal—you can just go back to the store again to get what you missed the first time around. If you begin the recruitment and selection process, however, without a clear idea of the qualifications that your successful candidate must ultimately possess, the stakes can be a bit higher.

Sometimes, our ideas about what the requirements for a particular position could unintentionally be tainted by other factors—for instance, the qualifications that the prior incumbent possessed, or the qualifications of the individuals who are actually applying for an open position. The best, most objective, and most legally defensible way to establish selection criteria is to do so objectively, within the context of the job-related information that has been generated through the job description, job specs, and the like. It's also critical to do this up front before you look at a single résumé.

Internal and External Recruiting

Once you've determined (in collaboration with your client) the selection criteria for a particular position, the next step is to decide whether to seek to create a candidate pool internally, externally, or through a combination of both approaches.

Recruiting Internal Candidates

Many—in fact, most—organizations embrace the idea of promoting current employees from within the organization. There are two primary mechanisms for seeking internal candidates for positions within the organization—job posting and job bidding.

Job Posting

Job posting systems announce position openings to current employees within the organization. Candidates who believe that they meet the minimum posted requirements of the position are invited to apply for positions—sometimes even before external candidates are sought.

Job Bidding

While the job posting process isn't "triggered" until a job opens, job bidding systems invite employees to express interest in positions at any time, even if a position is not currently available. Candidates who are determined to be qualified for a position in which they express interest will automatically be put into consideration when that position becomes available.

Skill Inventories

Organizations can and often do maintain a central database that captures the many KSAs possessed by its employees…even when those KSAs are not being used by an employee in his or her current position. When a position opens up, the organization can then generate a list of current employees who meet the minimum qualifications for the position

---

TIP

Skill inventory systems may identify individuals who meet the minimum qualifications for other positions, but who are not interested in applying for them. Assuming that an employee has not been specifically hired into a particular position as a "feeder pool" for a higher level position, it's important to ensure that there are no subtle or overt negative consequences for employees who decide not to pursue higher-level positions for which they have been identified as "qualified" through the skill inventory process. Every organization needs "Steady Eddies" and "Steady Bettys"—identify employees who are solid contributors in their current roles, who are happy and fulfilled in those roles, and who are not interested in "climbing the corporate ladder." Creating a culture in which promotion is the only acceptable career track devalues the contributions of these solid contributors, which can subsequently increase the likelihood that these under-appreciated employees may eventually leave the organization. It can also increase the likelihood of turnover because of unrealistic expectations that are not fulfilled. The bottom line is that not everyone in an organization can or even wants to be promoted—so it doesn't serve an organization well to imply that "moving up" is the only option available to its employees.

Replacement Charts

Replacement charts identify names of individuals who could potentially fill a particular position in the event that an opening occurs.

Internal Candidates: Advantages and Disadvantages

Recruiting internal candidates can benefit employees as well as employers. Employees can grow and develop without leaving the organization. Employers can select from a pool of internal candidates about whom they have more job-related knowledge than they would normally have about an external candidate. Both employees and employers can build upon the investments they have already made in each other, and may even experience an enhanced sense of loyalty and dedication to each other.

Recruiting internal candidates, however, also presents certain risks, such as

- ▶ Relying too heavily on performance appraisals that, for a variety of reasons, may not be reflective of actual past performance (see Chapter 5).

- ▶ Relying too heavily on performance appraisals that, even when accurate, may reflect KSAs that are not wholly relevant to the position for which the candidate is applying.

Particular "danger" exists when a position is posted for which a strong internal candidate has already been identified. If it is fully expected that a particular individual will be selected for an open position, this can significantly harm the integrity of the job posting or bidding system.

Policy Considerations

The organizational policies surrounding internal recruiting systems must be thought through carefully and administered consistently. For instance

- ▶ Is an employee who posts or bids for a position required to notify his or her current supervisor? Is the supervisor required to grant "permission" for the employee to post for another position?

- ▶ If an employee is selected for a position, how long must that employee wait before being allowed to start his or her new job? Must a replacement for the employee's former position be found before the employee can move on to his or her new position?

- ▶ Must an employee be performing satisfactorily in his or her current position in order to be considered for another position within the organization? Would certain areas of unsatisfactory performance be acceptable, such as those that are unrelated to the new position?

- ▶ Must an employee work for a particular period of time in one position before posting for a different position within the organization?

Any of these considerations, depending on how they are handled, can either strengthen or diminish the ultimate effectiveness of the job posting or bidding system.

EXAM ALERT

Be familiar with other advantages and disadvantages of techniques used to source internal candidates.

Recruiting External Candidates

There are a wide variety of options available for recruiting external candidates. Just a few of these options include

- Newspaper advertisement
- Radio advertisement
- .jobs websites
- Internet sites, such as hotjobs.yahoo.com or monster.com
- College and university career development offices
- Job fairs
- Open houses
- Alumni networks
- Former employees
- Walks-ins
- Professional organizations
- Referrals from current employees
- State unemployment offices
- Organizational website
- Prior applicants

CAUTION

Considering prior candidates for openings for which they did not specifically apply can have repercussions relative to who is considered an applicant, particularly with respect to EO 11246. Be familiar with these requirements before committing to candidates in their "rejection letters" that you will "consider them for any future job openings for which they may be qualified," or before digging through files to find a "great candidate" who you remember interviewing for a different position.

- Employment Agencies

    - **Employment Agencies—State**: Each state has a service through which unemployed individuals who are currently looking for work are often required to register, thus providing a potentially rich pool of candidates to employers. These public agencies will also provide preliminary screening and candidate referral services to employers.

    - **Employment Agencies—Temporary**: Many organizations utilize temporary agencies to secure services that are needed on a short-term basis. This allows organizations the flexibility to meet temporary, short-term, or unexpected needs. Some organizations also use a "temp to hire" model through which the organization "tries out" the employee before extending an offer of "regular" employment." This gives the employee the opportunity to "try out" the organization, as well, before deciding whether to make a commitment to a particular organization or position.

NOTE

This process was often referred to as "temp to perm." It is no longer advisable to use this language, since there is no such thing as permanent employment. Employers should be careful not to say anything that could potentially imply otherwise, or unintentionally create an implied contract.

    - **Private Employment Agencies (also known as private search firms)**: Employers may also enlist the services of private employment agencies to assist them in finding regular employees. There are two primary options:

        - **Contingency employment agencies/search firms**: The employer pays a fee to the firm only when a candidate is hired through its efforts. This type of agency would be selected more often for entry level professional or supervisory recruiting efforts.

        - **Retained employment agencies/search firms**: The employer pays a fee to the firm whether or not a candidate is hired. This type of agency would be selected more often for executive level recruiting efforts.

CAUTION

Different terms, conditions, and "guarantees" apply to different types of agencies. Terms can differ from employer to employer, or even position to position. It's important to negotiate knowledgeably, to finalize terms before beginning a search, and to review any agreements carefully before signing.

A Hybrid Approach: Employee Referral

Many organizations embrace employee referral systems—a recruiting technique whereby current employees are used as a source for recruiting external candidates into the applicant pool.

This approach offers distinct advantages—and potential disadvantages, as well. Some potential advantages include

▶ Candidates who are referred by current employees may have a better understanding of the culture and values of the organization.

▶ Current employees are more likely to refer individuals who they believe (rightly or wrongly) have a high likelihood of succeeding. This happens because current employees often believe that the performance of the person whom they refer will have an impact on how they are perceived by the organization.

▶ Employee referral programs—even those that offer rich rewards—are significantly more cost-effective than most other forms of recruiting.

Employee referral programs also have the potential for significant disadvantages:

▶ If the current organization is not particularly diverse (with respect to gender, age, race, education background, or a host of other factors), employee referral programs might perpetuate that lack of diversity.

▶ If an affirmative action plan is in place, and if there are areas of underutilization, an employee referral program is not likely to demonstrate "good faith efforts" to recruit candidates who are women or minorities.

▶ In organizations where there are prior patterns of hiring discrimination, employee referral programs are likely to reinforce those patterns.

In many cases, organizations will not rely exclusively on employee referral programs for creating pools of candidates. Instead, employee referral programs are often one of several techniques used to create a pool of qualified and, ideally, diverse candidates.

Other Non-traditional Staffing Alternatives

HR professionals also need to be familiar with other, more flexible, less-traditional staffing arrangements. These arrangements do not necessarily fall within "internal" or "external" sources, since these options could be offered to existing employees within the organization, or used as a way to attract candidates who are external to the organization, or could even result in the outsourcing of functions that were formerly handled within the organization.

Some of the non-traditional staffing arrangements that an employer might choose to implement involve securing the services of individuals who are *not* employees of the organization. Examples of this could include the use of temporary help, temp-to-hire arrangements, or consultants, as described previously. Current or newly hired employees can also participate in flexible programs through part-time employment, telecommuting, job sharing arrangements, or seasonal employment.

> **EXAM ALERT**
>
> Be familiar with the advantages and disadvantages of flexible staffing arrangements, as well as HR's role in implementing and executing these arrangements.

Measuring Recruiting Costs and Effectiveness

There are numerous ways to calculate the costs associated with recruiting as well as the overall effectiveness of the recruiting process. Some of those measures focus on the actual recruiting process (for instance, cost-per-hire, or time-to-hire), while others take a more forward-looking approach (for instance, turnover percentage for new hires within the first 3, 6, or 12 months).

The most critical point to keep in mind about measuring recruiting costs and effectiveness is this:

Do it, and do it consistently.

It is in situations such as this that HR professionals can become their own worst enemies by settling for subjective answers to the question "How am I doing?" The good news, however, is that herein lies yet another opportunity to be strategic. So, in conjunction with your HR leadership and with your clients, determine which measures are valuable. Ask questions such as

- ▶ Which recruiting sources yield the most applicants?
- ▶ Which recruiting sources yield the best qualified applicants?
- ▶ On that note, how will you define a "good applicant"? Is it one who meets the minimum qualifications of the position? Or, one to whom an offer of employment is extended? Or, one who accepts an offer of employment? Or, one who is still with the organization 3, 6, or 12 months after being hired?

▶ Which recruiting sources are the least expensive, on a cost-per-hire basis?

▶ How much time, effort, and attention does each recruiting source require from HR, or from the manager, during the recruiting process?

To calculate many of these measures, you'll need to calculate yield ratios. A yield ratio calculates the percentage of applicants from a particular recruiting source who advance to a particular stage in the recruiting process. For instance, one pertinent yield ratio might refer to the number of résumés from qualified candidates as a percentage of the number of total résumés received (from particular recruiting sources). It might also be helpful to compare this yield ratio for different recruiting sources.

Employment: The Selection Process

Once you've put together a pool of candidates who—at the very least—meet the minimum qualifications for the position, the recruiting process is essentially complete. At this point, the selection process can begin.

The Employment Application

In most cases, candidates submit résumés during the recruiting process (this may not be true for all positions, such as for certain entry level positions). From the candidate's perspective, résumés are essentially "advertisements" that are designed to get the candidate's foot in the door. This statement is actually quite literal, since the candidate's goal at this point is to be invited for an interview.

Résumés: Fact or Fiction?

A résumé is often written by someone other than the candidate who is submitting it; someone who may have great skill at presenting the candidate in the best possible light; someone who can perhaps make the candidate look stronger than he or she actually is. Résumés can also be created as the product of highly structured and pre-formatted software programs. These programs provide a host of possible qualifications, accomplishments, and responsibilities for hundreds of different positions that a candidate can choose to include in his or her résumé. Although software such as this can be very helpful in constructing a résumé, it can also enable candidates to craft résumés that are not wholly reflective of reality.

HR professionals and hiring managers must recognize that while résumés are intended to provide a record of candidates' employment and educational experiences, they are sometimes more "story" than "history." In addition, there is nothing on the résumé *itself* that requires the candidate to formally attest to the truthfulness of its contents—so relying on it to make employment related assessments (beyond selecting whom to interview) may be ill-advised.

Most organizations require candidates to complete an application form, usually before being interviewed.

> **CAUTION**
>
> At times, organizations may require some, but not all, candidates to complete an evaluation form before being interviewed. When this happens, individuals applying for "lower level" positions are often more likely to be required to complete the application before the first face-to-face interview, while applicants for "higher level" positions are sometimes more likely to be permitted to "postpone" that requirement until it is determined that they will move forward in the selection process. This is potentially problematic, on a number of levels. First, it is unfair and inconsistent. Second, if more women and people of color apply for lower level positions (and are therefore required to complete an application form), there could potentially be an adverse impact against women or people of color.

Like all other recruiting and selection tools, the application must seek information that is job-related and that is valid with respect to its ability to predict the applicant's ability to successfully perform the position.

> **NOTE**
>
> The EEOC considers the employment application to be a test—so be sure to scrutinize and assess it the same way you would scrutinize or assess any other test.

Types of Employment Applications

Employment applications provide a means for ensuring that all candidates present information about their work history, education, and experience—*in a consistent format*. The same organization, however, may operate in different states in which different laws might be in effect. In addition, different types of applications are sometimes used for different types of positions within the same organization. This practice is generally considered to be permissible, as long as similarly situated applicants are required to complete the same type of application at the same point in the selection process.

Short Form Employment Applications

Short form employment applications are "shorter" versions of an organization's standard employment application. In this sense, the word "short" is used in a relative sense; even the short form application could actually be several pages in length.

Short form employment applications may be used as a prescreening tool, or for "lower level" positions within the organization that require fewer, less complex, or less technical skills. Short form employment applications could also be used at an early phase in the selection process. In this case, candidates who progress to a later stage of the selection process might be required to complete a longer application at that time.

Long Form Employment Applications

Long form employment applications require candidates to provide more detailed and comprehensive information.

Job-specific Employment Applications

Job-specific employment applications are sometimes used when an organization does high-volume recruiting for a particular position, or for particular types of positions. In such cases, the application would be tailored to seek highly specific and relevant information pertaining to the specific position for which the candidate is seeking employment.

Weighted Employment Applications

Weighted employment applications are intended to facilitate the process of evaluating candidates' qualifications in a consistent and objective manner by assigning relative weights to different portions of the application. These different weights will vary depending upon the relative importance of each section, as determined by the requirements of the position.

> **CAUTION**
>
> Weighted employment applications are difficult and time consuming to create and maintain, as positions are almost constantly evolving and changing in some way. They can also run afoul of EEO guidelines (for instance, if extra "credit" is granted for factors that are not truly related to the job, or that are not as related as the weighting might imply).

Critical Parts of the Employment Application

Whatever type of employment application an organization chooses, there are a variety of elements that many applications share in common.

The application will often require the candidate to provide information relative to the following areas:

- Personal data (name, address, contact information)
- Education
- Training
- Credentials/certificates/job-related skills
- Employment history (including organizations, dates of employment, titles, supervisors' names, and reasons for leaving)
- Names of professional references
- The candidate's ability to provide proof during the first three days of employment of his or her identity and eligibility to work in the United States (in the event that he or she is hired)

The application also serves as a vehicle to seek permission from and/or communicate information to the candidate—and to require the candidate to acknowledge the granting of that permission and/or the receipt of that information by signing the application. Examples of this might include

- ▸ Permission to verify information provided on the application.

- ▸ Permission to check references (former employers, supervisors, and/or professional references).

- ▸ Employment-at-will statement. This statement articulates and reaffirms that in most states the organization can terminate the individual's employment at any time, with or without cause. Most employment applications also confirm and articulate that the employee also has the right to leave the organization at any time, with or without notice.

- ▸ EEO statement (and, if applicable, affirmative action statement).

- ▸ Acknowledgement that the organization reserves the right not to hire the candidate if it is determined that he or she has provided any information that is not truthful.

- ▸ Acknowledgement that the organization may, or will, terminate the candidate it is determined (after the candidate has been hired) that he or she provided any information on the application that was not truthful at the time the application was completed.

CAUTION

Whoever accepts applications from the candidate (whether electronically or face-to-face) must ensure that the application is fully completed *before it is accepted*. What this means in practice is that the candidate may not write the words "see résumé" on any portion of the application. It also means that all questions have been completed (sometimes candidates will leave a question that they do not wish to answer blank so that they can still attest to the truthfulness of the information they have provided on the application, and can thus attempt to avoid the sanctions that can accrue from lying on an application).

Interviews and the Interview Process

As stated previously, from the perspective of the candidate, the purpose of a résumé is to get a job interview. From the perspective of the organization, the purpose of a résumé is to decide whom to interview. Taking this a step further, the purpose of an interview is to collect information that will enable the interviewer and the organization to determine the degree to which each candidate possesses and demonstrates the knowledge, skills, abilities, and other job specifications required to successfully perform the position.

Interviewing is one of those skills that most people learn by observation or through practice. Unfortunately, however, this skill is too critical to be learned through osmosis—in other words, the "sink or swim" approach doesn't always work. Sometimes, what happens instead is that interviewers will learn to swim, but will swim poorly (and perhaps even risk drowning). In addition, sometimes the people who new interviewers observe (and emulate) may not be skilled in the process.

Increased knowledge about and skill in interviewing can have a significant impact on the quality of the selection process.

Styles of Selection Interviews

Interviews fall into two primary types of styles—directive and non-directive.

▶ **Directive Interviews**: These take a more structured approach by asking consistent questions of all candidates. The interviewer maintains control of the interview—despite the fact that candidates sometimes make significant attempts to seize that control away from them.

▶ **Non-directive Interviews**: These interviews are relatively unstructured. The candidate, not the interviewer, ends up guiding the interview, and therefore ends up controlling the flow and content of information.

To Direct, or Not To Direct

Which style is better to use in selection interviews—directive or non-directive? Generally speaking, a directive style is more effective and appropriate than a non-directive style, for a number of reasons:

▶ If a résumé is equivalent to a candidate's advertisement, giving a candidate control of the interview is like letting them perform their own "infomercial." Candidates will present and highlight information that is most flattering to them—but that information won't necessarily coincide with the information that the interviewer needs to collect and assess relative to each candidate's ability to perform the job. It also isn't likely to be consistent with information provided by other candidates, which can lead to unfair and even flawed comparisons between candidates.

▶ In order to conduct a fair, reliable, and legally defensible interview, interviewers must ask candidates consistent questions. This is exceedingly difficult, if not impossible, to accomplish during a non-directive interview.

Perhaps the most effective approach is a combination of *both* of these approaches—a combination that, in a sense, reflects the reality that selection interviewing is an art as well as a science. Developing a style that reflects a "structured conversation" ensures that all candidates are asked consistent questions, yet allows for related follow-up questions that keep the interaction lively, dynamic, revealing, and informative (all within a consistent and job related context).

Types of Selection Interviews

There are a variety of selection interviews. In this section, we'll look at some of the better-known types of pre-employment interviews:

▶ Phone interview

▶ Prescreen interviews

▶ Behavior-based interviews

▶ Stress interviews

▶ One-on-one and panel interviews

Phone Interviews

Sometimes, organizations choose to conduct a short phone interview before deciding whether to bring a candidate in for a face-to-face interview. This can be particularly helpful in identifying legitimate job-related "knock-out" factors that could either cause the employer to decide to eliminate the candidate from consideration, or that could cause the candidate to "self-select" out of the selection process. Factors that might be discussed could involve job requirements (such as overtime or work conditions), salary requirements, or basic technical knowledge or skill.

TIP

Phone interviews can be an efficient and effective way of showing respect for your candidates, your internal clients, and yourself. Just be certain to be consistent in the questions you ask each candidate—even at this point in the process.

Prescreen Interviews

In many organizations, HR conducts initial "pre-screening" interviews with candidates. The purpose of prescreen interviews is to determine which candidates meet specific job requirements—the same ones that were identified in advance. This can include the process of verifying that the candidate actually meets the minimum requirements for the position, as well as establishing whether the candidate meets other specific fundamental requirements.

TIP

Here too, the HR professional has an opportunity to partner with line managers. Don't make assumptions about what qualifications you should try to assess during a prescreen interview; instead, work collaboratively with your clients to etch out an effective, streamlined, cohesive strategy.

Behavior-based Interviews

Behavior-based interviews require the candidate to describe past experiences that demonstrate the degree to which he or she possesses the knowledge, skills, and abilities that are required to successfully perform the position for which the candidate is applying.

Behavior-based questions ask the candidate to describe a specific situation in which he or she demonstrated a particular job requirement. In their responses, candidates should describe the situation, the specific way in which the candidate behaved in the situation, and the outcome that resulted from his or her action.

TIP

Behavior-based questions are only effective if the candidate provides a thorough and complete answer. Candidates, however, often are not conditioned to respond in this way, so it's incumbent upon the interviewer to ask probing follow-up questions. Probing questions must focus on the original question and not allow the candidate to "stray" into a different area about which the candidate might prefer to speak.

Stress Interviews

During stress interviews, the interviewer (or interviewers) deliberately creates a high-stress environment in an effort to ascertain how the candidate would respond in a high stress work situation.

CAUTION

There are two primary concerns with respect to stress interviews. First, interviewers run the risk of jeopardizing the degree to which they can ascertain all of the *other* KSAs required for the position. In some jobs, where the ability to handle extreme levels of stress is absolutely essential and foundational (such as homeland security), this may be wholly appropriate. In other situations where extreme stress is a factor—but is not a constant, immutable, or defining element of a position—stress interviews may not be the most effective choice.

A second area of potential concern with respect to stress interviews is that the interviewer must be certain that a consistent level of stress is created in each employment interview. Otherwise, the "stress test" element of the interview could be found to be inconsistent and, therefore, unreliable. This could, in turn, increase the possibility of a legal challenge or allegations of unlawful discrimination.

One-on-One Versus Panel Interviews

Sometimes, for a variety of reasons, organizations choose to conduct panel interviews—interviews in which more than one interviewer interviews a candidate at the same time. Panel interviews can save time and money. They can also backfire. To help ensure that panel interviews are successful and productive, keep the following ideas in mind:

▶ Let the candidate know ahead of time that he or she will be participating in a panel interview. Eliminating the element of surprise will help prevent additional unnecessary anxiety.

▶ Plan—even choreograph—the interview in advance. Make sure all participants know their respective responsibilities. Plan who will ask which questions and how probing follow-up questions will be handled. Arrange for "hand offs" from one interviewer to another, much the same way as is done during a team-based television newscast.

▶ Consider the seating arrangements. If possible, interview in a room that has a round table. If you must interview in a room with an oval or rectangular table, position the chairs in a way that creates the feeling of a round table. At all costs, avoid placing all of the interviewers on one side of the table and the candidate on the other side of the table. It is also best to avoid placing the candidate at the head of the table when there are multiple interviewers, as this can lead to a "tennis match" need to continually look from one side of the table to the other.

Key Components of the Selection Interview

An interview is part science, part art, and part architecture. The interview process must be carefully structured to support its overall purpose: to provide the interviewer *and* the candidate with information that can be used to make accurate assessments and, ultimately, sound decisions. The interviewer needs to assess the degree to which the candidate possesses the qualifications for the position. The candidate needs information with which he or she can make an informed decision about whether to join the organization, in the event that an offer of employment is extended.

Though there is no single "best way" to structure an interview, the following presents one effective approach:

1. **Establish Rapport**—It's important to help the candidate to feel welcome at the beginning of the interview. Establishing rapport through a warm greeting, an offer of a glass of water, or brief "chit chat" about the weather can help the candidate to relax—and, in turn, hopefully provide more candid, honest responses.

CAUTION

Be careful that your "chit chat" does not stray into areas about which you should not be conversing with candidates. Avoid, for instance, discussions about children, hobbies, mode of transportation, world events, or political happenings. Don't allow the conversation to stray into "small talk" that would reveal information that is unrelated to the position. Instead, stay focused on the job, the candidate's experience, credentials, and qualifications.

In addition, recognize and remember that you will (hopefully) be interviewing a diverse pool of candidates, and may encounter individuals who dress, speak, behave, or interact in ways that are different from your own. A candidate, for instance, may choose not to shake your hand, or may choose not to make eye contact with you. Don't inappropriately read into these or any other potentially unexpected behaviors. Be open and inclusive of these differences, and make sure you base your assessments solely on job-related factors.

2. **Ask Primary and Probing Questions**—Primary questions are asked of all candidates for a particular position during a particular interview process. They are designed to elicit relevant information about how well the candidate possesses and could demonstrate the skills, knowledge, abilities, and other requirements of the position.

   Probing questions are the "follow up" questions to those primary questions. Since they are asked in response to each candidate's initial response to the primary question, probing questions will vary from interview to interview. Interviews can still ensure consistency, however, only asking probing questions that relate to the original primary question. Don't get derailed by an evasive candidate, an interesting tangent, or a candidate's inability to answer the original primary question.

3. **Invite the Candidate to Ask Questions**—Once you have finished asking your primary and probing questions, invite the candidate to ask you any questions he or she might have. It is important to provide this opportunity only after you have asked your questions, so as to ensure that the candidate does not obtain information from you that will enable him or her to better answer your questions. In other words, interviewers need to be careful not to "give away the answers" before they even ask the questions.

TIP

A candidate's questions can also provide insight into his or her motivations, professional interests, or the seriousness with which he or she is approaching the job search. Pay careful attention to what you hear.

4. **Realistically Describe the Position and the Organization**—Provide each candidate with complete, honest, realistic, and consistent information about the position and the organization. Ensure that you share information in a consistent manner with all candidates—those in whom you preliminarily think you might be more interested, as well as those in whom you think you might be less interested. "Pitching" the position more positively or enthusiastically to one candidate over another could potentially raise

questions later about why you did not share information in a consistent manner, and why you chose to encourage or discourage particular candidates.

5. **Close the Interview**—In that same spirit, end all of your interviews the same way. Let the candidate know what will happen next, and provide the candidate with a reasonable time frame during which he or she can expect to hear back from you. Make no promises, offer no assessment, and provide no "feedback" relative to how the candidate performed during the interview. An interviewer's role is one of "information gatherer," not career counselor.

Key Skills Required to Conduct an Effective Interview

Within this structure, interviewers must bring the interview to life. They must use their skills—interpersonal and otherwise—to attain a variety of goals, including ensuring that

- ▶ All needed information is obtained

- ▶ All interviews are conducted in a consistent manner and yield consistent information

- ▶ The interview does not assume a robotic tone

- ▶ The rapport that was established at the beginning of the interview is maintained—or, as necessary, rebuilt—throughout the interview

- ▶ They do not allow personal feelings or biases that are unrelated to the position to enter into the interview process

- ▶ They remain within both the letter and the spirit of the law

The following section highlights some of the skills essential for conducting an effective interview.

Intra- and Interpersonal Skills

Listen carefully, attentively, and effectively. Paraphrase what you hear the candidate saying. When you do, preface your statements with words like

▶ "What I think I hear you saying, correct me if I am mistaken, is…"

▶ "So what I'm getting from you on this point, and please let me know if I've heard this correctly, is…"

In this way, you actually give the candidate permission to correct your understanding (something that most candidates are probably reluctant to do). You ask them, essentially, to tell you if you're wrong. This will help you attain your objective of ensuring that you leave the interview with an accurate understanding of each candidate's qualifications for the position.

Nonverbals

Observe each candidate's nonverbal behavior. When you notice a significant change in that behavior, pay attention, and consider probing for more information around whatever question the candidate was answering when that change occurred. Be careful not to assign specific meaning to any specific gesture. For instance, folding one's arms across one's chest may not necessarily mean that a candidate is distant, aloof, or hiding something. It may mean that the candidate is cold (literally, not figuratively).

It's also important to be aware of the messages that you may be transmitting to candidates through your own nonverbal behavior. Try to ensure openness through your posture and movements. Use your nonverbals to encourage the candidate's engagement. Make sure you do not unintentionally convey any sort of judgment—either positive (for example, through nodding) or negative (for example, through a frown or furrowed brow).

Take Notes

During the interview, jot down key words or phrases that the candidate offers in response to your primary and probing questions. If you leave "white space" in between your list of questions, you'll have a convenient space in which to take notes that pertain to the specific questions you are asking. Be careful not to take too many notes—this could detract from your "connection" with the candidate.

TIP

It's important to let the candidate know at the beginning of the interview that you will be taking notes. Otherwise, the minute you jot something down, the candidate may assume that he or she said something "wrong," and may spend time and energy trying to determine what that was, and how they can back their way out of whatever they shouldn't have said. When you let the candidate know you will be taking notes, use it as a rapport building opportunity. Let them know, in your own words, that what you'll be discussing during the interview is important, and that you want to be sure that you accurately capture, and remember, what they tell you.

> **CAUTION**
>
> All notes must be strictly job-related. Do not use any sort of "code" that will help you recognize individual candidates. In addition, do not take any notes on the résumé; instead, use the white space that you have left between each of the primary questions you prepared.

Manage Your Biases—Individual, Organizational, and Societal

Although we all have the right to think or feel however we choose, we don't always have the right to act upon those feelings. This is particularly true with interviewers. Interviewers are human beings, and, like all human beings, we have biases. However, we should not make—and are often barred by law from making—assessments or decisions that are based on biases rather than on job-related factors.

As interviewers, it is incumbent upon us to vigilantly recognize how our individual biases could taint our assessments and decisions. Biases at the organizational level—and even at the societal level—could also affect our assessments, and must also be recognized and managed.

Interviewers must develop the ability to set aside factors that are not job related. These factors can relate to legally protected classes, such as a person's race or religion, or could relate to things that are (for the most part) generally unrelated to the law, such as a candidate's cologne, appearance, or even personal mannerisms.

Manage Your Biases—Interviewer Errors

Another category of interviewer bias also warrants attention. These biases essentially constitute "errors," or "errors in judgment" that are often made by interviewers. Interestingly, these errors are similar to those that are sometimes made by HR professionals or managers during the performance management and appraisal process, as well. Learning to address and prevent these up front, therefore, can yield benefits throughout the entire employment lifecycle. Table 4.2 describes some types of interviewing bias.

TABLE 4.2   Interviewing Bias or Errors

Type of Interviewing Bias or Errors	How It Manifests Itself in the Interviewing Process
Contrast	*The interviewer compares candidates to each other instead of comparing them to the requirements of the position.*
	Although it is essential to eventually compare candidates to each other, this comparison—by itself—can be misleading. Even the "best qualified candidate" won't necessarily meet the requirements of the position. Becoming professionally enamored with a candidate because he or she is "the best of the bunch" could result in a substandard hire, and, ultimately, an unsatisfactory hiring decision.

(continues)

TABLE 4.2   *Continued*

Type of Interviewing Bias or Errors	How It Manifests Itself in the Interviewing Process
First-impression	*The interviewer places an inordinate level of emphasis on the impression that the candidate makes on him or her during the first few minutes or even seconds of the interview.*
	It has been said that "first impressions last." While the impression may last, that impression may be incorrect. Interviewers need to remind themselves that good candidates, at times, get off to a slow start during the interview. So, too, poor candidates may initially appear quite polished and impressive.
Halo	*The interviewer evaluates the candidate positively on the basis of one outstanding qualification or characteristic.*
	This evaluation, however, is often incomplete and inaccurate. One positive quality or qualification—no matter how impressive it may be—is not reflective of all of the KSAs required to perform a position successfully.
Horns	*The interviewer evaluates the candidate negatively on the basis of one poor qualification or characteristic.*
	This evaluation, however, is often incomplete and inaccurate. One negative quality or qualification—no matter how unimpressive it may be—is not necessarily reflective of all of the KSAs required to perform a position successfully.
Leniency	*The interviewer applies an inappropriately lenient standard to one or more candidates, resulting in a higher overall assessment of the candidate.*
	Being "nice" to one or more candidates doesn't help the organization, and is unfair to the candidates, as well.
	Instead, an organization needs to hire qualified candidates in order to fulfill its mission and attain its overarching objectives. Extending offers to unqualified or less qualified candidates as a way of being "nice" undermines those efforts.
	In addition, it's important to keep in mind that a candidate who is invited to accept a position for which he or she is not truly qualified is, in one sense, being "set up to fail."
Strictness	*The interviewer applies an inappropriately harsh and demanding standard to one or more candidates, resulting in a lower overall assessment of the candidate.*
	Being "strict" with one or more candidates doesn't help the organization, and is unfair to the candidates, as well.

(continues)

TABLE 4.2 *Continued*

Type of Interviewing Bias or Errors	How It Manifests Itself in the Interviewing Process
	An organization needs to hire qualified candidates in order to fulfill its mission and attain its overarching objectives. Eliminating qualified candidates from consideration because of unrealistically high standards undermines those efforts.
	A candidate who is denied the opportunity to join the organization and perform a position for which he or she is truly qualified can end up with bad feelings towards the organization, and can potentially even damage the organization's reputation in the labor market.
Recency	*The interviewer recalls the most recently interviewed candidates more vividly than candidates who were interviewed earlier in the process.*
	Once again, this error allows unfairness to enter into the process. The random scheduling of candidate interviews should not unduly allow any candidate to be either favored or discounted.
Similar-to-me	*The interviewer evaluates a candidate on the basis of how much a candidate is similar to, or different from, him or her.*
	If interviewers recognize characteristics or attributes in candidates that they dislike about themselves, this recognition—whether conscious or unconscious—can have a negative affect upon how the interviewer evaluates the candidate. Conversely, if interviewers recognize characteristics or attributes in candidates that they like about themselves, this recognition—whether conscious or unconscious—can have a positive impact upon how the interviewer evaluates the candidate. Either way, the impression is personal in nature, unrelated to the candidate's qualifications, and is therefore inappropriate.

Showing Respect Throughout the Recruiting and Selection Processes

Sometimes, in the "heat" of the recruiting and selection process, HR professionals overlook the reality that candidates are not the only ones being assessed or interviewed during the selection process. At every stage of the recruitment and selection processes, candidates are paying careful attention to how the employees whom they have contact with treat them. As such, professionalism is essential—as is discretion and respect. It might be helpful to remember the "golden rule" when it comes to how you treat a candidate. So, throughout the recruiting and selection processes, try to empathize with the candidate. For

(continues)

(continued)

> instance, ask yourself…if you were a candidate, what kind of message would you like a potential employer to leave for you on your work voicemail? Would you want a telephone interviewer to just jump into his or her questions, or would you prefer him or her to set up a time that is mutually convenient? And always remember that when you participate in the recruiting and selection process, you are representing more than just yourself individually. To candidates, you represent and define—to a significant degree—the entire organization.

Legal Considerations for Interviewing and Selection

Interviewers need to be cautious not to wander intentionally or unintentionally into areas that present potential legal pitfalls.

The following tables provide some examples of questions that should not be asked during an interview, why they should not be asked, and questions that could possibly be asked instead. You'll start with Table 4.3, which covers inappropriate questions regarding sex discrimination, and then you'll cover Table 4.4, which discusses inappropriate questioning in regard to race and national origin discrimination. Next is Table 4.5, which covers religious discrimination; Table 4.6 covering age discrimination; Table 4.7 covering disability discrimination; and we wrap up with Table 4.8, which covers inappropriate questioning in regard to disability and worker's compensation discrimination.

TABLE 4.3   Inappropriate Questions Regarding Sex Discrimination

Don't Ask	Why	Ask This Job-Related Question Instead
Are you married? What is your marital status?	Sex discrimination	This is an illegal question. There is no way to reformulate it.
Do you wish to be addressed as Miss? Mrs.? Ms.? What is your spouse's name?	Sex discrimination	This is an illegal question. There is no way to reformulate it. Address the candidate either by his or her first name, or the prefix "Ms." or "Mr.", followed by the candidate's last name. Do not, however, address men by their first names and women by "Ms.", as this inconsistency could be interpreted as an effort to seek information relative to marital status.
Are you planning on starting a family?	Sex discrimination	This is an illegal question. There is no way to reformulate it.
How will your husband feel about your traveling overnight 30% of the time?	Sex discrimination	*This position requires 30% overnight travel. Can you meet this requirement of the position?*
How many children do you have?	Sex discrimination	This is an illegal question. There is no way to reformulate it.

(continues)

TABLE 4.3 *Continued*

Don't Ask	Why	Ask This Job-Related Question Instead
What childcare arrangements have you made?	Sex discrimination.	*Our hours are __ a.m. to __ p.m. Can you meet this requirement of the position?*
		This position requires approximately __ hours of overtime per week, often with little or no notice. Can you meet this requirement of the position?
		This position requires you to work shifts that can rotate on a monthly or even a weekly basis with little or no notice. Can you meet this requirement of the position?

TABLE 4.4 **Inappropriate Questions Regarding Race and National Origin Discrimination**

Don't Ask	Why	Ask This Job-Related Question Instead
Where are you from?	May get national origin information in response.	This is an illegal question. There is no way to reformulate it.
What languages do you speak?	Response may give national origin information.	Ask about specific language skills only if they are required for the position for which you are interviewing the candidate. *Can you speak _____ fluently?*
Do you own your home, or rent? How long have you lived at your current address?	Possible race or national origin discrimination.	*What is your address?* (This question is often included as part of the application.)
What type of military discharge did you receive?	May be acceptable if U.S. military related project. Otherwise, potential race discrimination.	*What job did you have in the military? Can you qualify for the security clearance?*
Have you ever been arrested?	Potential race discrimination.	*Have you ever been convicted of a crime?* (This question is often included as part of the application.)
What is your maiden name?	Sex or national origin discrimination.	*Have you ever worked for this company under a different name? Is additional information relative to change of name, use of a nickname, or assumed name necessary to enable a check on your work record? If so, please provide this information.*

TABLE 4.5   Inappropriate Questions Regarding Religious Discrimination

Don't Ask	Why	Ask This Job-Related Question Instead
What holidays do you require	Religious	*The required schedule for this position is Monday to Friday, from 9 a.m. to 5:30 p.m. Can you meet this requirement of the position?*

TABLE 4.6   Inappropriate Questions Regarding Age Discrimination

Don't Ask	Why	Ask This Job-Related Question Instead
How old are you?	Age discrimination	This is an illegal question. There is no way to reformulate it.
What is your date of birth?		

TABLE 4.7   Inappropriate Questions Regarding Disability Discrimination

Don't Ask	Why	Ask This Job-Related Question Instead
Is there any health-related reason why you may not be able to perform the job for which you are applying?	Disability discrimination	These are illegal questions. There is no way to reformulate them.
Have you ever been treated for a mental condition by a psychiatrist or psychologist?		
Are you taking prescription drugs?		
I see that you're a veteran; is that how you lost your arm?		
Will you always be confined to a wheelchair?		
How many days were you absent from work because of illness last year?		
Will you need a leave for medical treatment or for other reasons related to a disability?		
Will you need reasonable accommodation to get to the cafeteria?		

(continues)

TABLE 4.7 *Continued*

Don't Ask	Why	Ask This Job-Related Question Instead
Tell me about any restriction you have that would prevent you from lifting 30-pound metal sheets onto a conveyor belt for about four hours each day.	Disability discrimination	*This job requires lifting 30-pound metal sheets onto a conveyor belt for about four hours each workday. Can you meet this requirement of the position?*
The job requires visiting different company locations every week to conduct on-site compliance audits. If you need that cane to get around, you must be suffering from some sort of disability that would interfere with doing that much travel. What is your disability, and how bad is it?	Disability discrimination	*The job requires visiting different company locations throughout the country every week to conduct on-site compliance audits. Can you travel by airplane about six times a month?*

TABLE 4.8 **Inappropriate Disability and Worker's Compensation Discrimination**

Don't Ask	Why	Ask This Job-Related Question Instead
Have you ever had an on-the-job injury or filed a Workers' Compensation claim?	Likely to elicit information about disability discrimination, and is a violation of Workers' Compensation law	This is an illegal question. There is no way to reformulate it.
Have you ever had any job-related injuries?	Family and medical leave, worker's compensation, and disability discrimination	This is an illegal question. There is no way to reformulate it.
Do you or any one in your family have a serious illness that may require you to take time off from work?	Family and medical leave discrimination	This is an illegal question. There is no way to reformulate it.

Source: © Susan W. Brecher and Cornell University-ILR, 2005

> **CAUTION**
>
> Any pre-employment conversations that candidates have must adhere to all legal guidelines—regardless of whether the conversations were held with HR professionals, managers, or potential colleagues. This includes any "casual" conversations that take place over meals.

Realistic Job Previews (RJP)

At some point in the interview process, it is critical that candidates be given—and, perhaps more importantly, process and understand—a realistic picture of the position and the organization. This, in turn, will help the candidate make a realistic and accurate assessment of whether he or she will be willing and/or able to function effectively within the day-to-day realities of the position, the department or unit, and the organization.

Realistic job previews can be conveyed and communicated in a number of ways, including through

- Verbal descriptions of the work, the work environment, and/or the work conditions

- Facility tours

- The opportunity to read the employee handbook

- Opportunities to speak with current employees, particularly those who would be the incumbent's peers and/or colleagues

Different methods of communicating a realistic job preview can be used at different phases of the interview process. Whatever techniques are used, however, must be used at a consistent point in the interview and in a consistent manner for all candidates who are at that particular portion of the interview process.

Employment Testing

Employment tests are another way of ascertaining the degree to which a candidate possesses and can demonstrate the knowledge, skills, and abilities required to successfully perform the position. Any tests that are used must be job-related and valid (see the section on "validity" earlier in this chapter).

Some of the most commonly used types of pre-employment exams are seen in Table 4.9:

TABLE 4.9   Pre-employment Exams

Type of Test	Test Is Designed to Ascertain
Agility Tests	Whether the candidate can perform the physical requirements of the position.
Aptitude Tests	The candidate's ability to learn new skills and/or acquire knowledge.
Cognitive Ability Tests	A candidate's intelligence and/or current skill level with respect to a job-related function. Cognitive tests could be administered to assess skills such as typing, problem-solving, mathematical skill, or numeric ability.
Integrity, or Honesty, Tests	The degree to which a candidate would be likely to engage in behavior that is dishonest or that lacks integrity.
Personality Tests	Candidates' personality traits, motivation, discipline, and other characteristics.

Drug tests are another significant category of pre-employment testing conducted by many employers. Designed to detect the presence of illegal drugs in the candidate's system, drug tests are not considered to be medical exams.

Medical Exams

Medical tests, or exams, can only be conducted if the exam is job related and consistent with business necessity, and after an offer (or a conditional offer) of employment has been extended to the candidate.

An offer of employment cannot be rescinded simply because a medical test reveals that a candidate has a disability. Instead, in this situation, the employer would then determine the feasibility of extending a reasonable accommodation that does not cause undue hardship.

Employment: Background Checks

Once the interview process is complete and any appropriate and relevant tests have been successfully completed, the final candidate(s) should then be subjected to a rigorous background checking process.

In a sense, conducting a background check is almost like starting the interviewing process all over again. This is sometimes difficult to remember, especially since managers (and HR professionals) have invested a great deal of time, energy, and interest in the final candidate by this point in the process.

The person conducting a reference check must maintain—or regain, if necessary—a wholly objective perspective on the candidate. This person must be completely open to the fact that a reference check can yield a variety of possible outcomes. It could confirm, for instance, that the information that was collected through the interview and testing processes was accurate.

This is, of course, a good thing. Alternatively, the background check may reveal previously unidentified problems or concerns with the candidate's past performance or credentials. Since past performance is, in many ways, the best predictor of future performance, obtaining such information at any point before an offer of employment is extended is also a good thing.

Background checks can explore any or all of the following areas:

▸ **Work history**: Employers, dates of employment, titles, salaries, performance records.

▸ **Academic records**: Degrees, diplomas, certificates, certifications, and the dates when they were earned

▸ **Criminal background checks**: Many employers seek information relative to whether the final candidate(s) has been convicted of, pled guilty to, or pled no contest to a crime. In addition to identifying potentially serious performance issues, the organization may also discover convictions related to prior instances of violence in general, or prior instances of workplace violence.

> **TIP**
>
> In the event that you learn of a conviction at any point in the selection process, consult with senior HR leadership and counsel, as appropriate, before making any assessments, judgments, or decisions.

> **CAUTION**
>
> An arrest is not a conviction and cannot be treated as such. In our justice system, individuals are still innocent until proven guilty. Discriminating on the basis of arrest record could lead to adverse impact on the basis of race.

▸ **Driving history**: Employers may—and should—choose to review the motor vehicle reports for candidates who are applying for positions for which driving is an essential job function.

▸ **Credit history**: Employees who will have access to financial resources or who are entrusted with certain types of financial responsibility may be required to permit the potential employer to review their credit report.

> **CAUTION**
>
> Some organizations assert that there is a connection between one's integrity and one's credit rating. Other organizations assert that a candidate's individual financial habits provide insight into how that person would handle the organization's financial resources. Before implementing credit checking procedures, consult with senior HR leadership and counsel, as appropriate, to ensure that these assumptions—along with all other reasons for requiring candidates to submit to a review of their credit report—are accurate and defensible in the event of a challenge. It is also critical to ensure that all activities relating to credit checks are conduced in a manner consistent with the Fair Credit Reporting Act.

Employment: Extending the Offer

The story doesn't end when you decide whom you want to hire—you still need to extend the offer. The way you extend the offer will say a lot to the candidate about the organization—not just about you. (One of the exciting and challenging things about interviewing is that it is bigger than any of us, individually. "You" represent more than just "you.") The way you extend an offer will also have a big impact on whether the candidate accepts the offer.

Tips for Extending an Employment Offer

Many organizations extend a verbal offer of employment over the phone, and then follow that up with a formal written offer of employment. Other organizations meet with candidates personally and hand them an offer letter immediately upon extending an offer of employment.

Whichever method your organization uses, the manner in which an offer of employment is extended is important, and must be handled with the same degree of care with which the rest of the pre-employment process has been handled. The following are some particular considerations to keep in mind:

- ▶ Avoid expressing earnings in annual terms. Some organizations choose to indicate what the candidate would earn each pay period, while others choose to express earnings in monthly, daily, or even hourly rates.

- ▶ Avoid language that alludes to "guarantees" of earnings or employment, or dates through which the employee will be paid.

- ▶ Avoid language that hints of any sort of a long term employment relationship.

- ▶ Use the offer letter as an opportunity to reaffirm that the employment relationship is "at-will," and—if counsel agrees—define what that means.

▶ State that the only agreements or promises that are valid are those that are included in the offer letter.

▶ State the date by which the candidate must either accept or decline the offer of employment. Ensure that you permit a reasonable period of time—not too much time and not too little.

In short, an overly exuberant offer of employment can cause more harm that good. Such letters must be carefully crafted, and the template for such letters should be approved by counsel before implementation.

Employment Contracts

Some organizations use employment contracts for individuals in higher-level positions. The contract addresses and outlines different aspects of the employment relationship, and is binding upon the organization as well as the employee.

Some of the boilerplate items that would likely to appear in an employment contract are

▶ Identifying information and contact information for the employer and the employee.

▶ Position title, as well as the duties and responsibilities of the position.

▶ Duration of the contract, or a specific statement that the contract is indefinite.

▶ Type of compensation (salary, commission, and so forth), frequency of compensation, and formulas for calculating compensation (if appropriate).

▶ Benefits, including vacation allotment.

▶ Clauses covering terms of non-compete agreements, confidentiality, and non-solicitation of clients or customers.

▶ Termination clause, which could include conditions under which the employee could be terminated and/or mandatory notice requirements.

> **EXAM ALERT**
>
> Familiarize yourself with oral, written, implied and express contracts as they pertain to the employment relationship. More information on these topics can be found in Chapter 7 "Employee and Labor Relations."

Relocation

From time to time, an organization may choose to relocate employees. Some organizations relocate employees on an ongoing basis.

Relocation is one of the functions in HR that an organization may decide to outsource.

Employment: Employee Orientation

Employee orientation, also referred to as "onboarding," refers to the process by which an employee is supported as he or she transitions into the organization. This support can encompass a number of different factors including, but not limited to

- Introduction (or, assuming the interview process was conducted effectively, "reintroduction") to the goals and mission of the organization, and how this position supports those goals and that mission.

- Personal introduction to co-workers and peers.

- "Tour" around the facilities. Be sure not to forget the rest room, copy machine, printers, and fax machine—the little things can make a big difference, especially at the beginning of the employment relationship.

- Completion of required paperwork.

Unfortunately, many organizations still focus primarily or even exclusively on the completion of required paperwork, rather than on critical non-administrative elements, such as those listed previously. This is not to imply that paperwork is not important. It is. But it's not enough. Find ways to ensure that the employee is encouraged to feel comfortable. Work with managers to build an orientation program that will capture and channel the nervous excitement that new employees often experience on their first day in a new job. Get the employee off on the "right foot." Make sure the employee's first days, weeks, and months on the job are positive, memorable, and meaningful.

Terminations

Terminations reside at the other end of the spectrum of the employment life cycle. Terminations are often not given the degree of attention they deserve and require. Knowing how to effectively facilitate the process of employee terminations—whether voluntary or involuntary—is just as critical as knowing how to effectively facilitate the process of bringing employees into the organization. Whatever the reason, an employee's exit from the organization should be just as positive and respectful as the onboarding process for that employee's replacement will be.

Involuntary Terminations

Involuntary terminations—regardless of the specific reasons for the terminations—are challenging. There are several types of involuntary terminations.

Layoffs

Most HR professionals—at one time or another in their careers—will participate in the process of laying off employees. No matter what you call it—downsizing, rightsizing, reduction in force (RIF), or any of the other monikers—layoffs are never easy. Decisions to lay off employees should not be made lightly, and the manner in which the layoff is conducted is absolutely critical.

Determining Who Will Be Laid Off

Layoffs are handled differently in different organizations, and under different conditions. When the employment relationship is governed by a collective bargaining agreement, the terms and conditions governing who will be selected for layoff will likely be clearly spelled out, and are usually heavily weighted toward seniority ("last in, first out", or "LIFO"). In the absence of a collective bargaining agreement, decisions relative to who will stay and who will go may be based less on seniority and more on skills, potential, and/or past performance.

> **CAUTION**
>
> Before choosing to rely upon performance appraisal information or ratings when making employment decisions, it is critical to ensure the integrity and accuracy of the performance system. Any number of rater errors could significantly skew performance ratings, and could therefore diminish the legitimacy and defensibility of layoff decisions made under these assumptions.

The Role of HR in the Layoff Process

HR's role in the layoff process can vary greatly from organization to organization. Often, HR professionals help prepare for the layoff in an administrative and "paperwork" capacity. This may include calculating severance pay, vacation entitlements, or preparing COBRA paperwork. In addition, HR is often a primary source within the organization for information about outplacement services, in the event those services are being provided to assist employees as they transition out of the organization, and as they begin the process of seeking new employment.

HR's role often extends beyond administrative responsibilities. Sometimes, HR professionals participate in meetings that are held with employees who will be let go as a result of the layoff. These layoff meetings must be conducted with respect, consideration, empathy, and alacrity. This is a difficult situation for the employees who are leaving the organization, as well as for the employees who are staying. It is also a difficult process for the managers and HR professionals who are involved in the process.

NOTE

As difficult as it may be, HR professionals cannot allow themselves to become lost in the emotional dimensions of the layoff process. Ultimately, all layoffs should occur because of business necessity, and only after all other viable options have been considered. As strategic business partners, HR professionals are called upon to participate in even the most difficult parts of carrying out that business strategy. We can, however, commit ourselves to performing this role in a compassionate and professional manner.

Those Who Remain

It's critical not to overlook those employees who are still employed after the layoff. While these individuals have not been laid off, they did witness the layoff, and are therefore significantly affected by it. The impact on these individuals can be tangible as well as intangible. In a tangible sense, employees who are left behind may now face heavier workloads. They may also be concerned about what the future—both short term and long term—holds in store for them. "Waiting for the other shoe to drop" can be distracting, and can significantly diminish morale. Also, employees who remain after a layoff may feel some degree of uncertainty, and may even begin looking for employment elsewhere. If decisions relative to whom to lay off and whom to retain were made in part or in whole on the basis of performance, the organization risks losing its most valuable talent.

There is no single roadmap for handling this situation. Two tenets, however, should always be observed:

▶ Communicate clearly, frequently, and in a truthful manner. Credible communication about the layoff and the impact of the layoff on the organization is essential to rebuilding some sense of comfort and/or security.

▶ No matter how much you might want to, and no matter how much you believe it, do not offer any assurances or make any promises to the effect that the layoffs are over, or that no one else will be laid off. The reality of an employment-at-will relationship—particularly one that is not governed by a contract or other agreement—is that anyone can be let go at any time for any lawful reason. Make no promises that you cannot keep—and make no statements that could unintentionally create an implied contract.

> **CAUTION**
>
> There aren't too many "nevers" or "no brainers" when it comes to HR, but here's one: Never, under any circumstances, reveal the names of individuals who are on a layoff list unless and until you are explicitly directed to do so within the context of the overall communication strategy that has been developed. First and foremost, HR professionals cannot, under any circumstances, break the commitment to confidentiality with which they have been entrusted. Secondly, on a more practical note, such lists often change before the actual layoffs occur.

Other Involuntary Terminations

Many, if not most, employers have the legal right to terminate an employee at any time, for any lawful reason—or for no reason at all. In reality, however, using employment-at-will principles in a "willy-nilly" manner can seriously damage morale, diminish loyalty, increase turnover, and damage the employer's reputation in the labor market. It could also increase the likelihood of litigation.

Most of the time, the decision to terminate an employee is well-thought out, carefully scrutinized, and based on legitimate performance-related issues. It should also be made only after whatever progressive discipline process is in place within the organization has been followed.

Managers—HR's clients—make termination decisions. Sometimes (and ideally), they make these decisions in conjunction with HR. At other times, they make these decisions independently and only bring HR into the process when it comes time to execute the decision. In either scenario, HR can add value to this process. Sometimes, when it appropriate to do so, HR can suggest alternative approaches. HR can also ensure that the termination has been made in accordance with the organization's practices and that it is non-discriminatory. At times, HR can also point out information that has been overlooked, such as consistently positive performance appraisals in the file of a person who is being terminated for poor performance. In short, HR can provide another "set of eyes," and can help managers think through this all-important business decision.

Voluntary Terminations

There are a number of reasons why an employee might decide to voluntarily terminate his or her employment with the organization. Among these could be

- Accepting employment elsewhere ("other" employment, not necessarily "better" employment)

- Returning to school

- Retirement

- Avoiding an anticipated involuntary termination

- ▸ Dissatisfaction with the current employer, manager, or job
- ▸ Health- or disability-related reasons
- ▸ Enrollment in the military
- ▸ Personal reasons (birth or adoption of a child, illness of a family member)
- ▸ Early retirement

> **CAUTION**
>
> Early retirement can present an excellent way to downsize an organization, particularly if involuntary lay-offs are being considered. Early retirement, however, presents multiple risks—in particular, the possibility of allegations of age discrimination. Consult with counsel before implementing any retirement program to ensure that the program is lawful and defensible in the event of a challenge.

> **EXAM ALERT**
>
> Be familiar with how to conduct early retirements in a lawful manner that is consistent with the provisions outlined in the Age Discrimination in Employment Act.

Constructive Discharge

Constructive discharge does not fit neatly into either "voluntary" or "involuntary" terminations. It may, however, constitute a wrongful discharge. An employee who alleges constructive discharge asserts that he or she was subjected to such intolerable working conditions that remaining employed with the organization was an impossibility. Essentially, the employee is saying that he or she was forced to quit. Claiming constructive discharge, however, does not make it so—instead, this must be proven.

Exit Interviews

HR's responsibility extends beyond replacing an employee who has been terminated, either voluntarily or involuntary.

> **TIP**
>
> Replacing an employee should not be a "knee jerk" reaction in the wake of a termination. HR professionals are not order-takers, or order-fillers, and should not behave as such. Partner with your clients to explore creative options. Determine whether a position truly needs to be replaced. If it does, explore whether it should be replaced in its current format. Use terminations as an opportunity to revisit old assumptions and to support your clients by consider new and creative approaches.

HR professionals are often called upon to participate in the exit interview process. Exit interviews provide employers with an invaluable opportunity. If departing employees are assured—and if they believe—that their comments will not be attributed personally to them in any way, they can provide candid feedback relative to their employment experience with your organization.

Exit interviews should focus on job-related factors rather than feelings. An exit interviewer may want to ask for feedback relative to myriad topics, just a few of which could be

▶ The interview and selection process, and whether it provided a realistic and accurate depiction of the job

▶ The degree to which the employee felt as though he or she was making a valuable contribution that ultimately furthered, in some way, the mission of the organization

▶ The nature of the supervision received, and the employee's relationship with his or her supervisor

▶ Training opportunities, and the degree to which the employee was truly encouraged (and permitted) to take advantage of those opportunities

While some organizations conduct exit interviews using forms that the employee is asked to complete, many organizations find that in-person exit interviews yield more valuable results. The quality and the information provided will also be enhanced if the exit interviewer maintains a neutral and non-judgmental demeanor during the interview—regardless of what the departing employee might say. In fact, many of the same intra- and interpersonal skills that enhance the pre-employment interview process can also enhance the exit interview process.

Relevant Cases

HR professionals need to be familiar with key precedent-setting cases relating to EEO, workforce planning, and employment. The following summaries (presented in chronological order) describe the significance of some of those landmark cases.

Griggs v. Duke Power (1971)

Key issue: Adverse impact

Significance: Discrimination need not be deliberate or observable in order to be real. Rather, it can exist if a particular policy or practice has a statistically significant adverse impact upon members of a protected class. This is true even when the same requirement applies to all employees or applicants, as was the situation in this case. When a particular requirement does have an impact upon members of a protected class, the burden of proof rests with the employer to demonstrate that the requirement is, in fact, job-related and consistent with business necessity.

McDonnell Douglas Corp v. Green (1973)

Key issue: Disparate treatment/prima facie

Significance: The initial burden of proof for establishing a prima facie (Latin for "at first view") case of discrimination against an employer (or potential employer) under Title VII of the Civil Rights Act of 1964 rests with the employee (or applicant), who must be able to establish four key elements:

- ▶ The person is a member of a protected class.
- ▶ The person applied for a job for which the employer was seeking applicants.
- ▶ The person was rejected, despite being qualified for the position.
- ▶ After this rejection, the employer continued to seek other applicants with similar qualifications.

Once the employee establishes a prima facie case for disparate treatment, the burden of proof then shifts to the employer, who must then provide a non-discriminatory reason for its decision.

Albemarle Paper v. Moody (1975)

Key issue: Employment tests—job-relatedness and validity

Significance: Any tests that are used as part of the hiring or promotional decision making process must be job-related. This applies to any instrument that is used as a "test," even if that was not its original purpose. This case also established that employment tests must demonstrate predictive validity, consistent with the Uniform Guidelines for Employee Selection Procedures.

Washington v. Davis (1976)

Key issue: Employment tests—disparate impact

Significance: A test that has an adverse impact on a protected class is still lawful, as long as the test can be shown to be valid and job-related.

Regents of California v. Bakke (1978)

Key issue: Affirmative action

Significance: The Supreme Court ruled that while race could be a factor in college admission decisions, quotas could not be established.

Although this case was based on a college admissions program, its significance extended to workplace affirmative action programs.

This case falls under the category of "reverse discrimination," since it alleged race discrimination and was brought by someone who was not a minority/person of color.

United Steelworkers v. Weber (1979)

Key issue: Affirmative action

Significance: Affirmative action plans that establish voluntary quotas that have been jointly agreed to by an organization as well as its collective bargaining unit do not constitute race discrimination under Title VII of the Civil Rights Act of 1964 if they are designed to remedy past discrimination that has resulted in current underutilization.

This case falls under the category of "reverse discrimination," since it alleged race discrimination and was brought by someone who was not a minority/person of color.

Meritor Savings Bank v. Vinson (1986)

Key issue: Sexual harassment

Significance: This was the first ruling to establish that sexual harassment (whether quid pro quo or hostile environment) constitutes a violation of Title VII of the Civil Rights Act of 1964. In addition, the court ruled that it isn't enough for an organization to have a policy prohibiting discrimination. Instead, the ruling stated that "Reasonable care requires effective communication of policies and training. The employer has the burden of proof."

Johnson v. Santa Clara County Transportation Agency (1987)

Key issue: Affirmative action

Significance: Gender can be used as a factor in the selection process if there is under-representation in a particular job classification, as long as the AAP does not set forth a quota.

This case falls under the category of "reverse discrimination," since it alleged sex discrimination and was brought by a man.

Martin v. Wilks (1988)

Key Issue: Affirmative action

Significance: Current employees who are negatively affected by consent decrees that were established in an earlier time and which sought to resolve discrimination that was present in an earlier time may challenge the validity of such decrees.

This case falls under the category of "reverse discrimination," since it alleged race discrimination and was brought by individuals who were not minorities/people of color.

Harris v. Forklift Systems (1993)

Key Issue: Sexual harassment

Significance: The court clarified the standard relative to what constitutes a sexually hostile work environment: "This standard, which we reaffirm today, takes a middle path between making actionable any conduct that is merely offensive and requiring the conduct to cause a tangible psychological injury. Conduct that is not severe or pervasive enough to create an objectively hostile or abusive work environment—an environment that a reasonable person would find hostile or abusive—is beyond Title VII's purview. Likewise, if the victim does not subjectively perceive the environment to be abusive, the conduct has not actually altered the conditions of the victim's employment, and there is no Title VII violation."

Taxman v. Board of Education of Piscataway (1993)

Key issue: Affirmative action

Significance: The U.S. Court of Appeals for the Third Circuit ruled that—in the absence of under-representation as demonstrated and documented through an affirmative action plan—organizations cannot take race into account when making decisions relative to who will be laid off and who will be retained. Doing so would constitute a violation of Title VII of the Civil Rights Act of 1964.

This case falls under the category of "reverse discrimination," since it alleged race discrimination and was brought by a person who was not a minority/person of color.

St. Mary's Honor Center v. Hicks (1993)

Key Issue: Burden of proof

Significance: In order to ultimately prevail in an allegation of discrimination under Title VII of the Civil Rights Act of 1964, the charging party (meaning, the employee who filed the charge) must go beyond a prima facie case and *actually prove* that the employer's actual reasons for an employment action are, in fact, discriminatory.

McKennon v. Nashville Banner Publishing Co. (1995)

Key issue: After-acquired evidence

Significance: An employer will be held accountable for discriminatory employment actions even if it discovers evidence after taking the discriminatory employment action that would have led the employer to that same employment action for legitimate, non-discriminatory reasons.

Faragher v. City of Boca Raton (1998), and Ellerth v. Burlington Northern Industries (1998)

Key issue: Sexual harassment

Significance: If an employee *is* subjected to a tangible adverse employment action because of a supervisor's sexually harassing behavior, the employer is liable. The employer is also vicariously liable when its supervisors create a sexually hostile work environment even if the employee is not subjected to an adverse employment action. This is true whether or not the employer itself was negligent or otherwise at fault. However, if the employee *is not* subjected to tangible adverse employment action, the employer may be able to raise as a defense that he acted reasonably to prevent and/or promptly correct any sexually harassing behavior, and that the plaintiff unreasonably failed to take advantage of the employer's preventive or corrective opportunities.

Kolstad v. American Dental Association (1999)

Key Issue: Punitive damages under the Civil Rights Act of 1991

Significance: Punitive damages can only be awarded when the employer has acted with malice and reckless indifference to the employee's federally protected rights. This subjective standard was considered to be easier to establish than the more objective standard that would be required if employees had to prove that the nature of the actual behavior to which they had been subjected reached a level where it would be considered "egregious."

Grutter v. Bollinger and Gratz v. Bollinger (2003)

Barbara Grutter was applying for admission to the University of Michigan Law School, and Jennifer Gratz was applying for the University of Michigan as an undergraduate student. Lee Bollinger was the president of the University of Michigan.

Key issue: Affirmative Action

Significance: Race can be taken into account as an admissions factor since it furthers the establishment of diversity—a "compelling state interest"—as long as the admissions process is "narrowly tailored" to achieve the objective of achieving a diverse student body.

Interestingly, Supreme Court Justice Sandra Day O'Connor indicated that cases of this sort will likely be ruled differently in the future: "Race-conscious admissions policies must be limited in time. The Court takes the Law School at its word that it would like nothing better than to find a race-neutral admissions formula and will terminate its use of racial preferences as soon as practicable. The Court expects that 25 years from now, the use of racial preferences will no longer be necessary to further the interest approved today."

These cases fall under the category of "reverse discrimination," since they alleged race discrimination and were brought by people who were not minorities/people of color.

General Dynamics Land Systems v. Cline (2004)

Key Issue: Age Discrimination (Relative)

Significance: Younger employees (even if they are over the age of 40) cannot allege age discrimination because of the establishment of programs or decisions that favor older employees. As Justice David Souter wrote in the opening of his opinion, "The Age Discrimination in Employment Act of 1967 (ADEA or Act), 81 Stat. 602, 29 U.S.C. § 621 *et seq.*, forbids discriminatory preference for the young over the old. The question in this case is whether it also prohibits favoring the old over the young. We hold it does not."

Chapter Summary

Responsibilities relating to workforce planning and employment provide HR professionals with the opportunity to have a lasting impact upon the organization. Whether this impact is positive, however, depends in large part on the way in which HR professionals execute these responsibilities.

In order to function successfully with respect to the functional area of workforce planning and employment, HR professionals must develop an understanding or, and an appreciation for, equal employment opportunity (EEO).

It's also critical to understand the many laws and cases that shape this functional area. In addition, HR professionals must be prepared to contribute meaningfully to ensuring that the organization will be able to meet its future goals by making sure the right people, with the right skills, are in the right places, at the right times.

The ability to execute this functional area effectively is also predicated upon knowing and understanding the organization's strategic plan. HR professionals who have already earned a "seat at the table" in their organization are likely to have a good grasp of where the organization is going. HR professionals must proactively seek opportunities for learning about the organization's long-term objectives. Otherwise, our efforts may be less productive, less relevant, and less valued.

Ultimately, the choice of how we will perform in this area rests with us. The choice that we make will go a long way toward defining how we are perceived by the organization, our overall effectiveness in the organization, and the degree to which we will participate in a transformational manner within the organization.

Key Terms

- EEO (Equal Employment Opportunity)
- Protected class
- Discrimination
- Disparate treatment
- Disparate (or "adverse") impact
- Perpetuating past discrimination
- Harassment
- Sexual harassment
- Quid pro quo
- Hostile work environment
- Applicant
- Title VII of the Civil Rights Act (1964)
- Affirmative Action Plans (AAPs)
- Age Discrimination in Employment Act (ADEA) (1967)
- Rehabilitation Act (1973)
- Vietnam Era Veterans' Readjustment Assistance Act (VEVRAA) (1974)
- Pregnancy Discrimination Act (1978)
- Uniform Guidelines on Employee Selection Procedures (1978)
- Reliability
- Validity
- Content validity
- Criterion-related validity
- Construct validity
- Predictive validity
- Immigration Reform and Control Act (IRCA) (1986)
- I-9
- Worker Adjustment and Retraining Notification Act (WARN) (1988)
- Mass layoff
- Plant closing
- Americans with Disabilities Act (ADA) (1990)
- Qualified person
- Reasonable accommodation
- Undue hardship
- Disability
- Major life activities
- Civil Rights Act (1991)
- Congressional Accountability Act (CAA) (1995)
- The Delphi Technique
- Nominal Group Technique
- Trend analysis
- Ratio analysis
- Turnover analysis
- Simple linear regression
- Multiple linear regression
- Simulations
- Job analysis
- Job description

- Job specifications
- Job competencies
- KSAs
- Recruiting
- Selection
- Employer branding
- Selection criteria
- Internal recruiting
- External recruiting
- Job posting
- Job bidding
- Skill inventories
- Replacement charts
- Contingency employment agencies
- Retained employment agencies
- Employee referral
- Non-traditional staffing alternatives
- Employment application
- Short form employment applications
- Long form employment applications
- Job-specific employment applications
- Weighted employment applications
- Directive interviews
- Non-directive interviews
- Phone interviews
- Pre-screen interviews
- Behavior-based interviews
- Stress interviews
- Panel interviews
- Rapport
- Primary questions
- Probing questions
- Nonverbals
- Interviewing bias
- Contrast
- First impression
- Halo
- Horns
- Leniency
- Strictness
- Leniency
- Similar-to-me
- Realistic job previews
- Employment testing
- Agility tests
- Aptitude tests
- Cognitive ability tests
- Integrity, or honesty, tests
- Personality tests
- Drug tests
- Medical tests
- Background checks
- Employment contracts
- Relocation
- Orientation
- Involuntary terminations

- ▶ Voluntary terminations
- ▶ Constructive discharge
- ▶ Exit interviews
- ▶ Griggs v. Duke Power (1971)
- ▶ McDonnell Douglas Corp v. Green (1973)
- ▶ Albemarle Paper v. Moody (1975)
- ▶ Washington v. Davis (1976)
- ▶ Regents of California v. Bakke (1978)
- ▶ United Steelworkers v. Weber (1979)
- ▶ Meritor Savings Bank v. Vinson (1986)
- ▶ Johnson v. Santa Clara County Transportation Agency (1987)
- ▶ Martin v. Wilks (1988)

- ▶ Kolstad v. American Dental Association (1999)
- ▶ Harris v. Forklift Systems (1993)
- ▶ Taxman v. Board of Education of Piscataway (1993)
- ▶ St. Mary's Honor Center v. Hicks (1993)
- ▶ McKennon v. Nashville Banner Publishing Co. (1995)
- ▶ Faragher v. City of Boca Raton (1998), and Ellerth v. Burlington Northern Industries (1998)
- ▶ Grutter v. Bollinger and Gratz v. Bollinger (2003)
- ▶ General Dynamics Land Systems v. Cline (2004)

Apply Your Knowledge

This chapter focuses on issues relating to workforce planning and employment. Complete the following exercises, review questions, and exam questions as a way of reviewing and reinforcing the knowledge and skills you'll need to perform your responsibilities as an HR professional, and to increase the likelihood that you will pass the PHR examination.

Exercises

1. For some time, you've wanted to implement an exit interview process at your organization. You feel strongly that there's a lot of valuable information that can be gleaned from departing employees, and want to convince "the powers that be" of this, as well. You're ready to put together a proposal, and want to present the best possible arguments for establishing an exit interview program. Which of the following would be the strongest reason that you could include in your proposal to senior HR and line leadership?

   ○ **A.** If managers know that departing employees will have the opportunity to provide feedback as they are leaving the organization, they may be less likely to intentionally behave in ways that are problematic, or to treat employees in an unprofessional manner.

○ **B.** Since managers will be able to attribute comments made during exit interviews to specific employees, they will be better able to assess the validity of the feedback that departing employees provide.

○ **C.** Exit interviews provide an excellent opportunity to learn about how employees truly feel. Although employees may have been hesitant to express these feelings while employed with the organization, this same level of anxiety will not exist during the exit interview process—so departing employees can articulate their feelings more comfortably.

○ **D.** Exit interviews provide a unique opportunity to capture useful and relevant feedback from employees about a number of factors, such as the nature of the supervision that the employee experienced and the employee's relationship with his or her supervisor. This is information that in the absence of an exit interview process might never be obtained.

2. When you conduct employment interviews, you sometimes notice that candidates appear extremely nervous throughout the entire interview. So, to try to combat this, you've decided to rethink the way you begin your interviews and do more rapport building. Which of the following would be the best way to build rapport with your candidates?

○ **A.** Look at the candidate's résumé to see if you have anything in common with the candidate—such as hobbies, interests, former employers, place of residence, or any other shared commonality.

○ **B.** Place personal pictures—for instance, of your family members—within easy view of arriving candidates. This way, candidates can ask you about something that they know you'd be interested in talking about, thereby helping to "break the ice."

○ **C.** Talk about the weather. It's something that you know the two of you are certain to share in common, it's often changing, and it's neutral. If a blizzard or heat wave comes your way, you're certain to have rapport building for at least a week.

○ **D.** Choose a prominent current event—one that you are confident the candidate would know about—and refer to it in a somewhat general manner. This way, even if you and the employee are not in full agreement on the topic, the conversation will be superficial enough that no one will be offended, and you've still found something interesting to talk about (certainly more interesting than the weather).

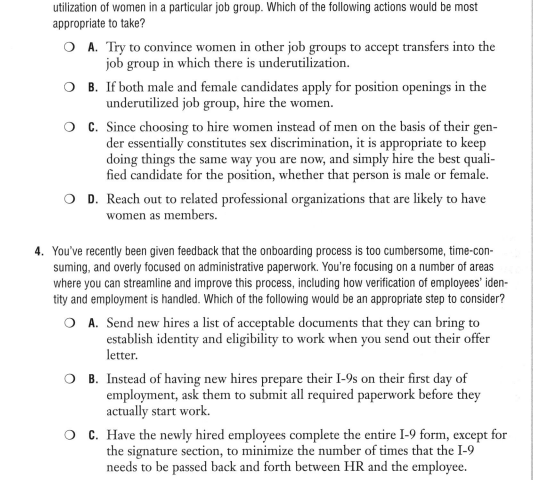

3. In reviewing your organization's most recent affirmative action plan, you notice that there is under-utilization of women in a particular job group. Which of the following actions would be most appropriate to take?

   - ○ **A.** Try to convince women in other job groups to accept transfers into the job group in which there is underutilization.

   - ○ **B.** If both male and female candidates apply for position openings in the underutilized job group, hire the women.

   - ○ **C.** Since choosing to hire women instead of men on the basis of their gender essentially constitutes sex discrimination, it is appropriate to keep doing things the same way you are now, and simply hire the best qualified candidate for the position, whether that person is male or female.

   - ○ **D.** Reach out to related professional organizations that are likely to have women as members.

4. You've recently been given feedback that the onboarding process is too cumbersome, time-consuming, and overly focused on administrative paperwork. You're focusing on a number of areas where you can streamline and improve this process, including how verification of employees' identity and employment is handled. Which of the following would be an appropriate step to consider?

   - ○ **A.** Send new hires a list of acceptable documents that they can bring to establish identity and eligibility to work when you send out their offer letter.

   - ○ **B.** Instead of having new hires prepare their I-9s on their first day of employment, ask them to submit all required paperwork before they actually start work.

   - ○ **C.** Have the newly hired employees complete the entire I-9 form, except for the signature section, to minimize the number of times that the I-9 needs to be passed back and forth between HR and the employee.

   - ○ **D.** Allow employees a full week to present their I-9 documents. In that way, the administrative responsibilities associated with onboarding can be spread over a longer period of time.

5. You strongly prefer to conduct directive interviews, because in your experience you end up with better information and can make better hiring recommendations to your client managers. At the beginning of one particular interview, the candidate pulls out a list of questions that she wants to ask you before she decides whether to proceed with the balance of the interview. Which of the following responses would be most appropriate?

○ **A.** Explain to the candidate that you use a directive approach to interviewing, and that it helps you make better hiring recommendations. As such, you'll be happy to answer her questions at the end of the interview.

○ **B.** Explain to the candidate that you will be happy to answer her questions at the end of the interview, once she has had an opportunity to answer the questions that you will be asking her.

○ **C.** Since there is nothing to be gained by getting into a confrontation with a candidate, you decide to answer her questions. Besides, in light of her approach, you've already decided to eliminate her from consideration for the position.

○ **D.** Since there is nothing to be gained by getting into a confrontation with a candidate, you decide to answer her questions. Besides, in light of her approach, you think she might have just the kind of spunk and tenacity that this organization needs.

Review Questions

1. Describe directive and non-directive interviews. In general, which is the preferred approach?

2. What are some of the factors that need to be taken into consideration when using performance as a criterion for determining who will be let go in a layoff situation?

3. What are some best practices with respect to taking notes during an interview?

4. Describe sexual harassment that takes the form of a hostile work environment.

5. Define and describe the differences between a mass layoff and a plant closing (according to WARNA).

Exam Questions

1. Which of the following forms of discrimination is not covered by Title VII of the Civil Rights Act of 1964?

○ **A.** Age

○ **B.** Color

○ **C.** Race

○ **D.** National Origin

2. Which of the following statements is true about quid pro quo sexual harassment?

    ○ **A.** It can be exacted by any employee on any other employee.

    ○ **B.** It creates a hostile work environment that can ultimately lead to constructive discharge.

    ○ **C.** It creates a situation in which an employee's terms and conditions of employment are affected by acceptance or rejection of sexual advances.

    ○ **D.** It cannot occur during the pre-employment selection process, since it refers to tangible or economic work-related consequences that, by definition, can only be experienced by current employees.

3. Which of the following employers would be required to prepare formal affirmative action plans?

    ○ **A.** Federal contractors who receive federal grants of any amount

    ○ **B.** Federal contractors with $50,000 or more in federal contracts

    ○ **C.** Federal contractors with at least 50 employees who have federal contracts of at least $50,000 per year

    ○ **D.** All federal contractors, regardless of the size or scope of the contract

4. In the event of a mass layoff or plant closing, WARN requires employers to notify all of the following individuals or entities except

    ○ **A.** Affected employees or their representatives (such as a collective bargaining unit)

    ○ **B.** The State Dislocated Worker Unit

    ○ **C.** The appropriate local government unit

    ○ **D.** The EEOC, which will conduct an adverse impact analysis before layoffs are implemented

5. A defining Supreme Court case for interpreting the Civil Rights Act of 1991 was

    ○ **A.** Kolstad v. American Dental Association

    ○ **B.** Grutter v. Bollinger and Gratz v. Bollinger

    ○ **C.** St. Mary's Honor Center v. Hicks

    ○ **D.** United Steelworkers c. Weber

6. Which of the following statements is true about the Delphi technique?

   ○ **A.** It looks at one particular factor, over a period of time, to track changes.

   ○ **B.** It requires all individual experts to present their own ideas to each other, without immediate discussion or assessment

   ○ **C.** It utilizes a neutral facilitator who compiles and condenses input

   ○ **D.** It is a structured, mathematical approach to forecasting

7. A properly conducted job analysis will produce all of the following except

   ○ **A.** Job competencies

   ○ **B.** Job postings

   ○ **C.** Job specifications

   ○ **D.** Job description

8. Which of the following is not one of the main elements in a job description?

   ○ **A.** Scope information

   ○ **B.** Physical work conditions and physical demands

   ○ **C.** Compensation rates

   ○ **D.** Minimum requirements

9. Which of the following would be least likely to be considered a job competency?

   ○ **A.** Communication skills

   ○ **B.** Facilitation skills

   ○ **C.** Teamwork skills

   ○ **D.** Interpersonal skills

10. All of the following represent benefits of employee referral programs except

   ○ **A.** Highly cost effective recruiting

   ○ **B.** Employees who are more likely to succeed

   ○ **C.** Demonstration of good faith efforts to remedy underutilization

   ○ **D.** Increased candidate familiarity with the organization

Answers to Exercises

1. **Answer D is the best possible response.** Employees are not likely to provide candid information about many dimensions of their employment experience—especially their relationship with their manager—while they are still employed with the organization. A well-structured exit interview process, therefore, can provide a one-time opportunity to glean information that might otherwise remain unspoken (at least to anyone within the organization who can actually use it in a productive manner). Answer A is not the best response, since the exit interview process will fail if it is used as a deterrent for management misbehavior, or in a threatening manner. Answer B is not the best response, since comments that an employee makes during exit interviews should be "sanitized," and should not be attributable to him or her. Answer C is not the best response, since—in order to be truly informative and effective—exit interviews should focus on facts, not feelings.

2. **Answer C is the best response.** Weather is a safe topic of discussion, and you can be certain that the candidate has some awareness of it. If you work in a windowless workspace, or if you haven't had a chance to go outside for a while, asking about the weather affords the candidate the opportunity to "update" you on something that is relevant to both of you. Also, when spoken about in an animated manner, even the weather can help to "break the ice" with a candidate. Answer A is not the best response, since interviewers should not discuss any factors that are not job-related (the weather, of course, is an exception to this)—including hobbies and interests. You never know what information candidates might reveal about themselves as they speak about their hobbies or interests, and it's much easier to avoid this discussion than to have to deal with unwanted information that the candidate has disclosed. Such discussions can also get the interview off track, or result in ceding control of the interview to the candidate. Answer B is not the best response, since positioning photos of family members in visible locations is equivalent to discussing your own family, which is akin to nonverbally inviting the candidate to discuss his or her own family. Answer D is not the best response, since discussing any prominent current event is likely to lead to issues that relate to politics, religion, personal beliefs, or a host of other topics that should not be discussed during an interview. Additionally, there is no way to be certain that a candidate is aware of the event that you bring up—no matter how prominent you think it is. And, even if the candidate is aware of the event, he or she may have no interest in or knowledge of it. This can result in increasing—rather than decreasing—the candidate's anxiety level.

3. **Answer D is the best response.** Reaching out to professional organizations that are likely to include women as members would likely constitute a good faith effort at address underutilization by creating a more diverse pool of candidates. Answer A is not the best response, since trying to convince women or minorities to change job groups

is not an appropriate way to address underutilization. Answer B is not the best response, because that approach as described would constitute sex discrimination. It would also be likely to result in hiring unqualified individuals, simply because those individuals happen to be women. Answer C is not the best response, since underutilization cannot simply be ignored. Additionally, while it is appropriate (and advisable) to hire qualified—if not the best qualified—candidates, an organization does have the obligation to make good faith efforts to create a pool of qualified candidates that includes women or minorities for those job groups where there is current underutilization.

4. **Answer A is the best response.** Although anyone who has started a new job since 1986 should be familiar with the requirement to present documents proving identity and eligibility to legally work in the United States, sending new hires a list of acceptable documents along with their offer letter gives them ample time to pull together the required materials. It also reaffirms that a wide range of documents is acceptable, and that none is preferred over any other. Answer B is not the best response, since the I-9 form specifically states that the form is to be "completed and signed by employee at the time employment begins." Answer C is not the best response, since certain portions of the I-9 must be completed by the employer. Answer D is not the best response, since the I-9 form must be completed within the first three business days of the new hire's employment.

5. **Answer B is the best response.** As the interviewer, *you—not* the candidate—are in control of the interview. There is no need to cede that control simply because a candidate asks you to. Answer B also responds to the candidate's request in a positive manner: You are not telling her "no"; instead, you are telling her "not now" (and you are managing to do so without even alluding to the word "no"). Answer A is not the best response, since it is not necessary to explain to the candidate why you have chosen to structure the interview in a particular way. Additionally, using technical terms (such as "directive interviews") adds no value to this discussion, and might even create distance between you and the candidate (distance that *no* amount of discussion about the weather will be able to bridge). Neither Answer C nor Answer D is the best response, for a couple of reasons. First, in both instances, you have ceded control of the interview to the candidate simply because she asked you to do so. In addition, in both scenarios, you made assumptions (one could even say "sweeping judgments") about this candidate based on a single behavior that is not necessarily accurate or reflective of how that candidate would behave in the workplace. An interview is a unique situation governed by unique "norms and mores." There are also a lot of people who make a living giving other people advice about how they "should" behave during an interview. Sometimes, that good advice just isn't good. At other times, it directs a candidate to behave in a markedly different manner from how he or she would act outside the interview...but it can be difficult to argue with so-called "experts" sometimes

(especially when you need or want to find a new job). Give candidates an opportunity to understand and comply with the expectations that you have of them for *your* interview process…and don't jump to conclusions too quickly.

Answers to Review Questions

1. Directive interviews take a more structured approach. The interviewer(s) asks the same questions of all candidates and maintains control of the interview. Conversely, non-directive interviews are more conversational and relatively unstructured. In a non-directive interview, the candidate—not the interviewer—ends up controlling the interview, and primarily determines what will be discussed.

   Generally speaking, a directive style is more effective and appropriate than a non-directive style, as it yields more consistent results, facilitates the process of comparing candidates to the job requirements and to each other, and is stronger in the event of a legal challenge. Although the directive approach is the better approach, however, the interview must still remain dynamic and interactive.

2. Before choosing to rely upon information about past performance to determine who should be laid off and who should be retained, the organization needs to carefully examine its performance appraisal system and assess its validity and overall worth. The system itself could be flawed, or even if it is sound, there could be problems with the way in which individual raters have executed it over time. Either factor could result in misguided assessments, which could consequently diminish the legitimacy (and defensibility) of layoff decisions made on the basis of employees' past performance.

3. At the beginning of the interview—perhaps at the end of the formal "rapport building" process—let the candidate know that you will be taking notes. The candidate may otherwise assume that he or she has said something wrong the minute your pen hits the paper. Letting the candidate know you will be taking notes can actually constitute another element of rapport building: You are interested in and care about what the candidate is going to tell you, and want to be certain that you remember it correctly.

   Note-taking should not interfere in any way with the interview process. It also should not harm the personal connectedness that the interviewer establishes with the candidate during the initial rapport building portion of the interview. Jotting down key words and phrases that the candidate offers in response to the interviewer's questions will help the interviewer to remember the candidate's responses after the interview is over. Interviewers can then go back after the interview is done and "flesh out" more details around each of the candidate's answers.

4. Sexual harassment that manifests itself as a hostile work environment exists when unwelcome sexual conduct unreasonably interferes with an employee's job performance

or creates a hostile, intimidating, or offensive work environment. A hostile work environment can be found to exist whether or not the employee experiences (or runs the risk of experiencing) tangible or economic work-related consequences.

Hostile work environment harassment is unrelated to any decisions that are made relative to the employee's employment. As such, hostile work environments can be created by virtually anyone with whom an employee might come in contact in the workplace or "workspace."

5. According to WARN, a "mass layoff" occurs when either of the following two events happens within a 30-day period at a single worksite:

▶ 500 full-time employees are laid off

▶ At least 33 percent of the workforce is laid off (if, and only if, that 33% includes 50-499 full-time employees)

A "plant closing" happens when a facility or operating unit is shut down for more than six months, or when 50 or more employees lose their jobs during any 30-day period at a single worksite.

Answers to Exam Questions

1. **Answer A is the best response.** Title VII of the Civil Rights Act of 1964 established five protected classes: color (Answer B), race (Answer C), national origin (Answer D), religion, and sex. Age did not become a protected class until 1967, with the passage of the Age Discrimination in Employment Act (ADEA).

2. **Answer C is the best response.** Quid pro quo harassment occurs when an individual's submission to or rejection of sexual advances or conduct of a sexual nature is used as the basis for employment-related decisions. Since this sort of impact can usually only be brought about by a supervisor or someone else in a position of authority in the organization, Answer A is not the best response. Answer B is not the best response, since quid pro quo harassment is a separate concept from hostile work environment harassment (although both types of harassment could potentially lead to constructive discharge). Answer D is not the best response, since either quid pro quo or hostile work environment harassment could occur during the recruiting or selection processes.

3. **Answer B is the best response.** Answer A is not the best response, since Executive Order 11246 does not use the awarding of federal grants as a factor that determines whether an organization needs to prepare a formal affirmative action plan. Answer C is not the best response, since this threshold refers to an organization's obligation to file annual EEO reports, not to the organization's obligation to prepare a formal affirmative action plan. Answer D is not the best response, since not all contractors are required to prepare formal affirmative action plans.

4. **Answer D is the best response.** There is no WARN requirement to notify the EEOC of impending mass layoffs or plant closings. The organization should, however, conduct an adverse impact analysis before making any layoff decisions. Answers A, B, and C are not the best responses since each one indicates individuals or entities who are required to be notified in the event that WARN is triggered.

5. **Answer A is the best response.** In this case, the court ruled that punitive damages can only be awarded when the employer has acted with malice and reckless indifference to "the employee's federally protected rights." Answers B, C, and D each address different legal principles.

6. **Answer C is the best response.** This neutral facilitator does not serve as an expert in this process, but does condense the submissions of the designated experts. Answer A is not the best response, since looking at one particular factor over time to track changes is trend analysis. Answer B is not the best response, since this is a description of a technique used in the nominal group technique. Answer D is not the best response, since the Delphi technique is a structured, *non*-mathematical approach to forecasting.

7. **Answer B is the best response.** A properly conducted job analysis will produce job competencies (Answer A), job specifications (Answer C), and a job description (Answer D). While information generated through the job analysis should be used to write a job posting, this is not one of the specific outputs of the job analysis process.

8. **Answer C is the best response.** Compensation rates are generally not included in a job description. Scope information (Answer A), physical work conditions and physical demands (Answer B), and minimum requirements (Answer C) do constitute important parts of the job description for each position.

9. **Answer B is the best choice.** Job competencies speak to broad categories of skills that are required to perform successfully in a particular position, department, or organization. Of the four choices, "facilitation skills" is least likely to be defined in this way, since it is more of a discrete, observable, and perhaps even measurable skill. Communication skills (Answer A), teamwork skills (Answer B), and interpersonal skills (Answer D) are all more likely to be considered "key success factors" or "performance factors."

10. **Answer C is the best response.** If underutilization exists within an organization, employee referral programs are not likely to remedy that problem. Answers A and D are not the best possible responses, since both of these represent benefits of employee referral programs. Answer B is not the best response, because although the employee who makes the referral may be believe that the candidate who they refer will succeed, that assessment is not necessarily accurate.

Suggested Readings and Resources

SHRM Website: www.shrm.org

Department of Labor Website: www.dol.gov

Equal Employment Opportunity Commission (EEOC) website: www.eeoc.gov

Department of Justice website: www.usdoj.gov

Other Internet Resources: Search the Web for any of the words listed in the "key terms" section of this chapter.

www.amazon.com: Search any of the words listed in the "key terms" section of this chapter.

CHAPTER FIVE

HR Development

Study Strategies

- ▶ Use index cards (ideally, of different sizes and different colors) to help you study:

- ▶ On small index cards, write the names of HRD related laws.

- ▶ Prepare large index cards for each of the laws. Make note of important facts, dates, and details relating to each law. On the back of the index card, write the name of the law in pencil.

- ▶ Prepare small index cards with the names of each of the theorists/gurus/experts mentioned in this chapter.

- ▶ Prepare small index cards with the name/title of each theory/philosophy/practice that is covered in this chapter that was developed by one of the theorists/gurus/experts covered in this chapter.

- ▶ On a third and slightly larger set of index cards, jot down key learning points associated with each philosophy/practice. Just like you did with the larger set of cards, write the name of each theory in pencil on the back of the card.

- ▶ Match the three sets of cards together. Of course, don't look at the back of the cards until you've matched all of the cards—then, check to see whether you've done so correctly.

- ▶ Try writing out your own multiple choice test questions. Writing out the questions—along with detailed answers—can go a long way toward reinforcing what you are studying. If you've got a study partner, trade questions with that person.

- ▶ Although the PHR exam is multiple choice, try writing and answering your own "essay-based" questions. Write open-ended questions that require a response of at least a full paragraph—and write your answers without looking back at your study materials. The process of actually writing down your answers will reinforce what you already know, and will highlight what you need to study more. It will also likely help you as you work to recall this same information when you answer related multiple choice questions on the actual PHR exam.

- ▶ As with each of the six functional areas of HR, determine what you already know and what you don't know. Then, work to prepare yourself. Conduct research. Use the Internet to find articles and white papers that highlight HR development. Peruse textbooks that provide guidance relative to those particular areas. Be sure to find several real-life examples of each responsibility to ensure that you gain a variety of perspectives and insights. This is particularly important for the skill-based, rather than fact-based, components of this functional area.

Introduction

Human resource development (HRD) can be defined, in its simplest terms—well…it actually isn't all that easy to define. A review of the research describes HRD in myriad and sometimes ambiguous ways. If you have had a chance to study and review HRD-related books, articles, and documents as part of your preparation for the PHR exam, and still aren't 100% clear in your understanding of where and how it fits within the broader field of HR, you are not alone. And, when you throw organization development (OD) into the mix, things can seem even a bit more unclear.

In an effort to lend as much clarity as possible to this critically important HR functional area, let's approach HR development with this working definition:

HRD consists of processes and initiatives that improve current—and prepare for future—organizational effectiveness by ensuring that those who work within the organization will be positioned to meet needed levels of performance through training, career development, and organization development initiatives.

In order to understand, appreciate, and begin to perform HRD more effectively, HR professionals need to be familiar with key foundational concepts as well as relevant legislation. HR professionals also need to be able to knowledgeably navigate the three primary areas of HRD:

- **Organization development (OD):** The development of effective and productive organizations that simultaneously develop, empower, and support their employees.

- **Training (also known as "learning and development"):** The transfer and learning of skills and knowledge that will enable an employee to perform his or her current job more effectively, thus contributing to overall organizational effectiveness.

- **Career development:** The deliberate preparation for, and unfolding of, the professional pathway each individual travels along during his or her adult working life.

It is worthwhile to note that although OD has more of an organizational focus, and training and career development are more individualized in nature, all three areas contribute significantly to the overall mission of HRD.

Two other areas that also contribute to the overall mission of HRD are leadership development and performance management. Although both areas are inextricably woven into the tapestry of HRD, each also maintains its own presence and uniqueness—even in those organizations that do not openly espouse HRD initiatives. As such, these two areas will be explored separately, but still as part of this chapter.

Related Legislation: Human Resource Development

In addition to the HR-related laws that are explored in the other HR functional areas, there are several other laws—ones that are not specifically HR-related—that need to be considered carefully because of the impact they can have on the way we perform our jobs. Here, we will look at

- ▶ Copyright Act of 1976

- ▶ Public domain

- ▶ Fair use

- ▶ U.S. Patent Act

Copyright Act of 1976

The idea of protecting the work of authors, artists, and others who create original materials dates back all the way to the Constitution. Article I, Section 8 of the United States Constitution states: "The Congress shall have Power… to promote the Progress of Science and useful Arts, by securing for limited Times to Authors and Inventors the exclusive Right to their respective Writings and Discoveries." Fast forward 189 years to the Copyright Act of 1976.

What's Covered, and What Rights Are Granted

A copyright grants certain rights to authors and others who create original works. According to Section 102 of the Act, this protection extends to "original works of authorship fixed in any tangible medium of expression, now known or later developed, from which they can be perceived, reproduced, or otherwise communicated, either directly or with the aid of a machine or device." Works of authorship that are protected include

- ▶ Literary works

- ▶ Musical works, including any accompanying words

- ▶ Dramatic works, including any accompanying music

- ▶ Pantomimes and choreographic works

- ▶ Pictorial, graphic, and sculptural works

- ▶ Motion pictures and other audiovisual works

- ▶ Sound recordings

- ▶ Architectural works (this category was added in 1990)

The Act grants copyright holders exclusive rights to six different specific activities. In so doing, the Act also prohibits those who do not hold the copyright from engaging in those activities without permission of the copyright holder. The six exclusive rights are

- The right to duplicate/reproduce/copy the work

- The right to create derivative works that are based on the original work

- The right to sell, lease, rent, or otherwise distribute copies of the work to the public

- The right to perform the work publicly

- The right to display the work publicly

- The right to digital performance in sound recordings

Copyright Holders

Most of the time, the author, artist, or individual who created the work owns the copyright to the work. The Copyright Act, however, does establish two important "work-for-hire" exceptions to this rule. These exceptions pertain specifically to work product created by

- **Employees**: The work product that an employee generates in the normal course of his or her employment is automatically owned by the employer.

- **Consultants/independent contractors**: Work product generated by a consultant or independent contractor is usually automatically owned by the organization with whom the consultant contracts. From the perspective of the organization that has contracted with the consultant, it is important to have a signed written agreement that states that a "work-for-hire" arrangement has been established, and that the organization owns all work product that is produced.

Copyright law covers only the particular form or manner in which ideas or information were first fixed. Copyrights do not, however, cover the actual ideas, concepts, or facts that are included in the fixed work.

Copyrights last for the lifetime of the author, plus 70 years. After that, the work passes into the "public domain." Anonymous works and works that were created under "work-for-hire" agreements enter the public domain 95 years after the first year of publication or 120 years after the year in which they were created, whichever comes first.

Public Domain

As previously indicated, copyrights—and the protections afforded by copyrights—eventually expire. Once a copyright for a particular work expires, that work enters the public domain.

This means that the copyright holder no longer enjoys the six rights cited previously, and that the works are available, and free, for all to use.

> **TIP**
>
> Work created by the federal government is, by definition, considered to be in the public domain. This provision of the Act can be very helpful to HR professionals, especially with respect to work product that is generated relative to legal and/or compliance-related issues.

> **EXAM ALERT**
>
> Familiarize yourself with the criteria that exist for determining whether a particular work is in the public domain.

> **CAUTION**
>
> Just because a work is "publicly accessible" does not mean that it is in the public domain. With access to countless numbers of websites, combined with the ability to copy, paste, and save text on almost any topic, the temptation may exist to incorporate existing materials into HRD/training presentations, handouts, or other work-related documents. For legal, professional, and ethical reasons, resist the temptation. Don't do it.

Fair Use

In addition to works that are in the public domain, HR professionals (and anyone else, of course) can use copyrighted works under certain circumstances. This is known as "fair use." According to the Copyright Act, portions of copyrighted works can be used without the permission of the author for purposes of "criticism, comment, news reporting, teaching (including multiple copies for classroom use), scholarship, or research." Even then, however, what constitutes "fair use" is contingent upon a number of factors:

▶ Whether the work will be used for commercial purposes, or for not-for-profit or educational purposes.

▶ The nature of the way in which the work will be used.

▶ How much of the work is used, both in terms of the overall "size" of the portion of the work that is being used, as well as the percentage of the total work that is being used.

▶ Whether the use could impact the potential market and/or the market value of the work.

U.S. Patent Act

In addition to being familiar with copyrights, HR professionals also need to have an understanding of patents.

Patents confer certain rights upon the individual to whom the patent is granted. Specifically, a patent holder has "the right to exclude others from making, using, offering for sale, or selling" the invention in the United States or "importing" the invention into the United States. Interestingly, a patent does not grant the patent holder the right to take any specific action relative to the patent that he or she has been granted, or relative to the invention for which the individual was granted the patent. Instead, it prohibits others from taking the preceding actions. The responsibility for enforcing those rights, however, falls squarely upon the individual to whom the patent has been granted (with no assistance from the US Patent Office).

There are three types of U.S. patents:

Type of Patent	Patent Issued to Individuals Who	Duration of Patent (from Date of Filing)
Utility	Invent or discover any new and useful process, machine, article of manufacture, or composition of matter, or any new and useful improvement thereof	20 years
Design	Invent a new, original, and ornamental design for an article of manufacture	14 years
Plant	Invent or discover and asexually reproduce any distinct and new variety of plant	20 years

HR professionals and the organizations for which they work need to understand and consider patent issues, particularly if employees might (or do) create inventions in the course of their work. To avoid costly and time-consuming litigation—which could even potentially impact the marketability of the invention—organizations should consult with counsel in advance, relative to drafting and implementing written agreements governing patent issues.

REVIEW BREAK

Although HRD isn't directly impacted by as many laws as the other functional areas of HR, it's still important to have a solid understanding of relevant laws—specifically, The Copyright Act of 1976 and the U.S. Patent Act. It's important to always remain cognizant of the fact that other HR-related laws (such as the Civil Rights Act of 1964) do apply, and must be carefully considered for their HRD implications.

Now, with the legal considerations tucked in the back of our minds, let's begin to look at some key HRD concepts, as well as their applications.

HRD: The Importance of ADDIE

While the ADDIE model can be applied in any of the functional areas within HR, it is perhaps most frequently referenced with respect to HRD (specifically, training and instructional design). Therefore, much of the information in this chapter (and, perhaps, on the PHR exam) relating to ADDIE use training-specific examples. As you move through the chapter, however, please keep in mind the broader applications of ADDIE.

ADDIE: An Overview

As mentioned in Chapter 2, the acronym "ADDIE" represents the following five steps:

- ▶ **A**: Analysis/assessment (of needs)
- ▶ **D**: Design
- ▶ **D**: Development
- ▶ **I**: Implementation
- ▶ **E**: Evaluation

Since this model is so integral to HRD—specifically in terms of instructional design—let's take a look at each of these steps more closely.

ADDIE: "A" Is for Analysis/Assessment

As we begin to explore needs analysis/assessment—the first step in the ADDIE model—it's helpful to keep in mind the kinds of questions that you might hear as you prepare for and work your way through this phase. In this way, you'll be better able to recognize these questions when you hear them, and more importantly, you can look for opportunities to ask them yourself. Some representative questions that might come up in the needs analysis/assessment phase might include

- ▶ Why is the HRD/training initiative being considered?
- ▶ If the HRD/training initiative is related to a performance problem, what is the reason for the substandard performance? (We need to recognize that reason before we can begin to determine whether a HRD/training initiative might constitute an appropriate intervention.)
- ▶ What level of subject-matter knowledge and skill do learners possess?
- ▶ What level of subject-matter knowledge and skill do learners need?

► What is the "gap" between current performance levels and desired or expected performance levels?

► What are the learning objectives that the HRD/training initiative would need to achieve in order to bridge that gap?

► What level of organizational/leadership support exists to bridge that gap? (This may be a function of how closely the skills or knowledge that is missing relates to the mission and goals of the organization.)

► By what date must the organization begin to address the gap?

► By what date must the organization resolve the gap?

► What are the costs of various HRD/training options, and what would be the benefits?

► What resources are available to address this gap? (Resources include, but are not necessarily limited to, people, money, and time.)

Analysis/Assessment: Theoretical/Scholarly Foundation

Before getting into the nuts-and-bolts of needs analysis/assessment, it's helpful and important to understand what's behind it.

EXAM ALERT

In addition to helping you perform your job better, questions about HR-related theory (such as this, for instance) will appear on the PHR exam.

In 1961, McGehee and Thayer identified three levels of HRD/training needs analysis and assessment. Their theory still constitutes an important tool for HRD/training needs analysis/assessment (although some of the terminology has evolved a bit over time, as indicated in the following table):

Level of Needs Analysis (1961 Verbiage)	Level of Needs Analysis (Contemporary Verbiage)	Definition/Description of the Level of Analysis	Examples of What the Analysis Looks At
Organizational analysis	N/A	Determine where HRD/training can and should be used within the overall organization	What is the organization's mission? What are its objectives? In the future, what KSAs will the organization's employees need to possess and demonstrate?

(continued)

Level of Needs Analysis (1961 Verbiage)	Level of Needs Analysis (Contemporary Verbiage)	Definition/Description of the Level of Analysis	Examples of What the Analysis Looks At
			What is the pool of skills currently available within the organization?
			What is the gap between those two?
			What is the organization's culture like?
Operations analysis	Task or work analysis	Collect data about a particular job or group of jobs	What are the performance standards for a particular job?
			What KSAs and behavior characteristics must an incumbent possess and demonstrate in order to achieve those standards?
Man analysis	Individual or person analysis	Assess performance of a particular individual	How well is a particular employee performing? Where does the employee's performance fall below the expected standards of the position? Is that lag attributable to skills or knowledge the employee needs to attain or develop? How might training or other HRD initiatives address any performance issues (areas in which actual performance does not match the level of performance required to attain established job standards)?

Needs Analysis/Assessment—Why Do It?

There are a number of reasons to conduct a needs analysis/assessment before embarking upon an HRD/training initiative. Some of those reasons are

▶ To identify—objectively and factually—performance-related problems within the organization. (Engaging in this process constitutes another manifestation of how HR can form an organizational partnership with its internal clients).

▶ To collect facts with which to establish a baseline level of performance. This baseline will then provide a valid basis of comparison for pre-training/post-training (or, more broadly, pre-HRD initiative/post-HRD initiative) assessments.

▶ To generate increased involvement with and, therefore, buy-in for the HRD/training solution that is ultimately implemented. Securing buy-in at all levels of the organization (especially at the senior leadership level) is critical.

▶ To ensure that your decisions and recommendations are based on facts, rather than on assumptions. This is another way to help to dispel the "fuzzy-wuzzy touchy-feely party-planning" stereotype, which many HR professionals are still wrestling to reinvent. This process provides HR professionals with an opportunity to enhance their reputation in the organization as legitimate business partners—not as people who rely on their ability to intuitively "read" a situation.

▶ To increase the likelihood of identifying a solution that will truly bridge the performance gap.

▶ To ensure that a legitimate cost-benefit analysis is conducted before a commitment is made to any particular HRD/training solution. The costs associated with implementing the HRD/training initiative must be compared to the costs that would accrue if the current situation were allowed to persist without implementing the HRD/training intervention.

An unintended, but potentially significant, benefit of conducting a needs analysis/assessment is that you may even identify other organizational issues that had previously gone unnoticed. Even if these concerns are not best addressed by an HRD/training-based initiative—and even if they do not fall within the purview of HR—you still will have made a meaningful contribution to the overall effectiveness of your organization.

Needs Analysis/Assessment—What Are the Risks of *Not* Doing It?

Having looked at the benefits of conducting a needs analysis/assessment, it's also important to look at the situation from a different perspective—specifically, the risks associated with *not* conducting a needs analysis/assessment. A few of these risks might be

- Misidentifying problems

- Overlooking problems

- Eliminating the only means of establishing a basis from which to make meaningful assessments of the impact of an HRD/training initiative.

- Risking the possibility of increased skepticism relative the value of—and necessity for—the HRD/training initiative.

- Damaging HR's reputation, either collectively or relative to specific individuals, by contributing to the impression that HR folks just try to "get a feel for things" instead of making rigorous, fact-based business decisions.

Needs Analysis/Assessment—How Do You Do It?

Though experts may differ on the specifics, and different models might include different steps, a well-constructed needs analysis should include the following four steps:

1. Gather data that will enable you to identify specific needs.

2. Determine which of those needs can be addressed through HRD/training interventions.

3. Propose/select a solution (depending upon HR's role in the organization and in this process) for those needs that are best addressed through HRD/training interventions.

4. Compare the costs of implementing an HRD/training initiative to the benefits that will accrue from delivering the HRD/training initiative.

NOTE

From time to time, HRCI may prescribe steps that differ slightly from research and recommendations that are available elsewhere. Essentially, however, "good practice is good practice," and most minor differences generally will not impact your ability to effectively carry out the function being described.

Step 1 of Needs Analysis/Assessment: Gathering Data

Data Collection Techniques	Sample Strengths	Sample Weaknesses
General surveys (closed ended questions)	Easier to tabulate (especially if done electronically). Confidentiality can be ensured, which may lead to greater candor of response.	Information may be overly general in nature, in part because of the nature of closed ended questions.
"Felt-needs" employee surveys (asking people to identify the areas in which they feel they need training)	Can reach a large number of employees in a short time frame.	Employees may identify "wants" instead of "needs." The training that the employees are requesting, therefore, may not directly translate into enhanced work performance that supports attainment of organizational objectives.
"Organizational challenges" employee surveys (asking employees to identify individual, group, or organizational performance issues)	Can reach a large number of employees in a short time frame. Ensures a focus on performance issues, which can then be translated by those who administer the survey into HRD/training solutions.	Since these questions are more open-ended in nature, results may take longer to tabulate.
Review of published business documents	Provides factual, objective data with which many decision makers should already be familiar (and in which they likely already have confidence).	Reflects past situations, which may not be reflective of more recent trends.
Interviews	Obtain in-depth information from individuals at all levels of the organization (thus providing a variety of valuable perspectives).	Time consuming. Labor intensive. Requires a skilled interviewer (who also can establish trust).
Focus groups	Provides a qualitative approach. A skilled facilitator may be able to extract particularly valuable information. The synergy present in a well-functioning group may generate more valuable and insightful data than would have been generated by the same members individually.	Labor intensive and time consuming. More difficult to reach large numbers of people, within a relative short time frame. Direction of discussion may be swayed by group dynamics, or by the presence and/or contributions of one or more influential individuals. It may be challenging to replicate identical conditions across various focus groups, which could theoretically taint/impact the consistency of the data that is collected. May be prohibitive because of limited resources (time, cost, or facilitator availability).

Step 1 *Continued*

Data Collection Techniques	Sample Strengths	Sample Weaknesses
Observation	Provides a realistic viewpoint, rather than one that might be "sanitized," obsequious, or self-serving.	Labor intensive and time consuming. Requires a trained observer (trained in making observations, as well as in the work that is being observed).
Performance appraisals	If done well, the performance management and appraisal process can establish criteria.	Performance appraisals—for myriad reasons—do not always provide an accurate reflection of actual performance (or of that performance as it compares to standards) (see "Performance Appraisal (and Management)— Pitfalls to Avoid"
Skills assessment	Results are easily quantified.	Does not measure whether the skills that are being assessed are actually being used on the job.

As indicated, each data gathering method has advantages and disadvantages. For this reason, a combination of two or more methods might be more effective.

Data gathering can be performed by someone within the organization, or with some level of support and assistance from external experts (consultants, and so on). Regardless of who gathers the data, establishing trust is absolutely essential. Otherwise, the overall objective of enhancing the organization could be overshadowed by mistrust or morale problems that poorly conducted data gathering can engender.

It's also essential to make a commitment to following through on this process beyond the data gathering phase, even if the organization ultimately decides not to launch an HRD/training initiative. In short, the first time that employees tell you about their concerns cannot be the last time that you communicate with them about those concerns. The very process of gathering data—especially through survey or focus group techniques—raises awareness, and thus raises expectations. Don't let those expectations be ignored—even if the answer ends up being that they will not be addressed through an HRD initiative at this time.

Step 2 of Needs Analysis: Identify Needs That Can Be Addressed Through Specific HRD/Training Initiatives

Organizations implement different HRD/training initiatives for a variety of reasons. Ultimately, however, these reasons can be categorized into two primary areas: to gain knowledge and to develop skills. Both of these, ultimately, are intended to change behavior, to enhance performance, and to achieve the organization's stated goals.

Knowledge

HRD/training initiatives that are implemented for the purpose of expanding upon employees' knowledge base will expose participants to a "body of information" they must know, or with which they must be familiar. Sometimes, knowledge training is even mandated by law (for instance, sexual harassment training in California). Knowledge training generally focuses more on "what" a person knows, rather than on "how" he or she applies that knowledge. Knowledge-based training can also be implemented to educate employees about organization-specific topics that are unrelated to specific skills or to general areas of knowledge. Either way, this acquisition of knowledge is directly intended to translate into desired behaviors (that employees now know more *about*), which in turn will produce desired results (that employees now know *how* to deliver).

Skills

As the name implies, skills training is designed to teach participants how to "*do*" something related to their job. That "something," however, can span a wide variety of possibilities.

Skills training can address certain specific, discreet functions that are important to the individual's ability to perform his or her job and that contribute to the organization's ability to attain its overall objectives. Skills training can also, however, address and cultivate behaviors that are reflective of the values of the organization, or that support demonstration of organizational competencies (see "Performance Management," later in this chapter).

Attitude Versus Behavior

Attitude is important to consider—particularly with respect to training and performance management. It's also exceedingly difficult to get one's hands around in any sort of concrete, consistent manner. Attitude, in short, is subjective and personal. By defining attitude behaviorally, however, an organization can accomplish two objectives: It can create a basis for designing HRD/training interventions that will cultivate behaviors that manifest desired attitudes, and it can provide a framework within which to evaluate employees in a more objective and more defensible manner (should the need arise).

For instance, consider the attitudinal characteristic "flexibility." This word can, of course, mean different things to different people—particularly to managers and their direct reports. By identifying "flexibility" behaviorally, however, within the context of the results that the employee is expected to produce, it's easier to discuss, address, and resolve "attitude problems." In this case, some behavioral definitions of flexibility might be

▶ The ability to display agility, openness, and responsiveness in the face of rapidly changing conditions

▶ The ability to perform a wide range of assignments accurately and efficiently

▶ The ability to successfully handle multiple projects simultaneously without experiencing a decline in quality or quantity of performance.

By framing and defining attitudes in terms of behaviors, therefore, they become easier to address, discuss, and resolve.

Step 3 of Needs Analysis: Propose/Select a Solution (Depending upon HR's Role in the Organization, and in This Process)

In proposing/selecting a solution, it is essential to use a logical, fact-based approach. One dimension of that approach will include comparing the resources that are available to the resources that are required to deliver each particular HRD/training initiative. Resources, in this context, could mean financial, human, temporal, and technological. If the resources required to implement a particular solution would be impossible to secure, it would be counterproductive to continue considering that solution. And that's the kind of information that you're better off knowing up front, before making a commitment to any particular course of action.

It is also critical to prepare a cost-benefit analysis as part of the process of proposing/selecting a solution. As with other dimensions of needs analysis, there is no one "right" way to conduct a cost-benefit analysis. Calculating "return on investment" (ROI), however, is essential. One way in which ROI can be calculated is

1. Calculate the costs associated with the current situation, as is, if no HRD/training intervention were to be conducted (in other words, the cost of *not* conducting the HRD/training initiative).

2. Calculate the costs associated with conducting the HRD/training intervention. Be sure to consider all direct and indirect costs, including (but not limited to)

   ▶ The trainer's/facilitator's salary (prep time, delivery, and follow up) and/or fees associated with an external trainer/consultant

   ▶ Wages and salaries paid to participants during the HRD/training session

   ▶ Lost revenue from non-production of goods or non-delivery of services during the HRD/training session

   ▶ Any overtime expenses that might result because of work that was not completed during the HRD/training session

   ▶ Food and beverages

   ▶ Materials

   ▶ Facility fees

   ▶ Travel

3. Calculate the financial gains that will accrue from conducting the HRD/training initiative. Financial gains could accrue from a variety of sources, such as

- ▶ The value of the skills that employees develop and the knowledge that employees gain through the HRD/training intervention (once those skills and that knowledge is applied in the workplace).

- ▶ Costs (or potential costs) that will not be incurred (or that will no longer be incurred) once the HRD/training initiative is delivered.

- ▶ Benefits that are less tangible (but no less real). Please note that some of these benefits might be more difficult to attribute directly to the HRD/training initiative (benefits such as increased morale, retention, and customer satisfaction).

4. Compare the costs of implementing the HRD/training initiative to the benefits that will accrue from conducting the HRD/training initiative.

   In doing this, it's important to keep in mind that the objective is not to "sell" anyone on a particular initiative—including ourselves. The objective is to make a well-informed decision that focuses on the meeting the needs of the organization.

In addition to conducting this analysis, many organizations use a measure referred to as "cost per trainee" or "cost per participant," which is calculated as follows:

$$\frac{\text{Total of all costs associated with the HRD/training initiative}}{\text{Number of individuals who participate in the HRD/training initiative}}$$

This formula can provide valuable information that can be used to make a wide variety of HRD/training related decisions. For instance, just a few of the decisions that this analysis could help you make might be

- ▶ Whether to sponsor an in-house HRD/training initiative, or to send participants to publicly offered training programs

- ▶ Whether to develop an HRD/training initiative internally, or purchase/license it externally

- ▶ If the HRD/training initiative will be secured through a source that is external to the organization:

  - ▶ Whether to purchase or license the product

  - ▶ Whether to have the vendor supply trainers, or to implement a "train the trainer" strategy

  - ▶ Whether to use the external product "as is," or to pay for customization

- ▶ The length of the HRD/training initiative

- ▶ Who will attend the HRD/training initiative

- ▶ The frequency with which HRD/training initiatives—on one particular topic, and across the board—will be delivered

- ▶ Whether to hold the HRD/training initiative on-site at the organization's facility, or to secure conference space at an off-site location, such as a hotel or conference center

By changing one or more than one variable, HR professionals will generate a variety of different scenarios for comparison. This will enable you to do a more effective job of making rigorous, business-oriented recommendations that will truly help bolster your role as a business partner.

EXAM ALERT

Be familiar with the specific strengths and weaknesses associated with developing and delivering an HRD/training initiative internally versus externally, and the factors that should be taken into account when making this decision.

REVIEW BREAK

In the design phase, you will plan—and prepare to build—an HRD/training initiative that will address the needs identified through the needs analysis/assessment phase. The deliverable that is most commonly associated with the needs analysis/assessment is just that—an actual HRD/training needs analysis/assessment. The balance of the ADDIE process will focus on designing, developing, implementing, and evaluating HRD/training initiative(s) that will grow out of that needs analysis/assessment.

ADDIE: "D" Is for Design

The design phase of the ADDIE process will generate a design plan. Looking at this phase of the process within the framework of the "5 W's and an H," some of the questions that are likely to be addressed during the design phase might include

- ▶ Who:
    - ▶ Who is the target population?
    - ▶ Who will develop the HRD/training initiative?
    - ▶ Who will deliver the HRD/training initiative?
    - ▶ Who will evaluate the HRD/training initiative?

- ▶ What:

  - ▶ What will the HRD/training initiative accomplish? In other words, what are the HRD/training objectives?

  - ▶ What content will be included to meet those HRD/training objectives?

  - ▶ What methodologies will be incorporated into the HRD / training initiative?

  - ▶ In what order will the various components of the HRD/training initiative be delivered?

  - ▶ What delivery method(s) will be used?

  - ▶ By what means and measures will the attainment (or non-attainment) of objectives be evaluated?

- ▶ When:

  - ▶ When will the HRD/training initiative be delivered?

  - ▶ When must the delivery of the HRD/training be completed (by what date, and/or before what organizational milestone)?

  - ▶ When will the HRD/training initiative be announced?

- ▶ Where:

  - ▶ Where will the HRD/training program be delivered?

- ▶ How:

  - ▶ Within each method, how will content specifically be addressed?

  - ▶ How will the learning objectives be attained through the HRD/training initiative?

Design—The Theoretical/Scholarly Foundation

What is design? Like so much of the information that can be found about ADDIE, the definition of the "design" component differs from "expert" to "expert." In 1992, Gagne described instructional design (ISD) as a systematic process with a strong planning component. He also identified three commonalities that exist. He found that most instructional design models

- ▶ Identify what the outcomes of the HRD/training will be

- ▶ Develop the actual instructional methods and materials

- ▶ Create a component that will serve to evaluate the effectiveness of a program/initiative

In 1998, Hannafin and Peck put forth that the instructional design process consists of a series of interrelated steps based on principles derived from educational research and theory. The three phases that they identify in their model (needs assessment, design, development/implementation) each involve a process of continual evaluation, reevaluation, and revision, *as the program is being developed.*

Design: The Steps

Combining the wisdom of these and other experts, let's look at the design process as consisting of four distinct steps:

1. Identify outcome objectives.

2. Identify learning methodologies.

3. Establish a time frame.

4. Gain agreement and sign-off.

Let's take a closer look at each of these individual steps.

Design—Identify Outcome Objectives

Similar to performance management applications, learning objectives should follow the acronym "SMART." While numerous definitions of this acronym exist, one particularly effective one is

- ▶ **S:** Specific

  The HRD/training objectives must be clearly articulated, unambiguous, and understood in the same way by everyone involved in the HRD/training process (the instructional designer, the manager, the facilitator, the participant, and so forth).

- ▶ **M:** Measurable

  If an HRD/training intervention is to be considered a valid solution that will truly support the overall performance objectives of the organization—and of the individuals in the organization—then the outcomes of that HRD/training initiative must be measurable and must be able to withstand the rigor to which those measures will ultimately be subjected through the assessment phase.

- ▶ **A:** Action-oriented

  Objectives should be written so that the behaviors/actions that the learner is expected to demonstrate at the conclusion of the HRD/training initiative are described using strong, robust, action verbs (for instance, generate, produce, resolve, demonstrate, complete, apply, and so on). Don't write objectives with verbs that are not as effective at articulating observable or measurable behaviors (such as understand, appreciate, value, and so forth).

▶ **R:** Realistic

Writing "realistic" training objectives means avoiding *both* ends of the "difficulty spec-trum." At one end of the spectrum, HRD/training objectives that are too easy to attain aren't challenging and may not hold the attention and interest of participants. Ultimately, overly easy objectives also might not generate desired results (if the results could be attained that easily, there would have likely been a less formal solution than a full-blown HRD/training initiative). At the other end of the spectrum, HRD/training objectives that are impossible to attain will only serve to discourage participants. Despite the belief that some individuals have that setting unrealistically high expecta-tions results in an overall higher level of attainment than would have been achieved if goals were set lower, the reality is often quite different. Setting objectives that are con-sistently unrealistically high will create a cycle of failure. Over time, this could result in employees feeling frustrated, resentful, and even manipulated or exploited. No matter what results have been attained through overly aggressive goal setting, they won't be worth the long-term negative repercussions of this approach—including (but not limit-ed to) morale issues, disengagement, and even high turnover (probably of your best employees, which is often the "bad" kind of turnover).

▶ **T:** Time-bound

Time is a valuable resource—at times, far more valuable than money. Ensure that the HRD/training objectives identify goals can be attained and applied to the position within the period of time that is acknowledged and agreed to in advance. This time frame should be determined collaboratively, taking the input of all stakeholders into consideration.

Design—Identify and Select Learning Methodologies

Identifying and selecting appropriate learning methodologies means deliberately choosing specific techniques and activities that will be most effective at giving participants the opportu-nity to learn and practice their new skills and apply their new knowledge. There are many methodologies from which you might choose, some of which include

▶ Lecture/"lecturette"

▶ Demonstration

▶ Reading

▶ Small group discussions/instructor-facilitated large group discussions

▶ Individual, small group, or large group activities/applications

- ▶ Case study

- ▶ Role play

Let's take a closer look at each of these methodologies.

Lecture/"Lecturette

Lectures/"lecturettes" (very short lectures) present information *to* participants. Often, this information is highly detailed or technical in nature. It often constitutes information that is substantially new to most of the learners, so they'll probably need some time to "absorb" it.

For those learners for whom note-taking is an effective means of reinforcing and retaining content, lectures/lecturettes afford the opportunity to take detailed notes. These notes can be taken "freely," without the expectation that learners will contribute to a topic about which they may not be very knowledgeable (yet). Lectures and lecturettes might also be particularly valuable for auditory learners.

When lectures/lecturettes are overused, participants may lose interest. Boredom (or even fatigue) can set in, in significant part because of the minimal degree of interaction permitted by most lectures/lecturette.

So, how long is too long for a classroom-based training lecture? In short, that depends. Some experts say—especially for online applications—that any lecture longer than 5 minutes is too long. Others assert that, in a classroom setting, lectures can last as long as 20 minutes without becoming excessive. Before deciding upon a particular length of time for a lecture/lecturette, however, it's important to weigh a variety of factors, a few of which are

- ▶ The nature and complexity of the topic

- ▶ The time of day

- ▶ How much time has passed since the last break

- ▶ What learning methodology preceded the lecture

- ▶ The overall effectiveness of the lecturer

- ▶ How the participants normally spend their day when they are actually performing their jobs (rather than participating in a training session)

- ▶ The overall percentage of lecture in the training program

Demonstration

Lectures are to demonstrations as *"tell me"* is to *"show me."* During a demonstration, the instructor/facilitator literally shows the participants how to perform a particular function, duty, or role.

Demonstrations are more engaging in nature than lectures, since something is "actually happening." The skill is not just being referenced—it is being exhibited. Visual learners, in particular, might benefit greatly from this aspect of demonstrations.

> **TIP**
>
> Demonstrations might be of even greater value if participants are also invited to try out—through an exercise or case study—what they are being shown. This multiple-step approach literally moves the activity from passive to active, and thus appeals to visual as well as tactile/kinesthetic learners.

Reading

In recent years, reading hasn't been used much during most training programs. In fact, it has often been given a "bad rap." Perhaps this is because some working adults still recall unpleasant experiences from grade school during which they were directed by a teacher to spend long periods of class time reading. Or, perhaps some participants think of reading as a "waste of time," since they feel that they could read on their own time.

Dedicating short periods of time during a training session to reading, however, can actually reap numerous benefits. First, it appeals to visual learners who effectively process and retain information through reading. Reading can also provide a welcome "change of pace" during a training session. For instance, if participants have completed some sort of self-analytical instrument, they may appreciate having a few minutes to read an interpretation that will help them begin to process what their results mean (particularly when compared to the option of sharing those results aloud, and having them interpreted in front of the rest of the group). Reading printed material can also be extremely helpful when it contains details that must be referred to more than once, such as instructions for a case study or role play.

Small Group Discussions/Instructor-facilitated Large Group Discussions

When considering discussions as a learning methodology, it may be helpful to think back to one of Knowles's tenets about adult learning: the role of learner's experience. This is the principle that says that adult learners believe that they have a significant amount of valuable experience from which they can draw to enhance their own learning—and from which others can learn, as well. Skillfully facilitated discussions will allow participants to do exactly that, and to feel more engaged in the learning experience. What's even better is that these feelings are legitimate. Participants can learn a great deal from small and large group discussions.

Individual, Small Group, or Large Group Activities/Applications

Hearing information is one thing; seeing it demonstrated is another...but following up one or both of those techniques with an activity that requires hands-on involvement can be an extremely effective way of reinforcing learning. Giving participants the chance to immediately apply the knowledge they have learned or the skills they have developed can also lead to significantly higher retention rates than lecture or demonstration alone.

Case Studies

Case studies draw upon two other Knowles theories:

- **Learner's self-concept**: "I'm an adult, and I can direct myself. That includes in a classroom setting, so please treat me that way."

- **Orientation to learning**: "What I learn today will help me solve problems in the workplace tomorrow—not at some unspecified time in the future."

Case studies present participants with a real-life situation that allows then to apply the knowledge they have learned and practice the skills they have developed during the training session. In the "safe" environment of the classroom, learners can try out their newly acquired knowledge and newly developed skills before they must return to the workplace (where it might not be quite as "safe" to make mistakes). Participants will benefit from receiving feedback from the instructor/facilitator relative to those aspects of the case study that were handled well. Participants will also benefit (perhaps even more) from receiving feedback from the instructor/facilitator relative to those aspects of the case study that could have been handled differently, or better. In both cases, the participant will be able to incorporate this feedback before transferring the knowledge and skills learned during the training back to the workplace. This can, potentially, increase the value of the training experience even more.

Role Plays

Role plays are similar to case studies, and can even be designed to be the natural "culmination" of a case study. Role plays, in one sense, take case studies one step further, in that participants actually "act out" the ways in which they would apply the knowledge and practice the skills in particular situations.

One of the advantages of role playing is that when well executed it provides the most realistic re-creation of workplace conditions that is possible in a training situation. It also presents participants with the opportunity to practice skills and apply knowledge—opportunities with which they otherwise might not have been presented for quite some time. This is particularly important since, as reviewed earlier, retention levels are higher if training is followed closely by opportunities to put that training into practice.

CAUTION

Role plays, however, can "backfire" if not handled delicately by the trainer. For instance, while feedback must be candid and honest, it also must be delivered in a way that does not diminish the self-esteem of the role-play participants, or negatively impact the way in which others will perceive that participant after the training ends. Role playing is, risky—for the participant, for the instructor, and ultimately for the HR or training professional who designed and "pitched" the training. Role plays should be led by skilled instructors/facilitators who are adept at providing positive and productive feedback in classroom settings, and who have the ability to defuse a variety of (potentially sensitive) situations.

Design—Establish a Time Frame

As explored previously, it's critical to make sure that HRD/training objectives are "time bound." At this point in the process, timing continues to be just as important. Establishing and agreeing upon a time frame for the development, implementation, and evaluation of the learning processes is critical. Establishing a time frame for implementing the entire project—as well as for reaching important milestones along the way—helps to ensure accountability, increase management support, and treat HRD/training with the same level of rigor as any other organizational initiative.

Design—Gain Agreement and Sign-off

Often, this step of the design may be minimized or even overlooked. However, without a signed agreement that specifies all of the elements and terms of the HRD/training initiative, you are more likely to experience misunderstandings (and all of the problems that go along with misunderstandings). There may be perceptions that you didn't deliver what you "promised," when you promised it, how you promised it. One incident like this can significantly damage your credibility (or the credibility of HRD/training initiatives, or even the credibility of HR in general). Don't allow room for misunderstandings; even if it may at first feel a bit formal, secure formal written agreement of the design plan before you begin the development phase of ADDIE.

ADDIE: "D" Is for Development

In this phase, you will develop (or oversee/participate in the development of) the design plan that was created in the previous phase. This will include the development of the actual instruction and materials. Alternatively, you may decide that the best way to execute the design plan is to purchase or license materials from a source outside the organization. Either way, during this phase, every exercise, resource, handout, activity, and/or training element is created, built, or otherwise secured. The outputs from this phase, therefore, will include program materials (for participants and instructors/facilitators) as well as instructional guides (for instructors/facilitators).

ADDIE: "I" Is for Implementation

By now, the HRD/training program has been designed and developed. You've made sure that it is practical rather than overly theoretical. It has been designed and built to deliver knowledge and skills that participants will be able to use in the workplace, *not just in the classroom*. Now, it's time to prepare for the actual launch—in the classroom, online, or through some blended combination of both.

Pilot Programs

By the time an HRD/training program is ready to be "implemented" (or "delivered"), a great deal of time, talent, and financial resources have probably been invested in the successful launch of the program. As such, it may be difficult (or even painful, at moments), to entertain the possibility that some dimension of the program, as conceived and/or designed, may need to be refined, overhauled, or even "scrapped." Yet it is precisely this possibility to which we must be open—and that we must even consciously invite.

It is for this reason that—assuming a program will be delivered more than one time—it is critical to run a pilot program before launching a full-fledged HRD/training initiative.

Options for Running Pilot Programs

A pilot program is generally delivered to a subsection of the population of individuals who would ultimately be expected to participate in the training initiative, as well as to decision makers, senior management (from whom you wish to re-secure buy-in), and other key stakeholders.

Pilot sessions can be run in a number of different ways, two of which are

- **Identical Program Format**: The pilot program is identical to the actual training program that you have designed and developed. In this way, the attendees of the pilot program will be able to experience and assess the same program that subsequent attendees will attend.

- **Abbreviated Program Format**: The pilot program enables participants to experience some, but not all, of the program elements. Some portions might be described, while others might be introduced, but not executed. Other portions of the program might be skipped entirely.

Ideally, a training pilot should be identical to the actual training program that subsequent participants will experience (the first option). Realistically, however, this will not always be possible, nor will clients always be open to this option. So, as an alternative, be prepared to implement the abbreviated format.

Collecting and Using Feedback from Pilot Programs

With either pilot program format, a critical component of the pilot involves receiving feedback from those who attend the pilot program. This feedback should be far more extensive than the single page forms (sometimes called "smile sheets") that workshop participants are often asked to complete at the end of training sessions. Ideally, pilot evaluation will afford the opportunity for a candid exchange of ideas with all stakeholders. Encourage your pilot participants to be open to a post-training feedback session, at which time they could present questions, comments, and thoughts that they jot down during the session. Be prepared, however, that your client may not be open to scheduling follow-up to the pilot. Instead, you may be asked to move "in" and "out" of role (instructor versus training designer/developer), as appropriate, during the actual training session.

Once pilot program participants have provided you with their feedback and insights, the next step is to review, assess, and incorporate (as appropriate) that feedback into the next iteration of the training program. This feedback—and even your own observations—may help you address issues relating to any number of potential concerns, such as (but not limited to): content, exercises, use of specific methodologies, pace, complexity, clarity, order in which the content is delivered, and so forth.

CAUTION

Yes, you've invested a lot of time and effort into the HRD/training initiative by this point. It can even be said that you have invested a lot of yourself. And yes, this process of "scrutiny" and review may feel a bit frustrating. But know that you are not wasting your time. Instead, you are being provided with insights and reaction that will make the time you have already invested pay off even more, since it will enable you to produce an even better training program.

Demonstrating defensiveness at this point in the process can harm you in two different ways—it can keep you from delivering the best training product possible, and it can diminish your credibility as an HR professional—something that goes well beyond the scope of even the broadest HRD/training initiative. So, as you are being provided with feedback, be sure to practice your active listening skills—even if it hurts. The end result, for all involved (including you), will be better because of your efforts, your willingness to listen, your flexibility, and your commitment.

Facilitator/Instructor

Another important dimension of effective implementation focuses less on the content, and more on the facilitator/instructor. Effective facilitation is an artful science, and a scientific art. There are myriad factors that can be taken into consideration when selecting a trainer. Different ones might be more relevant or important in different situations. The following items include a partial list of skills that are crucial to effective facilitation/instruction (and also provides a way to perform evaluation afterward):

Clarity of Presentation

The clarity of an instructor/facilitator's presentation refers to the effective use of practices that foster better understanding of the subject matter and prevent confusion. An instructor or facilitator who has strong clarity of communication would likely do the following:

▶ Provide a written outline of the key points that will be addressed during the workshop

▶ Regularly define new terms, concepts, and principles when they are introduced (rather than assuming a certain level of audience knowledge, or putting participants "on the spot" relative to who does or does not understand a particular concept)

▶ Explain why particular processes, techniques, or formulas are incorporated into the program (rather than just "throwing" information at participants)

▶ Use real-world examples to bring workshop concepts to life

▶ Relate new ideas and concepts covered in the program to more familiar ones, and/or to participants' own experiences

▶ Provide occasional summaries and restatements of important ideas, and ensures smooth transitions to new, yet related, topics

▶ Adjust the pace of delivery when introducing complex and difficult material

▶ Avoid excessive digressions from the outline and/or key topics

▶ Use materials and visual aids to support and clarify concepts

▶ Use well-organized and well-written handouts, workbooks, computerized presentations, and the like

Presentation Effectiveness

Some of behaviors that are indicative of presentation effectiveness would include

▶ Clearly stating the objectives of the workshop

▶ Presenting subjects in a logical order

▶ Allowing ample time for participants to grasp, explore, and practice concepts

▶ Periodically confirming with participants that they are "with you" (paraphrasing and asking discussion questions are far more effective ways of accomplishing this than asking participants if they are "with you")

▶ Designing and using exercises that are practical and helpful to participants, and that support concepts and objectives

▶ Referring to and utilizing training materials (including the participant manual) throughout the program

▶ Using videos, music, or other special audio/visual aids to enhance the learning experience and to appeal to auditory and/or visual learners

▶ Ensuring that writing on boards/easel pads is organized, legible, and captures important points of the subject matter

▶ Summarizing major points throughout, and at the conclusion of, the workshop (in an interactive manner, whenever possible)

Participant Dynamics

Effective presentations maintain participants' interest and strive for a high level of involvement. Instructors who are skilled with respect to engaging participants might do the following:

▶ Periodically modify the pace of the program to maintain—or recapture—participants' interest and engagement

▶ Use instructional techniques that promote interactivity

▶ Address participants by name (using "table tents" can help facilitate this)

▶ Encourage participant feedback

▶ Provide constructive feedback in a non-threatening and affirming manner

▶ Utilize activities and exercises that are challenging, and that encourage participants to reach above their previous level of skill or knowledge

▶ Utilize techniques, methods, and logic that can be applied back at the workplace

Question/Answer Technique

Effective presentations incorporate questions that challenge participants to analyze information and to apply their newly acquired (or enhanced) skills and/or knowledge. Effective question/answer facilitation techniques might include

▶ Ask factual questions to provide participants with the opportunity to demonstrate their knowledge

▶ Ask open-ended, thought-provoking questions that engage participants

▶ Ask questions that afford participants with the opportunity to apply information or principles addressed during the workshop

▶ Ask questions that challenge participants to exercise analysis or judgment to the instructional materials

▶ Ask follow-up questions to clarify and interpret instructional materials

▶ Allow ample opportunity (silence) for participants to think through their responses before answering a question

▶ Rephrase and repeat difficult questions, as appropriate

▶ Respond to unclear (or wrong) participant responses in an honest, yet affirming, manner

▶ Repeat participants questions and answers when they have not been heard by all participants (then addresses the reasons for this, acoustic or otherwise, at an appropriate time).

▶ Redirect participant questions to other program participants, as appropriate

▶ Defer difficult, irrelevant, or time-consuming questions or comments from participants for discussion outside the workshop (in other words, knows when to take a discussion "offline").

Verbal and Nonverbal Communication

Communicating effectively verbally and nonverbally (and combining those two means of communication in an effective manner) would require behaviors such as

▶ Speaking audibly

▶ Modulating voice level to ensure variety of emphasis

▶ Not using an excessive amount of "minimal encourages" speech fillers (okay, ah, uh-huh, um)

▶ Speaking with a pace of delivery that is neither too fast nor too slow

▶ Projecting excitement and enthusiasm about the program and materials

▶ Establishing and maintaining eye contact with class, as appropriate

▶ Moving throughout the room/area in an engaging (rather than distracting) way

▶ Using facial expressions and hand gestures to reinforce and emphasize verbal messages

▶ Listening carefully to participants' comments and questions

ADDIE: "E" Is for Evaluation

The evaluation phase allows for—and in fact mandates—a comparison of the results or outputs of the training to the learning objectives that were established during the needs analysis/assessment. In this way, the degree to which the specific HRD/training objectives were met can be ascertained through measurement, not guesswork. There will be no question, either way, whether the gap between actual performance (pre-training) and desired performance (post-training) has been bridged.

The Theoretical/Scholarly Foundation

The works of two experts—Donald L. Kirkpatrick and Robert Brinkerhoff—are particularly relevant to evaluation of training (and, through transferability, of other HRD) initiatives.

Kirkpatrick: Four Levels of Evaluation

Kirkpatrick's theory takes a "summative" approach to evaluation, in that it is predicated on the interpretation of data that is collected *after* the initiative has been implemented. Kirkpatrick's approach, therefore, allows for a complete analysis of the entire initiative on four different levels.

Kirkpatrick's Level 1: Reaction

Reaction level evaluation measures participants' responses and reactions to the program immediately after the program has been delivered. This level of evaluation often takes the form of a short survey that participants are asked to complete at the end of a training session.

Reaction level evaluation is fast, relatively easy, and frequently utilized. Its value lies in its ability to provide insights into participants' immediate reactions to instructor delivery, training environment, food, pace, and other immediately apparent factors.

CAUTION

Although post-evaluation training forms may ask participants to speculate relative to the degree to which the training will transfer back to the job, this process of speculation is not factual, nor is it necessarily accurate. Be careful not to assess the ultimate success of a training program on the results of those initial "smile sheets"—that success can only be determined by the long-term attainment of the learning objectives, the transfer of learning to the workplace, ROI, Kirkpatrick's remaining levels of evaluation, and the like.

Kirkpatrick's Level 2: Learning

Learning level evaluation measures whether and to what degree participants have mastered the skills or acquired the knowledge explored through the learning objectives. "Pre-tests" and "post-tests," which are frequently seen in elearning applications, are one means of assessing skills development and knowledge acquisition.

Kirkpatrick's Level 3: Behavior

Behavior level evaluation measures whether participants' on-the-job behaviors have changed in a manner consistent with training objectives. In short, it measures "transfer of training"—the degree to which participants apply the skills and knowledge covered in the training sessions in the workplace.

In conducting behavior level assessment, it is important to recognize that individuals can choose to change their workplace behavior for a variety of reasons—some of which are completely unrelated to the training in which he or she participated. A few of these reasons might relate to

▶ Positive reinforcement of the changed behavior

▶ Progressive disciplinary actions that are being pursued relative to the substandard behavior

▶ Performance management and/or appraisal activities that described the performance problem in explicit terms—terms that, to the employee, might ultimately prove to be motivational

Kirkpatrick's Level 4: Results

Results-level evaluation looks specifically at whether the business or organizational results that were expected to occur as a result of this training did, in fact, occur. This level of results-based evaluation is measurable, concrete, and usually of keen interest to the leaders of the organization, since results speak volumes.

As with Kirkpatrick's level 3 analysis, however, it is important to recognize the degree to which other factors (such as a direct competitor going out of business, for instance) could have affected the results. It's important that ROI calculations made as part of results level analysis truly reflects the implementation of HRD/training initiatives, not other unrelated factors.

EXAM ALERT

Be familiar with ways in which each of these levels of evaluations can be conducted.

Robert Brinkerhoff

As discussed previously, Kirkpatrick's model takes a "summative evaluation" approach that is implemented only after training has been delivered. Brinkerhoff's approach is different. Published in *Achieving Results Through Training*, Brinkerhoff's model incorporates "formative evaluation." With a formative evaluation model, evaluative feedback and input is sought *throughout* the development and implementation phases in an effort to strengthen the ultimate training initiative through real-time incorporation of evaluative feedback. Brinkerhoff's formative evaluation model mandates an iterative process, in which feedback, analysis, and assessment conducted at one phase of the process will be used to make enhancements in other stages, as well.

Brinkerhoff's model identifies six stages of evaluation:

1. Goals—What is really needed?
2. HRD design—What will work?
3. Program implementation—How is the training working?
4. Immediate outcomes—Did participants learn, what did they learn, and how well did they learn it?
5. Intermediate or usage outcomes—Are participants continuing to retain what they learned, and continuing to transfer that learning to the workplace?

6. Impacts and worth—Ultimately, did the training initiative make a difference to the organization? If so, did it make *enough* of a difference to be truly worthwhile?

REVIEW

ADDIE—A catchy acronym that delineates a critical process. Regardless of what kind of HRD intervention or HR program you are considering implementing, ADDIE can help you approach it in a more structured manner that, ideally, will lead to more predictable and productive results. With an understanding of ADDIE as a backdrop, let's begin to take a look at some of the key elements within HRD: organization development, training, career development, leadership development, and performance management.

Organization Development (OD)

Organization development (OD) refers to the process through which the overall performance, growth, and effectiveness of an organization is enhanced through strategic, deliberate, and integrated initiatives. The interesting and complex area of OD incorporates four academic disciplines: psychology, sociology, anthropology, and management.

OD does not happen haphazardly. Instead, it represents a systematic, planned, and usually multifaceted approach to organizational enhancement. OD interventions are intended to identify an organization's competitive advantages and to ensure the organization's success.

OD helps maintain the organization's focus on the truth that it is the people within organizations—literally, its "human resources"—who do the work of the organization. This, in turn, significantly impacts the overall success of the organization. In that sense, a big part of OD is human, or in this case, employee development, and is thus inextricably related to the HR function.

> **EXAM ALERT**
>
> Familiarize yourself with international issues (for example, culture, local management approaches/practices, societal norms) that might impact the ways in which you conduct OD (and, for that matter, any other HRD and HR) initiatives.

Elements of OD

Acknowledging that OD is a values-driven approach, R. T. Golembiewski identified and articulated important characteristics related to OD, some of which are

▶ Trust, openness, and collaboration are valued and emphasized.

▶ The needs of individuals as well as the needs of the organization and smaller units of the organization are important and relevant.

▶ Feelings, emotions, ideas, and concepts are important.

▶ Group interaction is emphasized and important with respect to change, as well as choice and problem identification and resolution.

Purposes of OD

OD serves a variety of purposes within an organization—purposes that have been defined differently by different individuals and organizations. Some of those reasons include, but are not necessarily limited to

▶ Enhancing the overall effectiveness of organizations

▶ Promoting openness toward differences, and to resolving the problems that can sometimes arise from those differences (diversity initiatives, in particular, would deal with questions and issues related to this)

▶ Aligning employee goals with unit and organizational goals

▶ Clarifying individual and organizational goals and objectives

▶ Encouraging, supporting, and facilitating collaborative working relationships between and among managers/leaders, individuals, and teams

▶ Improving decision-making, individually as well as organizationally

▶ Improving employees' work performance and promotability

▶ Supporting the development of new or replacement knowledge and skills

▶ Dealing more effectively with problems of a human, as well as a technical, nature

▶ Managing change more effectively

EXAM ALERT

Familiarize yourself well with specific human resource and OD theories and applications, as well as how they interrelate. Specifically, be familiar with how to develop, implement, and evaluate programs to address the unique needs of particular employees (for example, work/family programs, diversity programs, outplacement programs, repatriation programs, and fast-track programs).

Role of the HR Professional in OD

Sometimes, HR professionals are asked to consult with OD professionals. OD professionals may be employed within the organization, or may be brought in from outside the organization to work on a particular assignment. Alternatively, HR professionals may be assigned to work on a specific OD project without the assistance of specialized OD professionals (or, for that matter, specialized OD training). Either way, HR's role in the OD process is critical.

OD and Organizational Culture

An important topic when considering any OD intervention is the culture of the organization. Organizational culture can be, and has been, defined in myriad ways. Sometimes, it is referred to as "the way things are done around here." This seemingly flippant statement actually incorporates a number of important factors, such as

▶ The shared values of the organization

▶ The external environment in which the organization functions

▶ The way the organization responds to specific individual, group, and organization-level behaviors (punishment, reward, tolerance, and so on)

Organizational culture helps establish an organizational identity—one with which employees can relate, to which they can belong, and against which they can measure themselves as one way of ascertaining the degree to which they "fit" within the organization. The culture of an organization can entice candidates to join an organization, and can have a seemingly disproportionate impact on an employee's decision to leave an organization. The culture of the organization is a unifying force for those who work within it, and helps provide guidance with respect to the norms of the organization and the behavioral expectations—in short, helping employees figure out how they are supposed to act. Organizational culture helps shape organization goals, and is passed on from one "generation" of employees to the next through stories, publications, and the like.

Organization culture is powerful. It can be productive as well as counterproductive. It needs to be recognized, acknowledged, and understood by HR professionals who wish to increase the likelihood that OD interventions will be appropriate and effective.

Change Management

Successful OD initiatives will, by definition, bring about change within the organization. As such, it's important for HR professionals to have some basic understanding of "change management," the process by which that change is managed.

There are two types of change management theory with which HR professionals need to be familiar: change process theory and implementation theory.

Change Process Theory

Change process theory looks at the dynamics behind "how change happens" within organizations. Kurt Lewin took a close look at the change process, and is an important contributor in the area of change process theory. He identified two primary motivational sources of change:

1. Change that is driven within an individual, arising out or his or her own needs

2. Change that is imposed upon an individual from the environment

In this discussion of change management, we will focus on the second motivational source of change—environmental (meaning, external).

Lewin first described the change process as one that involves three stages: unfreezing, moving, and refreezing.

▶ **Unfreezing**: *"The bus is leaving, so get on board."* During the unfreezing stage, everyone who is involved with and impacted by the change must be brought to the point where they can understand and accept that a particular change *will* happen. (Understanding and accepting the change, however, does not necessary mean agreeing with the change—nor does it have to.) An important part of that acceptance involves letting go of behaviors that reflect resistance to change, or that actually can impede the change process.

▶ **Moving**: *"You've boarded the bus; now, let's get moving."* Moving represents the process through which people are brought to accept the change, and the process through which they are brought to the point where they actually experience the "new state" that the change was designed to bring about.

▶ **Refreezing**: *"You know, I almost can't remember a time when we **didn't** take this bus."* In this phase, what once represented a change has now become, in simplest terms, the norm.

Implementation Theory

The other change-related theory with which HR professionals need to be familiar is "implementation theory." Implementation theory focuses on carrying out specific strategies—in this case, OD interventions—that are designed to bring about the unfreezing, moving, and refreezing described previously.

Let's take a look at four different categories of OD interventions that might be executed as part of that implementation process:

▶ **Human processual interventions**: Seek to effect change and impact relationships within (and between) groups and individuals.

▶ **Technostructural interventions**: Focus on improving what work gets done, as well as the ways and processes through which the work gets done. It looks at job design, job redesign, job restructuring, work content, workflow, work processes, and the like.

▶ **Sociotechnical interventions**: Focus on groups in the workplace, and the ways in which those groups can become more (or semi-) autonomous with respect to the performance and execution of the work. Examples of this might include job enrichment, work rescheduling, and participative management.

▶ **Organization transformation change**: Focus on the organization as a complex human system that must be continually examined and reexamined. Leaders in organizations must, in turn, be able to take the vision of the organization and translate it into goals, which in turn should be the foundation for managing the organization and for distributing rewards.

Specific OD Interventions

While there are a wide variety of possible OD interventions, two specific ones that HR professionals should be familiar with are teambuilding and total quality management (TQM).

Teambuilding

Teambuilding exercises can take many forms, all of which share a common objective of helping the team learn to function more effectively so that it can attain its overall objective (which must link, of course, to the overall organizational objective). Teambuilding exercises will give teams the opportunity to explore topics such as trust, communication, problem solving, the role of the individual within the team, and the impact that the team has on the customer. Teambuilding exercises often provide scenarios through which participants can hone the same skills and learn about the same principles that it takes to function effectively in a team at the workplace.

Total Quality Management (TQM)

TQM is an OD intervention that is ultimately aimed at meeting or exceeding customer expectations through the commitment of everyone in an organization (often through a team-based approach) to continuous improvement of products and/or services.

Total Quality Pioneers

Several individuals factored prominently in the history of quality management:

▶ W. Edwards Deming, a true quality pioneer, began his focus on and study of quality in the 1940s, but, like most prophets, was not fully appreciated in his homeland of America. Deming then took his expertise to Japan in the 1950s, where he has been revered ever since. Deming reemerged as a strong business presence in America in 1980 after an NBC documentary featured him prominently. From that time until his death in 1993, Deming consulted extensively with American organizations, finally disseminating his 14-point quality management program in the nation of his birth.

▶ Joseph M. Juran was another giant in the area of quality. Like Deming, Juran focused on the perspectives and the needs of customers. His quality management ideas focused on three key areas: quality planning, quality improvement, and quality control. Juran's commitment to quality is still present today through the Juran Institute, whose stated mission is to "enable our clients to attain quality leadership by achieving sustainable breakthrough results. We focus on improving the 'customer experience' of our clients' clients!"

▶ Philip B. Crosby, a third quality guru, is well-known for his "zero defects" standard, as opposed to "acceptable quality levels" (AQLs). This management philosophy asserted that employees would perform at whatever level management sets for them. Settling for "goodness"—rather than the full attainment of objectives—would, therefore, effectively preclude the possibility of attaining those objectives. Crosby, however, raised the bar. He established four *absolutes of quality management*:

  ▶ Quality means conformance to requirements, not goodness.

  ▶ Quality is achieved by prevention, not appraisal.

  ▶ Quality has a performance standard of zero defects, not acceptable quality levels.

  ▶ Quality is measured by the price of nonconformance, not indexes.

▶ Kaoru Ishikawa believed in the idea of continued customer service—even *after* the customer purchases the product. He saw quality as a never-ending process, in that it can always be taken one step further. Ishikawa also believed strongly in the criticality of securing top-level management support, and dramatically increased worldwide awareness and acceptance of the idea of quality circles, originally a Japanese philosophy.

Quality Tools

As part of developing a basic understanding and knowledge of TQM, HR professionals need to be familiar with several important quality tools.

▶ Cause-and-effect, Ishikawa, or Fishbone diagram

Ishikawa developed an important quality tool called the cause-and-effect diagram, which is also known as an Ishikawa diagram, or the fishbone diagram. This tool presents a visual representation of factors that affect whether a desired outcome will be obtained. Ishikawa believed that, by presenting all of the possible factors that contribute to a particular result, any potential process imperfections can be identified in advance and eliminated. Figure 5.1 shows an example of an Ishikawa diagram.

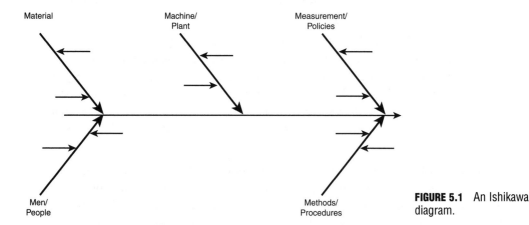

FIGURE 5.1 An Ishikawa diagram.

▶ Histogram

Histograms are graphs that depict information about a single factor. In addition to being used to graphically communicate information, they also sometimes can help identify patterns or explanations. See Figure 5.2 for an example.

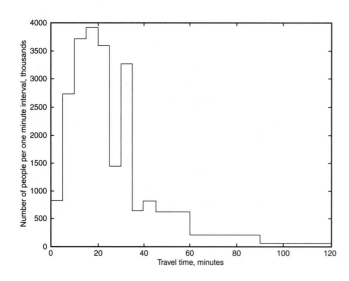

FIGURE 5.2 A histogram.

▶ Pareto Chart

The Pareto principle, also referred to as the "80-20 rule," asserts that 80% of effects result from 20% of causes. The Pareto principle and the chart that visually depicts it are intended to help individuals focus efforts where there is the greatest likelihood of maximizing the "payoff"—of bringing about positive change.

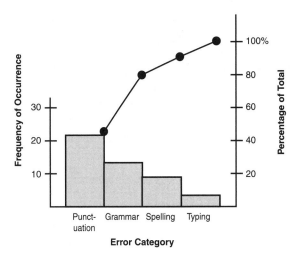

Courtesy of Professor Sid Sytsma, Ferris State University   **FIGURE 5.3**   A Pareto chart.

EXAM ALERT

Familiarize yourself with other quality tools (for instance, scattergrams, run charts, process control charts) and approaches (for instance, Theory of Constraints and Six Sigma).

Training

Once an overall strategy has been established for developing the organization and the individuals within the organization, training is one possible intervention that can be considered. Training is one way, but not the only way, to cultivate learning within an organization.

Learning organizations are ones in which individuals at all levels strive to acquire knowledge and develop skills that will enable them, individually and collectively, to attain higher levels of performance. The concept of a "learning organization" is fundamental to HRD, and is often supported through training initiatives.

To Train, or Not to Train

Training—or, as it is often called, "learning and development"—is a solution that can be easily overused or underused by organizations.

Training may be overused when it is used as a "cure all" for problems that may be unrelated to skills and/or areas of knowledge that are required to perform a particular task or function. It is not the act of experiencing a training program that improves individual or organizational performance; rather, it is the experience of participating in a program that will develop specific skills or impart specific areas of knowledge that are needed, at that moment, to support organizational success. Implementing a training solution when it is not appropriate to do so could diminish the likelihood that a training initiative would be accepted at a later date, when it might be more appropriate.

Training may be underused if an organization chooses not to avail itself of training options that could remedy performance issues relating to skills or knowledge deficiencies. There are also circumstances in which training may not be effective or helpful that reach beyond the question of whether individuals have specific skills or knowledge. Just a few of those might be

▶ When there are systemic issues that would exist even if all employees were fully proficient with the proposed content

▶ When there are underlying cultural issues or problems that the training would not address

▶ When there are leadership issues, such as lack of trust

▶ When organizational mission, vision, or values are either not clearly defined or are incongruous with each other, or with reality

▶ When training has been used before as a "flavor of the month" approach to problem solving

▶ When training is viewed as or has been used as a symbolic gesture rather than a means of creating real organizational change

In short, training is not a panacea. It is, however, an effective way of addressing issues involving skills development and transference of knowledge.

The Adult Learner

Even when training is an appropriate intervention, it can only be effective when it is learner-centered, and when the learners/participants are treated as adults.

Andragogy, the study and science of adult learning, is significantly different than pedagogy, the study and science of how children learn. One of the key contributors to andragogy was Malcolm Knowles. In 1978, Knowles stated:

"Andragogy assumes that the point at which an individual achieves a self-concept of essential self-direction is the point at which he psychologically becomes adult. A very critical thing happens when this occurs: The individual develops a deep psychological need to be perceived by others as being self-directing. Thus, when he finds himself in a situation in which he is not allowed to be self-directing, he experiences a tension between that situation and his self-concept. His reaction is bound to be tainted with resentment and resistance."

Based upon this observation, Knowles identified five key assumptions about how adults learn:

▶ Learner's need to know: "I understand why I need to learn this. It makes sense to me."

▶ Learner's self-concept: "I'm an adult, and I can direct myself. That includes in a classroom setting, so please treat me that way."

▶ Role of learner's experience: "I've got lots of valuable experience that I want to draw upon to help me as I learn. Maybe I can help others learn through that experience, as well."

▶ Readiness to learn: "I'm ready to learn this, because what I learn will help me function better in some way."

▶ Orientation to learning: "What I learn today will help me solve problems at my workplace tomorrow—not at some unspecified time in the future."

Learning Styles—How We Learn

It's also important for HR professionals to have an understanding of learning styles. Learning styles refer to different ways in which people learn and process ideas and information. There are three different learning styles:

▶ **Visual learners**: Visual learners learn most effectively through what they see. Visual learners might best benefit from videos or DVDs, the use of presentation software, easel pad notes, printed binders that include significant amounts of printed information, extensive note-taking, and the like.

PHR exam prep application: Reading this book, highlighting this book (perhaps with color coded highlighters), preparing study cards, using self-sticking color-coded flags).

▶ **Auditory learners**: Auditory learners learn most effectively through what they hear. Auditory learners might best benefit from lectures, facilitated discussions, "ask the expert" style lecturettes on elearning platforms, and the like.

PHR exam prep application: Audio recordings (self-made or otherwise) of materials from study guides.

▶ **Tactile/kinesthetic learners**: Tactile/kinesthetic learners learn best when they can be "hands on," in the most literal sense of the word. They like to touch, to feel, to explore, and to experience the world around them. Kinesthetic learners are most likely to enjoy—and learn best from—"role plays" that reinforce and synthesize key learning points. They like to move around during training sessions, and to be physically involved in the learning process. In studying for the PHR exam, tactile learners might be most likely to use note cards as a study tool (regardless of who created the cards).

EXAM ALERT

Learning curves refer to the patterns through which individuals learn new material. Be familiar with key learning curve patterns.

EXAM ALERT

Questions about motivation theories discussed in Chapter 2 are likely to appear on the PHR exam within the context of the HRD functional area. Refamiliarize yourself with those theories and with the applications of those theories.

Retaining What Is Learned

Effective trainers will incorporate all three styles into their programs, so as to increase participant involvement and improve the degree to which participants will retain what they experience. While this may vary from person to person, the following statement generally holds true: the greater the level of learner participation, the greater the level of retention

Learning Experience	Level of Retention
Lecture	5%
Reading	10%
A/V	20%
Demonstration	30%
Discussion	50%
Practical/application	70%
Teaching others	90%

Environmental Factors/Elements to Consider

There are some "nuts and bolts" considerations relative to training programs that, even though they may initially appear to be somewhat mundane in nature, can have a big impact on the ultimate success of a training program.

Seating Configuration

One of the factors that must be considered is how the training space will physically be set up. There are a variety of seating arrangements from which to choose. Figure 5.4 illustrates the symbols used in the models that follow.

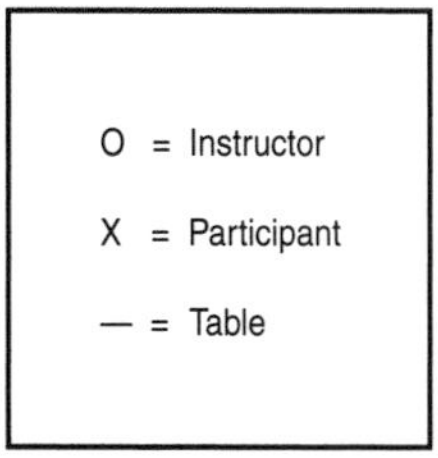

O = Instructor

X = Participant

— = Table

FIGURE 5.4 Instructor/participant legend.

Classroom/Theater

Classroom/theater style works well if there are a large number of participants in the training session (see Figure 5.5). By design, however, this style reduces the opportunity for participation by, and instructor interaction with, attendees. In some cases, especially when the size of the training group is particularly large and/or when the training is conducted in a room that has particularly bad acoustics, the instructor (who will likely become more of a "lecturer" in a setting like this) may require a microphone.

FIGURE 5.5 The classroom/theater seating style.

Chevron

Chevron style works well for narrower rooms (see Figure 5.6). It allows for more participation and interaction, and facilitates the process of participants working in small groups.

FIGURE 5.6 The chevron seating style.

U-shaped

The U-shaped style encourages interaction and participation through increased visual contact among participants and with the instructor (see Figure 5.7). Participants sit in chairs that are placed by tables (usually rectangular and narrow) that are set up in the shape of a letter "U."

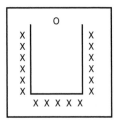

FIGURE 5.7 The U-shaped seating style.

By moving forward and backward in the U, an instructor may be able to move physically closer to individuals from whom he would be farther away in a classroom or chevron style. This movement and proximity may encourage engagement and interaction. While this style works particularly well with small groups, it may also provide a viable alternative (sometimes the *only* viable alternative) for long, narrow training spaces where there is no large center table.

Boardroom

The boardroom setup is similar to the U-shaped setup, except that there is a large table in the center of the room around which participants sit (see Figure 5.8). Sometimes, the boardroom setup may not be a "choice" at all, but rather may be the only option if training is to be held in a room with one large table.

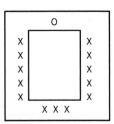

FIGURE 5.8 The boardroom seating style.

TIP

Most trainers have a "preferred" room setup, which may vary from program to program depending upon the nature, content, and level of interaction needed in each program. When possible, know what your preferred style is for a particular program and, when possible, request it. Recognize, however, that you may not have a choice relative to room configuration—sometimes, "it is what it is." Be prepared to train in a variety of settings. Also, be flexible—the training setup you expect may not be the training setup in which you must train, no matter how many times you follow up before the training session.

Room Temperature

Room temperature may be or may not be within your control. It's important to know this in advance. Also, as the instructor, you may be so involved in leading the training experience that you may not be aware of changes in room temperature. Be sensitive to cues that a temperature adjustment might be needed (participants putting on sweaters, or even jackets). If you have any degree of control over the temperature in the room, invite participants to tell you when the temperature needs to be adjusted. Just remember that you can't please everyone when it comes to room temperature; the best that you can do is to try to maintain the room temperature within a reasonable "range" that is acceptable to most people in the room.

Air Flow/Movement/Freshness

Know whether there are windows in the training room, and whether those windows can safely be opened. If there are no windows, determine whether the room has sufficient airflow. If not, determine whether you can bring a fan (a quiet fan) into the room to increase air movement.

Noise

Distracting noises can emanate from inside or outside the building in which you are conducting training. Unwanted noise can come from factors that are controllable, uncontrollable, or semi-controllable, depending upon the situation. Do what you can to anticipate possible noise distractions, and try to eliminate them in advance.

Breaks

Short breaks should be scheduled, ideally, once every 90 minutes. However, it's also important to create an environment where participants are free to leave the room if they need to (adults don't like to have to ask permission to use the bathroom or to get a drink of water). Allow enough break time during breaks to use the restroom, chat with a colleague, and perhaps check voicemail. Generally, 10 to 15 minutes is sufficient and appropriate. Allowing longer breaks might tempt participants to "steal away" to their desks or laptops—in which case, it may be difficult to get them back on time.

Telephones, Personal Technology, and Training Expectations

As communication technology has evolved, etiquette hasn't always evolved along with it. More and more, instructors are encountering situations in which beepers, cell phones, email devices, text messaging, pagers, handheld computers, and the like are being used during instructional portions of training sessions.

Communicate your expectations about electronic communication devices up front, at the beginning of the training program. Encourage participants to give themselves as well as those around them the gift of an uninterrupted training experience. Gently remind them that their organization wants them to be there, and

(continues)

(continued)

it is there that they should focus their attention. Also, however, let participants know that you recognize that life goes on outside of the training room, that emergencies do occur, and that you understand participants might need to be reachable during a session. Encourage participants to find the least disruptive way in which to do this—ideally, they will turn off their electronic devices and ensure that someone knows where to find them in the event of an emergency. If participants decide that they must keep their devices turned on, encourage them to set them to "vibrate," and to leave the room in the event they must take a call or respond to an electronic communication.

Food

Another decision that must be made is whether to provide meals, snacks, or beverages to participants. Different organizations have different philosophies on this topic. Some organizations feel that they should not have to "bribe" individuals to attend a program that will benefit them and the organization. Other organizations take a more "hospitable" approach, seeing training as an opportunity for them to demonstrate their appreciation while adding a bit of celebration and festivity (or, as some organizations say, "if you feed them, they will come").

To varying degrees, food-related decisions will be a function of organizational culture as well as of budgetary considerations. Whatever choice you make, try to make it one that the organization feels comfortable committing to for the foreseeable future (otherwise, you'll never stop hearing about how "we used to have such great lunches at training sessions, but now they expect us to buy our own lunch in the cafeteria"). Additionally, be aware that some people have dietary preferences and restrictions that relate to religion, health conditions, or other factors.

Career Development

One way of looking at OD is that it takes a "macro," overarching approach to the growth and development of the organization. Career development, on the other hand, takes a more "micro" approach in that it looks at the development of individuals *within* the organization. Those two "extremes" are linked together in that they both share the objective of developing the organization: Essentially, the growth and development of individuals within the organization contributes to the overall development and advancement of the organization as a whole.

Responsibility for an employee's career development is shared. Managers can support employees in their career development through coaching, counseling, and offering honest and candid performance feedback and appraisals. The organization can also support and encourage employees who actively seek to grow and enhance their skills through activities such as establishing a skills database or encouraging cross-training, transfers, and other opportunities for employees to expand their skills and knowledge.

Organizations can also ensure that resources are allocated to employee career development. In addition to financial resources, employees will also need time to develop new skills or attain new knowledge through cross-training or workshops. Organizations also need to ensure that psychological and/or emotional resources are not withheld—employees may be less likely to avail themselves of development opportunities if they feel that their current supervisors will want to hold them back, out of fear of "losing" them (in which case, of course, employees would already likely be halfway out the door so as to look for employers who will treat them less like property, and more like people).

Ultimately, however, each employee must take responsibility for his or her own growth and development. An organization cannot "force" an employee to grow. Learning can't be mandated, either. Each employee must determine how he or she wants to grow, and follow through on the opportunities that exist to do so.

> **EXAM ALERT**
>
> Be familiar with the stages of career development, as well as specific ways in which organizations, managers, and employees can contribute to that development.

Leadership Development

In order to understand leadership development, it's first necessary to grasp the concept of "leadership" and "management." Let's start by looking at how these two concepts are different, and how they can and should be intertwined and related.

> **EXAM ALERT**
>
> Chapter 2 of this book addressed various leadership models designed to provide a conceptual framework for understanding management and leadership. Though those two concepts were addressed within the framework of the 19 core competencies, revisit those theories and concepts. First, as an HR professional, you will be called upon to understand the how management and leadership differ and how those differences impact how you might apply these theories. Second, it is likely that you will be presented with questions relating to these theories and concepts when you take the PHR exam.

Management and Leadership: Bridging the Gap

Managers are seen as those individuals who manage the process or the activities of a department or organization. Leaders are those who provide the vision and direction that leads to a motivating force of accomplishment. To be an effective manager, you need to bridge both.

As described in a "leadership-management" model developed by Tony Panos (Statewide Director, Cornell University-ILR, and president, Performance Training, Inc.), "*Success is an anesthetic that dulls the drive for change.*" We see evidence of this phrase in many organizations and more specifically in many managers and potential leaders. As with employees, some managers feel that if things are going well, there is no need for change. Leaders who allow themselves to fall into the same trap are destined to a fate of mediocrity or failure.

According to Panos' model, there are five components to building the bridge between management and leadership:

▶ Commit to achieve

▶ "It's not about you."

▶ Establish credibility

▶ Align people

▶ Impact people significantly

Commit to Achieve

The first component to building the bridge between management and leadership is developing and embracing a commitment to achieve. This can be accomplished by understanding the organization's goals and striving with your staff to attain them, while being aware of and incorporating the personal goals and aspirations of the staff. Furthermore, and possibly more importantly is being honest with yourself about what kind of organization you want. There needs to be honesty of purpose and intent. Ensuring consistency between intent and reality will eliminate the confusion that occurs often between what employees signed up for and what is really going on.

"It's Not About You"

Next, it's important to remember that "it's not about you." Your focus must remain on the success of the employees, not on your success. That will come later. For now, spotlighting employees is the key. Leave the headlining for someone else, and give recognition to those who are excelling. When you allow your employees to do their jobs and do them well, they become responsible and empowered. And you, in turn, attain success.

Establish Credibility

To continue in this process you must establish credibility. This does not occur by the application of your authority; rather it comes from consistency, competence, dedication, and commitment. For you to lead, you must have the permission of the people whom you lead. You get that permission by the establishment of your credibility.

Align People

The next step is the alignment of people. Often, once the strategic planning is done, we put (hopefully) the right people in the right jobs to accomplish the plan. To properly align people you first must align them with the vision, mission, and values. Build staff that share common values. Align their professional needs with the organizations needs. Accomplishment of the strategic plan can be folded into everyone's common understanding of the needs and goals.

Impact People Significantly

Lastly, impact people significantly. How can you do that? Everyone is different, but through communication and understanding, you know what triggers people have. Without being manipulative, push the buttons. Be sensitive and responsive to their needs and tie them to the needs of the organization. Make the connections of how their interests, skills, talents, and developmental needs tie to the organization and vice versa.

According to Panos, managers provide direct reports with feedback, development, a sounding board, and help clear their path. Those who can bridge the gap between "leader" and "manager" do all of the above, and look out over the horizon to see where the next bump or opportunity is coming from. Leadership development, and the specific interventions that will accomplish it, should be aimed at attaining these end results.

One important tool that can be used to support the accomplishment of many of these objectives is effective performance management.

Performance Management

Though not always thought of as an HRD intervention, well-executed performance management is wholly consistent with the mission of HRD. Why? Individual performance directly impacts team, unit, and organizational performance. So performance management is a critical element of an organization's ultimate overall success.

Performance management is the process by which managers and their direct reports communicate about, plan for, and as the name implies, "manage" the individual performance of their direct reports.

NOTE

"Performance management" is sometimes confused with "performance appraisal." Though the two are related, there are important differences. Performance appraisal is, essentially, an "event." It is the form that is reviewed during the meeting that takes place at the end of the performance measurement period. During this meeting, the manager and the employee review the employee's performance during the prior year and look ahead to the next year.

Performance management, conversely, consists of a continuous flow of collaborative feedback, coaching, and communication opportunities in which the manager and the employee engage throughout the entire performance measurement period.

Performance Management—Its Organizational Roots

Effective performance management and appraisal can't take place in a vacuum. Instead, every step of the ongoing performance management process *must* be rooted in the organization's mission, vision, and values.

Performance Management and Organizational Mission

An organization's mission represents the reason why it exists: its ultimate purpose; the focus that drives (or should drive) every initiative, every employee; and, within the context of performance management, every goal. In short, goals cascade throughout the organization—beginning with the mission statement and moving through the hierarchy of the organization. Eventually, that mission statement should impact and link back to every goal for every employee in every position within the organization.

In turn, each employee's performance will be driven by the effort to attain his or her goals—goals that build and contribute to the successful attainment of objectives at every level of the organization, up through and including the mission. This combination of top-down/bottom-up goal setting and achievement helps ensure that time, effort, energy, and all other organizational resources are focused upon the "ultimate" objective—furthering the mission of the organization.

This is the practical, performance-focused definition of a mission-driven organization, illustrated in Figure 5.9.

Performance Management and Organizational Values

An organization's statement of values reflects its underlying philosophies, its guiding tenets, what it holds dear...in a sense, its soul.

The concept of "soul," however, can be difficult to define, and even more difficult to link to business objectives. The organization's values, however, must be explicitly clear for several reasons. First, the organization's values contribute significantly to defining the organization's culture. Culture, in turn, has a huge impact upon how the organization—and the individuals within the organization—functions on a day-to-day basis.

It is in thinking about this "day-to-day functioning" that a link can be made back to performance management. Values, if simply listed as catchy-sounding phrases, can be ambiguous. For instance, what does "integrity" look like? "Professionalism" is no easier to define, nor is "customer service" or "loyalty." From a performance management perspective, organizational values take on their true value when they are defined in behavioral terms. This can be done by providing specific behavioral examples of how each value might manifest itself behaviorally in a particular organization.

In addition to ensuring that an organization's values are truly lived out, the process of defining values behaviorally also provides a more objective, productive, and defensible basis from which to incorporate values-related considerations in the performance management and appraisal process. This is a critical consideration, since values-based performance management is one important way of addressing and appraising "how" work should be accomplished, instead of just "what" needs to be accomplished.

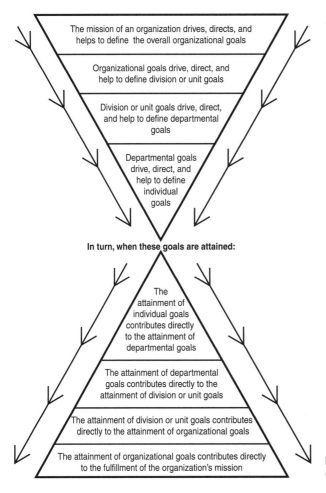

The mission of an organization drives, directs, and helps to define the overall organizational goals

Organizational goals drive, direct, and help to define division or unit goals

Division or unit goals drive, direct, and help to define departmental goals

Departmental goals drive, direct, and help to define individual goals

In turn, when these goals are attained:

The attainment of individual goals contributes directly to the attainment of departmental goals

The attainment of departmental goals contributes directly to the attainment of division or unit goals

The attainment of division or unit goals contributes directly to the attainment of organizational goals

The attainment of organizational goals contributes directly to the fulfillment of the organization's mission

FIGURE 5.9 The mission-driven organization. (© Gibson)

The Performance Management Process

With this foundation of mission and values, let's take a look at a typical performance management process.

Step 1: Setting and Communicating Performance Standards

Performance standards can be expressed in different ways, and through different measures:

- **Goals/objective**: Using the top-down/bottom-up model described previously, "performance goals" or "performance objectives" express and communicate expectations in terms of "what" should be produced. Just like any other OD goal, performance management goals and objectives must be SMART (see "ADDIE: "D" Is for Design"). The "M" in SMART—"measurable"—is particularly important with respect to setting and communicating performance goals and objectives.

- **Competencies**: Like values, competencies also describe "how" employees are expected to deliver the performance goals/objectives. Unlike values, however, competencies are generally rooted in skills. Competencies (also sometimes referred to as "success factors," "performance factors," or the like) are often the same for all employees who work in a particular organization. Some organizations also establish additional competencies that managers are expected to demonstrate. Examples of competencies for all employees (managers as well as non-managers) might be "communication," "customer focus," or "dependability." Examples of additional managerial competencies might be "staffing and development" or (even better) "performance management").

As with values, competencies must be expressed in terms of specific behaviors, rather than in terms of attitudes or personality traits. This is the best and perhaps the only way to ensure clarity and mutual understanding with respect to competency-based performance expectations. Failure to define competencies in behavioral terms can result in employee (and, sometimes, even managerial) frustration, confusion, resentment, and/or suspicion.

As an example, let's look at the competency "customer focus." An attitudinal or personality-based approach to customer focus might say that an employee should be "friendly" and "helpful." A behavioral approach to "customer focus" would look more like this:

- Demonstrates understanding of customers, as well as knowledge of their goals, needs, and wants.

- Accurately anticipates—and communicates understanding of —the spoken and unspoken needs of customers.

- Seeks out, obtains, and processes information that enables the employee to meet the needs of the customer.

▶ Responds to customer concerns in a timely, accurate, and thorough manner, and confirms that his or her response meets with the customer's satisfaction.

Sometimes, the ways in which competencies manifest themselves behaviorally are fairly easy to measure. At other times, however, competencies might manifest themselves through behaviors that are observable, but that do not lend themselves as easily to measurement. It is, in part, an organizational decision (that may, to a significant degree, be affected by organizational culture) whether "documented observation" is an acceptable way of measuring some of these harder-to-quantify competencies.

Step 2: Feedback and Documentation

Employees need feedback. So do managers (this would be the purpose of a 360-degree appraisal). Feedback relative to how the employee performed relative to the performance expectations that were set with/for him or her at the beginning of the performance measurement period should be delivered *throughout the performance measurement period*, not just at the end when it's time to complete the performance appraisal form.

Performance feedback serves a number of important purposes, including

▶ Recognizing (and thereby reinforcing) good performance

▶ Making the employee aware of performance problems

▶ Focusing attention on performance standards, not on personality or attitude

▶ Furthering the employee's development

▶ Supporting the larger performance culture

It's important for employees to understand (ideally, from the time they are initially interviewed as applicants), that they will be given feedback—positive as well as constructive—and that they are expected to actively participate in the process of discussing and implementing that feedback.

To be effective, feedback needs to be "BASIC":

▶ **B**: Behavioral: Measurable and/or observable, but not attitudinal

▶ **A**: As soon as Possible: This does not mean that feedback should be given immediately. Do not provide feedback when you are angry or upset, and in most cases, wait until you are alone to have a feedback discussion with employees. This always holds true for constructive feedback, and can hold true for positive feedback, as well.

▶ **S**: Specific and Single Subject: The performance expectations you established with and communicated to your employees were specific; the feedback you provide about the employee's performance as compared to those expectations should be specific, as well (remember the "S" in SMART). Also, don't let things "build up." Communicating about the employee's performance on a regular basis—*one behavior at a time*—helps increase the likelihood that feedback will be accepted and implemented, and that the employee will make the desired behavioral change.

▸ **I**: Interactive: Feedback is a two-way, dynamic interaction, not just a one-way monologue. Use feedback discussions (whether positive or constructive in nature) as an opportunity to collaboratively discuss and explore the employee's performance.

▸ **C**: Consistent: Be consistent in the way you provide feedback to different employees. Consistency, however, does not mean "sameness." Also try to behave and manage in a consistent manner, in general. Working for "Dr. Jekyll" and "Mr. Hyde" (and trying to figure out who will show up on any given day) can waste a lot of your direct reports' energy that could be better invested in working toward achieving performance expectations.

When you put all of this feedback into writing (assuming you do it well, and in accordance with the feedback principles listed previously), you've got documentation. Without documentation, feedback is merely opinion (Ron Katz, 2005). *With* appropriate documentation, feedback can provide the basis for a shared understanding of how performance compares to expectations. It also might just be what it takes to make your feedback "real" enough to motivate the employee to act upon it appropriately. It also creates a "paper trail" in the event that a performance-related decision is ever challenged.

> **NOTE**
>
> Don't let the previous paragraph fool you—documenting performance isn't always easy. Be sure to familiarize yourself with your organization's practices and policies on documentation (and progressive discipline).

Step 3: Performance Appraisal

Performance appraisals are often completed to evaluate and document the performance of one individual employee during a discrete period of time (the performance measurement period). They can also be completed, however, to evaluate the performance of a group of employees. Either way, the performance appraisal should be, in one sense, a non-climactic conclusion to an ongoing and continuous performance management cycle.

Performance appraisals look "backward" at the employees' performance over the performance measurement period, and they also look "forward" to short-term and long-term goals, as well as to development opportunities.

In some organizations, completed performance appraisals may contribute in part—or in whole—to decisions about salary or wage increases. Systems such as this are called "pay for performance." While there are many benefits to implementing "pay for performance" systems, it's critical that the discussion of "performance" does not get lost in the discussion of "pay" when a pay for performance system is in place.

Types of Performance Appraisals

There are three primary categories of performance appraisals.

Rating Methods

▶ **Rating scales**: Appraisers who use rating scales to appraise employee performance "rate" the employee on a variety of different categories using a three-, four-, or five-point scale. Those categories can consist of individual goals, individual competencies, multiple goals, groups of competencies, and the like. Each "point" on the scale corresponds to a different level of performance against standards. On a five-point scale, for instance, the numbers might correspond to the following language:

Rating	Description
5	Far Exceeds Standards
4	Exceeds Standards
3	Successfully Meets Standards
2	Does Not Fully Meet Standards
1	Unacceptable

Generally considered to be the least complex and most frequently used type of performance appraisal tool, rating scales can vary significantly in terms of reliability, objectivity, accuracy, and defensibility. This can depend on a number of factors, including the skill level of the person who developed the appraisal, as well as the skill level of the individual completing the appraisal. "Skill," in this case, does not refer to the goal or competency that is being evaluated; rather, it refers to the individual's ability to effectively appraise performance.

▶ **Checklist**: Appraisers who use checklist appraisals review a series of statements that could describe an employee's performance and literally "check off" those statements that are reflective of the employee's performance during the performance measurement period. Sometimes, checklists are weighted (called "weighted checklists"), in which case the weightings are used to generate a mathematically calculated score.

As with other performance appraisal methods, the value of a checklist appraisal is, in part, a function of the skill level of the person completing the appraisal, as well as that person's ability to recognize and manage any rater biases that he or she might have (see "Performance Appraisal (and Management)—Pitfalls to Avoid").

Comparative Methods

Comparative performance appraisal methods require the appraiser to compare employees to each other.

▶ **Ranking method**: Appraisers who use the ranking method literally rank their direct reports, in terms of overall performance, from "best" to "worst." While fairly simple to use, this method has several shortcomings. First, while it compares employees to each other, it does not compare them to the objective performance standards that were set for the position. So, while it might be nice to be able to know who your best performing employees are, it's much more important to know which of them meets or exceeds the requirements of the position. Conversely, with the ranking method it's also possible (though perhaps unlikely in larger groups) that even the lowest ranked employees might still be meeting the performance requirements of the position; they may just not be as stellar as those employees who were ranked higher.

▶ **Paired comparison method**: Appraisers who use the paired comparison method compare each employee in the group, one at a time, to every other employee in the group. Although this method provides more information than simple ranking, it still leaves out the all-important comparison of actual performance to performance standards.

▶ **Forced distribution**: Appraisers who use the forced distribution method (also known as "forced ranking") are required to rank or evaluate their employees according to a bell-shaped curve. Most employees, therefore, will be ranked or evaluated toward the middle of the curve, while a few will be ranked at the high and low ends of the performance spectrum. While this technique might be useful in helping to avoid (or at least identify) appraiser errors (see "Performance Appraisal (and Management)—Pitfalls to Avoid"), it is possible that the mandated ranking levels may not, in fact, reflect employees' actual performance levels. As such, evaluations are literally (and admittedly) being "forced" into categories that may not be accurate, which can lead to all sorts of complications (for instance, with respect to layoff decisions that are based on performance levels).

Narrative

Appraisers who use narrative methods write down their observations and assessments of each employee's performance.

▶ **Essay**: Appraisers who use the essay method write short essays describing and documenting each employee's performance during the performance measurement period. Some managers may prefer this method, since it gives them ample freedom to accurately and fully evaluate an employee's performance. The method, however, is highly time consuming, and requires considerable writing ability—perhaps in a different style than what the manager might be required to do in the normal course of performing his or her job. Better writers, therefore, might prepare more powerful or convincing performance appraisals. This, of course, does not necessarily make those appraisals more accurate. Also, because of the largely unstructured nature of an essay appraisal, it also might be easier for rater bias to creep in, if the appraiser does not carefully guard against that. "Short" essays can also become "long" (and thus time consuming) essays.

▶ **Critical incident**: Appraisers who use the critical incident method create and maintain documentation throughout the year relative to specific situations in which the employee met and did not meet the performance expectations of the position. The effectiveness of this method (which may or may not be combined with rating scales) will vary widely depending on how the appraiser defines "critical incidents." For instance, if an appraiser only documents extreme examples of behavior (ones that either far exceed or fall well below expected performance standards), those performers who are solid (but not outstanding) may receive little attention, and thus be provided with insufficient documentation. This method also requires that managers consistently and contemporaneously document critical incidents, which may not always be a realistic expectation. And, once again, this method relies on the writing skill as well as the objectivity of the appraiser.

▶ **Field review**: Field review appraisals are prepared by someone other than the employee's supervisor—for instance, someone from HR. One serious concern with field review appraisals is that they may unintentionally send a message that performance management and appraisal is an "extra" part of a supervisor's job, rather than an integral part of his or her day-to-day responsibilities. Instead of being valued as a way of getting work done more productively and in a manner that is consistent with performance expectations, the appraisal process may be perceived as separate, distinct, and therefore less relevant and valuable.

Behavioral Anchored Rating Scales (BARS)

An appraisal method known as "behavioral (or "behaviorally") anchored rating scales" (BARS) starts by identifying the most critical responsibilities or requirements of a position. Then, for each responsibility or requirement, "anchor" statements offering a specific description of a particular type of behavior (which corresponds to a particular level of performance) are written.

For instance, for a programmer analyst, a three-level BARS for responsibilities relating to organizing and planning might look like this:

Description of Behaviors

3. This person normally generates effective plans requiring at least a year of development and a budget of around $750,000. She almost always includes time for unseen emergencies in project timeliness and activities. On most projects she can schedule the team's activities to coincide with the activities of other teams, users, computer operations personnel, and so on. She normally makes long-term plans to use in effectively making schedule adjustments as a project progresses.

2. This person generally establishes his own goals and the steps to achieve them. She can generally organize a project or task into smaller tasks and time frames. She can generally plan his/her own and others' efforts on a project but may have difficulty organizing efforts on several concurrent projects. She may sometimes omit lesser elements from a plan that results in underutilization of resources or delays in project completion.

1. Generally, this person can handle one project, but not multiple projects. She has trouble breaking down a large project into smaller tasks and establishing time frames. She delegates tasks to others but not according to who is best qualified and may not properly coordinate activities with other teams or team members.

Results-based

Though several types of performance appraisals incorporate, to a greater or lesser degree, results as part of the measure of success, management by objectives (MBO) is driven almost exclusively by this measure.

▶ **Management by Objectives (MBO)**: MBO is a goal-centered OD intervention that focuses primarily on collaboratively generating individual employee objectives that align with organizational objectives. Measurement is an absolutely essential element of an MBO program. As follows logically, MBO is often used as a method of appraising performance, as well, due to its strong orientation towards goal establishment and attainment.

An MBO-based performance appraisal process will certainly ensure that individual objectives are aligned with organizational objectives. There are, however, some potential disadvantages. Since MBO focuses exclusively on results ("what" is produced or delivered), "how" goals are accomplished is not given any attention. This could potentially result in an employee choosing to engage in problematic behaviors to achieve goals, including behaviors that are inconsistent with the values of the organization. In addition, an MBO system is time-consuming to develop and maintain, since it must be continually updated to reflect the current expectations associated with each position. Since jobs change so quickly, this can become a daunting task.

Guidelines for Conducting Effective Performance Appraisal

Knowing the mechanics of performance appraisals is important. Even the best-designed performance appraisal will be rendered ineffective (and perhaps even harmful) if a performance appraisal meeting is executed poorly.

The following chart outlines some of the basic "do's" and "don'ts" of conducting an effective performance appraisal meeting:

DO's	DON'Ts
Listen actively	Talk too much
Maintain a professional tone	Behave in an overly "chummy" manner
Remain calm	Lose your composure, show anger, or behave emotionally—even if the employee does
Show empathy	Show sympathy
Treat employee with respect	Demean the employee
Listen for understanding	Psychoanalyze (even when you paraphrase)
Empower the employee	Don't make decisions for the employee, or try to solve his or her problems
Seek solutions	Argue
Stay focused on job-related issues	Pry into employee's personal life
Share appropriate information	Disclose confidential information
Be straightforward	Play games
Respect each employee's privacy	Discuss the performance of other employees
Be prepared	"Wing it"
Treat employees like adults	Infantilize employees

Performance Appraisal "Do's" and "Don'ts," © Gibson, Katz, and Cornell University-ILR, used with permission

Performance Appraisal and Management—Pitfalls to Avoid

In addition to these performance appraisal "do's" and "don'ts," there are other potential pitfalls to be aware of, as well. These other pitfalls relate more to the fact that we are all human and, as such, have biases, beliefs, and reactions that could potentially compromise our ability to manage and appraise performance effectively—that is, if we allow them that to happen.

You may recall that we addressed these same concerns in Chapter 4 during our exploration of interviewing and employment. We'll now look at them in terms of how they could potentially taint the performance management and appraisal process, as well:

Type of Performance Management and Appraisal Bias or Errors and Appraisal	How It Manifests in the Performance Management Process
Contrast	The appraiser compares the performance of each employee to the performance of other employees instead of comparing it to the performance standards that were established for the position at the beginning of the performance measurement period. Please note: This bias is, to a degree, inherent to ranking systems if not combined with other appraisal techniques linked specifically to performance expectations.
First-impression	The appraiser forms an impression of the employee's performance early in the performance measurement period (or even worse, early in the individual's employment) and places an inordinate level of emphasis on that impression. Please note: An employee's performance during each performance measurement period should be assessed separately from that employee's performance during any other performance measurement period. In addition, while it's important to recognize "performance trends" that an employee might demonstrate during a single performance measurement period, it's also critical to ensure that the performance appraisal reflects the employee's performance during the entire performance measurement period.
Halo	The appraiser evaluates the employee positively on the basis of one outstanding qualification or characteristic. This evaluation, however, is inherently incomplete and inaccurate. One particularly impressive skill, or one hard-fought goal, does not reflect the employee's overall performance.
Horns	The appraiser evaluates the employee negatively on the basis of one poor qualification or characteristic. This evaluation, however, is also inherently incomplete and inaccurate, in that it will not reflect the employee's overall performance.
Leniency	The appraiser applies an inappropriately lenient standard to one or more employees, resulting in a higher overall assessment of the employee's (or employees') performance. Being "nice" to one or more employees by "giving" "inflated" performance evaluations doesn't help the organization, and doesn't help

(continued)

Type of Performance Management and Appraisal Bias or Errors and Appraisal	How It Manifests in the Performance Management Process
	the employee, either. An organization needs to ensure that its employees are provided with honest feedback about performance if the organization is to fulfill its mission and attain its overarching objectives. Evaluating employees in an overly lenient (and thus dishonest) manner undermines those efforts. Employees who are, in fact, performing at or above expectations may be confused and/or demotivated if (we should actually say "when," in order to be realistic) they learn that other employees who perform at a level below them are given similar ratings. Those employees who are given inaccurate and overinflated ratings may cease any efforts to improve their performance—after all, they got a good rating. Since other appraisers in the organization will not apply this same degree of leniency, rating consistency across the organization is compromised. In addition to employee demotivation and morale issues, this can also create problems with respect to internal transfers, promotions, salary and wage increases, disciplinary actions, and layoff decisions. Please note: Generally speaking, when one speaks of performance ratings, it is more accurate and effective to say that an employee "earned" a rating rather than saying that an employee was "given" a rating. After all, performance management is intended to empower employees. When ratings are exaggerated, however, ratings truly have been "given," not earned.
Strictness	The appraiser applies an inappropriately harsh and demanding standard when evaluating the performance of one or more employees, resulting in a lower overall assessment of the employee(s). Being overly (and inaccurately) "strict" in one's assessment of the performance of one or more with one or more employees doesn't help the organization, and is unfair to employees, as well, for a number of reasons: An organization needs to ensure that its employees are provided with honest feedback about performance if the organization is to fulfill its mission and attain its overarching objectives. Evaluating

(continues)

(continued)

Type of Performance Management and Appraisal Bias or Errors and Appraisal	How It Manifests in the Performance Management Process
	employees in an overly strict (and thus dishonest) manner undermines those efforts, since it disconnects the employee's performance with any meaningful linkage to the organization's performance. Employees who are, in fact, performing at or above expectations may be confused and/or demotivated by unrealistically harsh ratings, in that such inaccurate (and manipulative) ratings will inevitably create a "cycle of failure"…a history of never being "quite good enough." Since other appraisers in the organization will not apply this same degree of harshness, rating consistency across the organization is compromised. In addition to employee demotivation and morale issues, this can also create problems with respect to internal transfers, promotions, salary and wage increases, disciplinary actions, and layoff decisions. Please note: Generally speaking, when one speaks of performance ratings, it is more accurate and effective to say that an employee "earned" a rating rather than saying that an employee was "given" a rating. After all, performance management is intended to empower employees. When ratings are diminished, however, ratings truly have been "given," not earned.
Recency	The appraisal places undue emphasis on the employee's most recent performance, rather than considering performance demonstrated throughout the entire performance measurement period. Appraisers who find themselves "under the gun" with a looming performance appraisal deadline might be more likely to fall prey to this error—especially if they have not maintained consistent documentation throughout the performance measurement period. But make no mistake: Just like children who are anticipating a holiday replete with presents brought by a magical judge (let's face it—those naughty and nice lists have to be based on something), many employees recognize that outstanding performance near the end of the performance measurement period might help to "make up for" less-than-stellar performance during the earlier portions

(continued)

Type of Performance Management and Appraisal Bias or Errors and Appraisal	How It Manifests in the Performance Management Process
	of the performance measurement period. Don't fall prey to the "Santa Claus" effect.
Similar-to-me	The interviewer evaluates an employee's performance on the basis of how much a candidate is similar to, or different from, him or her. If appraisers recognize characteristics, attributes, or performance patterns in an employee that they dislike about themselves, this recognition—whether conscious or unconscious—could cause the appraiser to evaluate the employee inappropriately negatively. Conversely, if appraisers recognize characteristics or attributes in an employee that they like about themselves, this recognition—again, whether conscious or unconscious—could cause the appraiser to evaluate the employee inappropriately positively. Either way, the impression is wholly unrelated to the employee's actual performance, and must be compartmentalized from the appraisal process.

Chapter Summary

Responsibilities relating to human resource development afford HR professionals with the opportunity to have a significant impact on the growth and development of the organization, and of the people within the organization.

In order to function successfully with respect to the functional area of workforce planning and employment, HR professionals must develop a working knowledge of related legislation. They also must develop facility with the key areas within HRD, specifically

- OD
- Training
- Career development
- Leadership development
- Performance management

As with every other functional area, the ability to execute HRD related responsibilities effectively is predicated upon knowing and understanding the organization's strategic plan, as well as its mission, vision, and values. Taking those "big picture" considerations and translating them into practical HRD applications will enhance the degree to which an HR professional can be effective within the organization.

Key Terms

- Human resource development (HRD)
- Copyright Act of 1976
- Public domain
- Fair use
- U.S. Patent Act
- Utility, design, and plant patents
- ADDIE (analysis/assessment [of needs], design, development, implementation, evaluation)
- McGehee and Thayer
- Organizational level analysis
- Operations (task or work) level analysis
- Man (person) level analysis
- Cost per trainee/cost per participant
- SMART (specific, measurable, action-oriented, realistic, time-bound)
- Lecture/"lecturette"
- Demonstration
- Reading
- Small group discussions/instructor-facilitated large group discussions
- Individual, small group, or large group activities/applications
- Case study

- Role play

- Pilot programs

- Donald L. Kirkpatrick

- Summative evaluation

- Reaction level evaluation

- Learning level evaluation

- Behavior level evaluation

- Results level evaluation

- Robert Brinkerhoff

- Formative evaluation

- Organization development (OD)

- R. T. Golembiewski

- Organizational culture

- Change management

- Kurt Lewin

- Change process theory

- Unfreezing

- Moving

- Refreezing

- Implementation theory

- Human processual interventions

- Technostructural interventions

- Sociotechnical interventions

- Organization transformation change

- Teambuilding

- Total quality management (TQM)

- W. Edwards Deming

- Joseph M. Juran

- Philip B. Crosby

- Zero defects

- Acceptable quality levels (AQLs)

- Four absolutes of quality management

- Kaoru Ishikawa

- Cause-and-effect, Ishikawa, or Fishbone diagram

- Histogram

- Pareto chart

- Learning organization

- Adult learner

- Andragogy

- Pedagogy

- Malcolm Knowles

- Learning styles

- Visual learners

- Auditory learners

- Tactile/kinesthetic learners

- Learning curves

- Classroom/theatre style

- Chevron style

- U-shaped style

- Boardroom style

- Career development

- Leadership development

- Performance management

- Performance appraisal

- Performance standards/expectations

- Goals/objectives

▶ Competencies

▶ Feedback

▶ Documentation

▶ BASIC (behavioral, as soon as possible, specific, interactive, consistent)

▶ Rating methods

▶ Rating scales

▶ Checklist

▶ Comparative methods

▶ Ranking method

▶ Paired comparison method

▶ Forced distribution method

▶ Narrative method

▶ Essay method

▶ Critical incident

▶ Field review

▶ Behavioral anchored ranking scales (BARS)

▶ MBO

▶ Contrast error

▶ First impression error

▶ Halo effect

▶ Horns effect

▶ Leniency error

▶ Strictness error

▶ Recency effect

▶ Similar-to-me effect

Apply Your Knowledge

This chapter focuses on issues relating to human resource development (HRD). Complete the following exercises, review questions, and exam questions as a way of reviewing and reinforcing the knowledge and skills you'll need to perform your responsibilities as an HR professional, and to increase the likelihood that you will pass the PHR examination.

Exercises

1. You've recently been hired as the HR manager within a unit of your organization that hasn't met its production goals (or, for that matter, hasn't even come *close* to meeting its production goals) in about 8 months. Turnover is high and getting higher, morale is low, revenues are plummeting, and stress is rising. You know you're facing a significant challenge, but you are "up for it." Shortly after you assume your new role, your managing director advises you that the situation is getting even worse, and something has to be done to change the situation—fast. She wants your input relative to what direction to take overall, and she's already made one decision: No training programs will be conducted "until the numbers improve." You understand that the situation is serious, and you're concerned about the decision to halt all training. Which of the following statements would summarize how you would respond to your managing director?

   ◯ **A.** Training is an important way for employees to position themselves for promotional opportunities, and the employees in this unit may need a "ticket out" of this underperforming unit.

   ◯ **B.** You'd like to have the opportunity to determine where the gap is between actual and desired performance, to see whether training might be an effective way of addressing the bottom-line performance issues in this unit.

   ◯ **C.** You accepted the position of HR Manager in this unit with the understanding that you'd be able to engage in training initiatives. You believe strongly that you should at least be given the opportunity to do so, until or unless those efforts prove to be ineffective.

   ◯ **D.** Historically, the employees in this unit have taken full advantage of the training opportunities with which they have been presented. Removing training opportunities now could damage morale even more than it already is, which would be the last thing this unit needs.

2. You've designed and developed a one-day training program on effective interviewing, and you're ready to deliver the pilot program. Your manager has told you that the senior leaders of your organization are interested in and supportive of what you've done, and will commit to give you two hours at their next meeting so you can deliver a pilot program to them. They're not, however, willing to participate in any role plays during the pilot. Which of the following statements would summarize how you would respond to your manager?

   ◯ **A.** You're glad that the organization's senior leaders are interested, and are confident that you can condense the training program pilot down to two hours for purposes of providing a high-level review.

   ◯ **B.** It's essential that the senior leaders of your organization experience the program in the same way in which the program participants will experience it, in order for the roll-out of the program to be successful.

   ◯ **C.** You'd like to present the senior leaders with a brief written comparison of the benefits of a two-hour pilot and the benefits of a full-length pilot, and will support the leaders' decision.

   ◯ **D.** You think it might be more valuable to carve out and deliver a two-hour portion of the training so that the leaders get a "feel" for it, rather than trying to condense the program down to two hours.

3. One of the new managers in your unit has had great success during the past year or so with motivating and inspiring employees in his unit. (The unit had been experiencing significant production and quality issues prior to this manager's arrival). His use of positive reinforcement, for instance, has been particularly well received by his direct and indirect reports. Employee satisfaction results are soaring, as well. This morning, you reviewed the final draft of the performance appraisals that he prepared for the employees in his unit, and noticed that all 100+ employees have been rated as meeting or exceeding performance expectations. Which rating error is this manager likely experiencing?

    ○ **A.** Halo effect

    ○ **B.** Leniency effect

    ○ **C.** Inflationary effect

    ○ **D.** Contrast effect

4. You're delivering a training program on supervising and managing people. It's highly interactive, and very well received. You've arranged for a U-shaped setup, which you've consistently found to be the most effective room setup for this program. You show up to deliver the program at an off-site location, and find that the room is set up with classroom-style seating. You try to get someone to rearrange the room for you, but you've been told that the tables are secured to the floor, and no other rooms are available. What would be the best step to take next?

    ○ **A.** Postpone the training. You know that it won't be effective with a rigid, classroom-style room setup, and you'd rather not deliver the training at all than deliver training that you know is likely to be unsuccessful.

    ○ **B.** Deliver the training, and hope for the best. You've made a commitment and will fulfill that commitment, since you don't want to earn a reputation as someone who doesn't keep his promises.

    ○ **C.** Speak to your client contact, if he or she is available, and describe the challenge you're facing. Ensure that he or she understands that you didn't get the setup that you had requested and been promised, and therefore cannot truly be responsible for attaining the training objectives.

    ○ **D.** Speak to your client content, if he or she is available, and describe the challenge you're facing. Tell the client the "backup" plan that you have in place for the situation, and see if he or she has any additional comments, suggestions, or ideas.

Review Questions

1. Describe some of the key differences between "performance management and "performance appraisal."

2. What does it mean when a document or work is in the "public domain"?

3. Why is it important that HRD/training objectives remain "realistic" (the "R" in the acronym "SMART")?

4. What are some of the benefits of the case study methodology?

5. Describe Brinkerhoff's formative evaluation approach.

Exam Questions

1. Which of the following rights is not granted to copyright holders by the Copyright Act of 1976?

   ○ **A.** The right to duplicate/reproduce/copy the work

   ○ **B.** The right to exclude others from making, using, offering for sale, or selling the invention in the United States

   ○ **C.** The right to display the work publicly

   ○ **D.** The right to sell, lease, rent, or otherwise distribute copies of the work to the public

2. All of the following are reasons for conducting needs analysis/assessment *except*

   ○ **A.** To identify performance related problems within the organization.

   ○ **B.** To increase the likelihood of identifying a solution that will truly bridge the performance gap.

   ○ **C.** To begin the initial creation of the HRD/training program before meeting with any organizational resistance that could slow progress

   ○ **D.** To ensure that a legitimate cost-benefit analysis is conducted before a commitment is made to any particular HRD/training solution

3. Which of the following statements about using reading as a training methodology is true?

   ○ **A.** It should be included at least once, whenever possible, in training programs, since ideally all training methodologies should be included in every training program.

   ○ **B.** It should be avoided in training programs unless truly necessary, since participants generally do not find it engaging or stimulating.

   ○ **C.** It represents a particularly effective methodology for auditory learners.

   ○ **D.** It should be included in training programs when participants would benefit from time to absorb and process detailed materials.

4. Which of the following statements does not reflect a statement by which the presentation effectiveness of instructors/potential instructors could be assessed/evaluated?

   ○ **A.** Summarizes major points throughout and at the conclusion of the workshop.

   ○ **B.** Refers to and utilizes training materials (including the participant manual) throughout the program.

   ○ **C.** Allows ample time for participants to develop concepts.

   ○ **D.** Scores consistently well on post-training evaluation forms.

5. Taking a "summative" approach to evaluation means that

- ○ **A.** The designer/instructor/HRD professional collects, summarizes, and incorporates feedback throughout the program development and implementation phases.

- ○ **B.** The designer/instructor/HRD professional collects, summarizes, and incorporates feedback at the conclusion of the program design and development phases.

- ○ **C.** The designer/instructor/HRD professional collects, summarizes, and incorporates feedback after implementing the HRD/training program.

- ○ **D.** The designer/instructor/HRD professional does not collect, summarize, and or incorporate feedback until summary data from a representative number of participants has been collected and analyzed.

6. All of the following statements about Kirkpatrick's behavior level evaluation are true *except*

- ○ **A.** It measures "transfer of training"—the degree to which participants apply the skills and knowledge covered in the training sessions in the workplace.

- ○ **B.** It measures whether and to what degree participants have mastered the skills or acquired the knowledge explored through the learning objectives.

- ○ **C.** It measures changes in behavioral that might be the result of factors unrelated to the HRD/training initiative.

- ○ **D.** It measures whether participants' on-the-job behaviors have changed in a manner consistent with training objectives.

7. Which of the following would *not* be considered to be a major purpose of OD?

- ○ **A.** Identifying and implementing more cost effective ways of increasing employee retention

- ○ **B.** Enhancing the overall effectiveness of organizations

- ○ **C.** Promoting openness towards differences

- ○ **D.** Aligning employee goals with unit and organizational goals

8. "Unfreezing" refers to

- ○ **A.** The process by which an instructor establishes rapport with a reticent group of participants.

- ○ **B.** The process by which resistance to change is addressed and "worked through."

- ○ **C.** The process by which managers are convinced to provide their employees with career development opportunities that could result in them leaving their current positions.

- ○ **D.** The process by which budgetary funds are released for allocation to HRD/training initiatives.

9. The Pareto principle says that

○ **A.** An organization's commitment to customer service must extend even beyond the point of purchase.

○ **B.** Quality is achieved by prevention, not appraisal

○ **C.** In organizations, individuals tend to be promoted up to their "level of incompetence."

○ **D.** 80% of consequences can be attributed to 20% of causes.

10. Of the following learning methodologies, which is likely to yield the highest level of participant retention?

○ **A.** Discussion

○ **B.** Demonstration

○ **C.** Application

○ **D.** Association

Answers to Exercises

1. **Answer B is the best response.** Communicate in terms of organizational results, and guide your suggestions and approaches accordingly. Answer A is not the best response, because giving employees "a ticket out" is not an appropriate focus for your attention at this point in time. Answer C is not the best response, because this is not about you. It is about addressing and resolving individual and collective performance issues in struggling unit, and that is where you must focus your efforts. Answer D is not the best response; your recommendations should not be motivated by avoiding difficult decisions that might upset employees. It must remain on attaining organizational and unit objectives and carrying out appropriate interventions (even difficult ones) in the most productive and positive way possible. In other words, don't just run away from tough situations and decisions.

2. **Answer C is the best response.** It's advisable at this point to help the managers understand the advantages and disadvantages of each approach, and to make their own decision on how they would like to proceed. Answer A is not the best response; part of taking a consultative approach means outlining choices and challenging the status quo, and then allowing others to make decisions based on the information you share. Answer B is not the best response; it represents a condescending, didactic, and closed-minded response. Answer D is not the best response; give the managers the choice of whether to "carve out" a portion of the program, condense it, or take some other approach—but don't make that decision for them.

3. **Answer B is the best response.** Although it is possible that all of the employees in this manager's unit performed at or above performance expectations during the performance measurement period, this is unlikely (particularly since the unit had been experiencing sub-standard performance levels with respect to productivity and quality before the manager came on board). More likely, the manager is rating his direct and indirect reports an overly lenient—and thus inaccurate—manner, in an attempt to avoid the possibility of demotivating them. Ultimately, however, this inherently dishonest (albeit well-intentioned) approach is counterproductive and problematic. Answer A is not the best response; the halo effect occurs when an appraiser evaluates a single employee (not necessarily a group of employees) on the basis of one outstanding dimension of performance. Answer C is not the best response, since there is no performance management rater error known as the inflationary effect. Answer D is not the best response; the contrast effect occurs when an appraiser compares the performance of each employee to the performance of other employees instead of comparing it to the performance standards that were established at the beginning of the performance measurement period.

4. **Answer D is the best response.** Communicating with the client is essential, as is being open to the client's ideas and suggestions. Maintain responsibility for the training program, and don't go to the client expecting him or her to solve your problems. Answer A is not the best response; although it is appropriate to know what setup is likely to be most effective, and to request that setup, trainers must also have the flexibility and wherewithal to "roll with the punches" and deliver a program in less-than optimal conditions (also, taking what could be considered a "diva-like" approach generally won't help to strengthen one's reputation within the organization). Answer B is not the best response, since it implies that you are leaving too much up to chance. "Hoping for the best" isn't enough—you need to actively prepare to excel even in conditions that are different from what you would have preferred or expected. Answer C is not the best response; while communicating with the client is essential, communicating in a manner that seeks to shed responsibility or assign blame is unprofessional and counterproductive. Respond to the situation in a responsible manner, demonstrate resilience, and move forward.

Answers to Review Questions

1. Performance appraisal is, essentially, an "event" or "form." It refers to the form that is completed and the meeting during which it is presented to the employee (usually at the end of the performance measurement period). During this meeting, the manager and the employee review the employee's performance during the prior year and look ahead to the next year. Performance management, on the other hand, is significantly different. It consists of a continuous flow of collaborative feedback, coaching, and communication opportunities in which the manager and the employee engage throughout the entire performance measurement period.

2. Copyrights—and the protections afforded by copyrights—eventually expire. Once a copyright for a particular work expires, that work enters the public domain. This means that the copyright holder no longer enjoys the six rights cited earlier in this chapter, and that the works are available and free for all to use. Work created by the Federal Government is also by definition considered to be in the public domain.

3. Writing "realistic" training objectives helps to ensure that those objectives are neither too easy to achieve, nor too difficult (or even impossible) to achieve. HRD/training objectives that are too easy to attain aren't challenging and may not hold the attention and interest of participants. Ultimately, overly easy objectives also might not generate desired results (if the results could be attained that easily, there would have likely been a less formal solution than a full-blown HRD/training initiative). At the other end of the spectrum, HRD/training objectives that are impossible to attain will only serve to discourage participants.

4. Case studies present participants with a real-life situation that challenges them to apply the knowledge they have learned and practice the skills they have developed during the training session. In the "safe" environment of the classroom, learners can try out their newly acquired knowledge and newly developed skills before they must return to the workplace (where it might not be quite as "safe" to make mistakes). Participants will benefit from receiving feedback from the instructor/facilitator relative to those aspects of the case study that were handled well. Participants will also benefit (perhaps even more) from receiving feedback from the instructor/facilitator relative to those aspects of the case study that could have been handled differently or better. In both cases, the participant will be able to incorporate this feedback before transferring the knowledge and skills learned during the training back to the workplace. This can potentially increase the value of the training experience even more.

5. Published in *Achieving Results Through Training*, Brinkerhoff's formative evaluation model espouses seeking evaluative feedback and input *throughout* the development and implementation phases in an effort to strengthen the ultimate training initiative through real-time incorporation of evaluative feedback. Brinkerhoff's formative evaluation model mandates an iterative process, in which feedback, analysis, and

assessment conducted at one phase of the process will be used to make enhancements in other stages, as well.

Answers to Exam Questions

1. **Answer B is the best response.** The right to exclude others from making, using, offering for sale, or selling the invention in the United States is granted to patent holders under the U.S. Patent Act. Answer A is not the best response, because the Copyright Act of 1976 does grant copyright holders the right to duplicate/reproduce/copy the work. Answer C is not the best response, because the Copyright Act of 1976 does grant copyright holders the right to display the work publicly. Answer D is not the best response, because the Copyright Act of 1976 does grant copyright holders the right to sell, lease, rent, or otherwise distribute copies of the work to the public

2. **Answer C is the best response.** The HRD/training initiative should not be created/developed until the needs analysis/assessment and design phases have been completed (and agreed to in writing). Answers A, B, and D are not the best responses, since each one articulates a legitimate reason for conducting a needs analysis/ assessment.

3. **Answer D is the best response.** Although reading is not always valued as a learning methodology, it does serve a number of valuable purposes, one of which is allowing participants the opportunity to absorb and process detailed information. Answer A is not the best response. Although it is important to use a variety of training methodologies, it is not necessary—and would not always be appropriate—to include all training methodologies in all training programs. Answer B is not the best response, since reading can serve a variety of valuable purposes in training programs. Answer C is not the best response, since reading can be a particularly effective methodology for visual learners, more so than for auditory learners.

4. **Answer D is the best response.** Scoring consistently well on post-training evaluation forms is not necessarily a valid measure of training effectiveness. That evaluation technique provides more insight into how well participants liked the trainer than to how effective the trainer was at ensuring that participants leave the program with the skills and knowledge they will need to bridge the performance gap. Answer A is not the best response, since summarizing major points throughout and at the conclusion of the workshop is one valid measure of presentation effectiveness. Answer B is not the best response, since referring to and utilizing training materials (including the participant manual) throughout the program is one valid measure of presentation effectiveness. Answer C is not the best response, since allowing ample time for participants to develop concepts is one valid measure of presentation effectiveness.

5. **Answer C is the best response.** "Summative evaluation" takes place at the end of the implementation phase. Answer A is not the best response, since it more closely describes the "formative evaluation" technique. Neither answer B nor answer D is the best response, since both describe evaluation techniques that are not espoused by recognized ISD or HRD experts.

6. **Answer B is the best response.** The degree to which participants have mastered the skills or acquired the knowledge explored through the learning objectives is a function of Kirkpatrick's learning-level of evaluation (level 2). Answer A is not the best response, since behavior level evaluation does measure "transfer of training"—the degree to which participants apply the skills and knowledge covered in the training sessions in the workplace. Answer C is not the best response, since behavior level evaluation could potentially measure changes in behavioral that might be the result of factors unrelated to the HRD/training initiative (these changes would "taint" the evaluation, and must somehow be accounted for). Answer D is not the best response, since behavior level evaluation does measure whether participants' on-the-job behaviors have changed in a manner consistent with training objectives.

7. **Answer A is the best response.** Although effective OD interventions might, in fact, result in increased retention of employees, that would not constitute a major purpose of OD. Answer B is not the best response, since enhancing the overall effectiveness of organizations is a major purpose of OD. Answer C is not the best response, since promoting openness toward differences is a major purpose of OD. Answer D is not the best response, since aligning employee goals with unit and organizational goals is a major purpose of OD.

8. **Answer B is the best response.** In Kurt Lewin's change process theory, "unfreezing" refers to the process by which everyone who is involved with and impacted by the impending change is brought to the point where they can understand and accept that a particular change *will* happen. An important part of that acceptance involves letting go of behaviors that reflect resistance to change, or that actually can impede the change process.

9. **Answer D is the best response.** The Pareto principle does assert that 80% of consequences can be attributed to 20% of causes. Answer A is not the best response, since the belief that an organization's commitment to customer service must extend even beyond the point of purchase is part of Kaoru Ishikawa's TQM philosophy, and is unrelated to causes and effects. Answer B is not the best response, since the statement that quality is achieved by prevention, not appraisal, is one of Philip B. Crosby's four absolutes of quality management. Answer C is not the best response, since the belief that individuals tend to be promoted up to their "level of incompetence" within organizations is the "Peter Principle" (Laurence J. Peter), not the Pareto principle.

10. **Answer C is the best response.** Application is likely to result in a 70% retention level. Answer A is not the best response, since discussion is likely to result in only a 50% retention level. Answer B is not the best response, since demonstration is only likely to result in a 30% retention level. Answer D is not the best response, since association is not a recognized instructional methodology.

Suggested Readings and Resources

Making Sense of Change Management: A Complete Guide to the Models, Tools & Techniques of Organizational Change, by Esther Cameron, Mike Green

Managing Change and Transition, by Harvard Business School Press

Organizational Development: A Process of Learning and Changing (2nd Edition), by W. Warner Burke

Telling Ain't Training, by Harold D. Stolovitch, Erica J. Keeps

The ASTD Training and Development Handbook: A Guide to Human Resource Development, by Robert L. Craig

Building a Career Development Program: Nine Steps for Effective Implementation, by Richard, L. Knowdell

Performance Appraisals, by Cathy Lee Gibson

The Center for Creative Leadership Handbook of Leadership Development, by Cynthia D. McCauley (Editor), Ellen Van Velsor

http://www.opm.gov/perform/measure.asp

CHAPTER SIX

Compensation and Benefits

Study Strategies

▶ On small index cards, write the names of laws related to compensation and benefits.

▶ Prepare large index cards for each of the laws. Make note of important facts, dates, and details relating to each law. On the back of the index card, write the name of the law in pencil.

▶ On a third and slightly larger set of index cards, jot down key learning points associated with each law. Just like you did with the previous set of cards, write the name of each law in pencil on the back of the card.

▶ Match the three sets of cards together. Of course, don't look at the back of the cards until you've matched all of the cards—then, check to see whether you've done so correctly.

▶ Try writing out your own multiple choice test questions. Writing out the questions along with detailed answers can go a long way toward reinforcing what you are studying. If you've got a study partner, trade questions with that person.

▶ Although the PHR exam is multiple choice, try writing and answering your own "essay-based" questions. Write open-ended questions that require a response of at least a full paragraph—and write your answers without looking back at your study materials. The process of actually writing down your answers will reinforce what you already know, and will highlight what you need to study more. It will also likely help you as you work to recall this same information when you answer related multiple choice questions on the actual PHR exam.

▶ As with each of the six functional areas of HR, determine what you already know and what you don't know. Then, work to prepare yourself. Conduct research. Use the Internet to find relevant articles and white papers. Peruse textbooks that provide guidance relative to those particular areas. Be sure to find several real-life examples of each responsibility to ensure that you gain a variety of perspectives and insights. This is particularly important for the skill-based, rather than fact-based, components of this functional area.

Introduction

It could be argued that the functional area titled compensation and benefits has been, in one sense, misnamed. This is because these separate areas, when joined together, represent an exponentially larger and more dynamic discipline that is often referred to as "total compensation."

Total compensation encompasses all of the "rewards" that an organization gives, grants, or otherwise bestows upon its employees in exchange for the services those employees have rendered through their employment. It includes more obvious items—such as wages and salaries—that would fall under the subheading "compensation," as well as mandatory and optional benefits such as social security contributions, health and welfare programs, and the like. It also includes items that some, but not all, employees enjoy, such as incentives, bonuses, stock options, and so on.

In this chapter, we'll look at foundational questions relating to C&B, starting with the most basic (and often overlooked) question: Who *is* an employee? We'll then look at the concept of total compensation before looking at its separate, more frequently recognized subdivisions—first compensation, and then benefits. In an effort to make this fact-rich chapter easier to digest, we will separate our scan of compensation-related legislation (which will appear at the beginning of this chapter) from our scan of benefits-related legislation (which will appear after we have completed our discussion of compensation-related items, and before we begin our discussion of benefits-related items). In addition to looking at legislation, we will examine each major component of C&B.

C&B Footing #1: Employee or Independent Contractor?

As indicated previously, one of the first steps that an organization needs to take is to ensure that individuals who contribute to the attainment of organizational objectives are accurately designated as either "employees" or "independent contractors."

As with most areas of HR, there is no immediate answer, no single test to determine the answer to the question of whether an individual is an employee or an independent contractor. To assist in this effort, the DOL has published a fact sheet citing Supreme Court rulings that offer the following seven factors, which will help to appropriately resolve the seemingly perpetual employee/independent contractor conundrum:

1. The extent to which the services rendered are an integral part of the principal's business.

2. The permanency of the relationship.

3. The amount of the alleged contractor's investment in facilities and equipment.

4. The nature and degree of control by the principal.

5. The alleged contractor's opportunities for profit and loss.

6. The amount of initiative, judgment, or foresight in open market competition with others required for the success of the claimed independent contractor.

7. The degree of independent business organization and operation.

The IRS also offers guidance at its website (www.irs.gov) with respect to properly classifying employees and independent contractors. According to the IRS, it is critical to examine the nature of the relationship between the worker and the organization. Specifically, all evidence of "control" and "independence" must be carefully considered. The IRS identifies three categories of "control" into which "facts" and "evidence" can be divided: behavioral control, financial control, and the type of relationship.

▶ Behavioral Control: Who controls and directs how the work is done? For instance, it could be argued that the business maintains behavioral control if it provides the individual with training, instructions, and so forth.

▶ Financial Control: Does the business have a right to control the financial and business aspects of the worker's job? More specifically

  ▶ To what extent does the worker have unreimbursed business expenses?

  ▶ What is the extent of the worker's investment in the facilities used in performing services?

  ▶ To what extent does the worker makes his or her services available to the relevant market?

  ▶ How does the business pay the worker?

  ▶ To what extent can the worker realize a profit or incur a loss?

▶ Type of Relationship: Is there a written contract in place? If so, to what extent does it describe

  ▶ the relationship the parties intended to create?

  ▶ the extent to which the worker is available to perform services for other, similar businesses?

- ▶ whether the business provides the worker with employee-type benefits, such as insurance, a pension plan, vacation pay, or sick pay?

- ▶ the permanency of the relationship?

- ▶ the extent to which services performed by the worker are a key aspect of the regular business of the company?

CAUTION

Exercise care in determining whether an individual is classified as an employee or as an independent contractor. Don't make this decision alone. There are many ramifications of misclassification, including the possibility of settlements that have cost some companies millions of dollars.

C&B Footing #2: Exempt or Non-exempt?

As mentioned earlier, FLSA addresses four different areas—minimum wage, record-keeping, child labor, and overtime. In this "footing #2" section, we will focus on the minimum wage and overtime provisions, since ascertaining exempt and non-exempt status is foundational to a discussion of total compensation.

On August 23, 2004, new minimum wage and overtime regulations to the FLSA were enacted.

NOTE

Interestingly, the DOL website specifically states that these revisions pertain to the overtime *and* minimum wage provisions of the FLSA. However, the $455 weekly threshold is more than twice the minimum wage that was in effect at the time these regulations passed, and no increase in the minimum wage was included with these revisions. The focus of the revisions, therefore, seems to be more on the overtime provisions of the FLSA, which is where we will maintain our focus here.

TIP

These provisions were hotly debated and widely discussed before implementation. Be alert to any changes that might be implemented.

Exemptions: The Basics

Known as FairPay, the 2004 revisions marked some significant changes relative to how determined whether an employee is exempt or non-exempt from the overtime provisions of the FLSA. According to these regulations, employees would be classified as exempt if they

▸ meet certain tests regarding their job duties

▸ are paid on a salary basis

▸ earn no less than $455 per week

Salary Basis

HR professionals need to have a solid understanding of what it means when an employee works on a "salary basis." According to the DOL, being paid on a salary basis means that

> "an employee regularly receives a predetermined amount of compensation each pay period on a weekly, or less frequent, basis. The predetermined amount cannot be reduced because of variations in the quality or quantity of the employee's work. Subject to exceptions listed below, an exempt employee must receive the full salary for any week in which the employee performs any work, regardless of the number of days or hours worked. Exempt employees do not need to be paid for any workweek in which they perform no work. If the employer makes deductions from an employee's predetermined salary, i.e., because of the operating requirements of the business, that employee is not paid on a "salary basis." If the employee is ready, willing and able to work, deductions may not be made for time when work is not available."

CAUTION

Job duties—*not* job titles—must be used to determine an employee's FLSA status. (In other words, don't use an employee's title to determine whether or not he or she is eligible to earn overtime—go by the work that an employee actually performs.)

It's important to be aware of a number of notable changes that were enacted with the FairPay provisions. These changes included

▸ The elimination of separate "short" and "long" tests (based on what an employee earned each week).

▸ Any employees earning less than $455 per week (equivalent to $23,660 per year) are automatically covered by the overtime provisions of the FLSA ("non-exempt")— regardless of the duties that they perform in their jobs. In other words, any employee who earns less than $23,660 is automatically eligible to earn overtime pay.

▸ The elimination of the long test resulted in the elimination of the well-known requirement that exempt employees cannot spend more than 20% of their time each week on non-exempt level activities.

Types of Exemptions: Non-computer Employees, Non-highly Compensated Employees, and Outside Sales Employees

> **NOTE**
>
> One concept that is integral to a discussion of FLSA exemptions is "primary duty," which refers to the principal, main, major, or most important duty that the employee performs.
>
> Determination of an employee's primary duty must be based on all the facts in a particular case, with the major emphasis being on the character of the employee's job as a whole.

Consistent with the 2004 FairPay revisions, employers must now apply one of the following four standard tests to employees (except those who do computer work) who are paid on a salaried basis, and whose salaries are between $23,660 and $99,999 per year.

Please note that in order to qualify for any particular exemption, an employee must meet all of the tests listed in that exemption.

Executive Exemption

▶ The employee's primary duty must be managing the enterprise, or managing a customarily recognized department or subdivision of the enterprise.

▶ The employee must customarily and regularly direct the work of at least two or more other full-time employees or their equivalent.

▶ The employee must have the authority to hire or fire other employees, or the employee's suggestions and recommendations as to the hiring, firing, advancement, promotion, or any other change of status of other employees must be given particular weight.

Administrative Exemption

▶ The employee's primary duty must be the performance of office or non-manual work directly related to the management or general business operations of the employer or the employer's customers.

▶ The employee's primary duty includes the exercise of discretion and independent judgment with respect to matters of significance.

Learned Professional Exemption

▶ The employee's primary duty must be the performance of work requiring advanced knowledge, defined as work which is predominantly intellectual in character and which includes work requiring the consistent exercise of discretion and judgment.

- ▶ The advanced knowledge must be in a field of science or learning.

- ▶ The advanced knowledge must be customarily acquired by a prolonged course of specialized intellectual instruction.

Creative Professional Exemption

- ▶ The employee's primary duty must be the performance of work requiring invention, imagination, originality, or talent in a recognized field of artistic or creative endeavor.

Types of Exemptions: Computer Employees

The Computer Employee exemption is slightly different with respect to pay. To qualify for the computer employee exemption, the following tests must be met:

- ▶ The employee must be compensated either on a salary or fee basis (as defined in the regulations) at a rate not less than $455 per week or, if compensated on an hourly basis, at a rate not less than $27.63 an hour.

- ▶ The employee must be employed as a computer systems analyst, computer programmer, software engineer, or other similarly skilled worker in the computer field performing the duties described below:

  1. The application of systems analysis techniques and procedures, including consulting with users, to determine hardware, software, or system functional specifications.

  2. The design, development, documentation, analysis, creation, testing, or modification of computer systems or programs, including prototypes, based on and related to user or system design specifications.

  3. The design, documentation, testing, creation or modification of computer programs related to machine operating systems.

  4. A combination of the aforementioned duties, the performance of which requires the same level of skills.

Types of Exemptions: Outside Sales

Unlike the other types of exemptions, a minimum salary is not required to establish an exemption on the basis of outside sales. The following criteria, however, must be met:

- ▶ The employee's primary duty must be making sales (as defined in the FLSA), or obtaining orders or contracts for services or for the use of facilities for which a consideration will be paid by the client or customer.

▶ The employee must be customarily and regularly engaged away from the employer's place or places of business.

Types of Exemptions: Highly Compensated Employees

FairPay defines highly compensated employees as those who

▶ Earn $100,000 or more annually (of which at least $455 per week must be paid on a salary or fee basis).

▶ Perform office or non-manual work.

▶ Customarily and regularly perform at least one of the duties of an exempt executive, administrative, or professional employee identified in the standard tests for exemption.

Other Key FairPay Items

HR professionals also need to be familiar with several important considerations relative to the overtime provisions of the FLSA that were clarified in the 2004 revisions.

Specific Non-exempt Designations

Non-exempt: Manual laborers and other "blue collar" workers who perform work involving repetitive operations with their hands, physical skill, and energy cannot be exempted from the overtime provisions of FLSA, no matter how much they earn. This would include non-management employees who work in maintenance, or who are carpenters, electricians, mechanics, plumbers, iron workers, and so on.

Police, Fire Fighters, Paramedics, and Other First Responders

The act also specifically identifies other positions that are likely to be non-exempt (in other words, positions that are likely to be eligible for overtime pay), although a case-by-case review is still needed. These positions include

police officers, detectives, deputy sheriffs, state troopers, highway patrol officers, investigators, inspectors, correctional officers, parole or probation officers, park rangers, fire fighters, paramedics, emergency medical technicians, ambulance personnel, rescue workers, hazardous materials workers and similar employees, regardless of rank or pay level, who perform work such as preventing, controlling or extinguishing fires of any type; rescuing fire, crime, or accident victims; preventing or detecting crimes; conducting investigations or inspections for violations of law; performing surveillance; pursuing, restraining, and apprehending suspects; detaining or supervising suspected and convicted criminals, including those on probation or parole; interviewing witnesses; interrogating and fingerprinting suspects; preparing investigative reports; or other similar work

Safe Harbor Provisions (from Improper Deductions from Salary)

Improper salary deductions can cause an employer to lose the FLSA exemption—and not just for the employee from whom the deduction was improperly made.

EXAM ALERT

Familiarize yourself with circumstances under which employers *can* make deductions from an employee's salary.

If it is found that an employer has "actual practice" of making improper salary deductions, *the employer will lose the exemption* during the time period of the deductions for employees in the same job classification working for the same managers responsible for the improper deductions.

Under the new safe harbor provision, however, an employer can protect itself from losing the exemption if the employer

1. Has a clearly communicated policy prohibiting improper deductions and including a complaint mechanism

2. Reimburses employees for any improper deductions

3. Makes a good faith commitment to comply in the future

C&B Footing #3: Compensation + Benefits = Total Compensation

An organization's total compensation philosophy represents far more than just the amount of cash it pays to employees, or even the "fringe benefits" that it provides. Instead, an organization's compensation philosophy speaks volumes about what the leaders of that organization value, the results they want to attain, the behavior they want to encourage, and their commitment to their employees.

In many ways, an organization's total compensation philosophy is a clear and direct expression of the organization's mission, vision, and values—*even if it is not deliberately intended to act as such*. Even the absence of a clearly defined compensation system or philosophy says something—and nothing can stop those messages from going through, loud and clear, to employees. Just as it is impossible for a person *not* to communicate, so too it is impossible for an organization's total compensation program (or absence thereof) not to send a clear message to employees and potential employees about what is important to the organization.

Objectives of a Total Compensation Program

Since an organization's total compensation program says so much, it's imperative that it be designed deliberately, intentionally, and with overarching as well as specific objectives in mind.

Those specific objectives will vary from organization to organization, from one portion of an organization's life cycle to another, and to some degree from position to position. Certain overarching objectives, however, should be kept in mind when crafting a total compensation program…objectives that can be addressed, at least initially, by asking the following questions.

How can—and will—we design a compensation system that…

- ▶ Supports and reinforces the mission, vision, and values of the organization?
- ▶ Is consistent with the culture of the organization?
- ▶ Attracts, motivates, and retains targeted/appropriate employees?
- ▶ Ensures internal equity between positions within the organization?
- ▶ Supports our philosophy toward the external labor market?
- ▶ Is affordable, sustainable, and cost effective?
- ▶ Is legally defensible in the event of a challenge?
- ▶ Is appropriate for the organization's current position in its life cycle?
- ▶ Is flexible and easily adaptable?

In an effort to better appreciate the nuances that need to be considered when crafting a total compensation philosophy, let's take a closer look at two of these questions.

Attracting, Motivating, and Retaining Targeted/Appropriate Employees

For some organizations, there may be great value in attracting, motivating, and retaining high-performing employees who (hopefully) are "in it for the long haul." In these situations, there may be important considerations that need to be factored in, such as long learning curves, sensitive and critical client relationships, and so on. For these organizations, there may be a great focus on designing a total compensation system that would be perceived as very competitive in the relevant labor market, and that would encourage high-performing employees to stay with the organization for the long-term.

Conversely, some organizations are perfectly comfortable with relatively high (or just plain high) levels of turnover. While these organizations might be interested in developing a total compensation program that will attract employees, motivating and retaining their employees might be of far less importance. Alternatively, those organizations whose employees do not require much training and/or whose employees form only transient relationships with customers might develop a compensation philosophy that positions them less competitively in the relevant labor market. By itself, neither approach is right nor wrong. If you were to switch the two compensation systems for these two types of organizations, however, the mismatch would create a significant disconnect—rendering both philosophies ineffective and even counterproductive.

Supporting Our Philosophy Toward the Relevant Labor Market

There are three primary approaches from which organizations choose when deciding how they want to position themselves relative to the external labor market with respect to total compensation. We'll look at those three approaches in a moment. First, however, it's necessary to understand the meaning of "relevant labor market."

The relevant labor market relates to the size and scope of the geographic area within which an organization would seek to attract qualified candidates. Even within the same organization, the relevant labor market for different positions can vary widely depending upon the skills, knowledge, abilities, and behavioral characteristics required to perform each position successfully. Other factors that impact how an organization defines the relevant labor market might be the degree of competition that exists among employers for particular skills and/or knowledge, and the degree to which certain skills and/or knowledge requirements are industry-specific.

Once the relevant labor market has been defined for a particular position, the organization must choose between the three approaches alluded to earlier—leading, lagging, or matching the market.

NOTE

It's critical to note that any of these three approaches could be adopted across an entire organization, or just for certain positions within an organization. It's important, however, to keep an eye on maintaining internal equity if different approaches (lead, lag, or match) are applied within the same organization.

Lead the Market

Organizations may choose to offer total compensation packages that are "better" than packages being offered by their labor market competitors. Organizations that lead the market may believe that higher compensation packages will attract higher-performing employees who will, in turn, "pay for themselves," and then some. In short, these organizations want the "best of the best," and are willing to pay for it.

Lag the Market

Organizations may choose—by design, or simply because of budgetary constraints—to offer total compensation packages that are "worse" (perhaps we should say "less attractive") than the total compensation packages that are being offered by their labor market competitors. Organizations that lag the market might offset this potential disadvantage by reinforcing and maximizing the intrinsic rewards that it offers—long-term potential growth opportunities, the ability to contribute to a particularly significant organizational mission, and so on.

Match the Market

Organizations may choose to offer total compensation packages that are comparable to the total compensation packages being offered by their labor market competitors. Organizations that match the market make a conscious choice to be "externally competitive" with respect to total compensation.

> **NOTE**
>
> It's important to keep in mind that how an organization addresses even the most overarching questions can vary considerably depending upon the organization itself, the phase of the business lifecycle in which the organization finds itself, and even the positions under consideration. As with all other areas of HR, therefore, there are no simple answers. (If you're tempted to say any situation is a "no brainer," look again—chances are you've missed something!)

Elements of a Total Compensation Program

Total compensation consists of a variety of elements, all of which can be divided into "direct compensation" and "indirect compensation."

Direct compensation refers to components that are presented to employees in the form of cash, and indirect compensation refers to components that are presented to employees in forms other than cash ("non-cash").

Some examples of direct compensation are

- Hourly wages/base salary
- Shift differentials
- Overtime pay
- Commissions
- Variable pay (such as short-term and long-term incentives)

Some examples of indirect compensation are

- Legally mandated benefits (such as social security)
- Medical insurance
- Dental insurance
- Long term disability insurance

▶ Vision coverage

▶ Vacation time

▶ Holiday time

▶ Long term disability insurance

▶ Recognition programs (such as peer recognition programs, non-cash spot awards, achievement awards, "pizza parties," desirable parking, and so forth)

▶ Perquisites (also known as "perks," such as company car, club memberships, financial planning, and so on)

NOTE

In addressing problems and questions that might come up, it's important to keep in mind is that what may initially appear to be a compensation problem may in fact not be one. Perhaps the problem under consideration is unrelated to compensation, or perhaps it is related to compensation *as well as* other issues, or perhaps it *is* truly a compensation problem. (Even then, it's important to think in terms of "total comp" and not just automatically "throw money" at a problem.) Without a doubt, your internal consulting skills will really come in handy here.

Communicating the Total Compensation Program

It's not enough to "walk the walk"—you've also got to "talk the talk."

Oftentimes, when we look around our organizations, our country, or even our world, we see people who "talk the talk" but don't "walk the walk." Or, to put it differently, people don't always "put their money where their mouths are." Interestingly, when it comes to compensation and benefits programs, the opposite tends to be true. Organizations often don't communicate enough with employees about the total compensation/benefits programs that they have in place, or about what those programs really cost.

For a number of reasons, it's important to change this practice, and to communicate with employees. Most employees simply do not know the real costs—let alone the actual value—of the benefits they receive. Also, in a very real sense, employees earn benefits, just like they earn cash compensation—and it's important to ensure that employees understand and recognize that. This holds true for benefits that are voluntarily provided by employers, as well as for benefits programs that are mandated by the government. Otherwise, even those benefits that are *not* entitlements may ultimately begin to feel like entitlements to employees.

There are myriad ways to communicate with employees about the benefits they receive, just a few of which are

▶ Employee meetings

▶ Newsletters

(continues)

(continued)

- ▶ DVDs
- ▶ Employee handbooks
- ▶ Annual total compensation and benefits statements
- ▶ Personal letters/emails
- ▶ Internet/intranet

Communicate early, and communicate often. Perhaps most importantly, don't rely on any single method to get your message across. Just as people learn differently in training programs (see Chapter 5, "HR Development"), people also process and absorb information differently.

REVIEW BREAK

At this point, we've laid a strategic and theoretical foundation that will provide us with a context within which to consider some of the fact-based and practical elements of compensation and benefits. Let's start with a review of some key compensation-related legislation.

Related Legislation: Compensation

Though many laws have some relevance to compensation, the following are some of the most important ones with which HR professionals need to be familiar.

Davis-Bacon Act—1931

The Davis-Bacon Act was the first piece of legislation to consider the topic of—and actually establish—a minimum wage. Davis-Bacon, however, was and still is limited to the construction industry, specifically those contractors and subcontractors on

- ▶ Any and all federal government construction contracts
- ▶ Non-federal government construction projects in excess of $2000 that receive federal funding

Contractors and subcontractors who meet either of these criteria are required to provide laborers and mechanics who are employed at the actual worksite with wages and benefits that are equal to (or better than) what workers on similar local projects receive.

Walsh-Healey Public Contracts Act (PCA)—1936

The next significant piece of compensation-related legislation was the Walsh-Healey Public Contracts Act (PCA), enacted in 1936.

The Walsh-Healey PCA requires contractors who have contracts with the federal government that exceed $10,000 to pay an established minimum wage to workers employed through that contract. In addition to minimum wage, Walsh-Healey PCA also addressed issues including overtime pay and safe and sanitary working conditions.

Fair Labor Standards Act (FLSA)—1938

> **NOTE**
>
> In the section titled "C&B Footing #2: Exempt or Non-exempt?" we explored the overtime provisions of the FLSA, particularly with respect to the 2004 FairPay revisions. Here, we'll focus on the other three provisions of the law, as well as some of the more technical aspects of the overtime provision.

Although it was initially enacted in 1938, the Fair Labor Standards Act (FLSA) still has a profound impact on employees today because of its wide scope and the degree to which it directly impacts the lives of nearly every American worker.

The FLSA covers full-time and part-time workers in the private sector and in federal, state, and local governments. It addresses minimum wage, overtime, equal pay, record keeping, and child labor standards (referred to by the government now as "youth employment standards"). For private enterprise employees, it is administered by the Wage and Hour Division of the DOL. For federal employees, the FLSA is administered either by the Wage and Hour Division or the U.S. Office of Personnel Management (which, interestingly, refers to itself as "The Federal Government's Human Resources Agency" on its website).

In looking at the FLSA, let's take a look at each of the areas it covers, in the order indicated (and the order they are listed at www.dol.gov):

- ▶ Minimum wage
- ▶ Overtime pay
- ▶ Record keeping
- ▶ Child labor standards (youth employment standards)

Minimum Wage

The FLSA established a federal minimum wage for private sector employees and for all other employees covered by the Act. From time to time, minimum wage has become a hotly debated issue in Congress, since it is Congress who has the responsibility for introducing legislation that will change the federal minimum wage. In our nation's system of checks and balances, however, that hotly debated congressional issue quickly becomes a hotly debated presidential issue, since it is the president who must either sign or veto legislation to increase the minimum wage.

EXAM ALERT

Know what the federal minimum wage is as of the date you take the exam. Also, be familiar with government-sponsored programs that enable employers to pay certain employees (full-time students, certain people with disabilities, and so on) at an hourly rate of pay that is less than the federal minimum wage.

NOTE

Many states have established a minimum wage that is higher than the federally established minimum wage. In these circumstances, employees would be entitled to the state minimum wage (in this case, the state law is more generous than the federal law, and thus supersedes the federal law).

Want a Good Tip?

Here's one—be sure your tipped employees earn at least the minimum wage.

The FLSA specifically addresses the question of employees who receive tips. According to the Act, an employer of "tipped employees" must pay those employees for every hour worked, even if the employees' tips alone would result in them earning more than the minimum wage. The minimum rate of pay that can be paid to tipped employees (available at www.dol.gov/esa), however, is substantially less than the minimum wage that must be paid to employees who do not receive tips. In order to be eligible to pay tipped employees this lower hourly rate, the employer must meet certain conditions, including (but not limited to)

▶ The employer must claim a tip credit against its minimum wage obligation.

▶ Each employee's tips combined with the hourly rate that the employer is paying must meet or exceed the federal minimum hourly wage. Otherwise, the employer must make up the difference.

Overtime

According to the FLSA, non-exempt employees must be paid at least the minimum wage for the first 40 hours worked during the workweek. If an employee works more than 40 hours during the workweek (commonly referred to as "overtime"), he or she must be paid those overtime hours at a rate that is at least 150% (commonly referred to as "time and a half") of his or her regular rate of pay per hour—which may be different from the employee's stated hourly wage rate.

In addition to the all-important questions of who is (and isn't) exempt from the overtime provisions of the FLSA, at least two additional pivotal questions related to overtime must be addressed:

1. How is the number of hours worked calculated?

2. What rate of pay must be used to determine the regular rate of pay per hour (which will, in turn, be used to calculate the overtime pay rate)?

Calculating the Number of Hours Worked During the Workweek

In order to calculate the number of hours worked during the workweek, it's first necessary to understand the government's definition of and rules regarding "workweeks":

▶ A workweek is any fixed and regularly recurring period of 168 hours (24 hours in a day, seven days a week).

▶ The employer can select any day (and any hour) of the "calendar week" on which to begin the "workweek." Once chosen, however, that day (and hour) must remain constant (hence the "fixed" and "recurring" requirement).

▶ The employer can establish different workweeks for different employees or groups of employees.

▶ The hours that an employee works during different workweeks cannot be "averaged" (to avoid overtime payments, or for any other reason).

Once you've got a handle on what a "workweek" is, the next step is to understand how to determine what "hours worked" really means.

First of all, "hours worked" means "hours worked"—*not* "hours paid." In other words, according to the FLSA, hours that have been paid but not worked (vacation time, sick time, holiday time, jury duty time, and the like) do *not* count towards the 40 hour threshold (although some organizations may voluntarily *choose* to count these hours toward the 40 hour threshold).

> **CAUTION**
>
> "Hours worked" also doesn't mean "hours approved to work." If an employer "suffers or permits" a non-exempt employee to work, that employee must be compensated for time worked. So, whether the employer requires the employee to work or simply allows the employee to work, the time counts as "hours worked," and must be compensated appropriately.

Calculating the Regular Rate of Pay

An employee's regular rate of pay includes more than just his or her hourly rate of pay; it would also include any incentives and commissions. It would not, however, include bonuses (which, unlike incentive programs, are discretionary), pay for time not worked, premium pay for weekend or holiday work, and the like.

CAUTION

It is critical that employers calculate overtime payments on the basis of each employee's *regular* rate of pay, not on each employee's *hourly* rate of pay.

NOTE

As with minimum wage, some states have established more generous overtime laws—for instance, laws that require overtime pay after an employee has worked eight hours in any one day, regardless of how many hours the employee works during the entire workweek. As is also the case with minimum wage, a more generous state law would supersede the federal law.

Child Labor

The child labor provisions of the FLSA restrict the number of hours (and the times of the day) that children under the age of 16 can work, as well as the types of work that children under the age of 18 can perform.

Under the Fair Labor Standards Act (FLSA)

- Children under the age of 14 years cannot be employed (different guidelines exist for certain jobs, such as for farm work or work performed for the child's parent).

- Hours worked by 14- and 15-year-olds are limited to

  - Non-school hours

  - 3 hours in a school day

  - 18 hours in a school week

  - 8 hours on a non-school day

  - 40 hours on a non-school week

  - Hours between 7 a.m. and 7 p.m. (except from June 1 through Labor Day, when evening hours are extended to 9 p.m.)

- Youth who are under 18 years of age may perform non-hazardous jobs. Youth who are 14 and 15 years of age are also restricted from performing manufacturing, mining, and hazardous jobs.

▶ Youth who are 16 years of age and older (and adults) may work an unlimited number of hours per day.

▶ The FLSA does not require work permits or working papers, but certain states do.

Record-keeping

Employers must maintain accurate and complete records for each non-exempt employee of hours worked and wages earned. Certain identifying information (such as social security number, address, and so forth) is also required. No specific method of time-keeping is required. See the Act for more specific information about these record-keeping (and retention) requirements.

> **NOTE**
>
> Employers are required to post the provisions of the FLSA.

Portal-to-Portal Act—1947

In May of 1947, the FLSA was amended by the Portal-to-Portal Act. Section 254(a) of the Portal-to-Portal Act offered clearer definitions of "hours worked" for purposes of minimum wage and overtime payments. According to the Act, employers are only required to compensate workers for working time that they spend on activities that relate to the performance of their job.

> **EXAM ALERT**
>
> This statement, while accurate, is also incomplete, in that it does not even begin to address the nuances of the Portal-to-Portal Act. The Act, for instance, addresses travel time (on public transportation, on private transportation, during work hours, outside work hours), pre-shift work, post-shift work, idle waiting time, overnight travel, training time, and many other considerations. Familiarize yourself with this Act before paying your employees and before taking the PHR exam.

Equal Pay Act (EPA)—1963

The EPA prohibits discrimination on the basis of sex in the payment of wages or benefits to men and women who perform substantially equal (but not identical) work, for the same employer, in the same establishment, and under similar working conditions. (An "establishment" generally refers to one specific physical location.) Similar to the way in which FLSA status is determined, "substantial equality" is determined by job content, not job titles. More specifically, the substantial equality of job content is assessed on the basis of the following four factors:

▸ **Skill:** The amount or degree of experience, ability, education, and training required to perform the job. Comparisons must be made on the basis of the skills that are required to perform the job—not on the skills that the incumbents happen to possess.

▸ **Effort:** The amount of physical or mental exertion rquired to perform the job.

▸ **Responsibility:** The degree of responsibility and accountability which an employer entrusts to and expects from a particular position.

▸ **Working Conditions:** The physical surroundings of the position, as well as any hazards that are associated with a particular position.

Employers can, however, set forth "affirmative defenses" to explain inequities in pay between men and women. These arguments can be based on—and must be proven to be—a function of

▸ Seniority

▸ Merit

▸ Quantity or quality of production

▸ Any factors other than sex

REVIEW BREAK

This section has provided an overview of some of the laws that are most relevant to compensation-related topics. Now, let's take a look at the actual building blocks that you can use to bring compensation principles to life within your organization.

Compensation: Job Evaluation

Job evaluation is the process through which every job in an organization is assessed and compared to other jobs in the organization. At the conclusion of the job evaluation process, you will be able to ascertain the relative worth of each job within the organization. When this is done, you will have generated an overall job worth hierarchy.

Job evaluation techniques fall into two categories: non-quantitative and quantitative.

Non-quantitative Job Evaluation Techniques

Non-quantitative job evaluation techniques, as the name implies, determine the relative value of jobs within the organization without using mathematical techniques. Instead, these methods focus on the "whole job" (which is why these techniques are also referred to as "whole job" methods).

Whole Job Ranking

In the whole job ranking techniques, jobs are "ranked" from lowest to highest, according to the importance that each job holds (or, stated differently, the value that each job brings) to the organization. In essence, a list is generated that reflects which jobs are more important to the organization, and which jobs are less important to the organization, in rank order.

Whole job ranking is easy to perform, and is also relatively inexpensive to maintain. It fails, however, to establish specific factors about each job that need to be taken into consideration when comparing jobs to each other, and can be prone to rater subjectivity. It also limits its comparison to elements of each job, rather than to any specific competencies or responsibilities that are universally valuable to each organization. This system can also be unwieldy to use if there are more than a few individuals working in an organization. Lastly, while the list that is generated through whole job ranking will show which jobs are most and least important, it will not demonstrate the *relative* worth of one job to another.

Job Classification

Job classification is a non-quantitative job evaluation technique that categorizes jobs into broad categories, or "levels," based on the level—and, ultimately, value to the organization—of the work that is performed by jobs within each job. Each level incorporates specific responsibilities and "benchmark statements" that describe the nature, complexity, autonomy, and so on of the work that is performed by positions in that level.

In addition to being inexpensive, job classification is relatively simple to implement and administer. One potential disadvantage, however, is that jobs may not match perfectly with the benchmark statements listed in each category. In this case, the evaluator would use his or her judgment (which can, of course, be imperfect and/or subjective at times) to choose the best possible classification. Another potential weakness of the job classification method is that raters are also more likely to evaluate jobs on the basis of the current incumbent, rather than on the basis of the jobs themselves, thus violating a key principle of job evaluation.

Job Slotting

Job slotting incorporates (or "slots") newly created or revised positions into an existing job hierarchy. This process of slotting is accomplished by comparing the new or revised job descriptions to job descriptions of positions that have already been evaluated and assigned within the hierarchy.

Like the other non-quantitative job evaluation methods, job slotting is inexpensive and simple to administer and implement. Job slotting can only be used, however, when a job structure is already in place. As with the other non-quantitative job evaluation methods, there is an increased possibility that rater error and subjectivity can "taint" the job evaluation process. It is also more likely that jobs will be evaluated on the basis of the current incumbent, rather than on the basis of the jobs themselves, thus violating a key principle of job evaluation.

Quantitative Job Evaluation Techniques

Quantitative (or "factor based") job evaluation methods identify the degree to which each position is responsible for or requires specific "compensable factors." Compensable factors are those skills, abilities, characteristics, or areas of responsibility that an organization values, and for which it is willing to pay. Some sample compensable factors include education, experience, financial responsibility, responsibility for contacts, and so on.

Factor-based methods generate a mathematical "score" that reflects the positions relative worth to the organization.

Point Factor

Point factor systems first identify specific compensable factors, and then establish levels of performance *within* each of those compensable factors. The relative importance of each compensable factor to the organization is then "weighted." A different point value is then assigned to each level within each compensable factor.

Once a point factor system has been established, each job is evaluated according to this system by determining which level within each compensable factor is most reflective of the position being evaluated, thus generating a point value for each compensable factor. The evaluator then adds up the points associated with each level to calculate a total point value. When the point values associated with each job are compared to each other, a mathematical depiction of the relative and absolute value of the jobs will emerge, thus indicating where the job falls within the established job worth hierarchy.

The point factor system affords greater reliability between different raters, and minimizes the impact of evaluator error or subjectivity. Developing a point factor system, however, can be time consuming and difficult; purchasing one can be expensive. In addition, using it properly requires some measure of training.

Factor Comparison

Factor comparison is a quantitative job evaluation technique that involves the ranking of each compensable factor. A monetary value for each level with each factor is subsequently identified. The appropriate level is then selected. Unlike the point factor method, however, a "dollar value" is associated with each compensable factor. When all of the levels that have been selected are added together, a pay rate will emerge for each job.

This system—while providing a degree of objectivity and reliability across raters—is difficult and expensive to develop. It also requires a great deal of monitoring and updating in order to ensure that the dollar value associated with each level remains appropriate, in a relative as well as in an absolute sense.

Compensation: Market Pricing

Market pricing involves looking at the relevant labor market to ascertain what the "going rate" or "market rate" is for a particular position. Market pricing can yield valuable pay data about "benchmark" jobs—jobs for which close "matches" can be identified in the relevant labor market.

Data collected through market pricing can be used in a number of ways. For example, market data can be obtained about a number of benchmark positions as part of a larger initiative. Market data can also help in the building of a job worth hierarchy, around which other positions can be placed using a whole job slotting technique. Market data can also be used to obtain information for one particular job, in combination with other job evaluation techniques that might be used.

Market Data Considerations

In preparing to collect market data, there are a number of considerations that need to be taken into account and a number of decisions that need to be made. Let's take a look at some of the questions that might be relevant.

What Is the Relevant Labor Market?

We first looked at the topic of relevant labor markets when we started considering the importance of the organization's compensation philosophy. Within the context of collecting market data, determining an appropriate relevant labor market for each position is foundational to ensuring that the market data we collect—and about which we will be making decisions—is truly relevant.

Who Are Our Labor Market Competitors in General, and for Specific Jobs?

Determining who your labor market competitors are within the relevant labor market is also critical. One important consideration is whether you are competing only within your industry for talent, or whether you are competing with organizations in different industries or sectors, as well.

What Sources of Market Data Are Currently Available to You, and What Sources Could You Secure?

Pay surveys provide one important source of market data. Pay surveys can be developed internally or secured externally (either by purchasing existing survey data or by contracting with an outside organization to develop a custom survey).

Market data can also be obtained through

▶ Government resources (the Bureau of Labor Statistics—www.bls.gov—is one excellent resource)

▶ Websites designed for this purpose (for instance, www.salary.com)

▶ Local economic development councils

▶ Professional associations

▶ Career development offices at college, universities, and /or tech training schools

▶ Employees (including departing employees) and managers

▶ Search firms and employment agencies

EXAM ALERT

Be familiar with the advantages and disadvantages associated with each of the different methods of securing market data—in particular, the advantages and disadvantages of survey based methods.

Which Matches Are Appropriate?

As mentioned earlier, matching benchmark positions to available market data provides valuable information. Not all of the positions we attempt to match, however, are benchmark positions. It simply won't be possible to find market data for some positions, in which case you may want to consider other options (for instance, internal job evaluation or benchmark market data combined with job slotting).

CAUTION

Match jobs on the basis of the duties and responsibilities that are performed—not on job titles. Job titles can be misleading or even inaccurate, which would in turn corrupt your analysis.

Does the Data Need to Be Adjusted in Any Way?

There are a number of ways to adjust market data, including

▶ **Aging**: Ideally, market data should be collected from multiple sources. It is likely that the dates on which these salaries were "effective" will be different for each different source of data, so it's necessary to adjust all the data to a common date (usually the date on which the market analysis is being conducted).

▶ **Quality of job match**: Sometimes (perhaps even "often"), it's impossible to make a perfect job match, especially for positions that are not benchmark jobs. This can occur because of differences in scope, work conditions, financial responsibility, or a variety of other factors. In situations like this, the best choice you can make is to find the best possible match, even if it is not ideal. Once you've made the best possible match, you can then "weight" different market data differently as a way of reflecting each source's relative value. "Weighting" market data means putting greater importance on certain data and less importance on other data when performing calculations with the data you've collected. This can help account for the imperfections that are sometimes inevitable with job matching.

Once the market data has been collected and appropriately aged, the conclusions that you'll draw on the basis of that data can support sound decision making. Those decisions may pertain to one particular position or may make a broader contribution toward developing a job worth hierarchy. It's also important to recognize that market data does not stand alone as the only factor that should be taken into consideration—ideally, it should be used in conjunction with existing job evaluation methods, pay structures, and so on. It is possible that externally generated data may present a different perspective than internally generated data, and it is important to consider and reconcile the two.

Compensation: Base Pay and Variable Pay

Once the overall compensation strategy is established, the next step is to determine how that strategy will come to life within the organization. As we discussed earlier, total compensation can be divided into direct (cash) and indirect (non-cash) elements. In this section, we'll consider two critical elements of direct compensation: base pay and variable pay.

Base Pay

Base pay refers to the fixed rate of pay that an employee receives for performing his or her job. Base pay does not, however, include earnings obtained through shift differentials, benefits, overtime, incentive premiums, or any pay element other than the employee's fixed rate of pay.

A number of factors go into setting base pay rates, including (but not limited to) the relative worth of the job to the organization, the market rate for a particular position, and other special circumstances (for instance, unique skills that are in great demand—also known as "hot skills").

Variable Pay

Sometimes, organizations choose to compensate employees through variable pay programs in addition to base pay programs. Variable pay is also known as "at risk" pay (but is not often referred to in those terms to employees, in that "risk" is not universally embraced).

There are a variety of different types of variable pay programs, each of which can be used on a standalone basis, combined with other variable pay programs, or customized to meet the needs and objectives of the organization's compensation philosophy.

Incentive Plans

Incentive plans establish specific financial and non-financial goals and targets for individuals, groups, and organizations. In order for incentive programs to be effective, employees need to believe that they can attain the goals that have been set as part of the incentive program, and that the reward that they would earn by attaining those goals is "worth it" (see "Vroom, Vroom, Expectancy Theory," in Chapter 2).

Incentive plans also need to be designed with an awareness of how much downside risk—as well as upside potential—exists for incentive plan participants. It's also critical to look at the design of the incentive program and the accompanying message that it sends to employees. For instance

▶ Are there "thresholds" in place, so that a partial incentive will be paid even if the goal is not fully attained? Or will employees/teams only be paid for meeting or exceeding objectives?

▶ Is the incentive program an "add on" to a current base pay program, or does it truly constitute "pay at risk"? Will participants' base pay be reduced, now or at some point in the future, as a function of participating in the incentive program?

▶ What is the overall degree of upside potential, and what is the overall degree of downside risk?

Regardless of the answers to these and many other questions, one thing is certain—any incentive program will speak volumes to employees about what your organization values.

There are a variety of different types of incentive programs, a few of which are described in the following sections.

Short-term Incentive—Individual

Short-term individual incentive programs are used to financially motivate individual employees to attain specific financial or non-financial objectives. Short-term incentive programs are usually one year or less in duration.

Short-term Incentive—Team/Group

Short-term team/group incentive programs are similar to short-term individual incentive programs, except that targets are set for groups of people instead of for individual employees. These incentive programs are intended to foster collaborative efforts and synergy among employees who are pursuing a common goal.

Gainsharing

Gainsharing incentive plans are designed to motivate (or, one could say, to "incent" or "incentivize") employees to reach specific goals relating to cost-cutting or revenue generation, and then to share a portion of that savings (or that increased revenue) with the employees who helped to achieve it. Gainsharing plans are based on team/group performance, not individual performance.

Profit Sharing

Profit sharing plans are organizationwide plans that establish an organizationwide profit goal. If the goal is reached, the profits are shared with employees. Profits can either be shared immediately (cash profit sharing plans) or later (deferred profit sharing plans).

Compensation: Building and Using Pay Structures

Once an organization has identified a total compensation philosophy, attention can be turned to building a compensation system to support that philosophy.

The overarching and specific total compensation goals that the organization has identified are brought to life through the organization's pay structures. Pay structures provide direction relative to wage and salary rates, pay increases, and incentive programs. They operationalize the organization's philosophies relative to internal equity and external competitiveness. In a very real sense, pay structures make strategy tangible.

EXAM ALERT

Pay structures provide a reminder about the criticality of effectively communicating with employees about the organization's compensation philosophy and programs. Familiarize yourself with ways to engage in meaningful and effective communication.

Elements of Pay Structures

Two important elements of pay structures are grades and salaries, both of which are often referred to as elements of a "salary administration" system.

Grades

Grades (also referred to as "job grades") represent a hierarchy of "levels" into which jobs of similar internal worth can be categorized. It may be helpful to liken "job grades" to "school grades"—just as students within a particular grade demonstrate similar levels of academic accomplishment, jobs within the same grade share a similar level of value or worth to the organization.

Different organizations will have different numbers of pay grades, with differing degrees of distinction between each of those grades.

Ranges

If grades provide the framework for clustering positions in accordance with their relative value within the organization, ranges provide corresponding compensation levels for each of those clusters.

Ranges specify the lowest ("minimum") and the highest ("maximum") compensation rates for which positions within each grade are generally paid. The halfway point between those two figures is known as the "midpoint" and is calculated as follows:

$$\frac{Maximum + Minimum}{2}$$

NOTE

As is often the case, exceptions can exist, for a variety of reasons. Employees who are paid above the maximum of the range are considered to be "red-circled"; employees who are paid below the minimum of the range are considered to be "green-circled."

The "range spread" is a percentage that is calculated by subtracting the minimum of the range from the maximum of the range and dividing that number by the minimum of the range. For instance

Range Minimum:	$40,000
Range Maximum:	$60,000
Range Spread:	$\dfrac{\$60,000 - \$40,000}{\$40,000} = \dfrac{\$20,000}{\$40,000} = 50\%$

Range spreads allow organizations to recognize and compensate employees within the same job and within jobs that are in the same grade, for different levels of skill, experience, or performance. Of course, how an organization compensates employees within each range will, to a degree, depend upon the total compensation philosophy of the organization.

There is no one "right" percentage for range spreads. Range spreads do, however, tend to grow wider at higher grade levels. Traditionally, range spreads are approximately

- 35% for non-exempt positions

- 50% for exempt positions

- 60% + for senior leadership positions

A series of ranges, along with their accompanying minimums, maximums, and midpoints, is known as a "range table." For identification purposes, numbers or letters are often assigned to each grade in a range table.

NOTE

Broadbanding

Sometimes, organizations choose to use a relatively small number of grades, an approach known as "broadbanding." Organizations might choose to use broadbands to bring about a cultural change (for instance, to support the implementation of a "flatter" organization), or to shift employees' focus away from traditional promotions and place it instead on career growth. Broadbands typically have range spreads of 100% or more.

Using Pay Structures for Decision Making

While it's important to build pay structures, just building them isn't enough. Organizations also need to develop the policies that will guide day-to-day decisions regarding pay. As alluded to earlier, these policies are a reflection of the compensation philosophies of the organization.

Pay guidelines can be based on seniority, performance, experience, effort, and a variety of other factors. One important consideration to keep in mind is that whatever factor(s) is used to determine how day-to-day decisions are made will be viewed as having great importance—and will likely become a key driver of employee efforts.

Pay guidelines also need to be developed to guide other types of increases (promotions, adjustments, general increases, cost of living increases, and so on) as well as the amount and timing of those increases.

Compa-ratio

Another important tool that can provide valuable information for decision making is the "compa-ratio."

The compa-ratio for each employee is calculated by dividing the employee's pay rate by the range midpoint for his or her position. For example, if an employee earns $40,000 per year, and the midpoint of his or her range is $50,000, the compa-ratio is calculated as follows:

$$\frac{\$40,000}{\$50,000} = 80\%$$

Compa-ratios can be a particularly valuable measure for organizations that seek to match the market, since in such systems midpoints are often considered to be a close approximation of the "market rate" for a position. By calculating the compa-ratio, therefore, it is possible to compare the employee's rate of pay with the market rate for his or her position. If you take this percentage in combination with length of service, time in job, performance level, and other employees' earnings, you'll end up with a significant amount of information to help you perform compensation management.

EXAM ALERT

In this section, we covered many areas related to the discipline of compensation—areas that are highly likely to show up on the PHR exam. There are other areas, however, that we have not touched upon directly, which are also included in the repertoire of responsibilities you need to perform and the cache of knowledge you need to possess as an HR professional. This (in a practical sense) means they also could appear on the exam. So, in addition to what's discussed here, be sure to review other sources in an effort to familiarize yourself with

HR-related Responsibilities:

▶ Analyze, select, implement, maintain, and administer executive compensation, stock purchase, stock options, and incentive and bonus programs.

▶ Analyze, develop, select, maintain, and implement expatriate and foreign national compensation and benefit programs.

▶ Develop/select and implement a payroll system.

▶ Administer payroll functions.

   HR Related Knowledge:

▶ Executive compensation.

▶ Noncash compensation methods (for example, stock option plans).

▶ International compensation laws and practices (for example, expatriate compensation, socialized medicine, mandated retirement).

REVIEW BREAK

At this point, we've covered a lot of ground including the question of who is (and who is not) an employee; FLSA status; total compensation; and a host of issues relating to compensation. Now, let's move into the other part of the total compensation equation—benefits.

As mentioned at the beginning of the chapter, we're going to take a slightly different approach to the way we look at benefits-related legislation. Instead of looking at it all together, we're going to divide benefits-related laws into two categories:

▶ Laws that exists for the purpose of regulating, governing, or guiding optional benefits programs

▶ Laws that actually created specific mandatory and optional benefits programs

In this way, we hope to make it easier for you to navigate the (relatively) heavily legislated discipline of benefits.

Related Legislation: Benefits— Laws That Regulate, Govern, and Guide Optional Benefits Programs

Many laws have an impact on the benefits that employers offer to their employees. Let's take a look at some of the most significant ones.

Employee Retirement Income Security Act (ERISA)—1974

The Employee Retirement Income Security Act is perhaps better known by its acronym, ERISA. ERISA's overall purpose is to protect the interests of those who participate—and the beneficiaries of those who participate—in employee benefit plans. ERISA applies only to programs established by private industry employers.

ERISA established minimum participation and vesting standards for retirement programs (ERISA covers defined benefit plans and defined contribution plans; see "Defined Benefit Plan"). ERISA also established minimum standards for welfare benefit (including health) plans.

NOTE

It's important to note that the private industry plans that ERISA is designed to regulate are *voluntary*. ERISA does not require private industry employers to establish any pension or health plans. It does, however, impose minimum standards on those employers who choose to do so—all in the interest of protecting plan participants.

A Few Words About Vesting: Cliff and Graded

Vesting is the process by which an employee earns a non-forfeitable right to the employer's contribution of his or her defined benefit/defined contribution plan. Organizations can choose between two vesting options for defined benefits and defined contribution plans: cliff vesting or graded vesting

In 2002, separate vesting rules were enacted for plans that provided for matching employer contributions, such as 401(k) plans.

Vesting Schedule for Defined Benefit/Defined Contribution Plans as of 2002

	401(k) Plans*	All Other DB and DC Plans**
Cliff Vesting	100% after 3 years	100% after 5 years
Graded Vesting	20% after 2 years	20% after 3 years
	40% after 3 years	40% after 4 years
	60% after 4 years	60% after five years
	80% after 5 years	80% after 6 years
	100% after 6 years	100% after 7 years

Participants are always 100% vested in their own contributions.

*Includes other plans with matching contributions

**Includes plans without employer matching contributions, such as profit sharing arrangements

The Protective Nature of ERISA

The safeguards established by ERISA have a strong, but not exclusive, focus on protecting participants with respect to the financial dimensions of plans. Here are two examples of requirements established by ERISA that demonstrate this effort to protect participants:

> ▶ **Under ERISA, participants must be provided with plan information, specifically about the features and funding of the plan**—For instance, when an employee (or beneficiary) becomes a participant in a retirement plan that is covered under ERISA, he or she is entitled to receive a summary plan description (SPD), at no cost, from the plan administrator. The SPD describes what the plan provides and how it operates. It also provides information relative to when an employee can begin to participate in the plan, how service and benefits are calculated, when benefits becomes vested, when and in what form benefits are paid, and how to file a claim for benefits. In addition to the

SPD, the plan administrator must automatically provide participants with a copy of the plan's summary annual financial report, which includes the same information that employers are required to file with the government on Form 5500.

EXAM ALERT

Be aware of ERISA participation rules for defined benefit and defined contribution plans. In general, an employee must be allowed to participate in a qualified plan after meeting the following requirements:

▶ The employee is at least 21 years old: An employee can be excluded for not having reached a minimum age (which cannot exceed age 21) but cannot be excluded for having reached a maximum age. In other words, no matter how old an employee is, he or she can still—and always—participate in the plan.

▶ The employee has at least one year of service: For qualified plans, a year of service is generally 1,000 hours of service performed during the plan year. Employees who do not perform 1,000 hours of service are not considered to have performed one year of service, even if services were performed for a 12-month period. (Please note: For plans other than 401(k), this requirement is two years, as long as the plan has fully vested after not more than two years of service.)

An employer may, however, choose to implement less restrictive eligibility requirements, such as a minimum age requirement that is younger than 21 or a service requirement of less than one year.

▶ **ERISA provides fiduciary responsibilities for those who manage and control plan assets**—ERISA establishes fiduciary responsibility for "persons or entities who exercise discretionary control or authority over plan management or plan assets, have discretionary authority or responsibility for the administration of a plan, or provide investment advice to a plan for compensation or have any authority or responsibility to do so are subject to fiduciary responsibilities." (www.dol.gov). Plan fiduciaries could include, for example, plan trustees, plan administrators, and members of a plan's investment committee.

Fiduciaries are charged with running the plan(s) for which they are responsible solely in the interest of participants and beneficiaries. They must ensure that the sole purpose of the plan is—and remains—providing benefits to participants and beneficiaries and paying plan expenses.

Fiduciaries must also act with skill, care, prudence, and diligence. For instance, they must protect plan participants by diversifying plan investments (in other words, just like any of us, they can't keep all of their financial "eggs in one basket"). In addition, they must follow the terms of plan documents to the extent that those terms are consistent with ERISA. They also must avoid conflicts of interest—and, many would argue, even the possibility of an appearance of a conflict of interest (the same standard to which HR professionals should hold themselves, as well).

All of this may sound simple…perhaps as though it should be common sense.

Common sense, however, is often somewhat uncommon. All it takes is a quick scan of recent headlines trumpeting the news of unethical behavior and defunct pension plans to appreciate that fiduciary responsibility is not something to be taken for granted. According to the Employment Benefits Security Administration (EBSA), ERISA enforcement yielded the following results:

ERISA Enforcement

Latest Enforcement Statistics	FY 2002	FY 2003	FY 2004
Prohibited Transactions Corrected	$398M	$460M	$2388.3M
Plan Assets Restored	$189.7M	$169.8M	$199.7M
Participant Benefits Restored	$125.3M	$105.4M	$47.8M
Plan Assets Protected	$168.2M	$662.1M	$141.6M
Voluntary Fiduciary Correction Program	$1.9M	$8.7M	$264.6M
Total Monetary Results	$883M	$1.4B	$3042M
Individuals Indicted	134	137	121

A sample of civil violations included

▶ Failing to operate the plan prudently and for the exclusive benefit of participants.

▶ Using plan assets to benefit certain related parties to the plan, including the plan administrator, the plan sponsor, and parties related to these individuals.

▶ Failing to properly value plan assets at their current fair market value, or to hold plan assets in trust.

▶ Failing to follow the terms of the plan (unless inconsistent with ERISA).

▶ Failing to properly select and monitor service providers.

▶ Taking adverse action against an individual for exercising his or her rights under the plan (for example, being fired, fined, or otherwise being discriminated against).

CAUTION

Plan administrators can be held personally liable for losses that result from breaching their fiduciary responsibility.

NOTE

ERISA also requires plans to establish a grievance and appeals process for participants and gives participants the right to sue for benefits and for breaches of fiduciary duty.

Administrative Responsibility for ERISA

Administrative responsibility for enforcement of ERISA is divided among three government agencies:

▶ **IRS:** The IRS focuses on tax-related dimensions of ERISA.

▶ **DOL:** Within the DOL, ESBA focuses on fiduciary responsibility and transactions that are prohibited by ERISA. Within the DOL, Employee Benefits Security Administratioin is responsible for administering and enforcing the fiduciary, reporting, and disclosure provisions of ERISA.

▶ **Pension Benefit Guaranty Corporation (PBGC):** The PBGC—a government corporation created by ERISA—functions as an insurer that provides a minimum guaranteed benefit for certain pension plans. PBGC protects participants in most defined benefit plans and cash balance plans (within certain limitations). So, for instance, if a covered plan is terminated, PBGC ensures that participants will receive payment of certain benefits.

PBGC is funded by insurance premiums that are paid by plan sponsors—not by general tax dollars. Funding also comes from investment income, assets from underfunded pension plans it has taken over, and recoveries from companies formerly responsible for those plans.

EXAM ALERT

ERISA is highly detailed and complex. If you do not have recent, in-depth, and first-hand experience with the application of ERISA, be sure to dig deeper. Be familiar with the rules under ERISA, the enforcement of ERISA, administrative requirements placed on employers by ERISA, the role of the PBGC, vesting guidelines, and so forth.

Retirement Equity Act (REA)—1984

The Retirement Equity Act (REA), an amendment to ERISA, incorporated a number of key revisions, many of which addressed the concerns of former (in the event of divorce) and surviving (in the event of death) spouses. Specifically, REA enacted a number of important provisions, seven of which are that the REA

1. Lowered the minimum age requirement for pension plan participation.

2. Increased the years of service that "count" for vesting purposes.

3. Allowed for longer breaks in service (with respect to vesting rules).

4. Prohibited plans from counting maternity and paternity leaves as breaks in service for participation and vesting purposes.

5. Required qualified pension plans to provide automatic survivor benefits and allow for waiver of survivor benefits only with the consent of the participant and the spouse.

6. Clarified that pension plans may obey certain qualified domestic relations (court) orders (QDROs) requiring them to make benefit payments to a participant's former spouse (or another alternative payee) without violating ERISA's prohibitions against assignment or alienation of benefits.

7. Expanded the definition of accrued benefits that are protected against reduction.

Consolidated Omnibus Budget Reconciliation Act (COBRA)—1985

The Consolidated Omnibus Budget Reconciliation Act (COBRA) is technically an amendment to Title I of ERISA, and is thus administered by EBSA. COBRA requires employers who employed 20 or more people during the prior year to offer continuation of group health care coverage to employees and their family members who experience certain "qualifying events"—events that would have otherwise resulted in the discontinuation of their health insurance benefits.

COBRA places certain requirements on plan participants who wish to extend coverage, and it places certain requirements on the plan provider—in particular with respect to notification requirements.

EXAM ALERT

Be familiar with specific COBRA notification requirements, which were updated as of May 2004.

COBRA Qualifying Events

Employees, their spouses, and their dependent children can experience qualifying events that would entitle them to continue group health insurance coverage under COBRA.

NOTE

Those who choose to extend coverage are responsible for paying the full cost of the health premium, plus a 2% administrative fee (if the plan sponsor chooses to charge one).

COBRA Qualifying Events for Employees

COBRA Qualifying Event	Length of Continuation Coverage Eligibility
Voluntary or involuntary termination of the covered employee's employment for any reason other than gross misconduct	18 months
Reduction in the hours worked by the covered employee	18 months

COBRA Qualifying Events for Employees' Spouses

COBRA Qualifying Event	Length of Continuation Coverage Eligibility
Voluntary or involuntary termination of the covered employee's employment for any reason other than gross misconduct	18 months
Reduction in the hours worked by the covered employee	18 months
Covered employee's becoming entitled to Medicare	29 months
Divorce or legal separation of the covered employee	36 months
Death of the covered employee	36 months

COBRA Qualifying Events for Employees' Dependent Children

COBRA Qualifying Event	Length of Continuation Coverage Eligibility
Loss of dependent child status under the plan rules	18 months
Voluntary or involuntary termination of the covered employee's employment for any reason other than gross misconduct	18 months
Reduction in the hours worked by the covered employee	18 months
Covered employee's becoming entitled to Medicare	29 months
Divorce or legal separation of the covered employee	36 months
Death of the covered employee	36 months

NOTE

Extensions of the length of continuation coverage may be available under certain circumstances, such as when a second qualifying event occurs.

COBRA is *not* available to employees, their spouses, or their dependent children when an employee is terminated for gross misconduct.

Older Worker's Benefit Protection Act (OWBPA)—1990

The Older Worker's Benefit Protection Act (OWBPA), passed in 1990, is an amendment to the ADEA that makes it illegal to discriminate against older workers with respect to benefits, or to target older workers for layoffs.

Title 2 of OWBPA prohibits individuals from waiving rights or claims under ADEA unless such a waiver is "knowing and voluntary." OWBPA established nine specific criteria for ensuring that such waivers are knowing and voluntary. One particularly important criterion states that employers must allow employees at least 21 days to consider any right-to-sue waivers that the employer offers in exchange for early retirement benefits.

Health Insurance Portability and Accountability Act (HIPAA)—1996

The Health Insurance Portability and Accountability Act (HIPAA) was a more recent amendment to ERISA. HIPAA has two main focuses: the security and portability of health care coverage, and privacy considerations.

Security and Portability of Health Care Coverage

One of HIPAA's two key purposes was to help workers experience greater security and portability with respect to health care coverage—even when an employee changes jobs. HIPAA also afforded significantly greater protections for employees who have or who have a family member with a preexisting medical condition.

> **NOTE**
>
> Under HIPAA, a preexisting condition is defined as one for which medical advice, diagnosis, care, or treatment was recommended or received during the 6-month period prior to an individual's enrollment date.

Under HIPAA, in the worst case scenario, employees (or their family members) with preexisting health conditions can have those conditions excluded from coverage for no more than 12 months (18 months for late enrollees). If an employee maintains health coverage continuously, he or she can reduce or even eliminate this period of exclusion.

HIPAA also prohibited employers from denying certain employees coverage—or from charging them higher premiums—because of existing health conditions. HIPAA affords protection to employers, as well, by mandating that health insurance providers must renew coverage for employers (as long as premium payments are made).

HIPAA Privacy Rule

HIPAA also addresses the issue of privacy for patients and healthcare consumers. While this rule is not specifically directed at employers, employers who offer group health insurance to employees may be considered a "covered entity" and thus be required to comply with HIPAA's privacy rule.

CAUTION

Employers should consult with counsel relative to compliance with the HIPAA privacy rule.

The primary purpose of the HIPAA privacy rule is to protect patients and other consumers of health care services from the unauthorized disclosure of any personally identifiable health information (protected health information, or PHI). Health information is considered to be personally identifiable if it relates to a specifically identifiable individual. The following items would generally be considered PHI (whether communicated electronically, on paper, or verbally):

- Health care claims or health care encounter information, such as documentation of doctor's visits and notes made by physicians and other provider staff

- Health care payment and remittance advice

- Coordination of health care benefits

- Health care claim status

- Enrollment and disenrollment in a health plan

- Eligibility for a health plan

- Health plan premium payments

- Referral certifications and authorization

- First report of injury

- Health claims attachments

If it is determined that an employer is a "covered entity" under the HIPPA privacy rule, the employer would need to take specific actions, some of which would include

- Enact written PHI privacy procedures

- Designate a privacy officer

- Require business associates to sign agreements stating that they will respect the confidentiality of PHI

▶ Train all employees in HIPAA privacy rule requirements

▶ Establish a complaint handling and resolution process for issues related to the HIPAA privacy rule

▶ Ensure that PHI is not used for making any employment-related decisions

> **EXAM ALERT**
>
> Like ERISA and COBRA, HIPAA is a highly complex and involved law. Don't let the apparent simplicity of the information presented here mislead you; it's necessary to dig much deeper to truly understand the nuances and subtleties of this law.

Mental Health Parity Act (MHPA)—1996

The Mental Health Parity Act (MHPA) prohibits group health plans providers, insurance companies, and HMOs that offer mental health benefits from setting annual or lifetime dollar limits on mental health benefits that are lower than any such dollar limits for medical and surgical benefits. This means that plans that don't impose annual or lifetime monetary caps on medical and surgical benefits *cannot* impose annual or lifetime caps on mental health benefits, either (benefits for substance abuse or chemical dependency are exempted). MHPA is under the jurisdiction of the Departments of Labor, Treasury, and Health and Human Services.

> **NOTE**
>
> MHPA *does not require* health plans to offer mental health benefits. It only applies to plans that do offer mental health benefits.

Under MHPA, plans can still dictate/define the terms and conditions of benefits provided under mental health plans (for instance, cost-sharing, limits on the number of visits or days of coverage, and so forth).

There are certain circumstances under which plan providers that offer mental health benefits are exempt from MHPA, including

▶ Small employers who have fewer than 51 employees

▶ Any group health plan whose costs increase 1% percent or more due to the application of MHPA's requirements (the increased cost exemption must be based on actual claims data, not on an increase in insurance premiums)

Sarbanes-Oxley Act (SOX)—2002

The Sarbanes-Oxley Act (SOX) was created in the wake of huge corporate accounting scandals, including Enron and Tyco, just to name two. Designed to protect investors, SOX enacted reforms designed to enhance corporate responsibility and financial disclosures and to combat corporate and accounting fraud.

There are a number of SOX provisions with which HR professionals needs to be particularly concerned, four of which are

▶ Prohibition against insider trading during certain pension plan blackout periods—section 306(a)

▶ Requirement that plan administrators must provide 30-day written notice in advance of blackout periods to individual account plan participants and beneficiaries—section 306(b)

▶ Requirement to disclose whether the company has adopted a code of ethics that applies to the company's key officers (at a minimum, this code must apply to the company's principal executive officer, principal financial officer, principal accounting officer or controller, or persons performing similar functions)—section 406

▶ Establishment of whistleblower protection in a wide variety of situations for employees who report fraud against shareholders—section 806(a)

REVIEW BREAK

At this point, we've completed a review of the major benefits related laws that govern existing benefits programs. As you continue your review and test preparation, be sure to review other benefits related laws that are less prominent than these (OBRA, Tax Reform Act, and so on).

Now, let's turn our attention to laws that actually created specific mandatory and optional benefits programs.

Related Legislation: Benefits—Laws That Created Mandatory and Optional Benefits Programs

Some of the laws that we'll look at created benefits programs that are optional, while others created benefits programs that are mandatory.

Worker's Compensation—*Mandatory Benefit Program*

Worker's compensation (also known as "worker's comp") laws were adopted by all states between 1911 and 1940. These laws were designed to provide medical care to injured employees and death benefits to families of those who died. Worker's comp is a "no fault" system—injured workers receive medical and/or compensation benefits regardless of who caused the job-related accident.

> **NOTE**
>
> Worker's compensation is mandatory in all states except for New Jersey and Texas.

Social Security Act (SSA), 1935—*Mandatory Benefit Program*

In August of 1935, President Franklin D. Roosevelt signed the Social Security Act into law. Social Security is a social insurance program (although some would define it differently) that is funded through payroll taxes. Approximately 96% of all workers are covered under the Social Security Act.

> **NOTE**
>
> Since the program's inception, Social Security has been designed so that employers and the workers they employ have contributed equal dollar amounts each pay period (originally 2% of the first $3,000 of the employee's earnings. That cap, along with that percentage, have been raised significantly over the decades). Independent contractors and self employed individuals are required to pay both the employer and the employee portions.

Social Security is also known as the Old Age, Survivors, and Disability Insurance program (OASDI), in reference to its three primary components, which are now referred to as retirement income, disability benefits, and survivor's benefits.

Retirement Benefits

Workers earn "credits" towards Social Security benefits. As of 2005, workers earned one credit for each $920 in earnings—up to a maximum of four credits per year. (The amount of money that a worker must make to earn one credit generally increases each year, but the four-credit-per-year maximum remains the same.) Workers born in 1929 or later need 40 credits in order to earn retirement benefits. Younger people need fewer credits to be eligible for disability benefits, or for their family members to be eligible for survivors' benefits.

Social Security tracks each worker's earnings throughout his or her life. It is the employee's record of earnings—combined with the age at which he or she retires—that determine the monetary amount of each worker's monthly benefit.

> **NOTE**
>
> The earliest age at which a worker can retire and still receive benefits is 62. These benefits, however, are reduced from what they would have been if the worker had worked until his or her full retirement age. "Full retirement age" ranges between age 65 (for those who were born in 1937 or earlier) and age 67 (for those who were born 1960 or later). Workers who work beyond their full retirement age will increase their monthly retirement—the longer they work past their full retirement age, the more their monthly retirement income will be (everyone must start receiving retirement benefits at the age of 70—including individuals who contiue to work).

Disability Benefits

Disability benefits were added to the Social Security Program in 1956. Under Social Security, workers who become "totally disabled" can receive benefits under Social Security. "Total disability," however, can be a fairly difficult standard to meet. Total disability cannot begin until after five full calendar months of continuous disability. Even then, in order to be considered totally disabled, the worker must be unable to continue in his or her previous job and unable to adjust to other work; in addition, the disability must be expected to last for at least one year or to result in the worker's death.

In addition to being deemed to have a total disability, the disability eligibility formula requires that the worker has earned a certain number of credits (during his or her entire working life), and that the worker must have earned a certain number of credits within the 10 years preceding the disability (younger workers who haven't had a chance to earn as many credits are held to more lenient requirements than older workers). Similar to the way in which retirement benefits are calculated, the actual disability benefit that the worker would receive depends upon the worker's age and how many credits the worker has earned.

Survivors' Benefits

When a person who has worked and paid Social Security taxes dies, his or her family members may be eligible to receive survivors' benefits. Depending on the person's age at the time of death, up to 10 years of work is needed in order for survivors to be eligible for benefits.

Social Security survivors' benefits can be paid to

- ▶ A widow or widower—full benefits at full retirement age, or reduced benefits as early as age 60

- ▶ A disabled widow or widower—as early as age 50

- ▶ A widow or widower at any age if he or she takes care of the deceased's child who is under age 16 or disabled, and receiving Social Security benefits

- Unmarried children under 18, or up to age 19 if they are attending high school full time (under certain circumstances, benefits can be paid to stepchildren, grandchildren, or adopted children)

- Children of any age who were disabled before age 22 and remain disabled

- Dependent parents age 62 or older

Medicare

Passed in 1965 as an amendment to the Social Security Act, Medicare provides hospital and medical insurance for the elderly and people with disabilities.

There are two parts to Medicare: hospital insurance (sometimes called Part A) and medical insurance (sometimes called Part B).

> **NOTE**
>
> Neither Part A nor Part B pays for all of a covered person's medical costs. In addition, the program contains deductibles and co-pays (payments due from the covered individual).

Medicare—Part A: Hospital Insurance

Part A helps pay for inpatient hospital care, skilled nursing care, and other services.

People age 65 or older are eligible for benefits under Part A of Medicare if they meet *any* of the following criteria:

- Receive Social Security or railroad retirement benefits

- Are not getting Social Security or railroad retirement benefits, but have worked long enough to be eligible for them

- Would be entitled to Social Security benefits based on a spouse's (or divorced spouse's) work record

- Worked long enough in a federal, state, or local government job to be insured for Medicare

People under age 65 are eligible for Part A Medicare benefits if they experience certain disabilities (for instance, Lou Gehrig's disease, permanent kidney failure) and meet other specified criteria (for instance, having worked long enough to receive disability benefits under Social Security).

Medicare Medical Insurance (Also Known As Part B)

Part B helps pay items such as doctor's fees, outpatient hospital visits, and other medical services and supplies.

Almost anyone who is 65 or older *or* who is under 65 but eligible for hospital insurance can enroll for Medicare medical insurance by paying a monthly premium. People over age 65 don't need any Social Security or government work credits for this part of Medicare.

Unemployment Insurance—*Mandatory Benefit Program*

The Federal-State Unemployment Insurance Program was established as part of the federal Social Security Act of 1935, and is administered at the state level. Federal rules are developed by the DOL.

In general, the maximum period for receiving benefits is 26 weeks, though the federal government may choose to extend the benefit period during difficult economic times.

Unemployment insurance is funded through employer taxes (except in three states, where employees contribute as well). Unemployment insurance is intended to help employees financially "bridge" the time between positions, when a position has been lost through no fault of their own.

Unemployment Insurance—Eligibility

There are a number of requirements for establishing eligibility, two of which are

▶ You must meet the state requirements for wages earned or time worked during an established (one year) period of time referred to as a "base period." (In most states, this is usually the first four out of the last five completed calendar quarters prior to the time when your claim is filed.)

▶ You must be determined to be unemployed through no fault of your own (determined under state law), and meet other eligibility requirements of state law.

Unemployment benefits are subject to federal income taxes.

Revenue Act, 1978—*Optional Benefit Program*

The Revenue Act brought with it many changes, including a reduction in individual income taxes, a reduction in corporate taxes, and so on. It also added two sections to the tax code that essentially resulted in the creation of two new—and ultimately very important—employee benefits.

Section 125

Section 125 created flexible benefits plans (often referred to as "cafeteria" plans). Section 125 plans can help employers as well as employees save money by reducing payroll taxes.

Before looking at the three types of Section 125 plans, let's consider some of the reasons that an organization might have for implementing a section 125 plan.

Reasons for Considering Section 125 Plans

Thinking back to where we started in this chapter, each organization's total compensation program communicates a great deal to employees—and to potential employees—about what the organization values. As such, Section 125 plans might be one way of communicating some of the following messages (to the degree they are appropriate) to employees:

▶ We recognize that not everyone's life is the same, and that everyone has different needs. Because of that, different employees may want to allocate—or spend—the money they earn in different ways. Section 125 plans are one way to acknowledge and support these different and changing employee needs.

▶ When it comes to benefits, *we* may not always know what's best for you, but *you* do. In this sense, our goal becomes to give you tools and information with which you can make benefits-related decisions that are right for *you*.

▶ We know you have a choice regarding the company for which you will work. Every day that you choose to remain employed with us, you are casting a vote. We know this, and we appreciate it. Giving you some choice regarding the benefits you select is one way we can say "thanks."

Types of Cafeteria Plans

There are three types of cafeteria plans

▶ **Premium Only Plans (POPs)**: With Premium Only Plans, the simplest and most transparent (from employees' perspectives) of the three Section 125 plans, employees pay for their portion of certain insurance premiums (health, dental, and so forth) on a pre-tax basis. The net effect is that each employee's taxable income is reduced, which is how employers and employees can reduce taxes—and save money.

▶ **Flexible Spending Accounts (FSAs)**: Flexible Spending Accounts take POPs one step farther. With FSAs, employees can set aside pre-tax dollars to pay for medical expenses that are not covered by insurance. FSAs can also be set up for dependent care. Employees decide how much money to set aside for the following year, and that amount is automatically deducted from the employee's pay on a pre-tax basis. After incurring and paying for eligible expenses, employees apply for reimbursement from the FSA.

> ▶ **Full Cafeteria Plans**: Employers who offer full cafeteria plans provide their employees with a specific amount of money they can use to pick and choose from a variety of benefits.

Although they offer distinct advantages, especially for employees, full cafeteria plans are the most administratively burdensome of the three Section 125 options.

Section 401(k)

The second employee benefit that was created by the Revenue Act is the 401(k) plan. A type of defined contribution plan, 401(k) plans allow employees to set aside pre-tax dollars to save for their retirement. This can be done through salary deduction, which may or may not be matched in part or (less frequently) in whole by employer contributions. 401(k) dollars can also be set aside through deferral of profit sharing income.

Family and Medical Leave Act (FMLA), 1993—*Mandatory Benefit Program*

The Family and Medical Leave Act (FMLA) entitles eligible employees (who work for covered employers) up to 12 weeks of unpaid, job-protected leave during any 12-month period for one or more of the following reasons:

▶ For the birth and care of the newborn child of the employee

▶ For placement with the employee of a son or daughter for adoption or foster care

▶ To care for an immediate family member (spouse, child, or parent) with a serious health condition

▶ To take medical leave when the employee is unable to work because of a serious health condition

Under some circumstances, leave can be taken intermittently.

The FMLA is administered and enforced by the DOL.

Employee Eligibility for FMLA

In order to be eligible to take FMLA leave, an employee must

▶ Work for a covered employer (public agencies, state, local, and federal employers, local education agencies [schools], and private-sector employers with 50 or more employees)

▶ Have worked for the employer for a total of at least 12 months (this time does not have to have been uninterrupted)

▶ Have worked at least 1,250 hours over the previous 12 months

▶ Work at a location in the United States or in any territory or possession of the United States where at least 50 employees are employed by the employer within 75 miles

FMLA—Employer Requirements

The FMLA places specific requirements upon employers before and during FMLA leaves. Specific requirements pertain to

▶ Posting requirements

▶ Notifying employees of their rights under FMLA

▶ Designating use of leave as FMLA leave

▶ Maintaining group health benefits

▶ Restoring an employee to his or her original job, or to an equivalent job with equivalent pay, benefits, and other terms and conditions of employment

FMLA—Employee Requirements

Employees are also subject to certain requirements under the FMLA:

- ▶ 30-day advance notice (when foreseeable and practicable).

- ▶ Employers may also require employees to provide

  - ▶ Medical certification.

  - ▶ Second or third medical opinions (at the employer's expense) and periodic recertification.

  - ▶ Periodic reports during FMLA leave regarding the employee's status and intent to return to work.

- ▶ For intermittent leaves, employees must try to "work around" the needs of the workplace.

FMLA Specific Terms

There are many terms used in FMLA, the definitions of which need to be carefully reviewed in order to ensure compliance with the law (and solid preparation for the PHR exam). For instance, be certain that you are familiar with the following terms:

- ▶ Job protected leave

- ▶ 12-month period

- ▶ Health care provider

- ▶ Key employee

- ▶ In loco parentis

As an example of the complexity and the criticality of understanding the language of the FMLA, let's look at one particular term, "serious health condition."

Serious Health Conditions

The Act defines a serious health condition as

"An illness, injury, impairment, or physical or mental condition that involves either:

- ▶ any period of incapacity or treatment connected with inpatient care (i.e., an overnight stay) in a hospital, hospice, or residential medical-care facility, and any period of incapacity or subsequent treatment in connection with such inpatient care; **or**

▶ continuing treatment by a health care provider which includes any period of incapacity (i.e., inability to work, attend school or perform other regular daily activities) due to:

1. A health condition (including treatment therefore, or recovery therefrom) lasting more than three consecutive days, and any subsequent treatment or period of incapacity relating to the same condition, that **also** includes:

   ▶ treatment two or more times by or under the supervision of a health care provider; **or**

   ▶ one treatment by a health care provider with a continuing regimen of treatment; **or**

2. Pregnancy or prenatal care. A visit to the health care provider is not necessary for each absence; **or**

3. A chronic serious health condition which continues over an extended period of time, requires periodic visits to a health care provider, and may involve occasional episodes of incapacity (e.g., asthma, diabetes). A visit to a health care provider is not necessary for each absence; **or**

4. A permanent or long-term condition for which treatment may not be effective (e.g., Alzheimer's, a severe stroke, terminal cancer). Only supervision by a health care provider is required, rather than active treatment; **or**

5. Any absences to receive multiple treatments for restorative surgery or for a condition which would likely result in a period of incapacity of more than three days if not treated (e.g., chemotherapy or radiation treatments for cancer)."

The paradox of the term "serious health condition" (and so many other FMLA terms) is that, despite the large amount of effort and large number of words dedicated to defining it, in practice its meaning remains somewhat ambiguous. As with all other aspects of the FMLA, HR-related law, and the HR profession in general, a significant amount of analysis (coupled with sound judgment and careful monitoring of relevant court interpretations) is essential.

NOTE

Be aware of special USERRA rules that apply for returning reservists.

Uniformed Services Employment and Reemployment Rights Act (USERRA), 1994—*Mandatory Benefit Program*

The Uniformed Services Employment and Reemployment Rights Act (USERRA) provides reinforcement rights for individuals who miss work because of "service in the uniformed services," which is defined as voluntary or involuntary uniformed service.

Employers are required to inform their employees of their rights under USERRA. This requirement can be met by displaying a poster that clearly outlines employees' rights and obligations under USERRA. An example can be downloaded at http://www.dol.gov/vets/programs/userra/poster.pdf.

REVIEW BREAK

We've looked at laws—those that guide and regulate as well as those that create certain benefits. Now, let's take a look at specific types of optional, or "voluntary," benefits (which therefore, by definition, are not government mandated).

Optional Benefits Programs

Let's now take a look at some of the different types of benefits programs organizations offer that are voluntary.

> **NOTE**
>
> Voluntary benefits are ones that the organization freely chooses to offer, perhaps because those benefits are consistent with designing a total compensation package that is consistent with the organization's total compensation philosophy.

Retirement Plans

By definition, retirement plans "defer" income—and therefore defer the tax that must be paid on that money until it actually becomes income, which occurs at the time of distribution. Here are some examples of specific retirement plans.

Defined Benefit Plan

Defined benefit plans represent a more traditional type of pension plan, in which the employer shoulders the balance of the risk. This risk stems from the non-negotiable fact that defined benefit plans promise to pay the employee a specified monthly benefit at retirement. This "specified monthly benefit" could be expressed as an actual dollar amount, or it could be calculated through some sort of formula (this is the more common method). Either way, the PBGC protects participants in defined benefit plans by ensuring that, within certain limitations, the promised benefits will be paid.

> **NOTE**
>
> Defined benefit plans tend to be more advantageous to longer term employees.

One interesting, and slightly different, type of defined benefit plan is the "cash balance plan." A cash balance plan is a defined benefit plan that expresses the promised benefit in terms of a stated account balance (similar to the way a defined contribution plan works). Most of the time, each participant's cash balance plan account is credited annually with a "pay credit" (the percentage of compensation that his or her employer contributes) and an "interest credit" (either a fixed or variable rate of interest).

Defined Contribution Plan

Unlike defined benefit plans, defined contribution plans do not "promise" a specific monthly benefit (or total benefit) at retirement. Instead, the employer and/or the employee contribute to the employee's individual retirement savings account. Those contributions are then invested—investments which can either make money, or lose money. In this way, defined contribution plans shift the risk away from the employer (which is where it rests for defined benefit plans) and back onto the employee.

NOTE

This "shift" may account for part of the reason why defined contribution plans are increasing in popularity, while defined benefit plans are decreasing in popularity (keep in mind that neither of these is legally mandated).

At the "end of the day" (meaning, at the time of retirement), what's there is there. No promises have been made, therefore no promises about total payouts can be broken. (This does not, of course, mean that the ERISA guidelines of fiduciary responsibility are waived—they absolutely apply to defined benefit plans as well as to defined contribution plans.)

NOTE

Defined contribution plans tend to be more advantageous to shorter term employees.

Examples of defined contribution plans include 401(k) plans, employee stock ownership plans, and profit-sharing plans.

Employee Stock Ownership Plan (ESOP)

An employee stock ownership plan (ESOP) is a type of defined contribution plan in which investments to individual accounts are made primarily in the form of employer stock. ESOPs offer certain tax advantages to employers, as well as to employees.

Profit Sharing Plan

A profit sharing plan is a type of defined contribution plan under which the organization makes contributions to its employees' accounts. These contributions often come from profits, and thus also serve as an incentive to performance.

Simplified Employee Pension Plan (SEP)

A simplified employee pension plan (SEP) allows employers to make contributions on a tax-favored basis to individual retirement accounts (IRAs) that employees set up for this purpose.

Health and Welfare Benefits

Organizations can choose from a wide array of health and welfare benefits, a few of which are explored here.

Medical Insurance

Employers and employees can choose from several different types of medical insurance plans.

Indemnity Insurance

The most traditional type of medical insurance plan, indemnity plans provide participants with (virtually) unrestricted choices relative to their doctors, hospitals, and other health care providers. Health care providers are paid a fee for the services they actually provide and perform. Hence, the more services that are provided, the greater the fees that will be paid. This is one reason why indemnity plans are usually one of the most expensive type of medical insurance programs from which employers and employees can choose.

Health Maintenance Organizations (HMOs)

Health maintenance organizations, or HMOs, offer a very different model of health care, one that is referred to as "managed care." One significant difference between HMOs and indemnity plans centers around "choice." While participant "choices" are nearly unlimited in indemnity plans, participant choices are more closely managed (and many would argue more limited) with HMOs.

For instance, with indemnity plans, participants make choices relative to which doctors they will go to and how often they will go. In an HMO, each participant chooses a primary care physician, or PCP, who serves as a gatekeeper. Participants must see their PCPs first, and the PCP then decides whether to refer the patient to a specialist or for additional tests.

In this sense, HMOs truly do "manage" participants' health care experiences. There are advantages and disadvantages to this approach. Some would argue that HMOs are beneficial in that they emphasize preventive care, and control health care costs. And since participants can change their PCP, there is still a critical element of choice inherent to the plan. In addition, HMOs provide a full range of health care including doctor's visits, specialist services, hospitalization, surgical services, and so on.

Others would argue that HMOs are overly restrictive. With an HMO, a referral from a primary care physician is required before a participant can see a specialist or get any tests done. In addition to being administratively burdensome (and inconvenient), some would argue that this disempowers participants about their own personal health care choices.

Another concern of HMOs centers around "capitation," the basis on which doctors are paid. What this means, essentially, is that each PCP is paid each month for every person who chooses that doctor to be his or her PCP—*not* for the actual amount of care that is provided. In short, providing more care won't generate more revenue—in fact, it dilutes the physician's earnings (not in terms of actual dollars, but in that the physician gets paid the same amount of money for doing "more work"). Some individuals do not feel this is problematic, while others believe it incents physicians to provide patients with fewer services.

Preferred Provider Organizations (PPOs)

A preferred provider organization (PPO) is a managed care health insurance plan that offers a network of health care providers who band together to offer services at a discounted rate to plan participants. PPOs resemble indemnity plans, in that network providers are paid when they render services and plan participants can choose which doctors they want to visit and when they want to visit them. Plan participants can also choose to avail themselves of doctors or other health care providers who are outside the network; however, the costs to the member will be higher than they would have been if the member had chosen a doctor within the network.

Point of Service (POS)

Point of service plans (POSs) are a combination of the HMO and PPO managed care models. Like the PPO model, there is a network of physicians and health care providers who have agreed to provide services at a discounted rate. Like the HMO model, there is a gatekeeper—a primary care physician who must provide plan members with referrals to specialists and for other services. Unlike the HMO model, however, referrals can be made to physicians who are either inside or outside the network. While out-of-network referrals will cost participants more, they are permissible.

Dental Insurance

Like medical insurance described previously, dental insurance can be offered through an indemnity program, an HMO network, or a PPO network. There are also some specific categories of coverage within dental plans, each of which is likely to offer a different level of reimbursement.

Preventive Care

"An ounce of prevention is worth a pound of cure"—that adage is perhaps no more apparent than in dental care (with, of course, the possible exception of performance management—see chapter 5). Preventive care includes things such as regular dental checkups, exams, cleanings, and sometimes X-rays. It is often reimbursed at 100% of cost (or at 100% of reasonable and customary (R&C) expenses), so as to encourage plan members to take advantage of measures that encourage good oral health and that potentially decrease long-term costs.

Restorative Care

Restorative care, as its name implies, refers to oral "repairs" that are usually of a relatively minor nature, such as cavities or root canals. The reimbursement for restorative care is generally less than the reimbursement rate for preventive care (perhaps 80% instead of 100%).

Major Restorative Care

For those readers who are thinking "you think a root canal is *minor*?" please understand that "minor" is a relative term that is used to describe the degree of restoration that is required, not necessarily the degree of discomfort that is experienced. By comparison, major restorative care—which would be reimbursed at an even lower rate (perhaps 50%)—refers to things such as bridgework and crowns.

Orthodonture

Orthodonture—braces, headgear, retainers, and the like—is a benefit that is often reimbursed at 50%. Unlike the other types of dental insurance discussed previously, orthodonture is often subject to a lifetime cap—perhaps in the vicinity of $1,000–$1,500. For multiple children (dependents under the age of 19) with multiple oral challenges, plan members can burn through this benefit relatively quickly. It still, however, represents a significant savings over full-cost orthodonture, and may be highly valued by that segment of your employee population with children to raise, palates to spread, and teeth to straighten.

Vision Coverage

Vision coverage is a little different from the other health and welfare benefits we've looked at so far. Unlike those other plans, an employer will typically offer vision coverage as a discount program (generally around 10%). Vision coverage generally includes items such as exams, contact lenses, and glasses.

Prescription Drug Coverage

As the cost of prescription drugs rises, prescription drug coverage is becoming an even more highly valued employee benefit. Some employers provide prescription drug coverage as part of their medical plan, while others provide this coverage under a separate plan. Plan members may be required to pay a co-pay, to purchase their prescriptions at certain pharmacies, to use generic drugs (when available), or to use "mail order" services for maintenance drugs (prescriptions that are prescribed for chronic, long-term conditions and that are taken on a regular, recurring basis). Even with these restrictions, prescriptions drug coverage can be a huge benefit to employees.

Life Insurance

Term life insurance is also considered to be a valuable benefit by many employees, as a way of ensuring that they can provide their beneficiaries and loved ones with income in the event of their deaths. Many employers offer a certain amount of life insurance at no cost to employees, and offer optional supplemental life insurance, as well.

Long Term Disability Insurance

Long term disability (LTD) insurance replaces a designated percentage of an employee's income that is lost through illness or injury.

> **EXAM ALERT**
>
> In addition to being familiar with different types of health and welfare plans, be sure to familiarize yourself with various funding options for those plans. such as fully insured plans, partially insured plans, administrative services only (ASO) plans, third-party administrator (TPA) plans, and self-insured plans. It's equally important to be familiar with cost-shifting and cost-containment strategies and options.

Pay for Time Not Worked

Pay for time not worked refers to situations in which employees receive compensation for sick days, vacation days, jury duty, personal time, designated holidays, floating holidays, bereavement leave, and the like.

> **NOTE**
>
> Pay for time not worked is a benefit that is highly valued by many employees, overused by some, and underused by a few others. "Free time" for employees, however, isn't "free of charge" to the organization. From the organization's perspective, pay for time not worked needs to be "costed out" just like any other benefit.

Work-life Programs

The same can be said for work-life (balance) programs. Programs such as flexible schedules, job sharing, telecommuting, and compressed work weeks can be a great advantage for employees, and a great way for employers to market themselves in the relevant labor market, as well. Still, don't institute any program without conducting careful analysis and assessment first (see "ADDIE: An Overview," in Chapter 5).

Chapter Summary

Compensation, benefits, and the synergies created by the combination of those two disciplines are both technically challenging and strategically impactful. Knowledge and insight in both of those areas is critical.

The specific areas we've looked at are

- C&B Footing #1: Employee or independent contractor?

- C&B Footing #2: Exempt or non-exempt?

- C&B Footing #3: Compensation + Benefits = Total Compensation

- Related Legislation: Compensation

- Compensation: Job evaluation

- Compensation: Market pricing

- Compensation: Base pay and variable pay

- Compensation: Building and using pay structures

- Related Legislation—Benefits: Laws that regulate, govern, and guide optional benefits programs

- Related Legislation—Benefits: Laws that created mandatory and optional benefits programs

- Optional benefits programs

HR professionals can enhance their value to the organization by enhancing knowledge and enhancing skills in these areas—even if they do not immediately appear to be relevant to our "primary functions." In addition, this is a crucial portion of the PHR exam. For that reason, start by learning what is here and then go beyond what is here. The value that will accrue to you, and to your organization, is unquestionably worthwhile.

Key Terms

- Compensation
- Benefits
- Employee
- Independent contractor
- Exempt
- Non-exempt
- Fair Labor Standards Act (FLSA)
- Minimum wage
- Overtime
- FairPay

- Salary
- Primary duty
- Executive exemption
- Administrative exemption
- Learned professional exemption
- Creative professional exemption
- Computer employee exemption
- Outside sales exemption
- Highly compensated employee
- Safe harbor provisions
- Total compensation
- Relevant labor market
- Lead the market
- Lag the market
- Match the market
- Direct compensation
- Indirect compensation
- Davis-Bacon Act, 1931
- Walsh-Healey Public Contracts Act, 1936
- Fair Labor Standards Act, 1938
- Workweek
- Hours worked
- Regular rate of pay
- Child Labor
- Portal to Portal Act, 1947
- Equal Pay Act, 1963
- Skill
- Effort

- Responsibility
- Working conditions
- Affirmative defenses
- Job evaluation
- Non-quantitative job evaluation techniques
- Whole job ranking
- Job classification
- Job slotting
- Quantitative job evaluation techniques
- Point factor
- Factor comparison
- Market pricing
- Market data
- Labor market competitors
- Job match
- Aging
- Base pay
- Variable pay
- Incentive plans
- Short-term incentives—individual
- Short-term incentives—team/group
- Gainsharing
- Profit sharing
- Pay structures
- Grades
- Ranges
- Range spread
- Broadbanding

- Compa-ratio
- Employee Retirement Income Security Act (ERISA), 1974
- Vesting
- Cliff vesting
- Graded vesting
- Plan administrator
- Summary plan description
- Fiduciary
- Fiduciary responsibility
- Pension Benefit Guaranty Corporation (PBGC)
- Retirement Equity Act, 1984
- Qualified Domestic Relations Order (QDRO)
- Consolidated Omnibus Budget Reconciliation Act (COBRA), 1985
- COBRA qualifying event
- Older Worker's Benefit Protection Act (OWBPA), 1990
- Health Insurance Portability and Accountability Act (HIPAA), 1996
- Preexisting condition
- HIPAA privacy rule
- HIPAA covered entity
- Mental Health Parity Act (MHPA), 1996
- Sarbanes-Oxley Act (SOX), 2002
- Worker's Compensation
- Social Security Act (SSA), 1935

- Old Age, Survivors, and Disability Insurance (OASDI)
- Retirement benefits
- Disability benefits
- Survivor's benefits
- Medicare
- Medicare—Part A
- Medicare—Part B
- Unemployment insurance
- Revenue Act, 1978
- Section 125
- Flexible benefits
- Cafeteria plans
- Premium-only plans (POPs)
- Flexible spending accounts (FSAs)
- Full cafeteria plan
- Section 401(k)
- Family and Medical Leave Act (FMLA), 1993
- Job protected leave
- 12-month period
- Health care provider
- Key employee
- In loco parentis
- Serious health condition
- Uniformed Services Employment and Reemployment Rights Act (USERRA), 1994
- Defined benefit plan

- Cash balance plan

- Defined contribution plan

- Employee stock ownership plans (ESOPs)

- Profit sharing plans

- Simplified employee pension plan (SEP)

- Health and welfare benefits

- Medical insurance

- Indemnity insurance

- Health maintenance organization (HMO)

- Primary care physician (PCP)

- Preferred provider organization (PPO)

- Point of service (POS)

- Dental insurance

- Preventive care

- Restorative care

- Major restorative care

- Orthodonture

- Vision coverage

- Prescription drug coverage

- Life insurance

- Long term disability insurance (LTD)

- Pay for time not worked

- Work life programs

Apply Your Knowledge

This chapter focuses on issues relating to compensation and benefits. Complete the following exercises, review questions, and exam questions as a way of reviewing and reinforcing the knowledge and skills you'll need to perform your responsibilities as an HR professional, and to increase the likelihood that you will pass the PHR examination.

Exercises

1. You've recently been promoted to a position as an HR generalist, and you're anxious to get down to work. One day, a manager who you haven't worked with before comes to you to talk about a problem he's having with one of his direct reports. The direct report happens to be an executive assistant, and is a highly trusted and valued member of the department. He handles confidential information, and is always looking to grow and to learn. The employee feels, however, that he has been "held back" because he's classified as non-exempt, and therefore can't join in with the team on special projects that require overtime or weekend work (there is no money in the budget for overtime hours). This employee ends up feeling excluded and less important. The manager wants you to help him find a way to reclassify the position as exempt. Which of the following responses would be the least appropriate?

    ○ **A.** The manager should help the employee understand that he truly is a valued member of the team.

    ○ **B.** Based on the information the manager has given you, the position should be upgraded, but the title would have to be changed.

    ○ **C.** The position should be evaluated to see how it has changed since the last review, and whether it should be upgraded.

    ○ **D.** The manager should have a conversation with the employee about his career objectives.

2. You work as the sole HR professional in a relatively small organization. Recently, the company conducted its first employee survey, and the results indicated that employers don't understand how the company sets its pay rates—in other words, they don't know *why* they are paid *what* they are paid. The company president, who happened to recently read an article during a cross-country flight about "total compensation philosophy," has asked you to draft one. He wants it "fast, good, and cheap." You know that no one source of information alone will give you everything that you need, but you've got to start somewhere. Which of the following do you think would be of greatest value to you as you put together this document?

    ○ **A.** A sample "total compensation philosophy" statement from a reputable HR-related website.

    ○ **B.** A "total compensation philosophy" statement from a local company that is well-known for being an "employer of choice."

    ○ **C.** Your organization's mission, vision, and values statement, along with the organization's employee handbook.

    ○ **D.** A brochure from a consulting firm that specializes in communicating with employees about compensation-related issues.

3. A manager who you know fairly well, and with whom you have a good working relationship, leaves a voice mail message for you, asking you to please call her back about a benefits question. You return her call, and she comes down to your office to speak with you in person. She explains that her former assistant, who left nearly a year and a half ago to go back to college, is about to run out of COBRA. She explains to you that he still is one semester away from earning his degree, and can't get decent health insurance through the college plan. She asks if you wouldn't mind leaving him on COBRA, just for a few more months. You know that you've got to formulate a response that accomplishes a number of things, including providing accurate facts. Which of the following facts would be the most appropriate to share?

    ○ **A.** You inform the manager that, under COBRA, former employees who are full-time students at the time that COBRA runs out are entitled to an extension for as long as the former employee remains a full-time student (up to 18 months).

    ○ **B.** You inform the manager that although COBRA only requires an employer to continue benefits coverage for 18 months, the employer has the option to extend COBRA benefits for an additional 18 months.

   ◯ **C.** You inform the manager that COBRA can be continued for another 18 months, as long as the employee pays the company 110% of the monthly premium costs.

   ◯ **D.** You inform the employee that COBRA cannot be continued beyond 18 months in this particular situation, but that there are other situations that would warrant an extension, and that you would be happy to share that information with her.

4. You're the HR manager at your organization, and report directly to the president (whose sister died of cancer about six months ago). One afternoon, an employee comes to you with a problem. Her sister (who lives out of state) has been diagnosed with a very aggressive form of cancer, and has less than six months to live. The employee wants to spend the last few months of her sister's life with her, to share time with her and to care for her in her final days. The employee has already requested a leave of absence, but was advised by an HR representative and her manager that this sort of leave isn't covered under FMLA. Your department is going into its "busy season," so her manager is unwilling to grant any other type of leave. She is concerned about how she will support herself while she is staying with her sister. She asks you whether it would be possible for the company to call this a layoff and approve of her getting unemployment insurance. Sadly, she knows that her sister won't live longer than six months, so unemployment insurance benefits would carry her through. After you express your concern and sympathy for her sister's condition, which of the following responses would be best?

   ◯ **A.** Tell the employee that it's up to the state, not the company, whether or not unemployment insurance will be granted, and that, while you do sympathize with her situation on a personal level, it's not possible for you to code the termination as a layoff.

   ◯ **B.** Tell the employee that it's up to the state, not the company, whether or not unemployment insurance will be granted. However, as long as the president approves (and you're pretty sure he will), you're willing to code the termination as a layoff.

   ◯ **C.** As HR, your role is that of employee advocate, and you are willing to advocate on her behalf to the president. You are fairly confident that he will approve this request, and will get back to the employee either way as soon as possible.

   ◯ **D.** You remind the employee, as gently as possible, that, as HR, your role is to ensure that all of the company's policies and procedures are followed, and falsifying the termination code would be a violation of policy. As such, you just can't code the termination as a layoff.

5. As the HR manager, you've been looking for creative ways to provide employees with greater benefits without incurring significant additional costs. Your company already has a POP in place. Which of the following would you be most likely to recommend?

   ◯ **A.** FSAs

   ◯ **B.** PCAs

   ◯ **C.** ESOPs

   ◯ **D.** PNGs

Review Questions

1. Describe the similarities and differences between defined benefit plans and defined contribution plans.

2. Why is it important to communicate with employees about their compensation and benefits programs?

3. Define what is meant by "total compensation" and "total compensation philosophy."

4. What is meant by the term "internal equity"?

5. What is meant by the term "relevant labor market"?

Exam Questions

1. Which of the following statements about workweeks is not true?

   ○ **A.** A workweek is any fixed and regularly recurring period of 168 hours.

   ○ **B.** The employer can select any day (and any hour) of the calendar week on which to begin the workweek.

   ○ **C.** The employer can establish different workweeks for different employees or groups of employees.

   ○ **D.** The hours that an employee works during different workweeks within the same pay period can be "averaged."

2. Which of the following would not be considered an affirmative defense under the Equal Pay Act?

   ○ **A.** Seniority

   ○ **B.** Diversity

   ○ **C.** Quality of production

   ○ **D.** Merit

3. Which of the following statements about the point factor method of job evaluation is true?

   ○ **A.** Point factor systems do not establish levels of performance within each compensable factor, since that would constitute making the error of evaluating the person instead of the position.

   ○ **B.** There is a greater likelihood of rater subjectivity with point factor methods of job evaluation than with whole job methods, since point factor systems require the evaluator to make more judgments.

○ **C.** The product of a completed job evaluation will generate information that will be helpful to establishing a job worth hierarchy.

○ **D.** While point factor systems address evaluative information about different compensable factors, they do not address the relative importance of each compensable factor.

4. Which of the following could generate a calculation that represents "range spread"?

○ **A.**
$$\frac{\$55,000}{\$61,000} = 90.1\%$$

○ **B.**
$$\frac{\$80,000 - \$50,000}{\$50,000} = \frac{\$30,000}{\$50,000} = 60\%$$

○ **C.** $100,000 - $40,000 = $60,000

○ **D.** None of the above

5. Which of the following was established by ERISA?

○ **A.** Enhanced protection for plan members with preexisting medical condition.

○ **B.** A clearer definitions of "hours worked" for purposes of minimum wage and overtime payments.

○ **C.** Whistleblower protection for employees who report fraud against shareholders.

○ **D.** Minimum participation and vesting standards for retirement programs.

6. Fiduciaries must do all of the follow *except*

○ **A.** Protect plan participants by diversifying plan investments

○ **B.** Act with skill, care, prudence, and diligence

○ **C.** Avoid conflicts of interest

○ **D.** Follow the terms of plan documents without deviation

7. Which of the following did the REA not accomplish?

○ **A.** Lowered the minimum age requirement for pension plan participation, and increased the years of service that count for vesting purposes

○ **B.** Prohibited plans from counting maternity and paternity leaves as breaks in service for participation and vesting purposes

   ○ **C.** Required qualified pension plans to provide automatic survivor benefits that could be waived only with the written consent of the plan participant

   ○ **D.** Clarified that pension plans may obey certain qualified domestic relations (court) orders (QDROs) without violating ERISA

8. "PHI" refers to

   ○ **A.** Health information that relates to a specific individual.

   ○ **B.** A managed care health option offered to federal and state government employees

   ○ **C.** Information that was used as part of the "long form" test under the old provisions of the FLSA

   ○ **D.** Information that must be maintained in according with the record-keeping requirements of the FLSA

9. Which of the following is not one of the three main provisions of the Social Security Act?

   ○ **A.** Retirement benefits

   ○ **B.** Pension protection

   ○ **C.** Survivor's benefits

   ○ **D.** Disability benefits

10. Which of the following is *not* required of covered entities by the HIPAA privacy rule?

   ○ **A.** Designation of a privacy officer

   ○ **B.** Creation of a code of ethics that applies to all employees who have access to health-related information

   ○ **C.** Establishment of a complaint handling and resolution process for issues related to the HIPAA privacy rule

   ○ **D.** Agreements signed by business associates stating that they will respect the confidentiality of patient information

Answers to Exercises

1. **Answer B is the best response.** First, reclassifying a position from "non-exempt" to "exempt" is a decision that must be made after much analysis—analysis that is grounded in actual job responsibilities, rather than because of a particular incumbent (or a particular incumbent's feelings). Also, FLSA status is determined on the basis of the responsibilities that are performed, not on the basis of job title. Lastly, it is best to refer to this process as "reclassifying," not "upgrading," in that the word "upgrading" seems

to reinforce the fallacy that it is better or more desirable to be exempt than it is to be non-exempt. Answer A is not the best response; it would be appropriate for the manager to help the employee understand how he contributes to, and is valued by, the team. Answer C is not the best response; it is possible that the position might have changed enough to warrant a reclassification, and a job evaluation would provide information that is necessary for making that assessment. Answer D is not the best response; this might be an appropriate opportunity for a manager to have a discussion with the employee about his career objectives.

2. **Answer C is the best response.** The first, and best, source of information that you can have when communicating with employees about compensation is any resource (written, or otherwise) that expresses, reflects, and articulates the mission of the organization. This is the only way to be sure that your comp philosophy truly aligns with, and will therefore help fulfill, your organization's "reason for being." Although other items are important, if you don't capture the essence of your own organization, any statement of compensation philosophy that you draft will likely be hollow and ineffective. Answer A is not the best response; while it may be useful to review (and perhaps even be inspired by) a sample total comp statement from a reputable HR-related website, "vanilla" statements aren't as valuable to you in this process as information about your own organization. Answer B is not the best response; a total compensation philosophy that works brilliantly for one organization (no matter how successful that organization might be) may be completely inappropriate for another organization. Answer D is not the best response; outside consultants may be able to develop a "good" statement "fast," but "cheap" might be a bit unrealistic. Give this a try on your own first—your organization will appreciate your efforts as well as your budget-sensitive approach.

3. **Answer D is the best response.** It is true that, according to the facts you have been given, COBRA can't be extended; however, it's also true that there may be other facts of which you're not aware. Be helpful, and also be factual and accurate. Answer A is not the best response; there is no provision under COBRA that states that an extension beyond 18 months is available for former employees who are full-time students. Answer B is not the best response; COBRA does not allow employers to continue benefits coverage beyond legally specified time frames. Answer C is not the best response; COBRA allows for participation to continue for up to another 18 months only under specific circumstances (and those circumstances cannot be "bought" with a 10% surcharge).

4. **Answer A is the best response.** First, it is important for the employee to understand how the process works, so it is appropriate to share that information with her. No matter how much you feel for her, however, and regardless of any other personal circumstances that might be "pulling at your heart strings," there are many reasons (ethical, legal, procedural, financial, and so on) why you would not falsify a termination code.

You don't, however, need to go into all those reasons with the employee (although you might want to consider following up with the manager to see if you can come up with any creative solutions). Answer B is not the best response; although the factual information at the beginning of this response is correct, there are many reasons (ethical, legal, procedural, financial, and so on) why you should not falsify the termination code. Answer C is not the best response; as HR, your role is to be a "truth advocate," not an employee advocate (and the truth, in this case, is that the employee wasn't laid off). Answer D is not the best response; prattling on about policies and procedures at this moment isn't the best approach, and might only serve to reinforce the notion of HR as the "personnel police."

5. **Answer A is the best response.** Like a POP (premium only plan), an FSA (flexible spending account) falls under Section 125. An FSA goes one step further than a POP, by allowing employees to set aside pre-tax dollars to pay for medical expenses that are not covered by insurance. This lowers the employee's taxable income, which benefits the employer as well as the employee. Answer B is not the best response; PCA refers to the Walsh-Healey Public Contracts Act (PCA), which was passed in 1936. Answer C is not the best response; an ESOP (employee stock ownership plan) involves the distribution of stock and are much more complex than establishing FSAs. Creating an ESOP has many implications, and would not constitute an appropriate solution for a problem such as this. Answer D is not the best response; "PNG" is not a commonly known acronym in HR.

Answers to Review Questions

1. Some of the differences and similarities between defined benefit and defined contribution plans are summarized in the following table:

	DB Plans	DC Plans
Nature of the plan	More traditional type of pension plan	Less traditional type of pension plan
More risk is shouldered by…	The employer	The employee
What will the plan pay out to the employee?	Promises to pay a specified monthly benefit at retirement	Makes no guarantees about the value of the plan as of the time of retirement

2. Organizations must communicate with employees about their compensation and benefits programs, with respect to each element of each program and to the program as a whole. First, employees may not truly understand all of the benefits that they enjoy as employees of an organization. This leads to a second reason communicating with employees about compensation and benefits is important—most employees simply do not know the real costs, let alone the actual value, of the benefits they receive (this

holds true for government mandated as well as optional benefits). In a very real sense, employees earn benefits, just like they earn cash compensation, and they should know what they are earning. Without this measure of communication, it is more likely that even those benefits that are *not* entitlements may ultimately begin to feel like entitlements to employees, rather than something they have earned in return for their services to the organization.

3. The term "total compensation" refers to all of the compensation- and benefits-related elements that employees within an organization earn and enjoy. An organization's total compensation philosophy, however, represents far more than just the amount of cash it pays to employees or even the "fringe benefits" that it provides. Instead, it speaks volumes about what the leaders of that organization value, the results they want to attain, the behavior they want to encourage, and their commitment to their employees. It is a clear and direct expression of the organization's mission, vision, and values—*regardless of whether that was the organization's intention.* Even the absence of a clearly defined compensation system or philosophy sends a very clear message, so be certain that it is the message that your organization truly wants to convey.

4. "Internal equity" refers to fairness (or "equity") within a department and/or organization with respect to the ways in which jobs are ranked and individuals are compensated.

5. The relevant labor market relates to the size and scope of the geographic area within which an organization would seek to attract qualified candidates. Even within the same organization, the relevant labor market for different positions can vary widely depending upon the skills, knowledge, abilities, and behavioral characteristics required to perform each position successfully. Other factors that impact how an organization defines the relevant labor market might be the degree of competition that exists among employers for particular skills and/or knowledge and the degree to which certain skills and/or knowledge requirements are industry-specific.

Answers to Exam Questions

1. **Answer D is the best choice.** The hours that an employee works during different workweeks cannot be averaged, even when those weeks are during the same pay period. Answers A, B, and C are not the best choices, since each one makes a true statement about the definition of a "workweek."

2. **Answer B is the best choice.** Diversity has not been designated as an affirmative defense under the equal pay act. Answers A, C, and D are not the best choices, since seniority, quality of production, and merit would all be considered affirmative defenses under the Equal Pay Act.

3. **Answer C is the best choice.** The information that is generated through the job evaluation process *will* provide information that is helpful to establishing a job worth

hierarchy. Answer A is not the best choice, since point factor systems *do* establish levels of performance within each compensable factor. (As long as evaluations are conducted relative to the performance expected of the position rather than on the basis of the incumbent's individual performance, the job evaluation will still be job-based rather than person-based.) Answer B is not the best response, since the potential for rater subjectivity is *lower* with the point factor job evaluation method than it is with whole job methods of job evaluation. Answer D is not the best choice, since point factor systems *do* address the relative importance of each compensable factor.

4. **Answer B is the best choice.** The formula to calculate range spread is

$$\frac{\text{Maximum} - \text{Minimum}}{\text{Minimum}} = \_\_\%$$

Answer A is not the best choice, since it represents a calculation that could generate a compa-ratio. Answer C is not the best choice, since it represents a calculation that could generate the numerator of the range spread formula. Answer D is not the best choice, because A was correct.

5. **Answer D is the best choice.** ERISA did establish minimum participant and vesting standards for retirement programs. Answer A is not the best choice, since enhanced protection for plan members with preexisting medical conditions was established by COBRA. Answer B is not the best choice, since a clearer definition of "hours worked" for purposes and minimum wage and overtime payments was established by the Portal-to-Portal Act. Answer C is not the best choice, since it represents a whistleblower protection for employees who report fraud against shareholders was established by Sarbanes-Oxley.

6. **Answer D is the best choice.** Under ERISA, fiduciaries must follow the terms of plan documents *to the extent that those terms are consistent with ERISA, not* simply without deviation. Answers A, B, and C are not the best choices, since they each state something that fiduciaries are required to do.

7. **Answer C is the best choice.** The Retirement Equity Act (REA) requires that the participant *and his or her spouse* must waive the provision that provides for automatic survivor benefits. (This provision cannot be waived independently by the plan participant, as answer C implies.) Answers A, B, and D are not the best responses, since each states an accomplishment of the REA.

8. **Answer A is the best choice.** PHI stands for "protected health information" that relates back to one individual. Answers B, C, and D are not the best choices, since each offers a fabricated definition that is wholly unrelated to PHI.

9. **Answer B is the best choice.** Pension protection is addressed through ERISA, not through the Social Security Act. Answers A, C, and D are not the best choices, since retirement benefits, survivor's benefits, and disability benefits are the three major provisions of the Social Security Act.

10. **Answer B is the best choice.** The HIPAA privacy rule requires creation of a code of ethics that applies to the company's key officers (within a "covered entity"). At a minimum, this code must apply to the company's principal executive officer, principal financial officer, principal accounting officer or controller, or persons performing similar functions. It does not, however, have to apply more broadly within the organization. Answers A, C, and D are not the best response, since each cites a requirement to which covered entities under HIPAA must adhere.

Suggested Readings and Resources

www.worldatwork. com—WorldatWork

International Foundation of Employee Benefit Plans (IFEBC)—CEBS (Certified Employee Benefit Specialist) Designation: www.ifebp.org/cebs/usprogram.asp

www.bls.gov—Bureau of Labor Statistics

www.ecornell.com—eCornell, offering online programs on compensation and benefits

The Compensation Handbook, by Lance A. Berger, Dorothy R. Berger

Employee Benefits: A Primer for Human Resource Professionals, by Joseph J. Martocchio

Employee Benefits, by Burton T. Beam Jr., John J. McFadden

Compensation, by George Milkovich, Jerry Newman

CHAPTER SEVEN

Employee and Labor Relations

Study Strategies

Although the PHR exam is multiple choice, try writing and answering your own "essay-based" questions. Write open-ended questions that require a response of at least a full paragraph and write your answers without looking back at your study materials. The process of actually writing down your answers will reinforce what you already know, and will highlight what you need to study more. It will also likely help you as you work to recall this same information when you answer related multiple choice questions on the actual PHR exam.

As with each of the six functional areas of HR, determine what you already know and what you don't know. Then, work to prepare yourself. Conduct research. Use the Internet to find articles and white papers that highlight employee relations and labor relations (particularly if you don't have experience working in an organized workplace). Peruse textbooks that provide guidance relative to those particular areas. Be sure to find several real-life examples of each responsibility to ensure that you gain a variety of perspectives and insights. This is particularly important for the skill-based, rather than fact-based, components of this functional area.

Introduction

Employee relations…labor relations…what are these topics all about, and why are they important to HR professionals? The answer to this question is sometimes presented in ways that are overly simple, and it is sometimes presented in ways that are exceedingly complex. In this chapter, we'll try to strike an appropriate balance between these two extremes.

Let's first take a look at employee relations, since all employees, whether members of a union or not, *are*, in fact employees.

> **NOTE**
>
> Although this may seem like an axiomatic statement, it warrants mention. Why? Because sometimes, in the midst of the complexities, challenges, and opportunities of dealing with organized labor, organizations (and the people within those organizations, including HR professionals) wrongly perceive "labor" as an amorphous entity, perhaps even an opponent, without a specific identity. In fact, quite the opposite is true. Labor is a group of employees who happen to be organized to speak with a collective voice.

In its most straightforward sense, the definition of "employee relations" can be found in the words "employee" and "relations." Within this context, employee relations can be described as

The way in which an organization responds to, handles, and/or addresses any issue that has impact on employees, and their relationships

- to and with other employees

- to and with managers

- to and with those outside the employment in the organization with whom they come in contact as part of their employment experience

For many, this is a new and unfamiliar way of looking at employee relations, since many individuals, HR and non-HR alike, are more accustomed to thinking of employee relations in "functional" terms. By this, we mean that employees may define "employee relations" in terms of what the "Employee Relations Department" does within their individual organization. All too often, this perspective can lead to a limited and/or a misguided definition of what employee relations is all about. Why? Because HR can end up being saddled with the reputation of being "party planners," "personnel police," "the terminators," and other unhelpful, incomplete, and inaccurate stereotypical imagery.

In thinking about this definition of employee relations, one might be left to wonder whether there is anything that *isn't* part of employee relations? The answer, as one might expect, is "that depends." In many ways, so much of what happens in our world, the states and localities in which we live, and the organizations in which we work has an impact, in one way or another, on the workplace and on the people who work there.

Let's now shift for a moment to "labor relations," which, in some ways, is a "subset" of employee relations. How? Because the term "labor relations" is most frequently used to refer to those individuals who are "organized"—or, in other words, who belong to and are represented by a union who will collectively bargain on their behalf.

When considering labor relations, it's particularly important to keep an historical perspective in mind, not only because the history of labor is so rich, but also because the history of labor has had such a significant impact on the lives of *all* workers—whether or not those workers happen to belong to a union.

EXAM ALERT

PHR test preparation warrants a review of some of the key people, events, and concepts that emerged in the historical timeline of labor history—a timeline that spans the history of our nation (and some would argue even prior to that). Some of the key people, events, and concepts with which you should familiarize yourself are

- ▶ Knights of Labor
- ▶ Great Uprising
- ▶ Samuel Gompers
- ▶ "Bread and butter unionism"
- ▶ Haymarket
- ▶ AFL
- ▶ Industrial Workers of the World (IWW)
- ▶ Mary Harris "Mother" Jones
- ▶ Triangle Shirtwaist Company
- ▶ Electric Auto-Lite Strike
- ▶ CIO
- ▶ UAW
- ▶ Walter Reuther
- ▶ AFL-CIO

Let's start our journey into employee relations and labor by looking at those principles that unite these disciplines. We'll then move into the distinctions that apply separately to these two areas.

Employee Relations/Labor Relations (ER/LR) Unifying Principle #1: EEO

Beginning with the passage of the Civil Rights Act of 1964 (the first major civil rights legislation), a series of laws has been enacted in an effort to end unlawful discrimination in all terms and conditions of employment. These laws fall under the broad category often referred to as related to as "equal employment opportunity," or EEO.

Key EEO-related Terms

In going through this section, and as you prepare for the PHR exam, there are a couple of terms that you'll need to be familiar with:

▶ **Charge**: A formal complaint, submitted to an agency, that alleges unlawful discrimination.

▶ **Charging Party**: A person who alleges that he or she has experienced unlawful discrimination (also called the "complainant").

▶ **Complainant**: A person who alleges that he or she has experienced unlawful discrimination (also called the "charging party").

▶ **Plaintiff**: A party who files a lawsuit alleging unlawful discrimination.

▶ **Respondent**: The person or party against whom a charge of unlawful discrimination has been filed.

▶ **Fair Employment Practices Agencies (FEPAs)**: State or local agencies that are responsible for enforcing EEO laws that are specific to their respective jurisdiction.

> **NOTE**
>
> At the state level, 47 states (all except Alabama, Arkansas, and Mississippi) have agencies that respond to charges of EEO violations.

Federal, State, and Local Jurisdictions

On the federal level, the agency charged with enforcing many of the laws that are aimed at eliminating discrimination is the Equal Employment Opportunity Commission (EEOC).

> **NOTE**
>
> More information about EEO laws can be found in Chapter 4.

Sometimes, charges can be filed under two or even three jurisdictions. For instance

- ▸ If a charge is filed with a FEPA and is also covered by federal law, the FEPA "dual files" the charge with EEOC to protect federal rights. In this scenario, the FEPA will usually maintain responsibility for handling the charge.

- ▸ If a charge is filed with EEOC and is also is covered by state or local law, EEOC "dual files" the charge with the state or local FEPA. In this scenario, the EEOC will usually maintain responsibility for handling the charge.

At other times, when a state or local EEO law is more protective than the corresponding federal law (or when a corresponding federal law does not exist), a charge may be filed only with the FEPA whose laws offer greater protection to employees.

Filing Charges: Time Limits and Related Restrictions on Filing Lawsuits

Different time limits and different rules apply to different EEO-related laws under different circumstances. Specifically, let's take a look at the rules surrounding filing charges of discrimination and private lawsuits for specific laws.

Title VII of the Civil Rights Act (Title VII)—ADA and ADEA

Before an individual can file a private lawsuit alleging unlawful discrimination under Title VII, the Americans with Disabilities Act (ADA), or the Age Discrimination in Employment Act (ADEA), he or she must first file a charge of discrimination with the EEOC.

- ▸ When there is no FEPA, charges must be filed with the EEOC within 180 days of the alleged discriminatory act.

- ▸ Where there is a FEPA, charges must be filed with the state or local agency. Charges may then be filed with the EEOC within 300 days of the discriminatory act, or 30 days after receiving notice that the state or local agency has terminated its processing of the charge, whichever comes first.

Equal Pay Act (EPA)

The rules are a little bit different under the EPA. Under this act, an individual is not required to file a charge with the EEO before filing a private lawsuit. For this reason, the time limits stated previously do not apply to claims under the Equal Pay Act. The EEOC, however, explicitly cautions individuals that "it may advisable to file charges under both laws within the time limits indicated" since many EPA claims also raise sex discrimination issues that would fall under Title VII.

EEOC—Handling Charges

Once a charge of discrimination has been filed, the EEOC sends a letter to the organization notifying the organization that a complaint has filed. At this point, some employers will decide to "settle." There are any number of reasons why an organization might decide to settle, just a few of which are

▶ To elude the requirement of providing information to the EEOC.

▶ To avoid allocating resources (financial, human, emotional, and otherwise) to the process of responding to a charge of discrimination, especially if it appears that the costs of fighting may outweigh the "benefits" (even if the organization believes that no unlawful discrimination has taken place).

▶ To prevent the possibility of bad press that can, at times, be generated even by the mere filing of a charge of discrimination.

▶ To seek a resolution to a situation where the employer believes that there may be exposure (in other words, where the charge of discrimination may be valid).

Alternatively, many employers choose *not* to seek a settlement agreement when a charge of discrimination is first filed. In such situations, there are four primary ways that the EEOC can handle the charge:

▶ **Investigate it**: Investigations can be designated as "high priority" or "non-high priority," depending upon the strength of the facts that have been presented in the charge. An EEOC investigation can take myriad forms, including written requests for information, in-person interviews, document reviews, and even a visit to the location where the discrimination allegedly occurred.

▶ **Settle it**: This can happen at any stage of the investigation if the charging party and the employer are both interested in reaching a settlement. If no settlement is reached, the investigation resumes.

▶ **Mediate it**: The EEOC offers a confidential mediation program as an alternative to a lengthy investigative process. In order for a charge to be mediated, the charging party and the employer must both be willing to participate. If the mediation process is not successful, the charge will be investigated.

▶ **Dismiss it**: A charge can be dismissed at any point in the process if the agency determines that further investigation will not be able to establish that the alleged unlawful discrimination actually occurred. When a charge is dismissed, a notice is issued in accordance with the law that gives the charging party 90 days within which to file a lawsuit on his or her own behalf.

EEOC Determinations

The EEOC determines whether there is "reasonable cause" to believe that unlawful discrimination has occurred.

If the EEOC determines that there is *no reasonable cause*, the case is closed, the parties are notified, and the charging party is given a "right to sue" letter. The charging party then has 90 days to file a private lawsuit.

If the EEOC determines that there *is reasonable cause*, the EEOC will attempt conciliation with the employer in an effort to develop a remedy for the discrimination. If the EEOC cannot conciliate the case, the EEOC will decide whether or not to take the case to court (this happens in a very small percentage of cases). If the EEOC does not take the case to court, it will close the case and issue the charging party a "right to sue" letter.

The charging party can also request a right to sue letter from the EEOC 180 days after the charge was filed (60 days for ADEA). Under the EPA, lawsuits can be filed within two years of the alleged discriminatory act (three years if the act was "willful").

> **NOTE**
>
> A charging party may not bring a case to court if the charge has been successfully conciliated, mediated, or settled.

> **NOTE**
>
> Different processing guidelines are in effect for federal employees.

EEO—Going to Court

If a case *does* proceed to court, HR's role will vary significantly depending upon a host of factors. For instance, in some organizations, HR may be called upon to assist in-house or outside counsel with responding to a complaint, or to collect data as part of the discovery process, and/or just to be available to assist and facilitate the process in any way necessary. Depending upon HR's role in the actual case, HR professionals may be deposed, testify, and/or represent the organization during the trial—in a sense, being the "face" of the organization to the jury and the judge.

> **NOTE**
>
> It is important to keep in mind the critical and unique role of juries. A "jury of one's peers" might be more likely to identify with a plaintiff than with an organization. In short, from the perspective of the organization, the stakes are higher, and the turf is a bit less friendly, than they were before 1991.

Remedies

When a plaintiff prevails, he or she may be awarded the following forms of "relief" or remedies (whether the discrimination was intentional or unintentional):

▶ Back pay

▶ Hiring, or front pay (instead of hiring the individual)

▶ Promotion

▶ Reinstatement, or front pay (instead of rehiring the individual)

▶ Reasonable accommodation

▶ Other actions that will make an individual "whole" (in the condition that he or she would have been but for the discrimination)

▶ Attorneys' fees

▶ Expert witness fees

▶ Court costs

Compensatory and punitive damages may also be available when the discrimination is found to be intentional (and in rare cases, even when the discrimination is unintentional).

NOTE

This highlights the reality that any situation could potentially devolve into a lawsuit. Sometimes, there is just nothing you can do to prevent that from happening. It's also not helpful to worry excessively about the possibility of litigation. The best thing that any of us can do is to ensure that we handle situations well (and consistently), that we seek to de-escalate situations whenever possible, that we invite employees to raise concerns internally, and that we—along with the clients with whom we consult—conduct ourselves in a manner that, if subject to scrutiny, will hold up.

CAUTION

HR plays various roles in the organization, one of the most important of which is the role of proactive observer. In short, if you believe that a situation has the possibility to produce a charge of discrimination or any other legal challenges, let counsel know. Depending on the culture of your organization, seek input from counsel as you go along. Also remember the fine line that HR cannot cross—HR professionals cannot practice law. We must, however, recognize then we need to call in someone who can (such as in-house or outside counsel). This can, at times, be a fine line to walk.

REVIEW BREAK

Now that we've had an opportunity to look at employee relations principles and EEO guidelines laws and regulations that apply to all employees—whether or not they are covered by a collective bargaining agreement—let's take a look at an equally fundamental premise that applies to employee relations as well as labor relations: the fact that "good employee relations is good employee relations."

Employee Relations/Labor Relations (ER/LR) Unifying Principle #2: "Good Employee Relations Is Good Employee Relations"

Good employee relations is good employee relations, *whether or not* the employees in question happen to belong to a union. In turn, good employee relations fosters enhanced morale, which in turn strengthens the organization's culture. A stronger culture impacts and shapes the kinds of employee relations initiatives that will be most effective. When well-handled, this circle of influence can evolve positively and productively.

Employee Relations: External Considerations

As mentioned earlier, it's hard to think of anything that *doesn't* have an impact on employee relations. This is just as true of external considerations as it is of internal considerations.

To demonstrate this, we chose a newspaper at random and scanned the headlines. Within minutes, we compiled a list of factors that can have a direct impact on employee relations (as defined earlier). Just a small portion of that list (in alphabetical order) included

- Aging workforce
- Climate changes
- Crime (corporate and otherwise)
- Drug use in schools
- Drug use in professional sports
- Economic conditions—national, regional, and local
- Energy prices
- Energy supplies
- Ethical breaches

- ▶ Executive compensation
- ▶ Globalization: management versus leadership
- ▶ Home prices
- ▶ Misappropriation of funds
- ▶ Organ donation
- ▶ Outsourcing/offshoring
- ▶ Same sex marriage
- ▶ Security/homeland security
- ▶ Social promotion (in schools)
- ▶ Sports
- ▶ Supreme Court
- ▶ Technology and technological developments
- ▶ Unemployment
- ▶ War/international unrest
- ▶ Weather events

Even with a cursory review of these items, it's relatively easy to make legitimate, meaningful connections that demonstrate how each of these topics could, in one way or another, impact employee relations, as defined earlier.

Even if the organization decides not to respond to factors such as those listed above, make no mistake, the organization is still making a decision. As is mentioned elsewhere in this book, "you can't not communicate." In that sense, employee relations is defined just as much by what an organization *doesn't* do as it is by what an organization *does* do.

Employee Relations: Internal Considerations

The considerations listed previously represent external elements that impact employee relations. While these are critical, it's also important to consider internal elements that can impact employee relations. Perhaps the most important internal consideration impacting employee relations is organizational culture.

Organizational Culture

Organizational culture casts an expansive, inclusive, and incredibly wide net. It encompasses historical events, current events, and future events (whether potential, likely, or simply rumored). More specifically, organizational culture reflects and embodies the norms, mores, values, beliefs, customs, and attitudes of the organization, and of those who work within the organization. It is thought of by some as the "soul" or "personality" of the organization.

Organizational Culture—What It Is

Sometimes, we don't fully recognize the importance that organizational culture has on the day-to-day workings of the organization. There is also sometimes a tendency to think of organizational culture of something nebulous. In reality, the opposite is true.

To begin to get a grasp on this idea, let's consider the work of Terrance E. Deal and Allan A. Kennedy, who have studied culture extensively for decades. Deal and Kennedy identified four specific dimensions of culture:

- **Values**: The beliefs that lie at the heart of the corporate culture

- **Heroes**: The individuals who embody those values

- **Rites and rituals**: Routines relative to the way that people interact that have strong symbolic qualities

- **The culture network**: The information system of communication, or the "hidden hierarchy of power" within an organization.

In this sense, Deal and Kennedy's definition of culture helps us recognize the tangible impact and manifestation of organizational culture. This hands-on expression of organizational culture is what employees see and experience every day. To employees, these four dimensions of culture provide a much more meaningful description of culture than any formal organizational communication strategy (by itself) ever could. It is for this reason, in part, that we as HR professionals do a disservice to ourselves and our clients if we limit our awareness to the "formal" definitions of culture.

In addition to Deal and Kennedy, Edgard Schein also sheds important insights into organization culture, which, when boiled down to its basics, is about shared assumptions, adapting, integrating, and assimilating new members. In short, Schein seems to be saying that organizational culture speaks to "the way we do things around here."

Like Deal and Kennedy, Schein reaches beyond the formal dimensions of culture to recognize the power and impact inherent in the more subtle dimensions of culture, which in turn begins to speak to the *importance* of organizational culture.

Organizational Culture—Its Importance

Schein was quite direct about the importance of organizational culture. In his 2004 book *Organizational Culture and Leadership*, Schein wrote about the possibility that a group's very survival could be threatened by the emergence of problems relating to its culture, and the resulting need for leaders to rise to the occasion and address those cultural issues.

At this point, some readers may be wondering, "Threatened survival? Isn't that a bit overly dramatic?" The answer, however, is a clear and unequivocal "no." Deal and Kennedy also identify culture as the single most important factor contributing to an organization's success or failure. And Deal and Kennedy are not alone in their assertion:

▶ In *Ideas Are Free*, Robinson and Schroeder explore the ways in which organizational culture can impact the ideas generated by the organization.

▶ In *HR from the Heart*, Sartain and Finney stress the criticality of culture as a business issue.

▶ In *Reinventing Strategy*, Pietersen links organizational culture to employee performance, and ultimately to the overall success or failure of the organization.

▶ In *The Fast Forward MBA in Business*, O'Brien looks at culture in terms of productivity, profitability, and overall performance.

If we can agree to the premise that culture is a significant factor contributing to the overall success of an organization, the next step that we as HR professionals must take is to focus on how we can use effective employee relations initiatives as a way of strengthening an organization's culture and, therefore, moving the organization closer to the attainment of its objectives. Two important ways this can be accomplished is through employee communication programs and employee involvement strategies.

Employee Involvement and Employee Communication

Employee communication and employee involvement are two separate, albeit closely interrelated, types of programs. Both are important components to effective employee relations, and neither is as effective without the other. In addition, when well executed, each can strengthen the role of the other.

Let's take a look at each of these topics, and more importantly the tools and initiatives that can bring them to life.

Employee Communication Strategies

One cornerstone, perhaps *the* cornerstone, of effective employee relations is effective communication. We'll look at communication in terms of communicating *with*—and not just communicating *to*—employees.

Handbooks

Employee handbooks are an important and frequently used method that organizations use to communicate information about policies, procedures, and rules. Handbooks provide, in a sense, the "rules of the road" in that they ensure that employees are fully informed (in writing) about the obligations and the benefits that are associated with being an employee.

Handbooks can vary widely in terms of the information they contain, their length, the topics they cover, and the tone in which they are written. The following topics represent a sampling of what employee handbooks can address:

▶ Introduction (for example, welcome, history, mission, vision, values)

▶ Statement relating to collective bargaining unit (if applicable)

▶ EEO-related policies (for example, statements and/or policies pertaining to equal employment opportunity (EEO) and/or affirmative action (AA); diversity and inclusion; employees with disabilities; sexual harassment; religious accommodation; employment eligibility and verification [I-9 form])

▶ Job performance (for example probationary period for new employees/transferred employees, performance management and appraisal, progressive disciplinary process)

▶ Behavioral expectations (for example, conduct and work rules, work behavior, appropriate attire, workplace equipment and supplies, absenteeism and tardiness)

▶ Positions (for example, job grading system, job regrading, non-exempt and exempt FLSA status)

▶ Benefits programs (for example, health plans, prescription drug plans, dental plans, retirement plans, flexible spending accounts, life insurance, disability insurance, child care, elder care)

▶ Pay (for example, compensation policy, overtime pay, comp pay, time reporting system, pay procedures, direct deposit)

▶ Workplace as community (for example, transportation, parking, public transportation, carpooling, cafeteria, health and fitness center, ATM, company store, travel agency, bowling league, softball league)

▶ Leave programs (for example, FMLA, jury duty, holiday/sick/vacation leave, and so on)

▶ Terminations (for example, voluntary [resignation, retirement]; involuntary [layoff, dismissal, job abandonment, failure to successfully complete probationary period])

▶ Employee records

▶ Conflicts of interest

▶ Substance abuse policy

- Smoking policy
- Inclement weather and other emergency conditions
- New hire/new transfer orientation
- Company ID cards
- Hours of work (workweek, meal/break periods)
- Safety and security
- Development and training
- Employee assistance programs
- Retirement programs
- Educational and tuition reimbursement benefits

While they do not necessarily have to be written in a legalistic manner (and may be even more valuable and effective if they are not), handbooks can have significant legal impact. In the event that an employment related decision (for instance, relating to discipline, termination, or other terms or conditions of employment) is questioned or challenged, the handbook will serve as a key piece of evidence that will be closely scrutinized by all parties.

One factor that will significantly impact whether the handbook will support the *employer's* position or the *employee's* position is the presence or absence of an "employee acknowledgement." From the perspective of the employer, every employee should acknowledge, either in writing or electronically, that he or she received, read, had the opportunity to ask, and in fact did ask any questions that he or she might have relative to the information contained within it. This, in effect, removes or greatly diminishes the effectiveness of the *"I had no idea"* defense. In addition, when policies are added or updated, organizations should strongly consider obtaining a written or electronic acknowledgement from each employee (that, once again, confirms that the employee received, read, had the opportunity to ask, and in fact did ask any questions that he or she might have relative to the new or updated policy).

> **NOTE**
>
> Cultural as well as legal considerations need to be weighted when deciding how to handle the distribution of and updating of employee handbooks. As is so often the case with HR, "how" we handle and communicate relative to a situation is just as important as "what" we handle or communicate.

"But What I *Meant* by That Was…"

Because handbooks can have such far reaching legal impact, it is critical that counsel review and approve handbooks, policies, and updates to either of these before they are distributed to employees. In this way, counsel can ensure that legal concerns do not unintentionally arise from the language that is used.

For instance, handbooks sometimes are written using language that can unintentionally create an implied contract that might jeopardize the employment-at-will relationship. The term "permanent employee," for example, can raise questions of this sort. For this reason, most attorneys advise that employees should be referred to as "regular," not "permanent." Equal care must be taken when the progressive discipline and probationary policies are crafted, for similar reasons.

In addition to all of the carefully crafted language that must be included throughout the handbook, organizations also often choose to have an attorney draft an overall statement that is included at the beginning of the handbook, on the signed acknowledgement sheet, or in both places. This statement would reconfirm that the employment relationship is "at will," that the handbook does not create a contract, and that no other oral or written agreements or statements can override the employment-at-will relationship unless they are specifically designated as such.

Despite all this apparent legalese, handbooks must be user friendly. If the culture is the organization's "soul" then the handbook is (in one sense) its voice. It is the document to which employees will refer over and over again, and needs to written in a clear and readable manner. It may even be appropriate to print the handbook in a variety of languages, depending upon the demographics of the workforce.

Town Hall/Department/Staff Meetings

In short, hold them routinely. Share information, and be open to receiving and acting upon feedback.

Newsletters, Emails, Intranet Communication

All of these methods represent potentially excellent ways of sharing information, and can be made even more effective if employees are encouraged to make these traditionally "one way" communication methods more dynamic. Create mechanisms through which feedback is sought and collected, and develop ways to encourage employees to actually partake in these mechanisms.

"Word of Mouth"

Don't waste your energy trying to deny that informal communications and methods exist. They do, and they can't be eliminated. Nor should they be, as long as they do not become destructive. Instead of trying to "wish away the grapevine," consider shifting your perspective. In other words, to the degree that is possible and appropriate, consider how you might be able to use those informal communication channels to your advantage.

Employee Involvement Strategies

The line between "communication strategies" and "employee involvement strategies" is cloudy, as, in many ways, it should be.

In order for an organization to practice effective employee relations, the employment experience can't just happen "to" employees. Such an approach implies detachment and disempowerment. Instead, HR professionals must seek to actively and meaningfully involve employees in the experience of their own employment.

There are a variety of employee involvement strategies. In this section, we'll focus on the following:

- Employee surveys
- Focus groups
- Employee participation groups
- Open door policy
- Suggestion programs
- Management by walking around (MBWA)

Employee Surveys

Employee surveys (also sometimes called "attitude surveys" or "climate surveys") provide employees with the opportunity to express their opinions and to share their perspectives. Sometimes, employee surveys can even provide a vehicle through which employees can truly contribute in a meaningful and significant way to their organizations by having a voice in shaping the policies, practices, and direction of their organizations.

In order for employees to fully participate in the survey process and to make truly valuable contributions, employees must fully and clearly understand the purpose of the survey, be assured anonymity, and receive feedback relative to the survey results.

Four functional reasons for organizations to conduct surveys are

- To gauge and measure employees' perceptions, viewpoints, and attitudes
- To take the pulse of specific employee current and/or potential issues
- To collect information that can be used by the organization to help set priorities
- To provide a benchmark—a "snapshot", in a way—of employees' viewpoints and perspectives. This will enable you to establish a baseline from which you can later draw comparisons.

> **NOTE**
>
> While they offer many advantages, surveys are not the only, nor are they necessarily the best, employee involvement tool for any particular situation. Before you choose whether to use a survey, be sure to consider the advantages and disadvantages of various employee involvement tools. If you work in an organization where a survey has been used in the past, be careful to look thoroughly into that process: what was done, how it was done, and what the outcomes were. This is particularly important since there is a great deal of disparity with respect to the methodology applied to and quality of employee survey administration.

If you decide that you are going to conduct an employee survey, there are 10 general steps to follow:

1. Secure management buy-in, starting with the senior levels of management

2. Determine the survey content

3. Determine the survey methodology (for instance, online, hardcopy, in person, mail, open-ended, closed-ended, and so forth)

4. Develop the survey

5. "Market" the survey

6. Conduct the survey

7. Calculate the results

8. Interpret the results

9. Share the results

10. Act upon the results

How a survey is designed and conducted are two critically important factors that will contribute significantly to determining the overall success or failure of the survey process. This design, and the actual survey, can be conducted within the organization or by consultants from outside the organization.

Either way, the process of simply conducting a survey isn't enough to make an employee survey a valuable involvement strategy. First of all, whether the survey is administered internally or through a consultant, it is absolutely essential to ensure that the survey is conducted in a confidential manner, and just as importantly that participants *believe* in the confidentiality of the process. Another critical element that will contribute significantly to determining the ultimate success of a survey is the degree of follow-up that occurs after the survey administered. This does not mean that all requests expressed through surveys must be granted. It does, however, mean that survey results must be reported back to participants, and that specific requests and recommendations must be acknowledged and addressed.

Focus Groups

Focus groups provide another means of communicating with and involving employees in the organization. A focus group consists of a small but representative sample of individuals within an organization. These group discussions are led by a neutral facilitator who seeks to elicit feedback and input on a specific subject. Focus groups can range in size, with an ideal number of participants ranging from 10 to 15 people. In determining the size of the focus group, the objective is to ensure that you have enough people to generate a dynamic and synergistic discussion, but not so many people that there is insufficient time for participants to meaningfully contribute their ideas. It's also essential to ensure "groupthink" does not derail the group from its mission.

Focus groups can be used independently or as a follow-up tool to an employee survey, since focus groups afford a degree of flexibility that a survey simply cannot provide. Successfully facilitating a focus group, however, does require a far greater level of interpersonal skill than is required for survey administration. In addition, while surveys require a significant level of trust if they are to be successful, focus groups require an even greater level of trust. This is true in part since anonymity is by definition impossible when people are participating together in a focus group.

If you decide to use a focus group, be sure to thoroughly address the five following "steps for success":

1. Develop the right questions

2. Involve/include all stakeholders

3. Determine how many focus groups you need to conduct (this may be a function of the size of the population involved, the scope of the issues involved, the number of distinct stakeholder groups, the amount of time you have, the amount of money you have, and the number of skilled and consistent facilitators at your disposal)

4. Arrange the logistics (who, when, where, how, how long, and so forth)

5. Conduct the meetings, select moderator/facilitator, establish and agree upon ground rules, ensure consistent participation, ask probing questions, ensure continuity across focus groups, and so on.

> **EXAM ALERT**
>
> Be familiar with the techniques, advantages, and disadvantages of focus groups. In addition, based on the potential strengths and weaknesses of surveys and focus groups, be prepared to identify situations in which a focus group would be the preferred employee involvement approach, situations in which a survey would be the preferred employee involvement approach, and situations in which a "combined" approach might be most effective.

Employee Participation Groups

Employee participation groups invite employees to participate actively in the process of managing the organization. Through these groups, employees can contribute ideas and provide feedback. Employee participation groups can also provide an excellent way of encouraging creative involvement and enhancing commitment.

CAUTION

Under the National Labor Relations Act (NLRA), *it is possible* that employee participation groups could be found to be "company dominated" and therefore be rendered illegal.

While employee participation groups are neither legal nor illegal by definition, the way in which they are administrated can have a huge impact on whether any particular group is deemed to be legal or illegal.

Open-door Policy

An "open-door" policy is just what its name implies—a "standing invitation" for employees to raise their concerns with managers and/or human resources, face to face. The use of an "open door" cannot result in penalties, formal or otherwise, against those employees who avail themselves of these resources.

"Betrayer? Me? I Was Only Doing My Job."

Open-door policies highlight another reason why we must not promise confidentiality, lest we end up being perceived as "betrayers of trust." There are times when *we are obligated* to reveal information that has been shared with us. Situations like this can crop up unexpectedly, especially in organizations where an open-door policy is in effect.

Ensuring discretion and reassuring that you will only reveal information on a "need to know basis" is one thing. Promising "confidentiality" is something entirely different.

Complaint handling and resolution is a skill, an art, and a discipline. Proceed with skill, knowledge, and caution to ensure that you do not unintentionally step into a situation that can damage your credibility, perhaps beyond repair.

Suggestion Programs

Suggestion programs invite employees to submit their ideas, usually anonymously, unless they choose to reveal their identity. Ideas are usually welcomed relative to any work-related topic, such as improving work systems, identifying or eliminating safety concerns, or even exposing unethical (or criminal) behavior.

Questions submitted through suggestion programs or "boxes" need to be responded to quickly, regardless of whether the suggestion is implemented. Employees must *be* heard, and *feel* heard, in order for any suggestion program to be successful.

Management by Walking Around (MBWA)

"Management by walking around" (MBWA) is an acronym that has been around for many years, and is just as valid now as it was years ago. Neither HR professionals nor managers can hide in their offices. If we isolate ourselves, we cannot be surprised when we end up being marginalized. It is up to each of us, individually and collectively, to make the choice to "get out there" and to keep our finger on the pulse of the workplace and the workforce.

Progressive Discipline as Employee Relations

Though not often thought of as an employee relations or employee involvement program, progressive discipline programs can be both. This is despite the fact that the word "discipline" evokes unpleasant associations for many if not most of us. For some, it may elicit thoughts of a relationship where there is an imbalance of power, a sense of disempowerment or helplessness, or even a tendency to judge or to blame. For others, it may simply conjure up images of "being in trouble," and therefore represent one or more steps along the path to termination. A third possibility is that it may simply equate to "punishment."

It is in this context that we must once again ensure that we fix the true definition of "employee relations" in the forefront of our awareness: *anything that impacts relationships with, among, or for employees.* For even through the disciplinary process, our focus on employee relations/relationship-building must be maintained.

It is also in this context that we can benefit greatly from remembering Dick Grote's idea of "discipline without punishment" (published in his 1995 book of the same name). Discipline is not a way to "pave a paper trail." Discipline must be seen as a way to give employees the opportunity to help themselves. More specifically, discipline can be used as a tangible way of supporting employees in their efforts to address and resolve their own performance issues. It can, in short, serve as a means to "turn around" employee performance so as to meet or even exceed performance expectations.

TIP

This vision may be consistent with the culture of your organization and the mindset of the managers whom you support. It is also important to recognize, however, that it might contradict the ideas of managers who might view discipline as a way to "pave a paper trail" that will enable them to terminate an employee. If you encounter that mindset, move cautiously. Remember your role—you are a consultant and a business partner. You are not there to say "no," nor are you there to enable behaviors that might prove to be problematic and/or counterproductive. Keep the ultimate objectives of the organization in mind as you work with your managers—you might be surprised to see just how far a collaborative problem-solving approach can take you.

It is in this spirit that the process of "progressive discipline" emerges as a truly untapped opportunity. Progressive discipline is a system that incorporates a series of steps, each more progressively "involved," advanced, or serious, than the last.

The progressive discipline process is predicated on the belief that—assuming that an employee is at least minimally qualified for the position for which he or she was hired—an employee can choose whether or not to perform his or her job satisfactorily. There are, of course, other factors involved—for instance, the very assumption that the employee is at least minimally qualified for the position for which he or she was hired.

> **NOTE**
>
> Like most of the general concepts that we're exploring in this section, the concept of progressive discipline generally holds true for employees who belong to a union as well as for employees who do not belong to a union. As always, however, specific progressive disciplinary steps that are outlined in a collective bargaining agreement could overrule the concepts explored here.

Principles of Progressive Discipline

There is no single "best approach" to the specific steps in progressive discipline; however, there are some important ideas to keep in mind.

Employees Choose to Discipline and Even Terminate Themselves

Technically speaking, it is true that either the employer or the employee can make a decision to terminate the employment relationship for any lawful reason (assuming, of course, the absence of an employment contract or collective bargaining agreement that stipulates otherwise). Within that range of possibilities, it's also true that an employer can choose to "fire" an employee who doesn't meet the performance standards of his or her position.

Another way of looking at this, however, is that, within the structure of progressive discipline, each employee makes choices relative to whether he or she will meet the expectations of his or her position. These choices can, ultimately, lead to a larger choice: whether to terminate him/her self.

What does this mean? Well, let's first say what it *doesn't* mean—we're not talking about employees who "see it coming" and quit before their employer terminates them.

Now, let's take a look at what it *does* mean. An employer's decision to terminate an employee is made, to a greater or lesser degree, because an employee will not, or cannot, bring his or her performance up to expected levels. Employees have some degree, perhaps even a large degree, of control over that decision. How? An employee may not perform at expected performance levels, for instance, because he or she chose

- ▶ Not to get additional training

- ▶ Not to turn to his or her manager for support or assistance

- ▶ Not to change specific behaviors

- ▶ Not to cease certain behaviors

- ▶ Not to begin certain behaviors

Ultimately, progressive discipline provides multiple opportunities at multiple decision points for employees to make choices that will result in them maintaining their employment. When applied appropriately, therefore, progressive discipline truly is an empowering process.

Fairness Isn't Sameness

When it comes to progressive discipline (and, for that matter, many other dimensions of the employment relationship), "fairness" doesn't mean "sameness." Or, to use other words, just because you're treating everyone "the same way" doesn't mean that you're treating everyone fairly.

An idea that needs to be taken into consideration during the progressive discipline process, as at other times, is referred to as "similarly situated employees." This term does have a legal meaning, and thus needs to be defined by lawyers. However, just for purposes of understanding the concept better, let's look at this concept in an admittedly non-legal manner. With that caveat, "similarly situated employees" are employees who are, in one way or another, in "the same boat." In terms of the ADEA, for instance, this could mean employees who are over 40 years of age, or who are under 40 years of age. In the context of Title VII of the Civil Rights Act of 1964, similarly situated employees might share the same gender, race, or color. The concept of "similarly situated employees," however, isn't limited to civil rights legislation. For example, employees who are being considered for a position and who possess similar credentials could, in one sense, be "similarly situated."

It's also possible, and often advisable, to look at progressive discipline in terms of whether different employees are similarly situated. In this context, being similarly situated could be a function, in part, of each employee's level of performance—ideally, in comparison to the SMART goals that were established for and with the employee at the beginning of the performance measurement period (see Chapter 5). In addition to performance against goals, it might also be important to consider other factors such as the length of time the employee has been employed with the organization, how long it has been (if ever) since the employee demonstrated any performance problems, whether there are extraordinary reasons for the performance issues, and the like.

To reiterate, looking at whether employees are "similarly situated" doesn't mean that we, as employers and HR representatives, should treat all employees the same. It does mean that we should be, in one sense, "consistently inconsistent." This is part of what makes our profession an art as well as a science.

> **CAUTION**
>
> Nothing in this section changes the fact that many organizations (whether unionized or not) identify specific behaviors that can, do, and will result in immediate termination. Those behaviors might be listed in an employee handbook, a collective bargaining agreement, or the like. It is also important to remember that it is not possible to enumerate every behavior that could result in disciplinary action or immediate termination, so situations must also be looked at—in concert with management and with counsel—with an open mind.

Progressive Discipline Steps

Often, progressive disciplinary processes will include the following steps:

1. **Discussion of problem ("coaching," rather than "counseling")**—If progressive discipline is truly an employee relations initiative, it must be grounded in open communication, collaboration, and an effort to achieve a common objective: the attainment of the organization's objectives, and the furtherance of its mission. And all of this can start with discussion. Sometimes, and there are those who would argue "often," this step, when performed well, may be able to preclude the need to engage in the balance of the progressive discipline processes, thereby taking less of a toll on the organization itself and on the employees who work within it.

2. **Verbal warning**—The next step in the progressive discipline process is verbal warning. This step moves a step beyond discussion, because the tone is closer to "counseling," rather than to "coaching." In other words, when the process moves to a verbal warning, there is a problem, not just a situation. There are those, however, who say that a verbal warning is "not worth the paper it's not written on." These individuals might assert that the most important aspect of a verbal warning is the message that is conveyed by the tone of the communication, rather than the actual words that are used. Once again, the idea or hope is that in response to the "escalation" from coaching to verbal warning, the employee will choose to bring his or her behavior up the stated performance standards.

3. **Written Warning**—At this point, the counseling is formal, as is the actual written warning. Sometimes, the reality of seeing a written warning is enough to help an employee recognize the gravity of a situation. In other words, sometimes messages do not truly seem "real" until they are written.

4. **Final written warning and/or suspension**—This is the final opportunity the employee has to change his or her behavior before the behavior, if continued, will result in termination. Some organizations will suspend employees with or without pay (FLSA considerations must be observed for exempt employees so as not to forfeit their

exempt status). Others will present the employee with a date by which he or she must make a commitment to bring his or her behavior up to the expected standards.

> **NOTE**
>
> Depending on the organization, this step could actually be broken into one, two, or even three sub-steps.

Either way, the written documentation accompanying this step will likely include language to the effect that continuing substandard performance will lead to further disciplinary action, up to and including termination.

> **CAUTION**
>
> Here again, it is particularly important to consult with counsel relative to the language that is used in any warning letters, and particularly in final written warning letters. Care must be taken neither to create any sort of implied contract that the employee's employment will continue for any period of time, nor to use language that can limit the employer's response to continued substandard performance.

5. **Involuntary termination**—There comes a point at which it is no longer advisable or productive to continue the employment relationship. It is at this point that managers, with the assistance and support of HR, end the employment relationship. Even this, however, must be done with respect, empathy, and dignity.

> **EXAM ALERT**
>
> Review best practices relative to progressive discipline and be prepared to answer questions related to those practices. For instance, tolerating substandard performance and/or inappropriate behaviors is unacceptable and ill-advised for a number of reasons. First, those employees who *are* meeting standards will get a message—a *troubling* message—loud and clear: *"Why should I work so hard, since nothing happens to those who aren't pulling their weight?"* Those who are not meeting standards will get a message, as well: *"I guess I can continue to act this way, or perform at this level, since no one seems to have a problem with it."*

Employee Relations—What's the Bottom Line?

Often, HR professionals think that the purpose or "bottom line" of effective employee relations is making employees happy. It isn't. Even setting aside the fact that no one can "make" anyone else happy, there are problems with this premise. First, using the goal of "making employees happy" as our benchmark of success merely reaffirms the erroneous perception of HR professionals as "people people" rather than as business people. Second, it ignores the organization's measures of success. It is against these organizational measures of success that we must be prepared to measure our employee relations initiatives. So, to be considered successful, an employee relations initiative must bring the organization closer to achieving its objectives, furthering its mission, and attaining its vision—all while remaining consistent with the organization's values. In short, the bottom line of employee relations must measurably support and reinforce the bottom line of the organization.

Measuring Employee Relations Initiatives

As with all other areas of HR, we need to be prepared to use measures when ascertaining the success of employee relations initiatives. Just a few of the measures that might be appropriate to determine the success of employee relations initiatives could be

▶ Turnover levels

▶ Absenteeism (particularly unplanned)

▶ Work-related accidents/injuries/"preventable" illnesses

▶ Productivity

▶ Quality

▶ Return on Investment (ROI)

▶ Customer satisfaction

▶ Employee survey results

REVIEW BREAK

Up through this point, we've focused on the commonalities that unite employee relations and labor relations. At this point, however, we'll begin to look at how these areas diverge, starting with laws and legal principles.

We'll start by looking at common law and the individual employee rights that accrue from common law. In the next major section of this chapter, we'll then focus specifically on labor law and the history of labor law.

Related Legislation and Legal Systems/Concepts: Common Law and Individual Employee Rights

"Common law" refers to refers to a system of law in which traditions, customs, and precedents have the same "force of law" as existing laws or statutes that have been enacted as a result of the full legislative process. With a common law system, laws and statutes are quite literally interpreted and reinterpreted on a case-by-case basis. The way this works is that each interpretation and each case sets a precedent, but can also be reinterpreted, thus setting a new precedent. As it evolves, this process results in rights being granted to employees on an individual basis.

> **NOTE**
>
> Although in a technical sense common law applies to all employees, in all workplaces, common law is eclipsed by the presence of an individual employment contract or collective bargaining agreement. In other words, if there is an employment contract in place, or if an employee belongs to a union that has negotiated an agreement, the terms that are outlined in that contract or agreement will take precedence over the precedents created by common law.

We'll start by looking at common law and the individual employee rights that go along with it. We'll then take a closer look at the legal doctrines associated with common law—tort doctrines and contract doctrines. Lastly, we'll look at some of the legal agreements that employees are asked to make in exchange for securing employment with the organization (specifically, mandatory arbitration agreements, non-compete agreements, and confidentiality agreements).

> **NOTE**
>
> Unionized employees might also be asked to adhere to one or more of these three types of agreements in which case they would constitute articles that are included as part of a larger collectively bargained agreement.

The common law system holds true at the federal and state levels (with the exception of Louisiana, which follows Napoleonic Law). It is composed of two "sub-types" of law: tort law and contract law.

Common Law—Tort Doctrines

Torts are wrongful acts committed against another individual's property or person. By definition, the commission of a tort infringes on another person's rights.

Torts can include anything from damage or injuries sustained in automobile accident, to malicious prosecution to false imprisonment—the list could go on and on. This section, however, will specifically address some of the major tort doctrines that affect individual employee rights in the absence of an employment or labor contract. Specifically, we'll take a look at

- ▶ Employment-at-will
- ▶ Wrongful termination
- ▶ Implied contracts
- ▶ Defamation
- ▶ Invasion of privacy
- ▶ Negligent hiring
- ▶ Negligent training
- ▶ Negligent retention
- ▶ Negligent referral

Employment-at-will

Under the employment-at-will doctrine, the employer and the employee are both granted broad rights, most of which focus around the right of either party to terminate the employment relationship at any time for any *lawful* reason. A number of important exceptions to the employment-at-will doctrine exist, some of which are discussed in the following sections.

Lawful Reasons

Although seemingly self-explanatory, "lawful reasons" deserves a second look. Employees cannot be fired, for instance, for engaging in protected concerted activity, or because they belong to a particular protected class.

CAUTION

While everyone involved in the hiring/employment/termination process shares in this responsibility, HR must be particularly diligent about ensuring that a lawful, legitimate, non-discriminatory reason exists and can be articulated when a decision is made to terminate an employee.

Public Policy Exception

Most states have adopted the "public policy exception," which holds that an employer may not terminate an employee if the termination would violate public policy. For instance, an employee cannot be fired for serving on jury duty, for engaging in protected whistleblower activity, or for reporting safety violations to OSHA.

Wrongful Termination

In certain circumstances, employees who believe that they have been terminated wrongfully—in a legal sense, that is—may pursue a tort action. One possible basis for wrongful termination could exist if an employee was terminated in violation of an individual employment contract in which specific requirements were articulated. Others might apply as well, but would vary from state to state.

Implied Contracts

Just because a formal written employment contract isn't in existence doesn't mean that a contract—specifically, an "implied contract"—is not in force.

There are two primary ways that an implied contact can be created; through documents that the employer has "published," and through oral statements.

Written Documents or Publications

Sometimes, the language that is used within employer-published documents (electronic or hardcopy) can actually be sufficient to create a contract between the employer and the employees. Oftentimes, this can happen because of language that is used in an employee handbook. For instance, language in a handbook stating that an employee will only be terminated for "good cause" or "just cause" could also be problematic, in that a court could then interpret that an employer may only terminate an employee when that standard is met.

> **CAUTION**
>
> Don't dismiss the possibility of an implied contract just because your counsel has determined that your handbook doesn't create one. Any document—whether it is directed toward just one employee, all employees, or anything in between—can be submitted as evidence in an effort to support the existence of an implied contract.

"Just Cause" or "Good Cause"

"Just cause" or "good cause" refers to a particular legal standard or "test" that is used to ascertain whether a specific disciplinary action was appropriate. Factors that may be considered in determining whether this standard was met could include, but are not necessarily limited to

▶ Whether the employee was warned in advance

▶ Whether the rule or standard that was violated was reasonable

▶ Whether a legitimate investigation looking into the totality of the circumstances around the alleged violation was conducted

▶ Whether reasonable "proof" as to the violation existed or was obtained through investigation

▶ Whether the rule has been applied consistently

▶ Whether the punishment is proportionate to the violation

Oral Contract

An oral contract can be created when an "agent" of the employer "promises" some benefit or right. The term "agent" is legal and involved, but the point is this—be careful what your supervisors, recruiters and others say to current, and especially to potential, employees. If you have your doubts as to the veracity of this statement, look back at the avalanche of oral contract claims that resulted from the "dot coms" that became "dot bombs"—even a cursory glance should dispel any doubts you might have.

CAUTION

Be particularly careful not to create implied contracts through your dealings with employees *or candidates*. This may hold particularly true if you find yourself trying to "sell" the company to a prospective employee, or "convince" a current employee not to leave for another employment opportunity (this process, by the way, which is sometimes accompanied by a "counter offer," may not always be advisable, and should not be made lightly).

Good Faith and Fair Dealing

"Good faith and fair dealing" is a somewhat less frequently recognized exception to the employment-at-will doctrine.

The good faith and fair dealing exception kicks in when a court decides that an employer has treated an employee unfairly or has failed to provide some benefit to that employee. Two examples of this might be an employer who terminates an employee to avoid paying stock options, or who terminates an employee right before his or her retirement benefits vest.

> **NOTE**
>
> If you have an employment contract with an employee, you have an obligation to treat the employee fairly. In other words, "good faith and fair dealing" would likely apply.

Defamation

Defamation is a legal term that, in a general and practical sense, refers to making a false statement that damages someone's character or reputation. Defamation that is in written form is referred to as libel, and defamation that is made through the spoken word is referred to as slander. An employee could sue an employer for libel or slander for a variety of reasons, such as the provision of a false reference to potential employers.

> **NOTE**
>
> A key requirement for defamation is that the "statement" (whether oral or written) must be false. This is particularly important with respect to providing references.

Invasion of Privacy

The right to privacy is a highly complex doctrine relating to several amendments of the U.S. Constitution, in particular the Fourth Amendment:

> The right of the people to be secure in their persons, houses, papers, and effects, against unreasonable searches and seizures, shall not be violated, and no warrants shall issue, but upon probable cause, supported by oath or affirmation, and particularly describing the place to be searched, and the persons or things to be seized.

The Fourth Amendment, however, only addresses and protects individuals against searches and seizures that are conducted by the government. Invasions of privacy by individuals who are not "state actors" (a person who is acting on behalf of the government) must be addressed through private tort law, which is why we are discussing it here.

Modern tort law includes four categories of invasion of privacy:

▶ Intrusion of solitude

▶ Public disclosure of private and embarrassing facts

▶ False light

▶ Appropriation of identity

Negligent Hiring

Negligent hiring refers to the process of hiring an employee without engaging in appropriate "due diligence" into that candidate's credentials, prior work experience, and the like. Negligent hiring tort claims might be filed after an employee who was hired through a flawed hiring process inflicts some sort of harm on another person—harm that could have been predicted (and therefore prevented) if the employer had conducted a background check. A hiring process can be flawed for a number of reasons. For instance, a sound hiring process that is applied in an unsound manner would be flawed, as would a hiring process that is designed in a flawed manner. Flaws could relate to inadequate or poorly conducted reference checks, job requirements that do not reflect the skills or credentials that are truly required for a position, and the like.

Example: Tallahassee Furniture Co. v. Harrison, 1991

Tallahassee Furniture Company hired a delivery person without interviewing him, having him fill out an employment application, or conducting any sort of background check. After entering a customer's home to deliver furniture, the delivery person stabbed and raped her. It was subsequently found that this employee had a long history of psychiatric problems (which had been serious enough to result in his hospitalization) as well as a history of drug abuse. The court ruled that the company should have conducted a background check before giving him a job that afforded him access to customers' homes, and awarded $2.5 million.

Negligent Training

Negligent training refers to an employer's failure to provide proper training to an employee when that failure results in some sort of unfit performance by the employee. A negligent training tort claim might be filed, for instance, when an employee inflicts some sort of harm on another person, harm that might not have been inflicted by that employee if the employer had provided him or her with appropriate training.

Negligent training can emerge as an issue either when an employee who was hired for one position assumes another position for which he or she may not be fully and appropriately trained, or when an employee's job duties and responsibilities change over time, thus requiring additional training if the employee is to continue performing the job in a fit manner.

Example: Gamble v. Dollar General Corp.

Heather Gamble went to a Dollar General Store in Purvis, Mississippi, to buy a shirt. At some point, Gamble left the store, returned to her car, and realized that a Dollar General employee had followed her out of the store. The employee subsequently followed Gamble to a Family Dollar store and parked behind Gamble. Gamble stepped out of her car and asked the employee why she was following her. Words were exchanged, and the employee—who decided that Gamble had not (as she had suspected) shoplifted anything from Dollar General—left Gamble in the parking lot of Family Dollar. During the trial, it was shown that although Dollar General had a written shoplifting policy that prohibited employees from leaving the store to pursue suspected shoplifters and from touching shoplifters, Dollar General had not provided its employees with training on how to handle actual or suspected shoplifting situations. The jury awarded Gamble $75,000 in compensatory damages and $100,000 in punitive damages, in part on the basis of a finding of negligent training.

Negligent Retention

Negligent retention refers to the continued employment of an individual who is performing in an unfit manner and therefore should have been terminated. Negligent retention tort claims might be filed when an employee who should have been terminated, but was not, inflicts some sort of harm on another person.

Negligent retention claims are often filed in conjunction with other tort claims, such as negligent training, intentional infliction of emotional distress, and the like.

Negligent Referral

Negligent referral refers to the failure of an organization to reveal truthful, negative information about an employee (or former employee) to a potential employer.

NOTE

Negligent referral highlights the complexities of navigating the choppy waters of tort litigation. The irony in this situation lies in the reality that many organizations confine their remarks about current and former employees to the employee's name, title, and dates of employment—often in an effort to avoid defamation claims. While this approach may limit the employer's liability for defamation claims, it could simultaneously increase the employer's liability with respect to negligent reference if the employer conceals truthful negative information about an employee.

Example: Randi W. v. Muroc Joint Unified School Dist., 1997

Officials at several school districts recommended a former employee, even though that employee had been the subject of several complaints relating to sexual misconducts with students. Two situations were so serious that the employee was forced to resign. Despite all of this, the employee moved from one school district to another, bolstered in large part by recommendations from the school districts for which he had worked. Letters from the former employers recommended the employee "for almost any administrative position he wishes to pursue," and commended his efforts to make "a safe, orderly and clean environment for students and staff." He was hired at another school district, and ultimately molested a 13-year-old girl in his office. The court found that these misleading employment recommendations amounted to "an affirmative misrepresentation presenting a foreseeable and substantial risk of physical harm to a third person," and that the student who filed the complaint had successfully established a prima facie case of negligent misrepresentation.

Common Law—Contract Doctrines

Another way in which common law directly impacts the employment relationship is through "contract doctrines." A contract is an agreement that is enforceable by law. Contracts can either be oral or written.

Employment contracts are made between an employer and an employee. They can include topics such as term or length of employment, compensation and benefits, job responsibilities, and termination.

> **NOTE**
>
> The terms and conditions under which an employee can be terminated constitute a critical element of any employment contract. Specifically, the contract should state whether the employee is employed under the "employment-at-will" doctrine, or conversely whether the employee can be terminated only for "just cause."

Employees are often asked to sign specific agreements in exchange for the opportunity to work for the employer. Three agreements that we'll look at in this section include

- ▶ Mandatory arbitration agreements
- ▶ Non-compete agreements
- ▶ Confidentiality agreements

Mandatory Arbitration Agreements

More and more, potential employees are being asked to agree in writing to mandatory arbitration. This means that, in return for the opportunity to be employed by the organization, the employee agrees to resolve employment-related issues through a neutral third party (the arbitrator/s) *instead of* filing a private lawsuit against the employer.

> **EXAM ALERT**
>
> Familiarize yourself with the advantages and disadvantages of mandatory arbitration agreements, from the perspectives of the employer *and* the employee.

The landmark Supreme Court case that confirmed the legality of mandatory arbitration agreements was *Circuit City Stores, Inc. v. Adams (2001)*, in which the court ruled that requiring employees to sign mandatory arbitration agreements as a condition of employment is legal, and that such agreements are enforceable under the Federal Arbitration Act (FAA).

Less than 10 months later, in *EEOC v. Waffle House, Inc.*, the court ruled that while the existence of a signed mandatory arbitration agreement precluded the employee from being allowed to file a private lawsuit, it did *not* preclude the EEOC from seeking its own independent action against an employer, since the EEOC cannot be bound by a private arbitration agreement to which it was not a party. More specifically, the EEOC is not required to "relinquish its statutory authority if it has not agreed to do so," and that, as "the master of its own case," the EEOC can independently determine whether it will commit resources to specific cases.

Non-compete Agreements

Non-compete agreements prohibit current and (within stated limitations) former employees from competing against the employer. "Competing" can manifest itself in a number of different ways, and must be defined within the agreement, with language similar to this:

The term "not compete" as used herein shall mean that the employee shall not own, manage, operate, consult, or be employed in a business substantially similar to or competitive with the present business of the company or such other business activity in which the company may substantially engage during the term of employment.

In return for signing the non-compete agreement, the employee is given the opportunity to work for the organization.

The strength, enforceability, and even legality of non-compete agreements depends on state and/or local laws, precedents that have been set by court cases, and a variety of other factors, such as

- ▶ Whether there is a time frame established in the agreement, and, if so, how long it is in effect

- ▶ The existence (and reasonableness) of any geographic limitation within which the employee cannot compete

- ▶ Whether there is anything in the agreement that would preclude the employee from earning a living in his or her chosen field

- ▶ Whether the employee is fairly compensated for signing the non-compete agreement, particularly if the employee was already employed at the time that he or she was asked to sign the agreement

Confidentiality Agreements

Confidentiality agreements prohibit employees from revealing any confidential information to which they might be exposed during the course of their employment. This could include trade secrets, patent information, and the like. It also prohibits employees from using confidential information in any way other than the purposes for which it was intended and is necessary within the context of the employee's job.

REVIEW BREAK

In this section, we looked at common law issues, including tort law and contract law, and the impact that they have on workplaces. As stated at the beginning of this section, however, these common law provisions are overridden by any situation where a labor or employment contract is in place. Let's take a look now at those laws that govern and have shaped labor and labor-management relations.

Related Legislation: Labor History and Labor Relations

We will be looking at a number of laws that have impacted and continue to impact labor and employee relations, including the following:

▶ Sherman Anti-Trust Act, 1890

▶ Clayton Act, 1914

▶ Railway Labor Act, 1926

▶ Norris-LaGuardia Act, 1932

▶ National Industrial Recovery Act, 1933

▶ National Labor Relations Act or Wagner Act, 1935

▶ Labor Management Relations Act or Taft-Hartley Act, 1947

▶ Labor Management Reporting and Disclosure Act or Landrum-Griffin Act, 1959

NOTE

All of these laws impact labor and labor relations. As specifically indicated in this section, however, some of them impact employees who do not belong to a union, as well.

Sherman Anti-Trust Act—1890

The Sherman Anti-Trust Act, named for its sponsor John Sherman of Ohio, was passed in an effort to curb the growth of monopolies. Under the Act, any business combination that sought to restrain trade or commerce would, from that time forward, be illegal. Specifically, the Act stated

▶ Section 1: "Every contract, combination in the form of trust or otherwise, or conspiracy, in restraint of trade or commerce among the several States, or with foreign nations, is declared to be illegal."

▶ Section 2: "Every person who shall monopolize, or attempt to monopolize, or combine or conspire with any other person or persons, to monopolize any part of the trade or commerce among the several States, or with foreign nations, shall be deemed guilty of a felony."

If, after reading the two sections cited here, you're feeling a bit bemused and confused, you share something in common with those who wrestled to interpret this law more than a century ago. The vague language of the Act, however, proved to be quite challenging—particularly terms such as "trust," "combination," "conspiracy," and "monopoly." This confusion opened the door for the Sherman Act to be used against labor unions by those who chose to define those unions as "monopolies." For instance, the Act allowed the use of injunctions—court orders that could be issued to restrict certain activities, such as strikes. The first example of this was when an injunction was issued against the American Railway Union in 1894 to end its strike against the Pullman Palace Car Company. George Pullman, the president of this company, decided to reduce his workers' wages. The company refused to arbitrate, and the American Railway Union called a strike, which started in Chicago and spread across 27 states. The attorney general sought and was awarded an injunction against the union.

NOTE

The Sherman Act also placed responsibility for pursuing and investigating trusts on government attorneys and district courts.

Clayton Act—1914

Passed in 1914, the Clayton Act was enacted to build upon and clarify the Sherman Act.

The provision of the Clayton Act that is most relevant to labor—and therefore to HR professionals—is that Section 6 of the act specifically exempted labor unions and agricultural organizations from the Sherman Anti-Trust Act:

The labor of a human being is not a commodity or article of commerce. Nothing contained in the antitrust laws shall be construed to forbid the existence and operation of labor, agricultural, or horticultural organizations, instituted for the purposes of mutual help, and not having capital stock or conducted for profit, or to forbid or restrain individual members of such organizations from lawfully carrying out the legitimate objects thereof; nor shall such organizations, or the members thereof, be held or construed to be illegal combinations or conspiracies in restraint of trade, under the antitrust laws.

This section rendered labor unions exempt from the Sherman Act, and effectively legalized boycotts, peaceful strikes, and peaceful picketing—thus rendering illegal injunctions of the sort that was filed against the American Railway Union during the Pullman strike.

Railway Labor Act—1926

In 1926, the Railway Labor Act (RLA) was passed. As its name implies, the Railway Labor Act applied only to interstate railroads and their related undertakings—at the time, the most critical element of the nation's transportation infrastructure. In 1936, it was amended to include airlines engaged in interstate commerce.

The Railway Labor Act was critical in that it provided what was perhaps the first "win-win scenario" for labor and management. Railroad management wanted to keep the trains moving, which meant they needed to end "wildcat" strikes. Railroad workers wanted to organize, to be recognized as the exclusive bargaining agent in dealing with the railroad, and to negotiate and enforce agreements.

The Railway Labor Act is also significant in that it is where the "work now, grieve later" rule originated. In an effort to keep the rails running, which Congress felt was in the public's interest, Congress mandated that when disputes arise in the workplace, transportation workers covered by the RLA must "work now and grieve later" (with a few exceptions, such as for safety).

Norris-LaGuardia Act—1932

The Norris-LaGuardia Act strengthened unions even more. First, it established the rights of labor unions to organize and to strike. Secondly, it prohibited federal courts from enforcing "yellow dog" contracts or agreements.

NOTE

A *"yellow dog" contract* is a contract or an agreement between an employer and an employee, the terms of which are essentially that the employer will give the employee a job, as long as the employee agrees not to join or have any involvement with a labor union.

National Industrial Recovery Act—1933

In 1933, Congress passed the National Industry Recovery Act (NRA). Title I of the Act guaranteed laborers the right to organize and bargain collectively. The Act also established that employees could not be required, as a condition of employment, to join or refrain from joining a labor organization.

In May of 1935, the National Industrial Recovery Act was held unconstitutional by the U.S. Supreme Court (*Schechter Poultry Corp. v. United States*). Although this decision was wholly unrelated to labor and collective bargaining, the Supreme Court decision rendered the labor-related provisions illegal, as well. The right to organize and bargain reverted, once again, back to railway workers—and no one else. This would not, however, be the case for long.

National Labor Relations Act (Wagner Act)—1935

Two months later, Congress passed the National Labor Relations Act (NLRA). Also known as the Wagner Act (named for Senator Robert R. Wagner of New York), the NLRA guaranteed "the right to self-organization; to form, join, or assist labor organizations; to bargain collectively through representatives of their own choosing; and to engage in concerted activities for the purpose of collective bargaining or other mutual aid and protection."

NOTE

Certain groups or categories of employees are excluded under the NLRA from membership in a bargaining unit. Examples would include managers, supervisors, confidential employees (essentially secretaries and administrative assistants to managers who can make labor relations decisions), and several others.

The NLRA also established procedures for selecting a labor organization to represent a unit of employees in collective bargaining, and prohibited employers from interfering with that selection. In addition, under the NLRA, the employer would then be required to bargain with the appointed representative of its employees. While "bargaining" does not require that either side agree to a proposal or even to make concessions, it does require each side to bargain in good faith. The NLRA also established regulations on what tactics (such as strikes, lockouts, picketing) could be employed during bargaining in an effort to bolster bargaining objectives.

The NLRA applied to all employers involved in interstate commerce with the exception of agricultural employees, government employees, and employees covered by the Railway Labor Act.

The Act also established the National Labor Relations Board (NLRB), a new federal agency that would be (and still is) responsible for administering and enforcing the rights established by the NLRA. As stated on its website, the NLRB has two principle functions:

▶ To determine, through secret-ballot elections, the free democratic choice by employees whether they wish to be represented by a union in dealing with their employers and if so, by which union.

▶ To prevent and remedy unlawful acts, called unfair labor practices, by either employers or unions.

NOTE

Initially, unfair labor practices (ULPs) were only identified for employers. Union ULPs were subsequently added through the passage of the Labor-Management Relations Act (also known as the Taft-Hartley Act) in 1947.

The NLRA identified five categories of employer unfair labor practices (ULPs):

▶ To "interfere with, restrain, or coerce employees" in the exercise of their rights to engage in concerted or union activities or refrain from them

▶ To dominate or interfere with the formation or administration of a labor organization

▶ To discriminate against employees for engaging in concerted or union activities or refraining from them

▶ To discriminate against an employee for filing charges with the NLRB or taking part in any NLRB proceedings

▶ To refuse to bargain with the union that is the lawful representative of its employees.

The terms of the NLRA originally permitted "closed shops" and "union shops." A closed shop is one in which an employer agrees to hire only union members. A union shop is one in which an employer agrees to require anyone hired to join the union. These practices were subsequently prohibited, however, through the next major piece of labor-related legislation, the Labor Management Relations Act (also known as the Taft-Hartley Act). Read on....

Labor Management Relations Act (Taft-Hartley Act)—1947

The Labor Management Relations Act (LMRA), also known as the Taft-Hartley Act, was an amendment designed to remedy what the Republican Congress saw as two major omissions in the Wagner Act: first, the identification of behaviors and practices that would be considered ULPs on the part of unions, and second, a provision that would allow the government to issue an injunction against a strike that threatened national interests.

Taft-Hartley identified the following unfair labor practices that could be committed by unions:

▶ Restraining or coercing employees in the exercise of their rights or an employer in the choice of its bargaining representative

▶ Causing an employer to discriminate against an employee

▶ Refusing to bargain with the employer of the employees it represents

▶ Engaging in certain types of secondary boycotts

NOTE

Secondary boycotts are defined as efforts to convince others to stop doing business with a particular organization that is the subject of a primary boycott.

▶ Requiring excessive dues

▶ Engaging in featherbedding

NOTE

Featherbedding agreements require the employer to pay union members wages whether or not their work is needed.

▶ Picketing for recognition for more than 30 days without petitioning for an election

▶ Entering into hot cargo agreements

NOTE

An employer who makes a hot cargo agreement agrees to stop doing business with another entity. Hot cargo agreements can thus help to protect union work by allowing union members to refuse to handle or process work produced by non-union entities.

▶ Striking or picketing a health care establishment without giving the required notice

In addition, the Act imposed these additional changes:

▶ Reaffirmed that employers have a constitutional right to express their opposition to unions, so long as employees are not threatened with reprisal for their union activities or promised benefits for refrain from such activities.

▶ Expressly excluded supervisors from coverage under the Act.

▶ Permitted employers to fire supervisors who engaged in union activities or did not support the employer's position.

▶ Outlawed closed shops, agreements that stated that employers could only hire individuals who were members of labor unions.

▶ Expressly permitted union shops, in which non-union workers must join the union within a certain amount of time after being hired.

NOTE

In "right-to-work" states, union shops are illegal. In other words, no employee is required to join the union.

▶ Established 60-day no-strike and no-lockout notice period requiring unions as well as employers to give each other 60 days' notice before strikes (on the part of the union) and lockouts (on the part of the employer) if either party wishes to change or cancel an existing collective bargaining agreement.

▶ Prohibited jurisdictional strikes

NOTE

A jurisdictional strike is a strike through which a union seeks to pressure an employer to assign particular work to its members, rather than to members of other unions or to non-union workers.

▶ Abolished the U.S. Conciliation Service and established the Federal Mediation and Conciliation Service (FMCS).

▶ Authorized the president to intervene in strikes or potential strikes that create a national emergency (a provision that President George W. Bush invoked in 2002 in connection with the employer lockout of the International Longshore and Warehouse Union during negotiations with west coast shipping and stevedoring companies).

Labor Management Reporting and Disclosure Act (Landrum-Griffin Act)—1959

By 1959, it became clear—painfully clear—that more guidelines were necessary. Senate committee hearings revealed improper activities by labor as well as by management, uncovered evidence of collusion between labor and management, exposed violent practices used by certain labor leaders, and uncovered the diversion and misuse of labor union funds by senior-level union leaders.

Enter the Labor Management Reporting and Disclosure Act (also known as Landrum-Griffin). Some of the protections instituted through this act are

▶ A requirement that unions submit annual financial reporting to the DOL, to document how union members' dues were spent

▶ A bill of rights for union members guaranteeing them freedom of speech and periodic secret elections

▶ The designation of every union official as a fiduciary

▶ Even stronger provisions relative to secondary boycotting and organizational and recognition picketing

Labor Relations: Understanding Unions and Union-Related Activities

HR professionals also need a solid understanding of unions, union structure, and union-related activities. To that end, this section will look at the following subjects:

▶ How unions are structured

▶ Union organizing ("the organizing process")

▶ Union decertification and deauthorization

▶ Protected concerted activities

▶ Strikes

How Unions Are Structured

Unions are structured democratically, in that union officers are elected. They are also hierarchical.

HR professionals need to be familiar with the following four types of union entities:

Local Union

Local unions are largely responsible for the day-to-day administration of the labor agreement and relationship with union members. "Locals" generally have an elected president and elected stewards who represent the workers in the workplace. Larger local unions might have a full-time paid business agent. Most locals belong to and are chartered by a larger national union.

National Union

National unions bring together all of the union locals who are scattered across the country. There are usually different hierarchical levels in between the local union and the national union. National unions have far more power with respect to bargaining and political influence than the union locals could have on their own. National unions also advise and guide local unions, and may also manage nationwide benefits programs (such as retirement programs and health insurance plans).

Federations

A federation is a group of national unions. Its many members speak with one voice, thus wielding even greater influence and lobbying power. Federations do not, however, get involved with bargaining or contract administration.

Until the summer of 2005, the AFL-CIO was, in many ways, a federation that was *the* voice of labor in America. During the summer of 2005, however, four major national unions quit the AFL-CIO:

- ▶ The Service Employees International Union
- ▶ The International Brotherhood of Teamsters
- ▶ The United Food and Commercial Workers
- ▶ Unite Here

Together, these four departing unions represented about 4.5 million workers—nearly 35% of the AFL-CIO's previous member of out of the previous total membership of 13 million workers.

International

International labor organizations operate on the international level in much the same manner as federations operate on the national level, only "bigger." For instance, the International Confederation of Free Trade Unions (ICFTU) is an international labor organization that has been in existence for more than 55 years and has a membership of 145 million people, across five continents and more than 150 countries. All member unions have a democratic structure. ICFTU consists of three major regional organizations:

- ▶ APRO for Asia and the Pacific
- ▶ AFRO for Africa
- ▶ ORIT for the Americas

The ICFTU is highly active. According to its website, IFCTU's five "priorities for action" include

- Employment and international labor standards
- Tackling the multinationals
- Trade union rights
- Equality, women, race, and migrants
- Trade union organization and recruitment

Union Organizing ("The Organizing Process")

Through the organizing process, a union seeks to become the recognized representative of a bargaining unit of individuals within an organization. Members of a bargaining unit share common interests with respect to items that are negotiated through a collective bargaining agreement. A bargaining unit can represent part or all of an organization's workforce (except supervisors, or others who are otherwise excluded from membership in unions).

There are five steps involved in this "union organizing" process:

1. **Make a Connection—Express Interest:** In this step, contact is established. Either the union initiates contact with employees in an effort to begin the process of exploring whether there is interest in forming a union, or one or more employees who have an interest in forming a union initiate contact with the union.

> **EXAM ALERT**
>
> Be familiar with reasons why unions might initiate contact with employees within an organization, and why employees within an organization might initiate contact with a union.

2. **Confirm Interest—Obtain Authorization Cards:** Once contact has been established and cultivated, unions confirm and demonstrate employees' interest by obtaining "authorization cards" signed by employees. Once 30% of the employees who would be in the collective bargaining unit have signed authorization cards, the union can petition NLRB to hold an election (the 30% threshold demonstrates a "showing of interest" to the NLRB). Oftentimes, however, unions may seek to obtain signed authorization cards from 50% or more employees before petitioning the NLRB, so as to ascertain the seriousness of employees' interest in joining a union once 30% have signed authorization cards.

In general, petitions from the union will not be accepted if an election has been held within the prior year, if a union has been certified within the past year but has not successfully negotiated a contract, or if there is a valid contract (not to exceed three years) in effect.

3. **Obtaining Recognition:** The next step in the process is for the union to gain recognition. There are a number of ways this can happen, both voluntary and involuntary.

Once the union has obtained recognition—regardless of the way in which that recognition is obtained—the employer must provide the NLRB with a list of the names and addresses of all of the employees who are eligible to vote in the union certification election (the "Excelsior List"). The NLRB will, in turn, provide that list to the union. The nickname "Excelsior List" is derived from the 1966 NLRB decision *Excelsior Underwear, Inc. v. NLRB*, in which the NLRB considered whether "a fair and free election [can] be held when the union involved lacks the names and addresses of employees eligible to vote in that election, and the employer refuses to accede to the union's request." The NLRB ruled that it could not. As a result, the employer must provide the list of employees' names and addresses within seven days after the NLRB has scheduled an election.

4. **The Campaign:** The NLRB will carry out a secret ballot election 30–60 days after the NLRB determines that an election will be held. As always, unfair labor practices, by employers as well as by unions, are prohibited during the union organizing campaign. See "Collective Bargaining: The Process," to review specific information about ULPs.

   The employer and the union are each permitted to engage in certain activities, and are prohibited from engaging in other activities, during the organizing and campaign processes.

5. **The Election:** The NLRB conducts the secret ballot election, usually at the workplace, between 30 and 60 days after the NLRB issues its decision. Management and the union are both permitted to have observers present at the election. Observers may object to a vote if they feel that a vote is being cast illegally. The NLRB is responsible for resolving all voter eligibility issues prior to the final vote count.

If a majority of the individuals vote in favor of the proposed bargaining unit, the unit will be established. Even if there is more than one union competing to represent the proposed collective bargaining unit, a simple majority vote is *still* required in order for a union to be recognized. If there is no majority vote then the top two choices will have an election, so as to generate a majority vote.

The NLRB can order a new election under certain circumstances if it is determined that the "laboratory conditions" of the secret ballot were disturbed in a way that impacted the outcome of the election.

In rare circumstances, the NLRB can require the employer to recognize and bargain with the union in the event that the employer conducted itself in such a seriously egregious manner that the NLRB deems "the holding of a fair election unlikely." This rare situation is referred to as a "bargaining order."

Permissible Union Activities

Some of the activities in which unions are permitted to engage are

▶ Inside organizing, where pro-union individuals can seek to influence others at the workplace (unless a no-solicitation rule in effect).

CAUTION

Employers must apply a no-solicitation rule 100% consistently in order for it to be upheld with respect to any form of inside organizing. Something as simple as selling cookie dough or wrapping paper can be enough to invalidate a no-solicitation rule.

▶ Mailing campaign literature to employees' homes

▶ "Leafleting"—distributing leaflets and flyers offsite or onsite

▶ Local media, such as newspaper ads or radio spots

▶ Dedicated websites

▶ Salting—a "salt" is a union organizer who seeks employment with the organization for the express purpose of actively organizing and campaigning within the organization.

▶ Organizational picketing—designed to generate interest on the part of employees to vote for union representation

Permissible Employer Activities

Like unions, employers have the right to engage in certain activities during a union organizing effort or campaign. Some of those activities include

- Voicing an opinion about unions and the unionization of its operation, as long as its communications carry no direct or implied threat toward employees, and as long as those communications are in no way coercive. This can be done in a number of ways:

  - Email

  - Hardcopy mail to home addresses

  - Payroll stuffers

  - Captive audience meetings: In the workplace, during regular working hours, the employer can hold mandatory presentations during which the employer can share its opinions relative to unions and the unionization of its operations. Unions do not have this opportunity. Captive audience meetings may not be held within 24 hours of the actual election.

- Secure the services of a consultant in its efforts to remain union-free.

Impermissible Union Activities

Like employers, unions are prohibited from engaging in unfair labor practices during a union organizing campaign. Some activities that would constitute an unfair labor practice on the part of a union would include

- Coercing

- Threatening

- Retaliating, or threatening to retaliate

Impermissible Employer Activities

So too, there are a number of activities in which employers cannot engage during a union campaign—activities that would constitute an unfair labor practice. Some of those activities include

- Telling workers that the employer will fire or punish them if they engage in any union activity

- Laying off or discharging any worker for union activity

- Granting workers wage increases or special concessions in an effort to bribe people from joining a union

- Asking workers about confidential union matters, meetings, members, and so on

- Asking workers about the union or about union representatives

- Asking workers how they intend to vote in a union election

- Asking workers whether or not they belong to a union or have signed up for a union

- Threatening or coercing workers in an attempt to influence their vote

- Telling workers that existing benefits will be discontinued if the employee is unionized

- Saying unionization will force the employer to lay off workers

- Promising employees promotions, raises, or other benefits if they get out of the union or refrain from joining it

- Spying on union gatherings

Union Decertification and Deauthorization

From time to time, employees may engage in an election process, vote in a union, and ultimately find that things didn't turn out quite the way they expected. It is in situations like this when decertification or deauthorization elections may be held.

Union Decertification

If employees decide that they no longer wish to be represented by their union, they must prepare for and hold another election. The process of removing the union's rights to represent the employees is called "decertification." This process is similar to certification, only in reverse. It starts with a petition requesting decertification that is signed by at least 30% of employees who belong to the bargaining union being sent to the NLRB. (Decertification cannot occur within the 12 months period following certification after a contract has been negotiated.) The NLRB will then conduct a decertification election if it decides that the petition is in order. If at least 50% of employees who vote (not 50% of the members of the CBU) vote to remove the union then the union will be officially decertified. The union will also be decertified if the vote is exactly even.

Union Deauthorization

Far less frequently, a deauthorization election may be held. Deauthorization revokes the security clause in the contract and effectively creates an "open shop" (see the section "Collective Bargaining: The Agreements (CBAs)"). Deauthorization requires a majority vote of the entire bargaining union, not just the members of the unit who vote in the deauthorization election.

Protected Concerted Activities

Protected concerted activity refers to associational rights that are granted to employee through Section 7 of the NLRA:

Employees shall have the right to self-organization, to form, join, or assist labor organization, to bargain collectively through representatives of their own choosing, and to engage in other concerted activities for the purpose of collective bargaining or other mutual aid or protection, and shall also have the right to refrain from any or all such activities.

CAUTION

Through this language, the NLRA protects associational rights for employees who do not belong to a union, as well as for employees who are unionized. This interpretation was confirmed by *NLRB v. Phoenix Mutual Life Insurance Co.* in 1948. As such, it is for this reason that employers need to be careful not to interfere with protected concerted activities even in non-unionized workplaces.

In order to not interfere with concerted activity, employers need to understand what concerted activity is.

Concerted Activity

Any activities undertaken by individual employees who are united in pursuit of a common goal is considered to be "concerted activity." In order for an employee's activity to be concerted, the activity must be engaged in with or on the authority of other employees, rather than just on behalf of the individual employee (*Meyers Industries*, 281 NLRB 882 [1986]).

Activity must be "concerted" before it can be "protected" by the NLRA.

Protected Concerted Activity

Section 8 of the NLRA specifically states that

It shall be an unfair labor practice for an employer to interfere with, restrain, or coerce employees in the exercise of the rights guaranteed in [Section 7].

Protected concerted activity can include activity aimed at improving employees' terms and conditions of employment. If an employee is engaged in protected concerted activity, an employer might be considered to have violated the NLRA if

▶ The employer knew of the concerted nature of the employee's activity

▶ The concerted activity was protected by the Act

▶ The adverse employment action in question (for instance, termination) was motivated by the employee's protected concerted activity

Remedies for unfair labor practices include reinstatement with full back pay plus interest. Employers also are required to post a notice to all employees detailing the violation and the remedy.

Example of Protected Concerted Activity

The following are specific cases in which employers were found to have committed an unfair labor practice by interfering with protected concerted activities:

▶ An employer fired a salesman for being an "outspoken critic" against two-hour meetings that sales personnel were required to attend (without compensation) before regular work hours. The employee was awarded reinstatement with full back pay plus interest (*NLRB v. Henry Colder Co.*, 1990).

▶ An employer fired two employees who composed a letter protesting a change to the compensation system. The employees were reinstated with full back pay plus interest (*NLRB v. Westmont Plaza*, 1990).

▶ An employer fired employees who mailed a letter to the employer's parent company complaining about working conditions and bonuses. (The employer's president was requiring employees to spend large amounts of time on the president's personal projects.) The employees were reinstated with full back pay plus interest (*NLRB v. Oakes Machine Corp.*, 1990).

A Few Words About Strikes

No dialogue about unions would be complete without some discussion of strikes.

There are two very different types of strikes (or work stoppages)—unfair labor practice strikes and economic strikes.

Unfair Labor Practice (ULP) Strikes

Sometimes, unions allege, correctly or incorrectly, that the employer has committed an unfair labor practice during contract negotiations and call a strike in response to those alleged ULPs. Employers cannot hire permanent strike replacements during a ULP strike, and the striking workers must be returned to their original positions once the strike is over.

The courts would need to determine that a strike was in fact a ULP strike, and not an economic strike "in disguise."

Economic Strikes

Any strike that is not directly tied to the employer's commission of a ULP is considered, by law, to be an "economic strike." Economic strikes are called in an effort to obtain some sort of economic concession from the employer during collective bargaining negotiations—

concessions relating to higher wages, better working conditions, low health insurance premiums, and the like.

> **NOTE**
>
> Economic strikers cannot be terminated except under highly limited situations, such as if they engage in serious misconduct during the strike. Economic strikers can, however, be "permanently" replaced by the employer.

> **TIP**
>
> Under the Mackay Doctrine, employers have the right to permanently replace workers who strike during an economic strike. This right and its nickname derived from the 1938 Supreme Court decision in *NLRB v. Mackay Radio and Telegraph Co.*
>
> While it is advisable to avoid using the word "permanent" when describing employment relationships, the term "permanent replacement" is used here, because it is the recognized vernacular with respect to strikes.

Perhaps the most renowned example of the use of permanent replacement workers occurred in 1981 when President Ronald Reagan replaced 12,000 striking air traffic controllers. This event had a chilling impact on economic strikes because of concerns relative to employees losing their jobs to permanent replacement workers.

> **NOTE**
>
> The historic impact of this strike was not diminished by the fact that workers who have been permanently replaced are entitled to priority status as the employer hires new employees.

> **NOTE**
>
> In 1952, there were 470 strikes; in 2001 there were only 29.

Strike-related Protected Concerted Activities

Economic strikes are considered to be a protected concerted activity under the NLRA. Other protected concerted strike-related activities include picketing and sympathy strikes.

Sympathy Strikes

Employees who are not directly involved in an economic dispute but who choose not to cross a picket line out of support for striking workers are engaging in a sympathy strike. Sympathy strikers do not need to be employed by the same employer as the employees who are actually on strike in order to engage in a sympathy strike.

Picketing

Picketing is an expression of free speech that takes place when people congregate outside a workplace. In order to be considered protected concerted activity, picketing must remain non-violent. Pickets can be used to inform the public, to discourage non-striking workers from entering the workplace (also referred to as "crossing the picket line"), and to encourage people to boycott the products or services of the employer who is the subject of the picket.

Double Breasting Picketing

Double breasting picketing, which is actually a type of secondary boycott, takes place when a company that owns or operates union as well as non-union operations shifts work to the non-union operation in an effort to diminish the impact of the strike. In this situation, the non-union operation to which the business has been shifted *can* be picketed.

Common Situs Picketing

Common situs picketing, which is actually a type of secondary boycott, occurs when members of a labor union picket a workplace in which multiple employers work—the employer with whom the labor union has the dispute, as well as one or more employers with whom the labor union does not have a dispute. Common situs picketing is legal as long as the picket signs indicate the name of the employer with whom the picketers have a dispute.

NOTE

Double breasting picketing and common situs picketing are both examples of secondary boycotts. Secondary boycotts are actions that are ultimately intended to impact a primary party through taking action against a secondary party. Depending upon the circumstances, secondary boycotts may or may not be legal.

One specific situation that can permit the union to conduct secondary boycott is the ally doctrine.

Strike-related Activity That Is Not Protected Concerted Activity

In addition to strike-related activity that is considered to be protected concerted activity, and which is therefore protected by law, there are certain strike-related activities that are not considered to be protected concerted activity.

Wildcat Strikes

If a collective bargaining agreement contains a no-strike clause prohibiting striking during the duration of the agreement, any strikes are considered "wildcat strikes." Wildcat strikes are no longer considered to be protected concerted activity.

Jurisdictional Strike

A jurisdictional strike is used to force an employer to assign work to bargaining unit employees as opposed to some other work group. Jurisdictional strikes constitute a ULP, and those who engage in a jurisdictional strike can experience discipline up to and including termination.

> **EXAM ALERT**
>
> Also familiarize yourself with other strike-related terms and conditions, such as work slowdowns, strike benefits, strike insurance, strike preparation, and the like.

> **EXAM ALERT**
>
> The area of striking, picketing, and boycotting is not as simple or direct as it appears (and, quite frankly, it doesn't appear all that simple to begin with). Be certain to familiarize yourself thoroughly with this area before sitting for the PHR exam.

Collective Bargaining: The Process

Collective bargaining is the process by which an employer and a labor union negotiate the terms of the collective bargaining agreement that will govern the employment relationship for those employees who are represented by the union.

This section will look at a number of specific dimensions of collective bargaining:

▶ Good faith bargaining

▶ Subjects of bargaining (mandatory, permissive, and illegal)

▶ Approaches to collective bargaining

Good Faith Bargaining

According to the Section 8(d) of the NLRA, the employer and the union are both required to bargain in "good faith." The failure of either the union or the employer to do so is considered to be a ULP. Determining what does and does not constitute good faith bargaining, however, isn't always clear or simple.

Bargaining in good faith *doesn't* mean that either side is *required* to reach an agreement or to make concessions. Instead, when ascertaining whether an employer has bargained in good faith, the NLRB will take a more comprehensive look at the activities in which each side has engaged, in their totality.

Sometimes, good faith bargaining is more easily defined by what it's not than by what it is. In other words, good faith bargaining can sometimes be defined by the absence of behaviors that are characteristic of "bad faith bargaining." The following behaviors, when demonstrated by either the union or the employer, could constitute bad faith bargaining:

▶ Failing to agree to meet at reasonable and convenient places and/or times

▶ Failing to show up at the agreed-upon places and/or times

▶ Repeatedly canceling meetings

▶ Failing to maintain an "open mind" during negotiations

▶ Surface bargaining: Going through the motions of bargaining, with no real intention of ultimately reaching agreement (in other words, keeping bargaining "at the surface," without moving toward true agreement)

▶ Repeatedly withdrawing previous positions/concessions

▶ Refusing to bargain on mandatory items, insisting on bargaining on permissive items, or attempting to bargain on illegal items (see "Illegal Subjects," later in this chapter)

▶ Committing any sort of ULP(s)

In addition to these items, all of which can be committed by either the employer or the union, there are other examples of bad faith bargaining that could be committed by the employer:

▶ Taking any action that is deliberately designed to weaken the union's status as the bargaining agent

▶ Presenting proposals directly to employees instead of the union bargaining team

▶ Instituting unilateral changes to wages, hours, and/or terms and conditions of employment while negotiations are in process

▶ Providing the union with insufficient information with which to make informed proposals and counterproposals

Subjects of Bargaining

The NLRB is empowered to categorize bargaining issues into three different categories: mandatory, permissive, and illegal (derived from the 1958 Supreme Court decision *NLRB v. Wooster Division of Borg-Warner Corporation*).

Required Subjects

Required subjects are those that must be bargained in good faith if either the employer or the employees' representative requests it. It's important to keep in mind, however, that according to the NLRA, bargaining in good faith does not require "either party to agree to a proposal or require the making of a concession."

Examples of required subjects include pay, wages, hours of employment, pensions for present employees, bonuses, group insurance, grievance procedures, safety practices, seniority, procedures for discharge, layoff, recall, or discipline, and union security.

> **NOTE**
>
> Sometimes, although a certain item may not be considered to be a required subject, implementing that item might have an impact on a required subject. The bargaining that would take place as a result of these impacts is referred to as "effects bargaining." For instance, an organization's decision to close a particular plant is not a required subject. The decisions that are made relative to how employees will be treated during and impacted by the closure *is* a required subject, and is therefore an example of effects bargaining.

Voluntary or Permissive Subjects

"Voluntary" or "permissive" subjects are topics that can be submitted to collective bargaining if and only if the employer and the employees' representative are willing to do so. Attempting to force bargaining on a voluntary or permissive subject constitutes a ULP.

For example, "voluntary" or "permissive" subjects could include closing plants, shutting down parts of the business, instituting pre-employment testing, and/or modifying retiree benefits

Illegal Subjects

Certain topics simply cannot be collectively bargained. These would include items that would constitute a violation of the NLRA, subsequent labor laws, or, for that matter, *any* law.

Examples of illegal subjects would include closed shop agreements, hot cargo clauses, or featherbedding.

Approaches to Collective Bargaining

This section will discuss three primary approaches to collective bargaining: distributive, integrative, and interest-based.

EXAM ALERT

Expect a question on approaches to collective bargaining.

Distributive Bargaining

Distributive bargaining takes an approach to bargaining in which each side sets forth its position and does its best to stick to it. By the end of the process, one side will have "won" some (or all) of what it wanted, and one side will have "lost" some (or all) of what it wanted.

Distributive bargaining is essentially adversarial in nature. It assumes that "there's only so much to go around." When you divide up the "pie," therefore, one side will end up with "more of the pie" and one side will end up with "less of the pie."

By its very nature, the distributive approach to bargaining tends to encourage stubbornness, and also has a greater likelihood of damaging the parties' relationship with each other.

Integrative Bargaining

The integrative approach to bargaining doesn't look at issues one at a time—instead, it looks at multiple issues as a whole (hence the term "integrative"). Integrative bargaining looks at the "pie," but in a different way: Instead of just splitting up the pie, it creatively considers how it might be able to "make the pie bigger." It looks at how the needs of both sides can be better met when looked at in their entirety, and at how a "win-win" solution can be explored, rather than settling for the "win-lose" scenario that will almost invariably result from distributive bargaining.

In essence, advocates of integrative bargaining believe that an agreement that renders one side "better off" does not necessarily have to result in the other side being "worse off." Instead, through creativity and cooperation, trade offs are sought that will ultimately benefit both sides.

Interest-Based Bargaining

Roger Fisher and William Ury, authors of *Getting to Yes: Negotiating Agreement Without Giving In*, assert that a "good" agreement is one that is wise and efficient and that ultimately results in everyone involved developing a stronger relationship with each other than they would have had if they had *not* gone through this negotiation process together.

Fisher and Ury set forth four principles of principled negotiation that can be used effectively in a variety of situations to resolve many types of disputes. Those four principles are

▶ Separate the people from the problem

▶ Focus on interests rather than positions

▶ Generate a variety of options before settling on one

▶ Resolve disagreements by focusing on objective criteria

Observing these principles throughout the entire negotiation process will enhance the process itself as well as the outcome that results from the process. Remaining aware of the other party's perspectives and perceptions throughout the entire process will also greatly strengthen the consensus building process.

Collective Bargaining: The Agreements (CBAs)

The output of successful collective bargaining is a collective bargaining agreement (CBA). The CBA contains provisions related to a variety of conditions of employment and also outlines the procedures to be used in settling disputes that may arise during the duration of the contract.

Typical Provisions of Collective Bargaining Agreements (Excluding Disciplinary and Grievance Procedures)

Most collective bargaining agreements will include specific guidelines around discipline and discharge, addressing topics such as

▶ Prohibiting discipline or discharge without "cause" or "just cause"

▶ Establishing a progressive discipline process (oral warning, written warning, suspension, discharge), and consideration of mitigating factors

▶ Listing acts that can result in immediate discharge

▶ A requirement to notify union of disciplinary actions

▶ Protecting whistleblowers

▶ Limiting methods that employers may use to conduct investigations (for instance, polygraphs)

▶ Notifying the employee that he or she has the right to union representation during a potential disciplinary interview, and a guarantee that the interview will not be held until union representation is provided (Weingarten Rights)

NOTE

Weingarten Rights, derived from the Supreme Court decision in *NLRB v. Weingarten* (1975), established the right of unionized employees to have union representation at an investigatory interview with management if the employee reasonably believes that discipline might result from that meeting. Although the NLRB reversed this decision in 2000 (*Epilepsy Foundation of Northeast Ohio, 331 NLRB 676*) and held that non-union employees also have the right to have a representative present at a meeting of this sort, in 2004 the NLRB returned to its original determination and held that non-union employees do not have the right to have a co-worker or other representative present in a meeting that the employee reasonably believes might result in discipline.

EXAM ALERT

Be prepared for a question on Weingarten Rights. Be sure that you verify whether the NLRB has issued any more opinions on Weingarten Rights (after the printing of this book) before you take the PHR exam.

The provisions that are contained within collective bargaining agreements will vary from employer to employer, from union to union, and from situation to situation. Some provisions of a collective bargaining agreement are relatively self-explanatory, while others are less self-evident.

NOTE

For those terms that are relatively self-explanatory, we have indicated either a description or, a bullet-point list of the types of stipulations that the provision would seek to address. For those provisions that are somewhat less self-evident, we have also included a definition as well as a sample clause.

The specific provisions that we'll present in this section are

▶ Preamble

▶ Duration of agreement

▶ Non-discrimination clause

▶ Union dues deductions

▶ Management rights clause

▶ Probation

- ▶ Seniority

- ▶ Bumping rights

- ▶ Hours worked/schedules/rest periods/workdays/overtime

- ▶ No strike/no lockout (also referred to as "continuous performance")

- ▶ Wage rates/wage increases

- ▶ Zipper clause

- ▶ Union security clauses:

  - ▶ Open shop

  - ▶ Closed shop

  - ▶ Union shop

  - ▶ Agency shop

  - ▶ Maintenance of membership

- ▶ Holidays

- ▶ Vacation and personal days

- ▶ Sick days

- ▶ Leaves of absence

- ▶ Performance evaluation

- ▶ Layoff and recall

Preamble

Definition: The introductory and first clause of the collective bargaining agreement. The preamble may articulate the purposes of the agreement, formally recognize the employees' representative, define terms that will be used in the agreement, and basically "set the stage" for the remaining provisions of the agreement.

Sample preamble clause:

This Agreement is between (the employer), hereinafter called the "Employer" and (the union), hereinafter called the "Union."

This Agreement has as its purpose the joint commitment to achieve the Employer's goals of teaching, research, and community service; promotion of harmonious relations between the Employer and the Union; the establishment of an equitable and peaceful procedure for the resolution of differences; and the expression of the full and complete understanding of the parties pertaining to all terms and conditions of employment.

The term "employee" when used hereinafter in this Agreement shall refer to employees represented by the Union in the bargaining unit unless otherwise stated. The term Human Resources Department shall mean "appropriate" Human Resources Department: coordinate Employee's Human Resources.

Any member of Employee's management referenced in this Agreement may specify a designee.

Titles of articles, sections and subsections of this Agreement are meant for ease of reading and may not be used to interpret or clarify the text of the language.

Duration of Agreement

Definition: Identifies the first date on which the contract is effective and the last date on which the contract is effective.

Sample duration of agreement clause:

This Agreement shall be effective as of 12:00 a.m. July 1, 2003 and shall continue in full force and effect until midnight, June 30, 2006.

Non-discrimination Clause

Definition: The contract expressly prohibits discrimination on various grounds such as sex, race, creed, color, religion, age, national origin, political affiliation or activity, disability, sexual orientation, or union activity. The non-discrimination clause might also specifically prohibit sexual harassment.

Sample non-discrimination clause:

There shall be no discrimination or intimidation by (the employer) or by (the employees' representative) against any unit member as a result of, or because of such Member's race, color, creed, sex, age, national origin, disability as qualified by law, or membership/nonmembership in the Union.

Union Dues Deductions

Definition: Employers agree to deduct and forward to the union dues amounts agreed to by workers. By law, employees must agree in writing to this deduction. There is some debate, litigious and otherwise, as to whether dues checkoff constitutes a union security clause.

Sample union dues deductions clause:

(The employer) agrees to deduct from the wages of any employee who is a member of the Union a deduction as provided for in written authorization. Such authorization must be executed by the employee and may be revoked by the employee at any time by giving written notice to both (the employer) and the Union. (The employer) agrees to remit any deductions made pursuant to this provision promptly to the Union together with an itemized statement showing the name of each employee from whose pay such deductions have been made and the amount deducted during the period covered by the remittance. Deductions shall be sent by the Board to the Union by separate check from membership dues and/or fair share fees.

Management Rights Clause

Definition: Management reserves the right, in terms that are either general or highly specific, to manage the organization as it sees fit, unless those rights have been specifically modified in the labor contract through a reserved rights doctrine.

Sample management rights clause:

The parties agree that only the written specific, express terms of this Agreement bind (the employer). Except as specifically and expressly provided in this written Agreement, (the employer) has full and complete discretion to make decisions and implement changes in operations including those affecting wages, hours, terms, and conditions of employment of members of the bargaining unit, without prior negotiation with or the agreement of the (employees' representative) except as to the effects of such decisions. The (employees' representative) expressly waives any and all right that it may have to bargain about the decision to make any change in operations, practices, or policies which affect wages, hours, and terms and other conditions of employment of employees in the bargaining unit. Any arbitrators used by the parties under Article (XX) shall give full force and effect to this section.

Probation

Definition: The length of the probationary period, the purpose of probationary period, and employee status and rights during probationary period.

Sample probation clause:

▶ A new employee shall be appointed on probation for a period of three months and may be extended for a further three months if deemed necessary by (the employer) in order to assess the employee's suitability or otherwise for confirmation in his appointment provided such extension shall be made at least one week prior to the completion of his probationary period.

▶ At any time during the probationary period, such employment may be terminated by either (the employer) or the employee on one day's notice being given without any reason being assigned for such termination.

▶ On completion of an employee's probation, (the employer) shall normally inform the employee in writing whether or not he is confirmed in his employment but in the event that (the employer) has omitted to do so, the appointment of the employee concerned shall be deemed to have been confirmed from the date of the completion of his probation and the period of probation shall be deemed as part of the employee's period of service.

Seniority

Definition: The length of time that an employee has been employed by the employer. Seniority can also be defined, however, as seniority within a position, seniority within a department, seniority within a location, and the like. In collective bargaining agreements, seniority can play an important role with respect to decisions such as promotions layoffs, shift bids, bumping right, and so on.

Sample seniority clause:

"It shall be the policy of the department to recognize the seniority principle. Seniority time shall consist of the total calendar time elapsed since the date of original employment with (the employer); no time prior to a discharge for cause or a quit shall be included. Seniority shall not be diminished by temporary layoffs or leaves of absence or contingencies beyond the control of the parties to this Agreement.

Bumping Rights

Definition: The process by which a more senior employee whose position is being eliminated may, instead of losing employment with the organization, choose to replace a less senior employee (assuming that the more senior employee is qualified for the position into which he or she is requesting being bumped). This can ultimately lead to a situation in which a person who was not originally slated for job elimination, in fact, loses his or her job.

Sample bumping rights clause:

A regular employee seniority who is to be laid off may elect to displace an employee with less service seniority where the laid off employee has the necessary skills, abilities, experience, education, qualifications, and certifications. Where an employee elects to displace another employee with less service seniority, he/she shall notify (the employer) within ten (10) days of his/her receipt of notice of layoff; or where an employee exercises his/her right to displace an employee with less service seniority, the (employees' representative) shall be notified in writing by copy of the acknowledgement letter to the employee.

Hours Worked/Schedules/Rest Periods/Workdays/Overtime

Definition: Clauses related to hours worked, rest period, workdays, and overtime help to further establish the tangible terms and conditions of employment. Topics including shifts worked and changes to scheduled shifts may also be addressed.

Sample hours worked/schedules/rest periods/workdays/overtime clause:

The standard workweek consists of seven consecutive days and shall begin at 12:01 a.m. Saturday. The standard work schedule for full-time employees shall be forty (40) hours per work-week, normally scheduled in shifts of eight (8) hours. Meal periods shall consist of thirty minutes and shall not count as time worked if the employee is completely relieved from duty. Employees who are completely relieved from duty shall not be required to be accessible during the meal period. Normal hours of work are from 7:00 a.m. to 3:30 p.m. Shifts are: Day, 7:00 a.m. to 3:30 p.m.; Swing, 3:00 p.m. to 11:00 p.m.; and Owl, 11:00 p.m. to 7:00 a.m. Rest periods not to exceed fifteen minutes, once during each half of an eight-hour shift, will be granted to employees. The time shall not be taken at the beginning or end of a work period, and rest periods shall not be accumulated. Rest periods shall be taken unless operational necessity requires that they be denied.

No Strike/No Lockout (Also Referred to As "Continuous Performance")

No strike—definition: The union agrees not to strike for the duration of the contract. Usually, a union will agree to a "no strike" clause in exchange for a clause to engage in binding arbitration in the event that an impasse is reached relative to administration of the contract.

Sample no strike clause:

No strike of any kind shall be instigated, encouraged, condoned, or caused by (the employees' representative) during the term of this Agreement.

No Lockout—definition: The employer agrees not to lock out employees for the duration of the contract. In this context, a lockout is defined as a situation in which the employer prevents some or all employees from working. Usually, an employer will agree to a "no lockout" clause only in exchange for a "no strike" clause.

Sample no lockout clause:

No lock out of employees shall be instituted by the Employer during the term of this Agreement.

Wages Rates/Wage Increases

Definition: How much, and when, employees will be paid for the various services they render. This clause can also address shift differentials, standby or "on-call" pay, reporting/call-back pay, and roll call pay.

Sample wage rates clause:

- ▶ (The employer) agrees to pay and the (employees' representative) agrees to accept the schedule of job classifications and wage rates attached hereto as Wage Schedule I and Wage Schedule II for the term of this Agreement.

- ▶ When an employee is temporarily assigned to a position having a lower rate of pay than his/her regular position, his/her rate of pay shall not be reduced during such temporary assignment. It is understood that this clause does not apply to any situation when the downward assignment has been as a result of a layoff within the Bargaining Unit.

▶ When an employee is temporarily assigned to a position having a higher rate of pay than his/her regular position, and such assignment is in excess of two (2) consecutive hours, he/she shall be paid at the higher rate of pay for the entire time served in such higher assignment.

Sample wage increases clause:

Wages for bargaining unit members are set forth in the Wage Schedule attached as Appendix A. "Steps" set forth in the wage schedule generally reflect a member's years of continuous service with (the employer) as a regular contract (employee in a particular position), unless placement in the wage schedule was modified upon the employee's initial hiring in accordance with provisions of this Article. Step increases shall be effective on the first day of July following the completion of one (1) year.

Effective July 1, 2002, all members shall advance to the next step in the wage scale each year in accordance with the terms of this Agreement.

Unit members who have transferred from other positions in (the employer) may be placed at any step on the wage scale not to exceed their years of service in the district.

Each member shall receive written notice of the wage schedule step he or she is placed at effective within thirty (30) days of (employer) approval of this Agreement, and thereafter shall receive written notice of the step he or she advances to each subsequent July.

Zipper Clause

Definition: Both parties agree that the agreement is an exclusive and complete "expression of consent"—in other words, that the only items that can be collectively bargained until the expiration of the agreement are the only ones that can be collectively bargained throughout the life of the agreement. Once the agreement is signed, new subjects cannot be added and existing subjects cannot be reopened for negotiation. The contract has been "zipped" closed.

Sample zipper clause:

All matters within the scope of bargaining have been negotiated and agreed upon. The terms and conditions set forth in this Agreement represent the full and complete understanding and commitment between (the employer) and (the employees' representative). During the term of this Agreement, there shall be no change in (the employer's) regulations or departmental policies on matters within the scope of negotiations without notice to the (employees' representative) and providing the (employees' representative) the opportunity to bargain the impacts and effects.

Union Security Clause

Definition: Union security clauses are included in some agreements in an effort to protect the interests, strength, and security of the union. Union security clauses regulate membership in the union and, consequently, relate to the payment of dues. Some of the more common types of union security clauses include

- **Open shop**—Employees are required neither to join the union nor to pay union dues. This is the *only* type of union security clause that is legal in right-to-work states (and for federal government employees).

- **Closed shop**—Employers can only hire employees who are already members of the union. Closed shops were ruled illegal by the Taft-Hartley Act; however, "hiring halls" do in one sense encourage a closed shop arrangement. A hiring hall is a union-operated placement office that refers registered applicants to jobs on the basis of a seniority or placement system.

- **Union shop**—Newly hired employees must join the union within a specified period of time, usually 30 days, and must remain a member of the union as a condition of employment. In a union shop, employers must terminate employees who are not union members.

  Union shops are illegal in "right-to-work" states.

- **Agency shop**—Employees are not required to join the union. They must, however, pay a monthly fee that is typically equivalent to union dues.

  Agency shops are illegal in right-to-work states.

- **Maintenance of membership**—Employees who voluntarily choose to join a union must maintain their individual memberships for the duration of the labor contract. Each employee then has a 30-day window at the beginning of the next contract period during which he or she may terminate membership. Maintenance of membership arrangements are illegal in right-to-work states.

> **NOTE**
>
> "Beck Rights" are the right for bargaining unit members to pay only that portion of union dues which is attributable to mainline union responsibilities (collective bargaining, organizing in the same industry, contract administration, and the like). It is up to the employee, however, to exercise his or her Beck Rights. These rights were established by the 1988 Supreme Court decision in *Communication Workers of America v. Beck.*

Holidays

Terms and conditions that could be delineated in the bargaining agreement clause might include

- Number of holidays granted per year
- Designated holidays (with specific dates) versus floating holidays

- ▶ Terms of pay for working on a holiday
- ▶ Right to equivalent time off for time worked on a holiday
- ▶ Procedures for assigning holiday work
- ▶ Special circumstances—for example, "one-time" holidays

Vacation and Personal Days

Terms and conditions that could be delineated in the bargaining agreement clause might include

- ▶ Number of vacation and personal days accrued per year and procedure for using
- ▶ Right to take accrued vacation
- ▶ Procedure and time of year for scheduling
- ▶ Role of seniority in scheduling vacations and personal days
- ▶ Right to carry over vacation to next year, and the amount that can be carried over
- ▶ Procedure for payment upon death, resignation, or retirement of employee
- ▶ Pro-rated vacation for part-time employees

Sick Days

Terms and conditions that could be delineated in the bargaining agreement clause might include

- ▶ Days accrued per year and maximum accumulation
- ▶ Right to use for doctor's appointments
- ▶ Right to use for ill family members
- ▶ Provision for cash out of sick leave
- ▶ Provision for sick leave bank
- ▶ Pro-rated sick leave for part-time employees
- ▶ Interaction of sick leave policy with Family and Medical Leave Act (FMLA) and Americans with Disabilities Act (ADA)
- ▶ Documentation required for sick leave; protections of employee privacy rights

Leaves of Absence

Terms and conditions that could be delineated in the bargaining agreement clause might include

- ▶ Right to take leave, administrative rules for requesting leave, duration of leave, pay during leave, continuation of benefits during leave, and reinstatement after leave
- ▶ Parental leave, including adoption leave
- ▶ Elder care leave
- ▶ Bereavement leave: relatives or household members covered, number of days, extra time when travel required
- ▶ Educational leave, leave to attend professional meetings, sabbaticals
- ▶ Leave for jury duty
- ▶ Military leave with responsibility of employer to hold open same job, shift, and other conditions
- ▶ Leave for union business
- ▶ Leave for voting
- ▶ Family and medical leave: benefits, if any, in addition to those in law (for example, longer period of paid leave than required by law), description of employee and employer rights and responsibilities under law

Performance Evaluation

Terms and conditions that could be delineated in the bargaining agreement clause might include

- ▶ Criteria for evaluations
- ▶ Frequency of evaluations
- ▶ Right of employee to receive copies of evaluations
- ▶ Right to rebut or grieve performance evaluations
- ▶ Limitations on use of performance evaluations (for example, not to determine pay, bidding rights, and so on)

Layoff and Recall

Terms and conditions that could be delineated in the bargaining agreement clause might include

▶ Procedures for layoff based on seniority provisions

▶ Prior notification to union of layoffs, right of union to offer alternative proposals or plans

▶ Rights of employees to bump into positions of less senior employees

▶ Procedures for recalling employees; duration of recall list

Discipline and Discharge, and Grievance Handling

"Discipline and discharge" and "grievance procedures" are two critical elements of the collective bargaining agreement that, in one sense, bring together all of the other provisions in the agreement. Together with mediation and arbitration, they form the basis for contract administration.

Because of the unique impact of these two types of contract provisions, we will introduce them briefly here before exploring them in greater detail later, in the section, "Contract Administration."

Discipline and Discharge

Management reserves the right to discipline (a more positive approach than "punishing" or "penalizing") employees for sub-par performance and/or non-performance. Discharge (the termination of the employment relationship by the employer) is the culmination of unsuccessful discipline—meaning discipline that does not result in the employee bringing her or his performance up to an acceptable level.

Grievance Handling

Grievance handling is the formal process established by the collective bargaining agreement through which disagreements arising from the administration of the labor agreement are resolved. These difficulties could arise from a number of courses, including but not limited to interpretation of contract language or alleged unfair or inconsistent application of employment provisions. Grievances most often arise out of decisions relating to discipline and discharge.

Contract Administration

As indicated earlier, the collective bargaining process results in a collective bargaining agreement. In many ways, however, the collective bargaining agreement is more of a beginning than an ending. It is a living document that provides the structure and framework within which the daily happenings of the employment relationship are brought to life. It also provides the language that will govern the employment relationship—language that is at times subject to different interpretations, thereby presenting challenges that need to be resolved.

Grievance Procedure

Each collective bargaining agreement outlines a grievance procedure for resolving these sorts of differences. This procedure establishes the formal process through which problems and challenges associated with the interpretation or application of the collective bargaining agreement will be addressed and resolved. Sometimes, challenges arise out of differences in opinion relative to the interpretation of the language that was used to craft the agreement. Challenges can also erupt when there is a perception that the contract has been applied in an unfair or inconsistent manner, particularly with respect to decisions relating to discipline and discharge.

Although management and labor both have the right to use the grievance process, management does not often choose to do so. Instead, the process is usually initiated by an employee who is a member of the collective bargaining unit or by the union itself. Either way, the grievance alleges that the labor contract has been violated in some way, and seeks resolution.

Although the actual grievance procedure will vary widely from one collective bargaining agreement to another, they are similar in that they consist of a series of prescribed steps, each of which has an accompanying time limit for action. The process by which appeals can be filed is also clearly delineated in the agreement.

Many, though not all, agreements outline a four-step grievance procedure:

1. Initiate a complaint.
2. Escalate the complaint internally.
3. Highest level of internal escalation.
4. Binding arbitration.

Step One: Initiate a Complaint

Either the employee or the union must initiate a complaint within a specified time frame after the date on which the alleged contract violation took place (or, alternatively, the date on which the employee or union became aware of the alleged violation). In some contracts, this step must be formally filed (in writing), while other contracts permit this initial complaint to be informal (verbal). This initial complaint is usually filed with the supervisor of the person who experienced the alleged violation. This first line supervisor then has a prescribed number of days within which to meet with the employee and the union steward to discuss the situation. In most cases, the supervisor will then have a prescribed number of days after that initial meeting to reach a decision relative to the situation. The supervisor can grant the requested relief in part, in whole, or not at all.

If the employee and/or the union decide to accept the resolution that the supervisor proposes, the grievance is considered to be settled. If the employee and/or the union decide not to accept the resolution, the union has a prescribed number of days within which to appeal the grievance to the next step.

> **NOTE**
>
> In many agreements, management's failure to abide by all prescribed time limits will result in the grievance being automatically appealed to the next level. On the other hand, the union's failure to abide by all prescribed time limits will often result in the immediate dismissal of the grievance and the termination of the grievance process.

Step Two: Escalate the Complaint Internally

Step two is similar to step one with respect to the actual process and the requirements to abide by prescribed time frames. An important difference at this step, however, is that the meetings occur between higher levels of union and management leadership. At step two, for instance, the president of the local union might meet with manager of the plant at which the employee works. If resolution is not reached at step two, an appeal can be made to move to step three.

Step Three: Highest Level of Internal Escalation

Step three is similar to step two, except that the level of the meetings that are being held have escalated even more. At this level, it is quite possible to find someone from the union's national office sitting across from someone from the organization's corporate headquarters.

If step three does not produce a resolution that is acceptable to the union, the union must decide (within a prescribed period of time, of course) whether to appeal to binding arbitration—the final step.

Step Four: Binding Arbitration

In this step, the disagreement is referred to an outside party—an arbitrator—who will render a decision that will be binding upon the union and management. Most of the time, the collective bargaining agreement will fully outline the arbitration process to which the parties will be held if the grievance is appealed to step four.

Arbitration that is used to resolve grievances during the administration of the contract (as is described here) is called "rights arbitration."

EXAM ALERT

For the PHR exam, it's important to be familiar with arbitration related terms and practices. In addition to the rights arbitration process described here, be prepared to respond to questions on

▶ **Interest arbitration:** Arbitration that is used to resolve conflicts around contract language during the collective bargaining process.

▶ **Arbitrator:** An individual selected to participate in the resolution of an agreement, and the rendering of a binding decision.

▶ **Arbitrator panels:** Panels that are usually composed of three arbitrators, one of whom is selected by management, one of whom is selected by the union, and one of whom is selected jointly (this person is the "neutral arbitrator").

▶ **Federal Mediation and Conciliation Service (FMCS):** A source that maintains lists of qualified arbitrators.

▶ **American Arbitration Association (AAA):** A source that maintains lists of qualified arbitrators.

▶ **Arbitration hearing:** A relatively formal process (not wholly unlike a court hearing) that can be conducted by an individual arbitrator or by a panel of arbitrators. The hearing includes the presentation of evidence, the testimony of witnesses, and opening and closing statements from both sides. Lawyers are often present, as well, which adds even more to the judicial "feel" of the hearing.

▶ **Permanent arbitrators:** An individual arbitration arrangement in which one arbitrator who is selected for a fixed period of time (often the duration of the contract) hears all arbitration cases that arise during that period of time. One advantage to this approach is that the arbitrator becomes very knowledgeable about the contract. One potential disadvantage could emerge if the union, management, or both are dissatisfied with the arbitrator for some reason.

▶ **Ad hoc arbitrators:** More frequently, each arbitration will result in the selection of an arbitrator. The arbitrator who is selected may specialize in the particular topic with which the arbitration deals, which can be a distinct advantage. Also, neither party will be "stuck" with an arbitrator with whom it is not happy.

▶ **Decisions:** Arbitrators must resolve grievances on the basis of an objective interpretation of the contract as it was written. In the event that the contract language is unclear, the arbitrator must then work to ascertain what the intent of the parties was at the time that the contract was written. Past practice is an extremely important element in this process, especially if the contract language is somewhat ambiguous.

Chapter Summary

Employee relations... labor relations

These are terms that encompass practices and responsibilities that are far reaching and of critical importance. They are also terms that evoke strong feelings and reactions.

In the beginning of this chapter, we described employee relations as

The way in which an organization responds to, handles, and/or addresses any issue that has impact on employees, and their relationships

▶ to and with other employees

▶ to and with managers

▶ to and with those outside the organization with whom they come in contact as part of their employment experience

During this chapter, we attempted to explore the myriad ways in which these "relationships" can manifest themselves, as well as the many factors that need to be taken into consideration when it comes to "relationships" with "employees." We also looked at the history, legality, processes, tools, and importance of labor relations.

It is our hope that, after having journeyed through this chapter, you will understand the true impact of your role more fully—and, therefore, be better equipped to perform it even more effectively. (We also hope that you perform exceedingly well in your role as PHR candidate, as well.)

> **EXAM ALERT**
>
> The PHR exam covers a wide range of information relating to employee and labor relations. Those topics have been explored in this chapter, with three exceptions:
>
> ▶ Public sector labor relations issues and practices (this includes federal, state, and local government employees)
> ▶ Expatriation and repatriation issues and practices
> ▶ Employee and labor relations for local nationals (for example, labor relations in other countries)
>
> As part of your preparation for the PHR exam, be certain to review matters pertaining to each of these areas.

Key Terms

- Employee relations
- Labor relations
- Knights of Labor
- Great Uprising
- Samuel Gompers
- "Bread and butter unionism"
- Haymarket
- AFL
- Industrial Workers of the World (IWW)
- Mary Harris "Mother" Jones
- Triangle Shirtwaist Company
- Electric Auto-Lite Strike
- CIO
- UAW
- Walter Reuther
- AFL-CIO
- Equal Employment Opportunity (EEO)
  - Charge
  - Charging party
  - Complainant
  - Plaintiff
  - Respondent
  - Fair Employment Practices Agencies (FEPAs)
  - Reasonable cause
  - Right to sue letter
  - Relief

- Remedies
- Organizational culture
- Employee handbooks
- Employee communication strategies
- Employee involvement strategies
- Employee surveys
- Focus groups
- Employee participation groups
- Open door policy
- Suggestion programs
- Management by walking around (MBWA)
- Progressive discipline
  - Common law
  - Tort doctrines
  - Employment-at-will
  - Wrongful termination
  - Implied contracts
  - Defamation
  - Invasion of privacy
  - Negligent hiring
  - Negligent training
  - Negligent retention
  - Negligent referral
  - Contract doctrines
  - Mandatory arbitration agreements
  - Non-compete agreements

- Confidentiality agreements
- Circuit City Stores, Inc. v. Adams (2001)
- Sherman Anti-Trust Act, 1890
- Clayton Act, 1914
- Railway Labor Act, 1926
- Norris-LaGuardia Act, 1932
- "Yellow dog" contract
- National Industrial Recovery Act, 1933
- Schechter Poultry Corp. v. United States
- National Labor Relations Act or Wagner Act, 1935
- National Labor Relations Board
- Unfair Labor Practice (ULP)
- Labor Management Relations Act or Taft-Hartley Act, 1947
- Secondary boycott
- Featherbedding
- Hot cargo agreements
- Right-to-work states
- Jurisdictional strikes
- Federal Mediation and Conciliation Service (FMCS)
- Labor Management Reporting and Disclosure Act or Landrum-Griffin Act, 1959
- Local union
- National union
- Federations

- International labor organizations
- APRO for Asia and the Pacific
- AFRO for Africa
- ORIT for the Americas
- Authorization cards
- No-solicitation rule
- Leafleting
- Salting
- Organizational picketing
- Captive audience meetings
- Union decertification
- Union deauthorization
- Protected concerted activities
- ULP strikes
- Economic strikes
- Mackay doctrine
- NLRB v. Mackay Radio and Telegraph Co.
- Sympathy strikes
  - Wildcat strikes
  - Picketing
  - Double breasting
  - Common situs picketing
  - Ally doctrine
  - Good faith bargaining
  - Required subjects
  - Voluntary subjects
  - Permissive subjects
  - Illegal subjects

- ▶ Distributive bargaining
- ▶ Integrative bargaining
- ▶ Interest based bargaining
- ▶ Collective bargaining agreement
- ▶ Weingarten rights
- ▶ NLRB v. Weingarten (1975)
- ▶ Zipper clause

- ▶ Union security clauses
- ▶ Open shop
- ▶ Closed shop
- ▶ Union shop
- ▶ Agency shop
- ▶ Maintenance of membership

Apply Your Knowledge

This chapter focuses on issues relating to employee and labor relations. Complete the following exercises, review questions, and exam questions as a way of reviewing and reinforcing the knowledge and skills you'll need to perform your responsibilities as an HR professional, and to increase the likelihood that you will pass the PHR examination.

Topics to Explore

In this chapter, we delved into many topics, and highlighted certain others with which you will need more familiarity in order to be an effective HR professional (and in order to enhance your preparation for the PHR exam). As you continue your study and preparations, be sure to review with the following terms, concepts, people, and events:

- ▶ Knights of Labor
- ▶ Great Uprising
- ▶ Samuel Gompers
- ▶ "Bread and butter unionism"
- ▶ Haymarket
- ▶ AFL
- ▶ Industrial Workers of the World (IWW)
- ▶ Mary Harris "Mother" Jones
- ▶ Triangle Shirtwaist Company
- ▶ Electric Auto-Lite Strike
- ▶ CIO
- ▶ UAW

- ▶ Walter Reuther
- ▶ AFL-CIO
- ▶ Voluntary recognition
- ▶ Involuntary recognition
- ▶ Strike preparation
- ▶ Work slowdowns
- ▶ Strike benefits
- ▶ Strike insurance
- ▶ Strike preparation
- ▶ Interest arbitration
- ▶ Arbitrators
- ▶ Arbitrator panels
- ▶ Federal Mediation and Conciliation Service (FMCS)
- ▶ American Arbitration Association (AAA)
- ▶ Arbitration Hearing
- ▶ Permanent arbitrators
- ▶ Ad hoc arbitrators
- ▶ Ally Doctrine
- ▶ Public sector labor relations issues and practices (this includes federal, state, and local government employees)
- ▶ Expatriation and repatriation issues and practices
- ▶ Employee and labor relations for local nationals (for example, labor relations in other countries)

Your research will pay off professionally as well as in terms of your preparation for the PHR exam.

Review Questions

1. Explore and discuss "discipline" within the context of its role as an employee involvement program.

2. Describe and compare local unions and national unions.

3. Compare and contrast distributive and integrative approaches to collective bargaining.

4. Describe negligent hiring.

5. If an employee EEO charge is not settled, what are the four primary ways that the EEOC can handle the charge?

Exam Questions

1. All of the following represent measures that could be helpful in measuring the effectiveness of employee relations initiatives except

   ○ **A.** Turnover

   ○ **B.** Absenteeism

   ○ **C.** Unionization

   ○ **D.** Work related accidents/injuries/"preventable" illnesses

2. FEPAs are

   ○ **A.** State or local agencies that provide employers and unions with lists of qualified arbitrators

   ○ **B.** State or local agencies that have anti-discrimination laws and agencies responsible for enforcing those laws

   ○ **C.** State or local agencies that are responsible for administering and enforcing the rights established by the NLRA

   ○ **D.** State or local agencies responsible for approving the recognition of union federations

3. The NLRA identified all of the following as unfair labor practices (for employers) except

   ○ **A.** To dominate or interfere with the formation or administration of a labor organization

   ○ **B.** To discriminate against employees for engaging in concerted or union activities or refraining from them

◯ **C.** To discriminate against an employee for filing charges with the FMCS or taking part in any FMCS proceedings

◯ **D.** To refuse to bargain with the union that is the lawful representative of its employees

4. Which of the following terms means the same as "charging party"?

◯ **A.** Complainant

◯ **B.** Plaintiff

◯ **C.** Respondent

◯ **D.** Defendant

5. The landmark Supreme Court case that confirmed the legality of mandatory arbitration agreements was

◯ **A.** NLRB v. Weingarten

◯ **B.** NLRB v. Phoenix Mutual Life Insurance Co.

◯ **C.** Circuit City Stores, Inc. v. Adams

◯ **D.** Excelsior Underwear, Inc. v. NLRB

5. "Featherbedding" refers to

◯ **A.** A requirement that anyone who is hired by the organization must join the union

◯ **B.** An agreement that requires the employer to pay wages to union members whether or not their work is needed

◯ **C.** A requirement to pay "prevailing wages" on federal government construction contracts and most contracts for federally assisted construction over $2,000

◯ **D.** An agreement that an employer will stop doing business with another entity (most frequently a non-union entity)

6. Weingarten Rights, derived from the Supreme Court decision in *NLRB v. Weingarten* (1975), established the right of unionized employees to

◯ **A.** Have union representative at meetings with supervisors/management if the employee chooses to do so

◯ **B.** Have union representation at investigatory meetings with management if the employee reasonably believes that discipline might result

◯ **C.** Have the EEOC take its own independent action even when a binding arbitration agreement is in place

◯ **D.** Pay only that portion of union dues that is attributable to mainline union responsibilities

7. Many, though not all, agreements outline a grievance procedure that includes all of the following steps except

   ○ **A.** Initiating a formal complaint

   ○ **B.** Notifying the NLRB of the complaint

   ○ **C.** Escalating the complaint internally

   ○ **D.** Participating in binding arbitration

8. Which of the following would be least relevant to determining the degree to which a non-compete agreement might be found to be valid:

   ○ **A.** Whether the agreement specified a time frame established in the agreement, and, if so, how long it is in effect

   ○ **B.** Whether the agreement specified any geographic limitations within which the employee cannot compete

   ○ **C.** Whether there is anything in the agreement that would preclude the employee from earning a living in his or her chosen field

   ○ **D.** Whether the employee was employed by the organization at the time that he or she was asked to sign the agreement

9. All of the following are important steps to take to ensure the success of a focus group except

   ○ **A.** Develop effective questions

   ○ **B.** Involve/include all stakeholders

   ○ **C.** Arrange the logistics

   ○ **D.** Conduct the survey

10. Which of the following would not be considered an employee involvement strategy?

   ○ **A.** Open door policy

   ○ **B.** Progressive discipline

   ○ **C.** Suggestion programs

   ○ **D.** Captive audience meetings

Answers to Review Questions

1. Progressive discipline programs can, in fact, function as a type of employee relations program, if we keep the true definition of employee relations in mind: anything that impacts a relationship with an employee. Even through discipline, there should be a

focus on building a relationship. Discipline can and should be seen as a way to give employees every opportunity to help themselves in their efforts to address their performance issues and, in short, "turn them around" so that they can meet or exceed performance expectations.

2. Local unions, which truly operate at the "local" level, are largely responsible for the day-to-day administration of the labor agreement and relationship with union members. Locals generally have an elected president and elected stewards who represent the workers in the workplace. Larger local unions might have a full-time paid business agent. Most locals belong to and are chartered by a larger national union.

   National unions, conversely, bring together all of the union locals for a particular group that are scattered across the country. There are usually different hierarchical levels in between the local union and the national union. National unions have far more power with respect to bargaining, and with respect to political influence, than the union locals could have on their own. They also advise and guide local unions, and may also manage nationwide benefits programs (such as retirement programs and health insurance plans).

3. Distributive bargaining takes an approach to bargaining in which each side sets forth its position, and at the end of the process one side has "won" some (or all) of what it wanted, and the other has "lost." Distributive bargaining is adversarial in nature. It assumes that "there's only so much to go around," so when you divide up the "pie," one side will get more and one side will get less.

   Integrative bargaining doesn't look at bargaining issues one at a time—instead, it looks at multiple issues as a whole (hence the term "integrative"). Integrative bargaining looks at "the pie" in a different way. Instead of just splitting up the pieces, it creatively considers how it might be able to "make that pie bigger"; how the needs of both sides can be better met when looked at in their entirety; and how a "win/win" solution can be explored, rather than settling for the "win/lose" scenario that will inevitably result from distributive bargaining.

   In essence, integrative bargaining is predicated on the idea that an agreement that renders one side "better off" does not necessarily have to result in the other side being "worse off." Instead, through creativity and cooperation, "trade offs" of some sort are sought that will ultimately benefit both parties to the agreement.

4. Negligent hiring refers to the process of hiring an employee without engaging in appropriate "due diligence" into that candidate's credentials, prior work experience, and the like. Negligent hiring tort claims might be filed when an employee who was hired through a flawed hiring process inflicts some sort of harm on another person—harm that could have been predicted and therefore prevented if the employer had conducted the background check. A hiring process can be flawed for a number of reasons, such as the application of a sound hiring process in an unsound manner, or the use of a

hiring process that was originally designed in a flawed manner. Flaws could relate to inadequate or poorly conducted reference checks, job requirements that do not reflect the skills or credentials that are truly required for a position, and the like.

5. Assuming that it is not settled, there are four primary ways that a charge can be handled by the EEOC, which can:

▶ Investigate it: Investigate either on a priority or non–high priority basis, depending on the strength of the facts that have been presented in the charge. An EEOC investigation can take myriad forms, including written requests for information, in-person interviews, document reviews, and even a visit to the location where the alleged discrimination occurred.

▶ Settle it: This can happen at any stage of the investigation if the charging party and the employer are interested in reaching a settlement. If no settlement is reached, the investigation resumes.

▶ Mediate it: The EEOC offers a confidential mediation program as an alternative to a lengthy investigative process. In order for a charge to be mediated, both the charging party and the employer must be willing to participate. If the mediation process is not successful, the charge will be investigated.

▶ Dismiss it: A charge can be dismissed at any point in the process if the agency determines that further investigation will not establish that unlawful discrimination occurred. When a charge is dismissed, a notice is issued in accordance with the law, which gives the charging party 90 days in which to file a lawsuit on his or her own behalf.

Answers to Exam Questions

1. **Answer C is the best choice.** The presence or absence of a union should not be used as a measure of the success or failure of employee relations initiatives. Unions provide a voice, and the right to join a union is afforded to most workers under the NLRA. The choice to exercise that right must not be used to draw unrelated conclusions. Answers A, B, and D are not the best choices, since turnover, absenteeism (especially unplanned), and work related accidents/injuries/"preventable" illnesses can all provide valid measures of the effectiveness of employee relations initiatives.

2. **Answer B is the best choice.** FEPAs (which stands for Fair Employment Practices Agencies) are state or local agencies responsible for enforcing anti-discrimination laws. Answer A is not the best choice, since there are no state or local agencies that provide employers and unions with lists of qualified arbitrators (the Federal Mediation and Conciliation Service [FMCS] and the American Arbitration Association [AAA] do provide this service, however). Answer C is not the best choice, since there are no state or

local agencies responsible for administering and enforcing the rights established by the NLRA (the NLRB, however, does do this on a national level). Answer D is not the best choice, since there are no state or local agencies responsible for approving the recognition of union federations

3. **Answer C is the best choice.** Discriminating against an employee for filing charges with the FCMS or taking part in any FCMS proceedings does not constitute an unfair labor charge. (FCMS stands for the Federal Mediation and Conciliation Service, and is a source that maintains lists of qualified arbitrators. Charges, therefore, cannot be filed with the FCMS.) Answers A, B, and D are not the best choices, since each one has been specifically identified as an unfair labor practices (ULP) by the NLRA.

4. **Answer A is the best choice.** Complainant means the same as charging party. Answer B is not the best choice, since a "plaintiff" in this context would refer to a charging party or complainant who has filed a lawsuit. Answer C is not the best choice, since the organization against whom the charging party files a charge is the respondent. Answer D is not the best choice, since a respondent against whom a lawsuit has been filed would be referred to as a defendant.

5. **Answer B is the best choice.** "Featherbedding" refers to an agreement that the employee will pay wages to union members whether or not their work is needed. Answer A is not the best choice, since a requirement that anyone who is hired by the organization must join the union refers to a "union shop." Answer C is not the best choice, since the requirement to pay prevailing wages on federal government construction contracts and most contracts for federally assisted construction over $2,000 refers to the Davis-Bacon Act. Answer D is not the best choice, since an agreement that an employer will stop doing business with another entity is a "hot cargo" agreement.

6. **Answer B is the best choice.** Wiengarten Rights refer to the rights of unionized employees to have union representation at investigatory meetings with management if the union member reasonably believes that discipline might result. Answer A is not the best choice, because unionized employees do not have the right to have a representative at a meeting with a supervisor/manager unless the employee reasonably believes that discipline might result from that meeting. Answer C is not the best choice, because the right of the EEOC to take its own independent action even when a binding arbitration agreement is in place refers to *EEOC v. Waffle House, Inc.*, not *NLRB v. Weingarten*. Answer D is not the best response, because the right of unionized employees to pay only that portion of union dues that is attributable to mainline union responsibility is known as to Beck Rights, not Weingarten Rights.

7. **Answer B is the best choice.** A grievance procedure would not include a requirement to notify the NLRB. Answers A, C, and D are not the best choices, since each represent a common step in many grievance processes.

8. **Answer D is the best choice.** Although the question of whether an individual was fairly compensated may be answered differently depending upon whether the individual who was asked to signed the agreement was employed at the time that he or she was asked to do so, the issue in that situation would be fair compensation, not employment status. Answers A, B, and C are not the best choices, since each represents an important consideration for determining the validity of a non-compete agreement.

9. **Answer D is the best choice.** Although focus groups can be used as follow-up to an employee survey, they can also be used independently from a survey. Answers A, B, and C are not the best choices, since each represents an important step that must be taken to ensure the success of a focus group.

10. **Answer D is the best choice.** Although captive audience meetings involve employees (in that the "captive audience" consists of employees), such meetings are held in response to efforts to organize and are not considered to be a true employee involvement strategy. Answers A, B, and D all not the best choices, in that each represents an employee involvement strategy.

Suggested Readings and Resources

www.eeoc. gov

www.dol.gov

An Eclectic List of Events in U.S. Labor History:

http://www.lutins.org/labor.html

"A Curriculum of United States Labor History for Teachers," sponsored by the Illinois Labor History Society: http://www.kentlaw.edu/ilhs/curricul.htm

Industrial Relations to Human Resources and Beyond: The Evolving Process of Employee Relations Management (Issues in Work and Human Resources) (Hardcover), by Bruce E. Kaufman (Editor), Inc. Industrial Relations Counselors (Corporate Author), Richard A. Beaumont (Editor), Roy B. Helfgoff (Editor), Roy B. Helfgott (Editor)

SPHR Exam Prep II, Larry Phillips

"Effective Employee Discipline: A Case of the Internal Revenue Service" An article from *Public Personnel Management*, by Cynthia J. Guffey, Marilyn M. Helms

Discipline Without Punishment/The Proven Strategy That Turns Problem Employees into Superior Performers (Hardcover), by Dick Grote

Labor Relations in the Public Sector (Public Administration and Public Policy), by Richard C. Kearney, David G. Carnevale

The Labor Relations Process, by William H. Holley

The Future of Human Resource Management: 64 Thought Leaders Explore the Critical HR Issues of Today and Tomorrow, by Mike Losey (Editor), Dave Ulrich (Editor), Sue Meisinger (Editor)

The Employment Relationship: Key Challenges for HR, by Paul Sparrow, Cary L. Cooper

The Common Law of the Workplace: The Views of Arbitrator, by Theodore St. Antoine, Theodore J. St. Antoine (Editor)

Getting to Yes: Negotiating Agreement Without Giving In, by Roger Fisher, William L. Ury, Bruce Patton (Editor), Bruce Patton

Getting Past No: Negotiating Your Way from Confrontation to Cooperation, by William Ury

CHAPTER EIGHT

Occupational Health, Safety, and Security

Study Strategies

▶ Prepare large index cards for each of the laws. Make note of important facts and details relating to each law, as well as of any relevant case law.

▶ Although this functional area accounts for a small percentage of the total PHR exam questions, there is a tremendous amount of data from which those questions can be selected. Make lists of terms, definitions, dates, and other factual information—and review them well.

▶ For many HR professionals, OHSS is the functional area in which we have the least amount of practical experience. As such, it's particularly important to carefully review the responsibilities relating to this functional area so that you can identify specific areas in which you don't have sufficient (or sufficiently valuable) experience. Once you've identified these areas, it's time to start doing your homework. Conduct research. Use the Internet to find articles and white papers that highlight OHSS. Peruse textbooks that provide guidance relative to those particular areas. Be sure to find several real-life examples of each responsibility to ensure that you gain a variety of perspectives and insights. This is particularly important for the skill-based, rather than fact-based, components of the functional areas.

Introduction

Like every other functional area in HR, Occupational Health, Safety, and Security (OHSS) has a wide-ranging impact on the day-to-day operations of the organization. This impact is real, direct, and important—even for those HR professionals who don't have formal responsibility for OHSS.

Productivity and performance can be derailed by health-related concerns, security breaches, or non-compliance with mandatory OHSS-related requirements. As such, OHSS issues are business issues...which means they are HR issues. As HR professionals, we must consider these issues from a proactive perspective, as well as from a reactive perspective. We must also recognize the specific ways in which an understanding of OHSS-related issues can bolster our efforts to advance the mission of the organization, and to achieve organizational objectives.

Related Legislation: OHSS

Each HR professional must have a solid understanding of—and familiarity with—key OHSS legislation in order to be able to effectively handle routine and non-routine health, safety, and security related situations.

Some of the laws that impact OHSS were crafted specifically around health and safety concerns, while others address these topics more tangentially (for instance, worker's compensation laws). Congress passed three laws created specifically to address health and safety issues on a national level:

▶ Occupational Safety and Health Act (OSH Act), 1970

▶ Mine Safety and Health Act (MSH Act), 1977

▶ Drug-Free Workplace Act, 1988

EXAM ALERT

Revisit other laws—such as the Americans with Disabilities Act (ADA) and the Fair Labor Standards Act (FLSA)—to reacquaint yourself with how they relate to health and safety issues.

Occupational Safety and Health Act (OSH Act), 1970

The OSH Act was the first law to establish consistent workplace health and safety standards. The Act's opening words communicate the reason for its creation—which is, essentially, to protect workers by ensuring safe and healthful workplaces.

According to a 2003 Department of Labor (DOL) report, the Act has been successful: Since its passage, workplace deaths have decreased by 62% and occupational injury and illness rates have dropped 40%—all while the size of the workforce has doubled.

The Act established three key mechanisms to ensure safe and healthful workplaces. Specifically, the Act

- ▶ Established a means of enforcement.

- ▶ Encouraged and assisted states to take steps to ensure safe and healthful workplaces.

- ▶ Provided for relevant research, information, education, and training.

> **EXAM ALERT**
>
> Familiarize yourself with OSHA's 13 specific objectives, as listed in Section 2 of the Act ("Congressional Findings and Purpose"—www.osha.gov).

The Act also called for the establishment of the Occupational Safety and Health Administration (also known as OSHA). Residing within the Department of Labor (DOL), OSHA administers and enforces the Act.

OSHA Coverage

The Act offers broad coverage. In a 1999 letter, OSHA defined its coverage as including "employees of an organization." Unlike most other employment laws, smaller employers are not exempt from OSHA. Exceptions do exist, however—for instance, family farms that do not employ anyone outside the family are not covered under OSHA. Also excluded from the Act are self-employed individuals, state government employees, and local government employees. State and local government employees, however, are often covered by state-sponsored OHSS legislation. Employees who work in specific industries (such as mining) that are covered by their own industry-specific laws are also exempt from OSHA.

General Duty Clause—Section 5(a)

The "General Duty Clause" of the Act identifies two primary duties for employers, and one for employees, upon which all subsequent requirements (called "standards") are ultimately built:

1. Employers must ensure a safe workplace. The Act defines "safe workplace" as one which is "free from recognized hazards that are causing or are likely to cause death or serious physical harm to his employees."

2. Employers must comply with all current and future OSHA-related standards.

The General Duty Clause comes into play when there are no existing standards covering a particular job or industry. Standards will be discussed later in this chapter.

The General Duty Clause also identifies a duty for employees—that that they must follow all safety and health-related rules stemming from the Act. This duty is defined broadly, as well, in that it would include

▶ Reporting hazardous conditions to their supervisor

▶ Immediately reporting any and all job-related injuries or illnesses to their employer

▶ Cooperating in the event of an OSHA inspection or investigation

Employee Rights under OSHA

The OSHA 3165 poster—which must be displayed in a conspicuous place that is easily visible to employees and applicants for employment—lists each employee's rights:

▶ You have the right to notify your employer or OSHA about workplace hazards. You may ask OSHA to keep your name confidential.

▶ You have the right to request an OSHA inspection if you believe that there are unsafe and unhealthful conditions in your workplace. You or your representative may participate in the inspection.

▶ You can file a complaint with OSHA within 30 days of discrimination by your employer for making safety and health complaints or for exercising your rights under the OSH Act.

▶ You have a right to see OSHA citations issued to your employer. Your employer must post the citations at or near the place of the alleged violation.

▶ Your employer must correct workplace hazards by the date indicated on the citation and must certify that these hazards have been reduced or eliminated.

▶ You have the right to copies of your medical records or records of your exposure to toxic and harmful substances or conditions.

▶ Your employer must post this notice in your workplace.

Employer Requirements Under OSHA—Recordkeeping, Reporting, and Posting

HR professionals must have a solid understanding of recordkeeping, reporting, and posting requirements under the OSH Act. The first step for any organization is to determine whether it needs to maintain such records.

Determining Whether an Employer is Required to Maintain Records

Most organizations with less than 11 employees are exempt from OSHA recordkeeping requirements. OSHA also publishes a list of specific low-risk industries that are exempt from this requirement, even if they employ more than 10 people.

Distinguishing Injury from Illness

For OSHA reporting purposes, OSHA defines a work-related "injury" as "any wound or damage to the body resulting from an event in the work environment." Identifying and classifying a work-related "illness" is somewhat more complicated. Illnesses can fall into any one of the following categories: skin diseases or disorders, respiratory conditions, poisoning, hearing loss, or a very broad category called "all other illnesses."

Determining What Must be Recorded

According to OSHA, an injury or illness must be recorded if it results in one or more of the following:

▶ Death

▶ Days away from work

▶ Restricted work or job transfer

▶ Loss of consciousness

▶ Medical treatment beyond "first aid," as defined in OSHA's directions.

EXAM ALERT

Familiarize yourself with medical interventions that come under the category of first aid, as well as with those that go beyond first aid.

▶ Work-related injuries or illnesses that are considered "significant," as defined in OSHA's directions, or that meet specific criteria outlined in those directions

Required Forms

Covered employers must maintain records using OSHA Form 300, OSHA Form 300A, and OSHA Form 301 for each worksite.

OSHA's Form 300: Injury and Illness Incident Report

OSHA's Form 300 is used to record the "what," "how," "when," "where," and "who" of work-related injuries and illnesses. The employer has six working days from the time it learns of a work-related injury or illness to record it on this form.

> **NOTE**
>
> Work-related deaths and/or inpatient hospitalizations of three or more employees resulting from a work-related incident must be reported to OSHA within eight hours.

> **CAUTION**
>
> Care must be taken to preserve employee privacy when completing these forms. Under certain circumstances—including upon employee request—the words "privacy case" should be substituted for the employee's name. In these cases, a separate document must be maintained matching case numbers with employee names (for identification purposes).

OSHA's Form 301: Injury and Illness Incident Report:

A separate Form 301 must be completed for each work-related injury or illness within seven calendar days of the date on which the employer learns of the work-related injury or illness. Completed forms must be maintained by the employee for five years following the year in which the incident or illness occurred.

OSHA's Form 300A: Summary of Work-Related Injuries and Illnesses

Employers use the Form 300A to record a numeric summary of all work related injuries and illnesses logged in OSHA's Form 300 over the course of each calendar year. This form indicates the number of cases, the number of workdays impacted, and the numbers and types of work-related injuries and illnesses. A worksheet is also available to assist employers in filling out this summary. Each year, a completed Form 300 must be posted conspicuously for three months (between February 1 and April 30).

> **TIP**
>
> Detailed instructions on how to complete these forms, as well as actual downloadable forms, can be found at www.osha.gov.

Optional Calculations

OSHA provides formulas for calculating incidence rates (see http://www.osha.gov).

An employer would then compare its incidence rate to incidence rates for other employers of similar size, or other employers in their industry.

Posting and Access Requirements

All employers covered by OSHA must display the OSHA 3165 poster (see "Employee Rights under OSHA").

In addition, all employers covered by OSHA must provide employees, their designated representatives, and OSHA with access to employee exposure and medical records (29 CFR 1910.1020). Exposure records must be maintained for 30 years, and medical records must be maintained for 30 years after the employee's period of employment ends.

Employer Responsibilities—Standards

OSHA's standards, or requirements, apply to one or more of the four industries designated by OSHA:

▶ General Industry

▶ Maritime

▶ Construction

▶ Agriculture

OSHA identifies six standards that apply to most general industry employers:

▶ **Hazard Communication Standard ("Employee Right-to-Know")**: This standard ensures that employers and employees have knowledge and awareness about hazardous chemicals located in the workplace, and that they know how to protect themselves. This is also referred to as "Employee Right-to-Know." Specifically, this standard requires all employers having hazardous materials at the workplace to implement a written Hazard Communication Program. Four important key elements of this program are Material Safety Data Sheets (MSDS), orientation, training, and container labeling requirements.

▶ **Emergency Action Plan Standard**: While recommended for all employers, an emergency action plan is mandatory only if required by a separate OSHA standard.

▶ **Fire Safety Standard**: While recommended for all employers, a fire safety plan is mandatory only if required by a separate OSHA standard.

▶ **Exit Routes Standard:** Mandatory for all employers, the exit route standard defines exit requirements and addresses maintenance, safeguarding, and operational dimensions of exit routes. OSHA defines an exit route as "a continuous and unob-structed path of exit travel from any point within a workplace to a point of safety" (Source: OSHA Fact Sheet, Exit Routes).

▶ **Walking/Working Surfaces Standard**: Mandatory in all permanent places of employ-ment (with few exceptions), this standard seeks to minimize or eliminate slips, trips, and falls in the workplace. Its coverage impacts surfaces such as floors, platforms, lad-ders, and steps.

▶ **Medical and First Aid Standard:** OSHA requires employers to provide medical and first aid personnel and supplies in accordance with the hazards of the workplace. The specifics of each program, however, will differ from workplace to workplace, and from employer to employer.

In a list that OSHA specifically describes as "not comprehensive," OSHA identifies nine addi-tional standards that may apply to workplaces. These are described in Table 8.1:

TABLE 8.1   Nine OSHA Standards

Standard	Employers May Be Covered If...
Machine Guarding	Employees operate machinery such as saws, slicers, power presses, and so on.
Lockout / Tagout	Employees work with equipment that can start up without warning, or that release hazardous energy.
Electrical Hazards	Any electrical systems are present.
Personal Protective Equipment (PPE)	Mandatory employer assessment determines that PPE is necessary. If so, the employer must provide, maintain, and require the use of PPE.
Respirators	Respirators are necessary to protect the health of employees. If so, the employer must provide respirators.
Hearing Conservation	Employees are exposed to excessive noise.
Confined Spaces	Employees work in confined spaces, thereby increasing the likelihood of entrapment, and/or placing the employee in close physical proximity to hazards (such as machinery with moving parts).
Bloodborne Pathogens	Employees are exposed to blood or other bodily fluids through the performance of their regular duties.
Powered Industrial Tools	Powered industrial tools, such as forklifts, are used.

The Needlestick Safety and Prevention Act of 2000

The Needlestick Safety and Prevention Act of 2000 was, essentially, a compliance directive for enforcing the Bloodborne Pathogens Standard. The Act added three key requirements to the existing standard:

▶ Evaluation and implementation of safer needle devices (as they become available). Reviews of—and searches for—such enhancements must be done annually.

▶ Actively involve employees who actually use needles and needle devices in this evaluation and selection process.

▶ Maintenance of a log of all injuries resulting from contaminated sharps.

EXAM ALERT

The PHR exam may cover any or all of these standards in greater detail. Increase your knowledge of all of them, especially if they do not apply to your particular industry.

OSHA—Inspections and Investigations

OSHA compliance officers can conduct inspections or investigations without prior notice or warning. Upon showing proper identification, a compliance officer is free to conduct "reasonable" inspections and investigations during regular working hours.

EXAM ALERT

There are special circumstances under which OSHA may give employers 24 hours advance notice. Visit www.osha.com for more information about these special circumstances.

Employer Rights

Employers have certain rights with respect to inspections, including the right to

▶ Request proper identification from compliance officers

▶ Ask the compliance officer for the reason for the inspection or investigation—and get an answer

▶ Have an opening conference with the compliance officer

▶ Accompany the compliance officer as he or she conducts the inspection

▶ Have a closing conference with the compliance officer

▶ File a "notice of contest" to dispute the results of the inspection

▶ Request an informal settlement agreement process after an inspection

▶ Protect the confidentiality of trade secrets

▶ Require the compliance officer to obtain a search warrant

OSHA Priorities

OSHA recognizes that its compliance officers can't be everywhere, all the time. For this reason, OSHA has established a tiered priority system for workplace inspections. Listed in order of importance (from highest to lowest), OSHA's priorities are

1. Imminent danger

2. Catastrophes and fatal accidents

3. Employee complaints

4. Referrals from other individuals, agencies, organizations, or the media

5. Planned inspections in high-hazard industries

6. Follow-up inspections

See www.osha.gov for additional information about each of these conditions.

OSHA Inspections

OSHA inspections consist of an opening conference, the physical inspection, and a closing conference.

EXAM ALERT

Know what happens during each of these phases of the inspection. Know what compliance officers look for.

EXAM ALERT

At times, OSHA will investigate an employee complaint with a "phone/fax investigation" instead of an on-site inspection. Know the circumstances under which this can happen, and know what an employer needs to do.

OSHA Violations and Penalties

OSHA has established five categories of violations—and five levels of accompanying penalties. Table 8.2 highlights these penalties.

TABLE 8.2 OSHA Violations and Penalties

Violation	Description of Violation of Standard	Penalty
Willful	Deliberate and intentional.	Up to $70,000 per violation. Will escalate in the event of employee death. Incarceration is possible.
Serious	Death or serious injury probable. The employer either knew or should have known about the violation.	Up to $7,000 for each violation.
Other-than-serious	Unlikely to result in serious injury or death.	Up to $7,000 for each violation.
De Minimis	No direct or immediate relationship to safety or health.	NA. They are documented, but are not included on the citation.
Failure to Abate Prior Violation	Violation continues beyond the prescribed abatement date.	Up to $7,000 per day
Repeat	Same or substantially similar violation as was found during a previous inspection.	Up to $70,000 for each violation.

EXAM ALERT

With the exception of those which are *de minimis*, violations result in citations. Know the process that must be followed upon receipt of a citation, and know the appeal process.

Mine Safety and Health Act (MSH), 1977

The MSH Act is the second piece of legislation created specifically to protect employee health and safety—this time, for underground and surface miners working in coal, as well as non-coal, mines. Unlike OSHA, inspections of mines are mandatory—at least four times a year for underground mines, and at least twice a year for surface mines.

NOTE

Check out www.msha.gov for additional information on the MSH Act.

Drug-Free Workplace Act, 1988

The Drug Free Workplace Act requires federal contractors (with contracts of $100,000 or more) and individuals and organizations who are awarded federal grants (of any size) to agree to maintain a workplace free from drugs. Like the OSH and MSH Acts, the Drug Free Workplace Act is administered and enforced by the Department of Labor.

The Act imposes three key requirements on employers:

▶ Publish a statement notifying employees that the manufacture, distribution, dispensation, possession, or use of a controlled substance in the workplace is prohibited. This statement must also include a description of the consequences of violating this policy.

▶ Establish a drug-free awareness program addressing the dangers of drug use in the workplace, the employer's drug-free policy (including the consequences of violating that policy), and information about programs that are available to employees who use drugs.

▶ Distribute a copy of the workplace substance abuse policy to all employees.

NOTE
Visit www.dol.gov for additional information on the Drug-Free Workplace Act.

Occupational Health

At their core, occupational health programs and initiatives help to ensure that workplaces remain healthy. Within that framework, organizations need to consider the physical, psychological, and emotional dimensions of health. Organizations also need to realize that while maintaining a healthy work *environment* is critical to maintaining a healthy *workplace*, it isn't enough. Employers also need to address—and be prepared to respond to—health-related issues that can develop in the workplace because of conditions, issues, or problems that don't originate in the workplace.

One area of responsibility related to occupational health involves identifying, preventing, and/or minimizing health hazards in the workplace. Another dimension involves developing appropriate responses in the event that a health hazard or health risk does emerge.

Health Hazards

A health hazard refers to anything in the workplace that creates or increases the possibility of work-related injuries. There are several types of health hazards with which HR professionals must be familiar.

Environmental Health Hazards

Environmental health hazards originate in—and exist because of—"something" in the workplace. Environmental health hazards refer to a wide spectrum of conditions, circumstances, objects and/or organisms in the workplace that can create or increase the likelihood of employee illness or injury.

Physical Hazards—Objects/Conditions

One type of physical health hazard results from actual, tangible "things" and/or conditions in the workplace that increase the risk of work-related illnesses or injuries. This type of hazard may be caused by or related to a variety of factors. Table 8.3 highlights some of these factors.

TABLE 8.3   Causes of Physical Hazards

Cause/Contributing Factor	Example
Failure to properly maintain or repair equipment or other physical objects	A tear in carpeting is not repaired, increasing the likelihood of trips and falls.
Failure to address and resolve potentially dangerous conditions	A puddle of water collects on the floor because of a leaking freestanding freezer unit, increasing the likelihood of slips and falls.
Poor process design	Bus drivers (such as for rental car companies) who enter information into portable computer terminals while in transit, increasing the likelihood of accidents.
Physical conditions *relating to* the actual performance of the job	A road paving crew installs or resurfaces asphalt in high heat conditions, increasing the likelihood of dehydration or heatstroke.
Physical conditions *resulting from* the actual performance of the job	MRI operators who are exposed to high noise levels, increasing the likelihood of temporary or permanent hearing loss.

Physical Hazards—Design

Physical hazards can also result from the way in which the workplace or workspace is designed (also referred to as ergonomics). Ergonomic problems can result from poor *workplace design*— for instance, doors in hallways that have no windows increasing the likelihood of accidents. Ergonomic problems can also result from poor *workspace design*—for instance, LCD monitors that are placed above eye-level increase the likelihood of back or neck injury since employees need to frequently look up.

Another significant area of concern involves work-related musculoskeletal disorders (MSDs). MSDs are perhaps better known as "repetitive stress injuries" (RSIs), "cumulative trauma syndrome" (CTSs), or "cumulative trauma disorders" (CTDs). Specific examples of MSDs are

▶ Carpal tunnel syndrome

▶ Trigger finger

▶ Chronic lumbar strain

- ▸ Tendonitis

- ▸ Bursitis

MSDs are caused, or exacerbated, by forceful exertions, awkward postures, repetitive movements, and/or exposure to extreme environmental conditions (for example, heat, cold, humidity or vibration). MSDs represent a serious and expensive workplace problem. In 1998, the National Academy of Sciences published a report estimating that financial costs from MSDs were in the vicinity of $20 billion annually.

OSHA has adopted a four-pronged approach to address MSDs and other ergonomics-related issues:

- ▸ Industry-specific or task-specific guidelines

- ▸ Enforcement

- ▸ Outreach and assistance (to businesses)

- ▸ National Advisory Committee

Chemical Health Hazards

Chemicals represent another potential workplace hazard. Many—and some would argue most—businesses need some type of chemicals to operate (for instance, gasoline at a service station, acetone at a nail salon, or certain cleaning supplies in an office). As required by the Hazard Communication Standard, employers must have MSDS sheets for all chemicals located in the workplace.

MSDS Sheets

In general, the MSDS must provide information about chemical hazards in the workplace, as well as protective measures that are available. Although OSHA does not mandate use of any specific MSDS format (unlike the I-9 form), the Agency does provide the following sample MSDS on its website. (This form, OSHA 174, does include and reflect all information that is required to comply with MSDS guidelines.)

Material Safety Data Sheet	**U.S. Department of Labor**
May be used to comply with OSHA's Hazard Communication Standard, 29 CFR 1910.1200. Standard must be consulted for specific requirements.	Occupational Safety and Health Administration (Non-Mandatory Form) Form Approved OMB No. 1218-0072
IDENTITY (As Used on Label and List)	
	Note: Blank spaces are not permitted. If any item is not applicable, or no information is available, the space must be marked to indicate that.

SECTION I

Manufacturer's Name   **Emergency Telephone Number**

Address *(Number, Street, City, State, and ZIP Code)*   Telephone Number for Information

Date Prepared

Signature of Preparer *(optional)*

SECTION II—HAZARDOUS INGREDIENTS/IDENTITY INFORMATION

Hazardous Components (Specific Chemical Identity; Common Name(s))	OSHA PEL	ACGIH TLV	Other Limits Recommended	% *(optional)*

SECTION III—PHYSICAL/CHEMICAL CHARACTERISTICS

Boiling Point   Specific Gravity (H_2O = 1)

Vapor Pressure (mm Hg)   Melting Point

Vapor Density (AIR = 1)   Evaporation Rate (Butyl Acetate = 1)

Solubility in Water

Appearance and Odor

SECTION IV—FIRE AND EXPLOSION HAZARD DATA

Flash Point (Method Used)   Flammable Limits   LEL   UEL

Extinguishing Media

Special Fire Fighting
Procedures

Unusual Fire and
Explosion Hazards

(Reproduce locally)   OSHA 174,
                                                                Sept. 1985

SECTION V—REACTIVITY DATA

Stability   Unstable   Conditions to Avoid

                                   Stable

Incompatibility
(Materials to Avoid)

Hazardous Decomposition
or Byproducts

Hazardous Polymerization   May Occur   Conditions to Avoid

                                   Will Not Occur

SECTION VI—HEALTH HAZARD DATA

Route(s) of Entry:	Inhalation?	Skin?	Ingestion?

Health Hazards
(Acute and Chronic)

Carcinogenicity:	NTP?	IARC Monographs?	OSHA Regulated?

Signs and Symptoms
of Exposure

Medical Conditions Generally
Aggravated by Exposure

Emergency and First Aid
Procedures

SECTION VII—PRECAUTIONS FOR SAFE HANDLING AND USE

Steps to Be Taken in Case Material is Released or Spilled

Waste Disposal Method

Precautions to Be Taken in Handling and Storing

Other Precautions

SECTION VIII—CONTROL MEASURES

Respiratory Protection *(Specify Type)*

Ventilation	Local Exhaust	Special
	Mechanical *(General)*	Other

Protective Gloves	Eye Protection

Other Protective Clothing or Equipment

Work/Hygienic Practices

* U.S.G.P.O.:
1986 - 491 - 529/45775

EXAM ALERT

Be familiar with required—and suggested—elements of MSDS sheets.

Teratogens

One specific group of chemicals, called teratogens, will not harm pregnant women—but do have the potential to harm unborn fetuses. To deal with this category of chemicals, some organizations (perhaps well-meaning, or perhaps just looking to minimize potential legal exposure) have developed fetal protection policies. These policies are *intended* to protect unborn fetuses from the possibility of being harmed by teratogens. The *impact* of most (if not all) these policies, as ruled by the Supreme Court, is unlawful gender discrimination.

The landmark case that resulted in this Supreme Court ruling was *Automobile Workers v. Johnson Controls* (1990). Johnson Controls manufactured batteries, a process that exposed employees to high levels of lead. The Supreme Court ruled that Johnson Controls's policy constituted a violation of Title VII of the Civil Rights Act of 1964, as amended by the Pregnancy Discrimination Act. The Act states that women cannot be discriminated against

> "because of or on the basis of pregnancy, childbirth, or related medical conditions; and women affected by pregnancy, childbirth, or related medical conditions shall be treated the same for all employment related purposes."

In the Johnson case, Supreme Court Associate Justice Byron White wrote in his opinion that "decisions about the welfare of the next generation must be left to the parents who conceive, bear, support, and raise them, rather than to the employers who hire those parents."

Biological Health Hazards

Biological health hazards can be introduced into the workplace by people—employees, customers, vendors, and so forth. Biological health hazards can also be caused by some factor other than person-to-person transmission.

Under the ADA, infectious diseases are considered to be disabilities. As such, employers must determine what reasonable accommodations—specifically, ones that do not cause undue hardship—must be afforded to individuals with infectious diseases. Infectious diseases also pose unique challenges, in that employers must take great care to ensure that the health of all individuals in the workplace is not threatened by possible person-to-person transmission. Essentially, the rights of people with infectious diseases must be balanced against the obligation to protect those who work with them.

CAUTION

Determinations relative to what constitutes "reasonable accommodation," "undue hardship," and "threat" must be made carefully. Such decisions cannot be made on the basis of misinformation, or co-workers' irrational—albeit genuine—fears. Employers should educate employees, as appropriate, while protecting the confidentiality of people with disabilities.

HR professionals need to be familiar with certain infectious diseases. In the following sections we will discuss HIV/AIDS, Hepatitis B and C, and tuberculosis.

HIV/AIDS

Human Immunodeficiency Virus (HIV) and Acquired Immune Deficiency Syndrome (AIDS) are transmitted person-to-person through blood or other bodily fluids. Transmission of HIV/AIDS is of particular importance in the health care industry, because of the nature of the work performed in that industry.

Employees with HIV/AIDS are afforded protection under the Americans with Disabilities Act. Like any other person with a disability, a person with HIV/AIDS may continue to hold his or her position as long as he or she can perform the essential functions of the position with or without reasonable accommodation (that does not cause undue hardship to the organization).

CAUTION

Bias against individuals with HIV/AIDS may exist in the workplace—and that bias is often based on misinformation. HR professionals must be alert to signs of such bias, and must be prepared to take appropriate action.

HBV

The Hepatitis B virus (HBV) causes Hepatitis B, a potentially serious (and potentially fatal) form of liver inflammation. People with HBV may experience a wide range of symptoms—anything from no symptoms to serious damage to the liver. Like HIV/AIDS, HBV is transmitted through blood and other bodily fluids, and is therefore of particular concern to those in the health care industry. Unlike HIV/AIDS, a vaccine for HBV exists—and must be made available to "all occupationally exposed employees." The term "made available" reflects the fact that an employee cannot be required to get an HBV vaccination.

HCV

The Hepatitis C virus (HCV) causes Hepatitis C, a viral infection of the liver. Transmitted by blood or bodily fluids, HCV has been identified by the Center for Disease Control and Prevention as the most chronic bloodborne infection in the United States.

While most people with HCV will experience no symptoms, over time that can change. After 10, 20, or as much as 40 years, people with Hepatitis C can develop cirrhosis or cancer of the liver. There is no vaccine for HCV, so the best protection is afforded through prevention, such as PPE (protective personal equipment).

Tuberculosis

Tuberculosis, or TB, is a highly infectious bacterial disease. While TB usually affects the lungs, it can also impact other organs.

TB can be spread by sneezing or coughing, and is thus an important workplace issue. An increase in drug-resistant strains of TB in the 1980s—along with an increased population of individuals with suppressed immune systems—led to a renewed focus on TB. The number of cases of TB has decreased dramatically in the last decade; in fact, according to OSHA, the number of cases of TB is now at its lowest level since reporting began in 1953.

Employee Assistance Programs

Employee assistance programs (EAPs) provide employees with help and resources on a variety of personal issues that can—and often do—have a direct impact on employee job performance. As such, EAPs—which are paid for by organizations—benefit employers as well as employees.

EAPs provide a variety of programs addressing topics that include (but are not necessarily limited to) financial, legal, and health issues. Areas of assistance can range from childcare, to elder care, to substance abuse. EAPs are also available as a resource for workplaces that have experienced difficult incidents, such the death of an employee or an act of workplace violence.

EAPs can be administered within the organization, through vendors who operate outside the organization, or through some combination of the two. Still others are provided through a consortium arrangement.

> **CAUTION**
>
> The degree to which employees perceive an EAP as confidential will play a key role in determining the degree to which employees will utilize its services—and, therefore, the degree of success that the EAP will ultimately achieve. Ensuring confidentiality is essential, but—by itself—is not enough. Ensuring that employees recognize and believe in the confidentiality of the program is equally important.

External EAPs are estimated to cost anywhere from $15 to $40 per employee, per year. EAPs, however, can pay for themselves many times over by attaining the following measurable contributions:

- ▶ Reduced turnover
- ▶ Decreased absenteeism and/or tardiness
- ▶ Increased productivity
- ▶ Increased employee satisfaction
- ▶ Decreased risk of workplace violence

Health and Wellness Programs

Health and Wellness Programs offer employees the opportunity to enhance the quality of their lives through healthier lifestyle choices. Health and wellness programs take a proactive approach to health of body, mind, and spirit.

While prevention is a key element, health and wellness programs can also provide assistance to employees who are dealing with existing health issues (for instance, weight problems or smoking).

EXAM ALERT

Be familiar with types, elements, and benefits of health and wellness programs.

Like EAPs, health and wellness programs benefit employers as well as employees. As with EAPs, HR professionals must be prepared to demonstrate the specific financial and non-financial benefits that would accrue to their employers as a result of implementing health and wellness programs.

Chemical Use and Dependency

The costs associated with chemical/substance use, abuse, and dependency are economically staggering to workplaces:

▶ According to the U.S. Department of Health and Human Services, in 1990, problems resulting from the use of alcohol and other drugs cost American businesses an estimated $81.6 billion in lost productivity due to premature death (37 billion) and illness (44 billion)—of which approximately $70 billion was attributed to drinking.

▶ The National Institutes of Health recently reported that alcohol and drug abuse cost the economy $246 billion in 1992.

▶ In 1992, the National Association of Treatment Providers in Laguna Hills, California, estimated that drug abuse results in 500 million lost workdays each year.

▶ According to results of a National Institute on Drug Abuse (NIDA) sponsored survey, employees who use drugs are 2.2 times more likely to request early dismissal or time off, 2.5 times more likely to have absences of eight days or more, three times more likely to be late for work, 3.6 times more likely to be involved in a workplace accident, and 5 times more likely to file a workers' compensation claim.

Substance Abuse Programs

According to the U.S. Department of Labor's Working Partners for an Alcohol- and Drug-Free Workplace initiative, a comprehensive substance program consists of the following five components:

- ▶ Drug-free workplace policy
- ▶ Supervisor training
- ▶ Employee education
- ▶ Employee assistance
- ▶ Drug testing

One more critical element (in many ways, the *most* critical element) must be added to this list: management buy-in and support. Without this, the likelihood that the program will be successful is greatly diminished—and HR is more likely to be seen as an enforcer, rather than as a strategic partner.

Symptoms of Chemical and Substance Abuse

HR professionals need to be able to recognize the warning signs of chemical and substance abuse:

- ▶ Sudden decline in quality or quantity or work performed, for no apparent reason
- ▶ Increased errors
- ▶ Increased accidents
- ▶ Inconsistent behavior
- ▶ Emotional unpredictability

It is important to note, however, that any of these symptoms could result from a variety of other factors, so guard against jumping to any conclusions.

Drug Testing

Drug testing in the workplace is a hotly debated topic. Some states restrict certain types of drug testing, and some federal laws require drug testing of certain employees. Drug testing programs must be administered fairly, and consistently, to similarly situated employees.

CAUTION

Consult with senior leadership—and with legal counsel—before implementing or changing a drug testing program. Such changes can have unforeseen legal and employee relations ramifications.

There are a variety of different types of drug testing programs, each of which has different goals and objectives. Table 8.4 highlights these programs further.

TABLE 8.4   Types of Drug Tests

Type of Drug Test	Purpose/Description
Pre-employment	Decrease the likelihood of hiring someone who is currently using/abusing drugs.
Pre-promotion	Decrease the likelihood of promoting an employee who is currently using/abusing drugs.
Annual physical tests	Drug testing is performed as part of each employee's annual physical exam to identify current drug users/abusers for assistance or disciplinary action.
Reasonable suspicion and for cause	For cause tests are conducted when an employee shows obvious signs of not being fit for duty. Reasonable suspicion tests are conducted when employee has a documented pattern of unsafe work behavior. These tests are conducted to protect the safety and well being of employees and co-workers, and to identify opportunities for rehabilitation.
Random	Unannounced tests are conducted at random, for reasons related to safety or security.
Post-accident	Employees who are involved in an accident or unsafe practice incident are tested to determine whether alcohol or some other drug was a factor. These tests are intended to protect the safety of employees (users and non-users) and to identify opportunities for rehabilitation.
Treatment follow up	Employees who return to work after participating in an alcohol or drug treatment program are periodically tested to ensure that they remain substance-free.

EXAM ALERT

Be familiar with drug testing techniques, as well as appropriate intervention strategies.

Work-related Stress

Stress is a significant workplace issue. In its 1999 report entitled *Stress at Work*, the National Institute for Public Safety and Health (NIOSH) defined stress as the "harmful physical and emotional responses that occur when the requirements of the job do not match the capabilities, resources, or needs of the worker." Stress can be more than disquieting—it can actually cause illness and injury. And stress is expensive. The American Institute of Stress estimates a $300 billion annual price tag for stress, which includes costs relating to accidents; absenteeism; employee turnover; diminished productivity; direct medical, legal, and insurance costs; workers' compensation awards; and tort and FELA (Federal Employers' Liability Act) judgments. In the book *Stress Costs*, author Ravi Tangri presents a formula for tabulating the actual costs of stress, which he asserts account for

▶ 19% of absenteeism

▶ 40% percent of turnover

▶ 30% percent of short- and long-term disability

▶ 10% percent of drug plan costs

▶ 60% percent of total workplace accidents

EXAM ALERT

Be familiar with the physical, psychological, and mental manifestations of stress.

HR professionals must also be able to identify, implement, and evaluate interventions designed to prevent or eradicate job stress. NIOSH outlines a valuable three-step approach to this in Stress at Work: http://www.cdc.gov/niosh/.

EXAM ALERT

Stress, left unchecked or unresolved, can lead to burnout. Know the symptoms of employee burnout.

Safety

Workplace safety can be defined in many different ways. In essence, a "safe workplace" can be defined as one in which employees are free from risks of injury or illness. Call it prevention…or call it avoidance…either way, workplace safety requires that companies take a proactive approach to accidents, injury, and illness:

1. First, organizations must minimize the likelihood that work-related injuries or illnesses will occur.

2. Second, organizations must proactively establish response plans in the event that injuries or illnesses do occur.

OSHA and Workplace Safety

OSHA, as its name implies, is the government agency charged with ensuring a safe and healthy workplace. OSHA recommends a four-module approach to safety and health management:

▶ **Module 1**: **Safety and Health Payoffs**—Work-related injuries are expensive, financially and otherwise. According to the National Safety Council, workplace injuries cost society $127.7 billion in 1997. The cost is also human—according to OSHA, nearly 16,000 workers are injured every workday.

▶ **Module 2**: **Management System—Safety and Health Integration**—Organizations must create and cultivate a culture of safety. Safety can't be separate from the culture; rather, it must be an integral component of the culture. Within this culture of safety, four specific elements can then be created, and integrated:

   ▶ Management Leadership & Employee Involvement

   ▶ Worksite Analysis

   ▶ Hazard Prevention and Control

   ▶ Safety & Health Training

▶ **Module 3: Conducting a Safety & Health Checkup**—Organizations must then assess their own safety and health—take a good hard look at themselves with respect to each of those four areas identified in module 2.

▶ **Module 4: Creating Change**—The roadmap is in place, and the self-analysis has been conducted. The next step is to implement necessary change. In order to do this, obstacles will need to be identified and overcome, and a process implementation strategy—beginning with the buy-in of top management—must be developed and implemented.

Safety Committees

Safety committees provide a means by which employees and managers can collaboratively work toward increasing workplace safety. Safety committees can also support HR professionals as they research, develop, select, and implement safety training and incentive programs.

> **EXAM ALERT**
>
> Familiarize yourself with different types of safety training and incentive programs, as well as effective ways to implement those programs within the organization.

Some of the purposes of safety committees are as follows:

- Building and maintaining interest in health and safety issues.
- Ensuring that managers and employees recognize that they are primarily responsible for preventing workplace accidents.
- Reinforcing safety as part of the fabric of the organization's culture.
- Providing a forum for discussing health- and safety-related issues.
- Informing, educating, and training employees about emerging safety-related information and/or guidelines.

Functions that safety committees might carry out in support of these objectives could include

- Analyzing accidents/incidents to identify trends, and to plan corrective action.
- Conducting periodic (such as monthly) safety inspections.
- Planning and carrying out training.
- Reporting and analyzing accomplishments as well as current safety concerns.
- Setting annual safety objectives.
- Ensuring that an effective safety program is in place.

> **EXAM ALERT**
>
> Carefully review the specified safety-related responsibilities and knowledge. In addition to reflecting upon your practical experience, seek out as much information as possible—anecdotal and otherwise—relative to each of those topics. This is particularly important if you have had limited practical experience with safety-related issues.

Security

Security refers to protection of the workplace and of the employees who work there. Security threats can come from a wide range of possible sources, just a few of which are

▶ Natural disasters, such as earthquakes

▶ Theft

▶ Workplace violence

▶ Terrorism (including biological terrorism)

▶ Identity theft

▶ Fire

▶ Flood

▶ Hazardous materials

▶ Computer viruses/hackers

HR professionals need a working knowledge of these and other threats that can jeopardize workplace security.

EXAM ALERT

Familiarize yourself with different types of safety training and incentive programs, as well as effective ways to implement those programs within the organization.

A cursory review of the above list reinforces the fact that security issues are business issues—ones that can jeopardize an organization's very existence. As such, it is critical for organizations to conduct a "SWOT" analysis—strengths, weaknesses, opportunities and threats—of security-related issues.

Threats are often perceived as coming from "outside" the organization. Overlooking "internal" threats, however, can be disastrous. For instance, a company's own employees can even present a security threat. Disgruntled employees, departing employees, or former employees can present threats in the form of sabotage, theft, espionage, or violence.

HR must partner with internal and/or external security experts to protect the tangible—and intangible—assets of the organization. Of primary importance are the organization's human assets—its employees. Other assets, such as technology, facilities, and financial assets, must also be protected.

When Prevention Isn't Enough

The criticality of emergency preparedness planning was perhaps among the most painful—and the most valuable—of the many lessons learned from the 9/11 terrorist attacks. On that day, the unthinkable became real. Now, it is a part of our shared history. As HR professionals, however, we must not allow any degree of complacency to creep back into our business operations. HR must work ceaselessly and collaboratively to develop emergency response plans should a situation arise in which security is breached. While the plans we collaboratively develop may never be utilized, failing to do so will surely place employers, employees, and all other assets at significant risk.

Chapter Summary

Knowledge and skill in the areas of occupational health, safety, and security present another significant opportunity for HR professionals to add value to the organization. As such, HR professionals must understand and be able to respond effectively to OHSS issues.

This holds true even if OHSS does not fall directly within an HR professional's formal "job description." HR professionals cannot be prepared to handle only those situations that are predictable or routine. We need look no further than the wake of the terror attacks of 9/11 to see examples of how HR professionals can—and will—be called upon to bring their knowledge and expertise to situations that are predictable, as well as situations that are unpredictable. Knowledge and skill in the areas of occupational health, safety, and security will ensure that we are poised to rise to the challenges with which we will inevitably be presented.

Key Terms

- Occupational Safety and Health Act (OSH Act), 1970
- Americans with Disabilities Act (ADA), 1992
- Mine Safety and Health Act (MSH Act), 1977
- Drug-Free Workplace Act, 1988
- General Duty Clause
- Standards
- OSHA 3165
- Work-related Injury/Illness
- OSHA Form 300
- Privacy Case
- OSHA Form 300A
- OSHA Form 301
- General Industry
- Hazard Communication Standard
- Material Safety Data Sheets (MSDS)
- Emergency Action Plan Standard
- Fire Safety Standard
- Exit Routes Standard
- Walking/Working Surfaces Standard
- Medical and First Aid Standard
- Machine Guarding Standard
- Lockout/Tagout Standard
- Electric Hazards Standard
- Personal Protective Equipment Standard
- Respirators Standard
- Hearing Conservation Standard
- Confined Spaces Standard
- Bloodborne Pathogens Standard
- Powered Industrial Tools Standard
- The Needlestick Safety and Prevention Act of 2000
- Willful Violation

- ▶ Serious Violation
- ▶ Other-Than-Serious Violation
- ▶ Repeat Violation
- ▶ Failure to Abate Prior Violation
- ▶ Health Hazards
- ▶ Environmental Hazards
- ▶ Physical Health Hazards
- ▶ Ergonomics
- ▶ Musculoskeletal Disorders (MSDs)
- ▶ Repetitive Stress Injuries (RSIs)
- ▶ Cumulative Trauma Syndrome (CTSs)
- ▶ Cumulative Trauma Disorders (CTDs)
- ▶ Teratogens
- ▶ Fetal Protection Policies
- ▶ Automobile Workers vs. Johnson Controls
- ▶ Biological Health Hazards
- ▶ Infectious Diseases
- ▶ HIV/AIDS

- ▶ HBV
- ▶ HCV
- ▶ Tuberculosis (TB)
- ▶ Employee Assistance Programs (EAPs)
- ▶ Health and Wellness Programs
- ▶ Substance Use/Abuse
- ▶ Drug Testing
- ▶ Pre-employment Drug Testing
- ▶ Pre-promotion Drug Testing
- ▶ Reasonable Suspicion Drug Testing
- ▶ For Cause Drug Testing
- ▶ Random Drug Testing
- ▶ Post-Accident Drug Testing
- ▶ Treatment Follow-up Drug Testing
- ▶ Stress
- ▶ Burnout
- ▶ Incident and Emergency Response Plans
- ▶ Safety Committees

Apply Your Knowledge

This chapter focuses on occupational health, safety, and security issues. Complete the following exercises, review questions, and exam questions as a way of reviewing and reinforcing the knowledge and skills you'll need to perform your responsibilities as an HR professional.

Exercises

1. One of the line managers with whom you consult has decided to terminate an employee for poor performance. This employee has been with the company for five years. A year ago, when a new manager (your client) took over the department, she soon realized that the employee's perform-ance was well below expectations (despite what had been written in the employee's earlier performance appraisals). The manager coached, counseled, and gave the employee every opportu-nity to improve his performance through the progressive disciplinary process. Still, his perform-ance was well below expectations. Now, the manager has asked you to help with the arrangements for the termination meeting. One of the items the manager wants your advice on is what to do about the employee's laptop computer equipment and files. Which of the following approaches would you recommend to the manager?

   ○ A. Arrange for the employee's access to all shared network files and email to be blocked or removed while the termination meeting is actually taking place. Then, out of cour-tesy to this long-term employee, allow him to take the laptop home overnight to remove any personal, non-network files.

   ○ B. Arrange for the employee's access to all electronic files and information to be blocked or removed while the termination meeting is actually taking place. Immediately after the meeting, retrieve the laptop from the employee.

   ○ C. After the termination meeting, arrange for someone to accompany the employee to his workstation. That person can watch discreetly while the employee takes a few minutes to remove personal files from his laptop.

   ○ D. Allow the employee a few minutes to privately copy or remove personal files from his laptop. This way, this long-term employee can "save face" and maintain his dignity during a difficult situation. Then, retrieve the laptop from the employee.

2. After putting together a detailed, multi-phased proposal—which included an impressive cost-benefit analysis—you have obtained approval to establish an EAP program at your organization. This the first opportunity you've had to introduce a new initiative at your organization, so you want to do everything possible to ensure its success. Which of the following factors will have the great-est impact on the ultimate success or failure of this EAP program?

   ○ A. Ensuring that employees believe that the program offers absolute confidentiality (assuming that belief is, in fact, true).

   ○ B. Ensuring that the program offers absolute confidentiality.

   ○ C. Administering the program by an outside vendor (instead of inside the organization).

   ○ D. Ensuring that you conduct a cost-benefit analysis annually to demonstrate the pro-gram's ongoing value, and to thereby secure ongoing management support.

3. An employee who just turned 18 two weeks ago—a day before she was hired—drops a box of materials on her foot, is taken to the emergency room, and is diagnosed with several broken bones. Which of the following has to happen?

  ○ **A.** OSHA must be notified within 8 hours.

  ○ **B.** The OSHA Form 300 must be completed within six working days.

  ○ **C.** The OSHA Form 301 must be completed and posted within seven calendar days of the date on which the employer learns of the work-related injury or illness.

  ○ **D.** The OSHA Form 300A must be completed within seven calendar days of the work-related injury or illness.

4. You've been selected to become the HR manager for your organization's new facility. This facility is the first "satellite" location—and in fact the *only* location other than the organization's very large world headquarters office. At WHQ, you operated as a compensation analyst, so this will be your first opportunity to function as a generalist. Since you've always been surrounded by experts from every HR discipline, you're not certain how to go about meeting safety requirements at the new location. You know that you need MSDS sheets, but you're not sure under what conditions. You do some research on the OSHA website, and learn that you must have MSDS sheets in place if

  ○ **A.** Any chemicals are accessible in the workplace.

  ○ **B.** Any chemicals are present in the workplace.

  ○ **C.** Any chemicals are stored in the workplace.

  ○ **D.** Any chemicals are used in the workplace.

5. You've accepted a position as the HR manager with a small manufacturing organization. You were acquainted with the former HR manager, since you were both active in the local SHRM chapter. He has decided to move out of state to be closer to his aging parents, and you're excited to be following in his footsteps at his former company. From everything he has told you, the company "has its act together" with respect to HR-related issues—including safety issues, EEO reports, I-9 documentation, and sound compensation practices, just to name a few. You're surprised, then, when you come across a document stating that the organization was cited for a "Serious Violation" three months earlier. You're concerned, because you know that a serious violation is

  ○ **A.** Considered by the EEOC to be deliberate and intentional.

  ○ **B.** Unlikely to result in death, but *is* likely to result in serious injury.

  ○ **C.** One that the employer either knew about or should have known about.

  ○ **D.** The most serious category of violation recognized by the Department of Justice.

Review Questions

1. What three employer requirements were added to the Bloodborne Pathogens Standard by the Needlestick Safety and Prevention Act of 2000?

2. In what way was the *Automobile Workers v. Johnson Controls* (1990) Supreme Court ruling significant?

3. The General Duty Clause identified three responsibilities: two for employers, and one for employees. What are they?

4. What is the best way to prevent Hepatitis C/HCV from being transmitted in the workplace?

5. What are the six critical components of a comprehensive substance program? Of these, which is the most important?

Exam Questions

1. Which of the following laws was not created specifically to address occupational safety and health issues?

   ○ **A.** Drug-Free Workplace Act

   ○ **B.** MSHA

   ○ **C.** OSHA

   ○ **D.** WARNA

2. Which of the following is exempt from coverage under OSHA?

   ○ **A.** Family farms that employ fewer than 11 employees

   ○ **B.** Federal government employees

   ○ **C.** Self-employed individuals

   ○ **D.** Certain low-risk industries specified by OSHA

3. Which of the following statements about health and wellness programs is most true?

   ○ **A.** They are of primary benefit to employers.

   ○ **B.** They are of primary benefit to employees.

   ○ **C.** They take a proactive approach to health and wellness issues.

   ○ **D.** They take a reactive approach to health and wellness issues.

4. All of the following are likely functions of a safety committee *except*

    ○ **A.** Investigating accidents and incidents.

    ○ **B.** Conducting inspections.

    ○ **C.** Instituting PPE enhancements.

    ○ **D.** Identifying safety concerns.

5. Which of the following is not a category of workplace drug testing?

    ○ **A.** Pre-employment

    ○ **B.** Reasonable Cause

    ○ **C.** Post-accident

    ○ **D.** Random

6. Which of the following statements does not reflect a security-related HR responsibility?

    ○ **A.** Develop/select, implement, and evaluate security plans to protect the company from liability.

    ○ **B.** Develop/select, implement, and evaluate record-keeping tools for reporting internal and external breaches of security to OSHA.

    ○ **C.** Develop/select, implement, and evaluate security plans to protect employees (for example, injuries resulting from workplace violence).

    ○ **D.** Develop/select, implement, and evaluate incident and emergency response plans

7. Which of the following is most likely to cause or contribute to the onset of an MSD?

    ○ **A.** Improper use of PPE.

    ○ **B.** Poor ergonomic design.

    ○ **C.** Poor ventilation.

    ○ **D.** Improper use of MSDS.

8. An employee who has just learned that he or she is HIV positive

  ○ **A.** Is entitled to continue performing his or her job as long as he or she can perform the essential functions of that job.

  ○ **B.** May continue to perform his or her job until he or she begins to develop visible or other outward symptoms.

  ○ **C.** Should strongly consider informing co-workers about his or her HIV status, so as to address any fears or concerns in a proactive manner.

  ○ **D.** Constitutes a direct threat to co-workers' health, and should therefore be strongly encouraged to take a leave of absence.

9. According to OSH Act, which of the following statements is true?

  ○ **A.** Employers must correct workplace hazards by the date indicated on the citation and must certify that these hazards have been reduced or eliminated.

  ○ **B.** Employees have the right to copies of medical records of co-workers who have been exposed to toxic and harmful substances or conditions.

  ○ **C.** Employers must submit a plan to reduce or eliminate workplace hazards by the date indicated on the citation.

  ○ **D.** Employees have the right to review, but not to photocopy, their medical records or records of their exposure to toxic and harmful substances or conditions.

10. Under OSHA, employees enjoy all of the following rights *except*

  ○ **A.** The right to notify their employer or OSHA about workplace hazards.

  ○ **B.** The right to ask OSHA to maintain your confidentiality.

  ○ **C.** The right to request an OSHA inspection if you believe that there are unsafe and unhealthful conditions in your workplace.

  ○ **D.** The right to file a complaint with OSHA within 45 days of discrimination by your employer for making safety and health complaints or for exercising your rights under the OSH Act.

Answers to Exercises

1. **Answer B is the best response.** Employees who are being terminated pose a potentially significant risk to the organization's technological, human, and financial resources—including proprietary information. This holds true for any employee—even long-standing ones. Don't take any chances. With respect to technical considerations,

access to all computer-based files and information should be blocked or removed during (but not before) the termination meeting. As appropriate, arrangements can be made for the employee to retrieve personal computer files at a later time. Answer A is not the best response, since the potential risk posed by terminated employees isn't limited to shared or network resources. Answer C is not the best response, since a great deal of damage can potentially be done under the seemingly "watchful eye" of a "discreet" observer. In addition, this could be embarrassing to and uncomfortable for the employee, as well. Answer D is not the best response, since a great deal of damage can be exacted in a very short period of time—even by those employees from whom we would not expect such behavior. Once again "better safe than sorry" is the best way to proceed—just ensure you maintain the employee's dignity and privacy to the greatest extent possible.

2. **Answer A is the best response.** Employees must believe and trust that an EAP provides absolute confidentiality in order to be willing to use it, and an EAP must be used if it is to be truly successful. Answer B is not the best response; while it is essential that the EAP offers absolute confidentiality, by itself, that isn't enough. The EAP will not be successful if employees do not *believe* that the EAP offers absolute confidentiality, even if it does. Answer C is not the best response, since the success or failure of an EAP is not contingent upon whether it is administered inside the organization, outside the organization, or by some combination of both methods. Answer D is not the best response; while it is important to conduct cost-benefit analyses to demonstrate the value of an EAP and to bolster ongoing management support, doing so will not directly impact whether employees choose to trust—and therefore use—a program. If a program isn't used, it's not successful—no matter what the "numbers" indicate.

3. **Answer B is the best.** Answer A is not the best response, since OSHA must be notified within 8 hours only in the event of a death or the inpatient hospitalization of three or more employees. Answer C is not the best response, since the OSHA form 301 requires a detailed account of each work-related injury or accident. Although it must be completed within seven calendar days, it is not posted. Answer D is not the best response, since the OSHA Form 300A is a summary report of all work-related injuries and illnesses that take place in a calendar year, and which therefore cannot be completed until after the end of each year.

4. **Answer B is the best response.** The presence of any chemicals in the workplace triggers the requirement for MSDS sheets. This is true even if chemicals are not accessible to employees (Answer A), and even if chemicals are stored—but not used—in the workplace (Answer C). Finally, the requirement is also triggered even if chemicals aren't actually being used in the workplace, but are still physically located or present within the workplace (Answer D).

5. **Answer C is the best response.** Answer A is not the best response, because "serious violations" are issued by OSHA, not by the EEOC. In addition, "willful"—not "serious"—violations are considered to be deliberate and intentional. Answer B is not the best response, because a serious violation *is* likely to result in death *or* serious injury. Answer D is not the best response, because "willful" violations are issued by OSHA, not by the Department of Justice. In addition, "willful"—not "serious"—violations are considered to be the most serious type of OSHA violation (and are the only type of violation that can result in mandatory imprisonment of an employer).

Answers to Review Questions

1. The Needlestick Safety and Prevention Act of 2000 added the following three employer requirements to the Bloodborne Pathogens Standard:

    ▶ Maintaining a log of all injuries resulting from contaminated sharps.

    ▶ Evaluating—and implementing—safer needle devices (as they become available).

    ▶ Involving employees who use needles and needle devices in the evaluation and selection of needles and needle devices.

2. The *Automobile Workers v. Johnson Controls* (1990) Supreme Court ruling established that most, if not all, fetal protection policies result in gender discrimination. It also affirmed that parents—not employers—bear the obligation of protecting unborn fetuses from chemical risk.

3. Employers are responsible for ensuring a safe workplace and for complying with all current and future OSHA-related standards. Employees are responsible for following all safety and health-related rules stemming from the Act.

4. Since there is no vaccine available for HCV, the best way to prevent the transmission of Hepatitis C/HCV in the workplace is to ensure the proper use of personal protective equipment (PPEs).

5. The six critical components of a comprehensive substance abuse program are

    1. Management buy-in and support

    2. Drug-free workplace policy

    3. Supervisor training

    4. Employee education

    5. Employee assistance

    6. Drug testing

    Of these, "management buy-in and support" is the most important.

Answers to Exam Questions

1. **Answer D is the best response.** WARNA, the Worker Adjustment and Retraining Notification Act, addresses plant closings and mass layoffs. The Drug-Free Workplace Act, MSHA (Mine Safety and Health Act), and OSHA (Occupational Safety and Health Act) were all created specifically to address issues of health and safety in the workplace.

2. **Answer C is the best response.** Answer A is not the best choice because family farms are only exempt from OSHA coverage if they do not employ anyone who is not a family member. Answer B is not the best response because federal government employees are covered under OSH Act (however, state and local government employees are not). Answer D is not the best response because although OSHA designates certain low-risk industries as exempt from OSHA reporting requirements; those industries are still covered by OSH Act.

3. **Answer C is the best response.** Health and wellness programs take a more proactive—rather than reactive—approach. Answer D is not the best response; although health and wellness programs do address some issues "reactively" (for instance, smoking cessation or weight loss), health and wellness programs are more frequently proactive in nature. Answers A and B are not the best responses, since health and wellness programs can significantly benefit employees *and* employers.

4. **Answer C is the best response.** While safety committees could very likely formulate recommendations relative to personal protective equipment (PPE) enhancements, they are far less likely to have final decision making authority. Safety committees, therefore, would not likely find themselves in a capacity to institute their own recommendations. Safety committees, however, do play an essential role relative to investigating accidents and incidents (Answer A), conducting inspections (Answer B), and proactively identifying safety concerns (Answer D).

5. **Answer B is the best response.** "Reasonable suspicion" is one category of drug test, and "for cause" is another. Pre-employment (answer A), post-accident (answer C), and random (answer D) are all categories of drug tests.

6. **Answer B is the best response.** OSHA requires most employers to maintain records and submit reports relative to work-related injuries and accidents, but not specifically in response to security breaches (unless, of course, those breaches result in work-related injuries or accidents). Answers A, C, and D do represent security-related HR responsibilities.

7. **Answer B is the best response.** Poor ergonomic design can result in employees assuming awkward postures, or having to move in problematic ways. In turn, and over time, this can lead to the development of an MSD (musculoskeletal disorder). Answers A and C are not the best responses, since neither use of PPE (personal protective

equipment) nor poor ventilation are identified as significant contributing factors to MSDs. Answer D is not the best response; although MSDS is a similar acronym, it refers to materials data safety sheets, which are generally unrelated to MSDs.

8. **Answer A is the best response.** A person who is HIV positive or who has AIDS is considered a person with a disability under the ADA (Americans with Disabilities Act) and is therefore entitled to perform the essential functions of his or her job as long as he or she can do so with or without reasonable accommodation (that does not cause undue hardship to the organization). Developing visible or outward symptoms (answer B)—as long as those symptoms are unrelated to the person's ability to perform the essential functions of his or her position—does not preclude an individual from continuing to work. Answer C is not the best response, as an employee who is HIV positive or who has AIDS is entitled to maintain confidentiality relative to either of those conditions. Answer D is not the best response, since the belief that a person who is HIV positive or who has AIDS poses a direct threat to co-workers is unfounded.

9. **Answer A is the best response.** Answer B is not the best response, because although each employee has a right to copies of his or her own medical records or records of his or her exposure to toxic and harmful substances or conditions, employees do not have the right to copies of co-workers' medical records. Answer C is not the best response, because employers must correct workplace hazards by the date indicated on the citation—not just create or submit a plan to do so. Answer D is not the best response, because an employee does have the right to photocopies of his or her medical records or records of his or her exposure to toxic and harmful substances or conditions.

10. **Answer D is the best response.** You have 30 days to file a complaint with OSHA if your employer has discriminated against you for making safety and health complaints or for exercising your rights under the OSH Act. Answers A, B, and C are not the best responses, as each identifies rights that employees enjoy under OSHA.

Suggested Readings and Resources

SHRM Website: www.shrm.org

Department of Labor Website: www.dol.gov

OSHA Website: www.osha.gov

Other Internet Resources: Search the Web for "OSH Act," "MSH Act," "Occupational Health, Safety and Security," "Drug Free Workplace Act," and other related terms.

www.amazon.com: Search for "occupational health," "workplace safety," "workplace security," and "OSHA" to find reference materials.

PART II
Apply Your Knowledge

Practice Exam

Practice Exam

1. Which of the following is not one of the four categories of invasion of privacy?

    ○ **A.** Intrusion of solitude

    ○ **B.** Public disclosure of private and embarrassing facts

    ○ **C.** Unbecoming light

    ○ **D.** Appropriation of identity

2. Which of the following is not mandated by the General Duty Clause?

    ○ **A.** Employers must ensure a safe workplace.

    ○ **B.** Employers must comply with all current and future OSHA-related standards.

    ○ **C.** Employees must report all work-related injuries resulting in hospitalization (emergency room or in-patient) to their employer.

    ○ **D.** Employees must follow all safety and health-related rules stemming from the OSH Act.

3. All of the following statements articulate beliefs that are reflected in the design of the balanced scorecard except:

    ○ **A.** Dissatisfied customers will eventually look to others who will meet their needs and expectations.

    ○ **B.** Employees need to continually grow and learn so as to be able to perform in a manner that will truly support the attainment of organizational goals.

    ○ **C.** In order to remain untainted and objective, measurement systems must be maintained separately from management systems.

    ○ **D.** The business process perspective ascertains performance levels through specific measures that are unique to each particular organization.

4. It's important for HR professionals to understand the differences and interplay between effectiveness and efficiency. Efficiency is

○ **A.** The degree to which goals are appropriate

○ **B.** Doing things right

○ **C.** Doing the right things

○ **D.** Impossible to achieve without effectiveness

5. The Retirement Equity Act enacted a number of important provisions, including

○ **A.** Increasing the minimum age requirement for pension plan participation

○ **B.** Requiring qualified pension plans to provide automatic survivor benefits and allow for waiver of survivor benefits without the consent of the participant or the spouse

○ **C.** Clarified that pension plans are prohibited from obeying qualified domestic relations (court) orders (QDROs) requiring them to make benefit payments to a participant's former spouse (or another alternative payee) if that order violates ERISA's prohibitions against assignment or alienation of benefits

○ **D.** Prohibited plans from counting maternity and paternity leaves as breaks in service for participation and vesting purposes

6. Which of the following is the least important factor in ensuring that an employee survey is a valuable employee involvement strategy?

○ **A.** Ensure confidentiality by administering the survey through an external consultant

○ **B.** Ensure that the survey input is maintained in a fully confidential manner

○ **C.** Ensure that employees believe in the confidentiality of the survey

○ **D.** Ensure management buy-in and support

7. Which of the following characteristics is most likely to first manifest itself during the development (or growth) stage in the organizational life cycle?

○ **A.** A core group of highly talented employees who focus fixedly on the founder for direction and inspiration

○ **B.** Resistance to OD and change initiatives

○ **C.** Resistance to the process of formalizing policies and procedures

○ **D.** An entitlement mentality towards pay and benefits

8. The scientific method includes all of the following steps except

    ○   **A.**   Question and observe

    ○   **B.**   Develop a hypothesis

    ○   **C.**   Design a method

    ○   **D.**   Assimilate existing data

9. Which of the following terms best describes transactional leaders?

    ○   **A.**   Enforcers

    ○   **B.**   Coaches

    ○   **C.**   Captains

    ○   **D.**   Directors

10. Of the following four types of pay that an employee could earn, which one would not need to be included in an employee's regular rate of pay?

    ○   **A.**   Overtime pay

    ○   **B.**   Premium pay (for weekend work)

    ○   **C.**   Bonus pay

    ○   **D.**   Incentive pay

11. All of the following statements about OD are true except

    ○   **A.**   OD refers to the process through which the overall performance, growth, and effectiveness of an organization is enhanced through strategic, deliberate, and integrated initiatives.

    ○   **B.**   OD incorporates the following four academic disciplines: psychology, sociology, anthropology, and management.

    ○   **C.**   OD helps maintain the organization's focus on the belief that the systems that have been enacted within organizations are ultimately responsible for whether the work of the organization is accomplished.

    ○   **D.**   OD interventions are intended to identify an organization's competitive advantages and to ensure the organization's success.

12. Which of the following statements about ULP strikes is untrue?

    ○ **A.** ULP strikes are called during contract negotiations.

    ○ **B.** Striking workers must be returned to their original positions after the strike is over.

    ○ **C.** ULP strikes are called when the employer has committed an unfair labor practice.

    ○ **D.** Employers cannot hire permanent strike replacements during a ULP strike.

13. All of the following are required by the Hazard Communication Standard except

    ○ **A.** Material Safety Data Sheets

    ○ **B.** Signed employee acknowledgement forms

    ○ **C.** Container labeling requirements

    ○ **D.** Training and orientation

14. Which of the following occurs during a jurisdictional strike?

    ○ **A.** Employees who are not directly involved in an economic dispute choose not to cross a picket line out of support for striking workers.

    ○ **B.** A union seeks to pressure an employer to assign particular work to its members, rather than to members of other unions or to non-union workers.

    ○ **C.** The strike occurs even though the collective bargaining agreement contains a no-strike clause prohibiting striking during the duration of the agreement.

    ○ **D.** A union seeks to pressure an employer to grant some sort of concession from the employer during collective bargaining negotiations.

15. Copyrights are granted for what period of time?

    ○ **A.** The lifetime of the author

    ○ **B.** The lifetime of the author, unless there are heirs to whom the copyright has been deeded

    ○ **C.** The lifetime of the author plus 70 years

    ○ **D.** The lifetime of the author plus 95 years

16. When conducting panel interviews, it is generally advisable to do all of the following except

○ **A.** Let the candidate know ahead of time that he or she will be participating in a panel interview. Eliminating the element of surprise helps prevent additional unnecessary anxiety.

○ **B.** Plan in advance who will ask which questions and in which order. Arrange for "hand offs" from one interviewer to another.

○ **C.** Consider the seating arrangements. If possible, interview in a room that has a round table. If you must interview in a room with an oval or rectangular table, position the chairs in a way that creates the feeling of a round table.

○ **D.** Place all of the interviewers on one side of the table and the candidate on the other, so that it is easier for the candidate to make eye contact with each of the interviewers.

17. According to OSHA, which of the following does not need to be recorded?

○ **A.** Days away from work

○ **B.** Injuries that result in bleeding

○ **C.** Restricted work or job transfer

○ **D.** Loss of consciousness

18. Protected concerted activity can include activity aimed at improving employees' terms and conditions of employment. If an employee is engaged in protected concerted activity, an employer might be considered to have violated the NLRA if all but which of the following conditions are met?

○ **A.** The employee and/or collective bargaining unit advised the employer of the concerted nature of the employee's activity.

○ **B.** The employer knew of the concerted nature of the employee's activity.

○ **C.** The concerted activity was protected by the Act.

○ **D.** The adverse employment action in question (for instance, termination) was motivated by the employee's protected concerted activity.

19. Henry Fayol was a guru in the area of

○ **A.** Quality

○ **B.** Management

○ **C.** Strategic human resources

○ **D.** Human behavior

20. *General Dynamics Land Systems* v. *Cline* (2004), a case that addressed age discrimination, established/clarified that

- ○ **A.** The ADEA prohibits favoring the old over the young.

- ○ **B.** The ADEA prohibits favoring the old over the young, and it also prohibits favoring the young over the old.

- ○ **C.** Younger employees (even if they are over the age of 40) cannot allege age discrimination because of programs that favor older employees.

- ○ **D.** Younger employees (even if they are over the age of 40) can allege age discrimination because of programs that favor older employees.

21. What method of job evaluation is this: "A non-quantitative job evaluation technique that categorizes jobs into broad categories, or levels, based on the level—and, ultimately, value to the organization—of the work that is performed by jobs within each level. Each level incorporates specific responsibilities and benchmark statements that describe the nature, complexity, autonomy, and so forth of the work that is performed by positions in that level."

- ○ **A.** Job classification

- ○ **B.** Job slotting

- ○ **C.** Whole job ranking

- ○ **D.** Factor comparison

22. An organization's total compensation program should do all of the following except

- ○ **A.** Support and reinforce the mission, vision, and values of the organization

- ○ **B.** Be consistent with the culture of the organization

- ○ **C.** Be competitive with the total compensation programs offered by labor market competitors

- ○ **D.** Attract, motivate, and retain targeted/appropriate employees

23. If a case does proceed to court, HR's role varies significantly depending upon a host of factors. HR professionals could conceivably find themselves performing any of the following functions except

- ○ **A.** Testify

- ○ **B.** Sit at counsel table during the trial

- ○ **C.** Collect data during discovery

- ○ **D.** Respond to the complaint

24. In determining whether outsourcing might be an appropriate option, which of the following considerations is least appropriate to take into consideration?

    ○ **A.** Vendors' technological resources and capabilities as compared to your project requirements

    ○ **B.** Internal abilities and talents versus abilities and talents available through outsourcing

    ○ **C.** The importance and complexity of the function that is being considered for outsourcing

    ○ **D.** The degree of variability in transaction volume of the function that is being considered for outsourcing

25. Your organization has decided to outsource its payroll function, and you're involved in the process of researching vendors. Which of the following actions would be least valuable to you?

    ○ **A.** Find out what each vendor's track record is over a long period of time by speaking with clients from several years ago (this would be akin to conducting a reference check in which you speak with former employers from a number of years ago).

    ○ **B.** Find out about each vendor's most recent performance by speaking with recent and/or current clients (this would be akin to conducting a reference check in which you speak with recent or current employers).

    ○ **C.** Find out whether each vendor has related experience, and ascertain how recently the vendor gained that experience. In addition, evaluate how closely that experience resembles the current project in terms of scope, complexity, and so forth.

    ○ **D.** Find out about each vendor's commitment to quality. Determine how it manifests itself and how can it be measured. Also, determine the average length of time that it takes each vendor to resolve concerns that originate from customers and/or clients.

26. Which of these individuals is least likely to create an oral contract?

    ○ **A.** A full-time recruiter

    ○ **B.** A hiring manager who interviews candidates for open positions in his or her area

    ○ **C.** An employee's current supervisor

    ○ **D.** An employee's current co-worker

27. According to equity theory, if an employee feels that he is being treated unfairly at work, he is least likely to take any of the following actions?

    ○ **A.** Encourage others to produce more

    ○ **B.** Encourage others to produce less

    ○ **C.** Recognize that life is not always fair, and start looking for a new job

    ○ **D.** Recognize that life is not always fair, and accept the situation as it is

28. Which case established the following relative to what constitutes a sexually hostile work environment: "This standard, which we reaffirm today, takes a middle path between making actionable any conduct that is merely offensive and requiring the conduct to cause a tangible psychological injury. Conduct that is not severe or pervasive enough to create an objectively hostile or abusive work environment—an environment that a reasonable person would find hostile or abusive—is beyond Title VII's purview. Likewise, if the victim does not subjectively perceive the environment to be abusive, the conduct has not actually altered the conditions of the victim's employment, and there is no Title VII violation."

   ○ **A.** *Taxman* v. *Board of Education of Piscataway*

   ○ **B.** *Meritor Savings Bank* v. *Vinson*

   ○ **C.** *St. Mary's Honor Center* v. *Hicks*

   ○ **D.** *Harris* v. *Forklift Systems*

29. Which of the following is true of Ishikawa's fishbone diagram?

   ○ A. Demonstrates how 20% of causes account for 80% of effects

   ○ B. Identifies factors that ultimately affect whether a desired outcome will be attained

   ○ C. Assesses the potential impact of utilizing quality circles in a particular situation

   ○ D. Depicts information about a single factor

30. All of the following statements about the Age Discrimination in Employment Act (ADEA) are true except

   ○ **A.** ADEA prohibits discrimination based on age, for individuals age 18 and above (so as to ensure that individuals are not discriminated against based on being too young, as well as based on being too old).

   ○ **B.** ADEA covers private employers with 20 or more employees, state and local governments (including school districts), employment agencies, and labor organizations.

   ○ **C.** ADEA does not establish an upper cap, or an age at which it once again becomes legal to discriminate against individuals based on age.

   ○ **D.** ADEA is subject to certain exceptions and places certain requirements on employers, particularly with respect to benefits plans, coverages, and early retirement incentives.

31. In the acronym KSAs, *A* refers to

   ○ A. An attitudinal predilection toward the type of work performed in the position

   ○ B. Specific information that the incumbent either needs to know or with which he or she needs to be familiar

   ○ C. The ability to perform a particular task

   ○ D. Specific traits required to successfully perform a position

32. A manager with whom you have not previously worked comes to you for help with implementing solutions she has come up with to address a turnover problem in her department. Your first response should be to

- ○ **A.** Communicate your commitment to implementing the manager's solution.
- ○ **B.** Offer alternative solutions based on experience you have had with similar situations.
- ○ **C.** Ask questions to obtain more information about the problems the manager is experiencing.
- ○ **D.** Ask questions to obtain information that will help you implement the manager's solution more effectively.

33. Of the following four options, the best way to avoid or minimize the likelihood of a negligent referral claim against the organization is to

- ○ **A.** Refuse to provide any employee references
- ○ **B.** Provide only titles, dates of employment, and final salary when providing references
- ○ **C.** Outsource the process of providing employee references to a third party
- ○ **D.** Require a signed release form from the employee or former employee before providing a reference

34. Which of the following statements about defined contribution plans is untrue?

- ○ **A.** Unlike defined benefit plans, defined contribution plans do not promise a specific monthly benefit (or total benefit) at retirement.
- ○ **B.** Defined contribution plans shift the risk away from the employer (which is where it rests for defined benefit plans) and back onto the employee.
- ○ **C.** Defined contribution plans are decreasing in popularity, while defined benefit plans are increasing in popularity.
- ○ **D.** Examples of defined contribution plans include 401(k) plans, employee stock ownership plans, and profit-sharing plans.

35. In which case did the Supreme Court rule that, in the absence of under-representation as demonstrated and documented through an affirmative action plan, organizations cannot take race into account when making decisions relative to who will be laid off and who will be retained (and that doing so would constitute a violation of Title VII of the Civil Rights Act of 1964)?

- ○ **A.** *Taxman* v. *Board of Education of Piscataway*
- ○ **B.** *Meritor Savings Bank* v. *Vinson*
- ○ **C.** *St. Mary's Honor Center* v. *Hicks*
- ○ **D.** *Harris* v. *Forklift Systems*

36. Which law implemented changes in two sections of the United States tax code that resulted in the creation of two new—and ultimately very important—employee benefits?

- ○ **A.** Consolidated Omnibus Budget Reconciliation Act (COBRA), 1985
- ○ **B.** The Revenue Act
- ○ **C.** Health Insurance Portability and Accountability Act (HIPAA)
- ○ **D.** Retirement Equity Act (REA)

37. A cash balance plan is

- ○ **A.** A defined benefit plan that expresses the promised benefit in terms of a stated account balance
- ○ **B.** A defined benefit plan that expresses the promised benefit in terms of a specific monthly benefit
- ○ **C.** A defined contribution plan that expresses the promised benefit in terms of a stated account balance
- ○ **D.** A defined contribution plan that expresses the promised benefit in terms of a specific monthly benefit

38. The balanced scorecard

- ○ **A.** Consists of a variety of non-financial measures of success, and is intended to be used as a tool to balance out other traditional financial measures of success
- ○ **B.** Consists of a variety of financial measures of success, and is intended to be used as a tool to balance out other tools that only incorporate one single financial measure of success
- ○ **C.** Consists of a variety of financial and non-financial measures of success, and is intended to balance them against each other within the scorecard
- ○ **D.** Consists of a variety of measures that are predicated on the evaluative ratings, or scores, collected from multiple stakeholders pertaining to multiple financial and non-financial measures of success

39. Which of the following statements about the Civil Rights Act of 1991 is untrue?

- ○ **A.** It expanded upon employees' rights.
- ○ **B.** It expanded upon employees' remedies.
- ○ **C.** It capped damages at $500,000 per employee.
- ○ **D.** It allowed for jury trials for discrimination cases.

40. McClelland's acquired needs theory focuses on one primary motivator, which is

- ○ **A.** Achievement
- ○ **B.** Recognition
- ○ **C.** Equity
- ○ **D.** Rewards

41. Joseph M. Juran's focus on quality addresses three key areas, which include all of the following except

- ○ **A.** Quality planning
- ○ **B.** Quality circles
- ○ **C.** Quality improvement
- ○ **D.** Quality control

42. Strategic planning is a step-by-step process through which an organization does all of the following except:

- ○ **A.** Ensures its individual and organizational readiness for the future
- ○ **B.** Generates a statement that articulates what the organization wants to become in the future
- ○ **C.** Identifies where it wants to be and what it wants to accomplish in the long-term (often 3–5 years)
- ○ **D.** Begins to map out how its vision and mission for the long-term will be attained

43. Which of these is not a type of legislation?

- ○ **A.** Concurrent resolution
- ○ **B.** Compound resolution
- ○ **C.** Joint resolution
- ○ **D.** Simple resolution

44. Which of the following factors is least relevant to creating and sustaining credibility during the implementation of a strategic plan?

- ○ **A.** Securing the support and commitment of senior leadership
- ○ **B.** Clear, complete, and appropriate documentation of the process
- ○ **C.** A commitment to follow through on every step of the process
- ○ **D.** Representative participation from all levels of the organization

45. For the set of numbers 5, 29, 194, 87, 645, 42, 29, 334, and 97, the mode is

   ◯ **A.** 162.4

   ◯ **B.** 645

   ◯ **C.** 29

   ◯ **D.** 87

46. A manager within your organization sends you an email asking you to help her with terminating an employee. This is the first time you've heard about the situation. The manager has specifically asked your help with pulling together the COBRA paperwork, calculating the final paycheck, and making sure that the employee turns over his company ID and corporate credit card. The manager tells you how much she needs and appreciates your help, and is glad she can count on you.

This manager probably views HR primarily in terms of the following dimension:

   ◯ **A.** Operational/Tactical

   ◯ **B.** Strategic

   ◯ **C.** Administrative

   ◯ **D.** Transformational

47. The difference between job posting systems and job bidding systems is

   ◯ **A.** Job bidding systems deal with jobs that are currently open, while job posting systems deal with jobs that might open at some point in the future.

   ◯ **B.** Job bidding systems are directed at internal candidates, while job posting systems are directed at external candidates.

   ◯ **C.** Job bidding systems deal with jobs that might open at some point in the future, while job posting systems deal with jobs that are currently open.

   ◯ **D.** Job bidding systems are directed at internal candidates, while job posting systems are directed at internal as well as external candidates.

48. According to the Older Worker's Benefit Protection Act (OWBPA), individuals are prohibited from waiving their rights or claims under ADEA unless such a waiver is "knowing and voluntary." OWBPA established nine specific criteria for ensuring that such waivers are "knowing and voluntary," one of which requires that employers must allow employees time to consider any right-to-sue waivers that the employer offers in exchange for early retirement benefits. How many days must an employer allow?

   ◯ **A.** At least one week

   ◯ **B.** At least two weeks

   ◯ **C.** At least three weeks

   ◯ **D.** At least one week for each year of service

49. The progressive discipline process is predicated on a belief that includes which of the following ideas/assumptions?

    ○ **A.** An employee decides whether to perform his or her job satisfactorily.

    ○ **B.** The employee, when hired, was at least minimally qualified for the position.

    ○ **C.** Both A and B.

    ○ **D.** Neither A nor B.

50. An organization conducts an employee survey and finds that many employees are bored with their jobs, unhappy with their pay, and feel as though they don't get enough vacation time. If the organization's primary goal is to motivate employees, what is the first step that should be taken?

    ○ **A.** Conduct an external survey to determine pay rates and vacation allotments among labor market competitors.

    ○ **B.** Identify ways in which employees' jobs can be enriched, and implement them.

    ○ **C.** Give everyone an across-the-board raise and an extra week of vacation, and let employees know that you will be conducting a salary/benefits survey to see if further adjustments are needed.

    ○ **D.** Before you take any action, conduct another employee survey to ensure that results of the second survey are consistent with the results of the first survey.

51. According to Hersey and Blanchard's model, effective leaders

    ○ **A.** Identify the leadership style that is best suited to them and use that style consistently.

    ○ **B.** Determine the quadrant into which each employee falls and manage employees in each quadrant according to the corresponding leadership style.

    ○ **C.** Place emphasis on ensuring that an employee has the ability to execute the technical, or functional, skills required to complete a task.

    ○ **D.** Utilize different leadership approaches, with different employees, at different times.

52. Which of the following was not one of Knowles's five key assumptions about how adults learn?

    ○ **A.** The learner's need to know

    ○ **B.** The learner's readiness to learn

    ○ **C.** The learner's self-concept

    ○ **D.** The learner's willingness to change

53. When would a plan provider that offers mental health benefits be exempt from MHPA?

   ○ **A.** If the plan provider is a small employer with fewer than 15 people

   ○ **B.** If a plan provider's costs (measured in terms of actual claims) increase 1% or more due to the application of MHPA's requirements

   ○ **C.** If a plan provider's costs (in terms of insurance premiums) increase 1% or more due to the application of MHPA's requirements

   ○ **D.** Never

54. Under COBRA, plan providers must offer plan participants the opportunity to continue participating in

   ○ **A.** Group healthcare plans, wellness programs, and long-term disability insurance

   ○ **B.** Group healthcare plans

   ○ **C.** All health and welfare plans for which the plan participant cannot secure coverage through another individual's group plan

   ○ **D.** All health and welfare plans

55. According to the Equal Pay Act, the substantial equality of job content is assessed based on four factors:

   ○ **A.** Working conditions, effort, skill, and scope

   ○ **B.** Effort, skill, responsibility, and working conditions

   ○ **C.** Scope, accountability, responsibility, and working conditions

   ○ **D.** Responsibility, skills, working conditions, and scope

56. An approach in which an organization chooses to utilize a relatively small number of grades is known as

   ○ **A.** Flattening

   ○ **B.** Growthbanding

   ○ **C.** Broadbanding

   ○ **D.** Gradesharing

57. Which of the following is not one of Philip B. Crosby's four Absolutes of Quality Management?

   ○ **A.** Quality means conformance to requirements, not goodness.

   ○ **B.** Quality is achieved by prevention, not appraisal.

   ○ **C.** Quality has a performance standard of Zero Defects, not acceptable quality levels.

   ○ **D.** Quality is measured by specific production indexes, not by customer satisfaction.

58. Which of the following statements is least reflective of an organization's statement of vision?

- ○ **A.** It is a descriptive and inspirational statement that articulates where the organization wants to be and what it wants to become in the future.

- ○ **B.** It gives employees an awareness that they have a meaningful opportunity to be part of something bigger than themselves.

- ○ **C.** It motivates and inspires employees to aspire to the legacy that the vision can create, and that it ultimately can leave behind.

- ○ **D.** It speaks to the nature of the organization's business or purpose, its customers, and sometimes even its employees and its role in the community.

59. After the House of Representatives and the Senate have approved a bill in identical form, the legislation will die unless

- ○ **A.** The president takes no action for 10 days while Congress is not in session

- ○ **B.** The president takes no action for 10 days while Congress is in session.

- ○ **C.** The president sends the legislation back for Conference Committee Action.

- ○ **D.** The president overrides Congress.

60. Pre-employment medical exams can only be conducted

- ○ **A.** If all candidates who apply for a position are required to partake in a pre-employment medical exam

- ○ **B.** If the medical exam is job related and consistent with business necessity

- ○ **C.** If the medical exam is conducted by a physician who is not employed or retained by the employer

- ○ **D.** If the candidate reveals that he or she has a disability that might require a reasonable accommodation

61. EO 11246 requires covered employers to develop and implement an auditing system that periodically measures the effectiveness of its total affirmative action program. This requirement could include all of the following actions except

- ○ **A.** Monitor records of all personnel activity, including referrals, placements, transfers, promotions, terminations, and compensation, at all levels to ensure the nondiscriminatory policy is carried out

- ○ **B.** Require internal reporting on a scheduled basis as to the number of charges of discrimination that have been filed based on race, gender, and veterans status during the length of each AAP degree to which equal employment opportunity and organizational objectives are attained

      ○ **C.** Review report results with all levels of management

      ○ **D.** Advise top management of program effectiveness and submit recommendations to improve unsatisfactory performance

62. Which of the following statements about trend analysis is true?

      ○ **A.** It can provide information that can be helpful in developing a better understanding of business cycles.

      ○ **B.** It can become the basis for a number of applications, including forecasting staffing needs.

      ○ **C.** It looks at how two variables have changed over time.

      ○ **D.** It looks at the relationship between one dependent variable and more than one independent variable.

63. WARN covers which employers?

      ○ **A.** Employers with 15 or more employees

      ○ **B.** 100 or more full-time employees.

      ○ **C.** All private employers

      ○ **D.** Private employers with 20 or more employees

64. Learning organizations are best described as those within which

      ○ **A.** The HRD/training budget is equivalent to (or exceeds) the merit budget.

      ○ **B.** Employees at all levels of the organization commit to attaining knowledge and skills that will enable them to perform better and attain more.

      ○ **C.** Employees at all levels of the organization participate in training initiatives—either individually or through organizational initiatives—at least annually.

      ○ **D.** Each employee's performance appraisal incorporates a goal relative to completing specific training and/or development activities.

65. Which of the following managers is most likely to experience the recency effect?

      ○ **A.** A manager who recently observed a direct report performing his or her position.

      ○ **B.** A manager who recently placed an employee on a performance improvement plan.

      ○ **C.** A manager who maintained consistent documentation during earlier portions of the performance measurement period.

      ○ **D.** A manager who has not consistently documented the direct report's performance during the performance measurement period.

66. For overtime purposes, hours worked includes

   ○ **A.** All hours for which an employee received compensation

   ○ **B.** All hours for which an employee was granted prior to, or subsequent to, approval to work

   ○ **C.** All hours during which an employee performed work

   ○ **D.** All hours during which an employee was required or allowed to perform work

67. The Equal Pay Act prohibits discrimination based on sex in the payment of wages or benefits to men and women who

   ○ **A.** Perform the same work for the same employer

   ○ **B.** Perform substantially equal (but not identical) work for the same employer

   ○ **C.** Perform substantially equal (but not identical) work for different employers within the same relevant labor market

   ○ **D.** Perform the same work for different employers within the same relevant labor market

68. Which of the following statements about job grades is not true?

   ○ **A.** Grades represent a hierarchy of levels into which jobs of similar internal worth are categorized.

   ○ **B.** Jobs within the same grade share a similar level of value or worth to the organization.

   ○ **C.** Jobs within the same grade are paid according to a corresponding compensation range.

   ○ **D.** Grades represent a hierarchy of levels into which jobs of similar external worth are categorized.

69. Which of the following statements about unemployment insurance is not true?

   ○ **A.** Unemployment insurance is a mandatory benefit program.

   ○ **B.** In general, the maximum period for receiving unemployment insurance benefits is 26 weeks.

   ○ **C.** Except in three states (in which only employers contribute), unemployment insurance is funded through employer and employee taxes.

   ○ **D.** Unemployment insurance was established as part of the federal Social Security Act, and is administered at the state level.

70. Which of the following is not a disadvantage of the non-quantitative job evaluation method known as job slotting?

○ **A.** Job slotting is somewhat expensive and difficult to administer.

○ **B.** It is more likely that jobs will be evaluated based on the person, not the position.

○ **C.** Job slotting can only be used when a job structure is already in place.

○ **D.** There is a greater chance that rater error and subjectivity can taint the job evaluation process.

71. Which of the following statements about protected concerted activities is not true?

○ **A.** Protected concerted activity refers to associational rights that are granted to employee through the NLRA.

○ **B.** The NLRA protects associational rights for employees who belong to a union.

○ **C.** The NLRA does not protect associational rights unless an employee belongs to a union.

○ **D.** Employees have the right to refrain from engaging in protected concerted activities.

72. When there is a FEPA, all of the following statements are true except

○ **A.** Charges must be filed with the EEOC within 180 days of the alleged discriminatory act.

○ **B.** The EEOC usually maintains responsibility for handling charges that are filed with it if the basis for the charge is also protected under state or local law.

○ **C.** The FEPA usually maintains responsibility for handling charges that are filed with it if the basis for the charge is also protected under federal law.

○ **D.** A charge may not be filed with the EEOC when state or local EEO law is more protective than the corresponding federal law.

73. COBRA (the Consolidated Omnibus Budget Reconciliation Act) covers employers who employed

○ **A.** 2 or more employees during the prior year

○ **B.** 15 or more employees as of the close of the most recent payroll period

○ **C.** 20 or more employees during the prior year

○ **D.** 50 or more employees as of the close of the most recent payroll period

74. Which of the following statements about Hepatitis B/HBV is untrue?

    ○ **A.** HBV is transmitted through blood and other bodily fluids.

    ○ **B.** A person with HBV is considered to be a person with a disability.

    ○ **C.** A vaccine for HBV exists, and must be administered annually to at-risk employees.

    ○ **D.** People with HBV might experience a wide range of symptoms.

75. The defining case for employment tests and disparate impact was

    ○ **A.** *McDonnell Douglas Corp* v. *Green*

    ○ **B.** *Griggs* v. *Duke Power*

    ○ **C.** *Meritor Savings Bank* v. *Vinson*

    ○ **D.** *Washington* v. *Davis*

76. Which of the following activities would be least likely to happen during onboarding?

    ○ **A.** Tour of the facility

    ○ **B.** Background investigation

    ○ **C.** Opportunity to meet with current employees

    ○ **D.** Review of the mission of the organization, and of how that mission relates to the position

77. Three of the following terms refer to the same sort of instrument or tool, and one does not. Which one of these terms means something different from the other three?

    ○ **A.** Employee surveys

    ○ **B.** Multi-rater surveys

    ○ **C.** Attitude surveys

    ○ **D.** Climate surveys

78. The AFL-CIO is an example of a

    ○ **A.** National union

    ○ **B.** Local union

    ○ **C.** Federation

    ○ **D.** International labor organization

79. The Labor Management Relations Act (LMRA), also known as the Taft-Hartley Act, was an amendment designed to remedy what the Republican Congress saw as two major omissions in the Wagner Act, including

   ○ **A.** The identification of behaviors and practices that would be considered ULPs on the part of employers

   ○ **B.** The identification of behaviors and practices that would be considered ULPs on the part of unions

   ○ **C.** The identification of behaviors and practices that would be considered ULPs on the part of employees

   ○ **D.** The identification of behaviors and practices that would be considered ULPs on the part of managers

80. The landmark Supreme Court case that confirmed the legality of mandatory arbitration agreements was

   ○ **A.** *NLRB* v. *Phoenix Mutual Life Insurance Co.*

   ○ **B.** *EEOC* v. *Waffle House, Inc.*

   ○ **C.** *Circuit City Stores, Inc.* v. *Adams*

   ○ **D.** *NLRB* v. *Henry Colder Co.*

81. OSHA did all of the following except

   ○ **A.** Establish relief for employees who suffer work-related injuries and illnesses

   ○ **B.** Establish a means of enforcement

   ○ **C.** Encourage and assist states to take steps to ensure safe and healthful workplaces

   ○ **D.** Provide for relevant research, information, education, and training

82. Change interventions that focus on improving what work is done, as well as the ways and processes through which the work is done, are considered

   ○ **A.** Human processual interventions

   ○ **B.** Technostructural interventions

   ○ **C.** Sociotechnical interventions

   ○ **D.** Organization transformation change interventions

83. Which of the following statements about the PBGC is not true?

   ○ **A.** PBGC is a government corporation created by ERISA.

   ○ **B.** PBGC is funded by a combination of employer and employee payroll taxes.

   ○ **C.** PBGC protects participants in most defined benefit plans and cash balance plans (within certain limitations).

   ○ **D.** PBGC ensures that participants will receive payments of certain benefits if a covered plan is terminated.

84. In conducting a SWOT analysis, the strengths and weaknesses portion of the analysis is directed

   ○ **A.** Internally

   ○ **B.** Externally

   ○ **C.** Both internally and externally

   ○ **D.** Neither internally nor externally

85. The landmark case *McKennon* v. *Nashville Banner Publishing Co. (1995)*, established that

   ○ **A.** An employer will be held accountable for discriminatory employment actions unless it discovers evidence after taking the discriminatory employment action that would have led the employer to that same employment action for legitimate, non-discriminatory reasons.

   ○ **B.** An employer will be held accountable for discriminatory employment actions even if it discovers evidence after taking the discriminatory employment action that would have led the employer to that same employment action for legitimate, non-discriminatory reasons.

   ○ **C.** An employer will not be held accountable for discriminatory employment actions if it discovers evidence after taking the discriminatory employment action that would have led the employer to that same employment action for legitimate, non-discriminatory reasons.

   ○ **D.** An employer will not be held accountable for discriminatory employment actions even if it discovers evidence after taking the discriminatory employment action that would have led the employer to a different employment action for legitimate, non-discriminatory reasons.

86. The Family and Medical Leave Act (FMLA) entitles eligible employees (who work for covered employers) up to 12 weeks of unpaid, job-protected leave during any 12-month period for all of the following reasons except

   ○ **A.** For the birth and care of the newborn child of the employee

   ○ **B.** For placement of a son or daughter for adoption or foster care with the employee

    ○ **C.** To care for an immediate family member (spouse, child, sibling, or parent) with a serious health condition

    ○ **D.** To take medical leave when the employee is unable to work because of a serious health condition

87. Which of the following statements about factor comparison is untrue?

    ○ **A.** Factor comparison provides a degree of objectivity and reliability across raters.

    ○ **B.** Factor comparison evaluates each job with respect to each compensable factor.

    ○ **C.** Factor comparison assigns a point value to each level within each factor.

    ○ **D.** Factor comparison involves ranking each compensable factor of each job.

88. The Drug-Free Workplace Act requires all of the following except

    ○ **A.** Establishing an EAP (employee assistance program) or equivalent program to which employees who use drugs can turn for assistance and rehabilitation.

    ○ **B.** Publishing a statement notifying employees that the manufacture, distribution, dispensation, possession, or use of a controlled substance is prohibited in the workplace.

    ○ **C.** Establishing a drug-free awareness program addressing the dangers of drug use in the workplace and the employer's drug-free policy, and information about programs that are available to employees who use drugs.

    ○ **D.** Distributing a copy of the workplace substance abuse policy to all employees.

89. Which of the following activities would not constitute an unfair labor practice on the part of an employer during a union organizing campaign?

    ○ **A.** Tell workers that the organization will fire or punish them if they engage in any union activity.

    ○ **B.** Grant workers wage increases or special concessions in an effort to bribe people from joining a union.

    ○ **C.** Require employees to attend presentations to listen to the employer's opinions about the unionization of its operations

    ○ **D.** Tell workers that existing benefits will be discontinued if the workplace is unionized.

90. An employer who makes a hot cargo agreement has done all of the following except

    ○ **A.** Agreed to stop doing business with another entity

    ○ **B.** Refused to stop doing business with another entity

    ○ **C.** Committed a ULP

    ○ **D.** Helped the union

91. Which of the following represents sound advice with respect to dealing with employees who remain with an organization after downsizing?

○ **A.** Let the employees who remain know when the final round of layoffs is done (so they can feel more secure and confident)

○ **B.** Communicate clearly, frequently, and in a truthful manner with the employees who remain

○ **C.** Encourage the employees who remain to be loyal to the organization, just as the organization has found a way to be loyal to each of them.

○ **D.** Minimize the amount and frequency of communication (to avoid the possibility of creating unrealistic expectations, or of saying something that might change).

92. All of the following statements about negligent hiring are true except

○ **A.** Negligent hiring refers to the process of hiring an employee without engaging in appropriate due diligence.

○ **B.** Appropriate due diligence includes looking into items such as the candidate's credentials and prior work experience.

○ **C.** An organization can prevent negligent hiring tort claims—or can ensure that it will prevail in any such claim—by performing due diligence on all employees before they are hired.

○ **D.** Negligent hiring tort claims might be filed after an employee who was hired through a flawed hiring process inflicts some sort of harm on another person.

93. Which of the following statements about focus groups is least true?

○ **A.** Skillfully facilitated focus groups can generate a great deal of valuable data.

○ **B.** The synergy of the group dynamics can contribute to a more valuable data collection experience.

○ **C.** When facilitated by the same individual, participants across multiple focus groups will have a similar data collection experience.

○ **D.** Focus groups can provide a qualitative approach to data collection.

94. Which of the following factors should have the least impact on how base pay for newly hired employees is set?

○ **A.** The relative worth of the job to the organization

○ **B.** Each incumbent's rate of pay in his or her current/most recent position

○ **C.** The market rate for the position in the marketplace

○ **D.** Whether the job requires hot skills

95. An agreement between an employer and an employee that states that the employer will give the employee a job, as long as the employee agrees not to join or have any involvement with a labor union is known as a

- ○ **A.** Yellow dog contract
- ○ **B.** Hot cargo agreement
- ○ **C.** Featherbedding agreement
- ○ **D.** Union shop agreement

96. Which of the following is the least likely reason that an organization might want to settle a charge of discrimination?

- ○ **A.** To save money
- ○ **B.** To avoid bad press
- ○ **C.** To avoid a strike
- ○ **D.** Because discrimination might have actually taken place

97. Which of the following would not describe a purpose of a safety committee?

- ○ **A.** Building and maintaining interest in health and safety issues
- ○ **B.** Satisfy the OSHA requirement that covered organizations establish cross-functional safety committees
- ○ **C.** Reinforcing safety as part of the fabric of the organization's culture
- ○ **D.** Providing a forum for discussing health- and safety-related issues

98. Which of the following cases established that gender can be used as a factor in the selection process if there is under-representation in a particular job classification, as long as the AAP does not set forth a quota?

- ○ **A.** *Johnson* v. *Santa Clara County Transportation Agency*
- ○ **B.** *Martin* v. *Wilks*
- ○ **C.** *Harris* v. *Forklift Systems*
- ○ **D.** *Taxman* v. *Board of Education of Piscataway*

99. Which of the following statements about diversity is true?

- ○ **A.** Diversity is a legally mandated program, similar to affirmative action.
- ○ **B.** Diversity initiatives require the preparation and filing of specific reports to the federal government on an annual basis.

○ **C.** Diversity can include attributes or characteristics such as communication styles, regional backgrounds, or affiliation with unions.

○ **D.** Diversity programs represent an extension of EEO programs, and thus should be limited to the same protected classes that are defined by EEO laws.

100. Which of the following statements about Social Security retirement benefits is untrue?

○ **A.** The earliest age at which a worker can retire and still receive benefits is 62.

○ **B.** Full retirement age ranges between ages 65 and 67.

○ **C.** Workers who work beyond their full retirement age will increase their monthly retirement—the longer they work past their full retirement age, the more their monthly retirement income will be.

○ **D.** There is no requirement to start receiving retirement benefits by any particular age.

101. An employee who was constructively discharged

○ **A.** Was forced to quit due to intolerable working conditions

○ **B.** Was terminated at the conclusion of a progressive disciplinary process

○ **C.** Was afforded the opportunity to resign (instead of being fired)

○ **D.** Was laid off through no fault of his or her own, and is eligible for rehire

102. Placement goals

○ **A.** Must be established for areas in which underutilization exists

○ **B.** Must be pursued through good faith efforts

○ **C.** Must be set at an annual percentage rate equal to the availability figure for women or minorities

○ **D.** Must be established for each specific minority group when underutilization is found to exist

103. McGregor's motivation theory

○ **A.** Is predicated on the idea that most employees will take on additional work if they think that work will be satisfying or rewarding

○ **B.** Is predicated on the idea that employees are uncommitted, uninterested, hesitant to assume any additional responsibility, and are essentially lazy

○ **C.** Assumes that different managers have different perspectives on employees

○ **D.** Laid the foundation for Maslow's hierarchy of needs

104. According to Hersey and Blanchard's situational leadership model, low task and low relationship dimensions correspond to which quadrant?

- ○ **A.** Telling
- ○ **B.** Selling
- ○ **C.** Participating
- ○ **D.** Delegating

105. Which of the following statements about correlation is true?

- ○ **A.** A negative correlation indicates that a relationship does not exist between two factors.
- ○ **B.** Correlation mathematically determines whether there is a demonstrated relationship between two factors or entities.
- ○ **C.** The correlation coefficient is a number between 0 and 1 that defines the strength of a relationship between two factors.
- ○ **D.** The closer the correlation coefficient is to 1, the greater the likelihood that there is a causative relationship between the two factors.

106. Which one of the following requirements must be met in order for an employee to qualify for an administrative exemption under the FLSA?

- ○ **A.** The employee's primary duty must be the performance of office or non-manual work directly related to the management or general business operations of the employer or the employer's customers.
- ○ **B.** The employee's primary duty must be the performance of work requiring advanced knowledge, defined as work which is predominantly intellectual in character and which includes work requiring the consistent exercise of discretion and judgment.
- ○ **C.** The employee's suggestions and recommendations as to the hiring, firing, advancement, promotion, or any other change of status of other employees must be given particular weight.
- ○ **D.** The employee may not spend more than 20% of work time performing functions that are non-exempt in nature.

107. The Fair Labor Standards Act established standards affecting full-time and part-time workers in the private sector and in federal, state, and local governments pertaining to the following four areas:

- ○ **A.** Minimum wage, overtime, recordkeeping, and child labor
- ○ **B.** Minimum wage, overtime, worker's compensation, and unemployment insurance
- ○ **C.** Minimum wage, overtime, child labor, and wage garnishments
- ○ **D.** Minimum wage, overtime, unemployment insurance, and wage garnishments

108. Which of the following is not a requirement under Sarbanes-Oxley (SOX)?

    ○ **A.** Prohibition against insider trading during certain pension plan blackout periods.

    ○ **B.** Establishment of whistleblower protection in a wide variety of situations for employees who report fraud against shareholders.

    ○ **C.** Plan administrators must provide 30-day written notice in advance of blackout periods to individual account plan participants and beneficiaries.

    ○ **D.** Requirement to disclose whether the company has adopted a company-wide code of ethics.

109. One potential problem with employee participation groups is that, under the NLRA, it is possible that employee participation groups could be found

    ○ **A.** To interfere with employees' ability to affiliate with a collective bargaining unit

    ○ **B.** To interfere with employees' associational rights

    ○ **C.** To be company dominated

    ○ **D.** To have an adverse impact upon members of a protected class

110. Which of the following four statements offers the best definition of slander?

    ○ **A.** A statement that damages someone's character or reputation

    ○ **B.** A false statement that damages someone's character or reputation

    ○ **C.** A false spoken statement that damages someone's character or reputation

    ○ **D.** A false written statement that damages someone's character or reputation

111. In the landmark case *Meritor Savings Bank* v. *Vinson*, the Supreme Court ruling stated all of the following *except*

    ○ **A.** Unwelcome sexual advances at work create a hostile work environment, which constitutes gender discrimination under Title VII of the Civil Rights Act of 1964.

    ○ **B.** The employer is responsible for the sexually harassing behavior of supervisors in its employ even if it didn't know about the behavior.

    ○ **C.** One way for employers to avoid liability is to prove that a sexually harassed employee had reasonable opportunities to take advantage of a good, clear complaint procedure (without fear of retaliation), but had failed to do so.

    ○ **D.** Employers are automatically liable for sexual harassment by their supervisors.

112. All of the following represent advantages of whole job ranking except

- ○ **A.** Whole job ranking is easy to perform.
- ○ **B.** Whole job ranking establishes factors about each job that need to be taken into consideration when comparing jobs to each other.
- ○ **C.** Whole job ranking is relatively inexpensive to maintain.
- ○ **D.** Whole job ranking produces a list that shows which jobs are most and least important.

113. Whether knowingly or unknowingly, incentive plan design is significantly by the work of

- ○ **A.** Vroom
- ○ **B.** Maslow
- ○ **C.** Skinner
- ○ **D.** Adams

114. There are five management functions, one of which speaks particularly to the ways in which the manager obtains and arranges resources. Those resources could include people, facilities, materials, and the like. While executing this function, the manager must also make decisions about reporting relationships within the organization. In short, the manager must work to establish linkages between people, places, and things. According to Henri Fayol, this management function is known as

- ○ **A.** Organizing
- ○ **B.** Controlling
- ○ **C.** Planning
- ○ **D.** Coordinating

115. An interviewer truly enjoys interviewing because he feels as though it gives him the opportunity to make a difference in the world by helping individuals who are unemployed find gainful employment. Which of the following four interviewer biases/errors might this interviewer be most likely to experience?

- ○ **A.** Compassion
- ○ **B.** Urgency
- ○ **C.** Leniency
- ○ **D.** Recency

116. Title VII of the Civil Rights Act of 1964 was a landmark piece of legislation prohibiting employment discrimination based on

- ○ **A.** Race, color, religion, sex, and national origin
- ○ **B.** Race, color, age, sex, and national origin
- ○ **C.** Race, age, sex, religion, and handicapping status (renamed to disability upon the passage of the ADA)
- ○ **D.** Race, religion, sex, and national origin

117. An undue hardship does all of the following except

- ○ **A.** Creates significant difficulty (enough to disrupt business operations)
- ○ **B.** Requires a financial outlay that exceeds 25% of the employee's annual salary
- ○ **C.** Changes something about the (essential) nature of the business
- ○ **D.** Results in a significant financial outlay

118. All of the following statements about teambuilding are true *except*

- ○ **A.** Building on the idea that there is no *I* in *team*, teambuilding exercises focus primarily on the role of the team, rather than on the role of each team member.
- ○ **B.** Teambuilding is an effective means through which team members can explore issues such as communication, problem solving, and trust.
- ○ **C.** Teambuilding exercises are most effective when they are linked directly and specifically to organizational objectives.
- ○ **D.** Teambuilding exercises can be of value even if the activity itself doesn't seem to bear any immediate resemblance to the actual workplace.

119. Taft-Hartley identifies all of the following unfair labor practices that could be committed by unions except

- ○ **A.** Striking or picketing an employer without giving the required notice
- ○ **B.** Picketing for recognition for more than 30 days without petitioning for an election
- ○ **C.** Causing an employer to discriminate against an employee
- ○ **D.** Refusing to bargain with the employer of the employees it represents

120. Some of the protections instituted through the Labor Management Reporting and Disclosure Act (also known as Landrum-Griffin) are all of the following except

   ○ **A.** A requirement that unions submit annual financial reporting to the DOL to document how union members' dues were spent

   ○ **B.** A bill of rights for union members guaranteeing them freedom of speech and periodic secret elections

   ○ **C.** The designation of every union official as an agent of the union

   ○ **D.** Even stronger provisions relative to secondary boycotting and organizational and recognition picketing

121. When a company that owns or operates union as well as non-union operations shifts work to the non-union operation in an effort to diminish the impact of the strike, this is referred to as

   ○ **A.** Featherbedding

   ○ **B.** Double breasting

   ○ **C.** Yellow dogging

   ○ **D.** Single roofing

122. The following formula calculates

$$\frac{\text{Total of all costs associated with the HRD/training initiative}}{\text{Number of individuals who participate in the HRD/training initiative}}$$

   ○ **A.** ROI

   ○ **B.** Cost per trainee

   ○ **C.** Cost per hire

   ○ **D.** Cost/benefit analysis

123. The Computer Employee exemption includes a different pay threshold before an employee might qualify for an exemption under the FLSA. To qualify for the computer employee exemption, the employee must be compensated either on a salary or fee basis (as defined in the regulations) at a rate not less than

   ○ **A.** The prevailing wage rate paid for comparable positions in the relevant labor market

   ○ **B.** $400 per week

   ○ **C.** $455 per week

   ○ **D.** $500 per week

124. The significance of *Martin* v. *Wilks* was

   ○ **A.** Current employees who are negatively impacted by consent decrees that were estab-lished in an earlier time and which sought to resolve discrimination that was present in an earlier time may not challenge the validity of such decrees.

   ○ **B.** Current employees who are negatively impacted by consent decrees that were estab-lished in an earlier time and which sought to resolve discrimination that was present in an earlier time may challenge the validity of such decrees.

   ○ **C.** Gender can be used as a factor in the selection process if there is under-representation in a particular job classification, as long as the AAP does not set forth a quota.

   ○ **D.** Gender can be used as a factor in the selection process if there is under-representation in a particular job classification, as long as the AAP does not set forth specific good faith efforts in which the organization will engage to attain that quota.

125. Organizations who lead the market

   ○ **A.** Choose to offer total compensation packages that incorporate a variety of indirect com-pensation components in addition to a competitive direct compensation component.

   ○ **B.** Choose to offer variable pay components with greater upside potential than those that are being offered by their labor market competitors, and offer base compensation com-ponents that are less competitive than what their labor market competitors are offering.

   ○ **C.** Choose to offer total compensation packages that are more generous than the total compensation packages being offered by their labor market competitors.

   ○ **D.** Choose to offer total compensation packages that are more innovative, creative, non-typical, and usually non-traditional than packages being offered by their labor market competitors.

126. Employers enjoy all of the following rights with respect to OSHA inspections *except*

   ○ **A.** The right to request proper identification from the compliance officer

   ○ **B.** The right to learn the reason for the inspection or investigation

   ○ **C.** The right to postpone an inspection until senior leadership is available

   ○ **D.** The right to decline admittance to certain areas that contain trade secrets

127. Under FairPay, highly compensated employees must

   ○ **A.** Earn $150,000 or more annually (of which at least $455 per week must be paid on a salary or fee basis)

   ○ **B.** Oversee office or non-manual work

      ○ **C.** Customarily and regularly perform at least one of the duties of an exempt executive, administrative, or professional employee identified in the standard tests for exemption

      ○ **D.** All of the above

128. Which of the following statements relative to HR's role in ethics is least true?

      ○ **A.** HR must play a leadership role in establishing, encouraging, and ensuring ongoing ethical behavior within organizations.

      ○ **B.** In its unique role as the conscience of the organization, HR should own the organization's ethical initiative.

      ○ **C.** Ethics must be operationalized so responsibility for ethics is dispersed throughout the organization.

      ○ **D.** The organization's code of ethics needs to address a variety of issues from a variety of perspectives.

129. The five distinct, yet overlapping, project management processes are (in order)

      ○ **A.** Establishing, developing, implementing, evaluating, controlling.

      ○ **B.** Initiation, planning, controlling, executing, closing

      ○ **C.** Planning, organizing, coordinating, directing, controlling

      ○ **D.** Initiation, planning, executing, controlling, closing

130. An HR audit is likely to yield information about all of the following *except*

      ○ **A.** The usefulness, appropriateness, and effectiveness of the employee handbook

      ○ **B.** Strategies for decreasing non-compliance with legal requirements

      ○ **C.** Grievances, their causes, and their impact

      ○ **D.** The degree to which the organization complies with legal requirements

131. Which of the following is a mandatory OSHA standard for all covered employers?

      ○ **A.** Emergency Action Plan Standard

      ○ **B.** Fire Safety Standard

      ○ **C.** Exit Route Standard

      ○ **D.** Hazard Communication Standard

132. Roger Fisher and William Ury, authors of *Getting to Yes: Negotiating Agreement Without Giving In*, assert that a good agreement is one that is wise, efficient, and that improves the overall relationship between the parties who are involved in working out (not hammering out) an agreement with each other. They set forth four principles of principled negotiation. Which one of the following is not one of the principles?

   - ○ **A.** Separate the people from the problem
   - ○ **B.** Focus on relationships rather than positions
   - ○ **C.** Generate a variety of options before settling on an agreement
   - ○ **D.** Insist that the agreement be based on objective criteria

133. The Mine Safety and Health Act (MSH Act)

   - ○ **A.** Applies only to underground mines
   - ○ **B.** Requires that all mines be inspected at least twice (and sometimes four times) a year
   - ○ **C.** Applies only to coal mines
   - ○ **D.** Provides protections in addition to those afforded by OSHA

134. An organization creates affinity groups. Which of the following of Maslow's needs does this initiative primarily address?

   - ○ **A.** Safety and security
   - ○ **B.** Belonging and love
   - ○ **C.** Esteem
   - ○ **D.** Self-actualization

135. Which of the following is not an example of direct compensation?

   - ○ **A.** Hourly wages/base salary
   - ○ **B.** Shift differentials
   - ○ **C.** Flexible spending accounts
   - ○ **D.** Variable pay

136. According to the FairPay guidelines, which of the following individuals cannot be exempted from the overtime provisions of the FLSA?

   - ○ **A.** Manual laborers and other blue collar workers who perform working involving repetitive operations with their hands
   - ○ **B.** Law enforcement officers, such as police officers, detectives, deputy sheriffs, state troopers, and highway patrol officers

C. Employees, regardless of rank or pay level, who perform work such as preventing, controlling, or extinguishing fires of any type

D. Employees who detain or supervise suspected and convicted criminals (correctional officers, parole or probation officers, and the like)

137. Which of the following does not represent a potential disadvantage of an employee referral program?

A. If the current organization is not particularly diverse (with respect to gender, age, race, education background, or a host of other factors), employee referral programs might perpetuate that lack of diversity.

B. If the organization needs to fill multiples openings for the same position during a short period of time, using employee referrals has the potential to significantly increase the cost-per-hire.

C. If an affirmative action plan is in place, and if there are areas of underutilization, an employee referral program is not likely to demonstrate good faith efforts to recruit candidates who are women or minorities.

D. If the organization has prior patterns of hiring discrimination, employee referral programs are likely to reinforce those patterns.

138. Job specs can be expressed as all of the following except

A. KSAs

B. Credentials (years of experience, educational requirements, and so forth)

C. Physical and or mental requirements

D. Qualifications possessed by the best qualified candidate

139. To what dimension of the organization is Edgard Schein referring when he writes

"…a pattern of shared basic assumptions that the group learns as it solved its problems of external adaptation and internal integration, that has worked well enough to be considered valid and, therefore, to be taught to new members as the correct way you perceive, think, and feel in relation to those problems."

A. Vision

B. Mission

C. Culture

D. Values

140. Managers who use performance appraisal systems based on rating scales

- ○ **A.** Rate employees against each other
- ○ **B.** Rate employees against performance expectations
- ○ **C.** Identify statements that are reflective of employees' performance
- ○ **D.** Write a narrative assessment of employees' performance

141. Which of the four cases listed resulted in the following ruling: "Title VII's prohibition in 703 (a) and (d) against racial discrimination does not condemn all private, voluntary, race-conscious affirmative action plans" and that "Congress did not intend to limit traditional business freedom to such a degree as to prohibit all voluntary, race-conscious affirmative action."

- ○ **A.** *United Steelworkers* v. *Weber*
- ○ **B.** *California* v. *Bakke*
- ○ **C.** *Johnson* v. *Santa Clara County Transportation Agency*
- ○ **D.** *Griggs* v. *Duke Power*

142. The key issues in *Albemarle Paper* v. *Moody* were

- ○ **A.** Job relatedness and validity
- ○ **B.** Disparate impact and disparate treatment
- ○ **C.** Reasonable accommodations and undue hardship
- ○ **D.** Negligent hiring and negligent retention

143. All of the following represent reasons to establish an ethics program except

- ○ **A.** To prevent or minimize aggression/violence
- ○ **B.** To prevent or minimize organizational politics
- ○ **C.** To prevent or minimize the erosion of trust
- ○ **D.** To prevent or minimize cynicism

144. Which of the following statements about the Uniform Guidelines on Employee Selection Procedures is not true?

- ○ **A.** One of its key purposes is to address the concept of adverse impact.
- ○ **B.** One of its key purposes is to address the concept of adverse treatment.
- ○ **C.** One important objective of the Uniform Guidelines is to ensure that interview and selection processes are reliable.
- ○ **D.** One important objective of the Uniform Guidelines is to ensure that interview and selection processes are valid.

145. What makes the outside sales exemption under the FLSA different from all of the other exemptions under the FLSA?

○ **A.** A maximum salary is imposed.

○ **B.** A minimum salary is not required.

○ **C.** Employers must reapply for the exemption annually.

○ **D.** None of the above.

146. The best way to prevent Hepatitis C/HCV from being transmitted in the workplace is by

○ **A.** Making the HCV vaccine available to all at-risk employees.

○ **B.** Ensuring proper use of PPEs.

○ **C.** Encouraging at-risk employees to wear masks over their mouths.

○ **D.** Including testing for HCV as part of the pre-employment physical.

147. The Davis-Bacon Act of 1931

○ **A.** Was the first piece of legislation to consider the topic of—and to actually establish—a minimum wage

○ **B.** Was rendered obsolete by the minimum wage provisions of the Fair Labor Standards Act of 1938

○ **C.** Applies only to federal contractors and subcontractors with contracts in excess of $20,000

○ **D.** Applies to construction projects that receive federal funding

148. Youth workers (also known as children) who are fourteen or fifteen years old may work

○ **A.** Up to 4 hours on a school day

○ **B.** Up to 20 hours during a school week

○ **C.** Up to 7 hours on a non-school day

○ **D.** Up to 40 hours during a non-school week

149. Which of these questions is the most appropriate to ask?

○ **A.** "Tell me about any restriction you have that would prevent you from lifting 30-pound metal sheets onto a conveyor belt for about four hours each day."

○ **B.** "This job requires lifting 30-pound metal sheets onto a conveyor belt for about four hours each workday. Do you have any problems doing this?"

○ **C.** "This job requires lifting 30-pound metal sheets onto a conveyor belt for about four hours each workday. Can you meet this requirement of the position?"

○ **D.** "Although it's technically not part of the job, the person who used to hold this job would help out everyone once in a while with lifting 30-pound metal sheets onto a conveyor belt. Can we count on you to follow in her footsteps, and help out if we needed you to do so?"

150. Which of the following statements about the Portal-to-Portal Act is not true?

○ **A.** The Portal-to-Portal Act offered a clearer definition of hours worked for purposes of minimum wage and overtime calculations.

○ **B.** It established that employers must compensate workers for the time that they spend performing their jobs, but not for time spent on activities that only relate to the performance of their job.

○ **C.** It addresses topics such as travel time, pre-shift work, post-shift work, idle waiting time, overnight travel, training time, and the like.

○ **D.** The Portal-to-Portal Act was an amendment of the Fair Labor Standards Act.

151. Common law refers to a system of law in which all of the following statements are true *except*

○ **A.** Traditions, customs, and precedents have the same force of law as existing laws or statutes.

○ **B.** Laws and statutes are, quite literally, interpreted and re-interpreted on a case-by-case basis.

○ **C.** Contracts, including employment, are eclipsed by the prevailing common law.

○ **D.** Each interpretation and each case sets a precedent, but can also be re-interpreted, thus setting a new precedent.

152. The key issue in *Griggs* v. *Duke Power* was

○ **A.** Replacing striking workers

○ **B.** Employment testing

○ **C.** Adverse treatment

○ **D.** Adverse impact

153. Taken together, the two 1998 landmark Supreme Court cases *Faragher* v. *City of Boca Raton* and *Ellerth* v. *Burlington Northern Industries* established all of the following *except*

    ○   **A.** If an employee is subjected to a tangible adverse employment action because of a supervisor's sexually harassing behavior, the employer is liable.

    ○   **B.** The employer is vicariously liable when its supervisors create a sexually hostile work environment even if the employee is not subjected to an adverse employment action.

    ○   **C.** If the employee is not subjected to tangible adverse employment action, the employer may be able to raise as a defense that he acted reasonably to prevent and/or promptly correct any sexually harassing behavior, and that the plaintiff unreasonably failed to take advantage of the employer's preventive or corrective opportunities.

    ○   **D.** If the employee is subjected to tangible adverse employment action, the employer may be able to raise as a defense that he acted reasonably to prevent and/or promptly correct any sexually harassing behavior, and that the plaintiff unreasonably failed to take advantage of the employer's preventive or corrective opportunities.

154. In order to be eligible to take FMLA leave, an employee must meet four requirements. Which of the following does not constitute one of those requirements?

    ○   **A.** The employee must work for a covered employer (public agencies; state, local, and federal employers; local education agencies [schools]; and private-sector employers with 50 or more employees).

    ○   **B.** The employee must have worked for the employer for a total of at least 12 months (this time does not have to have been uninterrupted).

    ○   **C.** The employee must have worked at least 1,250 hours over the previous 12 months.

    ○   **D.** The employee must work at a location in the United States or in any territory or possession of the United States where at least 75 employees are employed by the employer within 50 miles.

155. Which of the following considerations is least likely to factor into an assessment of whether the standard of just cause or good cause was met?

    ○   **A.** Whether the rule or standard that was violated was newly created or long standing

    ○   **B.** Whether a legitimate investigation looking into the totality of the circumstances around the alleged violation was conducted

    ○   **C.** Whether reasonable proof as to the violation existed or was obtained through investigation

    ○   **D.** Whether the punishment is proportionate to the violation

156. The ruling in the landmark case *Automobile Workers* v. *Johnson Controls* (1990) determined that

    ○ **A.** Employers have an obligation to establish policies to protect unborn fetuses from possible harm resulting from chemical exposure.

    ○ **B.** Most, if not all, fetal protection policies result in gender discrimination.

    ○ **C.** The government has the obligation to protect unborn fetuses from chemical risk even if the parents who conceived them do not choose to do so.

    ○ **D.** Most, if not all, fetal protection policies constitute a legitimate BFOQ.

157. The process of maintaining awareness of opportunities and threats is known as

    ○ **A.** SWOT analysis

    ○ **B.** Environmental scanning

    ○ **C.** Strategic planning

    ○ **D.** Contingency planning

158. The significance of *Regents of California* v. *Bakke* was

    ○ **A.** The permissibility of quotas in college admissions affirmative action programs is irrelevant and non-transferable to the workplace.

    ○ **B.** The permissibility of quotas in college admissions affirmative action programs is relevant and transferable to the workplace.

    ○ **C.** The impermissibility of quotas in college admissions affirmative action programs is irrelevant and non-transferable to the workplace.

    ○ **D.** The impermissibility of quotas in college admissions affirmative action programs is relevant and transferable to the workplace.

159. The employment application often requires the candidate to provide information relative all of the following areas *except*

    ○ **A.** Personal data (for example, name, address, contact information)

    ○ **B.** Gender/race (as required for EEO reporting)

    ○ **C.** Employment history (including reasons for leaving prior positions)

    ○ **D.** Names of professional references

160. In the acronym SMART, *M* stands for

○ **A.** Marketable

○ **B.** Meaningful

○ **C.** Measurable

○ **D.** Motivational

161. Generally speaking, what should be the first step in an effective progressive disciplinary process?

○ **A.** Verbal warning

○ **B.** Coaching

○ **C.** Ensuring consistency

○ **D.** Counseling

162. Out of the four following choices, which is the most effective way to deal with "the grapevine?"

○ **A.** Apply the motivation principle of extinction—in other words, ignore it.

○ **B.** Enact policies to prohibit employees from engaging in conversations about their pay and other confidential matters.

○ **C.** If you can't beat 'em, join 'em—use the grapevine as a way of disseminating information.

○ **D.** If you can't beat 'em, join 'em—use the grapevine as one way of collecting information.

163. During an organizing campaign, unions are permitted to engage in all of the following activities *except*

○ **A.** Inside organizing

○ **B.** Salting

○ **C.** Surface organizing

○ **D.** Organizational picketing

164. Which of the following statements about strikes is not true?

○ **A.** Employers cannot hire permanent strike replacements during an economic strike.

○ **B.** Employers cannot hire permanent strike replacements during a ULP strike.

○ **C.** Workers must be returned to their original positions after a ULP strike is over.

○ **D.** Workers cannot be terminated for participating in an economic strike.

165. Offshoring refers to

   ◯ **A.** Outsourcing to third-party providers whose corporate headquarters are located overseas

   ◯ **B.** Another term for outsourcing

   ◯ **C.** Outsourcing to third-party providers whose operations are located overseas

   ◯ **D.** Outsourcing to firms that primarily conduct business at their own worksite (rather than at the organization's worksite)

166. In order to ensure fair and consistent interviews, interviewers should

   ◯ **A.** Ask primary and probing questions that ascertain the skills, knowledge, skills, abilities, and behavioral characteristics that the candidate demonstrated in previous positions

   ◯ **B.** Ensure that primary questions remain consistent from interview to interview

   ◯ **C.** Modify primary questions to reflect a candidate's experience, as indicated on his or her résumé

   ◯ **D.** Ensure that probing questions remain consistent from interview to interview

167. Which of the following statements about focus groups is untrue?

   ◯ **A.** A focus group is more of a communication tool than an involvement tool.

   ◯ **B.** Focus groups consist of a representative sample of employees.

   ◯ **C.** Focus groups need to include enough people to generate a dynamic and synergistic discussion.

   ◯ **D.** Focus groups are led by a neutral facilitator.

168. Which of the following laws was not expanded to include employees of the legislative branch of the government through the Congressional Accountability Act?

   ◯ **A.** National Labor Relations Act

   ◯ **B.** Employee Polygraph Protection Act

   ◯ **C.** Worker Adjustment and Retraining Notification Act

   ◯ **D.** Americans with Disabilities Act

169. Which of the following considerations would be least valuable to ask while you are preparing to collect market data?

- ○ **A.** What is the relevant labor market for this position?
- ○ **B.** What sources of market data do you already have, and what additional sources could you get?
- ○ **C.** How does the position compare to others within the existing job worth hierarchy?
- ○ **D.** Who are our labor market competitors in general and for specific jobs?

170. A code of ethics will not be effective if

- ○ **A.** The organization adopts a one-size-fits-all approach.
- ○ **B.** It omits statements relative to how the code will be implemented and upheld.
- ○ **C.** The CEO does not write the introduction to and/or cover letter accompanying the code.
- ○ **D.** It includes components that could be perceived as threatening or punitive.

171. In general, the NLRB will not agree to accept a petition from a union for an election in all of the following situations *except*

- ○ **A.** A union has been certified in the past year but has not successfully negotiated a contract
- ○ **B.** An election has been held within the past year
- ○ **C.** There is a valid contract (not to exceed three years) in effect
- ○ **D.** There is a valid contract (of any duration) in effect

172. Of the following outputs, which is least likely to be supported by information that is generated from an HRIS?

- ○ **A.** Increasing overall employee productivity
- ○ **B.** Identifying and rewarding top performers
- ○ **C.** Increasing overall employee commitment
- ○ **D.** Placing the right people in the right jobs at the right times

173. You've been hired as the HR manager of a start-up company that produces a new type of alternative fuel. Which of the following conditions are you least likely to experience in your new role?

- ○ **A.** A request to publish an employee handbook
- ○ **B.** The need to offer cash compensation packages that lead the market
- ○ **C.** The need to offer cash compensation packages that lag the market
- ○ **D.** A high level of excitement and energy

174. In order to qualify for an executive exemption under the FLSA, an employee must meet all of the following requirements *except*

   ○ **A.** The employee's primary duty must be managing the enterprise, or managing a customarily recognized department or subdivision of the enterprise.

   ○ **B.** The employee must customarily and regularly direct the work of at least two or more other full-time employees or their equivalent.

   ○ **C.** The employee's primary duty includes the exercise of discretion and independent judgment with respect to matters of significance.

   ○ **D.** The employee must have the authority to hire or fire other employees, or the employee's suggestions and recommendations as to the hiring, firing, advancement, promotion, or any other change of status of other employees must be given particular weight.

175. An employee who prefers to learn about HR practices by attending a guest lecture series is probably a

   ○ **A.** Visual learner

   ○ **B.** Auditory learner

   ○ **C.** Kinesthetic learner

   ○ **D.** Vicarious learner

176. Which of the following statements does not constitute a consideration for determining what constitutes fair use?

   ○ **A.** Whether the work will be used for commercial purposes, or for not-for-profit or educational purposes

   ○ **B.** The nature or way in which the work will be used

   ○ **C.** How much of the work is used, both in terms of the aggregate amount of work that is being used, as well as the percentage of the total work that is being used.

   ○ **D.** Specific permissions that the copyright holder has previously granted, if those permissions are deemed to be precedent-setting in nature.

177. The most renowned example of the Mackay Doctrine in use was

   ○ **A.** In 2005, when President George W. Bush waived the requirement to pay a prevailing wage rate to government contractors and subcontractors involved in the rebuilding of New Orleans.

   ○ **B.** In 1996, when President Clinton signed legislation permitting employers to require all employees to agree to binding arbitration in exchange for the opportunity to be employed with the organization.

    ○ **C.** In 1992, when President George H. W. Bush passed an executive order that required more than 11,000 troops returning from the (first) Gulf War be reinstated to the positions that they would have held if they had not experienced a break in service due to their military service.

    ○ **D.** In 1981, when President Ronald Reagan replaced 12,000 striking air traffic controllers.

178. Which of the following is least likely to be considered an action-oriented program?

    ○ **A.** Recruiting at colleges or universities traditionally attended by minorities

    ○ **B.** Increasing the cash awards granted through the organization's employee referral program

    ○ **C.** Reaching out to professional organizations whose membership criteria is designed to attract women or minorities

    ○ **D.** Posting job openings at resource centers for displaced homemakers

179. An employee is hired as a telesales representative for a sports apparel company. She performs exceptionally well in that position and is promoted to the position of field sales manager. Two months later, this employee is injured in a serious automobile accident in which she loses both of her legs. To everyone's amazement, she is ready to return to work two months later. She is told, however, that she will not be able to return to her position as sales manager, but that she is welcome to return to her former position as telesales representative. Although she is not initially given a reason, she is finally told "off the record" that although the customers feel very bad for what happened to her, they just aren't comfortable having a wheelchair-bound field sales manager, and that, ultimately, the customer is always right. Would this decision likely be upheld as legal under EEO law?

    ○ **A.** Yes, because of the BFOQ exception to EEO laws.

    ○ **B.** No, because this would not qualify under the BFOQ exception to EEO laws.

    ○ **C.** Yes, because of the customer preference exception to EEO laws.

    ○ **D.** No, because there are no exceptions to EEO laws.

180. The following formula calculates

$$\frac{\text{\# of terminations during a specified period of time}}{\text{The average \# of employees in the workforce during that same period of time}}$$

    ○ **A.** Time to hire

    ○ **B.** Turnover

    ○ **C.** ROI

    ○ **D.** Cost per hire

181. All of the following statements offer sound advice to follow relative to offer letters *except*

    ○ **A.** State that the only agreements or promises that are valid are those that are included in the offer letter.

    ○ **B.** Use the offer letter as an opportunity to reaffirm that the employment relationship is at-will.

    ○ **C.** For exempt positions, avoid expressing earnings in weekly, bi-monthly, or monthly terms (depending upon your payroll cycle), so as not to jeopardize the non-exempt FLSA status.

    ○ **D.** Avoid language that hints of any sort of long-term employment relationship, or states that the employer is "like a family."

182. Which of the following types of tests is most frequently considered to be illegal on a pre-employment basis?

    ○ **A.** Agility tests

    ○ **B.** Aptitude tests

    ○ **C.** Honesty tests

    ○ **D.** Polygraph tests

183. FairPay defines highly compensated employees as those who

    ○ **A.** Earn $100,000 or more annually if single, or who earn $120,000 or more annually if married

    ○ **B.** Earn $100,000 or more annually (of which at least $455 per week must be paid on a salary or fee basis)

    ○ **C.** Earn $100,000 or more annually

    ○ **D.** Earn $150,000 or more annually

184. In order to be concerted, activity must be

    ○ **A.** Undertaken by individual employees who are acting in pursuit of an individual goal

    ○ **B.** Undertaken by individual employees who are acting in an independent manner

    ○ **C.** Protected before it can be concerted

    ○ **D.** Engaged in with or on the authority of other employees.

185. If an employer does not choose to seek a settlement agreement when a charge of discrimination is first filed, the EEOC can handle the charge in all of the following ways *except*

- ○ **A.** Investigate it
- ○ **B.** Settle it
- ○ **C.** Arbitrate it
- ○ **D.** Dismiss it

186. A protected class is best described as

- ○ **A.** A group of individuals who have, historically, experienced discrimination (for instance, women, people of color, people with disabilities, and so on)
- ○ **B.** A group of individuals who share a common characteristic, and who are protected from discrimination and harassment based on that shared characteristic
- ○ **C.** A group of individuals that has filed charges with the NLRB or taking part in any NLRB proceedings (ULP by an employer)
- ○ **D.** Employees who have engaged in an economic strike and who, therefore, under the Mackay Doctrine and who cannot be permanently replaced by the employer

187. If you notice a change in a candidate's non-verbal behavior during the interview

- ○ **A.** Probe for more information around whatever question the candidate was answering when that change occurred
- ○ **B.** Be familiar with what specific non-verbal communication cues mean (for instance, folded arms indicate aloofness), so you know how to interpret the behavior
- ○ **C.** Without assessing judgment, point out and describe the changed non-verbal behavior, and ask him or her to help you understand what it means
- ○ **D.** Mirror the candidate's non-verbal behavior, to see if he or she continues to display that behavior

188. Annual EEO reports must be filed

- ○ **A.** By employers with federal contracts or subcontracts of $100,000 or more
- ○ **B.** By employers with 100 or more employees
- ○ **C.** By federal contractors and subcontractors with contracts in excess of $10,000 during any one-year period
- ○ **D.** By all employers, with the exception of family farms, who do not employee individuals outside the family

189. Recruiting is

   ○ **A.** The process of creating a pool of candidates and selecting the final candidate

   ○ **B.** The process of attracting and creating a pool of qualified candidates

   ○ **C.** The process of identifying the candidate(s) to whom the position will be offered

   ○ **D.** The process of selecting the candidate to whom the position will be offered

190. After you decide that you are going to conduct an employee survey, what is the first step that you should take?

   ○ **A.** Select an internal or external consultant

   ○ **B.** Determine the survey methodology

   ○ **C.** Secure management buy-in

   ○ **D.** Decide upon the survey content

191. Union deauthorization

   ○ **A.** Is the process of removing the union's rights to represent the employees

   ○ **B.** Revokes the union security clause in the contract

   ○ **C.** Requires that 50% or more of those who vote during the union deauthorization election support the deauthorization

   ○ **D.** Is far more common than union decertification

192. Pre-employment realistic job previews can be conveyed and communicated in a number of ways. Which of the following is the least effective way of providing candidates with a realistic job preview?

   ○ **A.** Verbal descriptions of the work, the work environment, and/or the work conditions

   ○ **B.** The opportunity to read the employee handbook

   ○ **C.** The opportunity to speak with current employees, particularly those who would be the incumbent's peers and/or colleagues

   ○ **D.** The opportunity to interact with other candidates, and to compare perceptions of the organization with each other

193. On November 13, 2000, 41 CFR Part 60-2 (the portion of the federal register that addresses affirmative action) was significantly revised. Which of the following was not addressed or accomplished by these revisions?

   ○ **A.** Reduced the number of additional required elements of the written AAP from 10 to 4.

   ○ **B.** Reaffirmed that AAPs establish quotas that must be affirmatively pursued through good faith efforts.

○ C. Granted employers with fewer than 150 employees permission to prepare a job group analysis that uses EEO-1 categories as job groups.

○ D. Reduced the 8-factor availability analysis to 2 factors.

194. Which of the following statements about the nominal group technique is true?

○ A. It constitutes a non-mathematical forecasting technique that draws upon the insights of subject matter experts.

○ B. It is similar to the Delphi technique in that it affords experts the opportunity to interact with each other.

○ C. It is self-directing, self-governing, and relies upon the facilitative abilities of the experts who are participating in the forecasting process.

○ D. It permits and encourages discussion and collaboration throughout the forecasting process.

195. Which of the following statements about IRCA is inaccurate?

○ A. Prohibits discrimination against job applicants based on national origin.

○ B. Imposes penalties for knowingly committing recordkeeping errors.

○ C. Prohibits giving employment preference to U.S. citizens.

○ D. Imposes penalties for hiring illegal aliens

196. Which of the following statements about torts is not true?

○ A. Torts are wrongful acts.

○ B. Torts are committed against people, not against things.

○ C. The commission of a tort infringes on another person's rights.

○ D. Tort doctrine is associated with common law.

197. According to Fred Fiedler, all of the following are factors that contribute to determining a situation's level of favorableness for a particular leadership style except

○ A. Leader-member relations. This factor looks at how strong and how significant relationships between the leader and the team members are. It considers the degree to which those relationships make the leader more or less effective and influential.

○ B. Experience-expertise. This factor looks at the degree to which a leader's experience with a particular situation or task has contributed to developing true expertise. It also looks at the degree to which that experience-expertise connection is recognize, and appreciated by team members.

○ **C.** Task structure. This factor ascertains the degree to which the work that the team members perform is structured.

○ **D.** Position power. This factor looks at the degree to which the leader's position holds or can exert power or influence. It also looks at the degree to which the leader can ensure accountability for team members' performance, and the degree to which the leader has the authority to delegate.

198. All of the following are valuable guidelines for managing a vendor and a relationship with a vendor *except*

○ **A.** Giving the vendor constructive and positive feedback.

○ **B.** Setting clear and reasonable expectations.

○ **C.** Converting full-time vendors from independent contractors to employee to foster greater esprit de corps.

○ **D.** Incorporating upside potential and downside risk into your negotiated agreements with vendors.

199. The four Ps refer to

○ **A.** Priorities, posting, places, and people (the four Ps of recruiting)

○ **B.** Perception, perspective, proportion, and perseverance (the four Ps of employee relations)

○ **C.** Prospect, persistence, proposal, and project (the four Ps of project management)

○ **D.** Product, place, price, and promotion (the four Ps of marketing)

200. All of the following statements are true of weighted employment applications *except*

○ **A.** They are intended to facilitate the process of assessing each candidate's qualifications.

○ **B.** They facilitate and support compliance with EEO guidelines.

○ **C.** They can be difficult and time consuming to develop and maintain.

○ **D.** They assign relative weights to different elements of the employment application.

201. Which of the statements about common situs picketing is not true?

○ **A.** Common situs picketing is a type of secondary boycott.

○ **B.** Common situs picketing is generally legal.

     ○ **C.** Common situs picketing occurs when members of a labor union picket a workplace in which multiple employers work.

     ○ **D.** Common situs picketing is permissible when double breasting has occurred.

202. All of the following statements about essential functions are true *except*

     ○ **A.** In order to be considered essential, a function must be inherently fundamental and necessary to a position.

     ○ **B.** In order to be considered essential, a function must constitute part, or all, of the reason the job exists.

     ○ **C.** The elimination of an essential function would substantially alter the nature of the job.

     ○ **D.** They must be identified in the job description.

203. *McDonnell Douglas Corp* v. *Green (1979)* determined that the initial burden of proof for establishing a prima facie case of discrimination against an employer (or potential employer) under Title VII of the Civil Rights Act of 1964 rests with the employee (or applicant), who must be able to establish four key elements. Which one of these elements is not one of those four elements that the employee must be able to establish for a prima facie case?

     ○ **A.** The person is a member of a protected class.

     ○ **B.** The person applied for a job for which the employer was seeking applicants.

     ○ **C.** The person was rejected, despite being the most qualified for the position.

     ○ **D.** After this rejection, the employer continued to seek other applicants with similar qualifications.

204. An organization that utilizes the services of an employment agency/search firm must pay

     ○ **A.** A fee to a contingency employment agency/search firm whether or not an employee is hired through that agency's efforts

     ○ **B.** A fee to a contingency employment agency/search firm only if an employee is hired through that agency's efforts

     ○ **C.** A fee to a retained employment agency/search firm only if an employee is hired through that agency's efforts

     ○ **D.** Fees to a contingency firm as well as retained employment agencies/search firms whether or not an employee is hired through an agency's efforts

205. All of the following are possible reasons to conduct prescreen phone interviews *except*

   ○ **A.** To identify legitimate job-related factors that could cause the employer to decide to eliminate the candidate from consideration

   ○ **B.** To share (with every potential employee) job-related information that could lead one or more candidates to self-select out of the selection process

   ○ **C.** To interact with a candidate in a more informal manner so as to ascertain whether he or she is likely to be a good fit with the organization

   ○ **D.** To ascertain whether the candidate's desired salary/wage rate is close to the salary/wage range that the organization has established for the position

206. Which of the following situations would be least likely to result in disparate impact?

   ○ **A.** An employer requires all employees to live within a 30-mile radius of an employer, so as to ensure quick response in the event that employees need to report to work immediately.

   ○ **B.** An employer will not hire any candidates who have experienced a gap in employment.

   ○ **C.** An employer establishes a high potential program, in which all participants are required to relocate every 9–12 months until they have completed 5 rotational assignments in 5 different locations.

   ○ **D.** An employer creates a cross-training program in which all non-management employees who meet or exceed performance expectations of their current positions would be able to participate.

207. Although it is very difficult to establish good measures of validity, it is possible to make a case for validity if the interview process has certain characteristics. Which of these processes contributes the least to ensuring the validity of an interview process?

   ○ **A.** The same interviewer conducts every interview for a particular job opening.

   ○ **B.** The interview is based on job analysis.

   ○ **C.** The interviewer asks questions that provide evidence about important job-related skills.

   ○ **D.** The information shared, discussed, and collected during an interview is related to a specific job.

208. Skill inventories refer to

   ○ **A.** Pre-employment testing that ascertains the degree to which a candidate possesses specific skills required to perform the position.

   ○ **B.** A central database that captures the KSAs possessed by employees.

○ **C.** A performance management instrument that ascertains the degree to which the candidate demonstrates the competencies required by the position during the performance measurement period.

○ **D.** An online database used to create job descriptions.

209. An employee seems to be working diligently, but has been continually missing deadlines. After a great deal of coaching and counseling, this employee starts meeting deadlines—first sporadically, and then on a more consistent basis. In response, the employee's supervisor begins assigning additional work to this employee; he believes she's ready to handle more—specifically more than the job "originally" requires, and more than is required of other incumbents who held the same position. This is an example of

○ **A.** Negative reinforcement

○ **B.** Positive reinforcement

○ **C.** Punishment

○ **D.** Extinction

210. All of the following are elements of Vroom's expectancy theory except

○ **A.** Instrumentality

○ **B.** Proclivity

○ **C.** Valence

○ **D.** Expectancy

211. In behavioral leadership theories, the dimension of leadership behavior known as initiating structure or job-related refers to

○ **A.** The interpersonal relationships that managers must first establish with employees before attempting to ensure completion of the actual work

○ **B.** What employees need to do, and how they need to do it, in order to attain objectives

○ **C.** The training in which managers need to participate in order to develop the skills needed to be an effective leader

○ **D.** The degree to which an individual demonstrates an innate ability to being an effective leader

212. According to the Copyright Act of 1976, which of the following statements is true?

○ **A.** Most of the time, the employer owns/retains the copyright to the work product that an employee generates during the normal course of his or her employment.

○ **B.** Most of the time, an independent contractor owns/retains the copyright to the work product that he or she generates for the organization with which he or she has contracted.

    ○ **C.** Most of the time, an employee owns/retains the copyright to the work product that he or she generates in the normal course of his or her employment.

    ○ **D.** Most of the time, a consulting firm owns/retains the copyright to the work product that an employee generates for the organization with which he or she is consulting.

213. The formative evaluation model

    ○ **A.** Seeks feedback during and after the development and implementation phases

    ○ **B.** Uses feedback, analysis, and assessment conducted at one phase of the process to make enhancements in other phases

    ○ **C.** Was initially developed by Donald L. Kirkpatrick

    ○ **D.** Measures participants' responses and reactions to the program immediately after the program has been delivered

214. In order to qualify for the learned professional exemption under the FLSA

    ○ **A.** The employee's primary duty must be the performance of work requiring advanced knowledge, defined as work which is predominantly intellectual in character and which includes work requiring the consistent exercise of discretion and judgment.

    ○ **B.** The advanced knowledge must be in a field of science, learning, or other accredited profession.

    ○ **C.** Both A and B.

    ○ **D.** Neither A nor B.

215. Which of the following would not be considered a form of indirect compensation?

    ○ **A.** Legally mandated benefits (such as Social Security)

    ○ **B.** Vacation time

    ○ **C.** Perquisites

    ○ **D.** Vacation buyout programs

216. Which of the following statements about the MHPA is untrue?

    ○ **A.** MHPA requires employers that offer healthcare plans with medical benefits to offer mental health benefits.

    ○ **B.** Under MHPA, plans can still dictate/define the terms and conditions of benefits provided under mental health plans (for instance, cost-sharing, limits on the number of visits or days of coverage, and so forth).

    ○ **C.** Under MHPA, plans that don't impose annual or lifetime monetary caps on medical and surgical benefits cannot impose annual or lifetime caps on mental health benefits.

    ○ **D.** Benefits for substance abuse or chemical dependency are excluded from MHPA's requirements.

217. Generally speaking, when an employee handbook is submitted as legal evidence, which of the following factors is usually most important?

    ○ **A.** EEO/AA statement

    ○ **B.** Sexual harassment policy

    ○ **C.** Records retention policy

    ○ **D.** Employee acknowledgement

218. Which of the following is least likely to be a reason that an organization would conduct an employee survey?

    ○ **A.** To gauge and measure employees' perceptions, viewpoints, and attitudes

    ○ **B.** To take the pulse on specific current and/or potential employee issues

    ○ **C.** To collect information that can be used to address individual's employee relations

    ○ **D.** To collect information that can be used by the organization to help set priorities

219. In order for a bargaining unit to be established, which of the following has to happen during the election?

    ○ **A.** A simple majority of the voters must cast a vote in favor of the proposed bargaining unit.

    ○ **B.** A simple majority of the individuals who would be members of the proposed bargaining unit must cast a vote in favor of the proposed bargaining unit.

    ○ **C.** When there is more than one bargaining unit competing in the election, a proposed bargaining unit must obtain more votes than other bargaining units obtain.

    ○ **D.** At least 30% of the voters must cast a vote in favor of the bargaining unit.

220. Of the following situations, which one represents the highest priority for OSHA?

    ○ **A.** Referrals from the media

    ○ **B.** Planned inspections in high-hazard industries

    ○ **C.** Employee complaints

    ○ **D.** Catastrophes and fatal accidents

221. With respect to selection procedures, reliability can be defined as

○ **A.** The degree to which a selection procedure assesses a candidate's ability to perform representative and significant parts of the job.

○ **B.** The degree to which incumbents' scores or ratings on a particular selection procedure correlate with their actual job performance.

○ **C.** The degree to which a selection process or instrument is consistent, and generates consistent information that can be used for decision making.

○ **D.** The degree to which a clear relationship exists between performance on the selection procedure and performance on the job.

222. "The degree of responsibility and accountability which an employer entrusts to—and expects from—a particular position" refers to the definition of which of the four factors used by the Equal Pay Act to assess substantial equality?

○ **A.** Skill

○ **B.** Trust

○ **C.** Accountability

○ **D.** Responsibility

223. The Railway Labor Act of 1926 accomplished all of the following *except*

○ **A.** Established the grieve now, work later rule

○ **B.** Gave management additional tools to make sure the trains ran on time

○ **C.** Enabled railroad workers to organize and to have a collective bargaining agent

○ **D.** Created the first real win-win scenario for labor and management in American history

224. Taft-Hartley accomplished all of the following changes to the NLRA *except*

○ **A.** Reaffirmed that employers have a constitutional right to express their opposition to unions, so long as employees are not threatened with reprisal for their union activities or promised benefits for refraining from such activities.

○ **B.** Prohibited employers from taking adverse employment actions against supervisors who did not support the employer's position.

○ **C.** Outlawed closed shops, agreements that stated that employers could only to hire individuals who were members of labor unions.

○ **D.** Expressly permitted union shops, in which non-union workers must join the union within a certain amount of time after being hired.

225. The list of the names and addresses of all of the employees who are eligible to vote in the union certification election is known as

   ○ **A.** The Excelsior List

   ○ **B.** The Davis-Bacon List

   ○ **C.** The Hot Cargo List

   ○ **D.** The Waffle House List

Answers to Practice Exam

1. **Answer C is the best response.** Unbecoming light does not constitute one of the four categories of invasion of privacy; however, false light *does*. Answer A is not the best response; intrusion of solitude does constitute one of the four categories of invasion of privacy. Answer B is not the best response; public disclosure of private and embarrassing facts does constitute one of the four categories of invasion of privacy. Answer D is not the best response; appropriation of identity does constitute one of the four categories of invasion of privacy.

2. **Answer C is the best response.** Employees must report all work-related injuries to their employer—whether or not the injury results in in-patient hospitalization. Answers A, B, and D are not the best responses because each identifies responsibilities that are mandated by the General Duty Clause.

3. **Answer C is the best response.** The balanced scorecard manifests the opposite belief; it is, in fact, a management system that turns strategic planning into a hands-on, reality-driven, highly impactful tool. Answers A, B, and D are not the best responses; each reflects a belief that is embodied in the balanced scorecard.

4. **Answer B is the best response.** Efficiency can be described as doing things right—speaking, therefore, more to how something is accomplished than what is accomplished. Answer A is not the best choice; the degree to which goals are appropriate is a statement that is descriptive of effectiveness, not efficiency. Answer C is not the best choice; doing the right things is also a statement that is descriptive of effectiveness, not efficiency. Answer D is not the best choice; it is quite possible to achieve efficiency without achieving effectiveness—in other words, it's possible to do a good job of achieving goals that aren't appropriate (which, in the case of HR, could mean that the goals aren't strategically aligned with the goals of the organization).

5. **Answer D is the best response.** The Retirement Equity Act did prohibit plans from counting maternity and paternity leaves as breaks in service for participation and vesting purposes. Answer A is not the best response; REA lowered, rather than increased, the minimum age requirement for pension plan participation. Answer B is not the best response; REA required qualified pension plans to provide automatic survivor benefits and allow for waiver of survivor benefits *only with the consent of the participant and the spouse*. Answer C is not the best response; REA clarified that pension plans *may obey* certain qualified domestic relations (court) orders (QDROs) requiring them to make benefit payments to a participant's former spouse (or another alternative payee) *without violating ERISA's prohibitions against assignment or alienation of benefits*.

6. **Answer A is the best response.** Whether a survey is designed and conducted by someone from inside or outside the organization is not nearly as important as the other considerations that are listed in the other responses. A survey can be successful or unsuccessful whether it is conducted by someone inside, or outside, the organization. How the survey is designed and conducted is generally much more important. Answer B is the not the best response; ensuring that survey input is maintained in a fully confidential manner is an important determinant of the overall success of an employee survey. Answer C is not the best response; ensuring that employees believe in the confidentiality of the survey is an important determinant of the overall success of an employee survey. Answer D is not the best response; ensuring buy-in and support from management is an important determinant of the overall success of an employee survey.

7. **Answer C is the best response.** Answer A is not the best response; having a core group of highly talented employees focus on the founder is more likely to first manifest itself during stage 1 of the organizational life cycle (introduction or birth). Answer B is not the best response; resistance to OD and change initiatives is more likely to first manifest itself during stage 3 of the organizational life cycle (maturity). Answer D is not the best response; an entitlement mentality towards pay and benefits is most likely to first manifest itself during stage 3 of the organizational life cycle (maturity).

8. **Answer D is the best response.** The scientific method is a form of primary research, not secondary research. Primary research, by definition, goes to the source and, therefore, collects data, rather than assimilates data that been collected by others (existing data is assimilated as part of secondary research). Answers A, B, and C are not the best responses; each represents a step in the scientific method. The only step that is not represented here is the final one, which is to analyze data and reach a conclusion.

9. **Answer A is the best response.** Transactional leaders use a system built on the carrot and the stick method—and mainly the stick part of it. Answer B is not the best response; coaching is more characteristic of the transformational leadership style. Answer C is not the best response; the image of a captain might more closely reflect the role a leader plays in the selling quadrant of Hersey and Blanchard's situational leadership model. Answer D is not the best response; the image of a director could imply a wider variety of leadership approaches under transactional as well as transformational styles.

10. **Answer C is the best response.** Bonus pay (which, unlike incentive pay, is discretionary) would not be included in an employee's regular rate of pay.

11. **Answer C is the best response.** OD helps maintain the organization's focus on the belief that it is the people within organizations (not the systems within organizations) who perform and accomplish the work of the organization. Answer A is not the best response; OD does refer to the process through which the overall performance, growth, and effectiveness of the organization is enhanced through strategic, deliberate, and integrated initiatives. Answer B is not the best response; OD does incorporate psychology, sociology, anthropology, and management. Answer D is not the best response; OD interventions are designed to identify an organization's competitive advantages.

12. **Answer C is the best response.** A ULP is called when a union alleges that an employer has committed a ULP. This does not necessarily mean that the employer actually did, in fact, commit a ULP (the courts would need to subsequently determine that a strike was, in fact, a ULP strike, and not an economic strike in disguise). Answer A is not the best response; ULP strikes stem from an allegation that the employer has committed a ULP during contract negotiations. Answer B is not the best response; an employer must return striking workers to their original positions after the strike is over.

13. **Answer B is the correct response.** The Hazard Communication Standard has no requirement pertaining to obtaining signed employee acknowledgement forms, although it is *always* a good idea to obtain signed documentation that participants have attended a training session (especially when such training is required by law). This standard does, however, require MSDS (answer A), container labeling requirements (answer C), and training and orientation requirements (answer D).

14. **Answer B is the best response.** A jurisdictional strike is one through which a union seeks to pressure an employer to assign particular work to its members, rather than to members of other unions or to non-union workers. Answer A is not the best response; employees who are not directly involved in an economic dispute who choose not to cross a picket line out of support for striking workers are engaging in a sympathy strike, not a jurisdictional strike. Answer C is not the best response; a strike that occurs even though the collective bargaining agreement contains a no-strike clause is a wildcat strike, not a jurisdictional strike. Answer D is not the best response; a strike used by a union to pressure an employer to grant some sort of concession (namely, an economic concession) from the employer during collective bargaining negotiations is an economic strike, not a jurisdictional strike.

15. **Answer C is the best response.** Copyrights are granted for the lifetime of the author, plus 70 years (assuming that the work was not created anonymously). Answer A is not correct; the copyright does not end when the author dies. Answer B is not correct; copyrights cannot be deeded to heirs. Answer D is not correct; this response alludes to copyrights for anonymous works and works that were created under work-for-hire agreements that enter the public domain 95 years after the first year of publication or 120 years after the year in which it was created, whichever comes first.

16. **Answer D is the best response.** In general, placing all of the interviewers on one side of the table and the candidate on the other can unintentionally create an adversarial atmosphere, even if it is easier for the candidate to make eye contact with the interviewers. Answer A is not the best response; it is a good idea to let the candidate know ahead of time if he or she will be participating in a panel interview. Answer B is not the best response; it is a good idea to plan who will ask what questions in advance, and in what order. Answer C is not the best response; a round table will help create an atmosphere that is conducive to the exchange of information.

17. **Answer B is the best response.** As long as they fall under the category of "first aid," injuries resulting in bleeding do not need to be recorded unless they also result in death, days away from work (answer A), restricted work or job transfer (answer C), or loss of consciousness (answer D).

18. **Answer A is the best response.** The question of whether the employee and/or the collective bargaining unit advised the employer of the concerted nature of the employee's activity is irrelevant to whether the employer might be considered to have violated the NLRA. The only three requirements that would need to be met in order for an employer to be considered to have possibly violated the

NLRA are whether the employer knew of the concerted nature of the employee's activity (answer B), whether the concerted activity was actually protected by the Act (answer C), and whether the adverse employment action in question (for instance, termination) was motivated by the employee's protected concerted activity (answer D).

19. **Answer B is the best response.** Henry Fayol is known as the father of modern management. Answers A, C, and D are not the best responses; Fayol was not known as a guru in any of these areas.

20. **Answer C is the best response.** In *General Dynamics Land Systems* v. *Cline (2004)*, the Supreme Court ruled that younger employees (even if they over the age of 40) cannot allege age discrimination because of programs that favor older employees. Answer A is not the best response; *General Dynamics Land Systems* v. *Cline* established that the ADEA does not prohibit favoring the old over the young. Answer B is not the best response; although the ADEA prohibits favoring the *young over the old*, it does not prohibit favoring the *old over the young*. Answer D is not the best response; younger employees (even if they are over the age of 40) cannot allege age discrimination because of programs that favor older employees.

21. **Answer A is the best response.** Job classification is a non-quantitative job evaluation technique that categorizes jobs into broad categories, or levels, based on the level—and, ultimately, value to the organization—of the work that is performed by jobs within each level. Each level incorporates specific responsibilities and benchmark statements that describe the nature, complexity, autonomy, and so forth of the work that is performed by positions in that level. Answer B is not the best response; job slotting is a non-quantitative job evaluation technique that incorporates, or slots, newly created or revised positions into an existing job hierarchy. Answer C is not the best response; in whole job ranking techniques (non-quantitative), job are ranked, from lowest to highest, according to the importance that each job holds (or, stated differently, the value that each job brings) to the organization. Answer D is not the best response; factor comparison is a quantitative job evaluation technique that involves the ranking of each compensable factor of each job.

22. **Answer C is the best response.** The decision whether to lag, match, or lead the market with respect to total compensation is just that—a decision. It is not universally true that an organization's total compensation program should be competitive with (in other words, match) the total compensation programs offered by labor market competitors. Answer A is not the best response; an organization's total compensation program should support and reinforce the mission, vision, and values of the organization. Answer B is not the best response; an organization's total compensation program should be consistent with the culture of the organization. Answer D is not the best response; an organization's total compensation program should attract, motivate, and retain targeted/appropriate employees.

23. **Answer D is the best response.** Responding to the complaint is the responsibility of counsel. Although an HR professional might be asked to *assist* in this process, HR is not primarily responsible for this response. This is an important distinction to keep in mind, as HR professionals must be ever-vigilant not to cross the line and perform functions that can only be performed by an attorney. Answer A is not the best response; an HR professional may be called upon to testify during a trial. Answer B is not the best response; an HR professional may be called upon to sit at counsel table during the trial, thus being the face of the organization to the judge and jury. Answer C is not the best response; an HR professional is likely to be called upon to collect data during discovery.

24. **Answer A is the best response.** It would not be advisable or appropriate to consider vendor's technological resources and capabilities (as compared to the project requirements) until you have ascertained whether outsourcing is an appropriate option. Engaging in those sorts of comparisons at this point in the process is predicated on the assumption (perhaps an implicit one, and perhaps a faulty one) that outsourcing is an appropriate option. Instead, these comparisons should not be made until—and unless—you determine that outsourcing is, in fact, an appropriate option. Answer B is not the best response; comparing talents and abilities that are available internally to talents and abilities that are available through outsourcing is an appropriate consideration to engage in at this point in the process. Answer C is not the best response; the importance and complexity of the function that is being considered for outsourcing is an appropriate factor to consider at this point in the process. Answer D is not the best response; the degree of variability in transaction volume of the function that is being considered for outsourcing is an appropriate factor to consider at this point in the process.

25. **Answer A is the best response.** Less value can be gleaned from speaking with former clients from several years ago than from the choices offered through the other responses. Ascertaining a potential vendor's recent performance is more valuable than historical performance because performance can change (or erode) over time (answer B). Answer C is not the best response; information of significant value can be gleaned from comparing each vendor's experience to what is required by the project. Answer D is not the best response; information of significant value can be gleaned from exploring each vendor's commitment to quality.

26. **Answer D is the best response.** An oral contract can be created when an agent of the employer promises some benefit or right. The term agent is legal, and involved, but of the four individuals listed in the question, the one that is least likely to be considered an agent would be a co-worker. Answer A is not the best response; a full-time recruiter would be more likely than a co-worker to create an oral contract. Answer B is not the best response; a hiring manager—even if he or she interviews only for his or her open positions—is more likely than a co-worker to create an oral contract (it only takes one interview, and maybe even one comment, to create an oral contract). Answer C is not the best response; an employee's current supervisor is more likely to create an oral contract than an employee's current co-worker is.

27. **Answer D is the best response.** According to equity theory, employees are less likely to accept a situation that they perceive to be inequitable as is than they are to take some sort of action to rectify that inequity. Neither answer A nor answer B is the best response; according to equity theory, employees who feel they are being treated unfairly might seek to modify their inputs or outputs, or encourage others to modify their inputs or outputs. Answer C is not the best response; equity theory asserts that people who believe they are being treated unfairly will seek, in one way or another, to make a change that diminishes or eliminates that inequity.

28. **Answer D is the best response.** *Harris* v. *Forklift Systems* (1993) established the reasonable person standard. Answer A is not the best response; In *Taxman* v. *Board of Education of Piscataway*, the Supreme Court ruled that, in the absence of under-representation as demonstrated and documented through an affirmative action plan, organizations cannot take race into account when making decisions relative to who will be laid off and who will be retained (and that doing so would constitute a violation of Title VII of the Civil Rights Act of 1964). Answer B is not the best response; in *Meritor Savings Bank v. Vinson*, the Supreme Court ruled that a claim of "hostile environment"

sexual harassment does constitute a form of sex discrimination actionable under Title VII of the 1964 Civil Rights Act. Answer C is not the best response; in *St. Mary's Honor Center v. Hicks*, the Supreme Court ruled that, in order to ultimately prevail in an allegation of discrimination under Title VII of the Civil Rights Act of 1964, the charging party must go beyond a prima facie case and *actually prove* that the employer's actual reasons for an employment action are, in fact, discriminatory.

29. **Answer B is the best response.** Ishikawa's fishbone diagram (also known as the cause-and-effect diagram or the Ishikawa diagram) presents a visual representation of factors that impact whether a desired outcome will be obtained. Ishikawa believed that, by presenting all of the possible factors that can contribute to a particular result, any potential process imperfections can be identified in advance and eliminated. Answer A is not the best response; the Pareto Chart (based on the Pareto Principle) visually depicts the 80-20 rule. Answer C is not the best response; although Ishikawa dramatically increased worldwide awareness and acceptance of the idea of quality circles, quality circles are not directly related to his fishbone diagram. Answer D is not the best response; histograms depict information about a single factor, while the Ishikawa diagram depicts information about multiple factors.

30. **Answer A is the best response.** ADEA prohibits discrimination based on age, for individuals age 40 (not age 18) and above. Some states, however, have established age thresholds that are lower. Answer B is not the best response; the ADEA does cover private employers with 20 or more employees, state and local governments (including school districts), employment agencies, and labor organizations. Answer C is not the best response; the ADEA does not establish an upper cap, or an age at which it once again becomes legal to discriminate against individuals based on age (although it did at one time). Answer D is not the best response; ADEA is subject to certain exceptions, and places certain requirements on employers, particularly with respect to benefits plans, coverage, and early retirement incentives.

31. **Answer D is the best response.** The *A* in KSAs refers to abilities, which can be defined as specific traits required to successfully perform a position. Answer A is not the best response; the *A* in KSAs does not refer to attitude. Answer B is not the best response; this answer defines knowledge, the *K* in KSAs. Answer C is not the best response; this answer defines skill, the *S* in KSAs.

32. **Answer C is the best response.** HR adds value to this process by asking our clients questions

    ▶ That enable us to collect information

    ▶ That help us to collaboratively ascertain the underlying problems

    ▶ That can help us work with managers to distinguish problems from symptoms

    Answer A is not the best response; although a manager might be convinced of what the problem is and/or of what the solution should be, the manager's assessment is not necessarily 100% complete or correct, so it is not advisable to automatically commit to implementing it. (Instead, find another way to demonstrate your commitment to that manager, to her problem, and—ultimately—to building a relationship with her). Answer B is not the best response for a related reason; at this point, you don't truly know what the problem is, so it is not possible to suggest a solution. Additionally, if you use this approach, you are dismissing the manager's opinions and experience, and risk damaging your relationship with the manager (narcissism won't get you very far in your role as an HR professional). Answer D is not the best response; it assumes that the manager's assessment of the problem is 100% complete and correct, and that the proposed solution is the best possible intervention.

33. **Answer D is the best response.** In concert with counsel, develop a policy that requires that current and former employees sign a carefully worded release before information can be released to a third party. This might include designating what information can be released, as well as acknowledging what information must be released (for instance, to avoid a claim that the organization withheld truthful negative information about the employee). Answer A is not the best response; it could result in the employer concealing truthful negative information about the employee. Answer B is not the best response; providing only titles, dates of employment, and final salary information when providing references could still result in a tort claim alleging that the employer concealed truthful negative information about an employee. Answer C is not the best response; while outsourcing might anesthetize an organization to the fear of litigation, it will not immunize the organization from its consequences.

34. **Answer C is the best response.** Defined contribution plans are increasing, not decreasing, in popularity. Answer A is not the best response; it is true that, unlike defined benefit plans, defined contribution plans do not promise a specific monthly benefit (or total benefit) at retirement. Answer B is not the best response; defined contribution plans do shift the risk away from the employer (which is where it rests for defined benefit plans) and back onto the employee. Answer D is not the best response; 401(k) plans, employee stock ownership plans, and profit-sharing plans are examples of defined contribution plans.

35. **Answer A is the best response.** In *Taxman* v. *Board of Education of Piscataway*, the Supreme Court ruled that, in the absence of under-representation as demonstrated and documented through an affirmative action plan, organizations cannot take race into account when making decisions relative to who will be laid off and who will be retained (and that doing so would constitute a violation of Title VII of the Civil Rights Act of 1964).

36. **Answer B is the best response.** The Revenue Act of 1978 resulted in the creation of two very important employee benefits: section 125 plans and 401(k) plans. Answer A is not the best response; passed in 1985, COBRA requires employers who employed 20 or more people during the prior year to offer continuation of group health care coverage to employees and their family members who experience certain qualifying events—events that would have otherwise resulted in the discontinuation of their health insurance benefits. Answer C is not the best response; HIPAA has two main focuses: the security and portability of health care coverage, and privacy considerations. Answer D is not the best response; an amendment to ERISA, REA incorporated a number of key revisions, many of which addressed the concerns of former spouses (in the event of divorce) and surviving spouses (in the event of death).

37. **Answer A is the best response.** A cash balance plan is a defined benefit plan that expresses the promised benefit in terms of a stated account balance. Answer B is not the best choice; a cash balance plan is a defined benefit plan, but it doesn't express the promised benefit in terms of a specific monthly benefit (like other defined benefits plans do). Answer C is not the best response; a cash balance plan is not a defined contribution plan. Answer D is not the best response; a cash balance

plan is not a defined contribution plan, and it doesn't express the promised benefit in terms of a specific monthly benefit.

38. **Answer C is the best response.** The balanced scorecard does consist of a variety of financial and non-financial measures of success, and is intended to balance them against each other within the scorecard. Answers A, C, and D are not the best responses; none of them describes what a balanced scorecard truly is.

39. **Answer C is the best choice.** The Civil Rights Act of 1991 capped damages at $300,000 per employee, not at $500,000 per employee. Answer A is not the best choice; the Civil Rights of 1991 expanded upon employees' rights. Answer B is not the best choice; the Civil Rights Act of 1991 expanded upon employees' remedies. Answer D is not the best choice; the Civil Rights Act of 1991 did allow for jury trials for discrimination cases.

40. **Answer A is the best response.** McClelland's theory speaks to the need that certain individuals have to achieve. Answers B and D are not the best responses; recognition and rewards both relate to the consequences of achievement, rather than to the achievement itself. McClelland, conversely, asserts that individuals with a high need to achieve are focused more on the act of achieving, rather than on the consequences that result from having attained a particular level of achievement. Answer C is not the best response; equity is a primary motivator in J. Stacy Adams' equity theory, not McClelland's acquired needs theory.

41. **Answer B is the best response.** Quality circles were brought to the attention of the world by Ishikawa. Answers A, C, and D encompass Juran's three-point quality focus: quality planning, quality improvement, and quality control.

42. **Answer B is the best response.** The statement that articulates what the organization wants to become in the future is the vision statement. The vision statement should be one important tool used to guide strategic planning, rather than be a product of strategic planning. Answers A, C, and D are not the best responses; each one makes a true statement about strategic planning.

43. **Answer B is the best response.** Compound resolution refers to a type of medical imaging, not a type of legislation. Answer A is not the best response; a concurrent resolution is a type of legislation. Answer C is not the best choice; a joint resolution is a type of legislation. Answer D is not the best choice; a simple resolution is a type of legislation.

44. **Answer A is the best response.** Securing the support and commitment of senior leadership is critical to the strategic planning process, but with respect to *demonstrating commitment to the strategic planning process* rather than with respect to *creating and sustaining credibility*. Answer B is not the best response; clear, complete, and appropriate documentation of the process is particularly relevant to creating and sustaining credibility during the implementation of a strategic plan. Answer C is not the best response; a commitment to following through on every step of the process is particularly relevant to creating and sustaining credibility during the implementation of a strategic plan. Answer D is not the best response; representative participation from all levels of the organization is particularly relevant to creating and sustaining credibility during the implementation of a strategic plan.

45. **Answer C is the best response.** Answer A, 162.4, is the mean of the numbers in this set. Answer B, 645, is the highest number in this set. Answer D, 87, is the median of the numbers in this set.

46. **Answer C is the best response.** The paperwork-type functions described here are administrative and task-oriented in nature, and are reflective of the way HR was viewed in the past. Answer A is not the best response; the functions (as described) do not even rise to an operational or tactical level; they are purely administrative in nature. Neither answer B nor answer D is the best response; strategic and transformational dimensions of HR focus on a long-term, future-focused approach to the ways in which HR will work with the organization to attain its organizational mission. It looks at business and organizational issues, rather than so-called HR issues.

47. **Answer C is the best response.** Job bidding systems deal with jobs that might open at some point in the future, while job posting systems deal with jobs that are currently open. Answer A is not the best response; job bidding systems deal with jobs that might open at some point in the future, while job posting systems deal with jobs that are currently open. Neither answer B nor Answer D is not the best response; job bidding and job posting systems are both directed solely at internal candidates.

48. **Answer C is the best response.** Employers must allow at least 21 days to consider any right-to-sue waivers that the employer offers in exchange for early retirement benefits.

49. **Answer C is the best response.** The progress discipline process is predicated on the belief that (assuming that an employee is at least minimally qualified for the position for which he or she was hired) an employee can choose whether to perform his or her job satisfactorily. It is in this way that we establish the foundation for thinking of progressive discipline as an employee relations initiative.

50. **Answer A is the best response.** According to Herzberg's motivation-hygiene theory, motivation factors have a positive impact on an employee's motivation level *if, and only if*, hygiene factors are acceptable. In this situation, it appears as though neither motivation nor hygiene factors are acceptable. According to Herzberg's theory, it's important to address hygiene factors first to ensure that motivation factors will have a positive impact. Answer B is not the best response; it jumps straight to motivation factors. Answer C is not the best response; it takes a "ready, fire, aim" approach. Although employees have communicated that they are unhappy with their pay, that does not necessarily mean that pay levels are inappropriate, that they need to be increased, or that 5% would be the right number to use. Answer D is not the best response; although it will probably be necessary to collect more information (perhaps through follow-up meetings), it would not be effective (or even well-received) to ask employees to give you the same information, in the same way, through the same type of instrument.

51. **Answer D is the best response.** Hersey and Blanchard's situational leadership model is predicated on the idea that effective leaders are able to demonstrate different leadership styles, with different employees, at different times, under different circumstances. Answer A is not the best response; picking one leadership style and sticking to it in a resolute fashion violates that principle. Answer B is not the best response; the same employee can fall into two, three, or even four quadrants at the same time because quadrants are determined based on each employee's ability to perform a specific function or task, not based on an employee's overall performance. Answer C is not the best response; an effective leader focuses on an employee's maturity—the degree to which he or she possesses and demonstrates the non-technical skills required to bring the task to successful completion—as much as that leader focuses on the technical skills required to perform the function or task.

52. **Answer D is the best response.** Willingness to change is not one of Knowles's five key assumptions about how adults learn. Answer A is not the best response; the learner's need to know is one of Knowles's five key assumptions about how adults learn. Answer B is not the best response; the learner's readiness to learn is one of Knowles's five key assumptions about how adults learn. Answer C is not the best response; the learner's self concept is one of Knowles's five key assumptions about how adults learn.

53. **Answer B is the best response.** A plan provider that offers mental health benefits would be exempt from MHPA requirements if actual claims costs increase 1% or more due to the application of MHPA's requirements. Answer A is not the best response; a plan provider with fewer than 51 people (not 15 people) would be exempt from MHPA requirements. Answer C is not the best response; a plan provider's costs would need to increase more than 1% in terms of actual claims—not in terms of insurance premiums—in order for that plan provider to be exempt from MPHA.

54. **Answer B is the best response.** COBRA requires plan providers to offer plan participants the opportunity to continue participating in the plan provider's group healthcare plans. Answer A is not the best response; COBRA does not require plan providers to offer plan participants the opportunity to continue participating in wellness programs or long-term disability insurance. Answer C is not the best response; a plan participant's ability to join a different group healthcare plan is irrelevant to the plan provider's obligation to offer the plan participant the opportunity to continue participating in its group healthcare plan. Answer D is not the best response; COBRA does not require plan providers to offer plan participants the opportunity to continue participating in any benefit programs other than group healthcare plans.

55. **Answer B is the best response.** According to the Equal Pay Act, the substantial equality of job content is assessed based on effort, skill, responsibility, and working conditions (more often listed in the order of skill, effort, responsibility, and working conditions). Neither Answer A nor answer D is the best response; scope is not one of the four factors used by the Equal Pay Act to assess substantial equality. Answer C is not the best response; neither scope nor accountability is one of the four factors used by the Equal Pay Act to assess substantial equality.

56. **Answer C is the best response.** Broadbanding is an approach in which organizations choose to establish and use a relatively small number of grades. Answer A is not the best response; although one reason that organizations might choose to use broadbands could be to support the implementation of a flatter organization, this process or approach is not known as flattening. Answer B is not the best response; although one reason that organizations might choose to use broadbands could be to shift employees' focus away from traditional promotions and place it instead on career growth, this process or approach is not known as growthbanding. Answer D is not the best response; although the institution of broadbanding might result in the collapsing and combining of a large number of grades into a smaller number of grades, this process or approach is not known as gradesharing.

57. **Answer D is the best response.** Crosby's fourth Absolute of Quality Management states specifically that quality is not measured by production indexes; rather, it is measured by the price of nonconformance. Answers A, B, and C are not the best responses; each one identifies one of Crosby's four Absolutes of Quality Management.

58. **Answer D is the best response.** It is the mission statement, not the vision statement, that should speak to the nature of the organization's business or purpose, its customers, and sometimes even its employees and its role in the community. Answer A is not the best response; an organization's statement of vision is a descriptive and inspirational statement that articulates where the organization wants to be and what it wants to become in the future. Answer B is not the best response; an organization's vision statement should motivate and inspire employees to aspire to the legacy that the vision can create, and that it ultimately can leave behind. Answer C is not the best response; an organization's vision statement does speak to the nature of the organization's business or purpose, its customers, and sometimes even its employees and its role in the community.

59. **Answer B is the best response.** If the president takes no action for 10 days while Congress is in session, the legislation automatically becomes law. Answer A is not the best response; if the president takes no action for 10 days while Congress is not in session, the legislation dies (this is called a pocket veto). Answer C is not the best response; the president does not have the option of sending legislation back for more committee work. Answer D is not the best response; if Congress sends a bill to the president, there is nothing to override. In addition, the president cannot override Congress; rather, it is Congress who could override a bill that the president vetoes.

60. **Answer B is the best response.** Pre-employment medical exams can only be conducted if the medical exam is job-related and consistent with business necessity. Answer A is not the best response; an organization cannot require all candidates who apply for a position to take a pre-employment medical exam because an employer can only require a candidate to take a medical exam if an offer or conditional offer of employment has already been extended. Answer C is not the best response; the ADA does not specify who can or cannot conduct a pre-employment medical exam. Answer D is not the best response; a candidate's self-disclosures about a disability that might require a reasonable accommodation is unrelated to whether and when a pre-employment medical exam can be conducted.

61. **Answer B is the best response.** Employers covered under EO 11246 are not required to file internal reports relative to the number of charges of discrimination that have been filed based on race, gender, and veterans status during the length of each AAP (this might be a good moment to point out, once again, that affirmative action is different from, and should not be confused with, protections against discrimination afforded by EEO laws). Answer A is not the best response; the internal audit system does require covered employers to monitor records of all personnel activity, including referrals, placements, transfers, promotions, terminations, and compensation at all levels to ensure the nondiscriminatory policy is carried out. Answer C is not the best response; the internal audit system does require covered employers to review report results with all levels of management. Answer D is not the best response; the internal audit system does require covered employers to advise top management of program effectiveness and submit recommendations to improve unsatisfactory performance

62. **Answer A is the best response.** Trend analysis can provide information that can be helpful in developing a better understanding of business cycles. Answer B is not the best response; ratio analysis, rather than trend analysis, can become the basis for a number of applications, including forecasting staffing needs. Answer C is not the best response; ratio analysis, not trend analysis, looks at how variables can change over time. Answer D is not the best response; multiple regression analysis, not trend analysis, looks at the relationship between one dependent variable and more than one independent variables.

63. **Answer B is the best response.** WARN covers employers with 100 or more full-time employees (this is a somewhat oversimplified explanation; see www.dol.gov for more details). Answer A is not the best response; the ADA covers employers with 15 or more employees (this is somewhat oversimplified explanation; see www.eeoc.gov for more details). Answer C is not the best response; Title VII of the Civil Rights Act of 1964 covers all private employers, among others (this is a somewhat oversimplified explanation; see www.eeoc.gov for more details). Answer D is not the best response; the ADEA covers private employers with 20 or more employees, among others (this is a somewhat oversimplified explanation; see www.eeoc.gov for more details).

64. **Answer B is the best response.** In learning organizations, employees at all levels do strive to acquire knowledge and develop skills that will enable them, individually and collectively, to attain higher levels of performance. Answer A is not the best response; the size of an HRD/training budget does not necessarily correlate to the degree to which an organization is truly a learning organization. Answer C is not the best response; although learning organizations often manifest their commitment through training, training is not the *only* type of HRD initiative through which an organization can demonstrate that commitment. Answer D is not the best response; linking performance appraisal to training and development is not the only way in which an organization can demonstrate its commitment to being a learning organization (although it is often a good idea).

65. **Answer D is the best response.** Managers who have not consistently maintained documentation throughout the entire performance measurement period is less likely to rely upon recent events when preparing an employee's performance appraisal. Answer A is not the best response; while it *is possible* for a manager who has recently observed a direct report to experience the recency effect than a manager who did not maintain such documentation throughout the performance measurement period are even more likely to experience the recency effect. Answer B is not the best response, for a similar reason. Answer C is not the best response; a manager who maintained documentation during earlier portions of the performance measurement period is more likely to experience the first impression effect than the recency effect.

66. **Answer D is the best response.** For overtime purposes under the FLSA, hours worked would include all hours during which an employee was required or allowed (suffered or permitted) to perform work. Answer A is not the best response because the hours for which an employee receives compensation might include hours during which an employee was not suffered or permitted to work (such as vacation pay, jury duty pay, and so on). Answer B is not the best response; whether an employee was granted approval to work (prior or subsequent) is irrelevant to calculating hours worked. Answer C is not the best response; hours worked would include hours that an employee is suffered or permitted to work, not just those hours during which the employee actually performs work.

67. **Answer B is the best response.** The Equal Pay Act prohibits discrimination based on sex in the payment of wages or benefits to men and women who perform substantially equal (but not identical) work for the same employer and within the same establishment. Answer A is not the best response; the work in question has to be substantially equal, not the same or identical. Answer C is not the best response; the work in question must be performed for the same employer and within the same establishment. Answer D is not the best response; the work in question must be substantially equal (not the same or identical) and must be performed for the same employer and within the same establishment.

68. **Answer D is the best response.** Grades represent a hierarchy of levels into which jobs of similar internal, not external, worth are categorized. It is because of this distinction that answer A is not the best response. Answer B is not the best response; jobs within the same grade do share a similar level of value or worth to the organization. Answer C is not the best response; jobs within the same grade are paid according to a corresponding compensation range.

69. **Answer C is the best response.** Unemployment insurance is funded solely through *employer* taxes (except in only three states, where employees contribute as well). Answer A is not the best response; unemployment insurance is a mandatory benefit program. Answer B is not the best response; in general, the maximum period for receiving unemployment insurance benefits is 26 weeks (although the federal government may choose to extend the benefit period during difficult economic times). Answer D is not the best response; unemployment insurance was established as part of the federal Social Security Act of 1935, and is administered at the state level.

70. **Answer A is the best response.** Job slotting is not expensive or difficult to administer (in fact, its inexpensive cost and ease of administration are two of its advantages). Answer B is not the best response; job slotting increases the likelihood that a job will be evaluated based on the person, not the position. Answer C is not the best response; job slotting can only be used when a job structure is already in place. Answer D is not the best response; as with any non-quantitative job evaluation method, there is a greater chance with job slotting that rater error and subjectivity can taint the job evaluation process.

71. **Answer C is the best choice.** Section 7 of the NLRA does protect associational rights for employees who belong to a union as well as for those who do not. Employers need to be careful not to interfere with protected concerted activities even in workplaces that are non-unionized. Answer A is not the best response; protected concerted activity refers to associational rights that are granted to employee through the NLRA. Answer B is not the best response; the NLRA does protect associational rights for employees who belong to a union. Answer D is not the best response; employees have the right to refrain from engaging in protected concerted activities.

72. **Answer A is the best response.** Charges must be filed with the EEOC within 180 days of the alleged discriminatory act *when there is no FEPA*. Answer B is not the best response; the EEOC usually maintains responsibility for handling charges that are filed with it if the basis for the charge is also protected under state or local law. Answer C is not the best response; the FEPA usually maintains responsibility for handling charges that are filed with it if the basis for the charge is also protected under federal law. Answer D is not the best response; a charge may not be dual filed with the EEOC when state or local EEO law is more protective than the corresponding federal law.

73. **Answer C is the best response.** Passed in 1985, COBRA covers employers who employed 20 or more employees during the prior year.

74. **Answer C is the best response.** Although a vaccine for HBV does exist, that vaccine must be made available to at-risk employees; employers may not require employees to be vaccinated against HBV. Answers A, B, and D all reflect true statements about Hepatitis B/HBV.

75. **Answer D is the best response.** *Washington* v. *Davis, (1976)* determined that a test that has an adverse impact on a protected class is still lawful, as long as the test can be shown to be valid and

job related. Answer A is not the best response; the key issue in *McDonnell Douglas Corp* v. *Green* was disparate treatment and establishing a prima facie case. Answer B is not the best response; the key issue in *Griggs* vs. *Duke Power* was adverse impact. Answer C is not the best response; the key issue in *Meritor Savings Bank* v. *Vinson* was sexual harassment.

76. **Answer B is the best response.** Onboarding refers to the new hire orientation process, and a background investigation is far more likely to occur during the pre-employment reference checking phase than during the new hire orientation process. Answer A is not the best response; the onboarding process often includes a tour of the facility. Answer C is not the best response; the onboarding process often gives newly hired employees the opportunity to meet with current employees. Answer D is not the best response; the onboarding process should include a review of the mission of the organization, and of how that mission relates to the position.

77. **Answer B is the best response.** A multi-rater survey refers to a performance feedback and management tool in which one individual receives feedback on his or her performance from a variety of people, holding a variety of perspectives. A multi-rater, or 360-degree, survey is different from employee surveys (answer A), attitude surveys (answer C), and climate surveys (answer D), all of which refer to surveys that are distributed throughout the organization to collect information on a variety of topics that are relevant to the entire organization—not just to one single person.

78. **Answer C is the best response.** The AFL-CIO is an example of a federation, which is a group of national unions. Answer A is not the best response; the AFL-CIO is not a national union. Answer C is not the best response; the AFL-CIO is not a local union. Answer D is not the best response; the AFL-CIO is not an international labor organization.

79. **Answer B is the best response.** One of the two omissions that the Wagner Act sought to address was the identification of behaviors and practices that would be considered ULPs on the part of unions. Neither Answer A not answer D is the best response; the Wagner Act did identify behaviors and practices that would be considered ULPs on the part of employers/managers. Answer C is not the best response; an employee cannot commit a ULP unless he or she is acting on behalf of a union or an employer, in which case his or her role in that capacity would eclipse the significance of his or her role as an individual, and is therefore already addressed through the Wagner Act.

80. **Answer C is the best response.** In *Circuit City Stores, Inc.* v. *Adams, (2001)*, the court ruled that requiring employees to sign mandatory arbitration agreements as a condition of employment is legal, and that such agreements are enforceable under the Federal Arbitration Act (FAA). Answer A is not the best response; in *NLRB* v. *Phoenix Mutual Life Insurance Co.*, it was confirmed that union and non-union employees enjoy associational rights afforded under the NLRA. Answer B is not the best response; less than 10 months after the Circuit City case, the court ruled in *EEOC* v. *Waffle House, Inc.*, that while the existence of a signed mandatory arbitration agreement precluded the employee from being allowed to file a private lawsuit, it did *not* preclude the EEOC from seeking its own independent action against an employer. Answer D is not the best response; *NLRB* v. *Henry Colder* was a case in which an employer was found to have committed an unfair labor practice by interfering with protected concerted activities.

81. **Answer A is the best response.** Workers' compensation programs (not the OSH Act) are designed to enable workers to obtain relief (in particular, monetary relief) for work-related injuries. OSH Act did accomplish the items enumerated in answers B, C, and D.

82. **Answer B is the best response.** Technostructural interventions focus on improving what work is done, as well as the ways and processes through which the work is done. This category or OD intervention looks at job design, job redesign, job restructuring, work content, workflow, work processes, and the like. Answer A is not the best response; human processual interventions seek to effect change and impact relationships within (and between) groups and individuals, on more of an interpersonal level. Answer C is not the best response; sociotechnical interventions focus on groups in the workplace, and the ways in which those groups can become more (or semi-) autonomous with respect to the performance and execution of the work. Answer D is not the best response; organization transformation change interventions focus on the organization as a complex human system that must be continually examined and re-examined.

83. **Answer B is the best response.** The Pension Benefit Guaranty Corporation (PBGC) is funded by insurance premiums that are paid by plan sponsors, not by tax dollars (payroll or otherwise). Funding for the PBGC also comes from investment income, assets from underfunded pension plans it has taken over, and recoveries from companies formerly responsible for those plans. Answer A is not the best response; the PBGC is a government corporation created by ERISA. Answer C is not the best response; the PBGC protects participants in most defined benefit plans and cash balance plans (within certain limitations). Answer D is not the best response; the PBGC ensures that participants will receive payments of certain benefits if a covered plan is terminated.

84. **Answer A is the best response.** Assessing strengths and weaknesses is an inward-looking process. Answer B is not the best response because the external portion of the SWOT analysis refers to assessing opportunities and threats. By default, then, neither answer C nor answer D can be the best response.

85. **Answer B is the best response.** *McKennon* v. *Nashville Banner Publishing Co., (1995)* established that an employer will be held accountable for discriminatory employment actions *even if* it discovers evidence after taking the discriminatory employment action that would have led the employer to that same employment action for legitimate, non-discriminatory reasons.

86. **Answer C is the best response.** Although FMLA entitles employees to take job-protected leave to care for an immediate family member, siblings are not included in the definition of an immediate family member. Answer A is not the best response; FMLA does entitle employees to take job-protected leave for the birth and care of the newborn child of the employee. Answer B is not the best response; FMLA does entitle employees to take job-protected leave for placement of a son or daughter for adoption or foster care with the employee. Answer D is not the best response; FMLA does entitle employees to take job-protected leave when the employee is unable to work because of a serious health condition.

87. **Answer C is the best response.** Factor comparison assigns a monetary value, not a point value, to each level within each factor. Answer A is not the best response; the factor comparison method of job evaluation does provide a degree of objectivity and reliability across raters. Answer B is not the best response; factor comparison does evaluate each job with respect to each compensable factor. Answer D is not the best response; factor comparison involves ranking each compensable factor of each job.

88. **Answer A is the best response.** The Drug-Free Workplace Act does not require employers to establish EAPs. In the event an organization does have an EAP (or equivalent program), however,

information about that program must be included as part of the employer's drug-free awareness program (answer C). Answers B and D describe employer requirements mandated by the Drug-Free Workplace Act.

89. **Answer C is the best response.** Employers can require employees to attend mandatory presentations during which management will present its opinions about unions in general, and about the unionization of its operations. There are certain limitations to this, however, to which the employer must adhere (for instance, these captive audience meetings cannot be held within 24 hours of the actual election). It is also worth noting that while an employer can require an employee to attend captive audience meetings, the employer cannot truly require the employee to listen. Answer A is not the best response; telling workers that the organization will fire or punish them if they engage in any union activity would constitute a ULP. Answer B is not the best response; granting workers wage increases or special concessions in an effort to bribe people from joining a union would constitute a ULP. Answer D is not the best response; telling workers that existing benefits will be discontinued if the workplace is unionized would constitute a ULP.

90. **Answer B is the best response.** An employer who makes a hot cargo agreement has not refused to stop doing business with another entity; instead, it has agreed to stop doing business with another entity (answer A), thus helping to protect union work (answer D) by allowing union members to refuse to handle or process work produced by non-union entities. Answer C is not the best response; an employer who makes a hot cargo agreement has committed a ULP.

91. **Answer B is the best response.** Make no promises, and offer no assurances—just be open, honest, and credible in the way in which you communicate with the employees who remain. Answer A is not the best response; there is no way to know whether additional layoffs will occur, and making any statements to that effect could unintentionally create an implied contract with employees. Answer C is not the best response for the same reason. Answer D is not the best response; minimizing the frequency or amount of communication in which you engage with employees will only add to their feelings of uncertainty (and potentially mistrust).

92. **Answer C is the best response.** Although it is important to perform due diligence, performing due diligence does not insulate an organization from exposure relating from negligent hiring claims. One way in which this can happen is if stated job requirements for a particular position that are used as a guide through the hiring process do not reflect the skills or credentials that are actually required to perform a particular position. Answer A is not the best response; negligent hiring does refer to the process of hiring an employee without engaging in appropriate due diligence. Answer B is not the best response; appropriate due diligence could include looking into items such as the candidate's credentials and prior work experience. Answer D is not the best response; it is quite possible that negligent hiring tort claims might be filed after an employee who was hired through a flawed hiring process inflicts some sort of harm on another person.

93. **Answer C is the best response.** It can be challenging to replicate identical conditions across various focus groups, even when they are conducted by the same individual. These differences in conditions could taint/affect the consistency of the data that is collected. Answer A is not the best response; skillfully facilitated focus groups can generate a great deal of valuable data. Answer B is not the best response; the dynamics that exist in focus groups often can lead to a more synergistic and productive data collection experience. Answer D is not the best response; focus groups do, in fact, provide a qualitative approach to data collection.

94. **Answer B is the best response.** Although some organizations do choose to consider each incumbent's most recent salary or wage rate when setting base pay rates for new hires, this should be the least important of the four factors listed (if it is even factored in at all). Many variables could render the newly hired employee's most recent rate of pay irrelevant—for instance, the employee might have held a different position, in a different sector, in a different city, in a different industry, at a different time, and so on. Answer A is not the best response; the relative worth of the job to the organization is likely to affect how base pay for new hires is set. Answer C is not the best response; the market rate for the position in the marketplace is likely to affect how base pay for new hires is set. Answer D is not the best response; whether the job requires hot skills is likely to affect how base pay for new hires is set.

95. **Answer A is the best response.** A yellow dog contract is a contract or agreement between an employer and an employee that states that the employer will give the employee a job, as long as the employee agrees not to join or have any involvement with a labor union. Answer B is not the best response; an employer who makes a hot cargo agreement agrees to stop doing business with another entity (thus helping to protect union work by allowing union members to refuse to handle or process work produced by non-union entities). Answer C is not the best response; a featherbedding agreement states that the employer will pay wages to union members whether or not their work is needed. Answer D is not the best response; a union shop agreement exists when an employer agrees that anyone who is hired by the organization must join the union.

96. **Answer C is the best response.** Neither economic nor ULP strikes are related to the filing of an EEO charge, and are not likely to factor into the decision-making process of whether to settle a charge. Answer A is not the best response; an organization might decide to settle a charge to avoid the costs (financial as well as human) of responding to (fighting) that charge. Answer B is not the best response; an organization might decide to settle a charge to avoid bad press, which can harm business, even when no evidence is found to support the charging party's allegation of discrimination. Answer D is not the best response; an organization might decide to settle a charge of discrimination if it believes that there is a possibility that unlawful discrimination might have taken place, or when evidence exists that strongly supports that possibility.

97. **Answer B is the best response.** There is no specific OSHA requirement mandating the creation of a safety committee. Many organizations, however, do find that safety committees can make significant contributions toward achieving other health and safety objectives or mandates. Answers A, C, and D all describe legitimate and important purposes of safety committees.

98. **Answer A is the best response.** *Johnson* v. *Santa Clara County Transportation Agency, (1987)* established that gender can be used as a factor in the selection process if there is underrepresentation in a particular job classification, as long as the AAP does not set forth a quota.

99. **Answer C is the best response.** Answer A is not the best response; diversity is not legally mandated (although it makes sound sense from an organizational and business perspective). Answer B is not the best response; diversity initiatives do not have governmentally mandated reporting requirements. Answer D is not the best response; diversity can, and should, extend well beyond the boundaries of legally protected classes.

100. **Answer D is the best response.** Although there is no mandatory retirement age (with few exceptions, such as pilots who must retire from that particular position at age 60), there is a require-

ment that everyone must start receiving retirement benefits by age 70. Answer A is not the best response; the earliest age at which a worker can retire and still receive benefits is 62. Answer B is not the best response; full retirement age ranges between age 65 and age 67, depending upon the year of birth. Answer C is not the best response; workers who work beyond their full retirement age will increase their monthly retirement. The longer they work past their full retirement age, the more their monthly retirement income will be.

101. **Answer A is the best response.** An employee who alleges that he or she was constructively discharged asserts that he or she was subjected to such intolerable working conditions that remaining employed with the organization was impossible. Answers B, C, and D are not the best responses because none of those definitions accurately defines constructive discharge.

102. **Answer D is the best response.** Unless significant underutilization exists, placement goals are set for minorities (in total), unless significant underutilization exists (in which case it might be necessary to set goals for particular minority groups). Answer A is not the best choice; placement goals must be established for areas in which underutilization exists. Answer B is not the best response; placement goals must be pursued through good faith efforts. Answer C is not the best choice; placement goals must be set at an annual percentage rate that is equivalent to the availability figure for women and/or minorities.

103. **Answer C is the best response.** Answers A and B are not the best response; McGregor's theory recognizes that managers can ascribe to either of these perspectives; neither is necessarily primary across-the-board. Answer D is not the best response; Maslow's theory predated McGregor's theory.

104. **Answer D is the best response.** Answer A, telling, corresponds to high task and low relationship. Answer B, selling, corresponds to high task and high relationship. Answer C, participating, corresponds to high relationship and low task.

105. **Answer B is the best response.** Answer A is not the best response; a negative correlation *does indicate* that a relationship exists between two factors. Answer C is not the best response; the correlation coefficient is a number between −1 and 1 that defines the strength of a relationship between two factors. Answer D is not the best response; the correlation coefficient speaks to the strength of a relationship, not to causative dimensions of that relationship.

106. **Answer A is the best response.** According to the revised FLSA guidelines, in order to qualify for an administrative exemption under the FLSA, the employee's primary duty must be the performance of office or non-manual work directly related to the management or general business operations of the employer or the employer's customers. Answer B is not the best response; the requirement that "the employee's primary duty must be the performance of work requiring advanced knowledge, defined as work which is predominantly intellectual in character and which includes work requiring the consistent exercise of discretion and judgment" applies to the learned professional exemption, not the administrative exemption. Answer C is not the best response; the requirement that "the employee's suggestions and recommendations as to the hiring, firing, advancement, promotion, or any other change of status of other employees must be given particular weight" is one portion of one of the requirements under the executive exemption. Answer D is not the best response; FairPay revisions eliminated references to percentages of time spent performing exempt and non-exempt tasks.

107. **Answer A is the best response.** The FLSA established minimum standards affecting full-time and part-time workers in the private sector and in federal, state, and local governments pertaining to minimum wage, overtime, recordkeeping, and child labor. Answer B is not the best response; the FLSA does not address or establish standards relating to worker's compensation or unemployment insurance. Answer C is not the best response; FLSA does not address or establish standards relating to wage garnishments. Answer D is not the best response; the FLSA does not address or establish standards relating to unemployment insurance and wage garnishments.

108. **Answer D is the best response.** Sarbanes-Oxley (SOX) establishes a requirement to disclose whether the company has adopted a code of ethics that applies to the company's key officers, not to the company as a whole. Key officers include, at a minimum, the company's principal executive officer, principal financial officer, principal accounting officer or controller, or persons performing similar functions. Answer A is not the best response; SOX does prohibit insider trading during certain pension plan blackout periods. Answer B is not the best response; SOX does require the establishment of whistleblower protection in a wide variety of situations for employees who report fraud against shareholders. Answer C is not the best response; SOX does require plan administrators to provide 30-day written notice in advance of blackout periods to individual account plan participants and beneficiaries.

109. **Answer C is the best response.** One potential problem that HR professionals need to be aware of is the possibility that employee groups could be found to be company dominated and, therefore, be rendered illegal. Although employee participation groups are neither legal nor illegal by definition, the way in which they are administrated can have a huge impact on whether any particular group is deemed to be legal or illegal. Answers A, B, and D are not the best responses; none of these responses identifies a frequently identified potential problem with employee participation groups.

110. **Answer C is the best response.** Of the four choices in this question, slander is best defined as "a false spoken statement that damages someone's character or reputation." Answer A is not the best response; a statement must be false in order to be considered slanderous. Answer B is not the best response; "a false statement that damages someone's character or reputation" is more general in that it encompasses spoken and written statements and is therefore a better definition of the term *defamation* than it is of the word *slander*. Answer D is not the best response; "a false written statement that damages someone's character or reputation" constitutes libel, not slander.

111. **Answer D is the best response.** Answer B is not the best response; The Supreme Court found that an employer is responsible if its supervisors engage in sexually harassing others even if it didn't know about that behavior. The court did point out, however, that although it isn't enough for an organization to just have a policy prohibiting discrimination, one way for employers to reduce this liability is to prove that a sexually harassed employee had reasonable opportunities to take advantage of a good, clear complaint procedure (without fear of retaliation), but had failed to do so (answer C). Answer A is not the best response; in *Meritor Savings Bank* v. *Vinson*, the Supreme Court ruled for the first time that sexual harassment (whether quid pro quo or hostile environment) constitutes a violation of Title VII of the Civil Rights Act of 1964. The Supreme Court specifically rejected the lower court's view that employers are automatically liable for sexual harassment by their supervisors.

112. **Answer B is the best response.** Whole job ranking does not establish factors about each job that need to be taken into consideration when comparing jobs to each other (this is one of the disadvantages of whole job ranking). Answer A is not the best response; whole job ranking is easy to perform. Answer C is not the best response; whole job ranking is also relatively inexpensive to maintain. Answer D is not the best response; whole job ranking does produce a list that will show which jobs are most and least important.

113. **Answer A is the best response.** In order for incentive programs to be effective, employees need to believe that they can attain the goals that have been set as part of the incentive program, and that the reward that they would earn by attaining those goals is worth it. This model dovetails with Victor Vroom's expectancy theory that asserts that people will put forth effort when they believe that it will result in an outcome, and that that outcome is worthwhile.

114. **Answer A is the best response.** These functions describe the organizing management function. Answer B is not the best response; the controlling function is the one through which the manager assumes more of an oversight role and ascertains the degree to which the planning in which he or she engaged actually produced the desired results. Answer C is not the best response; planning consists of laying the groundwork for how managers will work towards accomplishing the organization's goals. Answer D is the not the best response; the coordinating function consists of activities through which the manager brings together all of the resources that he or she has organized to accomplish the stated plan.

115. **Answer C is the best response.** In the context of interviewing, the leniency bias/error occurs when an interviewer applies an inappropriately lenient standard to one or more candidates, resulting in a higher overall assessment of the candidate. Neither answer A nor answer B is the best response; neither is a legitimate and recognized interviewing bias/error. Answer D is not the best response; the recency error occurs when the interviewer recalls the most recently interviewed candidates more vividly than candidates who were interviewed earlier in the process.

116. **Answer A is the best response.** Title VII of the Civil Rights Act of 1964 established five areas of protection: race, color, religion, sex, and national origin. Answer B is not the best response; age did not become a protected class until the passage of the Age Discrimination in Employment Act (ADEA) in 1967. Answer C is not the best response; Title VII of the Civil Rights Act of 1964 did not address the question of disability (under any appellation). Answer D is not the best response; Title VII of the Civil Rights Act of 1964 included color as a protected class.

117. **Answer B is the best response.** The ADA describes an undue hardship as one that creates significant difficulty (enough to disrupt business operations) (answer A); changes something about the (essential) nature of the business (answer C); or requires a significant financial outlay (answer D), but it does not specifically define what significant financial outlay means, as answer B asserts.

118. **Answer A is the best response.** Although teambuilding is team focused, it also recognizes the criticality of addressing and enhancing the role of the individual within the team. Answer B is not the best response; teambuilding is an effective means through which team members can explore issues such as communication, problem solving, and trust. Answer C is not the best response; teambuilding exercises are most effective when they are linked directly and specifically to organizational objectives, or to the mission, vision, and/or values of the organization. Answer D is not the best response; parallels between teambuilding scenarios and their relevance to the workplace

might not always be immediately apparent. Sometimes teambuilding exercises are intentionally designed so they are not immediately recognized as being analogous to the workplace, so participants may gain greater insights after they do identify those similarities.

119. **Answer A is the best response.** Taft-Hartley was more specific, in that it identified striking or picketing a health care establishment (not just any employer) without giving the required notice as a ULP that could be committed by a union. Answer B is not the best response; Taft-Hartley did identity picketing for recognition for more than 30 days without petitioning for an election as a ULP that could be committed by a union. Answer C is not the best response; Taft-Hartley did identify causing an employer to discriminate against an employee as a ULP that could be committed by a union. Answer D is not the best response; Taft-Hartley did identify refusing to bargain with the employer of the employees it represents as a ULP that could be committed by a union.

120. **Answer C is the best response.** The Labor Management Reporting and Disclosure Act (also known as the Landrum-Griffin Act) specifically designated every union official as a fiduciary, not as an agent of the union. Answer A is not the best response; the Landrum-Griffin Act did institute a requirement that unions submit annual financial reporting to the DOL, to document how union members' dues were spent. Answer B is not the best response; the Landrum-Griffin Act did institute a bill of rights for union members guaranteeing them freedom of speech and periodic secret elections. Answer D is not the best response; the Landrum-Griffin Act did institute even stronger provisions relative to secondary boycotting and organizational and recognition picketing.

121. **Answer B is the best response.** Double breasting occurs when a company that owns or operates union as well as non-union operations shifts work to the non-union operation in an effort to diminish the impact of the strike. Answer A is not the best response; featherbedding occurs when an employer agrees to pay wages to union members whether or not their work is needed. Answer C is not the best response; there is no such expression as *yellow dogging* in labor relations (a yellow dog contract, however, is one in which an employer agrees to give the employee a job, as long as the employee agrees not to join or have any involvement with a labor union). Answer D is not the best response; there is no such expression as single roofing in labor relations.

122. **Answer B is the best response.** This formula calculates the cost per trainee, also known as the cost per participant. Answer A is not the best response; this formula does not yield a calculation of return on investment. Answer C is not the best response; this formula is unrelated to hiring costs. Answer D is not the best response; this formula does not represent a cost/benefit analysis.

123. **Answer C is the best response.** The employee must be compensated either on a salary or fee basis (as defined in the regulations) at a rate not less than $455 per week or, if compensated on an hourly basis, at a rate not less than $27.63 an hour. Answer A is not the best response; computer employees are not covered under the prevailing wage rate provisions of the Davis-Bacon Act.

124. **Answer C is the best response.** Current employees who are negatively impacted by consent decrees that were established in an earlier time and which sought to resolve discrimination that was present in an earlier time may challenge the validity of such decrees. Answer A is not the best response because it asserts the opposite. Answer C is not the best response; *Johnson* v. *Santa Clara County Transportation Agency* was the ruling that gender can be used as a factor in the selection process if there is under-representation in a particular job classification, as long as the

AAP does not set forth a quota. Answer D is not the best response because there is no case that resulted in this finding.

125. **Answer C is the best response.** The bottom line is this: Organizations who lead the market with respect to total compensation offer better total compensation packages than their competitors do. It's that simple. For purposes of determining whether an organization leads the market in this way, the balance of direct and indirect compensation pay components is not relevant (answer A), nor is the mix of variable and base pay (answer B), nor is the level of innovation or creativity of the total compensation package. All that matters is the total (and multi-faceted) value of the package.

126. **Answer C is the best response.** Although OSHA might give employers 24 hours notice under certain circumstances, employers may not request a postponement of an inspection. Answers A, B, and D all reflect employer rights with respect to OSHA inspections.

127. **Answer C is the best response.** In order to qualify for the highly compensated employee exemption under FLSA, an employee must customarily and regularly perform at least one of the duties of an exempt executive, administrative, or professional employee identified in the standard tests for exemption. Answer A is not the best response; in order to qualify for the highly compensated employee exemption under FLSA, an employee must earn $100,000 (not $150,000) or more annually (of which at least $455 per week must be paid on a salary or fee basis). Answer B is not the best response; in order to qualify for the highly compensated employee exemption under FLSA, an employee must perform (not oversee) office or non-manual work.

128. **Answer B is the best response.** Although it is true that HR is often viewed as the conscience of the organization, this role/reality should not result in HR owning the organization's ethical initiatives. (It is important to remember here that leading is different from owning—a key point for HR professionals to keep in mind.) Conversely, responsibility for ethics must be operationalized and dispersed throughout the organization (answer C). Answer A is not the best response; HR must play a leadership role with respect to establishing, encouraging, and ensuring ongoing ethical behavior within organizations. Answer D is not the best response; the organization's code of ethics does need to address a variety of issues from a variety of perspectives (for instance, employees, customers, shareholders, suppliers, and the community at large).

129. **Answer D is the best response.** The five distinct, yet overlapping, project management processes are initiation, planning, executing, controlling, and closing. Answer A is not the best response because establishing, developing, implementing, and evaluating are the four steps of strategic planning. Answer B is not the best response; although it cites the five project management processes, they are not in the right order. Answer C is not the best response because planning, organizing, coordinating, directing, and controlling are the five management functions.

130. **Answer B is the best response.** HR audits cannot yield strategies; conversely, they yield information that the organization can subsequently use to draw conclusions and develop strategies. Answers A, C, and D are not the best responses; each identifies an area about which an HR audit can generate information.

131. **Answer C is the correct response.** Answers A and B are not the best responses; although the Emergency Action Plan Standard and Fire Safety Standard are both recommended for all employers, they are not mandatory unless required under a separate OSHA standard. Answer D is not the

best response; the Hazard Communication Standard only applies to those workplaces where there are hazardous materials or chemicals.

132. **Answer B is the best response.** Interest-based bargaining advocates focus on interests rather than position, not on relationships rather than positions. Answer A is not the best response; interest-based bargaining does advocate separating the people from the problem. Answer C is not the best response; interest-based bargaining does advocate generating a variety of options before settling on an agreement. Answer D is not the best response; interest-based bargaining does advocate insisting that the agreement be based on objective criteria.

133. **Answer B is the best response.** MSH Act requires at least four inspections per year of underground mines, and at least two inspections per year of surface mines. Answer A is not the best response; MSH Act applies to underground and surface mines. Answer C is not the best response; MSH Act applies to coal and non-coal mines. Answer D is not the best response; employees who are covered by MSH Act are exempt from OSH Act.

134. **Answer B is the best response.** Affinity groups bring together people who share common interests, goals, and/or backgrounds. Although members might derive benefits that affect their esteem (answer C) or that enable them to self-actualize (answer D), affinity groups primarily address the need for belonging and love.

135. **Answer C is the best response.** Direct compensation refers to components that are presented to employees in the form of cash, and indirect compensation refers to components that are presented to employees in forms other than cash (non-cash). A flexible spending account is an example of a benefit, not an example of direct compensation. Answer A is not the best response; hourly wages/base salary is a form of direct compensation. Answer B is not the best response; shift differentials are a form of direct compensation. Answer D is not the best response; variable pay is a form of direct compensation.

136. **Answer A is the best response.** According to the FairPay guidelines, manual laborers and other blue collar workers who perform work involving repetitive operations with their hands, physical skill, and energy *cannot be exempted* from the overtime provisions of FLSA, *no matter how much they earn*. Answers B, C, and D cite positions that, although likely to be non-exempt, still require a case-by-case review.

137. **Answer B is the best response.** Employee referral programs can result in significant savings in cost-per-hire, not significant increases in cost-per-hire. Answers A, C, and D are not the best responses; each represents a potential advantage of employee referral programs.

138. **Answer D is the best response.** Just as it is critical to distinguish between the position and the incumbent, so too it is important not to confuse actual job requirements—such as KSAs (answer A), credentials (answer B), and physical or mental requirements (answer C)—with any particular candidate's or incumbent's qualifications.

139. **Answer C is the best response.** Schein recognized and appreciated the formal, as well as the informal, dimensions and expressions of culture. As HR professionals, so must we.

140. **Answer B is the best response.** Performance appraisal tools that use rating scales require managers (or any other appraisers) to evaluate employee performance on a variety of categories using

a multiple point scale (often three, four, or five points). Those categories can consist of individual goals, individual competencies, multiple goals, groups of competencies, and the like. Each point on the scale corresponds to a different level of performance against standards. Answer A is not the best response; performance appraisal systems that require managers to compare employees against each other are called ranking methods, not rating methods. Answer C is not the best response; the performance appraisal method that requires managers to indicate statements that are reflective of the employee's performance is called a check list method. Answer D is not the best response; the performance appraisal method that requires managers to write a narrative assessment of employee's performance is the essay method.

141. **Answer A is the best response.** The ruling in *United Steelworkers* v. *Weber, (1979)* was that affirmative action plans that establish voluntary quotas that have been jointly agreed to by an organization as well as its collective bargaining unit do not constitute race discrimination under Title VII of the Civil Rights Act of 1964. More specifically, the court ruled that "...Congress did not intend to limit traditional business freedom to such a degree as to prohibit all voluntary, race-conscious affirmative action." The ruling went on to say that, "It is not necessary in these cases to define the line of demarcation between permissible and impermissible affirmative action plans; it suffices to hold that the challenged Kaiser-USWA plan falls on the permissible side of the line. The purposes of the plan mirror those of the statute, being designed to break down old patterns of racial segregation and hierarchy, and being structured to open employment opportunities for Negroes in occupations which have been traditionally closed to them. At the same time, the plan does not unnecessarily trammel the interests of white employees, neither requiring the discharge of white workers and their replacement with new black hirees, nor creating an absolute bar to the advancement of white employees since half of those trained in the program will be white. Moreover, the plan is a temporary measure, not intended to maintain racial balance, but simply to eliminate a manifest racial imbalance."

142. **Answer A is the best response.** The key issues in *Albemarle* v. *Moody* were job relatedness and job validity. This case established that any tests that are used as part of the hiring or promotional decision making process must be job-related. This applies to any instrument that is used as a test, even if that was not its original purpose. This case also established that employment tests must demonstrate predictive validity, consistent with the Uniform Guidelines for Employee Selection Procedures.

143. **Answer B is the best response.** An ethics program cannot prevent or minimize organizational politics. Let's be real; there aren't many things that can prevent or minimize organizational politics. However, an ethics program *can* prevent or minimize *dysfunctional manifestations of organizational politics*—manifestations that can become destructive or even dangerous. Answers A, C, and D are not the best responses; each articulates a legitimate reason for establishing an ethics program.

144. **Answer B is the best response.** Adverse treatment was not one of the key topics that the Uniform Guidelines on Employee Selection Procedures was designed to address. Answer A is not the best response; one of the key purposes of the Uniform Guidelines was to address the concept of adverse impact. Answer C is not the best response; one important objective of the Uniform Guidelines is to ensure that interview and selection processes are reliable. Answer D is not the best response; one important objective of the Uniform Guidelines is to ensure that interview and selection processes are valid.

145. **Answer B is the best response.** A minimum salary is not required in order to qualify for the outside sales exemption under the FLSA. Answer A is not the best response; no maximum cap is imposed under the outside sales exemption. Answer C is not the best response; employers do not need to apply for any FLSA exemption.

146. **Answer B is the best response.** Preventing transmission of HCV by proper use of protective personal equipment is the best means of protection. Answer A is not the best response; there is no vaccine for HCV. Answer C is not the best response; HCV is transmitted by blood and other bodily fluids, not by airborne particles. Answer D is not the best response; a person with HCV is covered under the Americans with Disabilities Act, and therefore cannot be screened for or eliminated from consideration for employment solely because of HCV status.

147. **Answer A is the best response.** The Davis-Bacon Act of 1931 was the first piece of legislation to consider the topic of and actually establish a minimum wage. Davis-Bacon, however, was (and still is) limited to federal government construction projects, and non-federal government construction projects in excess of $2000 that receive federal funding (hence, neither answer C nor answer D is the best response). Answer B is not the best response; the Davis Bacon Act was not rendered obsolete by the minimum wage provisions of the FLSA; Davis-Bacon requires that covered contractors and subcontractors are required to provide laborers and mechanics who are employed at the actual worksite with wages and benefits that are equal to (or better than) what workers on similar local projects receive.

148. **Answer D is the best response.** Children who are fourteen or fifteen years old may work up to 40 hours during a non-school week. Answer A is not the best response; children who are fourteen or fifteen years old may work up to 3 (not 4) hours on a school day. Answer B is not the best response; children who are fourteen or fifteen years old may work up to 18 (not 20) hours during a school week. Answer C is not the best response; children who are fourteen or fifteen years old may work up to 8 (not 7) hours on a non-school day.

149. **Answer C is the best response.** As articulated, the question states the requirement in specific, measurable, job-related terms, and asks the candidate (in a closed-ended manner) whether he or she can meet that requirement of the position. Answer A is not the best response; as phrased, this question seeks information that may reveal the existence or nature of a medical condition and/or disability. Answer B is not the best response; using the phrase "Do you have any problems doing this" is more likely to elicit information relating to a disability than the very closed-ended phrase, "Can you meet this requirement of the position." Answer D is not the best response; as described, it does not appear as though this function would be considered "essential" (in fact, it does not even appear as though this responsibility falls within this function of this position at all). In addition, interview questions should be based upon the requirements of the job itself, not on the basis of the performance of prior incumbents.

150. **Answer B is the best response.** In actuality, the Portal-to-Portal Act clarified that employers are required to compensate workers for working time that they spend performing their jobs and for working time that they spend on activities that relate to the performance of their job. Answer A is not the best response; the Portal-to-Portal Act did offer a clearer definition of hours worked for purposes of minimum wage and overtime calculations. Answer C is not the best response; the Portal-to-Portal Act did address topics such as travel time, pre-shift work, post-shift work, idle

waiting time, overnight travel, training time, and the like. Answer D is not the best response; the Portal-to-Portal Act was an amendment of the Fair Labor Standards Act.

151. **Answer C is the best response.** In a common law system, contracts that govern the terms and conditions of employment (including employment contracts and collective bargaining agreements) take precedence over traditions, customs, and precedents. For example, a collective bargaining agreement could modify employment-at-will status, even though that concept exists in common law. Answer A is not the best response; in common law systems, traditions, customs, and precedents have the same force of law as existing laws or statutes. Answer B is not the best response; in a common law system, laws and statutes are interpreted and re-interpreted on a case-by-case basis. Answer D is not the best response; in a common law system, each interpretation and each case sets a precedent that can subsequently be re-interpreted, thus setting a new precedent.

152. **Answer D is the best response.** *Griggs* v. *Duke Power* established that discrimination did not need to be deliberate or intentional in order to be real. Instead, it can exist even when a particular policy or practice has a statistically significant adverse impact upon members of a protected class.

153. **Answer D is the best response.** If the employee is subjected to tangible adverse employment action, the employee may not raise a defense that it acted reasonably to prevent and/or promptly correct any sexually harassing behavior. Answer A is not the best response; Faragher and Ellerth did establish that an employer is liable if the employee is subjected to an adverse employment action. Answer B is not the best response; the employer is vicariously liable when its supervisors create a sexually hostile work environment even if the employee is not subjected to an adverse employment action. Answer C is not the best response; if the employee is not subjected to tangible adverse employment action, the employer may not be able to raise as a defense that he acted reasonably to prevent and/or promptly correct any sexually harassing behavior, and that the plaintiff unreasonably failed to take advantage of the employer's preventive or corrective opportunities.

154. **Answer D is the best response.** In order to be eligible to take FMLA leave, an employee must meet four requirements, one of which is that the employee must work at a location in the United States or in any territory or possession of the United States where at least 50 (not 75) employees are employed by the employer within 75 (not 50) miles. Answer A is not the not the best response; the employee must work for a covered employer—public agencies, state, local and federal employers, local education agencies (schools), and private-sector employers with 50 or more employees. Answer B is not the best response; the employee must have worked for the employer for a total of at least 12 months (this time does not have to have been uninterrupted). Answer C is not the best response; the employee must have worked at least 1,250 hours over the previous 12 months.

155. **Answer A is the best response.** Just cause or good cause refers to a particular legal standard or test that is used to ascertain whether a specific disciplinary action was appropriate. Of the four items that are listed, whether the particular rule that was violated was newly created is least likely to significantly impact the overall fairness of the action that was taken (this assumes, of course, that the employee knew about the rule, and was warned of the possible consequences before such action was taken). Answer B is not the best response; whether a legitimate investigation looking into the totality of the circumstances around the alleged violation was conducted is likely to factor into an overall assessment relative to just cause. Answer C is not the best response; whether reasonable proof as to the violation existed or was obtained through investigation is likely to factor

into an overall assessment relative to just cause. Answer D is not the best response; whether the punishment is proportionate to the violation is likely to factor into an overall assessment relative to just cause.

156. **Answer B is the best response.** Answer A is not the best response; the Supreme Court ruled that these sorts of decisions must be left to parents, not to employers. Answer C is not the best response; the Supreme Court ruling rendered the opposite ruling. Answer D is not the best response because few, if any, fetal protection policies would qualify for a bona fide occupational qualification exception.

157. **Answer B is the best response.** Environmental scanning refers to the process of maintaining awareness of opportunities and threats. Answer A is not the best response; although maintaining awareness of opportunities and threats is part of SWOT analysis, SWOT analysis also incorporates maintaining awareness of strengths and weaknesses. Answer C is not the best response; although conducting a SWOT analysis is an essential part of strategic planning, it does not encompass everything that is involved with strategic planning. Answer D is not the best response; although an organization's awareness of threats is likely to highlight the need for contingency planning, those two concepts are not synonymous.

158. **Answer D is the best response.** The Supreme Court ruled in *Regents of California* v. *Bakke* that race could be a factor in college admission decisions, but that quotas are impermissible. Although this case was based on a college admission program, its significance has extended to the workplace. Neither answer A nor answer B is the best response; those choices both assume that the Supreme Court ruled in *Regents of California* v. *Bakke* that quotas are permissible in college affirmative action programs. Answer C is not the best response; although it acknowledges that quotas are impermissible in college admission decisions, it asserts that this ruling is not transferable to the workplace.

159. **Answer B is the best response.** The actual employment application may not request information relative to gender, race, or any other information related to protected-class membership. Pull out sheets, however, that contain information needed for applicant flow data are generally considered acceptable when handled in an appropriate and legal manner. Answer A is not the best response; employment applications can request personal information such as the candidate's name, address, and contact information. Answer C is the not best response; employment applications can request information relative to a candidate's employment history, including reasons for leaving prior positions. Answer D is not the best response; employment applications can request names of professional references.

160. **Answer C is the best response.** Objectives—whether related to performance management or any other HRD (or, for that matter, HR) initiative—must be measurable. Answer A is not the best response; although goals should be marketable to the degree that they relate to the overarching objectives of the organization and are, therefore, hopefully widely embraced, marketability is not one of the key driving forces behind goal setting. Answers B and D are not the best responses, for similar reasons.

161. **Answer B is the best response.** If progressive discipline is truly viewed as an employee relations initiative, the process should start with the most foundational element of a relationship—communication. Coaching, or discussing the problem, is an appropriate way, therefore, to initially address

a performance issue. Answer A is not the best response; a verbal warning might be the second step in a progressive disciplinary process. Before you move to this step, give coaching a chance. It just might turn out that coaching, if performed well, can preclude the need to take any additional progressive disciplinary steps. Answer C is not the best response; when you notice a performance issue, speak to the employee before you do anything else. The employee might even provide you with information that could prove to be very valuable, particularly with the question of consistency. Answer D is not the best response; counseling resembles a verbal warning more closely than it resembles coaching, and therefore should not be the first step in a progressive discipline process.

162. **Answer D is the best response.** Don't waste your energy trying to deny that informal communications and methods exist. They do, and they can't be eliminated. Nor should they be as long as they do not become destructive. Instead of trying to wish away the grapevine, consider shifting your perspective. One possible way in which to do this is to be open to gathering information through informal, as well as formal, methods. Answer A is not the best response; ignoring the grapevine won't make it go away. In fact, if you are not open to gleaning information from time to time through the grapevine, you might find that you don't know about important items—items that you might have otherwise heard about if you had been open to less formal communication media. Answer B is not the best response; such an action might reinforce a reputation as the personnel police. It might also constitute a violation of the NLRA if it is found that your action has interfered with employees' associational rights. Answer C is not the best response; gleaning information from the grapevine doesn't mean that you should throw fuel on the fire. Starting rumors (let's face it, that's what it is) can seriously damage your credibility, as well.

163. **Answer C is the best response.** This is the best answer in part because there is no commonly recognized activity known as surface organizing. Rather, surface bargaining is an impermissible activity during the bargaining (rather than the organizing) process. Surface bargaining refers to going through the motions of bargaining, with no real intent of ultimately reaching agreement (in other words, keeping bargaining at the surface, without moving towards true agreement). Answer A is not the best response; unions may engage in inside organizing, an activity through which pro-union individuals can seek to influence others at the workplace, unless a valid no-solicitation rule is in effect 100% of the time. Answer B is not the best response; unions may engage in salting, the process through which a salt (a union organizer) seeks employment with the organization for the express purpose of actively organizing and campaigning within the organization. Answer D is not the best response; unions may engage in organizational picketing, which is designed to generate interest on the part of employees to vote for union representation.

164. **Answer A is the best response.** Employers can hire permanent strike replacements during an economic strike. This is different from ULP strikes, in which employers cannot hire permanent strike replacements (answer B). Answer C is not the best response; workers must be returned to their original positions after a ULP strike is over. Answer D is not the best response; workers cannot be terminated for participating in an economic strike.

165. **Answer C is the best response.** Offshoring refers to the process of outsourcing to third-party providers whose operations are based overseas. Answers A, B, and D all offer inaccurate definitions of offshoring and thus are not the best responses.

166. **Answer B is the best response.** Primary questions are based on the knowledge, skills, abilities, and behavioral characteristics required of a particular position, and therefore should remain consistent from candidate to candidate. Answer A is not the best response; it is important to ask primary and probing questions that ascertain the candidate's ability to demonstrate the knowledge, skills, and abilities required for the position for which the candidate is applying—whether or not those happen to correlate with the knowledge, skills, abilities, and behavioral characteristics that each demonstrated in his or her previous positions. Answer C is not the best response; as stated above, primary questions are based on the knowledge, skills, abilities, and behavioral characteristics required of a particular position, and therefore should remain consistent from candidate to candidate. Answer D is not the best response; because probing questions are asked in response to each candidate's response to primary questions, those probing questions will vary from interview to interview. Interviews can still ensure consistency, however, by only asking questions that relate to the original primary question.

167. **Answer A is the best response.** A focus group is an employee involvement tool as much as it is a communication tool. Answer B is not the best response; focus groups consist of a representative sample of employees. Answer C is not the best response; focus groups need to include enough people to generate a dynamic and synergistic discussion (but not so many people that not everyone has a chance to participate). Answer D is not the best response; focus groups are led by a neutral facilitator whose role is to elicit feedback and input on a specific topic.

168. **Answer A is the best response.** The National Labor Relations Act was not included among the 12 laws that were expanded to include employees of the legislative branch through the Congressional Accountability Act. Three of the 12 laws that were included in this expansion were the Employee Polygraph Protection Act (answer B), the Worker Adjustment and Retaining Notification Act (answer C), and the Americans with Disabilities Act (answer D).

169. **Answer C is the best response.** Asking how the position compares to others within the existing job worth hierarchy is a valuable question, but it pertains to internal, rather than external, considerations. That question is addressed through the job evaluation process, and is not as appropriate to ask because you are preparing to collect market data. Answer A is not the best response; it is valuable and appropriate to ask about the relevant labor market for a position when you are preparing to collect market data. Answer B is not the best response; it is valuable and appropriate to ask about what sources of market data you already have, and about what other sources you could get. Answer D is not the best response; it is valuable and appropriate to ask about labor market competitors in general, as well as for the specific job for which you are preparing to collect market data.

170. **Answer B is the best response.** Excluding statements relative to how the code will be implemented and upheld greatly diminishes the likelihood that the code will be effective. Doing so, in effect, robs the code of teeth. Answer A is not the best response; the code of ethics must be administered consistently if it is to be effective. Calling that a one-size-fits-all approach is just a negative way of saying that everyone will be held to the same standard—and that's a good thing. Answer C is not the best response; although it is advisable that the CEO write the introduction to and/or the cover letter that will accompanying the code of ethics, the ultimate effectiveness of the code of ethics is less contingent upon that than it is upon the consistent application of the code within the organization. Answer D is not the best response; it is quite possible that employees or others

might perceive certain elements of the code as threatening or punitive. That might simply be, however, another way of saying that the code will hold employees accountable, and that there will be consequences for failing to uphold the code—both of which add teeth to the code and increase the likelihood that it will be effective.

171. **Answer D is the best response.** In general, petitions from a union for an election would not be accepted if there is a valid contract in effect that lasts no longer than three years (answer C). Those circumstances would include situations in which a union has been certified in the past year but has not successfully negotiated a contract (answer A) and situations in which an election has been held within the past year (answer B).

172. **Answer C is the best response.** Although it is important to recognize and exploit (in the best sense of that word) the benefits that can ultimately accrue from an HRIS, it is equally important to recognize the limitations of an HRIS. There are points at which a line must be drawn, and at which technology becomes far less relevant and effective than human beings; increasing employee commitment is one of those points. Answer A is not the best response; an HRIS should provide information that can be used to increase overall employee productivity. Answer B is not the best response; an HRIS should provide information that can be used to identify and reward top performers. Answer D is not the best response; an HRIS should provide information that will support placing the right people in the right jobs at the right time.

173. **Answer A is the best response.** HR might or might not have a presence during the introduction or birth stage of the organizational life cycle. If you are fortunate enough to have a presence, you might find that the formalization of policies and procedures (as would be found in a handbook) is not the most valued or appreciated dimension of your role (give it time…). Answer B is not the best response; during the introductory phase of the organizational life cycle, employees might find themselves paid above market rates as a reflection of the founder's desire to lure them on board. Answer C is not the best response; struggling start-ups often find themselves searching for solid financial footing. In such situations, employees might earn less cash compensation, and have those diminished earnings offset by other non-cash rewards (equity, intrinsic rewards, and so forth).

174. **Answer C is the best response.** The executive exemption does not require that the employee's primary duty include the exercise of discretion and independent judgment with respect to matters of significance (however, this is one of the requirements for an administrative exemption). Answer A is not the best response; in order to qualify for an executive exemption under the FLSA, the employee's primary duty must be managing the enterprise, or managing a customarily recognized department or subdivision of the enterprise. Answer B is not the best response; in order to qualify for an executive exemption under the FLSA, the employee must customarily and regularly direct the work of at least two or more other full-time employees or their equivalent. Answer D is not the best response; in order to qualify for an executive exemption under the FLSA, the employee must have the authority to hire or fire other employees, or the employee's suggestions and recommendations as to the hiring, firing, advancement, promotion, or any other change of status of other employees must be given particular weight.

175. **Answer B is the best response.** Auditory learners learn most effectively through their sense of hearing. Answer A is not the best response; visual learners learn most effectively through their

sense of vision. Answer C is not the best response; kinesthetic (or tactile) learners learn most effectively through their sense of touch (or, in a more general sense, through hands-on experiences). Answer D is not the best response; vicarious learners are not among the three recognized learning styles. The term vicarious learner, however, does exist, and is defined as one who learns best by observing others participating in learning, which is not reflected in the scenario described in the question.

176. **Answer D is the best response.** When determining what constitutes fair use, any permissions that the copyright holder has previously granted are not relevant to a determination of fair use. Answers A, B, and C are all incorrect; each one constitutes legitimate considerations under the Copyright Act of 1976 for determining what does (and does not) constitute fair use.

177. **Answer D is the best response.** The most famous real-life example of the Mackay Doctrine occurred in 1981 when President Ronald Reagan replaced 12,000 striking air traffic controllers. Answer A is not the best response; President George W. Bush's decision to waive the requirement to pay a prevailing wage rate to government contractors and subcontractors involved in the rebuilding of New Orleans suspended the Davis-Bacon Act for the first time in its 74-year history (this action was wholly unrelated to the Mackay Doctrine). Answers B and C are not the best responses because actions such as these would not fall under the Mackay Doctrine, and because they never happened.

178. **Answer B is the best response.** Employee referral programs are not likely to bring in candidates who would address underutilization because employees are less likely to refer candidates who are of a different race or gender than they are to refer candidates who are of the same race or gender. Answer A is not the best response; recruiting at colleges or universities traditionally attended by minorities is likely to be considered an action-oriented program (if the job group or organization is underutilized with respect to race). Answer C is not the best response; reaching out to professional organizations whose membership criteria is designed so as to attract women or minorities is likely to be considered an action-oriented program. Answer D is not the best response; posting job openings at resource centers for displaced homemakers is likely to be considered an action-oriented program.

179. **Answer B is the best response.** The BFOQ (bona fide occupational qualification) exception to EEO laws would refer to certain job requirements that are mandated by business necessity that might have an unintended discriminatory (disparate) impact upon applicants or employees on the basis of gender, religion, or national origin. The scenario described in the question would not fall under that exception. Neither answer A nor answer C is the best response; this decision would not likely be upheld as legal under EEO law. Answer D is not the best response because there are certain permissible exceptions to EEO laws (for instance, BFOQ, professionally developed test of skill or ability, seniority systems, and piece rate systems).

180. **Answer B is the best response.** The formula used to calculate turnover is

$$\frac{\text{\# of terminations during a specified period of time}}{\text{The average \# of employees in the workforce during that same period of time}}$$

181. **Answer C is the best response.** Although it is advisable to express earnings in short-term increments, this has nothing to do with forfeiting the exempt FLSA status. Instead, this should be done

so as not to unintentionally create an implied contract. Answers A, B, and D all offer sound advice relative to how to craft an offer letter.

182. **Answer D is the best response.** With very few exceptions (such as for armored car services or pharmaceutical distributors), it is almost always illegal to administer polygraph tests on a pre-employment basis. Answers A, B, and D are not the best responses; each can be used, under specific circumstances, within specific prescribed parameters.

183. **Answer B is the best response.** FairPay defines highly compensated employees as those who earn $100,000 or more annually (of which at least $455 per week must be paid on a salary or fee basis). Answer A is not the best response; marital status is irrelevant when determining whether an employee is eligible for the highly compensated employee exemption. Answer C is not the best response; it does not include the important stipulation that states that at least $455 per week of that $100,000 must be paid on a salary or fee basis. Answer D is not the best response; FairPay sets the highly compensated employee threshold at $100,000, not $150,000.

184. **Answer D is the best response.** In order to be concerted, activity must be engaged in with, or on the authority of, other employees. Neither answer A nor answer B is the best response; in order to be concerted, activity must be undertaken by individual employees who are united in pursuit of a common goal. Answer C is not the best response; activity must be concerted before it can be protected by the NLRA (rather than the other way around).

185. **Answer C is the best response.** Arbitration is not one of the ways in which the EEOC can handle charges of discrimination. Mediation, however, is one possible option. Answer A is not the best response; the EEOC can handle a charge of discrimination by investigating it. Answer B is not the best response; settlement remains one possible, ongoing option, even if this option is not utilized (or successfully utilized) when the charge of discrimination is first filed. Answer D is not the best response; the employer can choose to dismiss the charge of discrimination.

186. **Answer B is the best response.** A protected class is a group of individuals who share a common characteristic, and who are protected from discrimination and harassment based on that shared characteristic. Answer A is not the best response; anti-discrimination laws protect everyone from discrimination based on the shared characteristic (for instance, women and men are protected from discrimination and harassment based on sex). Answer C is not the best response; employers may not discriminate against an employee who has filed charges with the NLRB or who has taken part in any NLRB proceeding, as this would be considered an unfair labor practice. These individuals would not, however, be considered members of a protected class as that term is traditionally defined. Answer D is not the best response; employees who have engaged in an economic strike can be permanently replaced by the employer (according to the Mackay Doctrine); however, this is unrelated to "protected class."

187. **Answer A is the best response.** A non-verbal communication cue could be an indicator of many things, only some of which might be job-related. If you notice a change, use job-related questions to probe for more information about the question that you were asking when you noticed the new or changed non-verbal communication cue. Answer B is not the best response; there is no one, single dictionary of non-verbal behaviors (and, even if someone claims to have written one, it is not advisable to apply it to employment or pre-employment interactions). Answer C is not the best response; it is not advisable to point out and describe the changed non-verbal behavior to the candidate, or to ask him or her to help you understand what it means (it won't do much to build

rapport, and it also won't help the interviewer obtain the information he or she needs). Answer D is not the best response; mirroring the candidate's non-verbal behavior to see if he or she continues to display that behavior will not yield any helpful job-related information, and might even create an uncomfortable interpersonal dynamic.

188. **Answer B is the best response.** EEO reports must be filed by employers with 100 or more employees (and by federal contractors with at least 50 employees and federal contracts of at least $50,000 per year). Answer A is not the best response; the filing requirement for federal contracts or subcontracts of $100,000 or more refers to the VETS-100, which is mandated by VEVRAA. Answer C is not the best response; the filing requirement for federal contractors and subcontractors with contracts in excess of $10,000 during any one-year period refers to requirements established by Executive Order 11246. Answer D is not the best response; family farms that do not employee individuals outside the family are excluded from coverage under OSHA.

189. **Answer B is the best response.** Recruiting—a separate and distinct process from selection—is the process of attracting and creating a pool of qualified candidates. Answer A is not the best response; recruiting does not include the process of selecting the final candidate. Answer C is not the best response; selection, not recruiting, involves the process of identifying the candidate to whom the position will be offered. Answer D is not the best response; selection, not recruiting, involves the process of selecting the candidate to whom the position will be offered.

190. **Answer C is the best response.** The very first thing that needs to be done after you decide to conduct an employee survey is to ensure that you have management support—up through and including top levels of management. Answers A, B, and D are not the best responses; although each represents an important step in the survey process, none of these should be the first step in that process.

191. **Answer B is the best response.** Union deauthorization revokes the union security clause in the contract, thereby effectively creating an open shop. Answer A is not the best response; the process of removing the union's rights to represent the employee is union decertification, not union deauthorization. Answer C is not the best response; union deauthorization requires that 50% or more of the members of the collective bargaining unit (not 50% or more of those who vote in the deauthorization election) support the deauthorization. Answer D is not the best response; union deauthorization is far *less* common than union decertification.

192. **Answer D is the best response.** Providing candidates with opportunities to interact with each other is not an effective way of providing a realistic job—and organizational—preview. Answer A is not the best response; providing verbal descriptions of the work, the work environment, and/or the work conditions can be a good way of providing candidates with a realistic job preview. Answer B is not the best response; providing candidates with the opportunity to read the employee handbook can be a good way of providing candidates with a realistic job preview. Answer C is not the best response; providing candidates with the opportunity to interact with current employees can be a good way of providing candidates with a realistic job preview.

193. **Answer B is the best response.** The November 2000 revisions confirmed that *affirmative action plans do not establish quotas*—instead, the revisions confirmed that AAPs establish *goals* that must be affirmatively pursued through good faith efforts. Answer A is not the best response; the

November 2000 revisions did reduce the number of additional required elements of the written AAP from 10 to 4. Answer C is not the best response; the November 2000 revisions did grant employers with fewer than 150 employees permission to prepare a job group analysis that uses EEO-1 categories as job groups. Answer D is not the best response; the November 2000 revisions did reduce the 8-factor availability analysis to 2 factors.

194. **Answer A is the best response.** The nominal group technique does take a non-mathematical approach to forecasting that draws upon the insights of subject matter experts. Answer B is not the best response; although it is true that the nominal group technique affords experts the opportunity to meet in person and process their ideas from the group, this is not a characteristic that is shared with the Delphi technique (in which the experts do not meet in person). Answer C is not the best response; the nominal group technique is led by a facilitator. Answer D is not the best response; although the nominal group technique permits collaboration at certain points of the process, collaboration is not permitted at all points in the process. Specifically, at the beginning of the meeting, each expert writes down his or her ideas, after which each expert presents those ideas to the group. Discussion of ideas is not permitted at this point, only presentation is acceptable.

195. **Answer B is the best response.** IRCA imposes penalties for recordkeeping errors whether those errors were committed knowingly or unknowingly. Answer A is not the best response; IRCA does prohibit discrimination against job applicants based on national origin. Answer C is not the best response; IRCA does prohibit giving employment preference to U.S. citizens. Answer D is the best response; IRCA does impose penalties for hiring illegal aliens.

196. **Answer B is the best response.** Although this chapter only talked about torts that can be committed against people, torts can also be committed against a person's property. Answer A is not the best response; torts are wrongful acts. Answer C is not the best response; the commission of a tort does infringe upon another person's rights. Answer D is not the best response; tort doctrine is associated with common law.

197. **Answer B is the best response.** Fiedler's theory does not address the concept of experience–expertise. Answers A (leader-member relations), C (task structure), and D (position power) are the only three factors that Fiedler identifies as contributing to situational favorableness.

198. **Answer C is the best response.** Vendors, by definition, are not employees. Whether to classify individuals as employees or contractors is a legal determination, not an emotional or psychological one. And while fostering an esprit de corps is essential, that sense of team is separate and distinct from whether an individual is an employee or an independent contractor. Answer A is not the best response; providing positive and constructive feedback is an important part of effectively managing relationships with vendors. Answer B is not the best choice; setting clear and reasonable expectations is an important part of effectively managing relationships with vendors. Answer D is not the best response; incorporating upside potential and downside risk into negotiated agreements with contractors is an important part of effectively managing relationships with vendors.

199. **Answer D is the best response.** The four Ps of marketing (or the marketing mix) are product, place, price, and promotion. These refer to the variables that need to be addressed and controlled in order to best satisfy customers in an organization's target market. Answer A is not the best response; there are no generally recognized four Ps of recruiting. Answer B is not the best

response; there are no generally recognized four Ps of employee relations. Answer C is not the best response; there are no generally recognized four Ps of project management.

200. **Answer B is the best response.** Weighted applications can conflict with EEO guidelines (for instance, if extra credit is granted for factors that are not truly related to the job, or that are not as related as the weighting might imply). Answer A is not the best response; weighted employment applications are intended to facilitate the process of evaluating each candidate's qualifications in a consistent and objective manner. Answer C is not the best response; weighted employment applications are difficult and time consuming to create and maintain because positions are almost constantly evolving and changing in some way. Answer D is not the best response; weighted employment applications do assign relative weights to different elements of the employment application.

201. **Answer D is the best response.** Common situs picketing is unrelated to double breasting because the employers in question with double breasting picketing share common ownership, while the employers in question with common situs picketing share a common work location. Answer A is not the best response; common situs picketing is a type of secondary boycott. Answer B is not the best response; common situs picketing is legal as long as the picket signs indicate the name of the employer with whom the picketers have a dispute. Answer C is not the best response; common situs picketing occurs when members of a labor union picket a workplace in which multiple employers work.

202. **Answer D is the best response.** The ADA states that "consideration shall be given to the employer's judgment as to what functions of a job are essential, and if an employer has prepared a written description before advertising or interviewing applicants for the job, this description shall be considered evidence of the essential functions of the job." Failure to have a job description in place, therefore, could diminish the strength of the employer's position in defending an allegation that an employee or applicant has been discriminated against based on disability. In short, employers can't make up (or look like they are making up) requirements after the fact. As such, an employer's case could be weakened if a job description designating certain functions as essential is not in place prior to the filing of a charge of discrimination. Identifying essential functions in a job description, however, is not specifically mandated by law.

203. **Answer C is the best response.** Although the person must be able to establish that he or she was qualified for the position, he or she does not need to be able to establish that he or she was the most qualified for the position in order to establish a prima facie case. Answer A is not the best response; the person must be able to establish that he or she is a member of a protected class. Answer B is not the best response; the person must be able to establish that he or she applied for the position for which the employer was seeking applicants. Answer D is not the best response; the person must be able to establish that the employer continued to seek other applicants with similar qualifications.

204. **Answer B is the best response.** An organization that utilizes the services of a search firm must pay a fee to a contingency employment agency/search firm only if an employee is hired through that agency's efforts. Answer A is not the best response; an organization that utilizes the services of a contingency employment agency/search firm does not pay a fee to that agency/firm unless an employee is hired through that agency's efforts. Answer C is not the best response; an organization

that utilizes the services of a retained employment agency/search firm must pay a fee whether or not an employee is hired through that agency's efforts. Answer D is not the best response; see the explanations for the other answers.

205. **Answer C is the best response.** Just like in-person interviews, prescreen phone interviews should be professional, consistent, and stick to job-related factors. An assessment of fit that is made through informal interactions is more likely to be based on factors that are not specifically related to the job-related knowledge, skills, abilities, and behavioral characteristics that are required for a position. Answer A is not the best response; a prescreen phone interview can be an effective way to identify legitimate job-related factors that could cause the employer to decide to eliminate the candidate from consideration. Answer B is not the best response; a prescreen phone interview can be an effective way to share job-related information (with every employee) that could lead one or more candidates to self-select out of the selection process. Answer D is not the best response; a prescreen phone interview can be an effective way to ascertain whether the candidate's desired salary/wage rate is close to the salary/wage range that the organization has established for the position.

206. **Answer D is the best response.** (For this discussion, keep the definition of disparate or adverse impact in mind: Disparate or adverse impact occurs when a seemingly neutral policy or practice has a disproportionately negative impact upon a member of a protected class.) Although it is conceivable that this could still result in adverse impact, of the four situations described it is least likely to have an adverse impact on a protected class. Answer A is not the best response; requiring employees to live within a certain radius of an employer could potentially have an adverse impact if it has the impact of screening out individuals based on membership in a protected class, for instance, race (this policy could also eliminate people from consideration based on socioeconomic status; although socioeconomic status does not constitute a protected class, it could be discriminatory depending upon the characteristics shared by individuals who have been eliminated because of this requirement. Employers would be better advised to consult with counsel relative to the appropriateness of requiring specific response times for specific positions). Answer B is not the best response; excluding candidates who have gaps in employment could potentially have an adverse impact upon women (who are more likely to experience a gap in employment than men) and individuals over the age of 40 (who are more likely to have experienced a layoff or other involuntary termination). Answer C is not the best response; any program that requires people to relocate frequently could potentially have an adverse impact based on gender or age.

207. **Answer A is the best response.** Of all these factors, having the same interviewer perform every interview contributes the least to ensuring that the interview process will have validity. Why? Because if the interview is not based on job analysis (answer B), if the interviewer (even if it is the same person) does not ask questions that elicit information about important job-related skills (answer C), or if the information that is shared, discussed, and collected during an interview does not relate to a specific job (answer D), having the same person conduct the interview isn't going to do anything to ensure validity. What will contribute to validity is if the interview(s) incorporates these processes into the interview process.

208. **Answer B is the best response.** A skill inventory system is a central database that captures the KSAs possessed by employees. When a position opens up, the organization can then use the skill

inventory system to generate a list of current employees who meet the minimum qualifications for the position. Answers A, C, and D are inaccurate definitions of skill inventories.

209. **Answer A is the best response.** The employee might, at some level, feel as though it isn't worth meeting her deadlines; it just results in getting more work (in this particular case, her visceral reaction might equate to an adage that says, "No good deed goes unpunished"). Answer B is not the best response; being given more work might not be considered a desirable result by the employee. Answer C is not the best response; the act of meeting deadlines is a desired behavior, and needs to be treated as such. Answer D is not the best response; the manager did respond in some way to the employee's changed behavior (whereas extinction occurs when a behavior does not elicit any response at all.

210. **Answer B is the best response.** Answers A, C, and D are all elements within Vroom's expectancy theory. Although addressed by certain motivation theories, the concept of proclivity is not specifically addressed by any of the motivation theories in this book.

211. **Answer B is the best response.** This dimension of leadership relates to the dimensions of leadership that speak specifically to ensuring that employees successfully perform the work associated with the position. Answer A is not the best response; it defines the other dimension identified through behavioral leadership theories, referred to as consideration or employee-centered. Answer C is not the best response; this does not reflect one of the two leadership dimensions. Answer D is not the best response; it articulates a belief that is ascribed to the trait leadership theories, not the behavioral leadership theories.

212. **Answer A is the best response.** Employers do normally own/retain the copyright to work product that is generated by an employee during the normal course of his or her employment. Neither answer B nor answer D is the best response; independent contractors/consulting firm do not normally own/retain the copyright to work product generated for the organization for which they are consulting. (From the perspective of the organization, however, it is important to have a signed written agreement that states that a work-for-hire arrangement has been established, and that the organization owns/retains all work product that is produced). Answer C is not the best response; an employee does not normally own/retain the copyright to the work product that he or she generates in the normal course of his or her employment.

213. **Answer B is the best response.** The formative evaluation model seeks feedback during and after the development and implementation phases. Answer C is not the best response; the formative evaluation model was developed by Robert Brinkerhoff. Answer D is not the best response; it refers to Kirkpatrick's reaction level analysis (which measures participants' responses and reactions to a program immediately after the program has been delivered).

214. **Answer A is the best response.** In order to qualify for the learned professional exemption under the FLSA, the employee's primary duty must be the performance of work requiring advanced knowledge, defined as work which is predominantly intellectual in character and which includes work requiring the consistent exercise of discretion and judgment. Answer B is not the best response; the advanced knowledge must be in a field of science or learning. Work that requires advanced knowledge in other accredited professions would not qualify under this exemption.

215. **Answer D is the best response.** A vacation buyout program (a program through which an employer will buy back a certain amount of unused vacation time) constitutes cash compensation, and therefore is not a form of indirect compensation. Answer A is not the best response; whether legally mandated or not, benefits are a form of indirect compensation. Answer B is not the best response; vacation time (or any program that grants employees paid time off) is a form of indirect compensation. Answer C is not the best response; perquisites (also known as perks), such as company car, club memberships, financial planning, and the like are a form of indirect compensation.

216. **Answer A is the best response.** MHPA (the Mental Health Parity Act) does not require health plans to offer mental health benefits; rather, it only applies to plans that *do* offer mental health benefits. Answer B is not the best response; under MHPA, plans can still dictate/define the terms and conditions of benefits provided under mental health plans (for instance, cost-sharing, limits on the number of visits or days of coverage, and so forth). Answer C is not the best response; under MHPA, plans that don't impose annual or lifetime monetary caps on medical and surgical benefits *cannot* impose annual or lifetime caps on mental health benefits, either. Answer D is not the best response; benefits for substance abuse or chemical dependency are excluded from MHPA's requirements.

217. **Answer D is the best response.** The single most important factor that is most likely to impact whether the handbook will support the *employer's* position or the *employee's* position is the presence or absence of a signed employee acknowledgement. Without it, even the most carefully crafted handbook—including one with a carefully (and effectively) written EEO/AA statement (answer A) or sexual harassment policy (answer B)—will be less relevant because it cannot be proven that the employee received, read, understood, and asked questions about it. Answer C is not the best response; employee handbooks usually don't include a records retention policy.

218. **Answer C is the least likely response.** In order to collect information that could be used to address individual's employee relations issues, the employee survey could not remain anonymous, rendering it useless and ineffective. Answer A is not the best response; an organization would conduct an employee survey to gauge and measure employees' perceptions, viewpoints, and attitudes. Answer B is not the best response; an organization would conduct an employee survey to take the pulse on specific employee current and/or potential issues. Answer D is not the best response; an organization would conduct an employee survey to collect information that can be used by the organization to help set priorities.

219. **Answer A is the best response.** In order for a bargaining unit to be established, a simple majority of those who choose to vote in the election must vote in favor of the proposed bargaining unit. Answer B is not the best response; a simple majority of voters (not of potential members) is required in order for a bargaining unit to be established. Answer C is not the best response; even when there is more than one bargaining unit competing in an election, a proposed bargaining unit must still obtain a simple majority of the votes (this is significant for two reasons: First, a runoff election might be required. Second, in that runoff election, the bargaining unit could find itself competing either with another bargaining unit or with the option of remaining union-free). Answer D is not the best response; at least 30% of the employees who would be in the collective bargaining unit must sign authorization cards before the union can petition the NLRB to hold an election. All of which takes place, of course, long before the actual election.

220. **Answer D is the best response.** Of the four choices listed in the question, catastrophes and fatal accidents would represent the highest priority, followed by employee complaints (answer C); referrals from the media or other individuals, agencies, or organizations (answer A); and planned inspections in high hazard industries (answer B). Imminent danger, however, poses an even higher priority for OSHA than any of the situations listed in this explanation.

221. **Answer C is the best response.** The degree to which a selection process or instrument is consistent determines the degree to which that instrument is reliable. Answer A is not the best response; the degree to which a selection procedure assesses a candidate's ability to perform representative and significant parts of the job measures its content validity, not its reliability. Answer B is not the best response, the degree to which incumbents' scores or ratings on a particular selection procedure correlate with their actual job performance measures its criterion-related validity. Answer D is not the best response; the degree to which a clear relationship exists between performance on the selection procedure and performance on the job measures (in a more general sense) its validity.

222. **Answer D is the best response.** With respect to the Equal Pay Act, the definition of responsibility is "the degree of responsibility and accountability which an employer entrusts to and expects from a particular position." Answer A is not the best response; with respect to the Equal Pay Act, the definition of skill is "the amount or degree of experience, ability, education, and training required to perform the job." Neither answer B nor answer C is the best response; the Equal Pay Act does not designate trust or accountability as one of the four factors used to assess substantial equality.

223. **Answer A is the best response.** The Railway Labor Act of 1926 established the work now, grieve later rule (there is not grieve now, work later rule). Answer B is not the best response; the Railway Labor Act of 1926 did afford management additional tools to make sure the trains ran on time. Answer C is not the best response; the Railway Labor Act of 1926 did enable railroad workers to organize and to have a collective bargaining agent. Answer D is not the best response; the Railway Labor Act of 1926 did create the first real win-win scenario for labor and management in American history.

224. **Answer B is the best response.** Taft-Hartley enacted provisions that permitted employers to (not *prohibited* employers from) fire supervisors who engaged in union activities or who did not support the employer's position. Answer A is not the best response; Taft-Hartley did reaffirm that employers have a constitutional right to express their opposition to unions, so long as employees are not threatened with reprisal for their union activities or promised benefits for refraining from such activities. Answer C is not the best response; Taft-Hartley did outlaw closed shops, agreements that stated that employers could only hire individuals who were members of labor unions. Answer D is not the best response; Taft-Hartley did expressly permit union shops, in which non-union workers must join the union within a certain amount of time after being hired.

225. **Answer A is the best response.** The list of the names and addresses of all of the employees who are eligible to vote in the union certification election is also known as the Excelsior List. This nickname comes from the NLRB decision *Excelsior Underwear, Inc.* v. *NLRB*, in which the NLRB considered whether "a fair and free election [can] be held when the union involved lacks the names and addresses of employees eligible to vote in that election, and the employer refuses to accede to the union's request…." The NLRB ruled that it could not. As a result, the employer must provide the list of employees' names and addresses within seven days after the NLRB has scheduled an election.

PART III

Appendixes

APPENDIX A

CD Contents and Installation Instructions

The CD features an innovative practice test engine powered by MeasureUp, giving you yet another effective tool to assess your readiness for the exam.

Multiple Test Modes

MeasureUp practice tests are available in Study, Certification, Custom, Adaptive, Missed Question, and Non-Duplicate question modes.

Study Mode

Tests administered in Study Mode allow you to request the correct answer(s) and explanation to each question during the test. These tests are not timed. You can modify the testing environment *during* the test by selecting the Options button.

Certification Mode

Tests administered in Certification Mode closely simulate the actual testing environment you will encounter when taking a certification exam. These tests do not allow you to request the answer(s) and/or explanation to each question until after the exam.

Custom Mode

Custom Mode allows you to specify your preferred testing environment. Use this mode to specify the objectives you want to include in your test, the timer length, and other test properties. You can also modify the testing environment *during* the test by selecting the Options button.

Adaptive Mode

Tests administered in Adaptive Mode closely simulate the actual testing environment you will encounter taking an adaptive exam. After answering a question, you are not allowed to go back; you are only allowed to move forward during the exam.

Missed Question Mode

Missed Question Mode allows you to take a test containing only the questions you have missed previously.

Non-Duplicate Mode

Non-Duplicate Mode allows you to take a test containing only questions not displayed previously.

Random Questions and Order of Answers

This feature helps you learn the material without memorizing questions and answers. Each time you take a practice test, the questions and answers appear in a different randomized order.

Detailed Explanations of Correct and Incorrect Answers

You'll receive automatic feedback on all correct and incorrect answers. The detailed answer explanations are a superb learning tool in their own right.

Attention to Exam Objectives

MeasureUp practice tests are designed to appropriately balance the questions over each technical area covered by a specific exam.

Installing the CD

The minimum system requirements for the CD-ROM are

▶ Windows 95, 98, Me, NT4, 2000, or XP

▶ 7MB disk space for testing engine

▶ An average of 1MB disk space for each test

To install the CD-ROM, follow these instructions:

> **NOTE**
>
> If you need technical support, please contact MeasureUp at 678-356-5050 or email support@measureup.com. Additionally, you'll find Frequently Asked Questions (FAQ) at www.measureup.com.

1. Close all applications before beginning this installation.

2. Insert the CD into your CD-ROM drive. If the setup starts automatically, go to step 6. If the setup does not start automatically, continue with step 3.

3. From the Start menu, select Run.

4. Click Browse to locate the MeasureUp CD. In the Browse dialog box, from the Look In drop-down list, select the CD-ROM drive.

5. In the Browse dialog box, double-click on Setup.exe. In the Run dialog box, click OK to begin the installation.

6. On the Welcome Screen, click MeasureUp Practice Questions to begin installation.

7. Follow the Certification Prep Wizard by clicking Next.

8. To agree to the Software License Agreement, click Yes.

9. On the Choose Destination Location screen, click Next to install the software to C:\Program Files\Certification Preparation.

> **NOTE**
>
> If you cannot locate MeasureUp Practice Tests through the Start menu, see the section later in this Appendix titled, "Creating a Shortcut to the MeasureUp Practice Tests."

10. On the Setup Type screen, select Typical Setup. Click Next to continue.

11. In the Select Program Folder screen, you can name the program folder your tests will be in. To select the default simply click next and the installation will continue.

12. After the installation is complete, verify that Yes, I want to restart my computer now is selected. If you select No, I will restart my computer later, you will not be able to use the program until you restart your computer.

13. Click Finish.

14. After restarting your computer, choose Start, Programs, MeasureUp, MeasureUp Practice Tests.

15. On the MeasureUp Welcome Screen, click Create User Profile.

16. In the User Profile dialog box, complete the mandatory fields and click Create Profile.

17. Select the practice test you want to access and click Start Test.

Creating a Shortcut to the MeasureUp Practice Tests

To create a shortcut to the MeasureUp Practice Tests, follow these steps.

1. Right-click on your Desktop.

2. From the shortcut menu select New, Shortcut.

3. Browse to C:\Program Files\MeasureUp Practice Tests and select the MeasureUpCertification.exe or Localware.exe file.

4. Click OK.

5. Click Next.

6. Rename the shortcut MeasureUp.

7. Click Finish.

After you have completed Step 7, use the MeasureUp shortcut on your Desktop to access the MeasureUp products you ordered.

Technical Support

If you encounter problems with the MeasureUp test engine on the CD-ROM, please contact MeasureUp at 678-356-5050 or email support@measureup.com. Technical support hours are from 8 a.m. to 5 p.m. EST Monday through Friday. Additionally, you'll find frequently asked questions (FAQ) at www.measureup.com.

If you'd like to purchase additional MeasureUp products, telephone 678-356-5050 or 800-649-1MUP (1687) or visit www.measureup.com.

Glossary

Numbers

80-20 rule (also known as the Pareto Principle) A principle that asserts that 80% of effects result from 20% of causes. The 80-20 rule, and the chart that visually depicts it, is intended to help individuals focus their efforts where there is the greatest likelihood of bringing about the desired change.

A

acceptable quality levels (AQLs) According to Phil Crosby's zero defect philosophy, acceptable quality levels refers to the acceptable level of errors that are sometimes permitted and that thus preclude the possibility of fully attaining quality objectives.

action-oriented programs Programs that are specifically designed to correct any areas of underutilization and, thereby, to attain established placement goals.

ADDIE A five-phase model that includes analysis/assessment (of needs), design, development, implementation, and evaluation.

administrative exemption An exemption under the FLSA. To qualify for an administrative exemption

▶ The employee's primary duty must be the performance of office or non-manual work directly related to the management or general business operations of the employer or the employer's customers; and

▶ The employee's primary duty includes the exercise of discretion and independent judgment with respect to matters of significance.

adverse impact (also known as disparate impact)   Occurs when a seemingly neutral policy or practice has a disproportionately negative impact on a member of a protected class. Adverse impact that results from policies or practices that are not job-related and that have a statistically significant impact on members of a protected class can constitute unlawful discrimination.

Affirmative Action Plans (AAPs)
Programs created under Executive Order 11246 to overcome the effects of past societal discrimination by identifying areas of underutilization. AAPs set forth (and document) good faith efforts to address and resolve that underutilization. Federal contractors and subcontractors with $50,000 or more in contracts during any 12-month period are also required to design and implement formal AAPs.

affirmative defenses   Legitimate explanations that employers can set forth to explain inequities in pay between men and women under the Equal Pay Act of 1963. These arguments can be based on—and must be proven to be—a function of

▶ Seniority

▶ Merit

▶ Quantity or quality of production

▶ Any factors other than sex

Age Discrimination in Employment Act, 1967   A law that prohibits discrimination on the basis of age, for individuals age 40 and above. There is no upper cap on age limit (although there initially was). The ADEA covers private employers with 20 or more employees, state and local governments (including school districts), employment agencies, and labor organizations.

agency shop   Employees are not required to join the union. They must, however, pay a monthly fee that is typically equivalent to union dues. Agency shops are illegal in right-to-work states.

agility tests   Preemployment tests that are used to ascertain whether the candidate can perform the physical requirements of the position for which he or she is applying.

aging   The process of mathematically adjusting market data collected during the market pricing process to a common date (usually the date on which the market analysis is being conducted).

agriculture   One of the major industries designated by OSHA.

AIDS (acquired immune deficiency syndrome)   An infectious disease that is transmitted person-to-person through blood or other bodily fluids.

Albemarle Paper v. Moody (1975)   Key issue: job-relatedness and validity of employment tests. Significance: any tests that are used as part of the hiring or promotional decision making process must be job-related. This applies to any instrument that is used as a "test," even if that was not its original purpose. This case also established that employment tests must demonstrate predictive validity, consistent with the Uniform Guidelines for Employee Selection Procedures.

ally doctrine   A doctrine that states that a union can expand on its primary picketing activity to include employers who are "allies" of the primary employer. One specific situation that can permit the union to conduct secondary boycott is the ally doctrine.

American Society for Personnel Administration (ASPA)   ASPA was renamed Society for Human Resource Management (SHRM) in 1989.

Americans with Disabilities Act (ADA), 1992   A law that guarantees equal opportunity for qualified individuals with disabilities in public accommodations, employment, transportation, state and local government services, and telecommunications.

andragogy   The study and science of how adults learn.

aptitude tests   Preemployment tests that are used to ascertain whether the candidate possesses the skills and/or knowledge required to perform the position for which he or she is applying.

attitude surveys (also sometimes called employee or climate surveys)   A vehicle through which employees can express their opinions or share their perspectives. Sometimes attitude surveys can even provide a vehicle through which employees can

truly contribute in a meaningful and significant way to their organizations by having a voice in shaping the policies, practices, and directions of their organizations.

auditory learners   Those who learn most effectively through what they hear.

authorization cards   Cards that, once signed by employees, demonstrate and confirm employees' interest in joining a union. After 30% of the employees who would be in the collective bargaining unit have signed authorization cards, the union can petition the NLRB to hold an election (the 30% threshold demonstrates a "showing of interest" to the NLRB). Often, however, unions seek to obtain signed authorization cards from 50% or more employees before petitioning the NLRB.

Automobile Workers vs. Johnson Controls   The case in which the Supreme Court ruled that Johnson Controls' fetal protection policy constituted a violation of Title VII of the Civil Rights Act of 1964, as amended by the Pregnancy Discrimination Act.

availability analysis   The section of an affirmative action plan that determines the availability of minorities and women for jobs in their establishments, compares incumbency to availability, declares underutilization, and establishes goals to eliminate the underutilization.

B

background check   A process through which the specifics of an individual's past history are explored and revealed.

balanced scorecard An approach to strategic management that seeks increased clarity and specificity by offering a clear and unequivocal prescription of what companies should measure to appropriately balance financial measures of success against nonfinancial measures of success.

base pay The fixed rate of pay that an employee receives for performing his or her job. Base pay does not include earnings obtained through shift differentials, benefits, overtime, incentive premiums, or any pay element other than the employee's fixed rate of pay.

BASIC (behavioral, as soon as possible, specific, interactive, consistent) An acronym that outlines the principles that should be followed when providing feedback to, and discussing feedback with, employees.

Beck Rights The right for bargaining unit members to pay only that portion of union dues which is attributable to mainline union responsibilities (collective bargaining, organizing in the same industry, contract administration, and the like). It is up to the employee, however, to exercise his or her Beck rights. Beck rights were established by the 1988 Supreme Court decision in Communication Workers of America v. Beck (1988).

behavior level evaluation Measures whether participants' on-the-job behaviors have changed in a manner consistent with training objectives. In short, it measures *transfer of training*—the degree to which participants apply the skills and knowledge covered in the training sessions in the workplace.

behavior-based interviews Interviews that require the candidate to describe past experiences that demonstrate the degree to which he or she possesses the knowledge, skills, and abilities required to successfully perform the position for which her or she is applying.

behavioral anchored ranking scales (BARS) A performance appraisal method that starts by identifying the most critical responsibilities or requirements of a position. Then, for each responsibility or requirement, "anchor" statements offering a specific description of a particular type of behavior (which corresponds to a particular level of performance) are written.

benefits Non-cash, or indirect, rewards provided to employees in recognition of and in exchange for the performance of their jobs.

bills Statutes, in their draft format, while they are on their way to becoming law.

biological health hazards Dangers of a biological origin or nature that are introduced into the workplace.

bona fide occupational qualification (BFOQ) Legitimate job requirements that are mandated by business necessity that can have an unintended discriminatory (disparate) impact on applicants or employees.

Brinkerhoff, Robert Brinkerhoff's evaluation model incorporates "formative evaluation."

broadbanding An approach to pay systems that includes a relatively small number of grades. Organizations might choose to use broadbands to bring about a cultural change (for instance, to support the implementation of a flatter organization) or to shift employees' focus away from traditional promotions and place it instead on career growth. Broadbands typically have range spreads of 100% or more.

business (or organizational) ethics A shared values-based system designed to inculcate within the organization's population a sense of how to conduct business properly.

business process perspective One of the four perspectives of the balanced scorecard. This perspective scrutinizes key internal business processes so as to measure and ascertain how well those processes generate business results (that is, products and services) that meet customer expectations. The business process perspective ascertains performance levels through specific measures that are unique to each particular organization.

C

captive audience meeting A mandatory meeting held by management, in the workplace, during regular working hours, during which the employer can share its opinions relative to unions and the unionization of its operations. Captive audience meetings cannot be held within 24 hours of the actual election.

career development The development of individuals within the organization.

case study A training method through which participants are presented with a real-life situation that allows them to apply the knowledge they have learned and practice

the skills they have developed during the training session.

cash balance plan A type of defined benefit plan that expresses the promised benefit in terms of a stated account balance (similar to the way a defined contribution plan does).

cause-and-effect diagram (also known as the Ishikawa or fishbone diagram) An important quality tool developed by Ishikawa that presents a visual representation of factors that impact whether a desired outcome will be obtained. Ishikawa believed that, by presenting all the possible factors that contribute to a particular result, any potential process imperfections can be identified in advance and eliminated.

certification The process by which HR professionals earn formal recognition by a professional certifying body (HRCI).

change management Activities involved in: "(1) defining and instilling new values, attitudes, norms, and behaviors within an organization that support new ways of doing work and overcome resistance to change; (2) building consensus among customers and stakeholders on specific changes designed to better meet their needs; and (3) planning, testing, and implementing all aspects of the transition from one organizational structure or business process to another" (as defined by the Government Accounting Office).

change process theory The theory that looks at the dynamics behind how change happens within organizations.

charge A formal complaint, submitted to an agency, that alleges unlawful discrimination.

charging party (also called the complainant) A person who alleges that he or she has experienced unlawful discrimination.

checklist A rating method type of performance appraisal in which the appraiser reviews a series of statements that could describe an employee's performance and literally checks off those statements that are reflective of the employee's performance during the performance measurement period. Sometimes checklists are weighted (called weighted checklists), in which case the weightings are used to generate a mathematically calculated score.

chemical health hazards Any chemical in the workplace for which evidence exists that acute or chronic health effects may occur in exposed employees.

child labor The child labor provisions of the FLSA restrict the number of hours (and the times of the day) that children under the age of 16 can work, as well as the types of work that children under the age of 18 can perform.

Circuit City Stores, Inc. v. Adams (2001) The landmark Supreme Court case that confirmed the legality of requiring employees to sign mandatory arbitration agreements as a condition of employment and that such agreements are enforceable under the Federal Arbitration Act (FAA).

Civil Rights Act of 1991 A law that significantly expanded employees' rights and remedies under Title VII of the Civil Rights Act of 1964. In addition to establishing the right for plaintiffs in Title VII cases to enjoy jury trials, it allowed for plaintiffs to be awarded compensatory and punitive damages.

Clayton Act, 1914 A law enacted to build on and clarify the Sherman Act. The provision of the Clayton Act that is most relevant to labor—and therefore to HR professionals—is that Section 6 of the act specifically exempts labor unions and agricultural organizations from the Sherman Anti-Trust Act.

cliff vesting A vesting arrangement in which an employee earns a non-forfeitable right to 100% of his or her employer's contributions after a specified number of years, but forfeits all rights to those contributions if his or her employment is terminated before he or she vests.

climate survey (also sometimes called attitude survey or employee survey) A vehicle through which employees can express their opinions or share their perspectives. Sometimes climate surveys can even provide a vehicle through which employees can truly contribute in a meaningful and significant way to their organizations by having a voice in shaping the policies, practices, and directions of their organizations.

closed shop Employers can only hire employees who are already members of the union. Closed shops were ruled illegal by the Taft-Hartley Act; however, hiring halls do, in one sense, encourage a closed shop arrangement. A hiring hall is a union-operated placement office that refers registered applicants to jobs on the basis of a seniority or placement system.

closing processes   Those processes (within project management) that mark the end of the project, including the sign-off process. As part of closing processes, stakeholders must determine whether, and to what degree, the project met its obligations. In general, closing processes are considered the fifth of five project management processes, although there can be considerable overlap between those five distinct processes.

COBRA qualifying event   Events that would have otherwise resulted in the discontinuation of health insurance benefits for employees, their spouses, and dependent children.

cognitive ability tests   Preemployment tests that are used to assess the candidate's intelligence and/or current skill level with respect to a job-related function. Cognitive tests could be administered to assess skills such as typing, problem-solving, mathematical skill, or numerical ability.

collective bargaining agreement (CBA)   The output of a successful collective bargaining process. The CBA contains provisions related to a variety of conditions of employment and outlines the procedures to be used in settling disputes that might arise throughout the duration of the contract.

common law   A system of law in which traditions, customs, and precedents have the same force of law as existing laws or statutes that have been enacted as a result of the full legislative process. With a common law system, laws and statutes are, quite literally, interpreted and reinterpreted on a case-by-case basis. The way this works is that each interpretation (and each case) sets a precedent but can also be reinterpreted, thus setting a new precedent. As it evolves, this process results in rights being granted to employees on an individual basis.

common situs picketing   A type of picketing that is actually a type of secondary boycott. Common situs picketing occurs when members of a labor union picket a workplace in which multiple employers work: the employer with whom the labor union has the dispute, as well as one or more employers with whom the labor union does not have a dispute. Common situs picketing is legal as long as the picket signs indicate the name of the employer with whom the picketers have a dispute.

Communication Workers of America v. Beck (1988)   The Supreme Court case that established the right for bargaining unit members to pay only that portion of union dues which is attributable to mainline union responsibilities (collective bargaining, organizing in the same industry, contract administration, and the like). It is up to the employee, however, to exercise his or her Beck rights.

compa-ratio   The compa-ratio for each employee is calculated by dividing the employee's pay rate by the range midpoint for his or her position. Compa-ratios can be a particularly valuable measure for organizations that seek to match the market because, in such systems, midpoints are often considered to be a close approximation of the market rate for a position. By calculating the compa-ratio, therefore, it is possible to compare the employee's rate of pay with the market rate for his or her position.

comparative methods Performance appraisal methods in which the appraiser compares employees to each other.

compensable factors Skills, abilities, characteristics, or areas of responsibility that an organization values and for which it is willing to pay. Some sample compensable factors include education, experience, financial responsibility, responsibility for contacts, and so on.

compensation Cash-based rewards provided to employees in recognition of and in exchange for the performance of their jobs.

compensation and benefits
Compensation and benefits speaks to HR's responsibility to ensure that the organization's total compensation and benefits programs, policies, and practices reinforce and support the short-term, long-term, emerging, and strategic objectives of the organization.

competencies Skills or behaviors that reflect how employees are expected to deliver performance goals/objectives.

complainant (also called the charging party) A person who alleges that he or she has experienced unlawful discrimination.

computer employee exemption An exemption under the FLSA. To qualify for a computer employee exemption:

▶ The employee must be compensated either on a salary or fee basis (as defined in the regulations) at a rate not less than $455 per week or, if compensated on an hourly basis, at a rate not less than $27.63 an hour;

▶ The employee must be employed as a computer systems analyst, computer programmer, software engineer, or other similarly skilled worker in the computer field performing the duties described below;

▶ The employee's primary duty must consist of:

1. The application of systems analysis techniques and procedures, including consulting with users to determine hardware, software, or system functional specifications;

2. The design, development, documentation, analysis, creation, testing, or modification of computer systems or programs, including prototypes, based on and related to user or system design specifications;

3. The design, documentation, testing, creation, or modification of computer programs related to machine operating systems; or

4. A combination of the aforementioned duties, the performance of which requires the same level of skills.

concerted activities Any activities undertaken by individual employees who are united in pursuit of a common goal are considered to be concerted activity. For an employee's activity to be concerted, the activity must be engaged in with, or on the authority of, other employees, rather than just on behalf of the individual employee (Meyers Industries, 281 NLRB 882 [1986]).

concurrent resolutions A legislative measure that addresses a concern that pertains to the Senate as well as the House of Representatives. Concurrent resolutions, however, are not submitted to the president and thus do not have the force of law.

confidentiality agreement A type of employment agreement that prohibits employees from revealing any confidential information to which they might be exposed during the course of their employment. This could include trade secrets, patent information, and the like. It also prohibits employees from using confidential information in any way other than the purposes for which it was intended, and which is necessary, within the context of their jobs.

Congressional Accountability Act (CAA), 1995 Expanded coverage of the following 12 laws to congressional employees:

- Fair Labor Standards Act (FLSA) (1938)
- Title VII of the Civil Rights Act of 1964, as amended
- Age Discrimination in Employment Act of 1967
- Occupational Safety and Health Act of 1970
- Rehabilitation Act of 1973
- Civil Service Reform Act of 1978
- Employee Polygraph Protection Act of 1988
- Worker Adjustment and Retraining Notification Act of 1988
- Americans with Disabilities Act of 1990
- Family and Medical Leave Act of 1993
- Veterans Reemployment Act of 1994
- Uniformed Services Employment and Reemployment Rights Act of 1994

Consolidated Omnibus Budget Reconciliation Act (COBRA), 1985 An amendment to Title I of ERISA that requires employers who employed 20 or more people during the prior year to offer continuation of group health care coverage to employees and their family members who experience certain qualifying events—events that would have otherwise resulted in the discontinuation of their health insurance benefits. COBRA places certain requirements on plan participants who wish to extend coverage and places certain requirements on the plan provider, in particular with respect to notification requirements.

construct validity The degree to which a selection procedure measures the degree to which the test-taker possesses a particular psychological trait (if, of course, it can be shown that the trait is required for successful performance of the position).

construction One of the major industries designated by OSHA.

constructive discharge An employee who alleges constructive discharge asserts that he or she was subjected to such intolerable working conditions that remaining employed with the organization would be impossible. Essentially, an employee who alleges that he or she was constructively discharged is alleging that he or she was forced to quit.

content validity The degree to which a selection procedure assesses a candidate's ability to perform significant parts of the job.

contingency employment agencies Search firms to whom an organization pays a fee only if that firm's efforts result in the organization actually hiring a candidate. The services of this type of agency are more often secured in an effort to fill entry-level professional or supervisory-level positions.

contract doctrines Another way in which common law directly impacts the employment relationship. A contract is an agreement that is enforceable by law. Employment contracts are made between an employer and an employee and can be either oral or written. They can include topics such as term or length of employment, compensation and benefits, job responsibilities, and termination.

contrast error/bias (interviewing) An interviewing error/bias that occurs when the interviewer compares candidates to each other instead of comparing them to the requirements of the position.

contrast error/bias (performance management) A performance management error/bias in which the appraiser compares the performance of each employee to the performance of other employees instead of comparing it to the established performance standards for the position.

controlling function Identified by Fayol as one of the five management functions, the controlling function is the one during which the manager ascertains the degree to which the planning in which he or she was engaged actually produced the desired results. If the manager determines that there is a gap between the targeted goals and the actual results, the manager must then focus on ways to bridge that gap.

controlling processes Those processes (within project management) that include managing the scope of the project and ensuring that the project stays in line with the original objectives. A significant degree of follow-up is required to carry out controlling processes. In general, controlling processes are considered the fourth of five project management processes, although there can be considerable overlap between those five distinct processes.

coordinating function Identified by Fayol as one of the five management functions. Through the coordinating function, the manager brings together all the resources that he or she has organized to accomplish the stated plan.

Copyright Act of 1976 A law protecting the work of authors, artists, and others who create original materials. This law also addresses fair use and public domain questions.

cost per trainee/cost per participant A formula that calculates:

$$\frac{\text{Total of all costs associated with the HRD/training initiative}}{\text{Number of individuals who participate in the HRD/training initiative}}$$

creative professional exemption An exemption under the FLSA. To qualify for a creative professional exemption:

▶ The employee's primary duty must be the performance of work requiring invention, imagination, originality, or talent in a recognized field of artistic or creative endeavor.

criterion-related validity   The degree to which a selection procedure correlates with employees' subsequent job performance.

critical incident   A narrative performance appraisal method in which the appraiser creates and maintains documentation throughout the year relative to specific situations in which the employee met, and did not meet, the performance expectations of the position.

Crosby, Philip B.   A quality guru known for his zero defects standard (as opposed to acceptable quality levels (AQLs)). This management philosophy asserts that employees will perform at whatever level management sets for them.

cumulative trauma disorders (CTDs) (also known as repetitive stress injuries [RSIs] or cumulative trauma syndrome [CTS])   Injuries that result from placing too much stress (often through overuse) on a part of the body.

cumulative trauma syndrome (CTS) (also known as repetitive stress injuries [RSIs] or cumulative trauma disorders [CTDs])   Injuries that result from placing too much stress (often through overuse) on a part of the body.

customer perspective   One of the four perspectives of the balanced scorecard. This perspective focuses on the criticality of customer focus and customer satisfaction.

Dissatisfied customers will eventually look to others who will meet their needs and expectations (often without ever sharing their reasons for doing so), which, if the numbers are large enough, can ultimately lead to organizational decline.

D

Davis-Bacon Act, 1931   The first piece of legislation to consider the topic of, and actually establish, a minimum wage. Davis-Bacon, however, was (and still is) limited to the construction industry, specifically those contractors and subcontractors on

▶ any and all federal government construction contracts

▶ nonfederal government construction projects in excess of $2,000 that receive federal funding

Contractors and subcontractors who meet either of these criteria are required to provide laborers and mechanics who are employed at the actual worksite with wages and benefits that are equal to (or better than) what workers on similar local projects receive.

decline   The fourth stage of the organizational life cycle, after which—if inertia has set in and if atrophy has begun—decline will not be far behind.

defamation   A tort doctrine that, in a general and practical sense, refers to making a false statement that damages someone's character or reputation. Defamation that is in written form is referred to as *libel*, and defamation that is made through the spoken word is referred to as *slander*. An employee could sue an employer for libel or slander for a variety of reasons, such as the provision of a false reference to potential employers.

defined benefit plan A more traditional type of pension plan in which the employer promises to pay the employee a specified monthly benefit at retirement. Under defined benefit retirement plans, employers shoulder more of the risk than employees.

defined contribution plan A type of retirement plan that does not promise a specific monthly benefit (or total benefit) at retirement. Instead, the employer and/or the employee contribute to the employee's individual retirement savings account. Those contributions are then invested, and these investments can either make money or lose money. In this way, defined contribution plans shift the risk away from the employer (which is where it rests for defined benefit plans) and back onto the employee.

The Delphi Technique A structured, nonmathematical forecasting technique in which opinions from a variety of experts are sought, distilled, and distilled again. An objective, neutral, uninvolved leader recaps what the experts submit, summarizes that information, and condenses it into a more concise format. (The leader is not one of the experts and does not inject his or her opinions or interpretations into the process.) This happens several times until a final position is identified, one that incorporates the input of many individuals but that does not unduly reflect any one position or viewpoint.

Deming, W. Edwards A true quality pioneer who, though unappreciated in America until the 1980s, brought his expertise to Japan, where he was revered until and long after his death. One of Deming's noteworthy contributions is his 14-point quality management program.

demonstration A training method during which the instructor/facilitator literally shows the participants how to perform a particular function, duty, or role.

design patents Granted for the invention of a new, original, and ornamental design for an article of manufacture.

designation of responsibility The section of an affirmative action plan that identifies the person who has overall responsibility for ensuring the successful implementation of the affirmative action plan.

development/growth The second stage of the organizational life cycle, during which the organization grows in so many ways. Market share, facilities, equipment, revenues, and the number of employees are all likely to expand, to varying degrees. Along with that growth, the organization is likely to experience some growing pains.

direct compensation Components of total compensation that are presented to employees in the form of cash.

directing function Identified by Fayol as one of the five management functions, the directing function is the one during which the actual work is performed—goods are produced or services are provided. In addition to ensuring that things go smoothly from a technical perspective, in the directing phase, the manager must also focus attention on leading and motivating the human resources who are actually performing the work.

directive interviews   Highly structured interviews in which interviewers maintain control, in significant part by asking consistent questions of all candidates.

disability   A medical condition or disorder that substantially limits a person's ability to perform major life activities.

disability benefits   One of the three primary components of the Social Security Act.

discrimination   Discrimination, in the truest sense of the word, is not necessarily illegal. To discriminate is to make a distinction or to discern. When distinctions or discernments are made on the basis of factors, traits, or characteristics that are protected by law, however, discrimination becomes unlawful.

disparate impact (also known as adverse impact)   Occurs when a seemingly neutral policy or practice has a disproportionately negative impact on a member of a protected class. Disparate impact that results from policies or practices that are not job-related and that have a statistically significant impact on members of a protected class can constitute unlawful discrimination.

disparate treatment   A type of unlawful discrimination that occurs when an employer intentionally treats applicants or employees differently on the basis of their race, color, sex, religion, national origin, age, disability, or any other characteristic that is protected by law.

distributive bargaining   An approach to collective bargaining in which each side sets forth its position and does its best to stick to it. By the end of the process, one side will have won some (or all) of what it wanted, and one side will have lost some (or all) of what it wanted. Distributive bargaining is essentially adversarial in nature. It assumes that there's only so much to go around. When you divide up the pie, therefore, one side will end up with more of the pie and one side will end up with less.

diversity   Diversity refers to process of recognizing, valuing, and embracing the many ways in which a group or organization embodies differences and leveraging those differences to enhance the overall performance of individuals and groups.

documentation   Notes maintained relative to an employee's performance.

double breasting picketing   A type of picketing that is actually a type of secondary boycott. Double breasting picketing occurs when a company that owns or operates union as well as non-union operations shifts work to the non-union operation in an effort to diminish the impact of the strike. In this situation, the non-union operation to which the business has been shifted can be picketed.

Drug-Free Workplace Act, 1988   A law that requires federal contractors (with contracts of $100,000 or more) and individuals and organizations who are awarded federal grants (of any size) to agree to maintain a workplace free of illegal drugs.

drug testing   Analysis that ascertains whether drugs are present within a person's body.

E

economic strike   Any strike that is not directly tied to the union's allegation that the employer has committed a ULP. Economic strikes are called in an effort to obtain some sort of economic concession from the employer during collective bargaining negotiations—concessions relating to higher wages, better working conditions, lower health insurance premiums, and the like. Economic strikers cannot be terminated except under highly limited situations, such as if they engage in serious misconduct during the strike. Under the Mackay doctrine, however, economic strikers can be permanently replaced by the employer.

effects bargaining   Bargaining that takes place when non-mandatory subjects would have an impact that does fall under the category of required subjects.

effort   One of the four factors used as a basis to assess the substantial equality of job content under the Equal Pay Act of 1963. *Effort* refers to the amount of physical or mental exertion required to perform the job.

Ellerth v. Burlington Northern Industries (1998) (along with Faragher v. City of Boca Raton [1998])   Key issue: Sexual harassment. Significance: If an employee is subjected to a tangible adverse employment action because of a supervisor's sexually harassing behavior, the employer is liable. The employer is also vicariously liable when its supervisors create a sexually hostile work environment, even if the employee is not subjected to an adverse employment action. This is true regardless of whether the employer itself was negligent or otherwise at fault. However, if the employee is not subjected to tangible adverse employment action, the employer might be able to raise as a defense that it acted reasonably to prevent and/or promptly correct any sexually harassing behavior and that the plaintiff unreasonably failed to take advantage of the employer's preventive or corrective opportunities.

employee   An individual who has been hired by an organization to perform work for that organization and who is compensated directly on that employer's payroll system.

employee and labor relations   Employee and labor relations encompass every dimension of relationships at the workplace, with the overall objective of balancing employee's needs and rights with the employer's need to attain short-term, long-term, emerging, and strategic objectives.

employee assistance programs (EAPs)   Employee assistance programs provide employees with help and resources on a variety of personal issues that can—and often do—have a direct impact on employee job performance. As such, EAPs, which are paid for by organizations, benefit employers as well as employees.

employee communication strategies   One cornerstone—perhaps *the* cornerstone—of effective employee relations. Effective communication can't happen by accident; it must be strategized and executed. Organizations must be deliberate about communicating with, and not just communicating to, employees.

employee handbooks   An important and frequently used method that organizations use to communicate information about policies, procedures, and rules. Handbooks provide, in a sense, the rules of the road in that they ensure that employees are fully informed (in writing) about the obligations and benefits that are associated with being an employee.

Handbooks can vary widely in terms of the information they contain, their length, the topics they cover, and the tone in which they are written.

employee involvement strategies
Deliberate efforts to actively and meaningfully involve employees in the experience of their own employment. HR professionals must seek to actively and meaningfully involve employees in the experience of their own employment.

employee participation groups   Groups through which employees are invited to participate actively in the process of managing the organization by contributing ideas and providing feedback. Employee participation groups can also provide an excellent way of encouraging creative involvement and enhancing commitment. While employee participation groups are neither legal nor illegal by definition, it is the way in which they are administrated that can have a huge impact on whether any particular group is deemed to be legal or illegal under the NLRA.

employee referral   A recruiting technique through which current employees are used as a source for recruiting external candidates into the applicant pool.

employee relations   The way in which an organization responds to, handles, and/or addresses any issue that has impact on employees, and their relationships

- ▶ to and with other employees
- ▶ to and with managers
- ▶ to and with those outside the employment in the organization with whom they come into contact as part of their employment experience

Employee Retirement Income Security Act (ERISA), 1974   A law that was established to protect the interests of those who participate, and the beneficiaries of those who participate, in employee benefit plans. ERISA applies only to programs established by private industry employers. ERISA establishes minimum participation and vesting standards for retirement programs and minimum standards for welfare benefit (including health) plans.

employee stock ownership plans (ESOPs)   A type of defined contribution plan in which investments to individual accounts are made primarily in the form of employer stock.

employee surveys (also sometimes called attitude surveys or climate surveys)   A vehicle through which employees can express their opinions or share their perspectives. Sometimes employee surveys can even provide a vehicle through which employees can truly contribute in a meaningful and significant way to their organizations by having a voice in shaping the policies, practices, and directions of their organizations.

employer branding   The process by and through which organizations deliberately and intentionally decide on the marketing strategy that will be used to promote the employer's brand within the labor market.

employment application   Documents/ forms (paper or electronic) that seek consistent job-related information from candidates relative to their work history, education, and qualifications.

employment-at-will   A common-law tort doctrine under which the employer and the employee are both granted broad rights, most of which focus on the right of either party to terminate the employment relationship at any time for any lawful reason. A number of important exceptions to the employment-at-will doctrine exist, including lawful reasons, public policy exceptions, wrongful terminations, and implied contracts.

Although everyone involved in the hiring /employment/termination process shares in this responsibility, HR must be particularly diligent about ensuring that a lawful, legitimate, nondiscriminatory reason exists and can be articulated when a decision is made to terminate an employee.

employment contracts   An agreement that addresses and outlines various aspects of the employment relationship and that is binding on the organization as well as on the employee.

employment testing   Preemployment tests, tools, or instruments used to ascertain the degree to which a candidate possesses and can demonstrate the knowledge, skills, and abilities required to successfully perform the position for which he or she is applying.

environmental health hazards   A type of health hazard that originates in and exists because of something in the workplace. Environmental health hazards refer to a

wide spectrum of conditions, circumstances, objects, and organisms in the workplace that can create or increase the likelihood of employee illness or injury.

environmental scanning   The process through which organizations maintain awareness of the opportunities and threats presented by the surroundings—both macro and micro—within which they operate.

Equal Employment Opportunity (EEO)   Laws, regulations, structures, and processes that are designed to ensure that all employment-related decisions are based solely on job-related factors and without regard to factors including race, color, religion, sex, age, national origin, disability, or other factors protected by law.

Equal Employment Opportunity Commission (EEOC)   The government agency responsible for enforcing Title VII of the Civil Rights Act of 1964 (Title VII), the Equal Pay Act (EPA), the Age Discrimination in Employment Act (ADEA), and the Americans with Disabilities Act (ADA).

Equal Pay Act, 1963   A law that prohibits discrimination on the basis of sex in the payment of wages or benefits to men and women who perform substantially equal (but not identical) work, for the same employer, in the same establishment, and under similar working conditions. (An *establishment* generally refers to one specific physical location.) Similar to the way in which FLSA status is determined, substantial equality is determined by job content, not job titles.

ergonomics   The way in which the workplace or workspace is designed.

essay method   A narrative performance appraisal method in which the appraiser writes short essays describing and documenting each employee's performance during the performance measurement period.

ethics   A shared values-based system that serves to guide, channel, shape, and direct the behavior of individuals in organizations in an appropriate and productive direction.

Excelsior List   The list of names and addresses of all employees who are eligible to vote in the union certification election. Once the union has obtained recognition, regardless of the way in which that recognition is obtained, the employer must provide the NLRB with this list, which the NLRB will in turn provide to the union. The nickname "Excelsior List" is derived from the 1966 NLRB decision *Excelsior Underwear, Inc. v. NLRB*.

Excelsior Underwear, Inc. v. NLRB (1966)   The NLRB case in which the NLRB considered whether "a fair and free election [can] be held when the union involved lacks the names and addresses of employees eligible to vote in that election, and the employer refuses to accede to the union's request." The NLRB ruled that it could not. As a result, the employer must provide the list of employees' names and addresses within seven days after the NLRB has scheduled an election.

executing processes   Those processes (within project management) that bring everything together, including the project's scope, objectives, and deliverables. In general, executing processes are considered the third of five types of project management processes, although there can be considerable overlap between those five distinct processes.

executive exemption   An exemption under the FLSA. In order to qualify for an executive exemption

- The employee's primary duty must be managing the enterprise or managing a customarily recognized department or subdivision of the enterprise

- The employee must customarily and regularly direct the work of at least two or more other full-time employees or their equivalent

- The employee must have the authority to hire or fire other employees, or the employee's suggestions and recommendations as to the hiring, firing, advancement, promotion, or any other change of status of other employees must be given particular weight

Executive Order 11246   EO 11246, the first employment-related EO, established two key requirements for federal contractors and subcontractors that have contracts in excess of $10,000 during any one-year period:

- First, these employers are prohibited from discriminating in employment decisions on the basis of race, creed, color, or national origin. This requirement reconfirmed the non-discrimination requirements established by Title VII of the Civil Rights Act of 1964.

- Second, these employers must take affirmative steps or actions in advertising open positions, recruiting, employment, training, promotion, compensation, and termination of employees to ensure the elimination of employment barriers for women and minorities (people who we might refer to today as "people of color").

exempt   An employee who is exempt from the overtime (and minimum wage) provisions of the FLSA.

exit interviews   Conversations with employees who are leaving the organization in an effort to obtain helpful, fact-based, job-related information about the departing employee's experience with the organization.

external recruiting   The process of creating a pool of qualified candidates who are not currently employed with the organization.

F

factor comparison   A quantitative job evaluation system that involves the ranking of each compensable factor of each job. A monetary value for each level with each factor is subsequently identified. Similar to the point factor method, each job is evaluated with respect to each compensable factor, and the appropriate level (with an accompanying dollar value) is selected. When all of the levels that have been selected are added together, a pay rate for each job will emerge.

Failure to Abate Prior Violation   A violation that continues beyond the prescribed abatement date. OSHA may propose a fine of up to $7,000 per day for each failure to abate prior violation.

fair employment practices agencies (FEPAs)   State or local agencies that are responsible for enforcing EEO laws that are specific to their respective jurisdiction.

Fair Labor Standards Act (FLSA)   A law that establishes standards with respect to minimum wage, record-keeping, child labor standards, and overtime pay.

FairPay   The nickname for the 2004 revisions of the FLSA.

fair use   The right to use copyrighted works without the permission of the author under certain circumstances, such as "criticism, comment, news reporting, teaching (including multiple copies for classroom use), scholarship, or research."

Family and Medical Leave Act (FMLA), 1993   The Family and Medical Leave Act (FMLA) entitles eligible employees (who work for covered employers) up to 12 weeks of unpaid, job-protected leave during any 12-month period for one or more of the following reasons:

▸ The birth and care of the newborn child of the employee

▸ Placement with the employee of a son or daughter for adoption or foster care

▸ Care for an immediate family member (spouse, child, or parent) with a serious health condition

▸ Medical leave when the employee is unable to work because of a serious health condition

Faragher v. City of Boca Raton (1998) (along with Ellerth v. Burlington Northern Industries [1998])   Key issue: Sexual harassment. Significance: If an employee is subjected to a tangible adverse employment action because of a supervisor's sexually harassing behavior, the employer is liable. The employer is also vicariously liable when its supervisors create a sexually hostile work environment even if the employee is not subjected to an adverse employment action. This is true whether or not the employer itself was negligent or otherwise at fault. However, if the employee is not subjected to tangible adverse employment action, the employer may be able to raise a defense that it acted reasonably to prevent and/or promptly correct any sexually harassing behavior, and that the plaintiff unreasonably failed to take advantage of the employer's preventive or corrective opportunities.

Fayol, Henri   Known as the father of modern management, Fayol identified five functions of a manager, now referred to as planning, organizing, coordinating, directing, and controlling.

featherbedding   An agreement that requires the employer to pay wages to union members whether or not their work is needed.

Federal Mediation and Conciliation Service (FMCS)   A resource that maintains lists of qualified arbitrators. FMCS was created by the Labor Management Relations Act (LMRA), also known as the Taft-Hartley Act.

federation   A formal group of national unions that choose to affiliate with each other. Its many members speak with one voice, thus wielding even greater influence and lobbying power. Federations do not, however, get involved with bargaining or contract administration.

feedback   Information that is provided to and discussed with an employee relative to his or her performance and the specific ways in which that performance is meeting or not meeting expectations.

fetal protection policies   Policies that are intended to protect unborn fetuses from the possibility of being harmed by teratogens. The impact of most (if not all) these policies, as ruled by the Supreme Court, is unlawful gender discrimination.

fiduciary   According to ERISA, a fiduciary is a person or entity "who exercise discretionary control or authority over plan management or plan assets, have discretionary authority or responsibility for the administration of a plan, or provide investment advice to a plan for compensation or have any authority or responsibility to do so are subject to fiduciary responsibilities." (www.dol.gov).

Plan fiduciaries could include, for example, plan trustees, plan administrators, and members of a plan's investment committee.

fiduciary responsibility   Fiduciaries are charged with running the plan(s) for which they are responsible solely in the interest of participants and beneficiaries. They must ensure that the sole purpose of the plan is and remains providing benefits to participants and beneficiaries and paying plan expenses. Fiduciaries must also act with skill, care, prudence, and diligence. For instance, they must protect plan participants by diversifying plan investments and must follow the terms of plan documents to the extent that those terms are consistent with ERISA. They also must avoid conflicts of interest, and, many would argue, even the possibility of an appearance of a conflict of interest (the same standard to which HR professionals should hold themselves, as well).

field review   A narrative performance appraisal method in which someone other than the employee's supervisor—someone from HR, for instance—prepares the performance appraisal.

financial perspective   One of the four perspectives of the balanced scorecard. The financial perspective is the most traditional of Kaplan's and Norton's four perspectives.

first-impression error/bias (interviewing) An interviewing error/bias that occurs when the interviewer places an inordinate level of emphasis on the impression that the candidate makes on him or her during the first few minutes, seconds, or even moments of the interview.

first-impression error/bias (performance management)   A performance management error/bias in which the appraiser forms an impression of the employee's performance early in the performance measurement period (or, even worse, early in the individual's employment) and places an inordinate level of emphasis on that impression.

fishbone diagram (also known as the cause-and-effect or Ishikawa diagram) An important quality tool developed by Ishikawa that presents a visual representation of factors that impact whether or not a desired outcome will be obtained. Ishikawa

believed that by presenting all of the possible factors that contribute to a particular result, any potential process imperfections can be identified in advance, and eliminated.

flexible spending accounts (FSAs)   A type of Section 125 plan. Flexible Spending Accounts (FSAs) enable employees to set aside pre-tax dollars to pay for medical expenses that are not covered by insurance. FSAs can also be set up for dependent care. Employees decide how much money to set aside for the following year, and that amount is automatically deducted from the employee's pay on a pre-tax basis. After incurring and paying for eligible expenses, employees apply for reimbursement from the FSA.

focus groups   An important vehicle for communicating with and involving employees in the organization. A focus group consists of a small but representative sample of individuals within an organization. Within each focus group, discussions are led by a neutral facilitator who seeks to elicit feedback and input on a specific subject.

for cause drug testing   Drug testing that is conducted when an employee shows obvious signs of not being fit for duty, in an effort to protect the safety and well being of employees and co-workers, and to identify opportunities for rehabilitation.

forced distribution method (also known as the forced ranking method)   A comparative performance appraisal method in which the appraiser ranks the performance of his or her direct reports so that, overall, the performance levels of all of the employees, when looked at together, reflect a bell-shaped curve.

forced ranking (also known as the forced distribution method) A comparative performance appraisal method in which the appraiser ranks the performance of his or her direct reports so that, overall, the performance levels of all of the employees, when looked at together, reflect a bell-shaped curve.

formative evaluation A process by which evaluative feedback and input is sought throughout the development and implementation phases in an effort to strengthen the ultimate training initiative through real-time incorporation of evaluative feedback.

four absolutes of quality management Phil Crosby's four absolutes of quality management include

1. Quality means conformance to requirements, not goodness.

2. Quality is achieved by prevention, not appraisal.

3. Quality has a performance standard of Zero Defects, not acceptable quality levels.

4. Quality is measured by the Price of Nonconformance, not indexes.

full cafeteria plan The most comprehensive and administratively burdensome of the three types of Section 125 plans. Employers who offer full cafeteria plans provide their employees with a specific amount of money from which they can use to pick and choose from a variety of benefits programs.

G

gainsharing Incentive plans that are designed to motivate employees to reach specific goals relating to cost-cutting or revenue generation, and that share a portion of that savings (or that increased revenue) with the employees who helped to achieve it. Gainsharing plans are based on team/group performance, not individual performance.

General Duty Clause Part of the Occupational Health and Safety Act (OSHA) that identifies two primary duties for employers (ensuring a safe workplace and complying with all current and future OSHA-related standards), and one for employees (following all safety and health-related rules stemming from the Act).

General Dynamics Land Systems v. Cline (2004) Key Issue: Age Discrimination (Relative). Significance: Younger employees (even if they are over the age of 40) cannot allege age discrimination because of the establishment of programs or decisions that favor older employees. As Justice David Souter wrote in the opening of his opinion, "The Age Discrimination in Employment Act of 1967 (ADEA or Act), 81 Stat. 602, 29 U.S.C. [section] 621 et seq., forbids discriminatory preference for the young over the old. The question in this case is whether it also prohibits favoring the old over the young. We hold it does not."

general industry One of the major industries designated by OSHA.

Global Professional in Human Resources (GPHR) The Global Professional in Human Resources certification, granted by and issued through HRCI.

goals/objectives Statements that express and communicate performance expectations in terms of "what" should be produced.

good faith bargaining Refraining from behaviors during the collective bargaining process that could constitute bad faith bargaining. The following behaviors, when demonstrated by either the union or the employer, could constitute bad faith bargaining:

- ▸ Failing to agree to meet at reasonable and convenient places and/or times

- ▸ Failing to show up at the agreed-upon places and/or times

- ▸ Repeatedly canceling meetings

- ▸ Failing to maintain an "open mind" during negotiations

- ▸ Surface bargaining: Going through the motions of bargaining, with no real intent of ultimately reaching agreement (in other words, keeping bargaining "at the surface," without moving toward true agreement).

- ▸ Repeatedly withdrawing previous positions/concessions

- ▸ Refusing to bargain on mandatory items, insisting on bargaining on permissive items, or attempting to bargain on illegal items

- ▸ Committing any sort of ULP(s)

graded vesting A vesting arrangement in which an employee earns a non-forfeitable right to an increasing percentage of his or her employer's contributions over a period of years.

grades (also referred to as pay grades or job grades) "Levels" into which jobs of similar internal worth can be categorized. Jobs within the same grade share a similar level of value or worth to the organization. Different organizations will have different numbers of pay grades, with differing degrees of distinction between each of those grades.

Griggs v. Duke Power (1971) Key issue: adverse impact. Significance: Discrimination need not be deliberate or observable in order to be real. Rather, it can exist if a particular policy or practice has a statistically significant adverse impact upon members of a protected class. This is true even when the same requirement applies to all employees or applicants, as was the situation in this case. When a particular requirement does have an impact upon members of a protected class, the burden of proof rests with the employer to demonstrate that the requirement is, in fact, job-related and consistent with business necessity.

Grutter v. Bollinger and Gratz v. Bollinger (2003) Barbara Grutter was applying for admission to the University of Michigan Law School, and Jennifer Gratz was applying for the University of Michigan as an undergraduate student. Lee Bollinger was the president of the University of Michigan.

Key issue: Affirmative action. Significance: Race can be taken into account as an admissions factor since it furthers the establishment of diversity—a "compelling state interest"—as long as the admissions process is "narrowly tailored" to achieve the objective of achieving a diverse student body.

Interestingly, Supreme Court Justice Sandra Day O'Connor indicated that cases of this sort will likely be ruled differently in the future: "Race-conscious admissions policies must be limited in time. The Court takes the Law School at its word that it would like nothing better than to find a race-neutral admissions formula and will terminate its use of racial preferences as soon as practicable. The Court expects that 25 years from now, the use of racial preferences will no longer be necessary to further the interest approved today."

These cases fall under the category of "reverse discrimination" since they alleged race discrimination and were brought by people who were not minorities/people of color.

H

halo error/bias (interviewing)   An interviewing error/bias that occurs when the interviewer evaluates the candidate positively on the basis of one outstanding qualification or characteristic.

halo error/bias (performance management)   A performance management error/bias in which the appraiser evaluates the employee positively on the basis of one outstanding qualification or characteristic.

Harris v. Forklift Systems (1993)   Key Issue: Sexual harassment. Significance: The court clarified the standard relative to what constitutes a sexually hostile work environment: "This standard, which we reaffirm today, takes a middle path between making actionable any conduct that is merely offensive and requiring the conduct to cause a

tangible psychological injury. Conduct that is not severe or pervasive enough to create an objectively hostile or abusive work environment—an environment that a reasonable person would find hostile or abusive—is beyond Title VII's purview. Likewise, if the victim does not subjectively perceive the environment to be abusive, the conduct has not actually altered the conditions of the victim's employment, and there is no Title VII violation."

hazard communication standard (also known as employee right-to-know)   Ensures that employers and employees have knowledge and awareness about hazardous chemicals located in the workplace, and that they know how to protect themselves. Specifically, this standard requires all employers having hazardous materials at the workplace to implement a written hazard communication program. Four important key elements of this program are Material Safety Data Sheets (MSDS), orientation, training, and container labeling requirements.

HBV (hepatitis B virus)   The virus that causes Hepatitis B, a potentially serious (and potentially fatal) form of liver inflammation.

HCV (hepatitis C virus)   The virus that causes Hepatitis C, a viral infection of the liver.

health and welfare benefits   A variety of non-retirement, non-mandatory benefits that can be effective ways of attracting, motivating, and retaining employees.

health and wellness programs   Programs that offer employees the opportunity to enhance the quality of their lives (usually proactively, but also reactively) through healthier lifestyle choices.

health hazards   Anything in the workplace that creates or increases the possibility of work-related injuries.

Health Insurance Portability and Accountability Act (HIPAA), 1996   An amendment to ERISA that has two primary focuses: the security and portability of health care coverage, and privacy considerations.

With respect to the security and portability of health care coverage, HIPAA was intended to help workers experience greater security and portability with respect to health care coverage, even when an employee changes jobs. HIPAA also afforded significantly greater protections for employees who have or who have a family member with a preexisting medical condition.

health maintenance organization (HMO)   A managed care model of health care and health insurance. In an HMO, each participant chooses a primary care physician, or PCP, who serves as a gatekeeper. Participants must see their PCPs first, and the PCP then decides whether to refer the patient to a specialist or for additional tests.

highly compensated employee exemption   An exemption under the FLSA. In order to qualify for a highly compensated employee exemption, an employee must

- Earn $100,000 or more annually (of which at least $455 per week must be paid on a salary or fee basis)
- Perform office or non-manual work

- Customarily and regularly perform at least one of the duties of an exempt executive, administrative, or professional employee identified in the standard tests for exemption

HIPAA covered entity   One of three groups of individuals or corporate entities (health plans, health care providers, and health care clearinghouses) that are covered by HIPAA's privacy rule, which thus requires specific actions regarding protected health information (PHI):

- Enact written PHI privacy procedures
- Designate a privacy officer
- Require business associates to sign agreements stating that they will respect the confidentiality of PHI
- Train all employees in HIPAA privacy rule requirements
- Establish a complaint handling and resolution process for issues related to the HIPAA privacy rule
- Ensure that PHI is not used for making any employment-related decisions

HIPAA privacy rule   Designed to protect patients and other consumers of health care services from the unauthorized disclosure of any personally identifiable health information (protected health information, or PHI). Health information is considered to be personally identifiable if it relates to a specifically identifiable individual.

histogram   A graph that depicts information about a single factor. In addition to being used to graphically communicate information, histograms can also sometimes help identify patterns or explanations.

HIV (human immunodeficiency virus) The virus that causes AIDS (acquired immune deficiency syndrome).

Horns error/bias (interviewing) An interviewing error/bias that occurs when the interviewer evaluates the candidate negatively on the basis of one poor qualification or characteristic.

Horns error/bias (performance management) A performance management error/bias in which the appraiser evaluates the employee negatively on the basis of one poor characteristic or dimension of performance.

hostile work environment A form of sexual harassment that occurs when unwelcome sexual conduct unreasonably interferes with an individual's job performance or creates a hostile, intimidating, or offensive work environment. Hostile work environment harassment can be found to exist whether or not the employee experiences (or runs the risk of experiencing) tangible or economic work-related consequences. By definition, hostile work environments can be created by virtually anyone with whom an employee might come in contact in the workplace.

hot cargo agreements An agreement entered into by an employer in which the employer agrees to stop doing business with another entity. Hot cargo agreements can thus help to protect union work by allowing union members to refuse to handle or process work produced by non-union entities. Hot cargo agreements were made illegal by the Landrum-Griffin Act.

hours worked "Hours worked" means "hours worked," not "hours paid." In other words, according to the FLSA, hours that have been paid but not worked (vacation time, sick time, holiday time, jury duty time, and the like) do not count towards the 40-hour overtime threshold (although some organizations may voluntarily choose to count these hours toward the 40-hour threshold). "Hours worked" also doesn't mean "hours approved to work." If an employer "suffers or permits" a non-exempt employee to work, that employee must be compensated for that time. So, whether the employer requires the employee to work or simply allows the employee to work, the time counts as "hours worked," and must be compensated appropriately.

HR audit The primary tool that many HR departments utilize to assess their own effectiveness and efficiency with respect to ascertaining how well they have aligned themselves with the organization's strategic objectives.

HRIS An integrated computer-based system that collects, processes, analyzes, stores, maintains, and retrieves information relating to all dimensions of the HR function.

human processual interventions OD interventions that seek to effect change and impact relationships within (and between) groups and individuals.

Human Resource Certification Institute (HRCI) An affiliate of SHRM, HRCI is the credentialing organization of the HR profession.

human resource development Human resource development employs effective training, development, change management, and performance management functions and initiatives to ensure that the skills, knowledge, abilities, and performance of the workforce will meet the short-term, long-term, emerging, and strategic objectives of the organization.

I

I-9   The form (mandated by IRCA) that documents an employee's identity and eligibility to legally work in the United States.

Identification of Problem Areas   The section of an affirmative action plan that provides an in-depth analysis of its total employment process to determine whether and where impediments to equal employment opportunity exist.

illegal subjects   Topics that simply cannot be the subject of collective bargaining. These would include items that would constitute a violation of the NLRA, subsequent labor laws, or for that matter any law.

Immigration Reform and Control Act (IRCA), 1986   A law that prohibits employers from discriminating against job applicants on the basis of national origin and from giving preference to U.S. citizens. IRCA also established penalties for those who knowingly hire illegal aliens (people who are referred to, by some individuals and organizations, as "undocumented workers," rather than "illegal aliens").

imminent danger   OSHA's highest priority for investigation, and defined in the Act as "any conditions or practices in any place of employment which are such that a danger exists which could reasonably be expected to cause death or serious physical harm

immediately or before the imminence of such danger can be eliminated through the enforcement procedures otherwise provided by this Act."

implementation theory   A theory that focuses on carrying out specific strategies— in this case, OD interventions—that are designed to bring about the unfreezing, moving, and refreezing through Lewin's change process theory.

implied contracts   A tort doctrine under which an employee can allege that a promise of employment has been created, even when that promise is not explicitly written or articulated. Sometimes, the language that is used within employer-published documents (electronic or hardcopy) can actually be sufficient to create a contract between the employer and the employees. An oral contract can be created when an "agent" of the employer "promises" some benefit or right. The term "agent" is legal and involved, but the point is this—be careful what your supervisors, recruiters, and others say to current, and especially to potential, employees.

incentive plans   Variable compensation plans that establish specific financial and non-financial goals and targets for individuals, groups, and organizations. In order for incentive programs to be effective, employees need to believe that they can attain the goals that have been set as part of the incentive program, and that the reward that they would earn by attaining those goals is worthwhile.

indemnity insurance   The most traditional type of medical insurance plan. Indemnity plans provide participants with (virtually) unrestricted choices relative to their doctors, hospitals, and other health care providers. Health care providers are paid a fee for the services they actual provide and perform.

independent contractor   An individual who has been retained by an organization to perform work for that organization and who is not compensated directly on that employer's payroll system.

indirect compensation   Components of total compensation that are presented to employees in forms other than cash.

individual, small group, or large group activities/applications   A training method during which the instructor provides participants with an opportunity to immediately apply the knowledge they have learned or the skills they have developed through hands-on application.

industrial relations   One of the earlier monikers by which the HR profession was known.

infectious diseases   Viral or bacterial diseases that can be transmitted from person to person.

initiating processes   Those processes (within project management) that secure approval and/or authorization to undertake the project. In general, initiating processes are considered the first of five project management processes, although there can be considerable overlap between those five distinct processes.

Injury and Illness Incident Report (also known as the OSHA Form 301)   A form that must be completed for each work-related injury or illness within seven calendar days of the date on which the employer learns of the work-related injury or illness, and must be maintained by the employee for five years following the year in which the incident or illness occurred.

integrative bargaining   An approach to collective bargaining that looks at multiple issues as a whole. Instead of just splitting up the pie, it creatively considers how it might be able to "make the pie bigger." It looks at how the needs of both sides can be better met when looked at in their entirety, and at how a "win-win" solution can be explored, rather than settling for the "win-lose" scenario that will almost invariably result from distributive bargaining. In essence, advocates of integrative bargaining believe that an agreement that renders one side "better off" does not necessarily have to result in the other side being "worse off." Instead, through creativity and cooperation, "trade offs" are sought that will ultimately benefit both sides.

integrity, or honesty, tests   Pre-employment tests that are used to ascertain the degree to which a candidate would be likely to engage in behavior that is dishonest or that reflects a potential lack of integrity.

internal audit and reporting system   An auditing system that periodically measures the effectiveness of an organization's total affirmative action program.

internal recruiting   The process of creating a pool of qualified candidates from individuals who are already employed with the organization. Two primary mechanisms for seeking internal candidates for positions within the organization are job posting and job bidding.

international labor organizations A formal group of labor organizations that operates on the international level in much the same manner as federations operate on the national level, only bigger.

interviewing error/bias Factors that are not related to a job that (when not identified and managed) can taint or impact an interviewer's assessment of a candidate.

introduction/birth The first stage of the organizational life cycle, during which excitement and energy are high, and cash flow may be low. Struggling start-ups often find themselves searching for solid footing, financially as well operationally. The core group of highly talented employees may focus fixedly on the founder as a source of direction, wisdom, and inspiration.

invasion of privacy The right to privacy is a key issue in the workplace and "work space" (meaning the electronic dimensions of the workplace as well as the physical ones). Modern tort law includes four categories of invasion of privacy, all of which employers need to be aware:

- ▶ Intrusion of solitude

- ▶ Public disclosure of private and embarrassing facts

- ▶ False light

- ▶ Appropriation of identity

involuntary terminations A decision, initiated by the employer, to end the employment relationship.

Ishikawa, Kaoru A quality guru committed to the idea of continued customer service, even after the customer purchases the product. Ishikawa also believed strongly in the criticality of securing top-level management support, and dramatically increased worldwide awareness and acceptance of the idea of quality circles, originally a Japanese philosophy.

Ishikawa diagram (also known as the "cause-and-effect" or "fishbone" diagram) An important quality tool developed by Ishikawa that presents a visual representation of factors that impact whether or not a desired outcome will be obtained. Ishikawa believed that, by presenting all of the possible factors that contribute to a particular result, any potential process imperfections can be identified in advance, and eliminated.

J

job analysis The process by which information about a specific position is collected, and through which three important outputs are generated: a job description, job specifications, and job competencies.

job bidding A system that invites employees to express interest in any internal position at any time, even if a position is not currently available.

job classification A whole job evaluation technique that categorizes jobs into broad categories, or "levels," based on the level—and, ultimately, value to the organization—of the work that is performed by jobs within each job level. Each level incorporates specific responsibilities and "benchmark statements" that describe the nature, complexity, autonomy, and so on of the work that is performed by positions in that level.

job competencies Broad categories of behavioral characteristics that are required to perform successfully in a particular position, department or organization. They are often referred to by organizations as "key success factors," "competencies for success," or "performance factors." They could include things such as "communication skills," "teamwork," and/or "judgment."

job description A document that contains information about a job, such as the essential functions, expected outputs, key accountabilities, requirements, and so forth of the position. This information is collected through the job analysis process.

job evaluation The process through which every job in an organization is assessed and compared to other jobs in the organization. At the conclusion of the job evaluation process, you will be able to ascertain the relative worth of each job within the organization. When this is done, you will have generated an overall job worth hierarchy.

job group analysis The section of an affirmative action plan that is used by non-construction contractors to begin the process of comparing the employer's representation of women and minorities to the estimated availability of qualified women and minorities who are available to be employed.

job match An external position to which an internal job is compared during the market pricing process.

job posting A system that announces position openings to current employees within the organization.

job slotting A whole job evaluation technique that incorporates or "slots" newly created or revised positions into an existing job hierarchy. This process of slotting is accomplished by comparing the new or revised job descriptions to job descriptions of positions that have already been evaluated and assigned within the hierarchy.

job-specific employment applications Employment applications that are tailored to seek highly specific and relevant information pertaining to one specific position.

job specifications The skills, knowledge, abilities, behavioral characteristics, and other credentials and experience necessary to perform a position successfully.

Johnson v. Santa Clara County Transportation Agency (1987) Key issue: Affirmative action. Significance: Gender can be used as a factor in the selection process if there is under-representation in a particular job classification, as long as the AAP does not set forth a quota.

This case falls under the category of "reverse discrimination" since it alleged sex discrimination and was brought by a man.

joint resolutions A resolution passed by the Senate as well as the House of Representatives that has the force of law once it has been either signed by the president, or passed over the veto of the president.

Juran, Joseph M. A giant in the area of quality who focused on the perspectives and the needs of customers, and whose quality management ideas focused on three key areas: quality planning, quality improvement, and quality control.

jurisdictional strikes A strike through which a union seeks to pressure an employer to assign particular work to its members, rather than to members of other unions or to non-union workers.

K–L

Kirkpatrick, Donald L. Kirkpatrick's theory takes a "summative" approach to evaluation, in that it is predicated on the interpretation of data that is collected after the initiative has been implemented. Kirkpatrick's approach, therefore, allows for a complete analysis of the entire initiative on four different levels: reaction, learning, behavior, results.

Knowles, Malcolm Identified five key assumptions about how adults learn:

- Learner's need to know

- Learner's self-concept

- Role of learner's experience

- Readiness to learn

- Orientation to learning

Kolstad v. American Dental Association (1999) Key Issue: Punitive damages under the Civil Rights Act of 1991. Significance: Punitive damages can only be awarded when the employer has acted with malice and reckless indifference to the employee's federally protected rights. This subjective standard was considered to be easier to establish than the more objective standard that would be required if employees had to prove that the nature of the actual behavior to which they had been subjected reached a level where it would be considered "egregious."

KSAs The minimally acceptable levels of knowledge, skills, and abilities required to successfully perform a position.

Labor Management Relations Act (also known as the Taft-Hartley Act), 1947 An amendment designed to remedy what the Republican Congress saw as two major omissions in the NLRA (Wagner Act): first, the identification of behaviors and practices that would be considered ULPs on the part of unions, and second, a provision that would allow the government to issue an injunction against a strike that threatened national interests. The Labor-Management Relations Act identified the following unfair labor practices that could be committed by unions:

- Restraining or coercing employees in the exercise of their rights or an employer in the choice of its bargaining representative

- Causing an employer to discriminate against an employee

- Refusing to bargain with the employer of the employees it represents

- Engaging in certain types of secondary boycotts

- Requiring excessive dues

- Engaging in featherbedding

- Picketing for recognition for more than 30 days without petitioning for an election

- Entering into hot cargo agreements

- Striking or picketing a health care establishment without giving the required notice

Labor Management Reporting and Disclosure Act (also known as the Landrum-Griffin Act), 1959 A law that created additional labor-management guidelines, including

- A requirement that unions submit annual financial reporting to the DOL, to document how union members' dues were spent

- A bill of rights for union members guaranteeing them freedom of speech and periodic secret elections

- The designation of every union official as a fiduciary

- Even stronger provisions relative to secondary boycotting and organizational and recognition picketing

labor market competitors Other employers with whom you are competing for talent.

labor relations Labor relations speaks to the many dimensions and facets of the relationship between management and groups of workers who happen represented by a labor union. In some ways, labor relations can be thought of as a subset of employee relations (see definition).

lag the market A compensation approach in which an organization chooses, by design, or simply because of budgetary constraints, to offer total compensation packages that are less competitive than the total compensation packages that are being offered by their labor market competitors. Organizations that lag the market might offset this potential disadvantage by reinforcing and maximizing the intrinsic

rewards that it offers—long-term potential growth opportunities, the ability to contribute to a particularly significant organizational mission, and so on.

Landrum-Griffin Act (also known as the Labor Management Reporting and Disclosure Act), 1959 A law that created additional labor-management guidelines, including

- A requirement that unions submit annual financial reporting to the DOL, to document how union members' dues were spent

- A bill of rights for union members guaranteeing them freedom of speech and periodic secret elections

- The designation of every union official as a fiduciary

- Even stronger provisions relative to secondary boycotting and organizational and recognition picketing

lead the market A compensation approach in which an organization offers total compensation packages that are "better" than packages being offered by their labor market competitors. Organizations that lead the market may believe that higher compensation packages will attract higher-performing employees who will, in turn, "pay for themselves," and then some. In short, these organizations want the "best of the best," and are willing to pay for it.

leadership development The strategic investment in the managers and leaders who work within the organization.

leafleting The on-site, or off-site, distribution of leaflets and flyers.

learned professional exemption   An exemption under the FLSA. In order to qualify for a learned professional exemption

- ▶ The employee's primary duty must be the performance of work requiring advanced knowledge, defined as work which is predominantly intellectual in character and which includes work requiring the consistent exercise of discretion and judgment

- ▶ The advanced knowledge must be in a field of science or learning

- ▶ The advanced knowledge must be customarily acquired by a prolonged course of specialized intellectual instruction

learning and growth perspective   One of the four perspectives of the balanced scorecard. This perspective looks at employee training, as well as attitudes toward individual and corporate growth. It emphasizes the criticality of the knowledge worker, of people as the organization's primary resource, and of the need for employees to continually grow and learn so as to be able to perform in a manner that will truly support the attainment of organizational goals.

learning level evaluation   Measures whether and to what degree participants have mastered the skills or acquired the knowledge explored through the learning objectives. "Pre-tests" and "post-tests," which are frequently seen in elearning applications, are one means of assessing skills development and knowledge acquisition.

learning organization   Ones in which individuals at all levels strive to acquire knowledge and develop skills that will enable them, individually and collectively, to attain higher levels of performance. The concept of a "learning organization" is fundamental to HRD, and is often supported through training initiatives.

learning styles   Different ways through which people learn and process ideas and information. There are three different learning styles: visual, auditory, and tactile/kinesthetic.

lecture/lecturette   A training method that includes presenting information to participants. "Lecturettes" are simply shorter versions of lectures.

leniency error/bias (interviewing)   An interviewing error/bias that occurs when the interviewer applies an inappropriately lenient standard to one or more candidates, resulting in a higher overall assessment of the candidate(s).

Leniency error/bias (performance management)   A performance management error/bias in which the appraiser applies an inappropriately lenient standard to one or more employees, resulting in a higher overall assessment of the employee's (or employees') performance.

Lewin, Kurt   Lewin first described the change process as one that involves three stages: unfreezing, moving, and refreezing.

life insurance   A health and welfare benefit that helps employees to provide their beneficiaries and loved ones with income in the event of their deaths. Many employers offer a certain amount of life insurance at no cost to employees, and offer optional supplemental life insurance, as well.

lobbying   The process of reaching out to elected officials to express beliefs and opinions with the hope of influencing a governmental body.

local union   A specific level of a union organization that is largely responsible for the day-to-day administration of the labor agreement and relationship with union members. "Locals" generally have an elected president and elected stewards who represent the workers in the workplace. Larger local unions might have a full-time paid business agent. Most locals belong to and are chartered by a larger national union.

Log of Work-Related Injuries and Illnesses (also known as the OSHA Form 300)   A form used to record the "what," "how," "when," "where," and "who" of all work-related injuries and illnesses and must be completed within seven calendar days from the time the organization learns of a work-related injury or illness.

long form employment applications   Employment applications that require candidates to provide more detailed and comprehensive information about their work history, education, and qualifications.

long-term disability insurance (LTD)   A health and welfare benefit that provides employees with the opportunity to replace a designated percentage of an employee's income that is lost through illness or injury.

long-term incentive programs   Incentive programs that area usually more than one year in duration.

M

Mackay Doctrine   The doctrine that grants employers the right to permanently replace workers who strike during an economic strike. This right and this nickname are derived from the 1938 Supreme Court decision in *NLRB v. Mackay Radio and Telegraph Co.*

maintenance of membership   Employees who voluntarily choose to join a union must maintain their individual memberships for the duration of the labor contract. Each employee then has a 30-day window at the beginning of the next contract period during which he or she may terminate membership. Maintenance of membership arrangements are illegal in right-to-work states.

major life activities   Include but are not necessarily limited to walking, seeing, hearing, breathing, caring for oneself, performing manual tasks, sitting, standing, lifting, learning, and thinking.

major restorative care   A category of dental care or coverage that includes more involved procedures such as bridgework and crowns, and that usually have a lower reimbursement percentage (perhaps 50%).

management by objectives (MBO)   A goal-centered OD intervention that focuses primarily on collaboratively generating individual employee objectives that align with organizational objectives. Measurement is an essential element of an MBO program. As follows logically, MBO is often used as a performance appraisal method due to its strong orientation toward goal establishment and attainment.

management by walking around (MBWA)   A management approach where a manager makes a commitment to spend a dedicated amount of time with employees on a regular basis. By increasing his or her visibility, the manager creates opportunities to provide feedback to and receive input from employees. Management by walking around also helps ensure that employees have increased access to "the boss," thereby increasing the potential for spontaneity, creativity, and synergy.

mandatory arbitration agreements   A type of employment agreement that stipulates that, in return for the opportunity to be employed by the organization, the employee agrees to resolve employment-related issues through a neutral third party (the arbitrator/s) instead of filing a private lawsuit against the employer.

maritime   One of the major industries designated by OSHA.

market data   Data that is collected through the process of market pricing. Market data can be obtained about a number of benchmark positions as part of a larger initiative, and can be used in a number of ways. For instance, market data can help in the building of a job worth hierarchy, around which other positions can be placed using a whole job slotting technique. Market data can also be used to obtain information for one particular job, in combination with other job evaluation techniques that might be used.

market pricing   A process of looking at the relevant labor market to ascertain what the "going rate" or "market rate" is for a particular position. Market pricing can yield valuable pay data about "benchmark" jobs—jobs for which close "matches" can be identified in the relevant labor market.

Martin v. Wilks (1988)   Key Issue: Affirmative action. Significance: Current employees who are negatively impacted by consent decrees that were established in an earlier time and which sought to resolve discrimination that was present in an earlier time may challenge the validity of such decrees.

This case falls under the category of "reverse discrimination" since it alleged race discrimination and was brought by individuals who were not minorities/people of color.

mass layoff   Occurs (under WARN) when one of the following two events happens within a 30-day period at a single worksite: 500 full-time employees are laid off, or at least 33 percent of the workforce is laid off (if and only if that 33% includes 50-499 or full-time employees).

match the market   A compensation approach in which an organization chooses to offer total compensation packages that are comparable to the total compensation packages being offered by their labor market competitors. Organizations that match the market make a conscious choice to be "externally competitive" with respect to total compensation.

material safety data sheet (MSDS)   Required (by the Hazard Communication Standard) for all chemicals located in the workplace.

maturity   The third stage of the organizational life cycle, during which the growing pains have passed and the culture is well-established. It's important to ensure that certain elements of the culture do not become a bit too well-established. If this were to happen, an "entitlement mentality" could begin to emerge relative to pay and/or benefits. The organizational structure could evolve in a somewhat rigid manner, and resistance to OD and change initiatives could be high.

McDonnell Douglas Corp v. Green (1973)   Key issue: Disparate treatment/prima facie. Significance: The initial burden of proof for establishing a prima facie (Latin for "at first view") case of discrimination against an employer (or potential employer) under Title VII of the Civil Rights Act of 1964 rests with the employee (or applicant), who must be able to establish four key elements:

▶ The person is a member of a protected class.

▶ The person applied for a job for which the employer was seeking applicants.

▶ The person was rejected, despite being qualified for the position.

▶ After this rejection, the employer continued to seek other applicants with similar qualifications.

Once the employee establishes a prima facie case for disparate treatment, the burden of proof then shifts to the employer, who must then provide a non-discriminatory reason for its decision.

McGehee and Thayer   Identified three levels of HRD/training needs analysis and assessment: organizational analysis, task or work (operations) analysis, and individual or person (man) analysis.

McKennon v. Nashville Banner Publishing Co. (1995)   Key issue: After-acquired evidence. Significance: An employer will be held accountable for discriminatory employment actions even if it discovers evidence after taking the discriminatory employment action that would have led the employer to that same employment action for legitimate, non-discriminatory reasons.

medical tests   Pre-employment medical tests, or exams, that can only be conducted if the exam is job-related and consistent with business necessity, and even then only after an offer (or a conditional offer) of employment has been extended to the candidate.

Medicare   An amendment to the Social Security Act that provides hospital and medical insurance for the elderly and people with disabilities. There are two parts to Medicare: Hospital Insurance (sometimes called Part A) and Medical Insurance (sometimes called Part B).

Medicare—Part A   The portion of Medicare that helps pay for inpatient hospital care, skilled nursing care, and other services.

Medicare—Part B   The portion of Medicare that helps pay for items such as doctor's fees, outpatient hospital visits, and other medical services and supplies.

Mental Health Parity Act (MHPA), 1996   A law that prohibits group health plans providers, insurance companies, and HMOs that offer mental health benefits from setting annual or lifetime dollar limits on mental health benefits that are lower than any such dollar limits for medical and surgical benefits.

Meritor Savings Bank v. Vinson (1986)
Key issue: Sexual harassment. Significance:
This was the first ruling to establish that
sexual harassment (whether quid pro quo or
hostile environment) constitutes a violation
of Title VII of the Civil Rights Act of 1964.
In addition, the court ruled that it isn't
enough for an organization to have a policy
prohibiting discrimination. Instead, the ruling stated that "reasonable care requires
effective communication of policies and
training. The employer has the burden of
proof."

**Mine Safety and Health Act (MSH Act),
1977** The second piece of legislation created specifically to protect employee health
and safety—this time, for underground and
surface miners working in coal as well as
non-coal mines.

minimum wage The lowest hourly rate of
pay that an employer can legally pay an
employee.

mission A statement that articulates, in
essence, the reason why the organization is
in existence. It may speak to the nature of
the organization's business or purpose, its
customers, and sometimes even its employees and its role in the community. A mission
statement should be broad (but not overly
generalized), brief, clear, unambiguous, and
designed to last for "the long haul."

moving The second stage in Lewin's
change process theory. Through the moving
stage, people are brought to accept the
change and experience the "new state" that
the change was designed to bring about.

multiple linear regression A mathematical technique that examines the past
relationship between several variables,
determines the statistical strength of that
relationship, and, on the basis of that analysis, projects future conditions.

musculoskeletal disorders (MSDs)
Work-related illnesses and/or injuries that
affect one or more parts of the musculoskeletal system.

N

narrative method Performance appraisal
method in which the appraiser uses a narrative format to write and record observations
and assessments of each employee's
performance.

National Industrial Recovery Act, 1933
A law that guaranteed laborers the right to
organize and bargain collectively (Title I).
The Act also established that employees
could not be required, as a condition of
employment, to join or refrain from joining
a labor organization. In May of 1935, the
National Industrial Recovery Act was held
unconstitutional by the U.S. Supreme Court
(*Schechter Poultry Corp. v. United States*).
Although this decision was wholly unrelated
to labor and collective bargaining, the
Supreme Court decision rendered the labor-
related provisions illegal, as well. The right
to organize and bargain reverted, once
again, back to railway workers, and no one
else. This would not, however, be the case
for long.

**National Labor Relations Act (also
known as the Wagner Act), 1935** A law
that guaranteed "the right to self-organization, to form, join, or assist labor
organizations, to bargain collectively
through representatives of their own

choosing, and to engage in concerted activities for the purpose of collective bargaining or other mutual aid and protection." Certain groups or categories of employees are excluded under the NLRA from membership in a bargaining unit. Examples would include managers, supervisors, confidential employees (essentially secretaries and administrative assistants to managers who can make labor relations decisions), and several others.

National Labor Relations Board (NLRB)
A federal agency created by the NLRA that is responsible for administering and enforcing the rights established by the NLRA. As stated on its website, the NLRB has two principle functions:

▸ To determine, through secret-ballot elections, the free democratic choice by employees whether they wish to be represented by a union in dealing with their employers and if so, by which union

▸ To prevent and remedy unlawful acts, called unfair labor practices, by either employers or unions

national union   A specific level of a union organization that brings together all of the union locals for a particular group that are scattered across the country. There are usually different hierarchical levels in between the local union and the national union. National unions have far more power with respect to bargaining and political influence than the union locals could have on their own. National unions also advise and guide local unions, and may also manage nationwide benefits programs (such as retirement programs and health insurance plans).

The Needlestick Safety and Prevention Act of 2000   A compliance directive for enforcing the Bloodborne Pathogens Standard that added three key requirements to the existing standard:

▸ Evaluation and implementation of safer needle devices (as they become available). Reviews of and searches for such enhancements must be done annually.

▸ Actively involve employees who actually use needles and needle devices in this evaluation and selection process of safer needle devices.

▸ Maintenance of a log of all injuries resulting from contaminated sharps.

negligent hiring   A tort doctrine that speaks to en employer's decision to hire an individual without engaging in appropriate "due diligence" into that candidate's credentials, prior work experience, and the like. In essence, negligent hiring claims arise after an individual is hired through a flawed hiring process. A hiring process can be flawed for a number of reasons. For instance, a sound hiring process that is applied in an unsound manner would be flawed, as would a hiring process that is designed in a flawed manner. Flaws could relate to inadequate or poorly conducted reference checks, job requirements that do not reflect the skills or credentials that are truly required for a position, and the like.

negligent referral   A tort doctrine that speaks to the failure of an organization to reveal truthful, negative information about an employee (or former employee) to a potential employer.

negligent retention   A tort doctrine that speaks to the continued employment of an individual who is performing in an unfit manner and, therefore, should have been terminated. Negligent retention tort claims might be filed when an employee who should have been terminated, but was not, inflicts some sort of harm on another person. Negligent retention claims are often filed in conjunction with other tort claims, such as negligent training, intentional infliction of emotional distress, and the like.

negligent training   A tort doctrine that refers to an employer's failure to provide proper training to an employee, when that failure results in some sort of unfit performance by the employee.

Negligent training can emerge as an issue either when an employee who was hired for one position assumes another position for which he or she may not be fully and appropriately trained, or when an employee's job duties and responsibilities change over time, thus requiring additional training if the employee is to continue performing the job in a fit manner.

NLRB v. Mackay Radio and Telegraph Co. (1938)   The Supreme Court case that established that employers have the right to permanently replace workers who strike during an economic strike.

NLRB v. Weingarten (1975)   Weingarten Rights, derived from the Supreme Court decision in *NLRB v. Weingarten* (1975), established the right of unionized employees to have union representation at an investigatory interview with management if the employee reasonably believes that discipline might result from that meeting. Although the NLRB reversed this decision in 2000

(Epilepsy Foundation of Northeast Ohio, 331 NLRB 676) and held that non-union employees also have the right to have a representative present at a meeting of this sort, in 2004 the NLRB returned to its original determination and held that non-union employees do not have the right to have a co-worker or other representative present in a meeting when the employee reasonably believes it might result in discipline.

nominal group technique   A non-mathematical forecasting technique that calls upon the expertise and predictive ability of experts who meet in person and process their ideas as a group. Led by a facilitator, the meeting begins with each expert writing down his or her ideas, after which each expert presents those ideas to the group. The group then comes together to discuss each others' ideas, after which each individual group member is called upon to independently rank the ideas. The meeting facilitator will then combine all of the individual rankings to determine which are the most important to the group.

non-compete agreements   A type of employment agreement that prohibits current and (within stated limitations) former employees from competing against the employer. "Competing" can manifest itself in a number of different ways, and must be defined within the agreement.

nondirective interviews   Relatively unstructured interviews through which the candidate, not the interviewer, guides and controls the flow and content of information.

non-exempt   An employee who is covered by the overtime (and minimum wage) provisions of the FLSA.

non-quantitative job evaluation techniques Job evaluation techniques that determine the relative value of jobs within the organization without using mathematical techniques. Instead, these methods focus on the "whole job" (which is why these techniques are also referred to as "whole job" methods).

nontraditional staffing alternatives Work arrangements that do not fall clearly within "internal" or "external" recruiting methods, since they could be used as a retention tool for existing employees, as a way to attract candidates, or as a way to outsource current assignments. Examples of non-traditional staffing alternatives could include the use of temporary help, temp-to-hire arrangements, or consultants. Current or newly hired employees can also participate in flexible staffing programs through part-time employment, telecommuting, job sharing arrangements, or seasonal employment.

nonverbals Also known as "body language," communication that is not based on spoken language.

Norris-LaGuardia Act, 1932 A law that strengthened unions even more by establishing the rights of labor unions to organize and to strike. It is also prohibited federal courts from enforcing "yellow dog" contracts or agreements.

O

occupational health, safety, and security Occupational health, safety, and security promotes employees' physical and mental well-being while maintaining a safe and non-violent work environment, all in support of the employer's short-term, long-term, emerging, and strategic objectives.

Occupational Safety and Health Act (OSH Act), 1970 The first law to establish consistent health and safety standards for the workplace.

Occupational Safety and Health Administration (OSHA) The federal agency created to administer and enforce the Occupational Safety and Health Administration Act (OSH Act).

offshoring A specific type of outsourcing that utilizes vendors that are located overseas.

Old Age, Survivors, and Disability Insurance (OASDI) (also known as the Social Security Act) Old Age, Survivors, and Disability Insurance program (OASDI) is a social insurance program (although some would define it differently) that is funded through payroll taxes. Its three primary components are retirement income, disability benefits, and survivor's benefits.

Older Worker's Benefit Protection Act (OWBPA), 1990 An amendment to the ADEA that makes it illegal to discriminate against older workers with respect to benefits, or to target older workers for layoffs.

onboarding (also known as orientation) The process by which a new employee is supported as he or she transitions into the organization.

open door policy A "standing invitation," and a genuine one, for employees to raise their concerns with managers and/or human resources, face to face. The use of an "open door" cannot result in penalties, formal or otherwise, against those employees who avail themselves of this resource.

open shop Employees are required neither to join the union nor to pay union dues. This is the only type of union security clause that is legal in right-to-work states (and for federal government employees).

operational/tactical HR Somewhere in between the administrative functions that must be performed to keep our organizations going and the inventive and creative life force that is part of strategic management lays the operational or tactical dimension of the HR function. The operational, tactical, or day-to-day performance and execution of the HR role can be accomplished in many different ways, some of which do more to define us toward the administrative end of the spectrum, and others that demonstrate more vividly how and whether the overarching strategic objectives of HR (and, therefore, of the organization) are being brought to life. Operational/tactical level HR is one leg of the HR stool—the other two legs are Strategic HR and transformational HR.

organization development (OD) The planned and structured process through which the overall performance, growth, and effectiveness of an organization is enhanced through strategic, deliberate, and integrated initiatives. The interesting and complex area of OD incorporates four academic disciplines: psychology, sociology, anthropology, and management.

organization transformation change OD interventions that focus on the organization as a complex human system that must be continually examined and reexamined.

organizational culture The "soul" of the organization; the "way things are done around here"; the formal and informal manifestation of what the organization "is all about." Organizational culture encompasses historical events, current events, and future events (whether potential, likely, or simply rumored). More specifically, organizational culture reflects and embodies the norms, mores, values, beliefs, customs, and attitudes of the organization and of those who work within the organization.

organizational display The section of an affirmative action plan that essentially provides an organization chart that depicts the contractor's workforce in terms of incumbents' race, gender, and wages. The organization display is the newer, shorter, and simpler version of the "workforce analysis."

organizational (or business) ethics A shared values-based system designed to inculcate within the organization's population a sense of how to conduct business properly.

organizational level analysis Level 1 of McGehee and Thayer's three levels of HRD/training needs analysis and assessment. Organizational level analysis determines where HRD/training can and should be used within the overall organization.

organizational life cycle Four evolutionary stages of birth, growth, maturity, and decline experienced by organizations over the course of time. These phases or stages are roughly approximate to the phases of life experienced by humans, thereby further bolstering the perspective of the organization as a living, breathing entity. Each phase of the organizational life cycle will warrant different HR systems or interventions.

organizational picketing Picketing that is designed to generate interest on the part of employees to vote for union representation.

organizational structure The various ways in which organizations can be designed to as to attain maximum levels of effectiveness and efficiency.

organizing function Identified by Fayol as one of the five management functions, organizing speaks to the ways in which the manager obtains and arranges the resources that he or she needs to implement the plans (the output of the "planning" function). Those resources could include people, facilities, materials, and so on.

orientation (also known as onboarding) The process by which a new employee is supported as he or she transitions into the organization.

orthodonture A specialty type of dental coverage that is often covered at a relatively low percentage (perhaps 50%) and that often has a lifetime cap per covered employee.

OSHA 3165 A poster that lists each employee's rights related to health and safety. This poster must be displayed in a conspicuous place that is easily visible to employees and applicants for employment.

OSHA Form 300 (also known as the Log of Work-Related Injuries and Illnesses) A form used to record the "what," "how," "when," "where," and "who" of certain work-related injuries and illnesses, and that must be completed within seven calendar days from the time the organization learns of a work-related injury or illness.

OSHA Form 300A (also known as the Summary of Work-Related Injuries and Illnesses) A form used to record a numeric summary of all work-related injuries and illnesses logged in OSHA's Form 300 over the course of each calendar year. This form indicates the number of cases, the number of workdays impacted, and the numbers and types of work-related injuries and illnesses. A worksheet is also available to assist employers in filling out this summary. Each year, a completed Form 300 must be posted conspicuously for three months (between February 1 and April 30).

OSHA Form 301 (also known as the Injury and Illness Incident Report) A form that must be completed for each work-related injury or illness within seven calendar days of the date on which the employer learns of the work-related injury or illness, and that must be maintained by the employee for five years following the year in which the incident or illness occurred.

other-than-serious violation A violation that is unlikely to result in serious injury or death. OSHA may propose a fine of up to $7000 for each other-than-serious violation.

outside sales exemption An exemption under the FLSA. Unlike the other types of exemptions, a minimum salary is not required to establish an exemption on the basis of outside sales. The following criteria, however, must be met:

▶ The employee's primary duty must be making sales (as defined in the FLSA) or obtaining orders or contracts for services or for the use of facilities for which a consideration will be paid by the client or customer

▶ The employee must be customarily and regularly engaged away from the employer's place or places of business

outsourcing   The reassignment of responsibilities, functions, or jobs that had been performed within the organization to now be carried out by resources that are outside the organization ("third-party contractors").

overtime   Hours worked in excess of 40 per week.

P

paired comparison method   A comparative performance appraisal method in which the appraiser compares every employee in the group, one at a time, to every other employee in the group.

panel interviews   Interviews in which more than one person interviews a candidate at the same time.

Pareto Principle (also known as the 80-20 rule)   A principle that asserts that 80% of effects result from 20% of causes. The Pareto principle and the chart that visually depicts it are intended to help individuals focus their efforts where there is the greatest likelihood of bringing about the desired change.

pay for time not worked   Programs that pay employees for time that they did not actually work (for instance, sick days, vacation days, jury duty, personal time, designated holidays, floating holidays, bereavement leave, and the like).

pay grades (also referred to as grades or job grades)   "Levels" into which jobs of similar internal worth can be categorized. Jobs within the same pay grade share a similar level of value or worth to the organization. Different organizations will have different numbers of pay grades, with differing degrees of distinction between each of those grades.

pay structures   The "building blocks" that are used to create compensation systems that will support the total compensation philosophy of the organization, and that will, in turn, support the attainment of the organization's objectives.

pedagogy   The study and science of how children learn.

Pension Benefit Guaranty Corporation (PBGC)   A government corporation created by ERISA that functions as an insurer that provides a minimum guaranteed benefit for certain pension plans. PBGC protects participants in most defined benefit plans and cash balance plans (within certain limitations). PBGC is funded by insurance premiums that are paid by plan sponsors, not by general tax dollars. Funding also comes from investment income, assets from underfunded pension plans it has taken over, and recoveries from companies formerly responsible for those plans.

performance appraisal   The form that is reviewed during the meeting that takes place at the end of the performance measurement period, during which the manager and the employee review the employee's performance during the prior year and look ahead to the next year.

performance management   Day-to-day activities in which managers engage with their employees as they work to collaboratively accomplish organizational objectives.

performance standards/expectations   The expectations that an organization has for an employee with respect to the ways in which the employee executes his or her position.

permissive subjects (also known as voluntary subjects)   "Permissive" subjects of bargaining are topics that can be submitted to collective bargaining if and only if the employer and the employees' representative are willing to do so. Attempting to force bargaining on a voluntary or permissive subject constitutes a ULP.

perpetuating past discrimination   Unlawful discrimination that occurs when an employer's past discriminatory practices are perpetuated through current policies or practices, even those that appear to be non-discriminatory. When linked in some way with past discrimination, seemingly nondiscriminatory practices can have a discriminatory effect.

person (man) level analysis   Level 3 of McGehee and Thayer's three levels of HRD/training needs analysis and assessment. Person (man) level analysis assesses performance of a particular individual.

personality tests   Pre-employment tests that are used to gather information about a candidate's personality traits, motivation, discipline, and other characteristics.

phone interviews   A telephone-based pre-screen interview that is used as one important tool to determine which candidates will be invited in for a face-to-face interview.

physical hazards—design   A physical hazard that results from the way in which the workplace or workspace is designed (also referred to as ergonomics).

physical health hazards   A type of health hazard that results from actual, tangible "things" and/or conditions in the workplace that increase the risk of work-related illnesses or injuries.

picketing   An expression of free speech that takes place when people congregate outside a workplace. In order to be considered protected concerted activity, picketing must remain non-violent.

piece-rate systems   Compensation programs under which individuals are paid according to their production volume.

pilot programs   A training program that is generally delivered to a subsection of the population of individuals who would ultimately be expected to participate in the training initiative. Others who might also participate in a pilot program could be decision makers, senior management (from whom you wish to secure buy-in), and other key stakeholders.

placement goals   The section of an affirmative action plan that establishes goals for areas in which underutilization exists.

plaintiff   A party who files a lawsuit alleging unlawful discrimination.

planning function   Identified by Fayol as one of the five management functions, planning lays the groundwork for how managers will work toward accomplishing the organization's goals. Through planning, managers decide what needs to get done, when it needs to get done, who will do it, how it will get done, and where it will be done.

planning processes   Those processes (within project management) through which objectives are established, along with the best alternatives that will support the attainment of those objectives. In general, planning processes are considered the second of five project management processes, although there can be considerable overlap between those five distinct processes.

plant closing   Occurs (under WARN) when a facility or operating unit is shut down for more than six months, or when 50 or more employees at a worksite lose their jobs during any 30-day period.

plant patents   Granted for the invention, discovery, or asexual reproduction of any distinct and new variety of plant.

point factor   A quantitative job evaluation system that first identifies specific compensable factors and then establishes levels of performance within each of those compensable factors. The relative importance of each compensable factor to the organization is "weighted," and a different point value is then assigned to each level within each compensable factor.

point of service (POS)   A type of managed healthcare plan that is a combination of the HMO and PPO managed care models. Like the PPO model, there is a network of physicians and health care providers who have agreed to provide services at a discounted rate. Like the HMO model, there is a gatekeeper, a primary care physician who must provide plan members with referrals to specialists and for other services. Unlike the HMO model, however, referrals can be made to physicians who are either inside or outside the network. While out-of-network

referrals will cost participants more, they are permissible.

Portal to Portal Act, 1947   An amendment to the FLSA that offered clearer definitions of "hours worked" for purposes of minimum wage and overtime payments. According to the Act, employers are only required to compensate workers for working time that they spend on activities that relate to the performance of their job.

post-accident drug testing   Drug testing that is conducted for employees who are involved in an accident or unsafe practice incident to determine whether alcohol or some other drug was a factor, to protect the safety of employees (users and non-users), and to identify opportunities for rehabilitation.

predictive validity   The degree to which the predictions made by a selection procedure actually manifest themselves through future performance.

preemployment drug testing   Drug testing that is conducted to decrease the likelihood of hiring someone who is currently using/abusing illegal drugs.

preexisting condition   Under HIPAA, a condition for which medical advice, diagnosis, care, or treatment was recommended or received during the six-month period prior to an individual's enrollment date.

preferred provider organization (PPO)   A managed care healthcare plan that offers a network of health care providers who band together to offer services at a discounted rate to plan participants. PPOs resemble indemnity plans, in that network providers are paid when they render services and plan participants can choose which doctors they want to visit and when they want to visit them. Plan participants can also choose to avail themselves of doctors or other health care providers who are outside the network; however, the costs to the member will be higher than they would have been if the member had chosen a doctor within the network.

Pregnancy Discrimination Act, 1978   A law that amended Title VII of the Civil Rights Act of 1964 to specifically prohibit discrimination on the basis of pregnancy, childbirth, or related medical conditions.

premium-only plans (POPs)   The simplest and most transparent (from employees' perspectives) of the three Section 125 plans. With POPs, employees pay for their portion of certain insurance premiums on a pre-tax basis. The net effect is that each employee's taxable income is reduced, which is how employers and employees can reduce taxes and save money.

prepromotion drug testing   Drug testing that is conducted to decrease the likelihood of promoting someone who is currently using/abusing illegal drugs.

prescreen interviews   An interview used early in the selection process to determine which candidates meet specific pre-determined job requirements.

prescription drug coverage   A health and welfare benefit that affords employees with discounted or (less frequently) free prescription drugs. Some employers provide prescription drug coverage as part of their medical plan, while others provide this coverage under a separate plan. Plan members may be required to pay a co-pay, to purchase their prescriptions at certain

pharmacies, to use generic drugs (when available), or to use "mail order" services for maintenance drugs (prescriptions that are prescribed for chronic, long-term conditions and that are taken on a regular, recurring basis).

preventive care   A category of dental care or coverage that includes things such as regular dental checkups, exams, cleanings, and sometimes X-rays. It is often reimbursed at 100% of cost or at 100% of reasonable and customary (R&C) expenses, so as to encourage plan members to take advantage of measures that encourage good oral health and that potentially decrease long-term costs.

primary care physician (PCP)   A member's primary physician, who in HMO and POS models is the "gatekeeper" who must provide plan members with referrals to specialists and for other services.

primary duty   The principal, main, major, or most important duty that the employee performs. Determination of an employee's primary duty must be based on all the facts in a particular case, with the major emphasis being on the character of the employee's job as a whole.

primary questions   Questions that are asked of all candidates for a particular position during a particular interview process. They are designed to elicit relevant information about how well the candidate possesses and would demonstrate the skills, knowledge, abilities, behavioral characteristics, and other requirements of the position.

primary research   A process that involves collecting data firsthand from the original source from which it emanates.

privacy case In an effort to preserve privacy, under certain circumstances (including upon employee request), the words "privacy case" should be substituted for the employee's name in the OSHA Form 300 (also known as the Log of Work-Related Injuries and Illnesses). In these cases, a separate document must be maintained that matches case numbers with employee names (for identification purposes).

probing questions The questions that an interviewer asks as a way of following up to the candidate's response to primary questions. Since they are asked in response to each candidate's initial response to the primary question, probing questions will vary from interview to interview. Interviews can still ensure consistency, however, by only asking probing questions that relate to each original primary question.

Professional in Human Resources (PHR) The Professional in Human Resources certification, granted by and issued through HRCI.

profit sharing Organizationwide incentive plans that establish an organizationwide profit goal. If the goal is reached, the profits are shared with employees. Profits can either be shared immediately (cash profit sharing plans) or later (deferred profit sharing plans).

profit sharing plans A type of defined contribution plan under which the organization contributes to its employees' accounts. These contributions often come from profits, and thus serve as an incentive to performance.

progressive discipline A system that incorporates a series of steps—each more progressively "involved," advanced, or serious, than the last—for addressing performance or behavior that does not meet expectations. Progressive discipline provides multiple opportunities, at multiple decision points, for employees to make decisions that will result in them maintaining their employment. When applied appropriately, therefore, progressive discipline can be an empowering process as well as an employee relations initiative.

project management "The application of knowledge, skills, tools, and techniques to a broad range of activities in order to meet the requirements of a particular project" (Project Management Institute).

protected class A group defined by a common characteristic that is protected from discrimination and harassment on the basis of law. People who share a common characteristic and who are protected from discrimination and harassment on the basis of that shared characteristic are said to belong to a protected class.

protected concerted activity Protected concerted activity refers to associational rights that are granted to employees through Section 7 of the NLRA. Protected concerted activity can include activity aimed at improving employees' terms and conditions of employment. Through this language, the NLRA protects associational rights for employees who do not belong to a union as well as for employees who are non-unionized. This interpretation was confirmed by *NLRB v. Phoenix Mutual Life Insurance Co.*, 1948. As such, employers need to be careful not to interfere with protected concerted activities even in workplaces that are non-unionized workplaces.

public domain Copyrights eventually expire, upon which the work enters the public domain. This means that the work is available and free for all to use.

Q

qualified domestic relations order (QDRO) Court orders that require employers to make benefit payments to a participant's former spouse (or another alternative payee) without violating ERISA's prohibitions against assignment or alienation of benefits.

qualified person A candidate who meets minimum job requirements (education, experience, licences, and so forth) and can perform the essential functions of the position with or without reasonable accommodation.

quantitative job evaluation techniques Job evaluation techniques that determine the relative value of jobs within the organization without using mathematical techniques. Quantitative (or "factor based") job evaluation methods identify the degree to which each position is responsible for or requires specific "compensable factors."

quid pro quo A form of sexual harassment that occurs when an individual's submission to or rejection of sexual advances or conduct of a sexual nature is used as the basis for employment-related decisions. Quid pro quo harassment, by nature, originates from a supervisor or from others who have the authority to influence or make decisions about the terms and conditions of the employee's employment.

R

Railway Labor Act, 1926 A law that provided what was perhaps the first "win-win scenario" for labor and management. Railroad management wanted to keep the trains moving, which meant they needed to end "wildcat" strikes. Railroad workers wanted to organize, to be recognized as the exclusive bargaining agent in dealing with the railroad, and to negotiate and enforce agreements. The Railway Labor Act addressed both issues. The Railway Labor Act is also significant in that it is where the "work now, grieve later" rule originated. In an effort to keep the rails running, which Congress felt was in the public's interest, Congress mandated that when disputes arise in the workplace, transportation workers covered by the RLA must "work now and grieve later" (with a few exceptions, such as for safety).

The Railway Labor Act applied only to interstate railroads and their related undertakings—at the time, the most critical element of the nation's transportation infrastructure. In 1936, it was amended to include airlines engaged in interstate commerce.

random drug testing Unannounced drug tests that are conducted at random, for reasons related to safety or security.

range spread The percentage that is calculated by subtracting the minimum of the range from the maximum of the range, and dividing that number by the minimum of the range. Range spreads allow organizations to recognize and compensate employees within the same job and within jobs that are in the same grade, for different levels of skill, experience, or performance.

ranges   A range of compensation rates that correspond to grades and that guide the pay rates for jobs within that grade. Ranges specify the lowest ("minimum") and the highest ("maximum") compensation rates for which positions within each grade are generally paid. The halfway point between those two figures is known as the "midpoint."

ranking method   A comparative performance appraisal method in which the appraiser literally "ranks" his or her direct reports, in terms of overall performance, from "best" to "worst."

rapport   The process of helping a candidate to relax and feel comfortable and welcome at the beginning of the interview.

rating methods   Performance appraisal methods in which the appraiser compares the performance of the employee against the expected behavior.

rating scales   A type of performance appraisal in which the appraiser rates the employee on a variety of different categories using a three-, four-, or five-point scale. Those categories can consist of individual goals, individual competencies, multiple goals, groups of competencies, and the like. Each point on the scale corresponds to a different level of performance against standards.

ratio analysis   A mathematical technique that examines changes, movements, and trends over a period of time. Instead of looking at just one variable alone, however, it looks at two variables and how the relationship between those two variables has evolved over time.

reaction level evaluation   Measures participants' responses and reactions to a program immediately after it has been delivered. This level of evaluation often takes the form of a short survey that participants are asked to complete at the end of a training session.

reading   A training method during which the instructor/facilitator directs the participants to read specific printed materials.

realistic job preview   A realistic picture of the position and the organization (that is provided to candidates). This, in turn, will help the candidate make a realistic and accurate assessment of whether he or she will be willing and/or able to function effectively within the day-to-day realities of the position, the department or unit, and the organization.

reasonable accommodation   A change in the way that one (or more) responsibilities relating to the execution of a position is performed, so as to enable a person with a disability to perform the essential functions of the position. Accommodations do not necessarily have to be adopted if they cause undue hardship to the organization.

reasonable cause   A determination made by the EEOC relative to whether discrimination has occurred. If the EEOC determines that there is no reasonable cause, the case is closed, the parties are notified, and the charging party is given a "right to sue" letter. The charging party then has 90 days to file a private lawsuit.

If the EEOC determines that there is reasonable cause, the EEOC will attempt conciliation with the employer in an effort to develop a remedy for the discrimination. If the EEOC cannot conciliate the case, the EEOC will decide whether to take the case to court (this happens in a very small percentage of cases). If the EEOC does not take the case to court, it will close the case and issue the charging party a "right to sue" letter.

reasonable suspicion drug testing   Drug testing that is conducted when an employee has a documented pattern of unsafe work behavior in an effort to protect the safety and well being of employees and co-workers, and to identify opportunities for rehabilitation.

recency error/bias (interviewing)   An interviewing error/bias that occurs when the interviewer recalls recently interviewed candidates more vividly than candidates who were interviewed earlier in the process.

recency error/bias (performance management)   A performance management error/bias in which the appraiser places undue emphasis on the employee's most recent performance, rather than considering performance demonstrated throughout the entire performance measurement period.

recertification   The process by which HR professionals who have earned PHR, SPHR, and/or GPHR certification maintain the currency of that status.

recruiting   The process of attracting and creating a pool of qualified candidates.

refreezing   The third and final stage in Lewin's change process theory. Through the refreezing stage, people come to experience that what once represented a change has now become, in simplest terms, the norm.

Regents of California v. Bakke (1978)
Key issue: Affirmative action. Significance: The Supreme Court ruled that while race could be a factor in college admission decisions, quotas could not be established.

Although this case was based on a college admissions program, its significance extended to workplace affirmative action programs.

This case falls under the category of "reverse discrimination" since it alleged race discrimination and was brought by someone who was not a minority/person of color.

regular rate of pay   An employee's regular rate of pay includes more than just his or her hourly rate of pay; it would also include any incentives and commissions. It would not, however, include bonuses (which, unlike incentive programs, are discretionary), pay for time not worked, premium pay for weekend or holiday work, and the like.

Rehabilitation Act (1973)   A law that prohibits discrimination on the basis of physical and mental disabilities.

Section 503 of the Act requires affirmative action and prohibits employment discrimination by federal government contractors and subcontractors with contracts of more than $10,000.

Section 504 of the Act states that "no otherwise qualified individual with a disability in the United States shall be excluded from, denied the benefits of, or be subjected to discrimination under" any program or activity that either receives federal financial assistance or is conducted by any executive agency or the United States Postal Service.

Section 508 requires that federal agencies' electronic and information technology is accessible to people with disabilities, including employees and members of the public.

relevant labor market   The size and scope of the geographic area within which an organization would seek to attract qualified candidates. Even within the same organization, the relevant labor market for different positions can vary widely depending upon the skills, knowledge, abilities, and behavioral characteristics required to perform each position successfully. Other factors that impact how an organization defines the relevant labor market might be the degree of competition that exists among employers for particular skills and/or knowledge, and the degree to which certain skills and/or knowledge requirements are industry-specific.

reliability   The degree to which a selection process or instrument is consistent.

relief   When a plaintiff prevails in an EEO lawsuit, he or she may be awarded various forms of "relief" or remedies.

relocation   The process of moving a current or existing employee's primary residence from one location to another.

remedies   When a plaintiff prevails in an EEO lawsuit, he or she may be awarded various forms of remedies or "relief."

repeat violation   A violation that is the same or substantially similar to a violation that was found during a previous inspection. OSHA may propose a fine of up to $70,000 for each repeat violation.

repetitive stress injuries (RSIs) (also known as cumulative trauma syndromes [CTSs] or cumulative trauma disorders [CTDs])   Injuries that result from placing too much stress (often through overuse) on a part of the body.

replacement charts   Tools that identify names of individuals who could potentially fill a particular position in the event that an opening were to occur.

request for proposal (RFP)   A request to potential vendors to propose solutions to address specific requirements identified in the RFP document.

required subjects   Subjects that must be bargained in good faith if either the employer or the employees' representative requests it. Examples of required subjects include pay, wages, hours of employment, pensions for present employees, bonuses, group insurance, grievance procedures, safety practices, seniority, procedures for discharge, layoff, recall, or discipline, and union security.

research   Finding answers to questions.

respondent   The person or party against whom a charge of unlawful discrimination has been filed.

responsibility   One of the four factors used as a basis to assess the substantial equality of job content under the Equal Pay Act of 1963. "Responsibility" refers to the degree of responsibility and accountability that an employer entrusts to and expects from a particular position.

restorative care   A category of dental care or coverage that refers to oral "repairs" that are usually of a relatively minor nature, such as cavities or root canals. The reimbursement for restorative care is generally less than the reimbursement rate for preventive care (perhaps 80% instead of 100%).

results level evaluation   Looks specifically at whether the business or organizational results that were expected to occur as a result of training did in fact occur. This level of results-based evaluation is measurable, concrete, and usually of keen interest to the leaders of the organization, since results speak volumes.

retained employment agencies   Search firms to whom an organization pays a fee whether or not the organization actually hires a candidate referred by the firm. The services of this type of agency are more often secured in an effort to fill executive level positions.

retirement benefits   One of the three primary components of the Social Security Act.

Retirement Equity Act, 1984   An amendment to ERISA that incorporated a number of key revisions, many of which addressed the concerns of former (in the event of divorce) and surviving (in the event of death) spouses.

Revenue Act, 1978   Among many other changes, the Revenue Act added two sections to the tax code that essentially resulted in the creation of two new and ultimately very important employee benefits: Section 125 plans and 401(k) plans.

right-to-know (also known as the employee hazard communication standard)   Ensures that employers and employees have knowledge and awareness about hazardous chemicals located in the workplace, and that they know how to protect themselves. Specifically, this standard requires all employers having hazardous materials at the workplace to implement a written Hazard Communication Program. Four important key elements of this program are Material Safety Data Sheets (MSDS), orientation, training, and container labeling requirements.

right to sue letter   A letter issued by the EEOC that entitles the recipient (the charging party) to bring a private lawsuit within the specified time frame.

right-to-work states   States in which union shops and closed shops are illegal. In a right-to-work state, no employee has to join the union.

role play   A training method that is similar to case studies and can even be designed to be the natural "culmination" of a case study. Role plays, in one sense, take case studies one step farther, in that participants actually "act out" the ways in which they would apply the knowledge and practice the skills in particular situations.

S

safe harbor provisions   Provisions under which an employer that has made improper salary deductions can protect itself from losing the exemption. In order to do so, the employer would be required to

- Have a clearly communicated policy prohibiting improper deductions and including a complaint mechanism
- Reimburse employees for any improper deductions

▶ Make a good faith commitment to comply in the future

safety committees A vehicle through which employees and managers can collaboratively work to increase workplace safety.

salary A predetermined amount of compensation that an employee will be paid per week.

salting Activity engaged in by a "salt," a union organizer who seeks employment with the organization for the express purpose of actively organizing and campaigning within the organization.

Sarbanes-Oxley Act (SOX), 2002 A law designed to protect investors, SOX enacted reforms designed to enhance corporate responsibility and financial disclosures, and to combat corporate and accounting fraud.

Schechter Poultry Corp. v. United States (1935) A Supreme Court case that rendered the National Industrial Recovery Act unconstitutional. Although this decision was wholly unrelated to labor and collective bargaining, the Supreme Court decision rendered the labor-related provisions illegal, as well. The right to organize and bargain reverted, once again, back to railway workers, and no one else. This would not, however, be the case for long.

scientific method A form of primary research that consists of a systematic approach of testing hypotheses and using the knowledge generated to strengthen the degree to which HR can support the overall objectives of the organization.

secondary boycott Efforts to convince others to stop doing business with a particu-

lar organization that is the subject of a primary boycott.

secondary research A process that involves collecting information "second-hand," meaning not directly from the original source of the data. Secondary research assimilates data that has already been collected by others, and thus allows the secondary researcher to "stand on the shoulders" of those who conducted the primary research.

Section 125 The tax code created by the Revenue Act of 1978 that created flexible benefits plans (often referred to as "cafeteria" plans). Section 125 plans can help employers as well as employees save money by reducing payroll taxes.

Section 401(k) The second employee benefit that was created by the Revenue Act. A type of defined contribution plan, 401(k) plans allow employees to set aside pre-tax dollars to save for their retirement. This can be done through salary deduction, which may or may not be matched in part or (less frequently) in whole by employer contributions. 401(k) dollars can also be set aside through deferral of profit sharing income.

security Protection of the workplace, and of the employees who work there.

selection The process of choosing the candidate(s) to whom the position will be offered.

selection criteria The "shopping list" of what you're looking for in the individuals who will populate your candidate pool (and, ultimately, the employees who will join the organization). This could and often will include KSAs, job specifications, behavioral characteristics, required credentials, and specific requirements stemming from job competencies.

Senior Professional in Human Resources (SPHR)   The Senior Professional in Human Resources certification, granted by and issued through HRCI.

seniority systems   Bona fide seniority or merit based systems that are not intended or designed to discriminate unlawfully.

serious violation   A violation that the employer either knew about or should have known about, and from which death or serious injury is probable. OSHA may propose a fine of up to $7000 per serious violation.

sexual harassment   A form of sex discrimination rendered illegal by Title VII of the Civil Rights Act of 1964. There are two categories of sexual harassment: quid pro quo and hostile work environment.

Sherman Anti-Trust Act, 1890   A law passed in an effort to curb the growth of monopolies. Under the Act, any business combination that sought to restrain trade or commerce would from that time forward be illegal. Specifically, the Act states that

- Section 1: "Every contract, combination in the form of trust or otherwise, or conspiracy, in restraint of trade or commerce among the several States, or with foreign nations, is declared to be illegal."

- Section 2: "Every person who shall monopolize, or attempt to monopolize, or combine or conspire with any

other person or persons, to monopolize any part of the trade or commerce among the several States, or with foreign nations, shall be deemed guilty of a felony."

The Sherman Act also placed responsibility for pursuing and investigating trusts on government attorneys and district courts.

short form employment applications   "Shorter" versions of an organization's standard employment application.

short-term incentive programs   Incentive programs that are usually one year or less in duration.

short-term incentives—individual   Variable incentive programs (usually one year or less in duration) that are used to motivate employees to attain specific individual financial or non-financial objectives.

short-term incentives—team/group   Variable incentive programs (usually one year or less in duration) that are used to motivate teams/groups to attain specific team/group financial or non-financial objectives. Short-term team/group incentive programs are intended to foster collaborative efforts and synergy among employees who are pursuing a common goal.

similar-to-me error/bias (interviewing)   An interviewing error/bias that occurs when the interviewer evaluates a candidate on the basis of how much a candidate is similar to, or different from, him or her.

similar-to-me error/bias (performance management)   A performance management error/bias in which the appraiser evaluates an employee's performance on the basis of how much a candidate is similar to, or different from, him or her.

simple linear regression A mathematical forecasting technique that examines the past relationship between two factors, determines the statistical strength of that relationship, and, on the basis of that analysis, projects future conditions.

simple resolutions A legislative measure that pertains to either the Senate or the House of Representatives. Simple resolutions offer a non-binding opinion, are not submitted to the president, and do not have the force of law.

simplified employee pension plan (SEP) A defined contribution plan that allows employers to contribute on a tax-favored basis to individual retirement accounts (IRAs) that employees set up for this purpose.

simulations A mathematical forecasting technique that creates scenarios through which different "realities" can be tested out to see what could happen under a variety of changing conditions.

skill One of the four factors used as a basis to assess the substantial equality of job content under the Equal Pay Act of 1963. "Skill" refers to the amount or degree of experience, ability, education, and training required to perform the job.

skill inventories A central database that captures the many KSAs possessed by its employees, even when those KSAs are not being used by an employee in his or her current position.

small group discussions/instructor-facilitated large group discussions A training method during which the facilitator encourages learning by drawing upon the experiences and insights of the participants. This is used as a way of reinforcing the adult learning principle that says that adult learners believe that they have a significant amount of valuable experience from which they can draw to enhance their own learning, and from which others can learn, as well.

SMART An acronym that can be applied to performance management (as well as other objectives that are developed and used within HR) that refers to specific, measurable, action-oriented, realistic, and time-bound.

Social Security Act (SSA), 1935 (also known as Old Age, Survivors and Disability Insurance [OASDI]) Social security is a social insurance program (although some would define it differently) that is funded through payroll taxes. Social security has three primary components, which are now referred to as retirement income, disability benefits, and survivor's benefits.

sociotechnical interventions OD interventions that focus on the ways in which groups can become more (or semi-) autonomous with respect to the performance and execution of the work.

St. Mary's Honor Center v. Hicks (1993) Key Issue: Burden of proof. Significance: In order to prevail in an allegation of discrimination under Title VII of the Civil Rights Act of 1964, an employee goes beyond a prima facie case and actually proves that the employer's true reasons for an employment action are, in fact, discriminatory.

standards   Requirements created by the Occupational Health and Safety Administration (OSHA) as a way of ensuring the health and safety of employees.

strategic HR   The transactions, the tasks, the procedural functions that need to be done. Strategic level HR is one leg of the HR stool—the other two legs are operational/tactical HR and transformational HR.

strategic management   Strategic HR management speaks to HR's overall commitment, in both word and deed, to meeting the ever-evolving short-term, long-term, and strategic objectives of the organization.

stress   According to Public Safety and Health (NIOSH), the "harmful physical and emotional responses that occur when the requirements of the job do not match the capabilities, resources, or needs of the worker."

stress interviews   Interviews in which the interviewer(s) deliberately creates a high-stress environment in an effort to ascertain how the candidate would respond in a high stress situation.

strictness error/bias (interviewing)   An interviewing error/bias that occurs when the interviewer applies an inappropriately harsh and demanding standard to one or more candidates, resulting in a lower overall assessment of the candidate(s).

strictness error/bias (performance management)   A performance management error/bias in which the appraiser applies an inappropriately harsh and demanding standard when evaluating the performance of one or more employees, resulting in a lower overall assessment of the employee(s).

substance use/abuse programs   A comprehensive program that consists of a drug-free workplace policy, supervisor training, employee education, employee assistance, and drug testing.

suggestion programs   Programs that invite employees to submit their ideas (often anonymously) relative to any work-related topic, such as improving work systems, identifying or eliminating safety concerns, or even exposing unethical (or criminal) behavior. Questions submitted through suggestion programs or "boxes" need to be responded to quickly, regardless of whether the suggestion is implemented. Employees must be heard and feel heard in order for any suggestion program to be successful.

Summary of Work-Related Injuries and Illnesses (also known as the OSHA Form 300A)   A form used to record a numeric summary of all work related injuries and illnesses logged in OSHA's Form 300 over the course of each calendar year. This form indicates the number of cases, the number of workdays impacted, and the number and types of work-related injuries and illnesses. A worksheet is also available to assist employers in filling out this summary. Each year, a completed Form 300 must be posted conspicuously for three months (between February 1 and April 30).

summary plan description (SPD)   A document that employees (or beneficiaries) who become participants in a retirement plan that is covered under ERISA are entitled to receive, at no cost, from the plan administrator. The SPD describes what the plan provides and how it operates. It also provides information relative to when an employee can begin to participate in the plan, how service and benefits are calculated, when benefits becomes vested, when and in what form benefits are paid, and how to file a claim for benefits.

summative evaluation   An approach that it is predicated on the interpretation of data that is collected after the initiative has been implemented. Summative evaluation allows for a complete analysis of the entire initiative on four different levels: reaction, learning, behavior, results.

survivor's benefits   One of the three primary components of the Social Security Act.

SWOT analysis (strengths, weaknesses, opportunities, threats)   An analysis that is conducted to ascertain the strengths and weaknesses that are inherent to an organization, as well as the opportunities and threats that it faces from external forces.

sympathy strikes   A type of strike that occurs when employees who are not directly involved in an economic dispute choose not to cross a picket line out of support for striking workers. Sympathy strikers do not need to be employed by the same employer as the employees who are actually on strike in order to engage in a sympathy strike. A sympathy strike is considered protected concerted activity.

T

tactile/kinesthetic learners   Those who learn most effectively when they can be "hands on," in the most literal sense of the word. They like to touch, to feel, to explore, and to experience the world around them.

Taft-Hartley Act (also known as the Labor Management Relations Act), 1947
An amendment designed to remedy what the Republican Congress saw as two major omissions in the NLRA (Wagner Act): first, the identification of behaviors and practices that would be considered ULPs on the part of unions, and second, a provision that would allow the government to issue an injunction against a strike that threatened national interests. Taft-Hartley identified the following unfair labor practices that could be committed by unions:

- Restraining or coercing employees in the exercise of their rights or an employer in the choice of its bargaining representative

- Causing an employer to discriminate against an employee

- Refusing to bargain with the employer of the employees it represents

- Engaging in certain types of secondary boycotts

- Requiring excessive dues

- Engaging in featherbedding

- Picketing for recognition for more than thirty days without petitioning for an election

- Entering into hot cargo agreements

- Striking or picketing a health care establishment without giving the required notice

task or work (operations) level analysis
Level 2 of McGehee and Thayer's three levels of HRD/training needs analysis and assessment. Task or work (operations) level

analysis collects and addresses data about a particular job or group of jobs.

Taxman v. Board of Education of Piscataway (1993) Key issue: Affirmative action. Significance: The U.S. Court of Appeals for the Third Circuit ruled that, in the absence of under-representation as demonstrated and documented through an affirmative action plan, organizations cannot consider race when making decisions relative to who will be laid off and who will be retained. Doing so would constitute a violation of Title VII of the Civil Rights Act of 1964.

This case falls under the category of "reverse discrimination" since it alleged race discrimination and was brought by a person who was not a minority/person of color.

teambuilding Exercises and initiatives that seek to help the team learn to function more effectively so that it can attain its overall objective (which must link, of course, to the overall organizational objective).

technostructural interventions OD interventions that focus on improving what work gets done, as well as the ways and processes through which the work gets done. It looks at job design, job redesign, job restructuring, work content, workflow, work processes, and the like.

teratogens A specific group of chemicals that will not harm pregnant women, but that do have the potential to harm unborn fetuses.

third-party vendor An entity or person outside the organization to whom work can be outsourced.

Title VII of the Civil Rights Act (1964) A landmark piece of legislation prohibiting employment discrimination the basis of race, color, religion, sex, and national origin.

tort doctrines Torts are wrongful acts committed against another individual's property or person. By definition, the commission of a tort infringes on another person's rights.

Some of the major tort doctrines that affect individual employee rights in the absence of an employment or labor contract are

- Employment-at-will
- Wrongful termination
- Implied contracts
- Defamation
- Invasion of privacy
- Negligent hiring
- Negligent training
- Negligent retention
- Negligent referral

total compensation All of the "rewards" that an organization gives, grants, or otherwise bestows upon its employees in exchange for the services those employees have rendered through their employment. It includes more obvious items, such as wages and salaries, that would fall under the subheading "compensation," as well as mandatory and optional benefits such as social security contributions, health and welfare programs, and the like. It also includes items that some but not all employees enjoy, such as incentives, bonuses, stock options, and so on.

total quality management (TQM)   An OD intervention that is ultimately aimed at meeting or exceeding customer expectations through the commitment of everyone in an organization (often through a team-based approach) to continuous improvement of products and/or services.

transformational HR   Takes a long-term, future-focused approach to the ways in which HR will work with the organization to attain its organizational mission. It looks at business and organizational issues, rather than "HR issues." It fosters and cultivates change and is dynamic, impactful, and ever-evolving.

treatment follow-up drug testing   Drug testing that is conducted periodically for employees who return to work after partici-pating in an alcohol or drug treatment program to ensure that they remain substance-free.

trend analysis   A mathematical technique that looks at and measures how one particu-lar factor changes over a period of time.

tuberculosis (TB)   A highly infectious bacterial disease that usually affects the lungs and that can also affect other organs.

turnover analysis   Measures the percent-age of the workforce that has left the organization during a specified period of time.

U

ULP strike   A strike called by a union that alleges, correctly or incorrectly, that the employer has committed an unfair labor practice during contract negotiations. Employers cannot hire permanent strike replacements during a ULP strike, and the striking workers must be returned to their original positions once the strike is over.

undue hardship   A hardship created by a requested accommodation that creates significant difficulty (enough to disrupt business operations), results in a significant financial outlay, or changes something about the (essential) nature of the business.

unemployment insurance   A program intended to help employees financially "bridge" the gap between positions, when an employee has lost his job through no fault of his own. Unemployment insurance was established as part of the federal Social Security Act of 1935, but is administered at the state level. Unemployment insurance is funded through employer taxes (except in three states, where employees contribute as well).

unfair labor practice (ULP)   Unlawful acts that can be committed by either employers or unions. The NLRA (Wagner Act) identified five categories of employer unfair labor practices:

- ▶ To "interfere with, restrain, or coerce employees" in the exercise of their rights to engage in concerted or union activities or refrain from them

- ▶ To dominate or interfere with the for-mation or administration of a labor organization

▶ To discriminate against employees for engaging in concerted or union activities or refraining from them

▶ To discriminate against an employee for filing charges with the NLRB or taking part in any NLRB proceedings

▶ To refuse to bargain with the union that is the lawful representative of its employees

Unfair labor practices that could be committed by unions were identified in 1947, in the Labor Management Relations Act (also known as the Taft-Hartley Act).

unfreezing   The first stage in Lewin's change process theory. Through the unfreezing stage, everyone who is involved with and impacted by the change must be brought to the point where he or she can understand and accept that a particular change will happen.

Uniform Guidelines on Employee Selection Procedures, 1978   A law that establishes a uniform set of principles relative to all elements of the selection process, including but not limited to interviewing, pre-employment testing, and performance appraisal. A key purpose of the Uniform Guidelines is to deal with the concept of "adverse impact" (also known as "disparate impact") as it pertains to the employment process, and to ensure that interview and selection processes are reliable (consistent) and valid.

Uniformed Services Employment and Reemployment Rights Act (USERRA), 1994   A law that provides reinforcement rights for individuals who miss work because of "service in the uniformed services," which is defined as voluntary or involuntary uniformed service.

union deauthorization   The revocation of the union security clause in the contract, which thereby creates an "open shop." Deauthorization requires a majority vote of the entire bargaining unit, not just the members of the unit who vote in the deauthorization election.

union decertification   The process by which employees vote to remove the union's rights to represent the employees. This process is similar to certification, only in reverse. Decertification requires a 50% (or more) of individuals who vote in the decertification election.

union security clauses   Articles that are included in some agreements in an effort to protect the interests, strength, and security of the union. Union security clauses regulate membership in the union and, consequently, relate to the payment of dues. Some of the more common types of union security clauses include

▶ Open shop

▶ Closed shop

▶ Union shop

▶ Agency shop

▶ Maintenance of membership

union shop   Newly hired employees must join the union within a specified period of time, usually 30 days, and must remain a member of the union as a condition of employment. In a union shop, employers must terminate employees who are not union members. Union shops are illegal in "right to work" states.

United Steelworkers v. Weber (1979)
Key issue: Affirmative action. Significance:
Affirmative action plans that establish voluntary quotas that have been jointly agreed
to by an organization as well as its collective
bargaining unit do not constitute race discrimination under Title VII of the Civil
Rights Act of 1964 if they are designed to
remedy past discrimination that has resulted
in current underutilization.

This case falls under the category of
"reverse discrimination" since it alleged race
discrimination and was brought by someone
who was not a minority/person of color.

U.S. Patent Act   Patents confer certain
rights upon the individual to whom the
patent is granted. Specifically, a patent
holder has "the right to exclude others from
making, using, offering for sale, or selling"
the invention in the United States or
"importing" the invention into the United
States.

utility patents   Granted for the invention
or discovery of any new and useful process,
machine, article of manufacture, or compo-
sition of matter, or any new and useful
improvement thereof.

utilization analysis   The section of an
affirmative action plan that compares the
percentage of qualified women and minorities available to be employed in a particular
job group to the percentage of women and
minorities who are actually employed in that
job group.

V

validity   The degree to which selection
processes measure skills that relate

meaningfully and clearly to the skills that
are required to perform a particular job.

values   Beliefs on which the organization
has been built. They are the tenets that
shape and guide strategic and day-to-day
decision making, as well as the behaviors
that are exhibited in the organization.
Organizations identify values, in part, as a
way to clearly guide those decisions and
behaviors. Values are often represented in
terms and principles such as integrity, honesty, respect, and so forth.

variable pay   Also known as "at risk" pay,
variable pay is cash compensation that fluc-
tuates and is tied, in some way, to the
employee's performance.

vesting   The process by which an employee earns a non-forfeitable right to the
employer's contribution of his or her
defined benefit/defined contribution plan.

VETS-100   The Federal Contractor
Veterans' Employment Report that must be
filed annually by those having federal contracts or subcontracts of $100,000 or more.

**Vietnam Era Veterans' Readjustment
Assistance Act (VEVRAA), 1974**   A law
that requires employers with Federal contracts or subcontracts of $25,000 or more to
provide equal opportunity and affirmative
action for Vietnam era veterans, special disabled veterans, and veterans who served on
active duty during a war or in a campaign or
expedition for which a campaign badge has
been authorized.

vision   A brief yet comprehensive descriptive and inspirational statement that articulates where the organization wants to be and
what it wants to become in the future.

vision coverage A type of health and welfare benefit. An employer will typically offer vision coverage as a discount program (generally around 10%). Vision coverage generally includes items such as exams, contact lenses, and glasses.

visual learners Those who learn most effectively through what they see.

voluntary subjects (also known as permissive subjects) "Voluntary" subjects of bargaining are topics that can be submitted to collective bargaining if and only if the employer and the employees' representative are willing to do so. Attempting to force bargaining on a voluntary or permissive subject constitutes a ULP.

voluntary terminations A decision initiated by the employee to end the employment relationship.

W–X

Wagner Act (also known as the National Labor Relations Act), 1935 A law that guaranteed "the right to self-organization, to form, join, or assist labor organizations, to bargain collectively through representatives of their own choosing, and to engage in concerted activities for the purpose of collective bargaining or other mutual aid and protection." Certain groups or categories of employees are excluded under the Wagner Act from membership in a bargaining unit. Examples would include managers, supervisors, confidential employees (essentially secretaries and administrative assistants to managers who can make labor relations decisions), and several others.

Walsh-Healey Public Contracts Act, 1936 The Walsh-Healey Public Contracts Act requires contractors who have contracts with the federal government that exceed $10,000 to pay an established minimum wage to workers employed through that contract. In addition to minimum wage, Walsh-Healey PCA also addressed issues including overtime pay and safe and sanitary working conditions.

Washington v. Davis (1976) Key issue: Employment tests and disparate impact. Significance: A test that has an adverse impact on a protected class is still lawful, as long as the test can be shown to be valid and job-related.

weighted employment applications Employment applications that assign relative weights to different portions of the application in an effort to facilitate the process of evaluating candidates' qualifications in a consistent and objective manner.

Weingarten Rights The right of a unionized employee to have union representation during a potential disciplinary interview.

whole job methods Non-quantitative job evaluation techniques that determine the relative value of jobs within the organization without using mathematical techniques.

whole job ranking A whole job evaluation technique that "ranks," from lowest to highest, according to the importance that each job holds (or, stated differently, the value that each job brings) to the organization. In essence, a whole job ranking is a list that reflects which jobs are more important to the organization, and which jobs are least important to the organization, in rank order.

wildcat strikes   A type of strike that occurs when a strike is called even when a collective bargaining agreement contains a no-strike clause that prohibits striking during the duration of the agreement. Wildcat strikes are not protected concerted activity.

willful violation   A violation that is deliberate and intentional. Deemed to be deliberate and intentional. OSHA may import a fine of up to $70,000 per willful violation (more in the event of the employee's death), and possibly incarceration.

Worker Adjustment and Retraining Notification Act (WARN), 1988   A law that mandates employer notification requirements under specific circumstances involving mass layoffs and plant closings, thus giving displaced workers time to make arrangements for other employment. WARN covers employers with 100 or more full-time employees.

worker's compensation   State laws intended to provide medical care to injured employees and death benefits to families of those who died. Worker's comp is a "no fault" system—injured workers receive medical and/or compensation benefits regardless of who caused the job-related accident.

workforce analysis   The section of an affirmative action plan that essentially depicts the contractor's workforce in terms of incumbents' race, gender, and wages. The workforce analysis is the older, longer, and more complex version of the "organizational display."

workforce planning and employment   Workforce planning and employment speaks to HR's responsibility to ensure integrated, seamless, and effective recruitment, hiring, orientation, and exit processes that support the short-term, long-term, emerging, and strategic objectives of the organization.

working conditions   One of the four factors used as a basis to assess the substantial equality of job content under the Equal Pay Act of 1963. "Working conditions" refer to the physical surroundings of the position, as well as any hazards that are associated with a particular position.

work-life programs   Programs that provide employees with the opportunity to combine or "balance" professional and nonprofessional dimensions of their lives, including flexible schedules, job sharing, telecommuting, and compressed work weeks. Work-life programs offer advantages for employees as well as employers who wish to market themselves in the relevant labor market.

work-related illness   Illnesses resulting from an event or condition in the work environment that fall into any one of the following four categories: skin diseases or disorders, respiratory conditions, poisoning, hearing loss, or "all other illnesses."

work-related injury   Any wound or damage to the body resulting from an event in the work environment.

workweek   A workweek is any fixed and regularly recurring period of 168 hours (24 hours in a day, seven days a week).

wrongful termination   A tort doctrine that speaks to the employer having ended the employment relationship for wrongful reasons. One possible basis for wrongful termination could exist if an employee was terminated in violation of an individual employment contract. Others could apply as well, and would vary from state to state.

Y–Z

"yellow dog" contract   A contract or an agreement between an employer and an employee in which the employer agrees to give the employee a job as long as the employee agrees not to join or have any involvement with a labor union.

zero defects   Phil Crosby's philosophy, which asserts that employees will perform at whatever level management sets for them. For that reason, settling for "goodness," rather than the full attainment of objectives, would effectively preclude the possibility of attaining those objectives.

zipper clause   A collective bargaining article through which both parties agree that the agreement is an exclusive and complete "expression of consent"—in other words, that the only items that can be collectively bargained until the expiration of the agreement are the ones that are actually included in the agreement. Once the agreement is signed, new subjects cannot be added, and existing subjects cannot be reopened for negotiation. The contract has been "zipped" closed.

Index

N

O

P

Q - R

W - Z

How can we make this index more useful? Email us at indexes@quepublishing.com